Needs of the Heart

RECENT TITLES FROM THE HELEN KELLOGG INSTITUTE FOR
INTERNATIONAL STUDIES

Scott Mainwaring, *general editor*

The University of Notre Dame Press gratefully thanks the Helen Kellogg Institute for
International Studies for its support in the publication of titles in this series.

Kevin Healy
*Llamas, Weavings, and Organic Chocolate: Multicultural Grassroots Development
in the Andes and Amazon of Bolivia* (2000)

Vikram K. Chand
Mexico's Political Awakening (2001)

Glen Biglaiser
Guardians of the Nation? (2002)

Sylvia Borzutzky
Vital Connections (2002)

Alberto Spektorowski
The Origins of Argentina's Revolution of the Right (2003)

Caroline C. Beer
Electoral Competition and Institutional Change in Mexico (2003)

Yemile Mizrahi
From Martyrdom to Power (2003)

Charles D. Kenney
Fujimori's Coup and the Breakdown of Democracy in Latin America (2003)

Alfred P. Montero and David J. Samuels
Decentralization and Democracy in Latin America (2004)

Katherine Hite and Paola Cesarini
Authoritarian Legacies and Democracy in Latin America and Southern Europe (2004)

Robert S. Pelton, C.S.C.
Monsignor Romero: A Bishop for the Third Millennium (2004)

Guillermo O'Donnell, Jorge Vargas Cullell, and Osvaldo M. Iazzetta
The Quality of Democracy (2004)

Arie M. Kacowicz
The Impact of Norms in International Society (2005)

Roberto DaMatta and Elena Soarez
Eagles, Donkeys, and Butterflies (2006)

For a complete list of titles from the Helen Kellogg Institute for International Studies,
see http://www.undpress.nd.edu

NEEDS
of the
HEART

A Social and Cultural History of Brazil's

Clergy and Seminaries

KENNETH P. SERBIN

University of Notre Dame Press
Notre Dame, Indiana

Library of Congress Cataloging-in-Publication Data
Serbin, Ken.
    Needs of the heart : a social and cultural history of Brazil's clergy
and seminaries / by Kenneth P. Serbin.
        p.   cm.
    "From the Helen Kellogg Institute for International Studies".
    Includes bibliographical references and index.
    ISBN-13: 978-0-268-04119-9 (cloth. : alk. paper)
    ISBN-10: 0-268-04119-9 (cloth. : alk. paper)
    1. Catholic Church—Clergy—Training of—Brazil—History.
2. Catholic theological seminaries—Brazil—History.
I. Helen Kellogg Institute for International Studies.   II. Title.
    BX910.B7S47   2006
    262'.14281—dc22

                                                        2006004728

For the seminarians and priests of Brazil.

For my parents.

For Regina and Bianca.

O padre furtou a moça, fugiu.
Pedras caem no padre, deslizam.
A moça grudou no padre, vira sombra,
aragem matinal soprando no padre.
Ninguém prende aqueles dois,
aquele um
negro amor de rendas brancas. . . .
— Carlos Drummond de Andrade, "O padre, a moça"

We have dissociated ourselves from the normal concerns of most people's lives under the pretext of thus becoming available for the preaching of the gospel. Many of us come from working-class families, and more than one cardinal has come from peasant stock. Our early entry into the seminary tears us away from our native environments and our families and offers us a way of life that represents a step up on the social scale. Our classical education alters our way of thinking and our vocabulary. The long training period in the cloister removes us from the real problems that affect the lives of everyone except the clergy and the rich. Is it possible at this point to build a bridge between our world and the world outside our ecclesiastical institutions?
— Frei Betto, 1970

Contents

Figures

Tables

AC -Acre
AL - Alagoas
AP - Amapá
AM - Amazonas
BA - Bahia
CE - Ceará
DF - Distrito Federal (Brasília)
ES - Espírito Santo
GO - Goiás
MA - Maranhão
MT - Mato Grosso
MS - Mato Grosso do Sul
MG - Minas Gerais
PA - Pará
PB - Paraíba
PR - Paraná
PE - Pernambuco
PI - Piauí
RN - Rio Grande do Norte
RS - Rio Grande do Sul
RJ - Rio de Janeiro
RO - Rondônia
RR - Roraima
SC - Santa Catarina
SP - São Paulo
SE - Sergipe
TO - Tocantins

Map of Brazil

Courtesy of Judy Bartlett.

Preface

Priests are crucial figures in Latin American history but are rarely studied as a group. *Needs of the Heart* recovers and interprets the history of the clergy's struggle with the many religious, political, and personal issues that have emerged from their experience in Brazil, home to the world's largest and arguably most dynamic branch of the Roman Catholic Church. Here the reader will learn how Brazil's priests participated in the colonization of Brazil, educated the elite and the poor in the faith, propped up the socioeconomic status quo, and reinforced the institution of slavery. Brazil's clergy lived in relative freedom from the authority of the Church. Earthy men, they sired families in violation of the rule of celibacy and became deeply involved in politics. Starting in the nineteenth century, the Church carried out a century-long reform of the clergy by seriously requiring for the first time that new candidates to the priesthood study in seminaries. Relying on strict discipline, the seminaries aimed to mold a new kind of priest—moral, isolated from politics and social entanglements, and, above all, obedient and celibate. Numbering in the hundreds and educating tens of thousands of men, the seminaries became one of Brazil's most important educational institutions.

The social, cultural, and religious upheaval of the 1960s, however, led a new generation of candidates to the priesthood to reject the seminary. Seminarians banded together in a movement to form a national union and fought for the right to experiment with new modes of clerical education. Students moved away from the seminaries and established greater contact with the public. Once again political activism came onto the agenda of ecclesiastical reform. The seminarians' movement helped spark the practice of liberation theology in Brazil. It also reflected the quest for professional and individual development, including the desire for optional celibacy. The Brazilian Church responded to the need for personalized education by attempting to build an ambitious program in liberation psychology.

These audacious experiments in clerical education coincided with the most critical development in modern Brazilian political history: the economically expansive but repressive military regime of 1964 to 1985. Experimentation in clerical education opposed authoritarianism and was ultimately severely curtailed by it. The story of this generation of seminarians and priests is intermingled with the challenges and fears posed by the dictatorship and its aftermath.

The seminarians' movement is a forgotten episode, overshadowed by the onset of militarism, ignored even in ecclesiastical writings, but nonetheless paramount for understanding the new directions in which the Latin American clergy and their flocks moved in the 1960s, 1970s, and 1980s. By studying the grass roots of the clergy we can achieve a clearer picture of priests' connections to the people, the evolution of religious beliefs in Brazil, socioeconomic modernization, and the emergence of liberation theology as an ideology and, more significantly, as a practice.

Needs of the Heart is a social and cultural history of Brazil's clergy and seminaries. The Church has been a cultural institution involving the daily lives of thousands of priests and seminarians who worked in relative anonymity. How these men lived, the words they preached, and the examples they set for their flocks were always central concerns of the organization, especially in the era of the seminaries. The drama of priests' lives touched on basic themes of humanity: love, sex, faith, the mind, discipline, and violence. Here I am thickening the description of Brazilian and Latin American Catholicism, topics addressed by many authors in recent decades. This is also a book about modern Brazil and Latin America, the link between religion and politics, popular religion, Church-state relations, the institutional Church, liberationist Catholicism, human rights, and the social history of psychology. A case study in ecclesiastical training, it sheds light on the construction of new models of the priesthood. Brazilian and U.S. clerics have much to learn from each other, and I hope that this book will stimulate dialogue between them.

Needs of the Heart is the result of nearly twenty years of research and reflection on the history of the Brazilian Church and its social and political roles. It is the second in a series of books. In *Secret Dialogues: Church-State Relations, Torture, and Social Justice in Authoritarian Brazil* (published in 2000 and issued in Brazil as *Diálogos na sombra* in 2001), I described behind-the-scenes meetings in which the country's top bishops and representatives of the military dictatorship negotiated the conflict that arose over radical priests and the Church's denunciation of socioeconomic inequality and human rights abuses. In a future project I will explore the social history of abortion in Rio de Janeiro, including its religious facets. *Needs of the Heart* is also informed by my various writings on the economic relationship between the Church and the Brazilian state and on the Church's involvement in democratic politics after the end of military rule in 1985.

The research for this book began serendipitously with a foreign-language stipend from the Mellon Fellowships in the Humanities program during the summer of 1986. Without that grant I would not have gone to Brazil, not improved my rudimentary Portuguese, and certainly not have met the courageous priests, nuns, and lay militants who introduced me to the practice of liberation theology in the favelas of São Paulo, Rio de Janeiro, Belo Horizonte, and Salvador. Because of that memorable visit I decided to write a dissertation on the Brazilian Church, the kernel of this book. The Mellon program additionally provided me with a prior grant to initiate Portuguese language studies in Lisbon, two years of support as a graduate student at the University of California, San Diego, and a third year of dissertation-writing assistance while residing in Rio de Janeiro. In Brazil I conducted field research with extremely generous support from the Comissão Fulbright in the form of a doctoral dissertation grant funded by the U.S. Institute for International Education and administered by Marco Antônio da Rocha and Terry McIntyre and their kind staff. I also received assistance from the Organization of American States and the History Department of the University of California, San Diego. During my graduate studies I obtained grants from the Tinker Foundation and the National Defense Education Act (Title VI) fellowship program. A residential fellowship at the Helen Kellogg Institute for International Studies at the University of Notre Dame furnished optimal conditions for advancing on the dissertation as well as a spectacularly collegial and stimulating environment of intellectual exchange. I thank the Reverend Ernest Bartell, C.S.C., Guillermo O'Donnell, and Scott Mainwaring for the opportunity to work at the Kellogg. I finished the dissertation while working as a Research Associate at the North-South Center at the University of Miami under the magnanimous direction of Ambassador Ambler Moss and Robin Rosenberg. From 1993 to 2004 I received a regular stream of research support from various units at the University of San Diego: the Office of the Dean of the College of Arts and Sciences, the History Department, and the Provost's Office. Many thanks go to Frank B. Lazarus, Patrick Drinan, James Gump, Iris Engstrand, Lisa Hoffman, Molly McClain, and the many members of the funding committees who evaluated my numerous research proposals.

This book was possible only because others before me dedicated themselves to the study of the Brazilian Church. I especially wish to acknowledge the influence of Scott Mainwaring, Thomas C. Bruneau, Ralph Della Cava,

Father Marcelo Azevedo, S.J., Riolando Azzi, Father Alberto Antoniazzi, and Pierre Sanchis.

At the University of California, San Diego (UCSD), generous intellectual and institutional support for my work came from Eric Van Young and Paul Drake. Without them this project would not have come to fruition. Their encouragement at each stage was invaluable. Peter Evans likewise displayed generosity and provided important contacts in Brazil. His perception of the research strategy was on point: penetrate the institutional Church. At UCSD additional assistance and encouragement came from Joe Foweraker, Aralia López-González, Manzar Foroohar, Michael Monteon, Leon Zamosc, and Peter Smith. Steven Topik of the University of California, Irvine, enthusiastically provided fine historical contextualization and contacts in Brazil. Eric, Paul, Michael, Peter, and Steven all provided incisive comments on the dissertation.

Father Antoniazzi read the entire book manuscript. Sadly, Father Antoniazzi died on Christmas Day, 2004, and was unable to see the final product of a work that he in so many ways helped make possible during our more than fifteen years of friendship. Andrew Chesnut and Thomas C. Bruneau lent their fine expertise to the manuscript. An early version of chapters 1 and 2 received a helpful critique from the informal but highly stimulating Fulbright discussion group in Rio de Janeiro. My thanks go to Peter Beattie, Sueann Caulfield, Jean Daudelin, Roger Kittleson, Brian Owensby, and other participants in the group. Dain Borges provided insightful commentary on chapters 1, 2, and 3 of the book manuscript, as did Margaret Keck and Marcelo Timotheo da Costa on parts of chapter 5, presented in the form of a conference paper at two international symposia, "The Cultures of Dictatorship: Historical Reflections on the Brazilian Golpe of 1964," University of Maryland, October 14–16, 2004, and "Brasil–EUA: Novas Gerações, Novos Diálogos," Fundação Casa Rui Barbosa, Rio de Janeiro, June 21–24, 2005. The initial conclusions that became chapters 3 and 4 were the subject of intense discussion at the regional meeting of the Comissão para o Estudo da Igreja na América Latina in São Paulo, September 9, 1991. Peter, Brian, and Sueann also furnished helpful remarks on a seminal version of chapters 3 and 4. Many of the ideas contained in chapter 6 were debated in sessions of the Grupo de Estudo do Catolicismo (GEC) of the Instituto de Estudos da Religião after oral expositions by the author: first, in preliminary form on April 5, 1991, and, second, upon the presentation of a paper, "A Difícil Entrada da Psicologia na Formação dos Padres Brasileiros: O Caso da Psicanálise, o Pe. Géza e o 'Christus Sacerdos,'" on October 4, 1991. These presentations were part of the GEC's larger debate in a collective research project entitled, "A Igreja Católica e a Crise da Modernidade," which resulted in the publication of Sanchis 1992a, 1992b, and 1992c. I extend my thanks to the participants of the GEC: Pierre Sanchis, Carlos Rodrigues Brandão, Nair Costa Muls, Telma de Souza Birchal, Father Matias Martinho Lenz, S.J., Father Mário França, S.J., Patrícia Birman, Raymundo Heraldo Maués, Father José Ivo Follman, S.J., Regina Novaes, Ana Maria Doimo, Pedro Ribeiro de Oliveira, Solange Rodrigues, Rubem César Fernandes, Samyra Crespo, Zélia Seiblitz, Ralph Della Cava, Cecília Mariz, Paula Montero, the late Francisco Rolim, and the late Carmen Cinira Macedo. A draft of this chapter was also discussed in an interdisciplinary research discussion group at the Kellogg Institute on March 6, 1992. Additional helpful comments on the book manuscript came from my students Sean Deshler, Pamela Espinosa, Kamea Hadar, and Veronica Perez.

Thanks to these many readers this work is much stronger than the initial version. Of course, any factual errors or faults of interpretation are my own.

In Brazil I received generous assistance from numerous individuals, especially from Father Celso Pedro da Silva, Celso Castro, Lúcia Lippi, Luiz Alberto Gómez de Souza, Lúcia Ribeiro, Father Virgílio Leite Uchôa, Sátiro Nunes, Magali Godoy, Maria Helena Moreira Alves, José Valentín, Célia Costa, Dulce Pandolfi, Aloysio de Oliveira Martins Filho, Rosângela Mello, the late Mons. Arnaldo Beltrami, Father João Panazzolo, Ivanildes Batista, Alexandre Brandão Martins Ferreira, Fátima Mesquita, Douglas Mansur, Eduardo Hoornaert, Fernando Novais, Romy Medeiros da Fonseca, Maria Isabel Baltar da Rocha, and the staffs of the Arquivo da Província Brasileira da Congregação da Missão, the Arquivo da Província Sul Brasileira da Companhia de Jesus, the Arquivo da Reitoria do Colégio Máximo Cristo Rei de São Leopoldo, the Arquivo do Instituto de Teologia do Recife, the Arquivo do Seminário Regional do Nordeste II, the Arquivo Nacional, the Arquivo Público do Estado do Rio de Janeiro, the Biblioteca Cardeal Câmara da Arquidiocese de São Sebastião do Rio de Janeiro, the Central de Documentação e Informação Científica "Professor Casemiro dos Reis Filho," the Centro de Pesquisa e Documentação de História Contemporânea do Brasil, the Instituto Brasileiro de Desenvolvimento and the Centro João XXIII, and the Instituto Nacional de Pastoral. Thanks go to the staff at Unidade 2 Artes Gráficas in São Paulo for their excellent work in scanning photographs.

Heartfelt thanks go to the scores of priests, nuns, seminarians, and bishops who received me in their residences, provided research tips and interviews, and supported my work in so many other ways. I especially wish to recognize

Dom Mauro Morelli, Dom Sinésio Bohn, Dom Nei Paulo Moretto, Dom Demétrio Valentini, Father Miguel of the Cristo Rei parish in São Paulo, Father
Luís Weel, Father Cláudio Sartori, Father Cleto Caliman, S. D. B., Father José
Oscar Beozzo, Father Jamil Nassif Abib, Father Carlos César dos Santos, and
the Jesuit community at the Colégio Anchieta in Porto Alegre. Most generous
assistance came from Dom Antônio Celso Queiroz and the staff of priests, sisters, librarians, and other employees at the headquarters of the Conferência
Nacional dos Bispos do Brasil in Brasília, where I lodged and studied several
weeks in a wonderful research setting. I am most deeply indebted to the Vincentian fathers of Rio de Janeiro and Belo Horizonte. I took many a meal with
the Lazaristas, as the Vincentians are known in Brazil, at their main house in the
Cosme Velho district of Rio de Janeiro and worked numerous hours in their
archive. I have fond memories of the late Father José Pires de Almeida, the late
Father Clóvis Duarte Passos, Father Lauro Palú, Father Célio Dell'Amore, and
the many other Lazaristas as well as ex-Lazaristas who assisted me. I am also
grateful to the Holy Spirit Missionary Sisters of São Paulo, Rio de Janeiro, and
Belo Horizonte for their hospitality, guidance, and inspiration. They provided
my very first lesson in liberation theology.

In Brazil friendship and additional support came from Fernando Ferreira
and Gláucia, Antero and Dirce Torres, Irany Arruda Costa, Fernanda Villasboas
and Ricardo, Soraia Jorge, Emílio and Ana LaRovere, Henri LaRovere, Elói Melo
Filho, Renato and Helena Nazaré, Ivan and Denise Bacellar, Heloísa and David,
Quélia Quaresma, Flávio dos Santos Gomes, Emanuelle de Oliveira, Raquel
Michelson, Célia Tavares, Carlos Alberto Baruki, Cecília Mariz, Nelly Boonen,
Dário Almeida Alves, Enildo Costa, Celina Tiemi Kirizawa, Heitor Frugoli, Anja
Kamp, Luciane and Amaury Meyer, Ciro Manzano, Regina Weber, Antônio and
Regina Gringo, Zizi Pereira and Roberto, Lucelena Barreira Novarino, Miriam,
Filemon Alves Filho, Maiby Castro Leal, Marco Aurélio Vannucchi Leme de
Mattos, Regiane Augusto, and many other friends and acquaintances.

Valuable assistance and support came from U.S. colleagues Timothy Power,
David Dixon, Jeffrey Lesser, Michael Weis, Michael LaRosa, Frank McCann, the
late Sheldon Maram, James Green, the late Jayne Spencer, Marshall Buelna,
Julie Edson, and Patrick Walls. Thanks go to Richard W. Fox for introducing
me to the passion of history. Paul Bass, Norman Oder, and Mark Prendergast
have also been sources of inspiration.

Barbara Hanrahan, the editor of the University of Notre Dame Press, provided special encouragement. Rebecca DeBoer and the staff of the press saw the
book through its final stages. Beth Wright expertly handled the copyediting.

This work would not have been possible without the love and support of longtime friends and my relatives: Stephen Downing, David Chappell, Stephen Prothero, Maryse Bacellar (minha mãe brasileira), Roberto Grimes, the late Mário Teodoro de Barros, Lourdes Alves Barros, Rogério Alves de Barros, Ricardo Alves de Barros; my parents, Paul and Carol Serbin; and, above all, my wife, Regina Barros Serbin, a fount of tolerance, patience, and love, and my daughter, Bianca, who was ever so patient waiting for her daddy to leave his office to play.

chapter one

Introduction

The Meaning of the Priesthood

The vocation of the Catholic priesthood embodies the most generous of human aspirations and the most profound human contradictions. Throughout history priests have sought to bring themselves and their flocks closer to God and to build a just society. For Catholics the priest is the way to salvation. For non-Catholics he symbolizes the Church's prominence as a religious, political, and social institution. Priests, the sociologist Father Andrew Greeley once wrote, have the special capacity "to take a constructive view of the nature of man."[1] Educated in a tradition stretching back to the start of Western civilization, they are a repository of the Judeo-Christian ethic. But in the name of God they have directed some of the most brutal campaigns against ideas, peoples, and individuals. Priests are expected to personify the divine while inhabiting imperfect bodies. Called upon to express the highest form of love, they must deny the basic drive for sexual pleasure, comfort, and freedom. These requirements bind priests together in a mysterious international brotherhood. Like a Greek tragedy, the story of the priesthood speaks about fundamental human issues.[2]

This account is a social and cultural history of the priesthood in Brazil, one of the world's largest and most religiously evocative places, nominally the world's largest Catholic country but in reality quite diverse in religious practice. I trace five centuries of continuity and change in the life of the clergy by focusing on the seminaries, the training schools in which young men—and only men—isolated themselves from the world in order to prepare for the ordained ministry of the Roman Catholic Church. Ethnicity, gender, politics, and economics come into focus. Just as important as these is religion, a dominant influence in the vast sweep of the history of civilizations.[3] Priests' social roles and the ways in which they struggled with the demands of their special station are the major underlying themes.

I was inspired to write this book in 1986, when, visiting Brazil for the first time, I learned that Rome had sentenced the famous liberation theologian Leonardo Boff, a Franciscan friar, to a year of silence because of his controversial critique of power in the Church. The Brazilian Church was also mourning the death of Father Josimo Morais Tavares, murdered in May 1986 because he assisted poor people who struggled against powerful landowners in the Amazon. The discovery of liberation theology and clerical activism refreshed my Catholic roots. Hearing priests denounce social evils during the first electoral campaign of post-dictatorial Brazil, I told myself, "*This* is what the Church should be doing everywhere!" The Brazilian Church stood in sharp contrast with the conformist, middle-class-oriented Church in the United States, where after Mass people raced to their new cars in the parking lot rather than contemplate a renewed life with God. The experience in Brazil led me to focus on the Church for my doctoral dissertation in Latin American history at the University of California, San Diego.

I commenced my research in 1987 on a balmy winter afternoon in Rio de Janeiro. I began by meeting with one of Brazil's most impressive clergymen, Father Marcello de Carvalho Azevedo, a Jesuit intellectual whose important book on the renowned Comunidades Eclesiais de Base (CEBs, or Grassroots Church Communities), faith, and culture had just appeared in English.[4] The CEBs had emerged in the 1970s, as the Church struggled to end Brazil's military dictatorship. Receiving me with his characteristic big smile, Father Marcello proceeded to outline verbally, in the space of about an hour and without notes, four possible dissertation topics. One of these topics—the training of priests in diocesan seminaries—had not been systematically studied by any social scientist or historian. "You can provide a great service to the Brazilian Church by doing a study on the seminaries," Father Marcello said.

Father Marcello received me in his office in Botafogo, one of the most interesting microcosms of modern Brazilian life. Located not far from downtown Rio, the Botafogo district hosted one of the greatest clusters of intellectual life in Latin America. Father Marcello and other key thinkers involved in the Progressive Church worked at the Instituto Brasileiro de Desenvolvimento (IBRADES, Brazilian Institute for Development), an influential Jesuit think tank that had trained a generation of Catholic grassroots activists. In 1970 agents of Brazil's military regime had invaded IBRADES, provoking a near rupture in the historic relationship between the Church and the state. Just around the corner stood the Instituto Brasileiro de Análises Sociais e Econômicos, where researchers under the leadership of former Catholic militant Herbert de Sousa (Betinho) organized a national anti-poverty movement in the 1990s. After our formal meeting Father Marcello and I walked briskly up the Rua São Clemente. Once graced with the elegant residences of the nineteenth-century Brazilian imperial nobility, when Botafogo sat idyllically on the city's outskirts, this street now bustled with traffic, shoppers, and pedestrians, many of whom resided in high-rise apartment buildings. Just a few steps up São Clemente one could find the cultural center known as the Casa de Rui Barbosa, the former home of the great Brazilian jurist, scholar, statesman, and abolitionist. Fernando Henrique Cardoso, an internationally renowned sociologist and Brazil's president from 1995 to 2003, grew up in Botafogo. Father Marcello pointed out the Colégio Santo Inácio, the Jesuit preparatory school that educated many of the members of Brazil's male elite. A bit further one encountered the Instituto Universitário de Pesquisas do Rio de Janeiro (IUPERJ), founded by Candido Mendes, the brilliant great-grandson of the senator who defended the Church against encroachment by the state in the 1870s. IUPERJ stood in the heart of Botafogo, on the Rua da Matriz, a short street that connected São Clemente and the neighborhood's other main thoroughfare. A stolid-looking stone church loomed at the far end of the Rua da Matriz, while on the São Clemente side the hills rose up to the Corcovado, the peak where the world-famous Christ the Redeemer statue spread its arms in a benevolent yet distant gesture to the people of Rio.

Life shifted dramatically on the hillside, where the favela Dona Marta sloped precariously upwards. Known by its inhabitants as Santa Marta, a name coined by a Jesuit father, the community gained national infamy in the 1980s as a lair for drug traffickers and their hit men. In 1996 it became a symbol of violence and First World-Third World tensions when pop singer Michael Jackson and movie producer Spike Lee produced a controversial music video there. Some Brazilian politicians opposed the filming, and Lee had to pay a bribe to the drug kingpin in order to assure security. That year Brazilian director Murilo Salles also made an acclaimed tragic action film based on children from the favela. It was titled *Como nascem os anjos* (How Angels Are Born). Joining cosmopolitan sophistication and class struggle, Botafogo and Santa Marta reflected the contradictions of postmodern underdevelopment.[5]

Father Marcello believed that foreign oppression caused this situation. He pointed to the noisy buses lurching up crowded São Clemente and belching out diesel pollution. The middle class avoided these buses, which were nothing more than transport trucks fitted with uncomfortable seats and rough, noisy turnstiles seemingly designed for animals. The residents of Santa Marta resigned themselves to a lifetime of commuting in these vehicles. "Look what the multinational corporations do here in Brazil," Father Marcello said. "They leave their worst technology for the poor countries of the world."

Our meeting resolved some central issues for me. Father Marcello not only helped me with an important career decision but also had charged me with an important mission. In Brazil the Church really mattered and, in the likes of individuals such as Father Marcello, truly seemed to care about the people. My work would be much more than an academic exercise. I would venture into faith, politics, and the fight for social change.

But a study of the seminaries would have to address more than the mainly political concerns expressed in most of the writings on the contemporary Latin American Catholic Church. In Father Marcello I had already observed that the life of the Brazilian clergy involved complex and sometimes contradictory demands. For instance, he belonged to the religious (or regular) clergy. These priests were grouped in orders, could serve anywhere in the world, and were subject to a bishop only if formally serving in a diocese, the Church's main territorial division. Yet he recommended that I study the diocesan (or secular) priests, who generally spent their entire careers subject to the local bishop. At first I decided to concentrate on the training of only diocesan priests. But in Brazil Jesuits and other orders had shouldered much of the responsibility for training the diocesan fathers. Rivalries developed between the religious and secular priests, and also among the many orders that came to Brazil from Europe. Tensions particularly developed along lines of national identity. Thus my study expanded to include research on the religious, and it went beyond the seminaries to give an overview of the clergy and other themes such as popular religion and the structure of the institutional Church. Whereas at first I hoped to examine only the post–World War II era, it became rapidly apparent that I could not explain the seminaries without returning to the colonial era.

Priests' struggles with celibacy became an inevitable part of my research. I discovered the personal side of things as I searched for the core of liberation theology among the activist priests of the Baixada Fluminense, a complex of hot, teeming working-class suburbs of Rio de Janeiro. Writing about and at times even assisting these men, I witnessed how they jumped into the political fray of Brazil's new democratic political system and, as a result, fell victim to oppression by the Church bureaucracy, threatened the pecuniary comfort of their clerical enemies, and challenged the standard model of the priesthood.

On a Friday night in July 1989, I ran into one of these priests at a Brazilian pop music dance concert held to benefit Luiz Inácio Lula da Silva, the presidential candidate of the Partido dos Trabalhadores (PT, or Workers' Party) in the country's first free presidential election in three decades. Father Nelson was wearing his usual jeans and holding the hand of a young woman. The three of us danced together and conversed a good while before I took my leave at midnight, but not before I offered them a room in my apartment. Getting back to the Baixada by bus was virtually impossible late on a Friday night. At 2:30 AM the doorbell rang, and I prepared a place for them on the living room floor. The next morning we ate breakfast together.

A year later Father Nelson and Ângela had their first child, a robust boy born only after the priest wrote a check to cover the cost of an emergency cesarean. To avoid bouncing the check Father Nelson got a loan from a friend who didn't question the priest's alleged need to help a needy "parishioner."

Father Nelson was highly popular. He was also a radical whose violation of celibacy became a pretext for his removal. His politics led his superiors to transfer him to a far-off diocese, but to no avail. His activism and denunciation of the local elite's abuse of power and privilege angered his new bishop. Father Nelson's flock gladly accepted his unofficial marriage to Ângela. They protested when the Church moved to use it as a reason to expel him from the parish and his religious order. The eight-month ordeal spilled into the pages of the press, including photos of Father Nelson and his family. His opponents ransacked his quarters and stole his personal Bible.

Unemployed and with a second child to support, Father Nelson worked as a janitor at a private recreational club before landing a position as an assistant to a PT city councilwoman. In his next job he assisted street children. Father Nelson then separated from Ângela and moved to another state, where he "married" again to an old friend. Father Nelson still considers himself a priest. He did not apply to the Vatican for release from his vows, and he still engages in pastoral activities. He hopes for a liberalization of the rules on celibacy so that he can return to the full practice of his ministry.[6]

Father Marcello's political stance and the tensions of Father Nelson's priesthood summarized key elements of the history of the clergy and Brazilian

Catholicism. The experiences of the clergy highlighted the link between religion and society as well as the struggles over beliefs, cultural values, and material resources spurred by the political evolution of the Brazilian Church. The seminaries were the starting point in this odyssey. The clergy formed the core of the Church, and the seminary its inner core.

Our story has panoramic dimensions. It covers the vast territory of Brazil, the transcontinental exchange of people and ideas, and the singular history of a two-thousand-year-old institution. The Catholic Church is a global organization with hundreds of millions of believers and more than a million functionaries, including hundreds of thousands of priests and nuns. Its vast network of dioceses is subdivided into a myriad of parishes. The Church is an ecclesiastical institution, but also the "People of God." The term refers to the clergy *and* the faithful. In Brazil the Church is the oldest institution. It played a central part in the development of Brazilian civilization. Only the military and the state have rivaled it in terms of organization and resources.

This is also a story of violence. The clergy were long the fulcrum on which much of Brazilian social life turned and, as a result, frequently stood at the center of conflict. Priests constantly needed to adapt to different pressures: from the elite, the people, and the Vatican. The colonial Church, for instance, sought to minister to the people but also exploited them. It legitimized the state and powerful economic interests, with the clergy generally enjoying great social comfort and privileges. In surveying the social roles, economic power, and ethnic background of the clergy of the colonial era (1500–1822), chapter 2 of this book pays particular attention to the social impact of the Church's missionary activity, its support for Brazilian slavocracy, and the repression of native and African culture. In contrast, in chapter 5 we will see how in the name of the people some clergy succored armed revolutionary movements seeking to overthrow the military dictatorship (1964–1985). These and other issues have divided the Church.

A central argument of this book is that patterns of Brazilian Catholicism from the colonial and imperial eras survived into the twentieth century. The famed transformation of the modern Brazilian Church into a progressive institution was deeply rooted in the historical experience of the clergy, and its causes long predated those identified by most scholars. Brazilian clerical nationalism—a factor often ignored in the explanation of progressivism— had beginnings in the colonial period. As chapter 2 illustrates, the political involvement of the clergy had numerous precedents in the First Empire (1822–1840). Father Diogo Antônio Feijó's campaign for an alternative model of the priesthood, including optional celibacy, formed a major plank of the nationalists' platform.

Another pattern is modernization. Scholars such as Richard Graham have focused on the economic progress and infrastructural improvements of the latter half of the nineteenth century as the key moment in Brazilian modernization.[7] In a broader sense, however, it had already started in the sixteenth century. Brazil began at the dawn of modernity and was thus essentially a modern project.[8] Brazil was colonized by the Portuguese, the leading seaborne nation of its time. Brazilian growers developed the world's most productive sugar plantations.

In addition to material progress, modernization brought shifts in attitudes about a host of changes that are all part of what we today call modernity: the new status of the individual, his or her evolving relationship to large organizations, the emergence of human consciousness, new notions of political participation (democracy, citizenship, and authoritarianism), the belief in rationality and scientific progress instead of medievalism's reliance on authority, the autonomy of the secular order, new women's roles, the need for constant cultural and technological innovation, personal innovation, and intensification of the search for truth. These flowed from such varied but interrelated developments as the Renaissance, the Enlightenment, the industrial revolution, the scientific revolution, the French Revolution, and the violent encounter of Europeans and Native Americans after 1492. Modernity is "humanity's adulthood" and "emancipation."[9] Modernity constructed its own utopia. But it also produced strong reactions such as Romanticism, which responded to modernity's degradation into a reductionist fundamentalism that was overly pragmatic and incapable of comprehending the spiritual and life's meaning.[10] As the twentieth century so tragically illustrated, modernity brought new methods of oppression and destruction.

The Brazilian Church's need to adapt to a constantly changing world caused it to undergo religious modernization. True, the Brazilian masses lacked most of the philosophical and political attributes mentioned above, and Brazil was the last country in the Americas to abolish slavery. Even at the start of the twenty-first century, Brazil still lagged terribly in terms of distribution of wealth and land and respect for the individual citizen. But Brazil orbited a European world in which social changes were taking place. Brazil began to experience them through religion, which played a major part in social and ideological evolution. Scholars of European history have described the Reformation and Counter-Reformation (and Catholic Reformation) as important determinants in the development of modernity. In colonial Brazil priests such as the Jesuits molded proto-modern culture by cultivating European Catholic ideas and practices and establishing an extensive system of missions, schools, plantations, and other institutions.

But the Counter-Reformation played out much more erratically in Latin America than in Europe. The Jesuits and other religious fathers—but generally not the diocesan clergy—worked to establish the norms established at the Council of Trent, the watershed meeting of Church fathers held between 1545 and 1563. Trent aimed to end the widespread laxity of the clergy and to strengthen loyalty to the institutional Church. Tridentine Catholicism represented the dominant religious values as put forth by the Church and royal governments in their subjugation of the Americas. In the Catholic world it was the most modern cultural proposal of its time. The institutional Church thus fomented the first of several waves of evangelization-cum-modernization. However, this campaign created religious and cultural conflict throughout Latin America. Popular religion, including many practices rejected by the official Church, resisted religious modernization and thrived everywhere, especially in Brazil. From the Church's standpoint the most serious shortcomings existed among the clergy. Combined with Brazil's vast territory and the chaotic development of colonial civilization, the lack of reform created an ambiguous situation in which priests routinely strayed from the modernized ecclesiastical standards.

The Counter-Reformation did not effectively take place in Brazil until the implantation of the diocesan seminaries in the second half of the nineteenth century. Catholic identity and the model of the Church were tightly linked to the identity of the priest. Through the seminaries the bishops hoped to transform the earthy, sexually active, and politicized clergy into a corps of socially superior, morally irreproachable, mainly apolitical pastors. The Church believed that a reformed clergy would foster institutional unity and obedience to the hierarchy's religious, political, and social dictates. The Church set out to change the model of the priesthood and to differentiate priests from the rest of the populace. To achieve this goal it isolated seminarians from the alleged dangers of the outer world. It also imposed control over their spiritual, physical, and emotional behavior.

Discipline was the key. It caused individuals to internalize ecclesial norms. For the Vatican, the bishops, and the heads of religious orders, discipline became the central issue of the Brazilian clergy. In Michel Foucault's assessment, modern Western discipline is rooted in the history of the Church. Although I do not embrace Foucault's philosophy as a universal explanatory theory, it provides a way to understand seminary life in its basic disciplinary elements, such as architecture and internal space, schedule of activities, surveillance of students, and regulation of bodily attitudes.[11] Discipline drove the mechanics of power, shaping individual behavior in the service of institutional goals: academic rigor, religious orthodoxy, compliance with celibacy, effective missionary action and moral leadership, obedience to the bishops and public authorities, and the preservation of the Church's male-controlled, monarchical structure. These goals formed part of a single package, a kind of religious Taylorism in which piety, celibacy, and moral norms were reinvented to make the Church more efficient. In the Church "discipline" became synonymous with the Tridentine seminary and Catholic tradition. Discipline was the millennial link between the distant Christian past and the modernizing present. For Brazil's bishops in the nineteenth and early twentieth centuries, it was the solution of the future.[12]

Clerical reform in Brazil amounted to a program of conservative modernization in which the Church sought institutional renewal, influence over its flock, and association with the state and networks of power. In the Second Empire (1840–1889) and First Republic (1880–1930) Brazil strengthened its ties to the international capitalist order, while its urban elite imported the fashions, customs, technology, and prejudices of Europe. Brazilians in the know wanted to look and act like Parisians. The coastal-oriented government in this period worked to consolidate its power vis-à-vis the backlands and the masses, whose lay-based Catholicism and resistance to oppression generated an alternative form of social organization and therefore a threat to the elite. In Rome the Church leadership felt increasingly besieged by the onslaught of modernization unleashed by the industrial revolution and the anti-clerical current of the French Revolution. Atheistic socialism and Communism represented another threat to the Church's traditional nucleus of power in Europe. The Vatican fought back by reasserting its authority, condemning both capitalism and Communism, and formulating a new Catholic social doctrine as the solution to the ills of modernization. Paradoxically, the Church sought to become modern by presenting itself as an alternative to the modern. This strategy included an effort to strengthen the Church's base overseas. Thus the Brazilian Catholic program of conservative modernization employed an international standard of seminary training determined by the Vatican and implemented through the importation of foreign priests. The Church also fortified European, clerically oriented religious devotions. Brazilian Catholicism thus underwent Romanization, or

Europeanization, a process that, like modernization, has lasted into the present. Like Brazil's elite, the clergy aped European ways. Romanization represented the second great wave of evangelization in Brazil. The institutional Church flourished, and, despite official separation of Church and state as decreed in 1890, attained a status as Brazil's quasi-official religion during the era of President Getúlio Vargas and post–World War II populism (1930–1964).

The Vincentian fathers epitomized the "grand discipline." Known in Brazil as Lazaristas, they built, standardized, and ran the country's most important seminaries in the so-called golden age—a feverish period of seminary construction starting in the 1840s and ending only on the eve of the momentous Second Vatican Council (Vatican II, 1962–1965). Chapter 3 features their extensive pastoral, organizational, and educational work.

Discipline went awry, however. This is the theme of chapter 4. By making discipline an end in itself, the Church diverted the clergy's energy from religious to institutional concerns. Tensions arose over celibacy, clerical nationalism, pedagogy, and other issues. The resultant institutional dysfunction hampered the clergy's ability to adapt to a rapidly changing society. Missionary activity faltered, and priests became more distant from the people. Like Karl Marx's description of capitalism's tendency to destroy its own successes to make way for new innovations, modernization created new levels of human achievement and increased demands on the individual, institutions, and society. In the case of the Brazilian Church conservative modernization failed to innovate beyond the implementation of discipline. Discipline instead became yet another layer of Catholic tradition. One crack in discipline harmed the Church: its failure to remove sexually abusive priests. The hierarchy's omission predated the infamous U.S. crisis by many decades and proved that problem priests were an international phenomenon.

The seminaries furnish an important case study of how cultural modernization proceeded in the Third World with the help of religion. In Brazil religion played a key role in the complex interplay of tradition and modernity, one of the central themes of twentieth-century Brazilian society. The seminaries stood at the nexus of religion, modernization, and state-building. The uneven development of religious modernization helps to explain other tensions in Brazil's overall modernization.

A new Catholic modernization after World War II spurred a movement in Brazil and Latin America for a Church based on the power of the laity and the struggle for social justice. Criticizing the military dictatorship, the Brazilian Church became the world's most radical branch of Catholicism. Liberation theology, the defense of human rights and democracy, and a critique of capitalism characterized the progressive wing of the Church in the 1970s and 1980s. Brazil gained international recognition for its leadership in theological and pastoral innovation.

Progressivism emerged as the Church's influence in the modern world diminished. Many pinpointed the difficulties in secularization. In Brazil the story was different. The Church's centuries-long religious monopoly began to erode in the face of industrialization and urbanization, but also a growing social and religious pluralism that was the by-product of a democratic political system as well as new social developments, including the mass media, consumer culture, and various new strains of Protestantism. As new groups emerged and as educational opportunities expanded, priests' leadership in politics, culture, and intellectual life decreased. Progressivism revealed innovation and vitality and, in the short run, breathed new life into the Church. But it also masked great insecurity. In the late 1960s the clergy plunged into a deep crisis of identity.

Acting as a modernizing vanguard, a large group of seminarians and priests pushed the Church leftward and rebelled against Tridentine discipline. In an effort to resolve their personal crises, they proposed a new model of the priest as social activist. Resistance to the military regime deeply affected this quest. Political opposition, the search for social justice, and the reform of ecclesiastical structures became intertwined. In the process the seminarians provided one of the first specific outlines for implementing the so-called preferential option for the poor, a new trademark of Latin American Catholicism. The redefinition of the vocation in the 1960s and 1970s reflected the Brazilian Church's attempt to renovate its social and religious mission.

There was no clear path for the seminarians. The challenge to discipline exacerbated the crisis of the clergy and produced widespread conflict, fear, and uncertainty for the Church everywhere. Here was another paradox of modernization. It fostered discipline but then critiqued it. As discipline dissolved, freedom to innovate expanded. All aspects of the priesthood came into question. Seminarians demanded a complete overhaul of the seminaries—and maybe even their destruction. This threatened the existence of the clergy and thus the very survival of the institutional Church. The Vatican and other sectors of the hierarchy at first stimulated, then quickly tried to control, and finally worked to stop much of the experimentation. The well-documented neoconservative reaction of the 1980s actually began in the 1960s. The crises of the clergy and the seminaries are examined in chapters 5, 6, and 7.

Seminarians saw discipline as an obstacle to becoming modern. While Church instructors still viewed the individual through the prism of neo-Thomistic philosophy and utilized a discipline developed in the sixteenth century, a rapidly industrializing Brazilian society was focusing increasingly on new forms of individuality. Seminarians no longer wanted to become the unique, Christ-like figures shaped in the seminaries. They wanted to be human. As a result, they advocated a more holistic approach in seminary training that included greater self-knowledge, individual fulfillment, and psychological well-being. This outlook provoked a revolutionary shift away from the traditional corporatist ideology of Catholicism. It also reflected the historical struggle within Catholicism between universality and particularity (including religious nationalism). New theology, student radicalism, and anti-regime protest captured the attention of this generation, but so did the idea of professionalism. The crisis of the clergy could be resolved by making the priesthood a more rewarding vocation. By taking the momentous step to work and live among the poor, seminarians broke through the impasse affecting both the institution and the individual. This theme is studied in both chapters 5 and 7. A model combining social justice and the modern shored up the declining status of the clergy. The option for the poor was political and religious, but also personal and occupational.

And it was romantic. The new Catholic modernity proposed in Latin America in the 1960s included powerful elements from the past. No matter how innovative seminarians' proposals might be, they were still working in a dense context of tradition. Seminarians endeavored to build a bridge between the demands of modern civilization and notions of community inherent in primitive Christianity.[13]

The personal side of the crisis involved the deepest needs of the clergy: sustenance, power, recognition, and sexual love, all of which governed the life of the Church as thoroughly and profoundly as they did any other human group. As Marc Bloch wrote, the historian has an obligation to explore such "secret needs of the heart."[14] The Church put men in seminaries to mold these impulses for institutional and spiritual goals. Successfully or not, Catholicism and especially its seminaries had always dealt in basic human psychology. In the 1960s seminarians and priests tried to break free of tradition in both an organizational and an emotional sense. Gripped by basic desires and fears, individual priests groped towards solutions to problems. It is a little studied fact, but not at all surprising, that the appeal of psychotherapy in the Catholic Church burgeoned at this time—precisely as the option for the poor emerged as the primary strategy of progressive Catholicism. Psychotherapy was a quintessentially modern approach. Chapter 6 discusses the rise of what I call "liberation psychology."[15]

My own psychotherapy proved to be an invaluable tool in exploring the primal motivations of priests. Traveling to Porto Alegre in August of 1989 to conduct research on the seminarians' movement and psychotherapy, I began reading *I'm OK, You're OK*, a best-selling book written in the 1960s to teach people how to conduct their own transactional analysis.[16] I was fascinated to learn that the book offered not only a handy way to manage emotional and social conflict but also reflections on the relationship between psychology and religion. Days later I began to interview a number of priests who had undergone psychoanalysis. I pored over the memoirs of Father Géza Kövecses, a masterful priest-psychoanalyst. While living with the Jesuits at the Colégio Anchieta, I became absorbed in a novel, partially autobiographical, written by a man who had left the order, married, and, in becoming a professional psychologist, continued to minister to the afflicted.[17] I became convinced of the transformative potential of psychotherapy. I contacted the Jesuit author, who put me in touch with a therapist who worked with a combination of techniques. Therapy clarified my deep feelings about Catholicism and the priesthood, to which I had aspired as a child. I arduously discovered that my research was a mere repetition of my childhood wish. Therapy enabled me to reconstruct more effectively the historical context of the psychoanalytic culture that emerged in Brazil in the 1960s just as the priesthood entered into crisis. As historian Peter Gay reports, psychoanalysis sharpens "sensitivity to the unconscious shared fantasies that underlie cultural styles, and to the potent, largely concealed currents of sexual and aggressive drives that give energy to action."[18] I now understood the social and religious pressures experienced by seminarians and priests. I also comprehended the tension between desire and vocation.

"I believe that . . . someone who is a writer is not simply doing his work in his books," Foucault stated shortly before his death, "but that his major work is, in the end, himself in the process of writing his books. . . . The historical-critical attitude must also be an experimental one."[19] One of Foucault's epistemological tools was the "limit-experience." In *The Passion of Michel Foucault* James Miller describes how the philosopher had a "personal fascination with experience." Foucault pushed "his mind and body to the breaking point, hazarding 'a sacrifice, an actual sacrifice of life,' as he put it in 1969, 'a voluntary obliteration that does not have to be represented in books because it takes place in the very existence of the writer.' "[20] Foucault, a gay man and sadomasochist, made sex his arena for extreme adventure. Employing the term "horizon experience,"

Garry Wills recalls how the French Jesuit Pierre Teilhard de Chardin served as stretcher-bearer in World War I in order "to conduct a laboratory test, as it were, in the crucible of his own body, on the concepts he had worked out in an abstract way."[21] Similarly, high-risk sports can bring a brush with death, as we know all too sadly from the case of Brazilians' beloved Ayrton Senna, the champion race driver killed in 1994. What else besides the vicarious thrill of danger can explain North Americans' fascination with football or hobbyists' love for guns and the history of warfare? I had a limit-experience flying to a clandestine gold mining camp's landing strip, a sliver of land carved into the Amazon rainforest. How many hubris-minded Western explorers, researchers, and missionaries have gone to the Third World with some sense of having a cultural limit-experience? But an academic or well-fed foreign tourist venturing into a favela is flirting with danger in a manner far different from the *favelado* who lives the far more daunting daily limit-experience of basic survival. Life-threatening illnesses are another form of limit-experience from which escape may be impossible, as Foucault, who died of AIDS, tragically learned. He was not unique — just privileged with greater intelligence and freedom in the exploration of human limits. His contribution was that he always strived to connect his experience "to a collective practice, to a manner of thinking." Foucault briefly tried psychoanalysis and employed Freudian ideas in much of his work. Going beyond Freud, Foucault posited that the dream was "the birth of the world," "the origin of existence itself." It was a key to the riddle of being. Psychoanalysis as limit-experience plunges the individual into the murky abyss of the subconscious, revealing the potential horror found in instinct and fantasy. As Foucault suggested, any of us could be mad if society chose to define us as such.[22]

The priesthood too is a limit-experience that sheds light on the human condition by revealing how discipline works in the extreme. In taking vows of poverty, obedience, and chastity, priests do what most humans avoid. They attempt to sublimate their desires in favor of the collective good of the Church and society. Free of family life, priests marry the Church. Historically they have strived to imitate Christ, who volunteered for the ultimate, Atlas-like limit-experience — crucifixion — in order to save humanity from sin and eternal death. The priest takes on the job of ultimate mediator, a "courier between the living and the dead."[23] In today's English vernacular, priests live on the emotional edge. They also seek the literal edges of society, aiding the sick and the downtrodden. In Brazil priests were tortured and murdered for their beliefs. Their imitation of Christ was revolutionary.

Many writers have pointed out that the Church changed Brazilian society. But society also changed the Church. I assess the meaning of the Catholic faith in Brazil by considering these reciprocal influences, which are clearly seen in the evolution of the seminaries' educational policies and in experiments such as those with psychotherapy. Our view is from inside the seminary looking out — and from the outside looking in.

Priests felt especially strong about celibacy. The Catholic ministry is a life-long commitment. Its most difficult requirement is the vow of chastity. Controversy over this directive preoccupied the Brazilian Church throughout its history. Brazil needed seminaries because its priests ignored celibacy. The Church attempted to prepare new generations of priests for celibate lives by isolating them from women (including female relatives) and other external stimuli considered dangerous. Some priests assumed celibacy as a personal commitment to the Church, but many saw it as an imposition of a system that exercised immense power over youths and children. After 1965 hundreds of priests quit the Church because they rejected obligatory celibacy.

Although some might categorize sexual matters as the history of private life, celibacy was at the center of a web connecting vocation, Church, and polity. It illustrated the tension between the priest's vocation and his humanity, between rationality and instinct. As the German Jesuit theologian Karl Rahner asserts, celibacy is so complex and central to life that it assumes dimensions as vast and mysterious as humankind and life itself.[24]

Sexual control exemplified sanctification: the elevation of the priest to a superior status by separating him from others and subjecting him to discipline. Celibacy reinforced isolation — literally, because the sexual act was forbidden, and symbolically, because the priest was a holy man, an *Alter Christus,* another Christ. Max Weber pointed out that in the West, where the Jesuits set the pattern, as well as in the East,

> the monastic procedural plan for attaining sanctification developed increasingly in the direction of rationalization. . . . Methodologies of sanctification developed a combined physical and psychic regime and an equally methodical regulation of the manner and scope of all thought and action, thus producing in the individual the most completely alert, voluntary, and anti-instinctual control over his own physical and psychological processes, and insuring the systematic regulation of life in subordination to the religious end.

As Weber further explained, the "relationship of religion to sexuality is extraordinarily intimate." Anti-erotic religions, including Catholicism, "represent substitute satisfactions of sexually conditioned psychological needs."[25] This phenomenon became especially evident among priests and nuns.

Two hostile attitudes toward sexuality stood out. According to Weber, the first was the conception of mystical flight from the world, which interpreted sexual abstinence as the central and indispensable instrument of the mystical quest for salvation through contemplative withdrawal from the world. From this view, sexuality, the drive that most firmly binds man to the animal level, furnishes the most powerful temptations to withdrawal from the mystical quest. The other basic position was that of asceticism. Rational ascetic alertness, self-control, and methodical planning of life are seriously threatened by the peculiar irrationality of the sexual act, which is ultimately and uniquely unsusceptible to rational organization.[26] Weber noted how the harsh restrictions on sexuality actually increased its social value. He affirmed that the

> preaching of Jesus, with its demand of absolute and indissoluble monogamy, went beyond all other religions in the limitations imposed upon permissible and legitimate sexuality. . . . At the level of the peasant, the sexual act is an everyday occurrence; primitive people do not regard this act as containing anything unusual, and they may indeed enact it before the eyes of onlooking travelers without the slightest feeling of shame. They do not regard this act as having any significance beyond the routine of living. The decisive development . . . is the sublimation of sexual expression into an eroticism that becomes the basis of idiosyncratic sensations and generates its own unique values of an extraordinary kind.[27]

Although Brazil's seminaries rationalized the training of priests, they did not fully contain or divert sexuality. The Church battled not only human instinct, but also the Brazilian cultural milieu, which led European priests to observe that Brazilian men were incapable of living celibately. Noncompliance undermined authority and the institution's social and political objectives. Priests lived the tensions of celibacy inwardly, but historically they also sparked social conflicts in the seminaries and in the community. It was more than just coincidence that celibacy became controversial during moments of difficult political transition. The history of the Brazilian clergy demonstrated repeatedly that celibacy was fundamentally a political question.

Women and concepts of femininity inevitably played important parts in the history of celibacy. In the colonial era the lack of clerical discipline facilitated contact with the opposite sex. The seminaries partially reversed this trend, making illicit contact with women publicly unacceptable. Women were portrayed as protectresses or temptresses. Seminarians cultivated devotion to Mary, the Mother of Jesus—pure, lovely, but unattainable. During the anti-Tridentine revolt priests and seminarians questioned celibacy, rediscovered real women, and witnessed a partial breakdown in the male monopoly on Church power— although women still could not be ordained or occupy positions in the hierarchy. Nuns from traditionally cloistered religious orders took a greater role in missionary work and even started teaching in the seminaries. For the first time women gained at least a modicum of recognition for their prominence in the Church. Catholic culture was changing.

The tensions described here—between other-worldly orientation and humanness, between rationality and instinct, between commitment to vocation and sexuality, and between the masculine and the feminine—stirred much conflict in Brazil's seminaries and became generalized among the clergy and the hierarchy in the period after World War II. Tensions also appeared in the dichotomies of contemplation versus action, institution versus mission, legalism versus pastoral practice, tradition versus modernity, and conservatism versus progressivism.

Additional conflict arose from the clergy's dual allegiances. The Church was a unique institution—perhaps the first multinational, multicultural organization in history. On the one hand, many of the clergy were native-born patriots. On the other hand, these men expressed loyalty to a foreign entity (the Vatican) and its leader, the pope. (Institutions such as the armed forces also absorbed foreign influences but had only Brazilians in their ranks.) Tridentine discipline enhanced a certain cultural dualism. Boys entered the seminary as Brazilians and left with a heavy grafting of European ideas and manners. Europeanization aided sanctification but also created cultural distance between the clergy and the people. Cultural frictions were exacerbated by the continual arrival of foreign priests to alleviate a shortage in vocations caused in part by Rome's demand for (European) cultural uniformity. Priests embraced nationalism and the faith. This phenomenon is crucial for understanding both the Church's millennial desire for unity and the nationalism of the Progressive Church.

Given Catholicism's multinational character, was there anything unique about the Brazilian Church's political transformation? After all, the Church was the quintessential borrower of personnel and ideas from the mother continent, taking cues from such European innovations as Catholic Action, the worker-priests, and humanistic theology. The flow of people and ideas to Brazil in the second half of the twentieth century constituted a third wave of evangelization in which the clergy once again acted as agents of modernization. Was progressive Catholicism just another colonial project—this time from the left instead of the right? Did allegiance to Rome ultimately cause nationalism to fizzle? These questions concern not only religion. They go to the heart of identity, which, in the complex multiethnic history of Latin America, is one of the central quandaries of everyday life.

The Brazilian Church did indeed make unique contributions by engaging in the Brazilian tradition of cultural anthropophagy: devouring European culture, assimilating its positive traits, rejecting the negative ones, and creating an original ecclesial culture.[28] The native and foreign elements of Brazilian Catholicism are inseparable. To be a Brazilian Catholic—or any Brazilian—is to partake of a complex cultural tradition involving Native, African, Euro-Western, and other influences. Progressive Catholic writers frequently cite poverty as the key historical and cultural context of their movement. Yet it is hard to see poverty as unique for the region or historical period. More important was the distance of Brazil and other Third World churches from the locus of European Church power. Because it did not play a major role in international Church politics, Brazil was a convenient proving ground for certain experiments. Innovation could fly loose—at least for a while. This was Brazil's greatest contribution. As Sydney Mintz has drawn the powerful conclusion that the industrial revolution began not in England but in the sugarcane processing plants of colonial Latin America,[29] so we can affirm that significant changes in world Catholicism developed not in Europe but in Brazil and other outposts of the neocolonial periphery. (Similarly, while working in China in an exile forced by the Jesuits, Father Chardin developed ideas that would shake the foundations of Catholicism.[30]) Moreover, cultural, intellectual, and political sharing flowed both ways. In some instances the intended transformers of Latin American religious culture became the transformed because of their profound experiences in the region.[31] And no matter how foreign the models, priests employed great creativity in adapting them to the local context.[32]

chapter two

To Be a Priest in Brazil

Since the 1960s numerous controversies have erupted in Brazil over the conduct of priests, signaling deep change in the Church. Priests have been praised
or castigated for defending the indigenous population, raising the political
consciousness of the poor, criticizing the military dictatorship, relying on the
European Church for personnel and resources, incorporating Afro-Brazilian
rituals into the Mass, and opposing celibacy. But these types of conflicts had
precedents in the period from 1500 to 1840. In analyzing the key institutive
trends and tensions of the distant past, this chapter contextualizes the recent
history of the priesthood and seminary training.

The Church itself carefully examines its past to define its current-day objectives. The appeal to a utopian myth is seen as purifying the Church of imper-
fection and breathing new spiritual life into its mission.[1] A prime example
of historical soul-searching took place at the Fourth General Assembly of the
Conference of Latin American Bishops in 1992 in Santo Domingo, Dominican
Republic, where the hierarchy debated a "new evangelization" of Latin America
in light of the achievements and atrocities of the colonial era.[2] In 2000 the
Brazilian Church reflected again on its past as clergymen protested traditional
historical interpretations of the country's quincentennial celebration. One pro-
Native bishop was jailed during a violent confrontation between protesting
Amerindians and the police. Shortly after the commemorations the CNBB (Na-
tional Conference of the Bishops of Brazil) met at Porto Seguro, Bahia, the scene
of Portuguese explorer Pedro Álvares Cabral's landing on April 22, 1500, and of
Brazil's first Catholic Mass. The bishops asked forgiveness for the missionaries'

role in the destruction of Native culture and voiced support for human rights and social justice.[3]

Our period can be divided into two parts. They differ from the standard split in Brazilian history marked by the transition from colony to independent empire in 1822.[4] The time frames used here more accurately describe the transformation of Brazilian religious and ecclesiastical history. The first, from 1549 to 1759, is known as Colonial Brazilian Christendom. During this era the religious orders dominated the Brazilian Church. It began with the arrival of the Society of Jesus, the Jesuits, and ended with their expulsion by the Portuguese crown. Dominican, Franciscan, and Benedictine fathers also established a firm foothold in Brazil. The regular clergy participated in the conquest and consolidation of the colony. Rigorously trained, the orders, especially the Jesuits, wrote the history of the colonial Church. The diocesan fathers, though more important than portrayed in many historical works, remained largely obscure, their biographies restricted to little "beyond a simple tombstone or perhaps scanty references," as one Brazilian priest-historian wrote.[5] One of the central goals of this book is to correct this lopsided view. The second part of our period, the Crisis of Brazilian Christendom, ran from 1759 to 1840 and was characterized by the rise of the secular fathers. As Brazil became an independent parliamentary monarchy in 1822, the diocesan clergy gave the priesthood a new, profoundly political stamp. They helped establish Brazil as a modern nation-state.

Our Father, Who Art in This Colony

The religious conquest of Brazil and the Americas became a major chapter in the history of Catholicism. The golden age of missionary work in the Western Hemisphere and Asia in the second half of the sixteenth century transformed the Church into a worldwide religion.[6]

The Church legitimized the colonial endeavor in Brazil by stamping Christian names on the territory. Brazil was first known as the Land of the True Cross, the symbol of both faith and military conquest emblazoned on the sails of Portuguese ships.[7] Tomé de Sousa, the first governor of Brazil, arrived in Salvador (the Savior), Bahia, with Father Manuel de Nóbrega and five others Jesuits in 1549. They sailed into the Bahia de Todos os Santos, All Saints' Bay, named after an important Catholic holy day. In 1554 the Jesuits founded the settlement of São Paulo (Saint Paul), today Brazil's largest city. Brazil abounds in such names.

The conquest took clerics into all spheres of Brazilian colonial life, lending an aura of omnipresence to the priesthood that reflected the situation in Portugal, in historian C. R. Boxer's estimation "probably the most priest-ridden country in Christendom, and only exceeded elsewhere in this respect by Tibet."[8] In the eighteenth century Portugal had as many as two hundred thousand clergymen and 538 ecclesiastical dwellings![9] Joining the Jesuits became fashionable among elite Portuguese men. In the early years of the order Portugal had its largest and fastest growing contingent.[10] In Brazil they were a versatile lot; among other occupations, Jesuits worked as physicians, botanists, soldiers, engineers, sailors, and statesmen. They wrote poetry too.[11] The clergy shared the lives of the Natives and the colonists. Jesuit missionary father José de Anchieta prepared his grammar lessons while lying in a hammock, that quintessentially American implement, and gathered his own firewood for the small house where he slept, ate, and taught. He also ministered to the Portuguese troops who fought bloody battles against French interlopers.[12] The clergy rapidly reconnoitered the vast expanse of Brazil, prompting the Natives to give one Jesuit the name of "Abaré bebé," "the priest that flies."[13] The ability of the Jesuits and other clerics to communicate with the diverse Amerindian groups through the creation of a *língua geral,* or lingua franca, helped the Portuguese to consolidate their grip on Brazil and to build its economic foundations. The Jesuits, stated the Brazilian historian João Capistrano de Abreu, "founded American linguistics." It is presumptuous, he added, to attempt to write the history of Brazil without including their critical contribution.[14]

Primary documents and the historiography of the colonial era make little mention of the secular clergy. Much of our knowledge comes from the Jesuit chroniclers, who usually denigrated their diocesan brethren. But the seculars were very active throughout the colony. Explorers, colonists, slaves, and others sailed to Brazil in the company of *capelães de bordo,* or sea chaplains, who celebrated Mass and performed general religious duties.[15] Priests worked in the *feitorias,* the militarized trading outposts set up along the Brazilian coast. Because the main requirement for entering the colony was a profession of the Christian faith, fathers boarded arriving ships to verify the religious beliefs of new colonists.[16] Other chaplains, usually secular priests, served as the everyday clergy in Brazil. They accompanied the rugged *bandeirantes,* or pathfinders, on expeditions into the interior.[17] As one priest-historian put it, the regular fathers implanted the faith, and the seculars maintained it.[18] The regular clergy controlled the missions established for the Amerindian population and the schools built in the cities for the children of the elite. The secular priests were charged with performing such rituals and obligations as Masses, baptisms, confessions, marriages, and funerals and seeing to the moral education of families. The secular priests taught catechism (in Latin, as opposed to the *língua geral*) and collected the royal tithe.[19]

The diocesan priests worked among the Natives and set up parishes in the royal captaincies, the colonial territories that preceded the establishment of the viceroyalty in 1549. Sponsored by the crown, the first parishes emerged in colonial villages and at military forts and sugar mills. Bishops set up their own parishes independent of the state. In these early religious communities the secular priests represented authority and commanded the people's respect. By the start of the eighteenth century, parishes had spread across the colony. Within the ranks of the seculars a hierarchy of so-called high clergy and low clergy developed based on ecclesiastical position, pay scales, and geography, with urban areas receiving preference.[20]

The canonical, sacramental view of the parish offered by traditional Church historians gives only a partial view of secular priests.[21] An alternative explanation of the parish deemphasizes its idealized religious purpose and places it in the context of the overall colonial project. In this sense the parish was "an advance post of a centralizing system, a system that seeks to extend its action as far as possible." As an arm of the Church and the crown, the parish developed alongside popular Catholicism, which revolved around hermits and *irmandades* (lay brotherhoods and sororities). Many priests ventured outside the parish structure to minister to these organizations, the *bandeirantes,* and the *engenhos,* or sugar plantations. Brazilian secular priests differed from the parish-bound *curas* of Spanish America, where the ecclesiastical hierarchy and structures were more carefully defined. The Brazilians belonged to a rural, family-oriented culture in which they acted as chaplains, *padres-mestres* (teachers), uncles, and godfathers. Many seculars viewed the priesthood as primarily a career. It was a refuge for intellectuals and a chance to become involved in public affairs. The seculars worked under the *padroado* (the system of royal patronage of the Church) as public employees and sought supplemental work to raise their standard of living.[22]

Priests' vast experience and knowledge gave them the capacity to shape events. Only the state and the elite could counter their power. At the same time they became ingrained in the structures of power. At the local level priests participated in the *cabido,* the diocesan governing body. Largely ceremonial, at times it could act as a check on the bishop, who was always carefully chosen by the crown. The members of the *cabido* earned great respect in the community. They served as witnesses to wills and important transactions and at times intervened in community affairs.[23] Under the *padroado* they became part of the state bureaucracy. Distance from Rome further encouraged the absorption of ecclesiastics into the state. Privy to the lives of the colonial elite, the clergy extended their influence to the highest levels of government. For example, the Jesuit missionary António Vieira became the chaplain and preacher to King John IV. Viera acted as the king's éminence grise, particularly on questions related to Brazil. He served in diplomatic missions to France, Holland, and Italy. Vieira was the most popular preacher in Brazil and Portugal in an age when sermons dominated public opinion.[24]

As colonists priests built a new civilization. They exercised great cultural influence through their monopoly in elite education. To this day Jesuit pedagogy serves as a major framework for Brazilian education.[25] The clergy worked to reproduce a system of ethics, family structure, marriage, sexuality, and other fundamental aspects of Western Christian civilization.[26]

Priests regulated customs and exerted a sort of moral police power. They could excommunicate and therefore ostracize individuals. Bishops could prohibit or censor books and theatrical productions.[27] Unlike their colleagues in Spanish America, priests in Brazil did not describe their surroundings as a new Garden of Eden. Brazil, whose name signified a red-hot ember, was an inferno populated with brutish, naked, cannibalistic, devilish Natives. The fathers, especially the Jesuits, imposed the Christian code on the indigenous peoples, forcing many to marry in the Church. Portuguese settlers who adopted the Brazilindians' errant ways were reprimanded. The crown made moral enforcement difficult, however, because of its desire to populate the colony at almost any cost, deporting to Brazil criminals, rapists, adulterers, priests' lovers, and other immoral individuals. Sin thrived everywhere, and everybody required punishment.[28]

But the conquest was often a bloody affair. In 1552 Brazil acquired its first bishop, Dom Pedro Fernandes Sardinha, whose seat was Bahia. Foreshadowing the complex and tumultuous relationship between Brazilian Catholicism and other beliefs, Dom Sardinha ingloriously fell victim to cannibals. Several Jesuits were also devoured.

Evangelization, the basic religious task of the priest, often led to the violent subjugation of the Amerindian population, the African slaves, and the masses of mixed-blood descendants. As Jean Delumeau has observed, Catholicism's expansion took place in a climate of fear about the end of the world. Missionaries rushed to convert as many people as possible with little attention to quality of teaching.[29] Conversion was driven by the tradition of Portuguese "warrior Catholicism," which had developed during the Crusades and intensified during the battles to rid the Iberian peninsula of the Arabs. The Arabs provided the Portuguese with the concept of holy war. Religious conquest fed on the zeal of the Counter-Reformation, the Inquisition, anti-Semitism, and an obsession with racial purity. Brazilian Catholicism evolved into a play on the fears of the people. In the words of Father Anchieta, for the unconverted "there is no better sermon than the sword and the iron rod." Priests were divine soldiers offering a choice between baptism and death. Colonization was a "sacred enterprise" with a unity of religious and political interests.[30]

The Church proceeded with the full backing of the state. This situation contrasted sharply with the United States, where the Pilgrims established an autonomous society after fleeing from state repression. And it came with a price. In Brazil Church-state relations were codified in the *padroado*. The *padroado* made evangelization official state business and therefore a form of domination that frequently overrode Christian ideals.[31] The *padroado* ostensibly offered privileges to the Church, but in reality it allowed a jealous state to guard its power. The pope had granted the Portuguese crown control over spiritual matters because of its success in expelling the Moors and converting new areas of the world. Paradoxically, while Portugal was one of the few countries to accept all of the provisions of the Counter-Reformation as dictated by the Council of Trent, its highly centralized state used the *padroado* to intervene frequently in the ecclesiastical realm. The king nominated bishops and even parish priests and chaplains. He could censor papal bulls, documents, and letters, which first passed through Lisbon on their way from Rome to the colony. The monarchy collected and managed the ecclesiastical *dízimos,* or tithes. Ecclesiastical administration became part of the royal bureaucracy, thus giving Portugal's rulers the ability to curtail the growth of the Church in Brazil. Early Brazil had only one diocese, Bahia. As late as 1750 the vast colony had only eight. Throughout the colonial era the crown allocated little money for seminaries.[32] The *padroado* guaranteed Catholicism's religious monopoly. Yet it restricted the institutional Church's growth and held Brazilians' contact with the Holy See to a minimum.

The difficulty of implanting a clergy in Brazil was complicated by the Church's attempt to end the long crisis of the European clergy, in decay since the Middle Ages and considered incompetent. European priests received little institutional training and practically no spiritual teaching. As a remedy the Council of Trent redefined ordination as a sacrament and created the institution of episcopal seminaries for educating diocesan priests.[33]

Trent definitively established the seminary in Catholicism. Only three centuries after the birth of Christianity bishops such as Saint Augustine began to organize communities of priests in training. From the sixth century until the Counter-Reformation most clerics were taught in the monasteries of religious orders, so-called cathedral schools, and universities. In stark contrast with the modern-day system, no central control existed over these institutions. Spiritual preparation was often lacking, especially in the universities. The decline of the clergy and Martin Luther's Reformation prodded the hesitant bishops of Trent to implement reform, with legislation on seminaries finally adopted only at the end of the council. This decree turned out to be Trent's most important step. But it was a mainly conservative measure that sought to prevent "the ordination of the unsuitable rather than providing suitable training." The Tridentine dicta concentrated on the administration of the seminary at the expense of pedagogy and intellectual training.

During the deliberations at Trent the Jesuits immediately recognized the need for clerical reform and opened two colleges in Rome, one for German seminarians and another for a more general ecclesiastical body. Within fifteen years the second college had nearly one thousand students. From then on the Jesuits would exert great influence in seminary training.[34]

After Trent each diocese was to have its own seminary, preferably located close to the local cathedral, thus facilitating supervision. Students were to be isolated from the outside world at an early age.[35] The council fathers put it simply: "If they are not well educated, young people are all too easily led astray by the pleasures of the world. Thus unless they are formed in piety and religion at the tenderest age, before vicious habits have entirely taken hold of them, it is impossible for them to persevere perfectly in ecclesiastical discipline without the special and powerful protection of almighty God."[36] Despite isolation, the fathers of Trent intended to keep the first seminaries close to the local community. As Celito Moro points out, people infrequently used the word "seminary" at the start of the Tridentine era. More often they spoke of the "collegium," a school.[37] As Catholicism's battle lines with the modern world became clearer, the seminary distanced itself further and further from daily life. In Spain, Italy, and other areas of Europe numerous seminaries opened shortly after the council and contributed decisively to the intellectual improvement of the clergy.[38]

In Brazil the Church only haphazardly implemented the Tridentine norms and failed to open seminaries. Brazil's enormity, the Church's fragility, the long absences of bishops, the crown's indifference to its financial obligations under the *padroado,* and the generally low level of education in the colony all undermined efforts at reform. Most of the burden of seminary training fell on the Jesuits, who educated their own as well as diocesan candidates to the priesthood in the order's private *colégios* in Bahia, Rio de Janeiro, Olinda, and other large towns. *Colégios* primarily taught lay pupils. In the eighteenth century the Jesuit Father Gabriel Malagrida opened several diocesan seminaries, but they closed after the order's expulsion from the colony. A mystic who clashed with the Enlightenment worldview of the influential Sebastião José de Carvalho, the future Marquis of Pombal, Malagrida became the last person to die in the flames of the Portuguese Inquisition.[39] The quality of ecclesiastical training remained terribly low until the installation of the Tridentine seminaries in the mid-1800s.

The weakness of the institutional Church also negatively affected the quantity and quality of the native clergy. But this did not make the clergy insignificant. It simply gave them a great deal of freedom from the hierarchy, which had little success in stopping clerical extravagances and promoting discipline. In fact, it opened the door to the clergy's wide involvement in social life. The clergy and the laity were left to practice the faith with little supervision. This independence helped make Brazilian Catholicism unique.

In the absence of a plentiful, well-trained clergy, religious practice among the laity acquired distinct, unorthodox shades. European Catholicism was clerical, emphasizing the priest's administration of the sacraments to a passive laity. During the Counter-Reformation (and the so-called Catholic Reformation) attempts by the European clergy to control popular piety led to confrontation with the laity.[40] In Brazil Catholicism took on a particular lay flavoring. Devotions, and not the sacraments, became the center of religious life: pilgrimages, processions, feasts, and the cult of the saints, including *promessas* and *ex-votos* (respectively the promises and objects offered to a saint in return for a favor).[41] The laity was especially active in the *irmandades.* But Brazil also had its share of conflict between the laity and the clergy. This fundamental tension became one of the underlying themes in the history of the Brazilian Church.[42]

The Church provided the main arena for social life. The Mass, processions, and other activities that took place in and around churches created opportunities for leisure, public recognition, and a modicum of freedom from the pall of slavery. So did the fraternities. The *irmandades* founded and ran the Santas Casas de Misericórdia (hospitals) and were associated with the so-called Third

Orders. Involving the profession of a vow and the payment of dues, membership in these orders brought prestige, a sense of community, and civic pride. Many members came from prominent families. While the Third Orders stressed racial purity, other *irmandades* catered solely to people of African descent, for example, the Brotherhood of Our Lady of the Rosary in Salvador. Friars from the First Orders, such as the Franciscans or Carmelites, could also participate in the Third Orders. Chaplains implemented the *irmandades'* policies, and the brotherhoods depended on priests for Masses and funeral services. Disputes often arose over fees and questions of jurisdiction, however.[43] Highly organized, the Third Orders engaged in philanthropy, guaranteed their members a Christian burial, and executed wills. Their religious festivities provided both entertainment and an opportunity to express the faith. During Holy Week, the commemoration of the order's patron saint, and other occasions the orders spent lavishly on floats and luxurious fabrics. The *irmandades'* religious *festas,* or festivals, were high points in Brazilian social life. These extremely baroque celebrations expressed the playful side of religion while reinforcing beliefs and piety, social hierarchy, and the intimate relationship between Church and state. Their carnival-like atmosphere served to defuse ethnic and class tensions.[44]

Brazilian popular religion was imbued with Messianism and millenarianism. Like warrior Catholicism, these dual phenomena were deeply set in the Islamic and Judeo-Christian traditions.[45] Settlers and especially priests carried these beliefs to Brazil. Messianism embodied the people's expectations of a coming savior who would establish paradise. Father Anchieta, revered for his miraculous conversions, cures, and visions in the second half of the sixteenth century, helped implant the Messianic tradition with his sermons, poems, plays, letters, and catechistic texts. In Brazil it came to involve a number of lay religious activities. For example, in the early colonial era, when the absence of shrines and village community life led to a focus on the family as a center for devotion to the saints, believers engaged in penitential rites, including self-flagellation and processions led by missionaries. After the death of the young King Sebastian in battle against the Moors in 1578, he became the awaited Messiah who would return from the dead to redeem Brazil.[46]

Messianism prepared the way for the rise of clerical nationalism. Father Vieira personified this development. In the 1660s he was imprisoned by the Holy Inquisition for pinpointing Brazil and in particular its Natives as the central point of biblical prophecies to be revealed to the world by the Portuguese. In his writings Vieira laid claim to the religious autonomy of the New World in relation to the metropolis. In his view it was Brazil and other branches of the Portuguese empire that supported the metropolis with their riches, and not vice versa. The ecclesiastical authorities were alarmed at Vieira's notion that the hierarchy was unnecessary for the realization of the imperial enterprise and its prophetic ramifications. Heavily influenced by missionary work among the Indians in the backlands of Maranhão, Vieira asserted that lived experience was more valuable than theological scholarship to understanding the mission of the Church. He praised the example of a humble cobbler, whose prophecies served as the basis for Vieira's own predictions about the empire. Vieira's ideas placed in doubt the political and religious authority of the Inquisition and of the entire Church. The belief that God directly revealed his intentions to ordinary people or through Brazilian Natives smacked of Protestantism. In 1667 the Inquisition ordered Vieira confined to Portugal, but Pope Clement X later granted him immunity. Returning to Brazil in 1681, he continued to produce provocative writings and sermons and worked to protect the Natives from the settlers.[47] Father Vieira was not alone in identifying Brazil's unique role in salvation. In 1744 Pedro Rattes Henequim, a former settler in Minas Gerais, was burned at the stake by order of the Inquisition in Lisbon for asserting that Brazil was the site of the original paradise.[48] Conflict with the hierarchy over an indigenous, Messianic theological proposition was to become a pattern in the Brazilian Church, particularly after the start of Romanization in the nineteenth century.

Nationalistic feelings had another cause. Portuguese skepticism about the abilities of clergymen born outside the homeland fanned the flames of resentment in the colonies.[49] As we will see below, ethnic impurity damaged one's chances of becoming a priest.

Priests, Plantations, and Slavery

Material life stood paramount in the history of the Catholic clergy. As Weber affirmed, economics figured in the very nature of the priesthood.[50] In colonial Brazil priests exercised considerable economic power. In fact, some priests went to Brazil simply to make a big profit and return quickly to Portugal.[51] These men differed little from the many colonists who dreamed of finding gold in the Americas as a basis for attaining noble status in Iberia.

Orders and individual priests cast their lot in a wide variety of enterprises. As usual, the Jesuits set the example. They constructed a vast network of sugar plantations, cattle and horse ranches, truck farms, brickworks, schools, seminaries, churches, religious retreats, and other facilities. Sugar mills were a major source of income. The Jesuits became the colony's largest landowner and the biggest holder of slaves in all of the Americas. The fathers' annual flotillas of canoes carried large supplies of spices and other products down the Amazon River basin to the Atlantic port of Belém. The Jesuits built their own ships and private ports to transport exports more economically. To deal in these goods they obtained royal licenses. The famed brazilwood, valuable as a source of dye, was one of their exports. The crown also granted the Society of Jesus large urban properties and exemption from all customs duties.[52] Commenting on the Jesuits' economic power, Capistrano de Abreu observed that the order's missions became not only "states within a state, but churches within a church," over which even the bishops had little control.[53] This was the golden age of the religious orders. From the mid-sixteenth to the mid-seventeenth century the Jesuit ranks grew from one thousand to fifteen thousand worldwide. They administered hundreds of residences and private schools.[54] In Brazil their success stirred the envy of the colonists and ultimately led to their expulsion.

Other orders and Catholic institutions participated as the money-lenders of the colony, which had no banks until 1808. In 1660, for example, one sixth of Benedictine income was from loan interest payments.[55] In the late colonial and imperial eras secular priests speculated in land, cultivated sugar and tobacco, sold goods, rented out slaves, and invested in shipping ventures. Of 190 secular priests in the diocese of Mariana in 1860, twenty-nine owned ranches.[56] Like the colonists, priests used slaves or others to perform manual labor.

In the eighteenth century priests and friars rushed to Minas Gerais to search for gold. The governors of Rio de Janeiro and Bahia complained constantly about the interference of friars and "bad clergymen" in the mining areas. Using their clerical immunity, which allowed them to avoid search at checkpoints, these ecclesiastics defrauded the royal fifths (a gold tax) and took part in the contraband trade on a massive scale. A favorite method was to hide gold dust in the hollow interior of the wooden image of a saint, the *santo de pau oco*. In 1711 the crown took the unprecedented measure of barring all religious orders from the mining region. In 1753 the bishop of Mariana asked the crown for permission to have four Jesuit fathers join another comrade as teachers in the diocesan seminary, but an official advised against the move in a letter to the king: "Between the evils of keeping the sons of Minas less educated than those of other captaincies, and permitting Religious Orders or colleges here, the first evil seems to me the lesser of the two." The crown granted the bishop's request but reversed itself a few years later under Pombal's anti-Church policies and for fear of losing more of the royal fifths. Gold fever among priests struck again during the big rush in Cuiabá.[57]

For the Brazilian clergy, faith and sugar were inseparable. Sugar and slavery formed the basis of the Brazilian colonial economy and gave rise to the paternalistic social relations that characterized Brazilian familial, social, and political life into the twentieth century. Many priests took up residence on the plantations under the patronage of *senhores de engenho,* the powerful sugar barons of the coastal region. Priests and religious orders became planters.

The life of priests on the *engenhos* revealed the economic dimensions of the ecclesiastical career. Priests moved to the forefront of sugar production and controlled some of the largest properties, such as the Jesuits' Engenho Sergipe do Conde, the "Queen of the Recôncavo" (the fertile area around Salvador) in the seventeenth century. The plantations supported the orders and their religious and educational activities. Ecclesiastical authorities as far away as Lisbon kept watch over *engenho* management and sometimes intervened in local disputes.[58]

Priests, usually secular chaplains, held great importance in the domain of the lay *senhores de engenho.* They sanctified the plantation. At the start of the harvest the parish priest or resident chaplain gave a blessing. Priests pressed the *senhores* to allow the baptism and religious indoctrination of the slaves, and they worked to overcome resistance to marriage. Slaveholders opposed the sacrament because it reduced the mobility and salability of their property. Africans rejected it as alien to their culture.

Interlocking relationships between priests and *senhores* strengthened the Church's social position but also increased its dependence on the plantation system. In Salvador sons of *engenho* owners attended the Jesuit college, where they studied theology, Latin, and other subjects. In the eighteenth century some priests worked as private tutors to *senhores'* children and oversaw the plantations' moral and spiritual life. A number of clerics supplemented their income by growing sugarcane or working as *engenho* administrators. Some *senhores de engenho* established benefices on their property in order to support the construction of a chapel, the celebration of Masses, or the establishment of a trust fund for clergymen. Planters' sons and relatives became priests, and clerics inherited cane farms. Because of the Bahia diocese's floundering endowment, ecclesiastics without family ties to sugar still relied on the *senhores* for financial help.

Working to exhaustion, African slaves cut, milled, and processed sugarcane with the holy approval of the priests. Although Church-owned plantations relied fully on slave labor, in both a moral and a business sense they tended to be more progressive than lay-owned *engenhos*.[59] Nevertheless, as one Jesuit father commented, "It is very difficult to deal with slaves with the piety necessary for a cleric." A few priests decried slavery, but the Jesuits and many other priests basically bought, sold, and worked the Africans just as any colonial planter did. The Jesuits actually encouraged the bondage of Africans and took part in the trans-Atlantic trade. Father Viera likened the predicament of slaves to the sufferings of the crucified Christ, to whom blacks should look for comfort.[60] In the nineteenth century religious orders classified their slaves as *bens eclesiásticos* (ecclesiastical property) and listed them in account books along with transactions in meat, fish, soap, manioc flour, horses, and oxen.[61] Diocesan fathers also depended heavily on slave labor. In the colonial era and the nineteenth century secular priests in the towns kept slaves as butlers, cooks, and servants and in the countryside put them to work in agriculture. In one group of sixty-nine diocesan priests in Bahia, fifty had slaves.[62]

As C. R. Boxer asks, why did the Jesuits champion the freedom of the Indians while encouraging the trade in blacks? Why did any priest at all own slaves, especially after papal pronouncements in 1639 and 1740 condemned the practice? Jesuit apologists attempt to justify the actions of their predecessors by noting that while Amerindians were born free, civil and canon law condoned the enslavement of Africans. The apologists have classified criticism of Jesuit slave-holding as a "modern mental anachronism."[63] After all, as one contemporary Jesuit writer asserts, the fathers sought to bring their slaves closer to God and to improve their lives in a model educational and social system, a "paradise of the slaves."[64] But moral indignation appeared long ago. It is hard to ignore the dissidents, including Jesuits, who spoke out against slavery.[65] Like the Natives, the Africans did not want to be slaves. Priests took slaves because, like the settlers, they participated in the colonial enterprise, needed labor, and failed to develop economic models in line with Christian ideals. Although European priests in earlier periods supported themselves and even begged to survive, the Iberian ideal of the American colonial era exempted priests from manual labor.[66]

"Whiteness of Skin and Purity of Soul"

Oppression of the Natives and Africans left haunting consequences for the priesthood. To be a priest in Brazil was not to be an indigenous or black man. To be a priest was to be white or to whiten oneself enough culturally in order to pass through the seminary doors. In a country with a large black and mulatto population and a perennial shortage of priests, the meager Afro-Brazilian contingent of clergymen is shocking. On one level, the Church faced enormous staffing demands. The Jesuit order needed not only evangelists, but teachers, confessors, administrators, and a whole host of personnel to perform the manual labor that made the religious enterprise possible.[67] But on another level the Church's broad participation in slavocracy and the development of racist attitudes not only blocked nonwhites from the priesthood, but produced an ecclesial culture that made vocations utterly unattractive to such individuals.

The roots of this shortage lay in what Dauril Alden describes as the "pertinacity of Eurocentrism." Creoles and even Portuguese fathers who had served long terms abroad lost prestige in the eyes of their European brothers. The Jesuits were notorious for their condescension toward the local clergy. European fathers thought Brazilians could not maintain a celibate life. In their opinion, a tropical climate made Brazilian clerics physically and mentally inferior. Lack of religious, ethnic, and phenotypic purity excluded such men from the priesthood. Brazilians consumed second-rate milk from the breasts of black and mulatto women, received inadequate discipline from parents, and were polluted with the blood of Africans and Amerindians. European Jesuits often came from the nobility; in Brazil, from the commoners. Among the Jesuits Brazilian-born members always remained a minority. The Jesuits at times relegated second-tier European recruits to the colonies, and non-European candidates faced more stringent standards for entrance to the order. New Christians (recently converted Jews) were also ineligible, according to a Jesuit decree of 1593. Other factors behind the shortage of Jesuits in Brazil included lack of sufficient financial resources, the issue of quality versus quantity of priests, political concerns, and the interference of the crown in Church affairs, for example, the barring by King Pedro II (1692) of foreign Jesuits from any administrative position in Brazil.[68] Another barrier to ordination came from defects in character inherited from socially inferior—and therefore immoral—parents.[69] Brazil also lacked nuns. Salvador did not have a convent until 1677, and only in 1749 did one open in Rio de Janeiro. The crown wanted to populate Brazil with white, marriageable women.[70]

Priests committed ethnocide by straightjacketing and even destroying Native culture.[71] From the start they tried to undercut the authority of indigenous religious beliefs. They misunderstood the Natives and demonized their customs, using, for example, theatrical presentations in which Natives appeared as devils. Ironically, priests even presented themselves as substitutes for the *pajés*, or indigenous medicine men.

Many Natives reacted violently to colonization, slavery, and the clergy. Some adopted the strategy of syncretistic appropriation of Catholic symbols. The Tupinambá leader Tamandaré, an ex-catechumen who had escaped from a Jesuit mission, actually proclaimed himself the real pope, named bishops, and made Natives saints.[72]

To be sure, some priests such as Vieira ardently attacked Amerindian slavery. As Célia Tavares observes, the Jesuits defended the faith but were flexible— allowing, for instance, Natives to attend Mass naked and allowing the use of interpreters in the sacrament of confession.[73] There was much give and take in the process of mission settlement.[74] Many conflicts erupted between ecclesiastics and the settlers over the use of indigenous labor. As proto-anthropologists, the Jesuits provided the moral and theological bases of crown Indian policy. They made the *senhores de engenho* uncomfortable with their questions about the use of Indian slaves. The fathers opposed the practice of encouraging free Natives to cohabit with or marry slaves as a way of increasing the supply of labor. When Portugal in 1609 decreed laws to protect the Amerindians, angry colonists in Bahia blamed the fathers and threatened to expel them. Two years later the crown retreated by passing laws that effectively permitted the enslavement of Natives to continue. The Jesuits thus felt that they had ample reason to gather the Natives into the *aldeias* or *reduções* (village missions) in order to protect them from slave-raiders and other colonists.[75]

Jesuit knowledge of the Natives was one-dimensional and simplistic, however. It focused on the spiritual and the moral and ignored much about their material existence. Most of what they learned came from a single source, the Tupinambá people. The Jesuits insufficiently understood the fragility of indigenous culture in the face of colonial assault and religious conversion. They shared the colonists' view of it as barbaric—a position unlike their more tolerant approach in India and China,[76] where the fathers more carefully pondered the wealth of these civilizations, which they saw as superior, and therefore developed respectful methods of evangelization.[77] But even in the East the Jesuits allowed few Native vocations. Everywhere Eurocentrism dominated the order's outlook.[78]

The *aldeias* proved disastrous for the Natives. The Jesuits hastened their demographic demise by taking them from their traditional home environments and exposing them en masse to foreign epidemic diseases. In the *aldeias* the Jesuits proceeded to "de-Indianize" the people by thoroughly eradicating their culture. They destroyed stories, styles of attire, aesthetics, artistic expression, symbolic orders, values, and architecture.[79] Catholic religious teachings and Christian communalism were alien concepts. The Jesuits prohibited such Native practices as polygamy, cousin marriages, and ritual cannibalism and warfare. The *aldeias* forcefully congregated people of disparate tribal and linguistic backgrounds, and the Jesuits' *língua geral* condemned Indian tongues to extinction. Counting, reading, and writing were repugnant to the Indians. The Jesuits attempted to skirt resistance by focusing their educational and evangelical energies on the children. The layout of the *reduções* disrupted the Indians' own village model, which represented their social and religious cosmos. Ultimately the *aldeia* system allowed the contracting of Indian labor to settlers.[80] The apocalyptic results of the Jesuit policy altered forever the indigenous perception of white culture.

In some parts of the colony the *reduções* had balder, more pragmatic purposes. In the Amazon, for example, the missions secured the borders against encroachment by French, Dutch, and Spanish interlopers. In southern missionary territory the Spaniards used the Jesuit *aldeias* as military garrisons in return for a reduction in tribute and exemption from the *encomienda* system of obligatory Indian labor.[81]

The Jesuit example was the best illustration of clerical control of the Amerindian population, but it was not the worst moral model. Other orders and secular priests were far less scrupulous. Parish priests had no qualms about accepting a royal policy that allowed them to obtain two captured Native slaves per year. Bishops also enjoyed the use of slaves,[82] as did Franciscan, Benedictine, Carmelite, and even Jesuit priests. The slave-raiding *bandeirantes* took priests on some of their expeditions.[83] The Jesuits had no monopoly on cultural control. Brazil's first bishop, Dom Sardinha, made naked converts wear clothing and recommended a Christian diet.[84] After the Jesuits' expulsion, the Natives lost their main protectors. By the end of the colonial period priests adhering to the Enlightenment defended a policy of extermination.[85] Clerical respect for the Amerindian had dropped into the moral abyss.

The Church explicitly barred Natives from the sacrament of Holy Orders. Both prejudice and ostensibly reasonable arguments played a role. The Jesuit superior general, for example, prohibited Brazilian-born men from entering the order. Portuguese men who had spent too much time in the colony were disqualified. The rest of the clergy had similar guidelines.

Substantial debate took place. Those against a Native clergy asserted problems of cultural inferiority. The Jesuits thought it inconceivable that a man could become a priest without a solid education in the classical culture that was an integral part of the Renaissance humanism of the fifteenth and sixteenth centuries. The cultural gap was practically insurmountable. Clerics believed that Amerindians were morally lax and incapable of renouncing cannibalism and polygamy and embracing celibacy, a practice unknown to the Indians. Racism furnished more pragmatic, nonreligious reasons against a Native priesthood. The Portuguese clergy knew that the inclusion of Amerindians, Africans, and *mestiços* would lower the prestige of the mainly white ecclesiastical caste. Loyal to the local community people, Native priests might even challenge colonial domination.[86]

Other clergymen argued in favor of Native vocations. In their view the Church's historically constructed barriers did not eliminate the possibility of some form of indigenous priesthood. An experiment had already been tried in the early years of New Spain. It was shut down for racist reasons. In Brazil the pro-Native school of thought maintained not only the viability but the urgency of developing a locally recruited clergy. Indigenous priests could serve as an effective intermediary between European Catholicism and the people and therefore facilitate transmission of the Christian message. Early Jesuit experiments at adapting the faith to Indian culture, however, were received with hostility by Dom Sardinha, who called Indian rites "pagan."[87] The failure to develop a Native clergy was both cause and effect of the Church's cultural myopia.

Harsh restrictions similarly walled off the African population from the priesthood. At the Council of Trent many bishops as well as Portuguese Dominican friars denounced slavery as a contradiction of Christian faith. Crown interests were stronger, however.[88] Portuguese law blocked blacks from religious vocations. Blacks, of course, were slaves and therefore kept uneducated and out of white institutions. African culture and religion came under assault, the victims of prejudice and misunderstanding. A key example was the repression of sexuality. Catholic morality redefined and unified the many variants of African kinship relations and sexual conduct. To ensure compliance the Church wielded the threat of punishment by the Inquisition.[89] Ignoring Church teachings, *senhores de engenho* had no interest in promoting stable slave marriages. Moral prudery and the illicit sexual activities of the captives—which, ironically, often took place in the beds of the *senhores*—"were ideologically projected into an eroticization of the African." Africans, one contemporary observer concluded, were "inclined by nature to the vice of sensuality."[90] Other forms of African expression offended the moral sensibilities of Europeans. In the nineteenth century, for example, foreign travelers frequently criticized the tolerance for Africans' loud music and noisy ways in public. They thought Afro-Brazilian dances were obscene. They were especially scandalized when whites joined in such festivities, particularly during religious holidays.[91]

As Ronaldo Vainfas observes, the Jesuits treated slaves in a highly contradictory manner. They tried to establish a regime embracing both slavery and Christian values. *Senhores* and slaves owed each other allegiance within a framework of patriarchy and monarchy. The Jesuits criticized the *senhores'* arrogance but expected the slaves to endure their miserable state. The Jesuits demonized African religion because it offended the Christian God, but also because it might foster an ethnic solidarity that could undermine the entire system.[92]

Another, more subtle factor was the Church's indecisiveness about black Christian religiosity. The Africans became Catholics, but they knew little about Catholicism. Most still believed in their native religions. Conversion through mere baptism brought blacks into the system but left them incapable of achieving a priest's intellectual level. Priests provided a cursory introduction to Catholicism and then simply sprinkled the slaves with holy water. Most often the *senhores de engenho* paid no heed to priests' exhortations to indoctrinate the slaves, particularly with regard to marriage.[93] The clergy showed little interest in comprehending or even repressing African witchcraft. Even whites, confused about what rituals were legitimate, adopted African practices.[94] The clergy's lackadaisical attitude encouraged syncretism.

Slavocracy created a strange and tragic paradox for the Church. Priests called the Africans to Catholicism and then stiff-armed them away from its core, the priesthood. Unlike their owners, the slaves were denied schooling. The Church's moral code tolerated the sexual abuse of slaves and the debilitation of the Afro-Brazilian family. Legitimate birth was doctrinally important, but as few as 1 percent of slave children were born in wedlock.[95] The slaves were black, but Jesus was always white, an aristocratic hero who belonged to the *casa grande* (the master's house), not the *senzala* (the slave quarters).[96] At Mass the nearest slaves got to the altar was the church door. Even free blacks attained only second-class status in the Church.[97]

The question of the ordination of nonwhites sprung up throughout the Portuguese empire and in the Spanish colonies, too. The decision for or against a black man depended on local circumstances, the particular needs of the

Church and the colonial power, and the degree of prejudice. In describing the situation in the Cape Verde Islands in 1652, Father Vieira revealed the prevailing ambivalence: "There are here clergy and canons as black as jet, but so well-bred, so authoritative, so discreet and so accomplished that they may be envied by those in our cathedrals at home." The majority of the clergy in Cape Verde and at São Tomé were mulattoes and free blacks, whose resistance to local diseases made them preferable to Portuguese clerics.[98] But prejudice and foot-dragging by the crown kept black and Native aspirants to the priesthood at a minimum. "Whiteness of skin and purity of soul" were linked, one Portuguese governor of Angola declared. Nonwhite seminarians and priests everywhere came under constant fire for their alleged incompetence.[99]

Despite the many objections against a local clergy, secular priests, including mixed-blood *mamelucos,* were already being ordained in Brazil just fifty years after the arrival of the Portuguese.[100] By no later than 1800 some mulattoes and blacks also pried their way into the priesthood,[101] most likely through *embranquecimento,* or cultural whitening. In the early nineteenth century official Church discrimination continued. Dark-skinned men had to pass as white or receive official dispensation from the hierarchy in order to enter the ministry.[102]

But the scant evidence about the number of dark-skinned priests for the colonial era and the empire indicates that they were few. Ecclesiastical historian Father Arlindo Rubert estimated that twenty-three black or mulatto priests existed at the end of the eighteenth century. The number of Amerindians was practically zero.[103] It is difficult to judge nonwhite priests' effectiveness or their degree of adherence to colonial domination. Training a local clergy would not automatically nullify the Church's struggle against Native and African culture. On the contrary, once within the Church, Native and black priests were more likely to identify with European ways.

Would Natives and blacks have even felt attracted to the priesthood? The destruction of their cultures by white colonists and priests was a horrifying disincentive. However, the people's readiness to imitate the colonizers and their rituals during times of peace suggested that some might have found the clerical career appealing. In all probability the Amerindians only vaguely understood the first Masses said in Brazil, although they did signal a kind of participation by performing spontaneous and original gestures of celebration. The residents of the first mission, abandoned by the Franciscans, continued to live in the style of the friars by adopting their own version of a monastery, priestly vestments, and practices.[104] The novelty of Catholicism and the influence of the clergy perhaps drew some Indians to the priesthood. After all, many tribes had their own *pajés,* shamans who exercised great influence. To a limited extent Catholic priests replaced the *pajés.*[105] The shallow roots of Africans' indoctrination did not necessarily signify a lack of interest in Catholicism. Some *quilombos* (runaway slave colonies) carried out evangelization and had black priests who baptized, married couples, and led the community in prayer. Other *quilombos* kidnapped white priests for the purpose of fulfilling people's religious needs. Blacks saw participation in the Church as an avenue to religious and social prestige and likely felt drawn to the priesthood. However, they were usually relegated to membership in the *irmandades.*[106]

Afro-Brazilians lived in a society in which their ordination was unthinkable. The dominant classes' view of life did not include a picture of a celibate black man wearing a cassock, speaking Latin, and displaying European mannerisms.

The Brazilian priesthood developed into a white aristocracy to which the most respectable families sought access as a proof of racial purity. Even to be the son of a priest was a great honor.[107] By the nineteenth century clergymen considered themselves to be on a par with the imperial nobility and the military, groups from which blacks and other social inferiors were generally excluded.[108] The prohibitions against nonwhites made Brazil dependent on the foreign, white clergy.

"Happy as a Priest's Son"

Denial of the priesthood to Amerindians and Afro-Brazilians resulted in part from Westerners' ethnocentric perception of these peoples' supposed inability to stay celibate. Paradoxically, to be a priest in Brazil was to be noncelibate. Many preachers had concubines, and even those fathers who remained virtuous were constantly exposed to temptation. In its early going Brazil lacked the repressive cultural paradigm of Europe. Amerindians and slaves initiated sexual contact with the settlers or were frequently abused.[109] "The environment in which Brazilian life began," wrote Gilberto Freyre, "was one of almost sexual intoxication."[110] But, as Ronaldo Vainfas has pointed out, it was really sexual *exploitation,* exacerbated by colonialism, slavery, and racism. For its part the Church tried to enforce the norm of the nuclear family blessed by the sacrament of marriage, an ideal of the Portuguese world strived for by members of the elite and social climbers but virtually inaccessible to the poor and outcast.[111] Notwithstanding official doctrine, Luso-Brazilian Catholicism was very erotic. The faithful might bless a saint's penis or pray to the famed Saint Anthony for help in finding a marriageable man—a practice still widespread in Brazil. During coitus women pronounced in Latin the words of the Eucharistic transubstantiation in order to guarantee the affection of their mates. In the 1730s a Carmelite father in Salvador used his semen to "cure" women suffering from melancholy or illness.[112]

It is difficult to ascertain the number of priests who were sexually active or lived with women, but contemporary sources indicate that they were legion. Oral tradition in Pernambuco referred to priests as "procreators." The popular Brazilian phrase "happy as a priest's son" survived into the twentieth century. It reflected the belief in the good luck of clerics' children, usually resulting in an advantageous social position.[113] The general increase in concubinage in Brazilian society contrasted with the tendency in Europe to adhere to the Counter-Reformation's emphasis on marriage. The Portuguese crown practically condoned priestly concubinage with slaves.[114] Priests often initiated sexual activity by soliciting women (and occasionally men) in the intimacy of the confessional.[115] Some took their slaves as lovers.[116]

The sacrament of penance and sex stood at the center of the Council of Trent's efforts to reform the clergy. Martin Luther's Reformation had rejected the notion of forgiveness of sins through the mediation of clerics. Trent responded by reinforcing the importance of the priesthood and confession. It created the modern confessional, which separated priest and penitent with a screen. With this new emphasis on the sacraments the Church aimed to remold popular piety by standardizing values and behavior, wiping out lingering paganism, and establishing a clear distinction between the sacred and the profane. It sought to abolish games, dances, songs, festivals, plays, and any other activity that might arouse people's sensuality and lead to fornication. Trent declared a battle against concubinage. The priest was fundamental—as moral guardian and example of upright conduct. However, in their parishes priests encountered resistance to the crusade against concubinage. Consensual union and high rates of illegitimacy were normal in Brazil. So was the priest who lived respectably with a woman and fathered children. The people's primary concern was not celibacy, but having priests who properly performed other sacramental and religious duties.[117]

The bishops and the Jesuits struggled unsuccessfully to enforce celibacy and improve the quality of the clergy.[118] (Ironically, Saint Ignatius's own brother, Pero, had earned a reputation as a dissolute priest in Spain.[119]) In Brazil the Church did not begin to implement Trent in earnest until the early 1700s, when

the gold rush and the colony's rising importance stimulated an interest in clerical reform on the part of the crown and the bishops.[120] In 1707 the bishops
issued the *Constituições Primeiras do Arcebispado da Bahia* (the First Constitution of the Archbishopric of Bahia), the first ever canonical legislation for
Brazil and the first attempt to apply Tridentine norms. The *Constituições* governed the administration of the sacraments, including confession, and set forth
the obligations of the clergy.[121] But the reform had little impact. Whereas the
Spanish American Church enjoyed strong and highly centralized organization,
in Brazil the *padroado,* lack of clerical discipline, and the strength of popular
religion hindered change.[122] At mid-century the Church attempted to increase
acceptance of penance by assuring its secrecy, improving the quality of confessors, and keeping amorous priests out of the confessional. But Trent was
cut short by the advent of the absolutist state of the Marquis of Pombal and
the expulsion of the Jesuits from the Portuguese dominions, followed by their
temporary suppression by the Vatican. The eighteenth century was merely
a relaxed rehearsal of the reforms to come one hundred years later under
Romanization.

The efforts to purify confession revealed that large numbers of priests
ignored celibacy. Of the 425 denunciations of sexual solicitation to the Holy
Office between 1610 and 1820, precise dates exist for 288. Three-quarters of
these occurred between 1730 and 1760, the height of reform. Unlike Spanish
America, Brazil had no local tribunal of the Holy Office, and visits by the Inquisition were rare (although the repression of crypto-Jews was rigorous until
the latter half of the eighteenth century). The Church encouraged the faithful,
priests, and even slaves to denounce errant fathers to members of the laity and
the Inquisition's clerical commissioners. The commissioners forwarded the
accusations to Lisbon and enforced the punishments of convicts returned to
Brazil. Priests themselves made the majority of the accusations about solicitation. Not surprisingly, many of the denunciations showed conflicting versions of events and were more frequently motivated by personal disputes than
by the desire to uphold priestly morality.[123]

The accusations contained steamy revelations about priests' sexual behavior,
their relationships with women, and the social life of the Church. Brazil's
patriarchal society kept women of respectable families under constant vigilance
and restricted public signs of affection to gestures, smiles, and furtive glances.
Ironically, the Mass, processions, and other religious ceremonies became occasions for flirting. The confessional afforded the greatest opportunity for
initiating a sexual liaison. It freed women from surveillance. Only a priest had

complete access to it. Inquisition witnesses testified to a wide variety of strategies for arranging trysts. Father João Ferreira Ribeiro, for example, received a love note from one Violante Maria. By way of a "mulatto confidante" the priest sent the woman a message directing her to meet him in the confessional after Mass. They agreed to meet in the woods, where the priest had "carnal access" to the woman. In 1753 Marciana Evangelha, a twenty-nine-year-old virgin from Maranhão, denounced Father José Cardoso, who had grabbed her breasts in the confessional and asked to see her nude. Nuns, prostitutes, slaves, poor women both white and black, and *donas* and *donzelas* of the elite all had romantic encounters with priests starting in the confessional. At times priests and women engaged in sexual foreplay or masturbation in the confessional. Preachers offered women money or absolution from sin in return for sex. On other occasions they employed purported magic in their attempt to charm women. Some fathers made sadistic comments or coaxed women into talking about sexual experiences.

The offending priests revealed that they mainly resembled the populace in terms of attitudes about sex, women, race, and social class. Similarly, the credibility of female witnesses before the ecclesiastical commissioners often depended on their skin color and social status. Because many women of lower station did not dare denounce priests, the number of soliciting fathers probably numbered higher than the Inquisition records suggest. The sad example of Father Sysnando Nunes de Quadros and Ignácia Duarte in mid-eighteenth century Bahia is a case in point. During confession the priest propositioned Duarte, who was married. When she threatened to report him, he remained calm and finished the confession. Later, seeking revenge, the priest sent two black men to assault the woman. The attack left her nearly blind and confined to bed.[124]

The Rise of the Secular Fathers and the Birth of Politics

During the Crisis of Brazilian Christendom (1759–1840) clergymen regained center stage in Brazil as revolutionaries and politicians. Brazil proceeded into the nineteenth century through fits of economic reform, regional revolutionary outbursts (first against Portugal and then against the imperial government), the start of a long boom in coffee production, and an increasing demand for African slaves. As the country gained independence (1822) and embarked on a project of nation-building, priests exerted less influence through the *engenho* and more by way of social movements and direct control of, or pressure on, the state. The secular fathers led the way.

Church-state conflicts became frequent. In the final years of the colony the crown eliminated privileges such as the exclusive ecclesiastical courts and tax exemptions, and in 1821 it abolished the Inquisition.[125] Throughout the empire (1822–1889) the secular fathers and the bishops encountered great difficulties in claiming their prerogatives under the *padroado.* The state took over part of the Church's patrimony. The first imperial government occupied monasteries to install its naval school, a law school, and the national archives. Troops billeted in churches. In 1837 Rio de Janeiro's São Joaquim seminary became the public school known as the Colégio Dom Pedro II.[126] Lacking funds, vocations, and clerical unity, the Church remained institutionally weak.

While the seculars had always worried about survival, their situation became even more critical after 1800. Religious priests enjoyed greater economic security because their members pooled resources and as a corporate entity accumulated many properties.[127] The rest of the Church's holdings diminished, however. As employees of the bureaucracy, diocesan priests depended on the state for their *côngruas,* or salaries, which came from tithes collected by the imperial administration. The rather meager *côngruas* discouraged vocations.[128] So did the rather low official remuneration for pastoral services.[129] Many seculars became corrupt, demanding extortionate rates for their services and in some cases amassing vast sums. Others collected payments even before administering sacraments or withheld bodies from burial until someone appeared with the proper emolument.[130] Some priests still relied on the *senhores de engenho,* who paid the religious fees.[131] On balance, however, the seculars still lived far better than most Brazilians.[132]

For the first time the clergy became more authentically Brazilian—and darker. Starting in the seventeenth century a minor relaxation of restrictions against Native vocations allowed for the ordination of some mulattoes, *mamelucos,* and blacks, the first, small hint of breakdown in the clerical aristocracy.[133] After the Jesuits' departure the floodgates of ordination opened. In one three-year period in the late 1700s, for example, 101 Brazilian men received Holy Orders.[134] Imperial curbs on the traditional religious orders hastened what I call the "Brazilianization" of the clergy. In 1828, for example, Father Diogo Antônio Feijó explained to the Chamber of Deputies the need to stop new religious priests from entering Brazil because they hailed from countries with absolutist governments.[135] This sentiment culminated in the 1855 imperial ban on new religious novices and on the entry of foreign religious priests.

By the 1872 census Brazil had 2,256 secular priests and only 107 religious fathers. For the first time in Brazilian history the majority of the clergy were seculars and native-born.[136]

Priests remained pivotal in society. After independence priests achieved great political power at the local level, particularly in the interior. Parishes kept records of land ownership, the basis of power in the countryside.[137] For the average Brazilian God reigned as the supreme judge and regulator of society. Fathers still intervened as moral arbitrators in people's most personal and delicate affairs.[138] Public administration was based on ecclesiastical territorial divisions, and elections, held in parish churches, were sacred affairs carefully regulated by the clergy. Priests participated in voter registration and on election boards, in the collection of statistics, and in mentoring new or inept justices of the peace.[139] Brazil was an elitist society far from democracy. Nevertheless, the clergy played a democratizing role by helping introduce Brazilians to new concepts such as the Constitution, laws, political parties, and the vote.[140] (The Church would play a similar role in the 1980s, as Brazil returned to democracy after twenty-one years of military dictatorship.) Priests acted as local judges and controlled the civil registry (the recording of births, deaths, and marriages). Catholic ministers during this period worked as musicians, researchers, scientists, journalists, poets, and essayists. A priest directed the imperial botanical garden, and another helped found the Instituto Histórico-Geográfico Brasileiro in 1838.[141] In 1826 Dom Romualdo Seixas, the archbishop of Salvador, supported an amendment in the Assembléia Geral (the General Assembly, the national legislature) to give parish priests the power to certify the conduct of members of their congregations. Though defeated, it revealed once again the perception of the Church as Brazil's moral judge.[142] Before the creation in 1827 of schools to educate bacharéis (professionals with college-level instruction) the clergy kept a virtual monopoly on intellectual life. Many sought the priesthood because it was the only avenue to higher education and intellectual prestige.[143] Priests maintained academic superiority until the second half of the nineteenth century.[144]

Priests led political agitation in the independence era. Political change and nationalistic feelings swept them into action. Rifts in the colonial system allowed debate about citizenship, the abolition of slavery, and freedom of the press to appear in the Brazilian public arena for the first time. Literary concerns became political ones, and ethnic and social tensions boiled over. Avid readers, priests accumulated large libraries and imbibed controversial ideas. The overwhelming influence of the French Revolution and liberal ideology, the example of France's pro-revolutionary clergy, frictions with the Portuguese, and resistance to the authoritarian attitudes of Emperor Dom Pedro I caused many fathers to rebel against the Portuguese crown and later against the imperial government. Inspired by the Enlightenment and opposed to tyranny, these fathers gave political movements ideological leadership.[145] Freemasonry, which in many respects resembled the *irmandades,* provided a channel for the spread of dissent and the formation of movements. The idea of upward mobility as witnessed in the U.S. republic appealed to Brazilian clergymen. Rebel priests were often the lowest-paid, least prestigious clergy. Like other unprivileged yet talented members of society, they were frustrated with the lack of opportunities for advancement.[146] Many priests eventually took up arms.

Nine priests took part in the Inconfidência Mineira of 1788–1789 (the failed independence plot in Minas Gerais), and five were imprisoned and then exiled from the colony. In the so-called *revolução de padres* of 1817 in Pernambuco, fifty-two of the 310 insurrectionists were priests. Some were put to death, and others committed suicide, among them Father João Ribeiro, a professor at the Seminary of Olinda whom the rebels tried to recruit for the presidency of their ephemeral republic. The authorities put his head on display as an anti-rebel trophy in the streets of Recife. Allied with Freemasons (many of whom were clerics) and influenced by the French Revolution, the padres set up a short-lived republican government and advocated the abolition of slavery. Priests took up the cause of revolution in Bahia, too, and in 1824 Pernambuco's rebellious Confederação do Equador, which actually stopped the slave trade, counted heavily on the leadership of fathers.[147] The clergy was dispersed, with many heading into exile.[148]

The legendary Frei Caneca symbolized the political transformation of the Brazilian clergy. Joaquim do Amor Divino Rabelo Caneca was a Carmelite friar who, like many of his brothers, ignored the vow of celibacy. He reportedly had between three and six children by a woman whom he passionately loved but whose name is unknown. But in all other ways Frei Caneca was a faithful Catholic intellectual who shunned activism and settled down to a tranquil life as a professor of philosophy, rhetoric, and geometry at the Carmelite order's convent in Recife. He did have a social conscience, however. Frei Caneca showed pride in his supposed indigenous roots, valued the African contribution to Brazilian civilization, and believed in the gradual abolition of slavery. Frei Caneca probably did not own slaves, although the Carmelite order certainly did. Unjustly imprisoned during the 1817 priests' rebellion, he spent four years in brutal detention in the province of Bahia. The horror of this experience awoke in Frei Caneca the progressive ideology he had absorbed at the Seminary of Olinda and from the liberal climate of his day, and his indignation inflamed his desire to resist the arbitrary rule of the Portuguese and after 1822 that of Pedro I, who had dissolved the Constituent Assembly in 1823 and imposed his own constitution on the nation. Frei Caneca took aim at the government with his oratorical skills and an outspoken newspaper. He upheld the need for a constitutional system based on the federalist, republican model of the United States. He wanted to combat the country's vast political and regional inequalities. In 1824 he became one of the principal leaders of the Confederação do Equador, only to be captured, stripped of his ecclesiastical garb and honors, and executed by a firing squad, despite the pleas of the Recife clergy that he be allowed to apply for clemency.[149]

If implemented, Frei Caneca's ideas would have shaken the foundations of Brazilian society. His political action and thirst for social justice resembled the struggle against authoritarianism and social inequality taken up by priests during Brazil's military dictatorship 150 years later. In both instances new political ideas and the repression of the clergy helped drive priests into activism.

The innovations at the Seminary of Olinda provided a major impetus for the rebellions of the northeast. Originally an important Jesuit seminary in the colonial period, the seminary was reestablished in 1800 by Dom José da Cunha de Azeredo Coutinho, who also shared in the governorship of Pernambuco. Dom Coutinho's objectives fit into the larger political project of the elite, in particular the Marquis of Pombal, to construct a new Luso-Brazilian empire. The Olinda seminary became one of Brazil's best educational institutions, a rare exception to the dearth of clerical schools. Dom Coutinho and a number of the professors had studied at Coimbra, which priests and members of the upper class routinely attended because of the astounding lack of a university in Brazil (another example of Portuguese royal jealousy). At Coimbra the Olinda clergymen imbibed Pombaline ideology and Enlightenment thought. Instead of the Tridentine model, the seminary of Olinda adopted a program focusing on the study of Brazilian social reality. The novel curriculum combined pedagogy, religion, and politics and included subjects usually not included in the ecclesiastical curriculum, for example, geography, botany, mineralogy, and other natural sciences. Although not interested in broad social transformation, the seminary taught priests about agriculture in the hopes of assisting the impoverished backlands population. Unlike the Tridentine seminaries of the 1800s and 1900s, Olinda did not require students to live at the school.[150] They lived at home. In fact, the pedagogy was antiauthoritarian.

Olinda respected the students' individual personalities and espoused egalitarian student-teacher relations. Those students freely participated in the independence movement.[151] A similar, radical model of clerical training would appear in Brazil in the 1960s and 1970s (see discussion in chapters 5 and 7).

Priests gained prominence in Brazil's new national political organizations. Their participation began in the Portuguese *cortes* (representative body) of 1821–1822; of eighty deputies elected, twenty-three were either bishops or priests. In the Brazilian Constituent Assembly of 1822–1823, twenty-two of the one hundred representatives were priests, including the bishop of Rio de Janeiro, who presided over the proceedings. In the twenty elected legislatures of the empire, two hundred seats were held by priests in the Chamber of Deputies. Others occupied seats in the Senate. As parliamentarians, priests demonstrated intellectual and political prowess in dealing with the wide range of problems that cropped up in the construction of a new nation.[152] Priests debated constitutional, electoral, and administrative reform, military service, colonization, prisons, censorship, contraband, industrial development, inflation, taxes, lotteries, and reforestation.[153]

Celibacy and the Quest for a National Church

Despite clerical eminence, ecclesiastics of different ideological stripes agreed that a pastoral crisis afflicted the Church. The bishops as well as the government believed that priests failed in their most important duty: the spiritual and moral guidance of the masses. Easy access to the priesthood, low educational standards, concubinage, and the decline of the religious orders hampered the Church's abilities. So did corruption and other forms of immoral behavior. In the north of Minas Gerais, for example, some fathers shirked their religious duties and gained reputations as swindlers, thieves, and libertines. Priests and their relatives employed slander and even violence to achieve their goals in ecclesiastical and municipal politics. Some fell in with prostitutes. One powerful vicar in Montes Claros was accused of establishing a "theocracy-oligarchy" of patronage, political control, and physical intimidation.[154] To complicate matters, the clergy needed to adapt to Brazil's new independent status and absorb the anti-clerical aftershocks of the French Revolution. Earthy and free of episcopal meddling, the clergy blended in with the people and their lay-based, familial Catholicism. Many priests walked the streets without cassocks (in violation of the requirement established in the sixteenth century), and some carried knives or daggers in their belts and played cards. Desacralized behavior caused confusion about the priest's role. He was both sacred and profane, an intermediary of the transcendent but also a human figure in the trenches of life.[155] Attempts to enforce Trent were nigh impossible for a Church institutionally emasculated by the state. But in the nineteenth century it became clear that the Church needed to renew its traditional role as social adhesive. In the 1820s and 1830s debates in the General Assembly and among ecclesiastical leaders demonstrated a consensus: the intellectual and moral reform of the clergy was essential for regenerating the Church. But *how* would the reform proceed?

Two camps formed. In one were conservatives, ultramonarchists, reactionaries, and ultramontanes (strong supporters of the papacy and centralized ecclesiastical authority); in the other, liberals, nationalistic revolutionaries, republicans, and Gallicans (advocates of close Church-state relations and greater national sovereignty in religious affairs).[156] A leading ultramontane, Dom Romualdo favored strict adherence to the dictates of the Vatican and the establishment of Tridentine seminaries for the training of priests. He promoted academic rigor, piety, and a return to the use of the clerical habit, which highlighted priests as sacred men distinct from the rest of the populace. Dom Romualdo also emphasized poverty, religious discipline, and especially celibacy.[157] He considered his opponent, the liberal Father Feijó, to be a "maniac."[158]

In the opposing camp stood Feijó and a group of São Paulo fathers known as the *grupo paulista*. Father Feijó epitomized the priest-politician of his time and embodied many of the characteristics attacked by conservatives. He openly disregarded Tridentine clerical norms. Born illegitimate, Feijó was most probably the son of a cleric, his "uncle." He shared illegitimate status with a number of other prominent clerics from across colonial Latin America, including other Brazilian political leaders.[159] After studying at Coimbra, he was ordained in 1808. Feijó could not receive Holy Orders, however, until nine witnesses had testified before an ecclesiastical tribunal that his unknown parents, whom they did not identify, came from good families and therefore had not passed on character defects.[160] He worked as a teacher and, as did other members of the clergy, founded a newspaper. In 1821 Feijó was chosen as a deputy to the *cortes* in Lisbon. Five years later he won election to the General Assembly, where he donned layman's clothing. As Minister of Justice (1831–1832) he stabilized the political climate in the wake of Dom Pedro I's abdication by creating the National Guard. In 1833 he was named senator. Feijó refused a state nomination in

1835 to become bishop of Mariana. He rose to the pinnacle of political power as regent from 1835 to 1837,[161] ruling in the stead of the minor Emperor Dom Pedro II during one of the most turbulent periods in Brazilian history. Feijó is remembered as one of the heroes of Brazilian national unity.[162] In 1842 he joined an unsuccessful rebellion against the central government that ended his political career.

Brazilian historiography and historical memory characterized Padre Feijó as a bad Catholic, even a heretic, because of his campaign to revoke obligatory celibacy. He also gained a pervasive image as a politician. In the century after his death interpreters of Feijó's life exhumed his body, measured his skull, painted numerous versions of his portrait, and repeatedly reformulated his biography in the attempt to redefine the political, ethnic, and moral identities of São Paulo and Brazil according to the needs of the moment.[163]

But Feijó was first and foremost a cleric—and a generally upstanding one. Except for keeping a mistress and fathering five children, the highly devout Feijó did not partake in the moral laxity of colleagues such as one Padre Pina, who violated the confidentiality of the confessional, stole holy ornaments from a church for his concubine, and allowed parishioners to die without receiving the sacraments. One biographer likened Padre Feijó to Abraham Lincoln. Feijó and a group of fervent fathers from Itu, São Paulo, known as the "Padres do Patrocínio," fashioned a kind of informal diocesan order based on the local devotion to Nossa Senhora do Patrocínio (Our Lady of Help).

The padres affectionately cared for the local church, dedicated to Our Lady, and sought to expand Itu's sacred patrimony. The proper training of priests was another primary concern. The Padres do Patrocínio emphasized many components of clerical discipline. Feijó, for instance, always carried his breviary. They gathered at the church to pray and issue moral judgments against the impious of Itu and the surrounding region. The padres upheld a morality and civic behavior that combined an emphasis on authority, the liberal doctrine of equality, the struggle against absolutism, and the protection of human rights. These attitudes confirmed the inseparable nature of politics and religion in the padres' mission, which gave rise to Feijó's involvement in government in Rio de Janeiro and Lisbon. The padres adhered to Gallicanism, but they defended what they believed to be the Church's interests and did not break with Rome. They were priests *and* citizens who fought for the independence of Brazil and the improvement of society.

In a nation swimming in titles of nobility Feijó refused to accept any, and as regent to Dom Pedro II he abolished the *beija-mão*, the ritual in which subjects kissed the hand of the emperor. As a matter of principle he refused an offer to become canon of the imperial chapel. Feijó believed in meritocracy, not favors. He did not hesitate to affront the imperial power and, as a result, was spied upon by the agents of José Bonifácio de Andrada e Silva, Dom Pedro I's prime minister. The padres' ideology aimed for concrete results. They preached to the slaves and advocated their education and a policy of gradual aboli- tion. They also proposed the stimulation of foreign immigration and a general defense of the oppressed. For them God was the supreme—and rational— legislator. These positions clashed with the fundamental values of Brazilian slavocracy. In the pages of their São Paulo newspaper *O Justiceiro* (1834), Feijó and his cousin, Padre Miguel Arcanjo Ribeiro, railed against slavery and cleri- cal celibacy and asserted the equality of all Brazilians. Feijó took a progressive stance with respect to other facets of Brazil's socioeconomic development. He maintained sugar plantations, where he experimented with the cultivation of coffee, the use of the plow, and free-wage labor. Historians have ignored Feijó's roots, but those roots infused his political activities and constantly drew him back to Itu.

Geography determined Feijó's politics and down-to-earth conduct. He rep- resented the interests of the clergy of the smaller towns and the countryside. The growth in the number of lawyers after the creation of Brazil's first law schools began to erode the clerical dominance of politics in the urban centers of the coast. But priests still held sway in the backlands. Despite his learned- ness, Feijó projected himself as an *homem do mato*, a man from the interior who held a certain resentment against the perceived falseness of urban civiliza- tion.[164] As Minister of Justice he wore sandals, and while regent he consulted with Dom Pedro II in a frock and boots.[165] As Roderick Barman has observed, Feijó's handwriting was frequently illegible and his Portuguese often rough and ungrammatical. He lacked tact, imagination, and social grace but pos- sessed a "grinding persistence, forthrightness, and zeal for his chosen cause."[166] He cultivated the image of the *homem do mato* to win over the sympathy of the powerful families of the interior, who maintained political dominance by sending their sons into the priesthood.[167] In parliament Feijó accused his fel- low representatives of knowing France better than their own provinces.[168] Feijó identified with the backlands clergy, men distant from the authority of Rome and steeped in traditions such as concubinage.

Feijó and the so-called *reformadores* largely concurred with the conserva- tives in their analysis of the Church's faults. For example, the liberals stated that reform depended on changing the priesthood. Priests needed to be dignified, cultured, and pastorally able to improve the people's morals.[169] But they radicalized on other points. Feijó and the *grupo paulista* wanted to establish a married clergy, an independent, national Brazilian Church, and an open system of clerical training. It was no wonder that their opponents compared them to Martin Luther.

General disregard for celibacy had reached new heights. The canonical and imperial laws of obligatory chastity were a "dead letter."[170] In Europe Brazil became known as the land of syphilis par excellence. One visitor affirmed that the disease devastated monasteries and convents.[171] In Crato in the province of Ceará at least five priests had substantial families. One fathered six children. His godson, who became a priest and a senator, had ten children, one of them the prominent novelist José de Alencar. At the Chamber of Deputies in Rio one cleric-politician appeared in the company of his daughter.[172] In one sample of Bahian priests as many as 51 percent declared they had children. This figure matches the percentage of single lay fathers who left wills. It again suggests that priests did not differ from other people. Priests tended to form families with more than one child, and practically nobody referred to a priest's son as a "bastard."[173] Priests rarely signed the birth register for their children. To avoid the stigma of illegitimacy, priests granted them the legally more favorable status of children of "unknown parents."[174] The papal nuncio accused some Brazilian priests of maintaining "harems."[175] Concubinage increased in large part because of the abolition of the Inquisition. An increasingly secularized civilian authority had little interest in punishing the relatively harmless infractions of such priests.[176]

Public display of attitudes about celibacy ranged from full compliance to the flaunting of lovers. In between these extremes were those priests with respectable families who discreetly presented their wives as *comadres* (godmothers) and their children as *afilhados* (godchildren) or nieces and nephews. Some priests took their partners to Mass.[177] Prudence was necessary because the priests were always vulnerable to being reported to the bishop.[178] Priests' sons had good jobs, and their daughters married middle-class men or lived well off the property accumulated by their fathers.[179]

Disobedience grew into open hostility. During the early years of the empire the liberals put forth a number of proposals to end obligatory celibacy. The very first came at the Constituent Assembly of 1822–1823, when deputy Ferreira França introduced a measure to outlaw friars and nuns and to abolish celibacy.[180] Feijó and the *grupo paulista* led the most spirited campaign. In 1827 the General Council of the Province of São Paulo, dominated by the *paulista* priests, asked the General Assembly to abolish the celibacy law. Feijó presented to the Assembly a report outlining the abuses and failures of obligatory celibacy over the centuries. He added theological and historical arguments against it.[181] Feijó stated that: (1) obligatory celibacy was not supported by the gospel; (2) the primitive Church had allowed married priests; (3) many priests of the early Church married after ordination; (4) Church discipline with respect to celibacy had become tighter over the ages but never uniform; (5) the Greek Orthodox priests continued to marry; and (6) scandals continued.[182]

Attracting great public attention, the debate over celibacy went on for seven years. The liberals presented revised, less radical proposals to both the General Council of São Paulo and the General Assembly. In 1834, for example, they proposed to the Council that in São Paulo the bishop be permitted to call married men to be "ministers of the altar, zealous pastors, as occurred in the primitive Church, as occurs today in the Greek Church and among the Reformed Christians." The *grupo paulista*'s aims were practical rather than theological. They wanted to alleviate the shortage of priests and stimulate population growth by presenting married pastors as examples for the people to emulate.[183] Feijó hoped that his own public career and advocacy of ecclesiastical reform might bring about the moralization of Brazilian society.[184] However, none of the *paulista* proposals passed in São Paulo or at the national level. Likewise, Feijó and his allies' plan for a national Church, including a national episcopal council and the freedom of each diocese to adopt local norms, went down to defeat.[185] Feijó also wanted the Brazilian government to nominate bishops and the provincial presidents to choose vicars and parish priests.[186] All of these ideas contradicted ultramontane centralization and uniformity.

The influential Dom Romualdo and other leading ecclesiastics in the General Assembly blocked serious discussion of Feijó's proposals. Despite public support, Feijó could not muster the necessary votes. Even some liberal sympathizers refused to back him for fear of breaking the Brazilian Church's traditional ties to Rome, being labeled schismatics, and endangering the country's delicate national unity.[187]

The liberal campaign epitomized clerical nationalism. On one level, Feijó and his clerical allies in the General Assembly reflected the regalist current of the Portuguese political tradition, exemplified by Pombal's expulsion of the Jesuits. They opposed the immigration of new foreign religious priests.[188] On another level, as liberals and republicans they identified with the ideas of the Enlightenment and the French Revolution. Feijó was also influenced by Jansenism. Theologically unorthodox, in France the Jansenist movement was

strongly anti-clerical. It criticized the papacy, the bishops, and a number of ecclesiastical practices and institutions.[189] In the wake of Brazilian independence,
Feijó and his allies shared their compatriots' nationalist sentiments. Proclaim-
ing the supremacy of the civil realm over the ecclesiastical, they distrusted Vatican interference in Brazil's religious affairs.[190] They sought the unification of the
Brazilian Church with the *Brazilian* state as a basis for building a stronger nation. "If the Brazilian nation does not have the strength and the power necessary to promote its prosperity, without the consent of the Roman Curia, then
it is not independent, it is not a nation," Feijó declared in a 1928 debate with
Dom Romualdo.[191]

As the basis for an autonomous Church and married clergy, the liberal
priests formulated a Brazilian ecclesiastical constitution. A likely model for this
document was the Civil Constitution of the Clergy of the French Revolution.
However, while the French document strongly advocated the secularization of
society, the Brazilian proposal displayed a more religious and sacral context,
a Brazilian Christendom sui generis.[192] Feijó always had Itu—not France—in
mind.[193]

The liberals' alignment with the state against Rome was another sign of nationalism. Relations between the empire and the Vatican became difficult because of the struggle over interests under the *padroado*. (The *padroado* remained in force after independence because Brazil was still a monarchy.) Feijó,
in fact, had (perhaps naively) tried to argue that the empire could use the *padroado* to pressure Rome to ease the rule of celibacy. Liberal-conservative strife
was exacerbated by the presence of the papal nuncio, who had arrived in Rio de
Janeiro with the royal entourage in 1808 after the court fled Napoleon Bona-
parte's Iberian incursion. The liberals perceived the nuncio as a meddlesome
foreign power.[194]

Significantly, the liberal proposal eliminated seminaries—an indispensable
part of the ultramontane program. The *reformadores* wanted future priests to
receive a kind of on-the-job training through contact with experienced clergymen. Meetings would take place at the diocesan headquarters. Parish priests
and the bishop would guarantee intellectual training through a series of conferences. Priests would be directly in charge of student discipline.[195] Instead of
standardized training, Feijó proposed exposing ecclesiastical students to local
conditions at an early stage. Like the system established earlier at the Seminary
of Olinda, this approach threatened the homogeneity and institutional unity
sought by the traditional hierarchy. The liberals viewed their proposal as an
effective way to weed out men lacking an authentic vocation. Feijó's comments

in the Chamber of Deputies in 1827 spoke to this point: "A young man enters (the seminary) and right away begins to have inclinations towards the ecclesiastical status; he has no other ideas. . . . And what is the result? That we see persons with ecclesiastical status that were perhaps not made for it . . . that if they had not acquired artificial inclinations, would have chosen another kind of life more useful to themselves and to society."[196]

Despite defeat, the Feijó group had set historical precedent. The nationalistic undercurrent of the *paulistas*' program would lead to opposition against Romanization,[197] and their critique of the Church and the seminaries would find echo in the nationalistic clerical movements of the 1960s and 1970s. At stake was the type of priesthood Brazil would adopt.

Conclusion

Priests contributed both positively and negatively—but always decisively—to the building of Brazilian civilization. Associating with the elites and mingling with the masses, consorting with *senhores* and sleeping with slaves, they were authentic men of the people.

Yet the clergy had failed to live up to its religious potential. In the 1820s everybody saw the need for change. The *reformadores* and their opponents wanted reform that would lead to revamping the institution as a whole according to the needs of Brazilian society. The liberals underscored nationalism. The ultramontanes wanted a less political, more compliant clergy in the mold of Trent. With the defeat of Feijó's proposals they would now have the chance to discipline the Brazilian clergy.

chapter three

Romanization and the Grand Discipline, 1840–1962

(or, Trent Comes to Brazil)

In the 1840s the Church took a definitive step to reform the wayward Brazilian clergy. The conservative, pro-Roman bishops established their authority and promoted the distinct social identity of the priesthood as a unified, collective body.[1] These bishops aimed to wrest priests from politics, the Enlightenment and Gallicanism, and the embrace of women. In their view Brazil needed ministers who would profess loyalty to the institution, purify popular religion, and preach Catholic morality. The key was education. The bishops replaced the haphazard setup of priestly training with an increasingly standardized Tridentine seminary that emphasized doctrinal orthodoxy, obedience to the hierarchy, and intellectual and spiritual rigor. Discipline governed this system, and celibacy was its ideal. Between the start of the Second Empire in 1840 to the eve of the momentous Second Vatican Council in 1962 the number of seminaries in Brazil increased from little more than a dozen to more than six hundred.[2] Pope Pius XII called this era the "golden century" of the seminaries.[3]

The new schools formed the bulwark of the Romanization (or Europeaniza-tion) of Brazilian Catholicism. Romanization dominated the Brazilian Church from 1840 to 1962 and in many ways continues to this moment. In contrast with the feeble reform efforts of the colonial period, it achieved compliance with Trent. The sacraments, morality, and clerical authority supplanted the autono-mous lay-based rituals and organizations of traditional Luso-Brazilian Catholi-cism as the main axis of the Church's life.[4] Romanization clericalized Catholi-cism and transformed the model of the priesthood. As a result, the institutional Church attained its strongest position ever.

This chapter traces the history of Brazil's seminaries and the clergy's new social roles by focusing on the Vincentian fathers, the prime agents of Ro-manization. Their work began under the leadership of Dom Antônio Ferreira Viçoso, a Portuguese Vincentian who implemented the clerical reform of the nineteenth century by introducing the Tridentine method. The Vincentians built and administered some of Brazil's greatest seminaries, where they trained hundreds of priests in the new disciplinary mold. They laid the foundation for the Church's institutional growth and political power in the twentieth cen-tury. They also worked to inculcate the populace with the ideals of Christian responsibility and morality. Zealous missionaries, spirited organizers, and able educators of the social and ecclesiastical elite, the Vincentians resumed the Je-suit goal of instilling the true faith in the people and piety in the priesthood.[5] Along with the Jesuits they were the Vatican's preferred choice for educating diocesan priests in Latin America.[6]

Romanization

Romanization sprouted from the Church's efforts to reassert its power and in-fluence amidst the vast changes wrought by the modern world. It came in the wake of the French Revolution's massive attacks on the clergy and the privi-leges, property, and doctrine of the Church. The most intense phase of Romani-zation began with the Pontificate of Pius IX in 1846 and extended to World War I.[7] Pius IX tried to shore up the Church's position in predominantly Catho-lic nations by concentrating ecclesiastical control in the papacy and by attack-ing liberalism and modernity. In 1864 he issued the famous "Syllabus of Er-rors," which denounced Freemasonry and the notion of independent national churches once preached by Feijó. The "Syllabus" asserted the Church's right to control science, culture, and education. In 1871 the First Vatican Council declared the infallibility of the pope (which applies to specific, formal doctrinal and moral statements only). In Brazil Pius IX's actions stirred both the ultramontanes and their opponents into action.[8]

Part of a general religious restoration,[9] Romanization involved a global campaign to expand the Church's influence. Before becoming pope, for instance, Pius IX visited Latin America and familiarized himself with the situation of the local Church. Lamenting the backwardness of Brazilian priests, he commented, "*Sicut populus sic sacerdos*" ("as go the priests, so go the people"). In 1858 Pius IX established the Pontificio Collegio Pio Latino Americano for the training of Latin American priests in Rome.[10] This came three centuries after the establishment of Roman collegios for the Germans, the Hungarians, and the English — yet another indication of how the implementation of Trent had lagged terribly in Latin America. North American priests started attending their own seminary the following year, and in 1899 a Portuguese collegio was opened. In the ensuing decades many Brazilian seminarians would study at the Collegio Pio Latino Americano. During his tenure as bishop of Mariana (1844–1876) Dom Viçoso sent nine priests to Rome, including three who later became bishops. In 1870 fifty Brazilians were studying in the Eternal City, where they were groomed to become seminary rectors, theology professors, and bishops in their homeland. These profoundly Europeanized priests became the vanguard of Romanization. Starting in 1934, Brazil's ecclesiastical students in Rome resided in the Colégio Pio Brasileiro, from which they commuted to the Gregorian University for classes.[11] This tradition of education in Rome lasted until Vatican II[12] and has since resumed. Catholic expansion occurred in North America and other regions. In the United States, for example, the number of diocesan and religious seminaries grew from eighty-two in 1910 to 409 in 1962.[13] Romanization also spurred an impressive increase in the number and membership of male and female religious orders comparable to the flowering of such groups in the Middle Ages. Though a religious movement, Romanization had important geopolitical ramifications. Catholicism sought to assert itself in a highly competitive political and military environment involving the European powers' scramble for new colonies and the zealous efforts of Protestant missionaries to gain converts in the Third World.[14]

In Brazil modernization transformed the social context in which Romanization occurred. The process was both progressive and highly disruptive. The Paraguayan War (1865–1870), the abolitionist movement, and resistance to change in the backlands sparked social conflict. New groups, especially the military, gained political prominence. Propelled by the vast expansion in coffee production, Brazil tied into a rapidly developing world economy dominated by Great Britain (and later the United States). Innovations such as the railroad spurred development, and in 1888 slavery was abolished in favor of the attempt to organize a system of free wage labor. In 1889 a military coup led by positivist (anti-religious and authoritarian), abolitionist officers and supported by republican politicians toppled the imperial regime, ending nearly four centuries of monarchy. But political control still lay in the hands of powerful planters and landowners. Hailing from Rio de Janeiro, São Paulo, and Minas Gerais, the coffee planters dominated the First Republic (1889–1930). The Revolution of 1930 finally ousted the planters and prepared the way for a half century of urbanization and industrial growth that surpassed the performance of most Third World countries but perpetuated Brazil's deep social inequalities and authoritarian political practices.

Romanization was the conservative modernization of Brazilian Catholicism. It was simultaneously a reaction against modernity and its product and promoter. Like socialism and nationalism, Catholicism sought to build new forms of community in the face of international capitalism's destruction of traditional ties. Along the way a greatly strengthened papacy sought to create the unity of the worldwide Catholic community.[15] As Austen Ivereigh observes, the Catholic revival of the nineteenth century bore "remarkable similarities to secular mass movements. . . . The rise of the modern state and the rise of the modern Church were contemporaneous and often coterminous."[16] Romanization simultaneously changed the Church and preserved its traditions. On the one hand, the Church sought to adapt to a new society. As Michel de Certeau wrote, Christianity in the modern world had to reemploy its past elements based no longer on religious concerns, but on social structure. The modern world imposed itself on the Church.[17] On the other hand, the Church defended orthodoxy, clerical authority, and the end of lay autonomy. The seminaries exemplified this dual process. They served as the foundation for both priestly reform and the renewal of traditional clerical power. The priest of the twentieth century was based on a model from the sixteenth century: Trent. In biblical terms, the seminaries were in the world but not of it. Brazil and its Catholic Church both modernized and remained steeped in religious tradition—a duality that still defines Brazil in the twenty-first century.

As we saw in the previous chapter, the Council of Trent endeavored to raise the moral level of the faithful and the clergy. The council and the seminaries, which were influenced by Jesuit pedagogy, fit into a larger socioreligious move-ment. Trent not only responded to Luther but was part of a dual Reformation, both Protestant *and* Catholic, that aimed to lift the people and their religious leaders out of theological ignorance. Had the council met earlier, it might even have avoided the Lutheran schism. Especially in Europe, Trent ignited a Catho-lic enlightenment in which the sacraments, regular attendance at Mass, par-ticipation in Easter, and the study of catechism disciplined believers in a new kind of standardized faith stripped of powerful pagan elements, superstition, magic, and witchcraft. As historian Jean Delumeau observes, "Tridentine Ca-tholicism gave the faithful a feeling of security by surrounding them with protective sacraments, and consequently giving the sacraments a new depth." Catholicism became increasingly based on scripture and an expanded, vastly improved theology. This shift satisfied the people's desire for clearer instruc-tion in the faith and necessitated the intellectual improvement of the clergy. Simultaneously Trent carried out a radical centralization of Church govern-ment with the creation of Vatican congregations, or commissions, that exist to this day. (In this respect Romanization resembled the centralization of pro-duction and management seen in modern industrial capitalism.) The Holy Office of the Inquisition was created in 1542, for example. Locally the episcopate took greater command over the institution and became more vigilant of the be-havior of their priests and the faithful. The bishops sought to root out priests who had concubines, abandoned their parishes, or neglected to wear a cassock. The Church assiduously improved clerical recruitment. The rationalization of Catholicism included a deepened emphasis on sin, painful asceticism, and per-sonal, methodical meditation, but also on education and charity. It linked the Church to modernity, although the Church rejected science and other aspects of the secular world. The Counter-Reformation restored sacredness to Catholi-cism but neglected to Christianize the profane. The implementation of Trent took place at different levels of intensity in different regions of Europe and reached a high point from the mid-seventeenth to the mid-eighteenth century, although its repercussions would continue into the twentieth century.[18] Trent also led to the appropriation of theology for state interests.[19]

In addition, Romanization was the "Europeanization" of Brazilian Catholi-cism. Indeed, it strikingly resembled the process of Catholic enlightenment described above, with the important exception that in Europe demand for re-form often flowed from the faithful to the hierarchy, but in Brazil usually from the hierarchy down.[20] The Church's attempts to control popular religion were part and parcel of the Europeanizing tendencies that took hold of Brazilian culture in the late imperial era and the First Republic. Pastors Europeanized religious customs by essentially seizing control of popular Catholicism, eliminating Luso-Brazilian lay practices considered to be unorthodox or even irreligious, and substituting them with uniform, clerically controlled rituals. In some instances the bishops ordered the actual destruction of unauthorized sanctuaries. The formation of a more homogenous religious community increased recognition of the Church as a distinct and highly unified social body. One of the most important new devotions paid homage to the Sacred Heart of Jesus. It had both religious and political significance. In Paris Catholics built the church of the Sacré-Coeur on the spot where the atheistic Communards had made their stronghold. Dom Viçoso and other Brazilian bishops consecrated their dioceses to the Sacred Heart. Another devotion arose to Our Lady of Lourdes, also of French origin, with the construction of replicas of her grotto in several Brazilian cities.[21] In Brazil the official Church raised the figure of Christ the King (Cristo Rei) above the popular pantheon of saints.[22] In 1915 the bishops issued the *Pastoral Coletiva* (a collective pastoral letter), which served as a guide for Church life until Vatican II. The *Coletiva* required bishops to "entrust to the religious congregations the principle diocesan sanctuaries, so that the abuses and excesses committed in pilgrimages and processions to the same will be gradually corrected."[23]

The parish, always controlled by a priest, replaced the lay sanctuaries, hermitages, and rural chapels as the center of Church activity, and clergymen and bishops fought to shut down lay organizations or subordinate them to the hierarchy. The clergy took charge of these organizations' substantial endowments and money-raising potential, which bishops used to support their seminaries and other activities. The sacraments became the most important rituals, and religious images and devotions of European origin gained favor. Emphasis on the Eucharist, or Holy Communion, especially grew with the organization of local and national Eucharistic congresses and the establishment of the highly popular First Communion celebration for children. Priests began keeping statistics on the number of communicants. The Church also tried to steer members of the elite away from European-inspired spiritism and Afro-Brazilian religions, which were growing in the cities.[24] In a modern effort to discredit spiritism, the Church adopted medical and psychological discourses, as opposed to strictly religious prohibitions.[25] Renewed emphasis on catechism, especially among women, became another key component of Romanization.[26]

As Europeanization proceeded, Brazilian Catholicism became more erudite and therefore more attractive to intellectuals and the urban middle sectors.

Overall lay dependence on the clergy increased. Dominated by European clerics and nuns, Romanization represented the second great wave of Catholic evangelization in Brazilian history. It split the Brazilian Church into two conceptual camps—a control-seeking, sacramentally oriented clergy versus grassroots, saint-oriented organizations such as the brotherhoods.[27]

Romanization made the average Brazilian familiar with basic Tridentine teachings and rituals regarding birth, marriage, procreation, and death. It led to the construction of the many churches and sanctuaries at which Brazilians still worship. Along with the first evangelization of the colonial era, Romanization is the reason for Brazil's historical character as a Catholic nation.

Through a variety of disciplinary measures the bishops endeavored to transform the identity of the clergy. They sharply reduced the number of priests who worked as civil servants and, aided by the rise of competing professions that eroded priests' relative intellectual dominance, pulled back the fathers from electoral politics. The bishops sought to instill the clergy with a new sense of mission that involved service to God and to the faithful.[28]

During the Second Empire (1840–1889) clerical reform created both elective affinities and conflicts between Brazilian state building and Church renewal. The Church and the state each wanted a more effective clergy, but with different purposes in mind. The Church needed better priests in its struggle for viability, whereas the state wanted the clergy to act as agents of social control, especially in the countryside, where priests held sway over the people along with the *coronéis,* or backlands political bosses. A Europeanized clergy in tune with the bishops and the Brazilian elite best served these goals.[29] In general, a well-disciplined, moral clergy helped build an orderly society by strengthening the social and material infrastructure at the local level. In rural areas lacking substantial public investment, for example, the construction or refurbishing of churches provided crucial social space used for religious rituals and schooling.[30] Festering Church-state tensions, however, often led to competing approaches. The Church emphasized the Romanizing aspects of reform, but the imperial government looked to control the clergy under the enduring *padroado.*

The lingering troubles of the older clergy underscored the need for change. In Bahia in the mid-1800s, for example, religious orders became the scene of murders and riots; slave rebellions took place on orders' plantations; and lawsuits were filed over convent debts. In the 1860s exercise of the sacrament of confession—a major plank of Trent—was still a cause of scandal, and as late as the 1920s some priests openly kept concubines and mistresses.[31] Priests stayed

TABLE 3.1
Number of Priests in Comparison with Other Occupations, 1872

Occupation	Number
Priests	2,363
Judges	986
Lawyers	1,674
Notaries and scribes	1,493
Physicians	1,732
Surgeons	238
Pharmacists	1,372
Teachers and *homens de letras* (journalists, etc.)	6,659
Military personnel	27,716
Slaves	1,510,806
Total population	9,930,478

Source: Beozzo 1983:96–97.

active in politics, in part because they still outnumbered several key political groups and maintained intellectual prominence in a society that was mainly rural, uneducated, and dependent on slave labor (see the 1872 census data in Table 3.1).[32] In the 1870s, for instance, priests participated in party politics, and preachers such as Father Cícero Romão Batista became virtual *coronéis*. Priests controlled voters' choices, selected and vetoed candidates, ran campaigns, and continued to compete for public office.[33]

Meanwhile, the religious orders plummeted in membership, abandoned their traditional pastoral duties, and fell into moral decay. Losing touch with the people, they focused on their internal activities and wealth. These fathers showed a remarkable conservatism by continuing to keep slaves while abolitionism grew. An 1870 imperial report showed that a small number of monks and friars held thousands of slaves on numerous plantations and ranches. Some leading clergymen militated for abolition, but on the whole Church opposition to slavery was weak.[34] In the context of world history the Brazilian Church failed miserably in not acting more vigorously.

The imperial government pressed for reform by changing, curbing, and even eliminating certain groups of priests. The government wished to restrict the power of the bishops and gain control of Church properties—in part to be able to fund the education of diocesan priests. Regalists, Freemasons, and anti-clerical political factions heightened the demands for control of the Church. An unenthusiastic Catholic, Emperor Dom Pedro II fully exercised the royal prerogatives of the *padroado*. He restrained the Church's organizational growth and prohibited publication of Pius IX's "Syllabus," for instance. His government issued detailed regulations on the conduct of the clergy and other religious matters. In addition, he encouraged Protestant missionaries to enter Brazil and favored the passage of a law permitting civil marriages (as opposed to Church-sanctioned unions).[35] Fulfilling its duties under the *padroado*, the Brazilian parliament grudgingly granted financial aid to the seminaries, including the payment of professors' salaries, but it also kept a tight rein on curricula and the movement of students. The government decided whether seminarians could study in Europe, for example. Provincial governments supported seminaries and joined in the vigilance of curricula and budgets.[36]

One of the most sweeping imperial measures was Decree No. 839 of 1851. It confirmed funds for all seminaries but allowed the government to intervene in the creation of new schools, the selection of teachers and foreign professors, and even the ordination of priests. In 1863 the government created additional controls. When the bishops rejected these intrusions, the government suspended seminary teachers' pay. At least one bishop complained to Dom Pedro II and reobtained salaries for his teachers, but other seminaries had to look elsewhere for resources. In 1879 the Church and the imperial government reached a modus vivendi that functioned until the start of the republic. But the Church remained dissatisfied. Echoing earlier complaints by Dom Romualdo Seixas, in 1888 the parliamentarian Father Mâncio Caetano Ribeiro decried the fact that the public Colégio Dom Pedro II enjoyed support four times greater than that of the country's twenty-four seminaries combined. He claimed the "right" to more aid.[37]

In 1855 the imperial government issued a historic decree on the religious orders. It prohibited the acceptance of new novices until improvements in the clergy could be made. This decree was provisional. Permanent changes in the status quo awaited negotiation of a concordat with the Vatican, under which the state also hoped to take over the orders' properties. Chilly relations between the Vatican and the empire prevented an agreement, however. The 1855 decree remained in effect, thus condemning the Brazilian orders to a slow death. In 1870 the empire issued an additional order prohibiting men from returning to Brazil if they entered a religious order in a foreign country.[38]

In 1857 another important decree aimed once again to foster clerical reform. It upheld the prohibition on appeals to the crown by unruly clergymen
punished by their bishops.[39] This measure underscored state support for Romanization.

Struggle over the clergy underlay one of the most important political events
of the Second Empire, the so-called *Questão Religiosa* (the Religious Question, 1872–1875). During the Religious Question the government jailed Dom
Vital Maria Gonçalves de Oliveira and Dom Antônio de Macedo Costa for ignoring a government order allowing Masons to belong to the *irmandades*.
The Masons included priests and public officials and were influential in the *irmandades*, but the bishops rejected Freemasonry because of papal prohibitions against it. Typifying Romanization, Dom Vital and Dom Antônio had
received training in France and become ultramontanes. The Religious Question galvanized episcopal solidarity and played a part in the downfall of the
empire and the subsequent separation of Church and state.[40] This oft-cited
episode, however, must be seen in the context of the greater, ongoing tensions
over clerical reform discussed above as well as Church-state conflicts at the
local level. Unlike the *Kulturkampf* in Germany (1871–1887), where the imprisonment of bishops led to the mobilization of the Catholic Masses, the Religious Question did not involve the Brazilian populace.[41]

Ironically, the Church resolved the crisis of the Brazilian priesthood by im-
porting European clerics, mainly from the religious orders. A key exception to
the 1855 decree, this move contradicted the profound regalist fears about the
orders. It superbly illustrated how the necessities of state-building and clerical reform dictated a major break with the general policy of control over the
Church. The leadership of the Second Empire displayed a dual policy. On the
one hand, it repressed the existing clergy, whom it considered to be corrupt, immoral, and ineffectual. On the other hand, it permitted the entrance of missionaries whose presence strengthened the state but also the institutional Church.
The new missionaries were of the desired Romanized cut and, because they
were foreign, would ostensibly have greater difficulty in accumulating properties. The selective application of the 1855 decree kept out priests potentially disruptive to imperial political stability and hindered the formation of the kind of
state within a state run by the Jesuits.[42]

A Europeanizing Brazil and the Vincentians made a good match. The Vincentians were members of the Congregation of the Mission, founded in France
in the seventeenth century by Saint Vincent de Paul to evangelize the poor and
to renovate the priesthood. Saint Vincent was the great Tridentine reformer of

a decayed French clergy that had failed to improve during the turbulent first century of the Counter-Reformation. During his life France led the way in seminary reform in the Catholic world. The son of poor farmers and a student of Franciscan friars, Saint Vincent entered the priesthood to combat the ignorance of the clergy. He started with a small band of itinerant preachers and became the leading pioneer of charitable techniques of his era. The congregation eventually established missions in the Far East, the Middle East, Africa, and the United States. Saint Vincent considered sending missionaries to Brazil, but the plans failed to materialize. He also founded the Daughters of Charity, a female religious confraternity whose first representatives arrived in Brazil in 1849. Significantly, the Daughters were not cloistered. They were to work in society by educating girls and assisting the poor, the sick, and abandoned children. Saint Vincent had the Daughters dress in plain, gray habits in order to resemble common women. In fact, the Daughters were not officially considered nuns. Administered in conjunction with the Vincentian fathers, the Daughters cultivated thousands of vocations in Brazil under Romanization. They also helped spread popular devotion to the Medalha Milagrosa, a reputedly miraculous medal. Other Vincentian organizations included the Ladies of Charity and services for the care of abandoned children, a ministry for prison inmates, aid to victims of war, and the rescue of slaves from non-Christian captors.[43] Saint Vincent and his followers venerated the black virgins of France. This devotion perhaps prompted Father Antonio Fiat, the superior general, to order the release of its Brazilian slaves in 1879.[44]

Another key influence on Saint Vincent was Jansenism, which, redefining grace and ignoring human free will, emphasized a "spirituality of sin" and a view of human nature as completely corrupt.[45] Opposed to the more tolerant views of the Jesuits, Jansenism caused a deep split in the Church in the 1600s and 1700s. Several popes condemned the movement. It opposed the more frequent consumption of Holy Communion advocated by the Jesuits. Saint Vincent and the Jansenists feared the power of orders such as the Jesuits and Dominicans and, sometimes operating in a proto-democratic vein, worked to safeguard the independence of the bishops from the papacy and the crown. Jansenism shared many points with Protestantism. It upheld the right of the faithful to read the Holy Scriptures in the vernacular, for instance. In France the Jansenists increasingly pitted themselves against the absolute monarchy, helping open the way to the French Revolution.[46]

The Vincentians distinguished themselves for their emphasis on humility. Saint Vincent restricted preaching to the poor of the countryside. While a

number became bishops, none served at the upper levels of the Vatican bureaucracy. None became a cardinal.[47]

The first Vincentians in Brazil belonged to the Portuguese branch of the congregation and probably arrived in search of exile along with Dom João VI, who
had fled from the Napoleonic wars.[48] The Vincentians enjoyed great prestige at
the Portuguese court. Unlike the Jesuits and other orders, they avoided politics.[49] In Brazil the Vincentians became known as "Lazaristas," a name taken
from the former priory of Saint Lazarus, the order's first residence in Paris.[50] In
1819 the crown called to Brazil two more Portuguese Lazaristas, Father Leandro
Rebelo Peixoto e Castro and Father Antônio Ferreira Viçoso, the future reform
bishop of Mariana. They aimed to perform missionary work in the province
of Mato Grosso, but with royal approval they installed themselves at Caraça, a
colonial religious sanctuary tucked in the mountains of the gold-mining region of Minas Gerais and presided over by its legendary founder, Brother Lourenço, who had just died. Lourenço was believed by some to be a fugitive who
belonged to the noble Távora family, many of whose members were burned to
death as suspects in an assassination attempt against King John I in 1758. More
likely he was a wealthy diamond prospector. The people of the region revered
him as a saint.[51]

At Caraça the Lazaristas established a mission and also the first of several *colégios*. This *colégio* became the most prestigious of the empire. Its many
prominent graduates entered politics and the professions and included two
presidents of the republic, Afonso Pena and Artur Bernardes. At different times
Caraça was also a seminary for both Lazarista and diocesan candidates to the
priesthood, and it served as a staging area for Vincentian expansion into other
parts of Brazil.[52] The Lazaristas' educational prominence extended to a number
of key diocesan seminaries, run mainly by French Vincentians who began arriving in Brazil in the 1850s and dominated the order for nearly a century.

Minas formed the nucleus of the so-called Província Brasileira da Congregação da Missão (PBCM). Prohibited by imperial legislation from maintaining contact with their superiors in Paris and Rome, the missionaries in Brazil
had no choice but to form their own province. Only in 1845 did the PBCM receive permission to renew its European ties, thus allowing the immigration of
the French fathers.[53] As more fathers arrived and local recruitment evolved, the
PBCM expanded its scope to include work in parishes and the establishment
of a network of hospitals and lay charitable organizations. Vincentians from
other European nations eventually came to Brazil. At the end of the 1800s Polish fathers joined their immigrant compatriots in Paraná and Santa Catarina.

Later Dutch Vincentians disembarked in Pará, Maranhão, and Ceará. Both the Polish and the Dutch eventually formed their own provinces.

The Vincentians' success resulted partly from their good relationship with Dom Pedro II. Under him they obtained exemption from the severe 1855 decree and, along with the Capuchins, avoided the closed-door policy against the orders. The Lazaristas' goals of religious and clerical reform, support for the social order, and exclusion of priests from politics pleased the government and won applause from the ultramontane bishops. Dom Romualdo Seixas greatly admired the Vincentians and entrusted them with his seminary in 1856.[54]

Social control was the prime directive of the state and the elite. Europeanization progressed quickly in the more developed urban areas, but people in the demographically and territorially predominant countryside did not always react peacefully to religious and social changes. Cooperating often with the central state or local *coronéis,* the Romanized clergy worked vigorously for religious reform in the rural areas. At mid-century, for example, the government invited Italian Capuchin missionaries, specially trained in Rome and Angola, to help quell disturbances among small-scale, free agriculturalists fighting oppression by the state and large landowners in the northeast.[55] In the Amazonian province of Pará the authorities called in missionaries to resume the Catholic indoctrination and social control exercised by the Jesuits a century earlier. In the Tapajós region the Capuchins once again separated Natives into missions run by priests. In the 1870s the rubber boom and increased demand for labor led the provincial government to send Capuchins to set up a mission among the Munduruku people. Natives who left the mission to work for the friars' nonindigenous competitors in exchange for *aguardiente* (alcohol) met with violent punishment. The Capuchins ultimately failed and left in 1882. In 1903 German Franciscans started working among the Natives. They gave way to North American friars who came at the end of World War II to work at Henry Ford's rubber plantations.[56]

Prompted by the Vatican and modernization, Brazil's bishops began to develop a systematic response to Brazil's social problems. Pope Leo XIII's historic encyclical *Rerum Novarum* (1891) marked the start of a more progressive Catholic social doctrine, a so-called third way between socialism and capitalism. Leo asked Catholics to work within democratic structures, for instance.[57] Romanization gradually spawned an ideology of neo-Christendom, under which the Church strived to build a moral society based on Catholic teachings. In line with the Church's hierarchical, corporate model of society, the clergy worked to instill in the masses order, good citizenship, and obedience to authority.

The *Pastoral Coletiva* preached "due respect to the constituted powers, as de-
positories . . . of the authority of God, for from Him emanates all power." Priests
were to teach their flocks a moral code based on the doctrine of individual salvation, regard for the state, and discipline. The Church wanted to promote good
behavior, respect for private property, love of work, and contentment with a
modest life. It opposed strikes. However, the *Pastoral Coletiva* also urged those
in positions of power to be "scrupulous in administering justice." The *patrão*
(boss) should pay a just salary, provide for the needs of the workers' families,
allow free time for the practice of religion, avoid burdening children and preg-
nant women with excessive tasks, and protect their employees from accidents
and "occasions of sin."[58] Romanization defended the Catholic notion of the
family as another of its central tenets.[59] As Brazil modernized, its political and
ecclesiastical leadership appealed to traditional ideas about sexual honor as a
way of civilizing the people. Honor buttressed the family, the basis of national
identity, political authority, and social order.[60]

The *Pastoral Coletiva* typified conservative modernization. Its counsel about
labor came on the verge of violent repression of Brazil's workers and union
movements and long predated the social legislation of the 1930s, and it demonstrated that sectors of the Brazilian Church pondered these difficult problems long before the radicalization of the 1970s. Following the lead of *Rerum
Novarum*, the exceptional social advocate and Vincentian-trained priest Júlio
Maria declared that the Church should help "subject the despotism of capital
to the laws of equity; demand of capital not only charity, but the justice which
is the right of the worker."[61] Yet the *Pastoral Coletiva* upheld the status quo.
The bishops' instructions echoed the words of Brazil's Foreign Minister Felix
Pacheco, an advocate of good relations with the Vatican: "Brazil needs the cooperation of all the living forces of the nation in order to remake itself in discipline, in respect for authority, in the practice of virtues, in obedience to the
law, in loyalty to public responsibilities, in useful work, and in responsible independence without hate."[62] Like the motto on Brazil's republican flag, Romanization envisioned "order and progress."

Romanization disarmed the threat of popular religion to the social order.
Both Church and state sought to control and even violently repress the inward-
looking, millenarian communities of popular Catholicism such as Canudos,
founded in the interior of Bahia by Antônio Conselheiro, opposed by the
bishops, and destroyed by the Army in 1897 in one of the definitive moments
of Brazilian history. Two reformist, ultramontane bishops helped stir sentiment against Conselheiro and his New Jerusalem. One was Dom Luís Antônio

dos Santos, the Roman-educated disciple of Dom Viçoso. In 1859 he became the bishop of Ceará, where he founded a Tridentine seminary immediately entrusted to the Vincentians. Upon becoming archbishop of Bahia in 1880 Dom Luís quickly voiced his opposition to Conselheiro's independent activities. In 1887 he complained to a Bahian official about the "subversive" Conselheiro, who was "distracting the common people from performing their daily tasks." The bishop unsuccessfully requested that Conselheiro be condemned to a mental hospital for religious fanaticism.[63] In 1895 a new archbishop, Dom Jerônimo Thomé da Silva, followed the advice of the governor of Bahia and sent a delegation of Italian Capuchins to Canudos in an unsuccessful attempt to convince Conselheiro and his followers to disperse. The archdiocese subsequently published a report denouncing Canudos as a "political-religious sect" that was resisting the government.[64] Thus the Romanized Church sealed the fate of the New Jerusalem—accommodating the Vatican, the state, and Brazil's coastal, Eurocentric population.

Priests' contact with the people usually entailed less drama and violence, but it had a deep and long-lasting effect on the practice of the faith and social relations. The *santas missões,* or itinerant missions, were a prime example. Prescribed by Trent and carried out in Brazil since the arrival of the first Jesuits, these Catholic revivals reimposed orthodoxy and reawakened the people's faith. They largely fell into disuse after 1759 with the decline of the religious orders, but returned with new vigor during Romanization. The missions became major events in the villages, ranches, and other areas of the vast interior and addressed the people's beliefs, hopes, and afflictions. These remote spots usually lacked a parish priest, but the people's thirst for salvation remained strong. The revivals combined religious expiation with festivity and an important social component: the mobilization of the populace for the construction of churches, cemeteries, dams, wells, and roads.[65] As in Europe, where early itinerant missionaries sometimes burned books and jewelry,[66] they could take on a fire-and-brimstone atmosphere. They also provided assistance to the poor and the sick. Some missionaries achieved saintly status among the people, for example, Vincentian Father Jerônimo Gonçalves de Macedo, a physician who cured the ill.[67] The *santas missões* could be used for explicitly political purposes. In 1842 they helped quell popular discontent in Minas Gerais after the province's failed anti-government rebellion.[68]

The Vincentians developed their missionary model among France's poor. The Vincentians' official name—Congregation of the *Mission*—revealed their primary goal. It was the first of its kind. Saint Vincent created the missions to compensate for the uneducated parish clergy primarily in the countryside. He exhorted his priests to avoid centers of established ecclesiastical and public authority. The saint advised the missionaries to establish a schedule that fit the rhythm of peasant life. To impress the Christian message on unsophisticated minds they employed a direct, simple approach to preaching. One goal was to teach the Our Father. The missions featured spectacular representations, including destruction of superstitious objects, the planting of crosses, and processions with pictures recalling key scenes from the Bible and saints' lives. People easily remembered the hymns because the missionaries put them in the vernacular and set the melodies to popular music. Like other European missions, the French Vincentians carefully designed theirs to maximize contact with the people, instill basic lessons, and lead as many individuals as possible to confession.[69]

The Lazaristas applied the same techniques in Brazil, starting in Minas Gerais. Effective methods included sermons that resonated with the simple spirituality of eighteenth-century *mineiro* (of Minas Gerais) popular religion.[70] The preachers moved the people with an unsophisticated but visceral understanding of the faith, and their Jansenist exhortations pressured or even terrorized listeners into seeking moral perfection by threatening eternal damnation. In 1860 one Vincentian described his success in a letter to his superior in France: "Speak a little loud, announce the great truths of religion, speak of the evil intent of sin: hanging on your words, the people fall to their knees and beat their breasts, shouting, 'Mercy! Mercy!' Speak of the punishments of the afterlife reserved for sinners, and to the cry for mercy they add, 'Ave Maria,' as if taking refuge in her arms. . . . Give them the hope of enjoying happiness of heaven, the calm of virtue, and they shout even more, 'Amen! Amen!'" The Lazaristas' missions spread across Minas Gerais and into Bahia, Pernambuco, and Ceará. In Bahia alone, for example, the preachers conducted 745 large revivals between 1858 and 1920, during which they gave the Eucharist to almost a million people.[71]

While most people welcomed the missionaries, some spurned them. In the early 1800s they became unpopular in some quarters because their hell-and-brimstone style of preaching bluntly pointed out the contradictions between the Christian message and individuals' immoral behavior. Others feared that the Vincentians could be "Jesuits in disguise" intent on accumulating vast wealth and power.[72] One parish priest in Minas Gerais refused to cooperate with the Vincentians, whom he viewed as competitors.[73] In the 1870s and 1880s the Lazaristas clashed with Freemasons who tried to disrupt revivals.

Liberal politicians attacked the Vincentian seminary professors and their bishops. In the early 1900s the fathers encountered resistance within the Church from a small schismatic group that still advocated a nationalistic, noncelibate clergy.[74]

The *santas missões* personified Romanization. The fascinating *livros das missões* (mission journals) left by the Lazaristas beautifully depict the revivals, their social and geographic contexts, and the life of the fathers and their reception by the people. They prepared these reports immediately upon returning to mission headquarters and read them aloud during meals.[75] Vincentians in Europe had begun the practice of portraying mission life in the seventeenth century.[76] In Brazil, Belgian, Italian, and French priests and their occasional Europeanized Brazilian companions rode the interior in search of a lost flock. On the trail the fathers dressed in clerical black, an ecclesiastical hat, and spurred boots. They carried a whip and used shiny, shoe-like stirrups.[77] The harsh conditions and violence of the backlands made the trip a tiring, challenging, and hazardous experience. The fathers' journeys through northern Minas demanded hardiness, skill on a horse, and a certain familiarity with the lay of the land—all acquired outside the bookish life of the Tridentine seminary. The fathers crossed mountains, swamps, and rivers to reach the mission sites. On occasion they traveled at night. Sometimes the fathers covered more than fifty kilometers without seeing a house or days without encountering other travelers. The circuit riding out of Caraça took eight months. At the mission site they embodied a modern Catholicism trying to recover a people long abandoned to folk Catholicism and its admixture of Native and Afro-Brazilian beliefs. The priests celebrated large outdoor Masses on the ranches and in hamlets. They led the multitude in the stations of the cross, the Rosary, offices to Our Lady, processions, and candlelight vigils. The mission usually ended with an evening procession in which the people carried a large cross, which was planted in a highly visible area of the village.[78] The missions became a key staple of religious life in twentieth-century Brazil. In outlying areas the arrival of missionaries was the greatest event of the year. They sometimes provoked moments of gripping collective catharsis.[79] They taught basic Catholic moral precepts and boosted the prestige of the clergy. The *santas missões* sanctified the Church's role as a pillar of Brazilian social structure. They also illustrated the barriers to Romanization and the contradictions between morality and actual behavior.

During the Second Empire and the First Republic the Vincentian itinerant preachers stressed moral behavior, obedience to the Church, and the sacraments as the means to eternal salvation. Christopher Abel's observations about

FIGURE 1. Father Henrique Lacoste, a French Vincentian itinerant missionary, 1890. Courtesy PBCM (Província Brasileira da Congregação da Missão).

Romanization in Colombia apply to the Brazilian missions: "Priests reinforced the prevalent view that status was defined not by an economic but by a spiritual differential."[80] The missions increased exposure to the sacraments, which the priests administered at a frenzied pace to hundreds and even thousands of people in just a few days. Every entry in the Vincentians' Diamantina mission books recorded the number of people who had received a particular sacrament. In general, the more rituals performed, the more enthusiastically priests commented on a mission. During their travels the fathers occasionally met men over the age of seventy who had yet to make a confession or take Holy Communion. The distances traveled by some *sertanejos* (backlanders) to the missions indicated deep faith in God and the Church, but the rituals in and of themselves required no changes in attitude or behavior. The priests lamented the spread of superstition, drinking, and gambling. They corrected the *sertanejos'* attitudes and behavior and commanded veneration of the institutional Church and its ceremonies, buildings, and clergy. The priests frequently witnessed concubinage and marital separation, which violated the Church's prohibition against divorce. They accordingly made great efforts to increase understanding and acceptance of the sacrament of Holy Matrimony. In line with Romanization, the fathers believed that only the training of more priests could lead to people's proper education in the faith.

In a world of hierarchical social relations the Romanized itinerant preachers almost always stood with powerful landowners and backlands political bosses. The fathers often lodged with the *fazendeiros* (ranchers), *capitães* (bosses), or other prominent backlanders. This was more than a question of comfort and efficiency. The priests depended on the local rulers to facilitate access to communities in order to preach the missions. The respect and approval of the local authorities contributed to the success of a mission. It was no wonder that the preachers wanted a judge, a *fazendeiro*, or some other *principal* to confess and then partake of the Eucharist in public. In turn many rulers of the *sertão* (backlands) depended on the missions and the Church to keep order. The bosses showed great esteem for the men who preached good moral behavior and hard work. By emphasizing respect for authority the missions reinforced state-building and the status quo.

Priests were not blind to social injustices, however. Revivals provided a measure not only of spiritual life, but also of material existence and political conditions. In the mission books the Vincentians noted the products of local economies. In their eyes the practical blessings of laboriousness and prosperity flowed from the sacraments and good moral behavior. But poverty reigned. The

FIGURE 2. Vincentian fathers with mission participants, Diamantina. Courtesy PBCM.

inhabitants of the missionary region suffered epidemic diseases such as malaria. The Vincentians' trails included northern Minas, the western stretches of the São Francisco River, and the valleys of the Rio do Jequitinonha and the Rio Doce—to this day one of Brazil's least developed areas. During the First Republic infant mortality rates in Minas reached more than 50 percent, and life expectancy in the state was among the lowest in the nation.[81] Powerful *fazendeiros* and clan politics dominated the mass of poor *posseiros* (small landholders) and Afro-Brazilians. Historically this region had seen no serious attempt to redistribute land or alleviate precarious social conditions. Concern for the *sertanejos* inevitably led the priests to raise social issues and cast judgment on the violence and corruption of backlands politics. The unfavorable political climate became institutionalized as the Brazilian state strengthened its control over municipal governments but failed to provide the money and personnel necessary for ethical administration and protection of the citizenry. Hiring mercenaries, local leaders politicized violent crime.[82] One entry in the mission books for Minas stated that "politics is at the boiling point, hatred is scorching, the *chefes* (bosses) promise worlds of things but do nothing. This evil is ruining entire families and is the cause of the backwardness and decay of so many places of the northern *sertão*. The worst is that this kind of politics is becoming a veritable idolatry." Another sign of social sensitivity came in the Vincentians' praise of the steadfast dedication of the secular fathers of the *sertão*, who often sided with the poor, emphasized social questions, and provided material and spiritual comfort in times of crisis.

To be a priest in this situation was to reconcile the ideals of vocation with the harsh realities of Brazilian social life. The Lazarista missionaries frequently performed a delicate balancing act between the powerful and the mass of the faithful. At times their presence even provoked confrontations. Their primary goal, however, was social harmony based on participation in the sacraments. Romanization was moral, even indignant, but always orderly.

The Vincentians' itinerant missions gradually lost importance as the PBCM increasingly put its resources into the seminaries. By 1932, for instance, the "perpetual" mission based at Caraça closed. The Curitiba and Espírito Santo missions also closed.[83] As discussed in the next chapter, this shift in strategy undermined the Church's ability to remain close to the people. Nevertheless, some missionaries continued their work until the years just before Vatican II. In particular the Diamantina missionaries strode on through the 1950s.[84]

Institutional Growth and the "Moral Concordat"

The critical organizational phase of Romanization occurred during the First Republic. The positivist-inspired military officers who toppled the monarchy in 1889 separated Church and state, wrote religious freedom into the Constitution of 1891, and generally undermined the Church's position in Brazilian society. Catholicism lost its historic claim as Brazil's official religion. Church leaders were ambivalent about the rupture. Religious freedom made Catholicism legally no different from Protestantism, and the state ended the Church's control over the birth registries, marriage, and cemeteries. It also removed religious education from public schools. Religious clergy who took a vow of obedience forfeited the right to vote. Moreover, the Church lost its *côngruas* and other state subsidies, although a political agreement after 1891 enabled at least some Catholic charitable organizations to continue receiving public funds.[85] Disestablishment, however, meant freedom from the burdensome *padroado*. The Church began an unprecedented expansion. Before 1889 Brazil had only twelve dioceses. Between 1890 and 1930 it opened fifty-six additional dioceses, eighteen prelatures, three apostolic prefectures, and numerous seminaries.[86] The government could no longer interfere in the nomination of bishops or block cooperation between the Brazilian Church and the Holy See, which supported the Brazilians by sponsoring national and regional meetings of the hierarchy. In 1901 the pope appointed a nuncio, and in 1905 Brazil gained its first cardinal, Dom Joaquim Arcoverde de Albuquerque Cavalcanti, also the first in Latin America.[87] The Vincentians were especially well-equipped to deal with the new model of Church-state relations. The French fathers who dominated after 1850 had come from a country in which Church and state had long been separated and an ultramontane clergy was engaged in reasserting itself vis-à-vis the public sector.[88]

Significantly, the removal of state barriers speeded Europeanization of the clergy by allowing a veritable flood of foreign religious fathers into Brazil. As Table 3.2 illustrates, the religious priests had almost completely disappeared by the 1872 census. The subsequent growth in the number of foreign religious far outstripped the increase in Brazilians. Between 1880 and 1930 more than three dozen male religious orders entered Brazil, and all but one of the orders traditional to Brazil had been restored. Twelve came from Italy, ten from France, four each from Holland and Germany, and three from Spain, with the rest arriving from various other nations. Although the 1920 census did not distinguish between religious and diocesan fathers, most of the foreigners were likely religious priests, as additional statistics indicate. In 1960, for example, 85.9 percent of the religious fathers came from abroad. In short, the Brazilian Church under Romanization returned to the dependence on foreign religious personnel characteristic of the colonial period.[89] The French Vincentians, for instance, doubted the quality of local vocations and constantly replenished their staff with European clergy. Between 1849 and 1900 the congregation had a total of 228 priests and brothers in Brazil. One hundred were French, compared with only thirty-eight Brazilians. Italians, Germans, and Portuguese also figured prominently.[90] The "denationalization" of the clergy led to the definitive decline of the uniquely Brazilian priesthood developed during the later colonial era and championed by Father Feijó.[91] It marked the end of dominance by the secular clergy and the start of a new phase in the history of Brazilian Catholicism. Reform brought these priests to Brazil, but some also came because of growing religious persecution at home. The governments of

TABLE 3.2
Religious Personnel in Brazil

Year	Secular Priests	Religious Priests	Brazilian Priests	Foreign Priests	Nuns
1872	2,256	107	–	–	286
1920	–	–	3,218	2,838	2,944
1935	2,466	2,028	–	–	8,826
1946	2,964	3,419	–	–	–
1960	4,180	6,971	6,440	4,711	–
1970	5,040	8,052	7,654	5,355	40,660

Sources: 1872 and 1920 census data and 1935 Church statistics cited in Beozzo 1983:97, 105, 108–10; 1946 statistics cited in Bruneau 1974:33; 1960 Brazilian census data cited in Perez, Gregory, and Lepargneur 1964:15–16. Data for 1970 are from www.ceris.org.br.

Germany, France, and Portugal put thousands of religious personnel under stricter control or forced them to emigrate.[92] Once again, to be a priest in Brazil was to be white. Old prejudices about Brazilians' inadequacy for the priestly life reappeared.

The growth in the number of nuns was even more impressive. From 1880 to 1930 ninety-six female orders set up in Brazil. The total number of women religious jumped from only 286 in 1872 to 8,826 in 1935. (By 1970 Brazil had more than forty thousand nuns—roughly three times the number of priests.) Most orders came from France and Italy, but nineteen local organizations were also created. Significantly, in the 1920 census a shade less than 60 percent of the religious women were Brazilian. The female religious vocation was more Brazilian than the male.

The new personnel served as the shock troops of Romanization, assisting in administration, the "re-Christianization" of the people, clerical reform, and education. The expanding network of Catholic, foreign-staffed colégios built the Church enormous prestige among the coffee bourgeoisie, the nascent industrial elite, and the emerging urban, Europeanized middle sectors. By the 1930s the Church had achieved a near monopoly in secondary education. Funds from the middle sectors underwrote Catholic altruism.[93] Tentative efforts to build a base among the working classes also took place.[94]

The organization of new dioceses within state borders helped the Church renew its prestige and power. The *estadualização* of the Church involved hard political calculations, with the bishops and priests of each diocese forming interlocking relationships with local and regional political bosses. This strategy was particularly effective in the less developed states of the northeast, where traditional oligarchies held sway.[95]

Under Romanization the bishops ruled their dioceses like fiefs and made the important political decisions. In the northeast, however, the independent political activism of individual priests did not completely disappear. Fathers stayed active as office-holders, government and partisan bureaucrats, ascetic reform-mongers, and spokesmen for Catholic political and social groups. These clerics were most successful in the *sertão,* which had few professional politicians and less vigilance by the hierarchy. Priests such as Father Cícero continued as *coronéis* and became embroiled in wars between rival clans.[96]

Regional characteristics shaped Romanized Catholicism. Minas Gerais, frequently referred to as the most Catholic state, displayed a mixture of Romanization and eighteenth-century baroque religion based on the colonial mining culture. The influence of the new foreign clergy shone in the architecture of churches such as the French Vincentians' edifice at Caraça.[97] In addition to Minas, Romanization's greatest advances occurred in São Paulo, Espírito Santo, Paraná, Santa Catarina, and Rio Grande do Sul. Large numbers of European fathers arrived to minister to many of the 3.5 million immigrants who disembarked mainly in these states. In the far south, Catholic rituals especially intermingled with immigrant culture. The new arrivals and their descendants continued to speak their native tongues well into the twentieth century. Uprooted by social and political strife in their homelands, the German and Italian immigrants received aid from their home governments, private concerns, and the Church to smooth the transition to life in Brazil.[98] Santa Catarina and Rio Grande do Sul became the *celeiro* (breadbasket) of priestly vocations. The Church in Rio Grande do Sul developed into a political powerhouse by setting up cooperatives among the *colonos* (small farmers), maintaining the loyalty of industrialists and merchants, and establishing a system of schools, *colégios,* and hospitals that surpassed the services of the state government. The Church cultivated good ties with the military and local politicians. In the 1970s the southern priests and bishops of Italian and German heritage formed the leadership of the Progressive Church. The northeast attracted far fewer foreign priests. Romanization had an impact in the coastal cities, where foreign clergy often located, but had difficulty making inroads in the backlands. Some priests of the *sertão* remained isolated from Romanization and continued to practice the traditional rustic Catholicism of the people. In the Amazon the foreign clergy remained in the majority.[99]

Romanization reinvigorated the institutional Church. Minas Gerais was at the epicenter. During the Second Empire European Lazaristas and Italian Capuchins had stirred the local Catholic revival. Later the first Archbishop of Mariana, Dom Silvério Gomes Pimenta (1896–1922), personally recruited Dutch and Belgian priests to assist with institutional buildup. A protégé, godson, and biographer of Dom Viçoso, Dom Silvério was one of the few black bishops in Brazilian history (although some would classify him as a mulatto). He founded the newspaper *O Bom Ladrão* (The Good Thief) to fight the traditional Church's enemies: Masons, liberal Catholics, freethinkers, atheists, and Protestants. Dom Silvério successfully engineered a campaign to reinstate religion classes in the public schools. Minas Gerais also renewed public subsidies to the Church.[100] Catholic activism in Minas provided a model for the Church's eventual realignment with the national government.[101]

By the late 1920s the Church's highly educated cadres were directing numerous social and religious activities throughout the country. The Lazaristas were one example. By the 1950s they affirmed that "thousands and thousands" of women were involved in the Ladies of Charity and other Vincentian-inspired groups. Their statistics showed a total of 2,907 Saint Vincent de Paul societies with more than forty-five thousand members. These societies aided the poor.[102] The Daughters of Charity became active in a wide variety of social projects such as child-care centers, orphanages, and leper colonies. The Catholic press and publishing industry burgeoned, becoming important new, professional missionary tools. In 1901, for example, the Franciscans in Salvador started the newspaper *O Mensageiro da Fé*, perhaps the most widely circulating periodical of its time. In the 1930s the Church increased its work in the field of mass communication. In line with the papal encyclical *Vigilanti Cura* parishes and *colégios* established cinema clubs to show doctrinally sound films to students and workers. Catholic review boards judged the moral qualities of movies.[103] In 1922 Dom Sebastião Leme da Silveira Cintra, archbishop of Olinda and Recife (1916–1921) and later Rio de Janeiro (1930–1942), encouraged the prominent intellectual and former atheist Jackson de Figueiredo to found the Centro Dom Vital (named for one of the bishops imprisoned during the Reli-

FIGURE 3. The church and colégio at Caraça. Courtesy PBCM.

gious Question). The center published the important Catholic journal *A Ordem*, became the seed of Brazil's first Catholic university, and served as a staging ground for Alceu Amoroso Lima, the greatest Catholic thinker of twentieth-century Brazil. Its membership coordinated numerous Catholic organizations that served as the Church's political base. Dome Leme also set up Ação Católica Brasileira (ACB, Brazilian Catholic Action), a group of lay organizations that the archbishop and the clergy used to mobilize the faithful.[104]

The Church's political capital grew substantially. Reorganization reinforced the ideology of neo-Christendom, which envisioned a Catholic religious monopoly and a central role for the Church in society. The Church worked to achieve these goals by attracting the support of the state and the middle and upper classes. Neo-Christendom thrived under such leaders as Dom Leme. He reaffirmed Brazil's Catholicity and upheld the social order by supporting the authorities, re-Christianizing the secularized upper classes, and maintaining a conservative, paternalistic outlook toward the poor.[105] Brazil's leaders paid notice to the Church's growing strength and acknowledged it as a bulwark of social stability.

President Getúlio Vargas (1930–1945, 1951–1954) and the Church relied on each other in developing their respective projects of institutional centralization. As C. F. G. de Groot observes, Brazil's national political unification stimulated ecclesiastical unification. Vargas fostered a more cohesive nation-state, and the Church created a national Catholicism that overrode the local interests of the brotherhoods, sanctuaries, and other expressions of popular belief. For the first time in its history the Brazilian Church now spoke with a national voice.[106] The clergy considered themselves patriots.[107]

Vargas and the Church established an informal pact of cooperation. A *gaúcho* (native of Rio Grande do Sul), Vargas ousted the coffee elite and seized power in the Revolution of 1930 with the full blessing of the powerful Church of his home state, including the participation of military chaplains and Catholic activists. To garner support for his regime, Vargas cultivated the national Church. He appeared with Dom Leme and other bishops at the inauguration of the statue of Cristo Redentor, Christ the Redeemer, at Rio de Janeiro's Corcovado peak.[108] A symbol of official Catholicism and Church-state cooperation, the Cristo Redentor had originated with a French Lazarista stationed in Brazil.[109] The Vargas-Church pact amounted to practical reestablishment of Catholicism as Brazil's official religion. Referring to the formal agreements, or concordats, that the Church signed with other countries, one bishop described this agreement as a "moral concordat."[110] This development paralleled the rise of corporatism in Western nations such as Italy, where the Church enjoyed important privileges under its concordat with Mussolini. It resonated with the Church's self-perception as a perfect institution. In Brazil the Church offered the state ideology, moral content, and models of social discipline, and it backed Vargas's corporatist system by aiming to "respiritualize culture" and foster cooperation among social classes.[111] The Church sought state support in the cultural and religious arenas. It backed and benefited from Vargas's cultural policy, namely the restoration of historic church buildings that symbolized the Luso-Catholic component of Brazilian national identity.[112] The Church obtained promulgation of the Constitution of 1934 in the name of God, prohibitions on divorce, pro-Catholic labor legislation, and more general Catholic demands such as female suffrage and freedom of education (in other words, religious education in the public schools and support for private Catholic schools).[113] The Church and the armed forces also experienced vast improvement in their relations.[114] Prohibited during the republic, military chaplaincies were reinstituted by the government, and religious images and crucifixes were placed on the walls of rooms in public buildings.[115]

While Vargas crushed other political organizations during his dictatorial Estado Novo (1937–1945), he permitted a semi-independent, nationally co-ordinated Catholic movement, the Círculos Operários (Workers Circles), to thrive alongside state-controlled unions. The Círculos were not a labor movement per se; they concentrated on the educational and cultural development of working-class people in an attempt to influence the labor movement and the state. The Círculos and the government united in their opposition to class struggle, Communism, and liberalism. As a product of Romanization, the Círculos aimed to forge a disciplined and patriotic workforce. The Círculos sought to harmonize labor-capital relations and to maximize the responsible involvement of employers in the lives of the workers. They personified the Church's quest for social justice by establishing cooperatives, literacy classes and other educational programs, leisure activities, social welfare projects, housing programs, and other initiatives designed to uplift the moral character and socio-economic status of working-class people. This strategy enabled the Church to undercut Communist utopianism. Furthermore, the Círculos' projects operated in areas neglected by the state. In effect, the Círculos (and the many other Catholic initiatives of this period) renewed the Church's traditional role as a social arm of the state. Modeled on the hierarchical structure of Catholic Action, the Círculos operated under the strict control of the clergy.[116]

Further Church-state cooperation came with the selection of Waldemar Falcão, a Catholic Action militant, as the Minister of Labor, Industry, and Commerce in 1937. Falcão used his post to forward the goals of re-Christianization. During this period the Church placed images of Our Lady of Aparecida and other Catholic symbols in the workplace to propagate unity and order.[117]

The moral concordat thrived under President Eurico Gaspar Dutra (1946–1951), the second government of Getúlio (1951–1954), and the terms of Juscelino Kubitschek (1956–1961), Jânio Quadros (1961), and João Goulart (1961–1964). This unwritten agreement lasted into the early years of the military regime. It fit into a larger set of mutual political goals, principally the fight against leftism in the union movement. Aspects of the moral concordat survive to this day.

Throughout this era government subsidies flowed to a panoply of religious activities and social programs. The aid helped the Church expand its role in building Brazil's social infrastructure. It also created a system of patronage and financial dependence. Politicians granted funds in exchange for the moral and electoral support of bishops, priests, nuns, and influential laymen. The Church used the funds for hospitals, orphanages, nursing homes, charitable organizations, libraries, child-care centers, housing projects, and educational entities (schools, convents, universities, and seminaries) that educated hundreds of thousands of people in the twentieth century. Strictly ecclesiastical projects also benefited. In 1954, for example, the Brazilian Congress voted five million *cruzeiros* for the construction of the National Basilica of Aparecida, a major attraction for pilgrims and a symbol of Brazilian national identity and devotion to Our Lady.[118]

Subsidies to seminaries epitomized the moral concordat. The seminaries educated candidates to the priesthood as well as tens of thousands of boys and men who eventually chose other careers. The Lazaristas' seminaries obtained resources through an impressive array of economic activities, collections, and donations from both the wealthy and the poor. And they pioneered the acquisition of public subsidies. Beginning with Vargas, federal, state, and municipal agencies provided funds to the Vincentians.[119] Many other seminaries soon received their share. Documents from the archive of Gustavo Capanema, Vargas's Minister of Education and a protégé of Alceu Amoroso Lima, demonstrate that he and his aides contemplated making subsidization of the seminaries an explicit policy of the Brazilian state during the Estado Novo.[120] This was a modern version of the colonial *padroado,* which, not coincidentally, intellectual priests studied with care in the 1930s.[121] Funding to seminaries increased over the next three decades. The outstanding example was the Colégio Pio Brasileiro. State help began as early as Vargas's second term and continued into the early 1970s. In 1961 the seminary received a subsidy of 120,000 dollars for a class of eighty-three students—an average of 1,500 dollars per student, a hefty sum for the time.[122]

As Brazil industrialized and its workforce specialized, the moral concordat's formula for social peace grew more complex. The Church gradually modernized its Ação Católica membership, and in 1952 it founded the CNBB, the national bishops' conference. The CNBB organized the Church rationally and nationally, cooperated with the authorities on economic development projects, and brought greater attention to social inequality. The Conferência dos Religiosos do Brasil (CRB, or Conference of Brazilian Religious, founded in 1954) grew along similar lines. Both would affect clerical training. In 1955 the Church hosted the prestigious Thirty-sixth International Eucharistic Congress, the apex of Romanization and the moral concordat. Held in Rio de Janeiro, the congress drew more than a million participants, including pilgrims from throughout the Catholic world. The Church received abundant public resources to stage the event. In return it backed Brazil's policy of nationalist developmentalism and anti-Communism by promoting tourism and class harmony. The splendor of the congress contrasted starkly with the poverty of Rio's burgeoning favelas, prompting Dom Hélder Câmara, the event's organizer, to intensify the Church's efforts to assist the poor.[123]

The Vincentian Seminaries: Disciplined Passage to Another World

Romanization ultimately depended on improved training of priests. In Europe the Tridentine seminaries had achieved remarkable results. An initially skeptical Alexis de Tocqueville commented that the French clergy of the late 1700s were virtuous, faithful, and enlightened.[124] In Brazil the seminaries strengthened the Church by establishing a new, standardized priesthood based on Europeanization and discipline. The Church aimed for, and frequently achieved, the graduation of well-educated, obedient, devout, celibate fathers. The growth of the seminaries increased the number of priests, which the Church saw as the most important factor in its success.

Discipline pervaded the seminaries and dominated the lives of the students. It governed hierarchy, students' and teachers' bodily attitudes, the system of vigilance, the architecture and internal spaces, the seminaries' schedule of activities, the curriculum, and religious activity and belief, including spirituality, obedience, and celibacy. Brazil's diocesan seminaries came to resemble monasteries for religious orders rather than schools for pastoral training. This system harked back to the traditions of the Middle Ages.[125] But it obviously represented the Catholic Reformation too. Saint Ignatius, whose rigorous spiritual exercises helped remake modern Catholic piety, inspired Saint Vincent and other reformers of the sixteenth and seventeenth centuries.[126]

In the early 1890s one seminarian taciturnly summarized Caraça, one of the models for the basis of the Vincentian system, as an "educational establishment whose raison d'être is its traditional and intangible discipline. . . . Here nothing is created, nothing is changed, nothing is transformed. What exists here has always existed, and will exist forever." The Vincentians took discipline so seriously that they decided to close Caraça after a student brawl provoked by a prankster who put his pince-nez on the replica of the Pietà located in the church. Only the intercession of less radical diocesan priests convinced the fathers to retract their decision, but not until two students were expelled and several others struck with the spatula-like *palmatória*.[127]

Discipline built esprit de corps and institutional loyalty, tightening the chain of command from Rome to the parish to the people. The monastic existence sanctified Brazilian priests, making them distinct from the rest of the populace—a stark contrast with the earthy clergy of previous eras. Theologically speaking, clerics were superior because they represented God and thus had supernatural qualities and responsibilities. In sociological and historical terms sanctification meant isolation from the world and its contaminating influences, which could threaten holiness. It echoed clerical paternalism. In the 1940s and 1950s priests writing for the prestigious *Revista Eclesiástica Brasileira* referred to themselves as saviors, heroes, and examples of an *Alter Christus* whose word equaled God's. One 1943 article stated that "the salvation of Brazil depends on the education of a good clergy."[128]

The disciplinary revolution began at Mariana, where Dom Viçoso overhauled the seminary with help from his fellow Vincentians. Originally founded in 1748 by the Jesuit missionary Gabriel Malagrida, this seminary was the first educational institution in Minas. After the expulsion of the Jesuits it operated only sporadically, however. It contributed little to the improvement of the clergy.[129] Named bishop of Mariana by Emperor Pedro II, Dom Viçoso took control of the seminary in 1844. He found no teachers and only one student in the school, which had served as a barracks during the recent liberal uprising. In 1845 Dom Viçoso reopened a newly remodeled and expanded facility. By the end of the decade French Vincentians began arriving to help run the program. In 1859 Dom Viçoso and the superior general of the Congregation of the Mission in Paris, Father João Batista Etienne, concluded a contract giving the Vincentians formal control of the seminary.[130] The involvement of Father Etienne, credited with restoring discipline in the congregation, left no doubt about the direction of affairs at Mariana. The Vincentians considered the training of wise and holy priests necessary to their mission.[131] Dom Viçoso ruled Mariana until his death in 1876. His work proved especially notable because he had to overcome the nettlesome *padroado* and rise above the unresolved debate over clerical reform wrought between liberals and ultramontanes like himself.[132]

Dom Viçoso screened men before they even set foot in the seminary. Complying with Trent, he carefully examined candidates' family and moral background and determined whether they were born legitimate. This last requirement did not automatically exclude an individual. It was part of a larger inquiry known as *De genere et moribus,* whose last stage resembled a wedding banns.

FIGURE 4. Dom Antônio Ferreira Viçoso, bishop of Mariana. Courtesy PBCM.

Upon pain of excommunication the priest and the faithful of a candidate's parish had to declare any of his faults, including physical defects, criminal activity, the practice of concubinage or bigamy, infrequent attendance at the sacraments, or former status as a slave. Although the seminary registered no slaves under Dom Viçoso, he accepted pious blacks such as the future Dom Silvério. *De genere et moribus* apparently became standard procedure in Brazil during the First Republic, although in the diocese of São Paulo it was used only for seminarians over age fifteen,[133] when the end of innocence presumably left individuals susceptible to character defects.

The cassock provided a distinguishing mark of the new seminarian. The return of the black, robe-like garment differentiated seminarians and priests from their lax predecessors and from their lay contemporaries. The donning of the cassock amounted to a rite of passage, the crossing of a psychological barrier in which the external appearance and the internal attitude of the individual underwent drastic change. The importance of this piece of clothing gave rise to the phrase "the cassock makes the monk," a rather superficial description of Romanization but nevertheless an indication of the cassock's power to symbolize. Joaquim de Salles recalled how a colleague at the Diamantina seminary become so attached to his cassock that he believed he should wear it to bed. The impressionable Salles wondered whether seminarians showered in their cassocks! Later, as he prepared to depart for the children's seminary at Caraça, Salles saw the cassock as "the eternal good-bye to my life as a child. . . . The cassock . . . is not the proper uniform for catching birds or digging for worms to put on fishhooks. It would be for praying, perhaps for studying." He profoundly admired the garment: "I courted it. . . . Every now and then, while I was at home, I would go to my room to see it, to check that it was still in the same place, all clean, wrapped up. . . . In a few days I would be a little priest, and that expectation filled my soul with jubilation and strengthened my heart." For the next three years he would wear only cassocks.[134]

Other items of clerical attire distinguished priests and denoted their place in the ecclesiastical hierarchy. The average priest wore a black hat, black socks, and black shoes. Next up the rung was the canon, whose socks and cassock buttons were red. His hat included a red tassel. The monsignor used a red cassock and hat and wore a large ring. Members of the *cabido*, the diocesan council, displayed a small poncho over their shoulders.[135]

A longer time at seminary was another key part of Dom Viçoso's program. For example, the famed Olinda seminary of the independence era had required only one year of residence. The Lazaristas required a minimum of eight years, giving them more than ample opportunity to train and evaluate candidates.[136] Later, with the introduction of minor seminaries for children and adolescents, clerical training could last up to fifteen years.

To foster order and morality Dom Viçoso and the Vincentians established detailed rules and regulations. Silence and cleanliness became paramount. Drinking, sexual activity, and unruliness were strictly prohibited and usually led to expulsion. All activity was governed by a detailed routine. The boys slept in large, barrack-like dormitories patrolled by superiors.

Dom Viçoso and the Lazaristas stressed academic achievement. Students took a large number of subjects in the classical tradition: Latin and other foreign languages, rhetoric, geography, geometry and algebra, sacred history, music, scriptural studies, and philosophy and theology, the two most important elements of seminary training. During the week seminarians spent seven hours in class or independent study per day.[137] In the philosophy program the professors taught the Aristotelian-Thomist Scholastic tradition.[138] Caraça was the Vincentians' pedagogical jewel. Learning took on as much importance as discipline. The director of the school read grades aloud in a solemn public ceremony. The fathers sought to inculcate knowledge in all phases of student life. During recess students challenged one another with questions about Latin grammar and other subtleties of language. Most of Caraça's graduates could speak Latin fluently, and some studied Greek and Hebrew.[139] Latin fell into disuse after Vatican II, but during research in the late 1980s I met elderly priests such as Father Clóvis Duarte Passos, a former director of Caraça, who could speak Latin, French, and English. Such academic excellence made the seminaries one of the top educational programs in Brazil.[140] In this respect Brazilian Catholicism outshone the U.S. Church, where seminary education aped American anti-intellectualism and produced few top-notch scholars.[141]

The rhythm of studies, silence, and prayer caused seminarians to absorb Tridentine values and to acquire a sense of dedication to the Church. Many of the readings at Mariana reinforced ultramontanism. Activities included reading the breviary (the priest's prayerbook) several times each day and attending Mass, retreats, and other observances and devotions. Frequent confession of sins shaped seminarians' habits and encouraged virtue. A later Vincentian manual included a chart on which the seminarian could record daily meditation, attendance at Mass and confession, and spiritual readings. Priest-confessors and in particular the seminary's spiritual director oversaw spiritual development and assisted with personal difficulties. As a counselor to whom seminarians were encouraged to reveal their innermost thoughts, the director engaged in a kind of psychotherapy at a time when the Church rejected modern psychology. He and the confessors held great power over students. Hoping to purge inadequate candidates, Dom Viçoso exhorted his students to examine their talents and motives. The spiritual director aided in this self-analysis.[142]

Dom Viçoso faced resistance from liberal, regalist priests. They rejected the new clerical morality. Despite the bishop's prohibitions against political activity, many priests still served in provincial legislatures. The populace, too, only slowly adhered to the new norms. Many saw no scandal in a priest living with a woman. In 1855 Dom Viçoso refused to accept Dom Pedro II's nomination of Father José de Sousa e Silva Roussim to the cathedral of Mariana because the priest was not celibate. Well-educated and ordained in 1835, Roussim had served in the provincial assembly. Although the Council of State overturned Dom Viçoso's decision, he kept the priest out of the post until 1872. Roussim accused the bishop of persecuting him for political reasons while promoting other clerics who were adulterers or had concubines and children.[143]

But on the whole Dom Viçoso's reforms marked a turning point. New priests were more ascetic and spiritual than their predecessors, and celibacy became a central issue in their lives. Better discipline and obedience improved the diocesan administrative structure, and loyalty to Dom Viçoso increased as he gave important positions to men whom he had ordained. Dom Viçoso successfully denied vicarages and benefices to unchaste or recalcitrant priests. In 1873, for example, he wrote to one vicar who had a concubine, "In order to avoid a great calamity in this parish I find myself obliged to suspend you. . . . Find another place far away, and beware of taking your bad influences along with you. I will make sure that the same fate will befall you everywhere as long as you do not give your whole heart to God." Increased allegiance also gave the bishop control over priests' ties to the state. In the brotherhoods Viçoso's men replaced independent religious devotions with Romanized ones.[144] Among the people the priests insistently preached moral reform. Rather than being pastors immersed in the people's lives, secular priests became like the itinerant preachers:[145] This new generation kept a social distance from their flocks. The altar—not the ranch or the seats of parliament—became their main stage.[146] Dom Viçoso's priests served the Brazilian elite's quest for "order and progress," or what Foucault would call the "society of discipline" intrinsic to modernization.[147]

In 1904 Dom Silvério commented on the new clergy: "The best [clerics] we have in the diocese are results of the work and care of [the Lazaristas]. If we compare the clergy of 1849 . . . with the clergy of today, the difference is so large that it appears we are living in another world. In the instruction, the habits, the zeal, the work for the salvation of souls, thanks be to God, the progress has been palpable."[148]

In the twentieth century the model of Dom Viçoso and other reform bishops became the standard.[149] Italian Capuchins, German Jesuits, and other foreign religious orders also worked in the seminaries,[150] but the Lazaristas were preeminent in this field. The Vincentian reforms had spread from Minas to other areas of Brazil through the work of Dom Viçoso's collaborators and disciples. Dom João Antônio dos Santos opened a seminary in Diamantina, Dom Pedro Maria de Lacerda another in Rio de Janeiro, and Dom Luís Antônio dos Santos in Fortaleza and Crato. Dom Silvério, the first archbishop of Mariana, kept the local seminary strong. Dom José Afonso de Morais Torres, another disciple, founded a seminary in Manaus in 1848. Finally, Dom Cláudio Ponce de León, a Lazarista who had studied in France, reopened the seminary of Campo Belo after becoming bishop of Goiás. The Lazaristas ran all of these schools.[151] Later they took command of seminaries in São Luis do Maranhão, Salvador, Curitiba, Botucatu, and other towns. In 1890 the order opened its own internal seminary in Petrópolis to train Brazilian Vincentians destined to work in seminaries or the itinerant missions. The Vincentians started or directed more than twenty seminaries in all.[152]

Vincentian graduates demonstrated the order's success. The Lazaristas trained well over a thousand Brazilian secular priests from the mid-nineteenth to the mid-twentieth century. Dom Viçoso and his successors Dom Benevides and Dom Silvério alone ordained 734 men from 1844 to 1922.[153] In addition, the PBCM ordained 248 of its own priests between 1819 and 2005.[154] By 2000, 158 of Brazil's modern bishops had studied under the Lazaristas, with more than forty having spent at least some time at Mariana. Five became cardinals.[155] Leading Lazarista students were Dom Hélder Câmara, the father of Brazilian Catholic progressivism; Dom Lucas Moreira Neves, who rose to cardinal-archbishop of Salvador and primate of Brazil; and Dom Eugênio de Araújo Sales, a confidante of popes and arguably the most powerful Brazilian churchman of the twentieth century (see Table 3.3).[156] A number of Lazaristas also became bishops. As in Brazil's military, education and esprit de corps became keys to institutional success.[157]

TABLE 3.3
Leading Brazilian Bishops Who Attended Vincentian Seminaries

Name	Comments
Dom Antônio dos Santos Cabral	Archbishop of Belo Horizonte and supporter of the controversial Liturgical Movement of the 1940s and 1950s (see chapter 5). Deceased 1967.
Dom Carlos Carmelo de Vasconcellos Motta	Archbishop of São Paulo and cardinal-archbishop of Aparecida. Deceased 1982.
Dom Manoel Pedro da Cunha Cintra	Apostolic visitator to Brazil's seminaries (1944–1956) and bishop emeritus of Petrópolis (see chapter 4). Deceased 1999.
Dom Oscar de Oliveira	Archbishop of Mariana and, ironically, responsible for the Lazaristas' departure from that city during the crises of the 1960s (see chapter 5). Deceased 1997.
Dom Hélder Câmara	Auxiliary Bishop of Rio de Janeiro, 1952–1955. Founder of CNBB. Coadjutor archbishop of Rio de Janeiro, 1955–1964. Archbishop of Olinda and Recife, 1964–1985. Persecuted by military regime for his defense of human rights (see chapter 7). Deceased 1999.
Dom Lucas Moreira Neves, O.P.	Auxiliary bishop of São Paulo, 1967–1987. Archbishop of Salvador, 1987–2000. Made cardinal 1988. President of CNBB, 1995–1998. Secretary of Sacred Congregation of Bishops, Rome, 1979–1987. In 1990s considered a possible successor to Pope John Paul II. Deceased 2002.
Dom Eugênio de Araújo Sales	Auxiliary Bishop of Natal, 1954–1962. Apostolic administrator of Natal, 1962, and Salvador, 1964. Archbishop of Salvador, 1968–1971. Made cardinal 1969. Archbishop of Rio de Janeiro, 1971–2001.
Dom Paulo Eduardo A. Ponte	Bishop of Itapipoca, 1971–1984. Archbishop of São Luis do Maranhão, 1984–present. Vice president of CNBB, 1987–1991.
Dom Serafim Fernandes de Araújo	Archbishop of Belo Horizonte, 1986–2004. Vice president of CNBB, 1991–1995. One of three presidents of the Latin American bishops' assembly at Santo Domingo, 1992. Made cardinal in 1998.
Dom José Maria Pires	Bishop of Araçuaí, 1957–1965. Archbishop of João Pessoa, 1965–1995. Important leader of the Church's progressive wing. One of Brazil's few black bishops.

TABLE 3.3
Leading Brazilian Bishops Who Attended Vincentian Seminaries (*cont.*)

Name	Comments
Dom José Falcão Freire	Bishop of Limoeiro do Norte, 1967–1971. Archbishop of Teresina, 1971–1984. Archbishop of Brasília, 1984–2003. Made cardinal in 1988. Key leader of the Church's conservative wing.
Dom Valfredo Bernardo Tepe	Auxiliary bishop of Salvador, 1967–1971. Bishop of Ilhéus, 1971–1995. Headed CNBB's division for seminary education. Pioneer in clerical training, especially in the use of psychological techniques (see chapter 6). Deceased 2003.
Dom Raimundo Damasceno de Assis	Auxiliary bishop of Brasília, 1986–2004. Archbishop of Aparecida, 2004–present. Secretary General of CNBB, 1995–2003. Secretary General of CELAM.

Sources: J. Zico 1988:252–54; J. Zico 2000:330–33; CNBB 1984b; CNBB 2002; www.catholic-hierarchy.org.

Institutional Growth and Recruitment

Seminaries functioned first and foremost for the social reproduction of the clergy. They were crucial to institutional buildup. Reflecting the big increase in the number of dioceses, the expansion of the seminary network made the priestly vocation accessible to more youths and opened careers for rectors, vice-rectors, teachers, spiritual directors, treasurers, and other personnel. Rectors frequently could expect promotion to bishop.[158] At the major seminaries candidates studied philosophy and theology and prepared for ordination. Often a prerequisite to the major seminary, minor seminaries, whose numbers expanded even more, focused on the academic and religious preparation of children and adolescents. The category of minor seminaries included novitiates and scholasticates for the regular clergy and so-called pre-seminaries for the youngest children. Table 3.4 illustrates the growth in the number of seminaries per decade. (A large increase in the number of seminaries also occurred in the United States.[159]) The Brazilian system took on the shape of a funnel, with large numbers of students entering the minor schools, a smaller number

TABLE 3.4
Seminary Growth in Brazil per Decade, 1880–1960

Decade	Number of Seminaries Opened
1880–1890	5
1891–1900	9
1901–1910	16
1911–1920	14
1921–1930	49
1931–1940	86
1941–1950	102
1951–1960	221

Source: adapted from Pérez, Gregory, and Lepargneur 1964:174–98. (Note: institutions for the preparation of lay brothers are not included.)

passing onto the major seminaries, and still fewer choosing ordination. A similar profile occurred in Brazilian secular education in the twentieth century.

To encourage standardization, the Vatican established the Sacred Congregation for Seminaries and Universities in 1915. Like the pope, the Congregation issued specific instructions for reinforcing discipline and requirements such as the study of Latin. In 1917 the Vatican decreed a new Code of Canon Law (*Codex Iuris Canonici*). For priests it legislated Tridentine ideals such as regular confession, retreats, and the prohibition on political activity. It also delineated the seminaries' institutional structure and defined the responsibilities of the rector and other positions. Rome required regular reports from the seminaries, and in the 1930s it nominated "visitators," or special inspectors, to assure compliance with rules. The seminaries remained under the central control of Roman bureaucrats until Vatican II.[160] Quipping about uniformity, one father recalled how a Brazilian seminary relied on a manual written for China.

The Roman collegios became the ultimate means of standardization. In addition to the aforementioned nationalities, Greeks, Scots, Irish, Belgians, French, Poles, Armenians, Bohemians, Spaniards, Ukrainians, Russians, Ethiopians, and other regional and ethnic groups all had their own colleges in Rome. Between its founding in 1858 and 1950 the Pio Latinoamericano trained approximately 1,500 priests. Of those, 173 would become bishops, and seven would rise to the cardinalate. The Brazilians became the largest single representation. Between 1859 and 1934 the Latinoamericano received 433 Brazilian students, producing 277 priests, ten bishops, three archbishops, and two cardinals. Cardinal Arcoverde studied at the Latinoamericano, as did his successor Dom Leme. The Church required that each diocese in Brazil send two seminarians to Rome. When Mexico's violent Church-state crisis of the late 1920s caused the Latinoamericano to overflow with Mexican students, the Vatican dusted off old plans to construct an exclusively Brazilian college, the Pio Brasileiro. The Brazilians welcomed this opportunity to speak Portuguese (as opposed to Spanish) and express their own culture. At the Gregorian University, where some 2,300 students from fifty-six nations studied, the Brazilians displayed their nation's colors by wearing green sashes with yellow stripes. The Pio Brasileiro would somewhat ameliorate the difficulties that many dioceses in Brazil had in making seminary education available. The Vatican entrusted the Pio Brasileiro's administration to the Jesuits. Discipline was Tridentine, with emphasis on the Ignatian examination of conscience, carried out twice daily.[161] Between 1934 and 1961 the Pio Brasileiro trained three hundred priests. Fourteen became bishops, and three attained the level of archbishop.[162]

The Vatican prohibited local theological innovation. The Pio Brasileiro had no equivalent—a national-level seminary—within Brazil. Before Vatican II Rome accredited only one Brazilian institution the right to grant theology degrees recognized by the Holy See: the Faculdade de Teologia Nossa Senhora da Assunção, operated in conjunction with the Central Seminary of Ipiranga in São Paulo.[163]

Good recruitment was essential for reform. It occurred in the context of a perceived shortage of clergymen. Indeed, as Table 3.5 demonstrates, Brazil's priest-parishioner ratio seriously lagged behind the ratio in other Catholic countries. The big expansion in seminaries gave the Church many candidates, but it still needed to develop strategies to ordain more men. So the Church devoted more energy to improving recruitment than to pastoral innovation. Recruitment involved sheltering potential seminarians even before they decided on the vocation, which was often described as a "germ" or "seed" needing cultivation. The word "seminary" means "seedbed" or "sowing."[164] The Church developed a system of attracting and orienting newcomers that involved priests, the community, and the seminary. Vicars tried to keep possible seminarians away from dangerous diversions such as movie houses and dances. The Brazilian Church copied European tactics and implemented Rome's dictates. Parish priests directed local vocational groups such as the *Obra das Vocações Sacerdotais* (OVS, or Works for Priestly Vocations), which raised money for seminaries and exalted the priesthood. Priests looked for potential seminarians among

TABLE 3.5
Number of Inhabitants per Secular Priest in Various Catholic Countries

Country (Year)	Inhabitants per Priest
Spain (1859)	401
France (mid-1870s)	639
Cologne (Germany) (1872)	839
Belgium (1880)	909
Ireland (1871)	1,560
Mexico (1895)	3,523
Brazil (1872)	4,202

Source: de Groot 1996:46–47.

their altar boys, parochial school pupils, and catechism students. In his first pastoral letter as the bishop of Patos de Minas in 1955, Dom José André Coimbra wrote that "the pious altar boy, constant in his service at the altar, a friend even of the sacrifice of rising early to open the church, ring the bell, and prepare to help at the holy Mass, will be a beautiful candidate to the priesthood."[165] Vocational publicity material presented the priest as a local hero to be emulated. It pointed to the family as the vocation's first line of defense. Episcopal and papal statements complemented the vocational strategy. By Vatican II the Church treated recruitment as a kind of psycho-social science. Priest-sociologists studied the problem intensely, as in the book *O problema sacerdotal no Brasil*, which contained dozens of graphs and tables about students, priests, and seminaries. The Church believed that the shortage of priests and high seminary dropout rates were technical problems to be solved with the right mix of good public relations and pastoral persuasion.[166]

   The Brazilian Church concentrated its efforts among the poor and in rural areas, thus complying with the Tridentine preference for the poor.[167] In 1890 Dom Macedo Costa, the bishop of Pará, summed up vocational philosophy: "Priestly vocations are not harvested in the great population centers. This is a phenomenon common to all countries of Christendom. Good vocations are recruited among the rural populations, in the interior zones still more or less preserved from the contagion of the evil of civilization."[168] Throughout the twentieth century the Church depended on the rural sector for roughly half its vocations. In the First Republic Brazil's bishops were generally sons of the old aristocratic families of the empire, of impoverished or declining families of the rural patriarchate, or of outright poor families. The Church virtually adopted poor boys when they entered the seminary. Having a priest son brought social prestige to humble families.[169] Even as Brazil rapidly urbanized, vocations continued to flow in from the countryside. For the period from the 1950s to the 1980s, for example, two Church studies demonstrated that seminarians of rural origin, often sons of small-scale, independent farmers, formed the largest group of students. In the early 80s more than half of the seminarians were still from families of rural origin. The seminarians' fathers generally earned no more than five times the minimum wage—a level of income ranging between utter poverty and lower-middle class.[170]

The Church's avoidance of certain types of boys illustrated its need for submissive people. For instance, German Franciscans who served in Mato Grosso after 1938 avoided sons of cattle ranchers, prospectors, and gatherers of mate leaves, because none of these groups had a fixed residence. Father Servácio Schulte observed: "Here in Mato Grosso people are right when they say that a boy who is good on a horse and rides on the heels of cattle with a lasso in hand has already passed the point of the priestly vocation. The reason is that cattle-raisers have independent, indomitable, and often proud personalities formed on the range, under an open sky, in the intimate proximity of the cattle." Schulte recommended that the Franciscans look for seminarians among families of *pequenos agricultores* (small farmers) and *colonos*, who were tied to the land. "In such families there is generally the dominance of a good religious faith, simplicity, respect for parents, and honesty in dealings with people of the opposite sex. The sons of *colonos* also do not refuse to work and have above all love for their vocation." During most of the twentieth century recruitment was especially effective in the deep south and Espírito Santo, areas with large numbers of *colonos* of German and Italian immigrant stock. Minas Gerais and Ceará provided many vocations because they had undergone clerical reform under the Vincentians. These recruitment patterns often gave Brazil's seminaries a certain rusticity.[171]

In some outlying areas, however, Europeanization's incompatibility with local culture discouraged vocations. In the Amazon, for instance, the ongoing reliance on foreign clergy underscored the inability—or unwillingness—to cultivate native vocations.

Nuns often recruited more assiduously than the mainly foreign male religious orders, perhaps because the religious life now allowed young women to work in education and social services—a stark contrast from the previous seclusion of female religious.[172] Women perhaps found easier entree to the Church because of the second-class status accorded to nuns in the patriarchal structure. In general, Brazilian women participated in the Church more than men. The Church did, in fact, preach a more active role for religious women as Romanizing agents of popular religion.

Father Francisco Lage Pessoa, a Vincentian father who became a political activist in the 1950s, recalled in his memoirs how his early contacts with priests led him to the ministry. His experiences both confirmed and diverged from the Church's vocational ideal. As a boy during the 1920s in Ferros, Minas Gerais, a town not far from where he would later ride the missionary circuit, Lage met Father Modesto Paiva, a recently ordained black priest in the archdiocese of Mariana. A good catechism teacher, Padre Modesto started an informal course to teach Lage and other altar boys Latin and French. Lage learned these subjects so well that he easily passed the first year at the Mariana minor seminary. Lage became Padre Modesto's apprentice, helping care for the church's roses and recording baptisms and deaths in the parish record books. To this point their relationship appeared to match the Church's criteria. But Padre Modesto was more than a kind vicar who liked to converse with parishioners about flowers. He took pride in having been a *peão*, a ranchhand who handled a horse well, and he invited Lage along on one of his pastoral visits, perhaps inadvertently exposing the potential priest to the dangers of the world. They strode into Ferreiros, the first large town Lage had seen and where for the first time he heard people talk about the wonders of the cinema. They also visited Gomes, which was celebrating the feast of its patron saint. The *cachaça* was flowing, and after Mass Padre Modesto had to disarm two drunken men who had gotten into a knife fight. He sent young Lage off alone into the night to notify the police in Ferros.[173]

Mothers usually nourished vocations. Parish priests sometimes tried to make them an "accomplice" in encouraging a potential seminarian.[174] The Church believed that women were the protectors of the family. Mothers' influence comes out frequently in priests' recollections. Priests of the pre–Vatican II era who underwent psychoanalysis in the 1960s expressed a dependence on the Church as a mother figure (see chapter 6).

Raimundo Caramuru de Barros, a key aide to Dom Hélder in the 1950s and 1960s, wrote of his mother's decisive influence. Caramuru grew up in the 1930s in Camocim, Ceará, an important Atlantic port, railway terminal, and stopover for flights from the United States to Rio. The abundance of longshoremen and railroaders led to the formation of a strong local Communist Party.

Caramuru's father took him regularly to see North American films. Despite its cosmopolitan air, Camocim was a devout community, located in the diocese of Sobral, traditionally a strong source of vocations. Through participation in the Marian Congregation and other religious activities the young Caramuru became devoted to the Mother of God. With the aid of a prayer book in Portuguese, Caramuru's mother helped him to understand the Latin Mass. Caramuru later became an altar boy, and his family participated in Lazarista and Franciscan revivals. At one revival the family obtained a copy of the New Testament, which the young Caramuru read. Caramuru's mother discussed her son's desire to become a priest with Dom José Tupinambá da Frota, the bishop of Sobral. Caramuru followed Dom Frota's recommendation to read a daily prayer asking for the seven gifts of the Holy Spirit. In 1941, after he completed primary school, Caramuru's mother arranged for her ten-year-old son to enter the minor seminary of Moçoró in the backlands of Rio Grande do Norte state. The rector was Father Jaime de Barros Câmara, the future cardinal and archbishop of Rio.[175]

Although the Church filled its seminaries, the overwhelming majority of students dropped out because of lack of interest, failure to adjust to the disciplinary regime, or misbehavior (including sexual misconduct). Highly selective, the superiors did not hesitate to expel a student considered inapt. Whereas some countries had dropout rates of 60 to 80 percent, Brazil's rose from 88 percent to 95 percent by the early 1960s.[176] A poor, historically agrarian society with minimal public education, Brazil offered few career opportunities outside the elite professions of medicine, law, and politics. During the First Republic the Church was practically the only institution that provided long-term schooling to people who failed to enter the *faculdades superiores,* or schools of law, medicine, pharmacy, and engineering.[177] Poor boys found in the seminaries an attractive springboard to higher education and a secular career. Most dropouts conveniently left before entering the major seminary. The Vincentian seminary at Mariana boasted three state presidents among its former students, including Delfim Moreira da Costa Ribeiro, vice-president of the republic in 1918 and 1919. The father of Gustavo Capanema, Vargas's education minister, also studied there.[178]

Juscelino Kubitschek de Oliveira, president of the Republic from 1956 to 1961, was Brazil's most prominent ex-seminarian. Juscelino's paternal grandfather converted from anti-clerical Freemasonry to respect for the Church and taught religious history.[179] Because of his family's meager resources and the lack of local public schools, Juscelino studied at the Lazaristas' minor seminary at

Diamantina between the ages of twelve and fifteen (1914–1917). Claiming hard-
ship, Juscelino's mother tried to have tuition waived for her altar boy son,
who had made a good impression on some Lazaristas. However, Father Vicente
Péroneille, a French Vincentian and the rector, gave only a small discount because Juscelino admitted that a medical career was his aim. "Those enormous
corridors, those very large halls. It was a sad place, but I found the atmosphere
of the seminary to be a happy one because I was studying," Juscelino once recalled in an interview. As mayor of Belo Horizonte in the 1940s, Juscelino lauded
the Lazaristas' educational work during a public tribute to the congregation by
former students, including doctors, lawyers, teachers, and magistrates.[180]

Although the Church kept no statistics on the number of ex-seminarians, it
was clearly in the tens—if not hundreds—of thousands during the golden
century.[181] Because of their peculiar training, many faced great difficulties in
adapting socially, professionally, and sexually. Many grouped into mutual
aid associations. Men such as Juscelino and former Finance Minister Roberto
Campos recalled the difficulty of having their studies recognized by other institutions, a common problem for ex-seminarians caused by the lack of government accreditation of seminaries. Campos described himself as "informally
erudite" but "legally illiterate." Key Church leaders believed that accreditation would only exacerbate the use of the seminaries as professional stepping-
stones.[182] Many ex-seminarians of the golden age probably landed jobs as teachers, as did those who quit after Vatican II.[183] By educating thousands of men
and by supplying schools with teachers trained in the rigorous classical tradition, the seminaries served as an escape valve for a state that neglected public
education.[184] This fact helps to explain why the state subsidized seminaries.

The dropout statistics did not discourage the Church. In theory candidates
could back out until the end of their theological studies, but in reality seminary personnel often pressured students to make the priesthood seem an obligation. In *O seminarista,* ex-seminarian Bernardo Guimarães's novel about
a Vincentian-run school in nineteenth-century Minas, seminarian Eugênio is
pushed to his psychological limits by the disciplinary regime, which forces
him to renounce a lifelong love affair. This and other fictional accounts could
apply to many real seminaries of the twentieth century. Once across the thresh-
old and wearing a cassock, the boy became a "mini-priest." Methods of persuasion included retreats, meditations, inspirational or threatening lectures,
prohibition of discussion about other careers, the use of older seminarians
as "guardian angels," and the spiritual director's persistent examination of the
seminarian's conscience.[185]

FIGURE 5. The seminary at Diamantina. Courtesy PBCM.

Canon law and the hierarchy's edicts forbade vocational coercion. In the 1940s and 1950s, however, an old polemic revived between "liberals," who demanded freedom of choice, and "obligationists," who insisted on the inevitability of the vocation. Anxious to increase vocations, the Vatican conveniently steered clear of the controversy, but it did stress selectivity.[186] For example, during his inspection at Mariana in 1946 the apostolic visitator Monsignor Manoel Pedro da Cunha Cintra told the staff that "rectors should not be afraid to remove students not ideal for the priesthood." The rector was required to have periodic discussions with each candidate for a sincere evaluation of his progress.[187] The obligationists held sway, however. In the Olinda minor seminary, Zilda Rocha observed that when his brother Zenaldo decided to quit, the superior expedited a secret departure in order to discourage others from having the same idea. "To leave the seminary in those days demanded greater courage . . . than is demanded of a priest today in leaving the ministry," Rocha wrote in 1972.[188] One prominent priest referred to the Tridentine system as the equivalent of the "abduction of minors."[189]

The Disciplinary Regime, 1900-1955: The Nuances of Continuity

Brazil's seminaries changed little between the consolidation of Dom Viçoso's model in the early 1900s and the 1950s—a tribute to his success but ultimately a symbol of the Church's tragic insularity.[190] After Vatican II Brazilian priests referred to the golden age as the era of the *seminário fechado,* the "closed seminary," or the *grande disciplina,* the "grand discipline."[191] The Church was "self-contained, eternal, outside culture."[192] Priests propagated a sense of timelessness and the idea of the Church as a "perfect society." The institution demanded unconditional obedience to the pope, an impeccable clergy, and defense of the faith against Protestantism, the modern world, and Freemasonry. Until the early 1960s seminarians had to profess an anti-modernist oath in the last days before ordination.[193] The Church was pure, society sinful. Denial of the world required that members of religious orders adopt pseudonyms. Many seminarians used the tonsure.[194] In sum, the Church and its seminaries stood above history.

But were seminaries "total institutions," as some have suggested? Erving Goffman used this term to describe places of residence and work in which a large number of people are separated from society for long periods of time and subject to formal administration.[195] At first glance seminaries fit this description. As in prisons and the military, discipline clearly dominated the lives of seminarians. The mere thought of sex was prohibited.

Teachers often used physical punishment to reinforce discipline. In Fortaleza in the 1940s the Vincentians still struck students' hands with the *palmatória.* Students learned quickly to observe even the least significant rules. Caramuru recalled that shortly after he entered the minor seminary the prefect made him stand in a corner during recess for two days because his eyes had wandered during the burial of a priest.[196] At Petrópolis the Lazaristas required the recitation of the Tridentine catechism by heart. When a novice presented a more modern text, the professor made him kiss the ground ten times. A month later he left.[197] In 1987 I experienced the "grand discipline" in an interview with Dom Oscar de Oliveira, the retired archbishop of Mariana and a firm traditionalist. When I failed to perceive his offer of a rare copy of Father Freitas's *Aplicação no Brasil do decreto tridentino,* Dom Oscar scowled and slapped me on the back of the head before thrusting the book into my hands.

While they were certainly authoritarian, it is easy to overdraw the interpretation of the seminaries as "total institutions." Such a view can skew our understanding and produce a Manichaean history in which the golden century is only criticized and the post–Vatican II era seen as utopic. Reality rarely conforms to the model. Seminarians were complex individuals dwelling in a complex, history-laden institution. We will see in chapter 4 how Romanization and discipline faced very serious limits. The Tridentine regime was a framework in which individuals could develop, maneuver, and negotiate.[198] Within continuity there were many nuances. Without these the seminaries would not have achieved the great cultural heights for which they were remembered.

For every harsh aspect of the regime there was a kind of antidote that made it livable. The seminaries were serious, austere, and controlling, but they had moments and spaces where students could take things less seriously and even have fun. Joaquim de Salles remembered his time at Caraça in the 1890s as years of intellectual growth and building bonds of friendship with other boys and priests. Some clergymen fixated on discipline, employing a "pedagogy of violence" that gave Caraça a reputation for excessive rigor. But other priests treated the boys with respect and kindness. The beloved rector, Father Luís Gonzaga Boavida, was said to have two hearts. Leaders such as Dom João Antônio, the bishop of Diamantina, tolerated a sense of humor in their seminarians. At Caraça and other Vincentian establishments priests offered wine to students, including children.[199] More recently former Vincentian João Batista Ferreira spoke of his days swimming, exploring caves, and reading the classics at Caraça as the happiest of his life.[200] Other priests expressed similar sentiments. Some found subtle ways to subvert the system. Repressed sexuality often found release through sport, intellectual development, and deep bonds of friendship and, in religious orders, a strong camaraderie and even a sense of family. The boys became intellectually isolated, especially after World War II, but the system also revealed substantial permeability caused by the more open-minded teachers. The rigorous training in the classics, philosophy, and theology put Brazil's priests in the stratosphere of Brazilian intellectual life. Discipline, silence, meditation, and ritual opened up possibilities for profound spiritual development that most of the Brazilian populace had little hope of achieving.

In his memoirs Zildo Rocha described how he became an ascetic by savoring acts of self-denial, such as refusing to slake his thirst with an orange after a game of soccer. "Without wanting to argue with myself, I . . . threw away the orange. I immediately experienced a profound sensation of well-being which introduced me to another rank of pleasures, those of the spirit, so real and even more consistent than those of pure feeling." This discovery introduced Rocha to "mortification," to show God "our submission and our love through acts contrary to our 'sensory appetites.' I frequently forsook drinking water

during moments of thirst or conversing with agreeable colleagues during recess, or I even lost at ping-pong on purpose."[201]

Entering the seminary was a decisive moment that marked the seminarian for life. The new student renounced friends, relatives, and parents until
ordination—a period of up to fifteen years. Boys became men under the tutelage of the seminary's superiors. "I prayed to God. . . . He relieved me of my
affection for my parents," Saint Vincent once stated.[202] "The monthly report
cards shall not be sent home to the parents. The aspirants are ours: we must
separate them from their families," Father Orlando Chaves, the provincial of
the Salesians, wrote in 1937. The Church put seminaries on the outskirts of
small towns in order to reduce exposure to society.[203] Outsiders were barred,
and parents could enter only on special occasions. For example, the 1929 statutes
of the Diamantina seminary restricted parental visits to a few hours on Thurs-
days for the major seminary and Sundays for the minor seminary. Seminarians
could go outside only with the rector's permission.[204] Even in the 1950s seminarians who were cousins could be expelled for greeting each other.[205] Only students and priests could enter the inner rooms, where space, time, studies, and
all other activities assumed a sacred character that added to the aura of socioreligious superiority.[206]

Young Caramuru immediately understood the consequences of becoming
a priest. The day of his arrival in Moçoró, the rector, Father Jaime, asked if he
would like to spend that night in the seminary, as classes had already started.
Caramuru recalled:

> I told him that I didn't want to enter that same day. At night I intended
> to go to the movies. For me it would be the last film of my life. . . . Dom
> Jaime respected my decision.
>
> Actually, for me entrance into the seminary implied the renunciation
> of everything that had occupied my childhood world: family life, the
> sea, the frolicking of infancy, the surroundings of my hometown. In a
> way I was becoming an adult at the age of ten. . . .
>
> For someone who was used to running freely across beaches and
> dunes, to facing the risks and immensity of the sea, to living in a local
> society of somewhat liberal attitudes, the discipline of the seminary be-
> came a kind of straightjacket.[207]

Separation was not all negative. The seminary frequently served as a surro-
gate family. Father Luiz do Amaral Mousinho, the rector of the Olinda semi-

FIGURE 6. The seminaries shaped personalities by taking in ever younger candidates, as seen here at the Vincentians' Escola Apostólica Vicente de Paulo in Fortaleza, 1955. Courtesy PBCM.

nary, became a father figure whom eleven-year-old seminarian Zildo Rocha sought to please at all times. "Without the shadow of a doubt the great motivations that impelled me, aside from life in the seminary, to which I adapted without much difficulty, were the friendship and affection that I felt from and for my superiors," Rocha wrote in his memoirs. "The need to have their attention made me strive to obtain progress in the classroom and in 'spiritual life.'"[208]

Seminarians learned a new culture. Boys shed their country ways for more refined ones. In 1924 Father Pedro Rota, the provincial of the Salesian order, exhorted his colleagues to educate students of coarse manners "in the fundamental norms of urbanity, impressing on them the habits of discipline, obedience, and respect for authority."[209] Proper deportment was decidedly European. The Lazaristas' seminary in Petrópolis was based wholly on French customs. Clashes between native and European values revealed nationalistic feelings among the Brazilians (discussed in chapter 4). Seminarians were also exposed to ecclesiastical politics. By observing priests and the machinations of the hierarchy, they got their first lessons in ascending the ladder of power in this global organization.

Hazing existed in some seminaries. At the Mariana minor seminary in the 1930s older pupils addressed incoming colleagues as "*novato*" for an entire year and played pranks on them. The superiors acquiesced in these traditions. At the Pio Brasileiro newcomers were taken into Rome and then abandoned to find their way back alone.[210]

The seminary's schedule both reinforced discipline and helped students adapt to it. The Lazaristas' list of activities (see Table 3.6) was typical. It resembled the schedule of Brazilian Army cadets in the late nineteenth century.[211] The sacred suffused daily life: prayers, reflections, the benediction of the Eucharist, and a reading from the work of Louis Tronson, a seventeenth-century French priest and seminary spiritual director who emphasized renunciation of the world. During this last ritual the students at Petrópolis lay head down on the ground in meditation—or, on occasion, in sleep, as Padre Lage recalled.[212] A bell signaled a change of activities. There was little time for idleness. Students kept silent during meals while listening to a fellow student read from religious publications. In Fortaleza, for example, major and minor seminarians heard selections from *A Ordem, Vozes de Petrópolis,* and other Catholic periodicals. The readings sometimes revealed the latest theological debates, which students would discuss during recess. "We fed our minds, not just the body," Father Celso Pedro da Silva recalled.[213]

The seminary measured the seasons by the liturgical calendar with its saints, celebrations, and holy days. Crucifixes and other holy images reinforced the sense of the sacred.[214] The discipline of time remained with a priest. One father continued to make out a daily schedule and used five alarm clocks to assure that he awoke on time. In the 1980s an elderly Vincentian paced the halls in the afternoon reading his breviary as prescribed in the pre–Vatican II era.[215]

Sports and hikes broke the routine of seminary life and provided fun. In Mariana the Vincentians took the boys on a *sueto,* or outing, every Thursday afternoon after the 1:30 coffee break. The practice predated Dom Viçoso. Padre Lage recalled how he and others in the 1930s got to know the railroad, the nearby town of Ouro Preto, and "every nook" of Mariana during these walks. They filched oranges from residents' yards. After catching a seminarian with the nickname "Santo Inácio," one indignant *dona* shouted: "Is this what you call a saint?" Soccer—always played in a cassock!—was another popular activity in the seminaries.[216]

Vacations at home were dangerous. They broke the sacred cycle and exposed students to the outside world. The Church therefore limited vacations and established special rules. Seminarians had to avoid women, including cousins.

TABLE 3.6
Daily Schedule of the São José Major Seminary

Mariana, 1934
(For days with four classes: Monday, Tuesday, Wednesday, Friday, and Saturday)

Time	Activity
05:00	Arise
05:30	Prayer and meditation
06:00	Mass (followed by breakfast and recess)
07:30	Study
08:00	First class
09:00	Study
09:30	Second class
10:25	End of second class
10:30	Lunch and recess
12:00	Rosary and reading of Tronson
12:30	Study
13:30	Coffee break and recess
14:00	Third class
15:00	Recess
15:15	Study
16:00	Fourth class
17:00	Supper and recess
18:30	Angelus and study
19:30	Coffee break
20:00	Spiritual reading or Benediction of the Blessed Sacrament
20:30	Evening prayer and short visit to the Blessed Sacrament
21:00	In bed
21:05	Lights off

Source: "Horário do Seminário Maior de São José da Archidiocese de Marianna," PBCM, 8 (3) CM/6, ED-29.

Students regularly visited the parish priest and had to behave as if at the semi-nary.[217] The Diamantina minor seminary required students to return with an *atestado de conduta,* or behavioral report card, from the parish priest.[218] One from the Diocese of Jacarezinho, Paraná, asked about attendance at Mass, vis-its to local priests, obedience, modesty in contact with women, and recreational activities. The *atestado* could not guarantee good behavior, especially if a semi-narian lived far from his school or befriended the vicar. During his annual two-month vacation Caramuru resumed his playful ways while the parish priest "looked the other way."[219] To reduce such risks, in the 1920s and 1930s the Vatican pressured the Lazaristas to cut vacation time. Some dioceses built vacation homes in the countryside to avoid sending seminarians home.[220] After vacations seminaries held spiritual retreats to ease the return to discipline. In the Mariana minor seminary, students spent the entire semester preparing for "Day Nine"—December 9, the last day of classes. "Day Nine" was taboo for the staff, which reprimanded the students for scribbling the phrase on the walls. At Diamantina in 1939 "Day Nine" became impossible because the Holy See ex-tended the semester to the day after Christmas![221] Many seminarians simply did not visit home because of the cost and time of the trip. Once he entered the major seminary at São Leopoldo, Rio Grande do Sul, Caramuru did not go home for seven years. João Batista Ferreira spent eleven years in the Vincentian system without a vacation.[222]

Ironically, despite the emphasis on academic excellence, intellectual life posed another potential threat to discipline. To preserve orthodoxy the Church carefully controlled reading selections. According to the 1929 Diamantina statutes, a pupil could be expelled for bringing in "immoral books." The rules stated that "students may not receive from the outside, nor have in their pos-session, without authorization, magazines, books, or other objects."[223] All mail passed through the rector's hands, and political activity and the discussion of politics were prohibited.[224] As Father José Pires de Almeida remembered, in Pe-trópolis at mid-century only a few students dared ask for extracurricular read-ings in the library. In the classroom students concentrated on reciting the the-ses of Saint Thomas Aquinas, the basis of Tridentine philosophy and theology. At times the professor himself would simply read the texts out loud. The rigid orthodoxy caused the Lazaristas' best students and teachers to leave.[225]

Brazilian seminarians had little access to the news, although there were ex-ceptions. During the First World War, which divided the Vincentians at Dia-mantina, the pro-German Father José Edwards Jardim spread the news about

battles through the seminary and showed magazine articles to interested seminarians who gathered about him during recess.[226] Padre Lage's experience was
probably closer to the norm. He remembered that in Petrópolis the fathers cut
out the items about Brazil and the world before handing the papers to the
seminarians. "To pick out literary or movie reviews from among the ads while
sitting in the bathroom was the kind of exercise that caused us a good half
hour of cultural constipation," Lage quipped. Listening to the radio was also
prohibited.[227]

The stifling of intellectual creativity contributed to the creation of a Catholic fortress mentality.[228] Scholasticism cut off seminarians (and therefore the
faithful) from understanding the relationship between Brazilian culture and
the Christian message. Seminarians read the Gregorian University's dogmatic
manuals and did not consult the original texts of the Bible and Church fathers,
or even those of Saint Thomas himself, Scholasticism's founder. Scholasticism
considered taboo any attempt at ecclesial renovation. This situation heightened
the tensions between the nascent conservative and progressive camps of the
1930s. While the Church had gained freedom from state domination after 1889,
the seminaries' break from civil society isolated them from general cultural
trends. State monitoring of seminary education gave way to Roman monitoring. Thus not until 1954 did minor seminary studies gain state accreditation, and
only in 1970 did such recognition come for philosophical studies.[229]

Pedagogical isolation deepened neglect of practical pastoral training.[230] The
curriculum lacked pastoral courses, and students acquired no experience with
the people. "The weak point of the formation received in my seminary was
the social part. In my time there was not one professor with a passionate interest in the great problems of humanity," Dom Hélder wrote of the Lazaristas
in Fortaleza from 1923 to 1931. He later reflected in an interview:

It's odd: in those days, when I was in the seminary, we thought it perfectly
normal that we should prepare ourselves to serve the people by keeping
our distance from them for years and years.... We bore the stamp of the
Counter-Reformation. We in the Church lost a great deal of time because
we were so preoccupied with defending ourselves. We were very good at
justifying our religion, but it was above all a defensive justification....
When I left the seminary I had only one idea about social matters.... The
world was increasingly divided into two opposing camps: capitalism and
communism.[231]

A similar estrangement occurred at the prestigious Pio Brasileiro and Gregorian University. "I spent seven years in Rome without learning which was Italy's form of government. No concern in appreciating the socio-political reality of my time," recalled Zildo Rocha.[232] In the words of one North American bishop, "The ecclesiastical seminary is not a school of intellectual culture, either here in America or elsewhere, and to imagine that it can become the instrument of intellectual culture is to cherish a delusion."[233] Father Theodore Hesburgh, the former president of the University of Notre Dame, confirmed the "rigid and unimaginative" methodology of the Gregorian, although he recognized its ability to instill intellectual discipline and the opportunity it provided for a more cosmopolitan education as compared to training in the home country.[234]

Dom Hélder's relationship with the French Vincentian rector Father Tobie Dequidt revealed the motives behind censorship and the ability of students to negotiate. Dom Hélder wrote poetry while at Fortaleza, where the rector had keys to the students' desks. When seminarian Hélder discovered his poems missing, he confronted Father Dequidt, himself a poet. "Will you condemn poetry when you are a poet yourself?" he asked the rector. The Lazarista replied, "But that's exactly why I must do it! I see you as a priest: I sense that you have a vocation, and I know the dangers poetry led me into. I want to protect you from them: from your imagination! . . . Poetry takes us so far, so much further than we may want to go!" The two struck a pact: Hélder would not write poetry until ordained, and Father Dequidt would stay out of the seminarian's desk. On another occasion Dequidt assented to Hélder's request to break the rule of silence in order to form study groups of seminarians. Dequidt also gave Hélder access to controversial theological writings freshly arrived from Europe.[235]

Conclusion

Dom Viçoso and his disciples were acute analysts of the crisis of the Brazilian priesthood. By revolutionizing seminary training they changed the public image of the pastor. He was no longer a man of the people, but a moral guide and savior hewn from a European model. The Romanized clergy transformed Catholicism into a religious, intellectual, and social force.

Reform created a dilemma. On the one hand, the bishops proudly believed that Brazil would become more Christian with the construction of each new seminary. On the other, spiritual superiority became social paternalism. The solution to this dilemma always lay in the appeal to orthodoxy and authority. The Church modernized, but only to a point. The results were a lack of intellectual curiosity and a pastoral monotony in which the sacraments and morals provided the only answers to life's difficulties. The Church grew, but it also became a bureaucracy.

chapter four

The Costs of Discipline

The grand discipline produced spectacular results. But it also had costs. In the long run discipline became an end in itself, a self-perpetuating system that forced the Church to concentrate more on internal matters than on the people. Michel de Certeau's observation about truth applies to the disciplinary doctrine that governed the clergy: "Truth appears less as what the group defends and more as what it uses to defend itself: finally, truth is what it *does*, it is its style of fashioning, of diffusing, and of centralizing what the group *is*."[1] Paradoxically, through conservative modernization the Church eventually lost its ability to adapt to the new developments of modernity. The inflexible disciplinary regime, exacerbated by Roman interference, favored strict obedience and a dogmatically Jansenist uniformity. It stifled individuality and creativity.[2]

The seminaries exacted an enormous drain on the energy of the institutional Church. Like Foucault, the anthropologist Richard Newbold Adams is concerned with flows of power and its relationship to social structure. He has demonstrated that the construction of complex human systems, including religion, is subject to the laws of thermodynamics. All activities require energy: "the forging of steel, the dry cleaning of a suit, or the dusting of a bookcase; the eating of nuts, the cultivation of rice, or the mining of ores; the playing of chess, the building of a skyscraper, or the arranging of books on a shelf." Once expended, human energy is irrecoverable.[3] We can add to the list any number of ecclesiastical functions: the distribution of communion, the hearing of confession, the building of churches and seminaries, the preaching of specific kinds of moral dicta and religious rites to the people, and compliance with those dicta. The imposition of discipline required large psychological expenditures on the part of priests and students. They wrestled with celibacy. As one observer of the clergy comments, priests each day spent enormous amounts of psychic energy to "combat and dominate" the basic human impulse to marry and form a family. Over a lifetime abstinence left profound marks on a clergyman's personality.[4] As Romanization emphasized the organization, the clergy's collective mental and physical exertions caused institutional dysfunction by diverting energy from the central objectives of indoctrination and salvation of the populace. Institutional inertia reinforced the static, paternalistic model of pastoral relations increasingly evident in the 1940s and 1950s (see chapter 5).[5] Scholars of Latin American religion have focused ever more intensively on the deepening erosion of the Catholic Church's religious monopoly.[6] The sluggishness of the seminaries helped cause the pastoral elitism responsible for the loss of the faithful.

This chapter illustrates institutional dysfunction by examining problems and conflicts in the Brazilian priesthood in the latter decades of Romanization: the shortage of priests, nationalistic sentiments, and the political use of disciplinary infractions and sexual misconduct. It is primarily based on priests' and bishops' private correspondence from the Vincentian archive. These documents allow us to examine the details of discipline and to demonstrate its profound significance for Brazilian Catholicism. They hold a wealth of information that contradicts official ecclesiastical pronouncements, and they reveal a repressed clergy's feelings about the doctrinally delicate, often hidden matter of sexuality.[7] Priests' memoirs are another key source.

The Limits of Romanization

Romanization undisputedly changed Catholicism, but it did not completely transform Brazil's syncretistic religious culture or even Catholicism itself. Romanization was a complex and uneven process. Local culture and history shaped its course. European Catholicism influenced some groups, but not all. Peasants and urban workers, for instance, remained marginal to the Church's elitist thrust.[8] Sometimes Romanization's Europeanizing tendencies actually worked in reverse, as in the suppression of German-language rites during World War II.[9] The tension between official and popular religion most often impeded Romanization.[10] The Church rejected beliefs in superstitious cures and condemned spiritism, but it failed to stop many popular practices and attracted only a minority of Brazilians to its new movements. In Europe the Church battled secularization and could afford to emphasize reenchantment of the world; in Brazil the ultramontanes battled superstition and worked toward *dis*enchantment. As a result, the Church relied more on sociopolitical theatrics than on charisma.[11] In resorting to government help to rebuild the Catholic community, the Church subordinated itself to the state and neglected the interests of the people.[12] Messianism further hampered Romanization and at times created powerful religious movements and social convulsions, as exemplified by the aforementioned Canudos (see chapter 3), the "Holy Cities" of Santa Catarina (1910–1916), and the Pedro Batista movement that began in the 1930s.[13] The Church's victories over popular religion were often Pyrrhic.

Romanization was not always combative. In religiously ornate Brazil it often tolerated and even reinforced many forms of popular religious practice. Vincentian seminarian Joaquim de Salles's picturesque memoir of faith and ritual in the small *mineiro* town of Serro in the 1880s reveals how Catholicism permeated all social classes. It sacralized social life and public order while stimulating a festive, at times even carnivalesque atmosphere that rivaled the emerging Carioca (Rio de Janeiro) carnival in creativity and revelry, complete with fireworks, delicious food, African music, costumes, and kings and queens. "In Serro heaven and earth live in a constant harmony of men and God. They are allies in all circumstances, in all activities, in sadness and in happiness," Salles wrote. Contradicting the usual portrayal of Brazilians as uneducated in the faith, the people fervently demanded the performance of clerical ritual. In Serro most people insisted on death-bed confessions. The faithful venerated images and statues, accompanied priests in the Stations of the Cross, watched dramatic representations of Christ's death, and walked in processions. Many religious moments erupted into collective celebration.[14]

Romanization encountered another important limit among the Afro-Brazilian population. The massive influx of clergy coincided with the abolition of slavery and a reflorescence of Afro-Brazilian religions, especially in the cities. Whereas Romanization proceeded along intellectual and literary lines, the *terreiros* (religious locales) of the Afro-Brazilian religions depended on oral tradition. The former slaves found little welcome in the Church, which, after all, had done little to oppose slavery. The black *irmandades* stagnated as Romanization combated the autonomy of lay organizations and cast suspicion over their customs and festivals. Clerics regarded the Afro-Brazilian religions cults as superstitious. These religions opened up greater opportunities for women than did the patriarchal Church. The Church's failure to tap into the energy of the Afro-Brazilian community stunted recruitment of a local clergy.[15]

The Church's official embrace of Our Lady of Aparecida, a black Madonna whose image had been found by fishermen during the colonial period, apparently contradicted Europeanization. However, her selection as Brazil's patroness was an astute tactic in the hierarchy's plan for religious unity. Devotion to Mary flourished in the Marian Congregations, a prominent Church movement controlled by the Jesuits. As the Mother of God Aparecida had strong appeal among the people. She later became a symbol of the struggle against Communism.[16] Aparecida brought together Catholicism and nationalism in a clerically controlled, centralized, well-disciplined devotion—as opposed to a loosely organized, decentralized lay piety.[17] By compromising, Romanization successfully channeled popular religion's force toward the Church's needs. Aparecida represented the syncretization of Romanization.

The "Shortage" of Priests

Romanization intensified a fundamental problem in the Church known as the *escassez de padres,* the "shortage of priests." As chapter 2 discussed, this problem originated in the colonial period. The Church of the nineteenth and twentieth centuries faced an even greater need for personnel. Father Pascoal Lacroix defined the modern shortage as the most serious difficulty facing the Church and the Brazilian nation. Father Lacroix personified Romanization. Born in France in 1879, he studied at seminaries in Belgium, Luxembourg, and Holland and in 1907 was ordained a priest in the order of the Sacred Heart of Jesus. He served as a missionary in the Congo before going to Brazil in 1915. He worked in a parish in Brusque, Santa Catarina, a town of European settlement that became a major training center for Sacred Heart fathers as well as diocesan priests. He was later a pastor in Minas Gerais, São Paulo, and Rio de Janeiro.[18] In a 1936 book Father Lacroix decried the weak social position of the clergy. Brazil needed to emulate France, "which, struggling to compensate for the losses suffered among the clergy during the war [World War I], has achieved an increase of 3,500 in the number of its priests in the last ten years." Brazil, Lacroix concluded, required thousands more priests—and more seminaries.[19]

In the 1950s Church sociologists produced a slew of studies on the shortage in various Latin American countries, and it was a frequent topic in the pages

TABLE 4.1
Ratio of Priests to the Population

Year	Number of Priests	Brazilian Population	Inhabitants per priest
1872	2,363	10,112,061	4,279
1920	6,056	30,635,605	5,059
1960	11,151	70,191,370	6,295
1970	13,092	93,139,037	7,114
2000	16,772	169,799,170	10,124

Sources: for 1872–1970, table 3.2, for the number of priests; www.ibge.gov.br for population. For 2000, www.ceris.org.br.

of the *Revista Eclesiástica Brasileira* (*REB*), Latin America's premier theological review.[20]

As Table 4.1 illustrates, the ratio of priests per inhabitant worsened dramatically in the twentieth century. Growth in vocations failed to keep pace with Brazil's rapidly expanding population. Between 1872 and 2000 the number of priests grew by a factor of seven, but Brazil's population grew by a factor of almost seventeen. Seminary dropout rates also rose in the decades before Vatican II. Immigration of foreign clergymen during the First Republic (see chapter 3) and again after World War II prevented an even more dire situation.

But was there really a shortage? Initially the very redefinition of priests' roles automatically increased the demand for priests. A geographically expanding, clericalizing Church simply required more manpower. Most interpretations viewed the shortage from the perspective of the priest-abundant Church in Europe and North America and ignored Brazil's peculiarities—for example, the inadequacy of public education and other cultural infrastructure. Clerics focused solely on the quantitative and not qualitative causes. The Church failed to delegate at least some tasks to the laity and to nuns. (Only a few limited experiments along these lines took place in the 1950s. The famed CEBs, which allowed more lay participation, did not multiply substantially until the 1970s.) The potential was enormous. By the early 1970s the number of nuns had topped forty thousand—more than three times the number of priests.[21] As Brazil urbanized, the Church insisted on recruiting seminarians in small towns and rural areas. It refused to devise new vocational strategies for the cities. In addition, the Church made little effort to cultivate Afro-Brazilian vocations. Meanwhile, bishops from across Latin America sent hundreds of seminarians to study in Europe without creating national or regional centers for strengthening cultural awareness and a Latin American priestly tradition. Eurocentrism blinded the Church to local solutions. In short, the shortage was at least partially self-inflicted.

Some will argue that the Church should not be anachronistically judged, because it was historically a patriarchal, Eurocentric institution in which women, married men, and blacks could not conceivably have served as pastors, ordained or otherwise. Such reasoning is faulty. Clerical dissenters had pointed out the immorality of slavery since the colonial era. Two hundred years after the French Revolution the world was replete with examples of social and national liberation and organizational innovation. Brazilian women were enfranchised in 1933 as Getúlio Vargas forged a modern, bureaucratic state. The Church was not oblivious to change. In fact, it fought for women's suffrage. But it resisted many other aspects of modernity. The grand discipline tragically precluded an imaginative approach to the Church's difficulties.

To be a priest in Brazil was to be white. Racial discrimination deepened under Europeanization.[22] The Lazaristas at best were extremely cautious about blacks. In 1928 a young tailor well-known at the Diamantina seminary wanted to become an unordained Vincentian brother. One Lazarista described him as "very prudent" and "ready for any job." However, "the only defect that can be noted in him is his color. . . . If he were to study [at the Lazarista's internal] seminary and return here right after, this accident would not be important, because a brother spends much of life indoors." The writer was clear: a black brother in public would tarnish the Lazaristas' image.[23] A similar case took place ten years later in Mariana, when another tailor, who had spent a short time in the diocesan seminary and had good references, also asked to become a brother. A priest noted that he was "not very light" in color.[24] The 1927 admissions flyer of the Vincentian-run diocesan seminary in São Luís do Maranhão stated bluntly that candidates had to be "*de cor branca*" (white).[25]

As we have seen, some blacks such as Father Modesto of Minas Gerais did enter the priesthood. A black youth might gain access to the seminary through Brazil's renowned *embranquecimento,* or cultural whitening. Nevertheless, while no statistics on black ordinations exist for the pre–Vatican II era, they were undoubtedly rare. The 1940 census listed more than six million blacks in Brazil— almost 15 percent of the population.[26] Photographs of seminarians demonstrate that whites and *pardos* (mixed-blood, dark-skinned people) predominated in the seminaries. The presence of blacks ranged from none to a small minority. A photograph of some seventy São Luís seminarians published in *O Seminário* in 1931 contained only four individuals who might be seen as black—less than 6 percent of the total.[27] A 1939 photograph of more than sixty São Luís seminarians revealed mainly *pardos,* about a dozen whites, and no blacks. A photograph of seminarians at Mariana had almost no blacks. The overwhelming majority were white (see figure 7). A 1934 photograph of more than one hundred seminarians in Diamantina included nine blacks, twenty-two whites, and the remainder *pardos.*

Discrimination was not a Lazarista monopoly. Silent, the Church was remiss. One of the few official mentions of the issue indicated that discrimination pervaded Catholic organizations. In 1960 the *REB* reported that an assembly of religious superiors had debated the topic of recruitment among "the element of color." The fathers carefully worded their conclusions. They urged pastoral work against prejudice and wanted Catholic schools and organizations opened to all people. For religious communities and seminaries, however, the assembly merely recommended an "intelligent explanation" of the issue in order "to eliminate possible racial prejudices." Color could not be a factor in the selection of priests. The superiors added that "due to the social level to which the majority of blacks or persons of color belong, special caution is recommended in the selection of these candidates, as it also is for all those of the same level. . . . Recruitment among the element of color must be courageously but prudently stimulated." At this time the leading historian of Brazil's Jesuits, Father Serafim Leite, sought in several publications to rationalize his order's historical support for black slavery.[28] The Brazilian clergy was not ready to swing open its doors to blacks.

The "shortage" and the Cold War kept up the drumbeat for more priests in Latin America and money from wealthy Catholic nations to underwrite the effort. Shut out by the Chinese Revolution, priests in the Far East looked to serve elsewhere. The Cuban Revolution prompted the Church to rush forces into Latin America to block the spread of Communism. It mobilized international resources such as the Pio Latinoamericano and the Pio Brasileiro. Special seminaries in Spain, Italy, and other countries trained priests for work in Latin America. Other European programs concentrated on anti-Communist ideology. To stimulate vocations the Vatican established hundreds of scholarships for Latin American students. Papal statements exhorted the Latin American bishops to work for more vocations, and Rome ardently appealed to the European and North American bishops to transfer fathers to South America.

FIGURE 7. Seminarians at Mariana. Courtesy PBCM.

The foreigners arrived with guarantees of good jobs in Church administration, seminaries, universities, and secondary schools. They imposed European pastoral and pedagogical techniques. Romanization was again at work.[29]

In Brazil the bishops hoped to alleviate the shortage by building more seminaries. But the Church became caught in a vicious cycle: the more seminaries it built, the more vocations it needed. Coupled with the lengthiness of the educational program, the expansion of seminaries created a demand for hundreds of additional priests to work as rectors, spiritual directors, and teachers. It drained personnel from pastoral work in the parishes, private schools, missions, and hospitals. Even so, the Church still experienced difficulty in supplying the seminaries with adequately trained men.

The Lazaristas struggled with the heavy teaching load. Bishops and the rectors of the Vincentian-run diocesan seminaries sent a constant barrage of requests for more priests to the order's Brazilian superior and even to its international headquarters. They complained that the Vincentian teachers received little pay and worked to the point of exhaustion. In 1926, for example, Dom Helvécio Gomes de Oliveira, the archbishop of Mariana, requested five more Vincentians because of the Holy See's requirement that the major and minor seminaries be housed in separate facilities.[30] Many priests shunned the demanding job of spiritual director. In Vincentian-run seminaries students went long periods without these counselors.[31] The Lazaristas resorted to the use of upperclassmen, former seminarians, and even lay teachers to fill gaps in the teaching schedules. These emergency measures violated the ideal of an all-priest staff.[32] At times even the rectors, already burdened with many administrative and pastoral duties, had to give more than twenty hours of classes per week.

Father José Dias Avellar lived such a taxing existence. A *mineiro* Lazarista, Father Avellar had completed his studies in France before ordination in 1922. In 1926 the congregation placed him in the Diamantina seminary. He won praise for his teaching ability and management of economic affairs from Archbishop Dom Joaquim Silvério de Sousa. Dom Joaquim asked Avellar's superior in Rio de Janeiro to reduce the young priest's schedule in order to conserve his health. However, in 1936, when Avellar stepped up to the rectorship under a new archbishop, he taught as many as twenty-five classes per week and several hours of musical instruction. He had also been "morally obliged" to help edit the local ecclesiastical bulletin. In less than a year the stress led him to request a replacement. "The only reason for my proposal is that I am very afraid of being on the path to hell, as the responsibility is very large," Avellar wrote his superior in Rio de Janeiro. The pace did not slow. By 1938, when he turned forty, Avellar had added to his seminary duties the posts of ecclesiastical censor, archdiocesan assistant for Catholic Action, director of the local Marian Congregation, and leadership of a youth aid program. He ran the Saint Thomas Aquinas Academy, which he himself founded, and had a hand in three other Marian associations. Other rectors had similar workloads.[33] At times the bishops increased the workload, but they also tried to lighten it by sending in diocesan priests to help. The seculars, however, shied away from teaching because of the low pay.[34] The Vincentians cited work as the cause of ailments or as reasons for visiting medical specialists in larger cities. "I think that all these miseries of the body are the consequence of the excessive work of this house. I still have 21 classes per week, much ministerial work, and services," wrote one priest with kidney and eye problems.[35]

The perceived priest shortage sparked ecclesiastical rivalries. Lazarista rectors vied with one another to wrangle additional priests from the superior. They lamented their own priests' exhaustion while accusing other seminaries of maintaining idlers.[36] The Lazaristas and the bishops, many of whom had studied in the Vincentian seminaries, generally maintained cordial or at least businesslike relations. The two groups shared the goal of solid training. But the

Vincentians and secular fathers often competed over vocations and for control of the seminaries. The seminary was a base of power. Despite the low salary, service in a seminary offered prestige and a chance at promotion. Bishops influenced the appointment of rectors and professors or tried to block the transfer of their favorite teachers.[37] At times acting arrogantly, the Vincentians tried to channel diocesan seminarians into the congregation.[38] The seculars sometimes bypassed Lazarista colleagues to report the congregation's local problems to the Vincentian superior in Rio de Janeiro.[39] In 1937 the archbishop of Diamantina found it necessary to issue a set of regulations for his diocesan collaborators in the Vincentian-operated seminary, including an order of obedience to the Lazarista rector.[40] The competition heightened as the Lazaristas lost ground to other orders and diocesan priests during the boom in seminary expansion in the 1940s and 1950s. The Lazaristas had difficulty matching new pretenders to seminary leadership precisely because they lacked enough priests. For example, under pressure from the archbishop primate to bring in a better team to correct disciplinary lapses, in 1947 the Lazaristas relinquished control of the important central seminary of Salvador to diocesan priests. After sixty years in Bahia the congregation decided to concentrate its personnel in other, traditionally more successful seminaries in Minas Gerais and elsewhere. The outgoing rector feared the retreat would cause the Vincentians' national reputation to become tarnished.[41]

In 1956 the Lazaristas learned of a plot, hatched during a retreat by the leading priests of the diocese of Curitiba, to take control of the local seminary from the Vincentians. Ironically, the plot failed for lack of priests. In the same year the Lazaristas debated internally whether to cede control of their seminaries in the north to Dutch Vincentians. As in Bahia, the move would permit the PBCM to protect its best schools from diocesan colleagues who, in the words of one Vincentian, were "dangerously threatening our position in the seminaries." According to the same priest, the archbishops of Curitiba and Fortaleza tolerated the Lazaristas in their seminaries for lack of alternatives. In Fortaleza the diocesans were "making war" against the Lazaristas.[42]

The Vatican complicated the shortage by overburdening the Brazilian Church with unreasonable norms. Rome's representative in the seminaries was the apostolic visitator. A Brazilian priest or bishop, this official had direct access to the pope,[43] transmitted orders to the rectors, and made periodic inspections. The seminaries struggled to comply. In the mid-1930s, for example, the visitator, Monsignor Alberto Teixeira Pequeno, informed the Lazarista rectors of new curricular requirements based on a reform carried out in Italy. These included new subjects, such as Italian, that not all professors were prepared to teach. The changes created a need for more professors. The Lazaristas had neither the necessary quantity nor the necessary quality of personnel. In one case Pequeno hinted that he would try to negotiate the changes with the pope, but he later insisted that the rectors follow the orders. The modifications ignited discontent among the rectors. "It's tough for the professors and the students, but I'm doing it out of obedience," wrote the São Luís rector, Father Luis de Gonzaga Cunha Marelim. In Diamantina Father Avellar threatened to close the seminary if he did not receive another priest.[44] The Vatican would not even consider the possibility of a Brazilian counter-proposal. Monsignor Pequeno implemented a partial solution, again based on European experience, by designating three "central seminaries" (in Salvador, São Paulo, and São Leopoldo) to take in students from undermanned diocesan seminaries. Many students took their philosophical and theological courses at these super-seminaries.[45] In the state of São Paulo, for instance, the dioceses of Botucatu, Campinas, and Taubaté had to close their new seminaries, originally built at the insistence of Rome, in order to comply with the Vatican's new dictate.[46] This makeshift solution only rearranged the problem geographically and made seminary training even more impersonal. Dom Manoel Pedro da Cunha Cintra, the apostolic visitator during the 1940s and 1950s, later concurred that the Brazilian Church did not have the resources to copy the European model of priestly training.[47]

Rome's Reach

The visitators flexed Rome's muscles in Brazil. They reached from the pope's chambers to the seminaries' inner quarters, where future priests felt their disciplinary effect in the most intimate details of their lives. This mechanism afforded a view of how Rome controlled a Third World Church. It also provided a measure of the enormous time and energy invested in priestly training and dissipated in intramural conflict.

Like a modern business organization, the Catholic Church centralized the command of its workforce and maintained surveillance over it. Romanization meant standardization at all costs, with the Vatican issuing uniform regulations for all seminaries. Overriding local filters, communication was direct.

The visitor informed rectors of decisions personally or by mail. The Vincentian superior in Rio de Janeiro and even bishops had no foreknowledge of orders.[48] The papal nuncio and a Commission of Vigilance also kept watch over the seminaries. For instance, the Lazaristas had to inform them about the selection of seminary teachers.[49] These had to be approved by the Vatican's Sacred Congregation for the Seminaries, after the pope the highest authority for priestly education. The nuncio also pressured dioceses to conform to the Holy See's norms.[50]

The practice of the apostolic visit in Brazil began around 1900. Later Pequeno and his successor, Monsignor Manoel Pedro da Cunha Cintra, conducted veritable marathons across Brazil. They were extremely thorough. Pequeno, the fourth of Brazil's visitors, saw all of Brazil's sixty major and minor diocesan seminaries from 1934 to 1937. He routinely met with the rector, the spiritual director, and each student. He concluded a visit with a speech to everybody in the seminary chapel. The visitor left a detailed report with criticisms and recommendations. Many were related to discipline: the necessity of study during vacation, the removal of inadequate students, the ban on newspapers, the avoidance of women and townspeople, the need for more exercise and showers, and the separation of younger from older students. Pequeno then spent three months in Rome conferring with Vatican officials and the pope, who issued a summary to Brazil's bishops.[51]

A visit left rectors apprehensive. They carefully prepared the seminary for the occasion and tried to hide unsavory incidents such as the sexual advances of a priest toward seminarians.[52] Pequeno once promised not to mention a scandalous priest to the Vatican if Father Avellar removed the man from the Diamantina seminary.[53] Pequeno could name seminary personnel and order an array of changes.[54] Such power, however, required that the visitor act with great prudence.

In September of 1987 I ventured into the imposing seminary at Petrópolis for an interview with Dom Cintra, then the archbishop emeritus of the city. He received me in his cassock. Extremely formal and a bit cold, Dom Cintra complained that in the post–Vatican II era people in the Church argued instead of simply accepting authority. Dom Cintra kept the interview short, probably suspicious of a young researcher examining the many changes in institutions that he had fought to protect from modernity. As the voice of the pope he had wielded incontestable power to maintain discipline. He once expelled ten minor seminary students whom he thought inappropriate for the priesthood. On another occasion a bishop refused to implement one of Dom Cintra's curricular decisions. The bishop relented after Dom Cintra threatened to go directly to the Holy Father.[55]

The work of the visitator served more than the Vatican's interests, however. The Lazarista priests used him as leverage in internal political disputes. Padre Lage, for example, maintained contact with Monsignor Cintra as he worked to be relieved as spiritual director at the Mariana seminary.[56] One Vincentian conspired against another during one of Cintra's visits.[57] In 1950 the rector at Mariana averred that one of his subordinates threatened to complain to Cintra about the seminary being overloaded with classes. Another Mariana teacher sent Cintra a letter criticizing fellow priests, and Cintra wrote the diocese's auxiliary bishop about the matter.[58] The attempts to manipulate the system negated the idea of the seminaries as a total institution. At the same time, however, complaints from priests reinforced discipline by providing the visitator with intelligence.

The visitator's conclusions became the grist of Church politics for bishops and seminarians. In 1947 Dom Augusto da Silva, the archbishop primate, used evidence about disciplinary lapses in Dom Cintra's report to justify his campaign to oust the Vincentians from the central seminary at Bahia.[59] At the Mariana minor seminary a student had successfully lobbied with Cintra for the removal of a troublesome priest. The seminarian, whom the rector tried to block from moving on to philosophical studies, had the support of Archbishop Dom Helvécio.[60]

Sometimes collective, head-on resistance could defuse the visitator's actions. In the early 1940s the Diamantina seminary moved to the brink of a major crisis because of politicking priests and an imminent breakdown in discipline.[61] Monsignor Pequeno proposed the drastic measure of removing the Vincentians. Archbishop Dom Serafim Gomes Jardim reacted immediately. "I declared my repugnance to this," he wrote. "And afterwards, to tell the truth, would I be able to find better preceptors? And will others be exempt from irregularities? Do I have enough secular clergy to, without damage to pastoral care, direct the seminary . . . ?"[62] Dom Serafim and the Lazaristas were able to ward off Pequeno's charges.

In another incident at Diamantina Monsignor Cintra decided to remove a Lazarista who allegedly tried to cover up the faults of a favorite student during the official visit. Furious, the priest wrote a letter of protest to his superior. The tone of the letter and the vehemence of the priest's denials suggested that he was affectively involved with the student, or at least this was the impression one of his accusers hoped to pin on him. He brazenly accused Cintra of prejudice, slander, and irresponsibility. He urged the superior to confront Cintra with the emotional letter, in which he directly addressed the apostolic visitator:

> Mons. Cintra reputes to me an infamy. Ponder well, Monsignor, what you do as a result of the imprudence due to bad information and the imprudent acts you yourself committed when you went around telling what you heard and saw in the seminaries. What need do others have to know of what Your Excellency learned in your scrutiny of consciences in the seminaries? Only to foment intrigue and disgust? . . . I ask if this is what should be expected of the visitator to the seminaries. I have resolved to file a complaint against you, Monsignor, before the nunciature.[63]

These words testified to the fear, controversy, and conflict swirling around the apostolic visitator.

With all his many responsibilities, the Church's maximum authority, Pope Pius XI, took time to learn about measures for adolescent seminarians in far-off Brazil. Cardinal Caetano Bisletti, the head of the Congregation for the Seminaries, had been pressing Dom Helvécio to separate the Mariana minor seminary students from the major seminary in order to maintain discipline. Dom Helvécio discussed the matter with Bisletti during his obligatory *ad limina* (periodic) visit to Rome in 1925. He also met with the pope. The diocese and the Lazaristas, Dom Helvécio explained, would "second the wishes clearly expressed by the Holy Father."[64] Discipline was truly at the heart of the Church's concerns.

Nationalism

Romanization produced a nationalistic reaction in Brazil. Brazilians were becoming preoccupied with questions of national identity, ethnic hierarchy, and the essence of what it meant to be Brazilian.[65] The redefinition of religious identity was linked to this process. As in the past, the Church made Catholicity a significant part of Brazilian identity.

The agents of Romanization frequently catalyzed new tensions. Some of the European seminary teachers echoed colonial-era missionaries' doubts about Brazilians' vocational capabilities. The phrase "brasileiro não dá para padre"

("Brazilians don't make good priests") became popular among foreigners,[66] including the Vincentians. It implied that Brazilians could not be celibate. Father Lacroix stressed that seminaries should be staffed with foreign fathers because they best resisted sexual temptation.[67]

Ecclesiastical neoimperialism fanned the embers of nativism surviving from the time of Feijó. The seminarians at Caraça rejected the first French Vincentian professors in Brazil because of their inability to speak Portuguese and their disdain for some attributes of Brazilian culture. These fathers eventually left Brazil. Mariana seminarians too reacted with patriotic indignation against their French teachers.[68] In 1858 people in Salvador staged revolts against the French Daughters of Charity, who tried to impose more rigid discipline on girls living in the local Santa Casa. The old Brazilian monks resented the new wave of regular priests from Europe, accusing them of racism and high-handedness.[69]

New Brazilian priests did not raise the old separatist banner. They were patriots *and* deeply loyal to the Church. Nevertheless, their sentiments about Brazil caused conflict. Nationalism pitted ministers against the laity, bishops against pastors, and priests against priests.

Padre Cícero embodied the new clerical nationalism. In 1889 he presided over a supposed miracle in which the communion host that he gave to a *beata* (a devout woman) in Joaseiro do Norte, Ceará, turned into the blood of Jesus Christ. The idea of a miracle occurring on *Brazilian* soil was unacceptable to the ultramontane hierarchy and especially to priests such as the French Vincentians, who controlled the key seminary in Fortaleza, the capital of Ceará. The Church launched an investigation into the veracity of the miracle. Brazilian priests of the most impeccable ecclesiastical credentials, including one who had studied at the Collegio Pio Latinoamericano, reported the miracle to be true. During the decade-long polemic that ensued, Padre Cícero was suspended from preaching, hearing confessions, and counseling the laity. The investigation came to involve the Holy Inquisition. Father Cícero traveled to Rome to make an unsuccessful appeal of his suspension and the archbishop of Fortaleza's declaration that the miracle was not valid. The faithful ignored the official pronouncements. Thousands of *beatos* and others flooded into Joaseiro do Norte. Padre Cícero became one of the most powerful *coronéis* of the northeastern *sertão*, brokering his followers as laborers and as political leverage. He was one of the most revered Brazilian clerics of all time.[70] While Cícero stimulated clerical nationalism, he nevertheless strove to stay within the institution. He kept the dual loyalty—to Rome and to *pátria*—required of Brazilian priests.

Other churchmen carried the nationalistic baton in the twentieth century. Cardinal Arcoverde, the archbishop of Rio de Janeiro, worried along with other bishops about Romanization's corrosion of the Brazilian Catholic identity. Between 1900 and 1920 he frequently proposed the founding of a strictly Brazilian male religious order. The Sacramentinos finally started up in 1928.[71]

In 1910 a group of leading bishops castigated immigrant priests whose comments in foreign press articles were "unjust" in their criticisms of the "customs and character of our people and the qualities of our clergy."[72] The same year Dom Joaquim, the archbishop of Diamantina, and other bishops composed a letter seeking interethnic peace. It recommended that foreign regular fathers carefully study Portuguese and select colleagues familiar with Brazilian culture for work in the itinerant missions, confession, and journalism. The letter advised "due respect for the institutions and authorities of the country" and the naturalization only of priests who had "the sincere purpose of adopting Brazil as a homeland." The bishops wanted the regulars to improve relations with the native seculars. "Exercise care, then, in treating them with the same benevolence that the founders of the religious orders so zealously recommend. And there shall be no criticisms or disdain of them, not only when you are among the faithful but also among other priests."[73]

Dom Duarte Leopoldo e Silva, bishop of Curitiba and later archbishop of São Paulo, advocated the cultural integration of European immigrant populations and their priests. He demanded that missionaries learn Portuguese and restricted them to certain areas within his jurisdiction. "We must never separate patriotism and religious sentiment," the archbishop declared in his 1922 pastoral letter commemorating the role of the clergy in Brazil's independence. Just as nationalistic, the immigrants stubbornly worked to preserve their cultures. Clergy from different countries even competed for pastoral territory, as the French Capuchins and Italian Scalabrinians did in Rio Grande do Sul.[74] Rising Brazilian nationalism fomented violent reactions against German religious orders during the First World War, forcing foreign congregations to open their ranks to Brazilians and to transfer provincial (intermediary) headquarters from Europe to Brazil.[75]

Clerical nationalism took new forms after the 1920s. Most bishops supported the quasi-fascist, nationalistic Integralista movement (Integralism) of the 1930s. Hundreds of priests joined its ranks and stirred up support among the populace.[76] A 1951 *REB* article reacted against the tendency of new foreign priests to land plum jobs. It held up the journal as a source of clerical and national pride. After ten years in existence the *REB* had more than two thousand subscribers. It dealt "a blow to the feeling of inferiority, all too frequent among us and which puts little confidence in national values while exalting, at times excessively, the foreign elements."[77]

Foreign priests and their Brazilian allies retorted that the critics of the Europeans had adopted "provincialism" and a "false nationalism, which, because of antipathy towards foreigners, rejoices in disrespecting, discrediting, and vilifying the very priests who came from abroad." This "sick nationalism" was a form of "egoism." It incorrectly labeled religious orders as "foreign." "It is scary that there are still Brazilian Catholics who prefer the abandonment of thousands of souls instead of the entrance of the foreign clergy," one defender of the missionaries wrote. Another insisted that foreign priests had "nothing to do with Protestant pastors, . . . but are true brothers, sons of the same Father and Mother, and they want to help save our people by leading our country to true civilization in search of its glorious destiny in the concert of nations."[78]

The French held numerical superiority in the PBCM from the mid-1800s through the early 1900s. In 1909 the seminary at Diamantina was headed by Father Henri Lacoste, a Frenchman. Of the seven other fathers posted there, only one was Brazilian, Father Antônio José dos Santos. There were two other Frenchmen, a Tirolean, a Dutchman, a Prussian, and a Finn. A Brazilian and a Frenchman divided mission responsibilities. In all, of ninety-two Lazaristas in Brazil only fourteen were natives.[79] After the start of World War I, however, the main house in Paris stopped sending new missionaries to Brazil. As the PBCM matured, native vocations emerged and gradually outnumbered the foreigners. Until 1945 only French fathers served as superiors of the PBCM. That year the province named its first native superior, Father Francisco Godinho. Of 275 priests and brothers in 1960, 209 were Brazilian and only thirty-three French.[80]

Ethnic tensions brewed in the archdiocese of Diamantina. Not long after the French arrived in 1849, seminarians boycotted the classes of a priest because of his different customs, lack of Portuguese, and accented pronunciation of Latin.[81] In 1908 Dom Joaquim tried to halt rumors that he would oppose the appointment of another Frenchman to replace the outgoing rector. "I do not put any emphasis at all *on the nationality* of the priests in my seminary," the archbishop stressed in a letter to Father Pedro Dahaene, the French superior in Rio. "I am completely hostile to the idea of provincialism. In the event that you have resolved to change the rector—something I did not request— my only wish . . . is that you have a substitute up to the job."[82] In 1914 Dom Joaquim would lobby hard with a new, less experienced French superior to block the nomination of yet another European as rector.[83] Into the position stepped Father Santos, a hunchbacked man who had served as a teacher since 1901. However, his status was only provisional; his predecessor, Father Vicente Péroneille, one of Juscelino Kubitschek's teachers, had left for France because of World War I.[84]

When word came from Paris in 1917 that Péroneille would return, the seminary become entangled in an ugly imbroglio involving resentment against European control. Father Santos was bitter. Noting that Dom Joaquim perhaps would not accept the change, he demanded that the superiors in Paris decide between himself and Péroneille. He wrote:

> There is much to be sad and discouraged about when Paris does not want to take the situation of this house into consideration, principally because the Holy See is showing itself to be very careful with the seminaries. In the queries it sent directly to the archbishop and in those sent to us by way of the nunciature, I figure as the true rector. The archbishop holds me as such, and so do the students and the people. . . . [Péroneille] wants to enter just as he left; on the way out he humiliated me before the archbishop, my fellow priests . . . and the director of the *Jornal do Brasil.* . . . For the Reverend Father Péroneille I am but a *nullity.*[85]

The determination of the French superiors prevailed, however. Santos, favored by the archbishop, moved up to the newly created position of auxiliary bishop on Dom Joaquim's recommendation to the Vatican, which evidently granted the promotion as a peacemaking gesture.[86]

The career of another Brazilian Lazarista offers a fascinating glimpse of Brazilians' personal struggles to fit into foreign-dominated congregations. Father Antônio Monteiro de Barros was obsessed with proving the connection between European prejudice and the shortage of native vocations. Branded by his superiors and colleagues as deranged, the recalcitrant Father Barros fell outside the paradigm of discipline and obedience. He badgered his superiors, writing, for example, a thirty-eight-page critique of the Lazaristas' performance at the Diamantina seminary in the 1930s.[87] Precisely because he may have been unstable—or extremely audacious—Barros perhaps dared say what other Brazilians would not. The irregular path of his career suggests that he paid a price for his candidness. In the context of ethnic tensions his statements ring true. At least one of his collisions with authority was not surprising, because it was with the controversial Father Péroneille. Father Barros's testimony is also important because he played a part in the crisis that nearly resulted in the ouster of the Vincentians from Diamantina by Monsignor Pequeno. His life and thought reflect the intricacies of clerical nationalism.

Born in 1896, Barros studied at Caraça, where, as he recalled, the superior frequently chastened him without reason. Barros later referred to Caraça as a "barrack of quixotic discipline." In 1917 he entered the Vincentian congregation. Two years later the congregation sent Barros to the Dax seminary in Paris for his philosophical and theological studies along with other as yet unordained Lazarista brothers, including Godinho.[88]

Motivated by nationalistic sentiment, the French Vincentians had closed the congregation's seminary in Petrópolis in the late 1890s and transferred all of its students to Paris. Father Júlio José Clavelin judged Brazilians in their own milieu to be incapable of achieving the necessary discipline for religious life. Brazilians could not speak Portuguese in the presence of French seminarians, nor could they go out without a French chaperone. Despite their prejudices, the French priests demonstrated ample knowledge about Brazilian affairs. They even ministered to the exiled royal family, which had left Brazil after the overthrow of Dom Pedro II.[89]

Barros first expressed enthusiasm about Paris, but over time his attitude changed. In a letter to Brazil two years later he complained about his health, the cold weather, and his "extremely difficult and almost impossible moral acclimation: the character and the mentality of people here are rather different from our own." According to Barros, other Brazilians experienced similar difficulties. He praised the teachers of the Paris seminary but noted that some of its French students were "impolite." "I have no prejudices of nationality," Barros wrote. "On the contrary, I condemn the conduct of certain Brazilian Lazaristas. It is for that very reason that I dare to speak to you with such frankness. What I most ask for from God in my prayers is the grace of a good organization for the seminary so that true sons of St. Vincent can walk through its doors."[90] Soon Barros returned to Brazil to complete his studies in the reopened Petrópolis seminary, but he was then transferred to a diocesan seminary. The Vincentians labeled him as "mischievous," continued to punish him for disciplinary shortcomings, and eventually decided to ordain him only "by indulgence." Refusing this condition, on his own Barros arranged for a bishop to grant him holy orders in 1928.[91]

Barros's problems in the early 1920s revolved around Father Péroneille, who had become rector at Petrópolis. In his recollections Barros criticized the French priest's incomprehension and unjust treatment of Luso-Brazilians.

From his standpoint, politics, the priest shortage, and ethnic prejudice guided Péroneille. Barros had refused to accept the rector's authority and denounced him to the superior general in Paris. He maintained that he tried to get along with the Frenchman, but to no avail. The Lazarista superior in Brazil then wrote to Paris warning that Barros should not be believed because he was insane. In support of his own position Barros wrote that "'the Bolshevist and diabolical revolutionary party of Senhor Barros,' as Father Péroneille calls it, has become legion and, whatever happens, it will not be long before the day breaks in which native Brazilians will definitely acquire, in their fatherland, the right to say the last word about everything that is of their interest." Barros added that the "extremely dangerous tension between Brazilians and Europeans" among the clergy was growing daily. Among the Vincentians an "uneasiness" originated in "the useless and brutal effort to extirpate, instead of guiding, the feelings of Brazilians; in the natural reaction of inferiors who do not always discover the right path, in the preoccupation of superiors in wanting only colleagues who submit themselves to their exclusive point of view, as if this view always had in mind the best interests of the establishment which they direct." The Petrópolis seminary, Barros concluded, had become "an ice-box of undesirables."[92]

Barros penned this analysis in 1940, shortly after the congregation banished him from the Diamantina seminary and relegated him to work in the itinerant missions and parishes.[93] The curious allusion by Péroneille to Barros's "party" had come as Brazilian nationalist sentiment grew in the 1920s. In 1922 Brazil commemorated a century of independence from Portugal. That same year nationalistic Army officers tried to overthrow the central government. The Brazilian Communist Party was founded, and intellectuals and artists sought new, Brazilian forms of expression under the auspices of the Modern Art Week in São Paulo. The Church celebrated its own participation in the independence movement by holding its first National Eucharistic Congress and inaugurating the construction of the Christ the Redeemer monument atop the Corcovado mountain in Rio de Janeiro. Among the Vincentians Brazilian vocations were on the rise. They sought equality with, and later autonomy from, their French superiors.

The troubled Barros's rereading of his turbulent past was undoubtedly influenced by a more recent association with nationalist fury as reported by Father Avellar: Barros fervently identified with the nationalist Integralista movement.[94] Barros argued that nationalism was an antidote to European insensitivity in the seminaries. In his eyes a nationalistic orientation would end the priest shortage, improve relations between foreign and native clergy, and foster a less harsh, more culturally flexible application of discipline. He urged an overhaul of the Diamantina seminary's personnel.[95] Barros's politics disrupted the disciplinary regime. His infamy no doubt contributed to Monsignor Pequeno's attempt to substitute the Lazaristas at Diamantina.

In the 1950s Francophile customs and discipline still dominated seminary life in its smallest details. At Petrópolis Brazilian innovations were practically nonexistent. Despite the tropical climate, seminarians were prohibited from drinking water during meals and had to walk downtown instead of taking the bus. In the recollection of former Vincentian Hugo Paiva, the desire of some students to replace the French style of napkin placement with the Brazilian one constituted "a revolutionary act."[96]

The Dark Side of Discipline: Celibacy, Sexual Repression, and Scandal

The manipulation of discipline damaged the Church. Priests abused the power of discipline and diverted discipline to personal purposes often unrelated to the Church's mission. The consequences could escape the control of the institution and spill over into the community. The Church's rules became weapons in a game of disciplinary one-upmanship. The basis of the Tridentine seminary, discipline triumphed by causing the vigilance of all by all. But that victory undermined the Church. Discipline became a means that smothered the ends.

Sexuality provided the most striking example. Sexual discipline—control, denial, or repression of the sex drive—was the raison d'être of the seminaries. At first glance it might appear that celibacy and sexual misdeeds involving priests and seminarians had no connection to other aspects of discipline or the social, religious, and political activities of the clergy. The casual observer might underestimate celibacy as merely a spiritual requirement. But, as I have argued, celibacy was central to Romanization. And it was a political matter. If the Tridentine seminary did not achieve priests' full compliance with celibacy, it certainly did change both the priests' and the public's image of the priesthood. Acceptance of the nineteenth-century "uncle priest" surrounded by children gave way in the twentieth century to institutional and public persecution of the cleric not careful or lucky enough to hide his amorous activity. Celibacy was the disciplinary measure par excellence.

Did celibacy alone cause unethical activity by priests? Alternatively, was discipline the cause? Or the seminary system itself? Or were these men just psychologically maladjusted or "bad priests"? As Frei Antônio Moser argues, the environment of the seminary alone does not cause sexual activity or perversion. If such were the case, then every seminarian and priest would automatically become a "pervert."[97] I maintain that it was the peculiar requirement of *obligatory* celibacy—whose significance is harmfully multiplied by an exaggerated disciplinary regime—as well as societal, psychological, and moral conditions that contributed to the distortion of sexuality and led to unethical sexual practices. As we will see, an insensitive hierarchy, primarily interested in power, also held responsibility.[98]

Celibacy was universal in the human experience and often viewed as natural. Pagans, Jews, Hindus, Buddhists, Jains, and Native Americans practiced it, for example. People became celibate not only for religious reasons. Hindu men avoided sex because they believed that semen contained special powers. Many males shared in the reverence for semen as an invigorating element. Celibacy had a strong utilitarian purpose, too. Men could shun fatherhood and dedicate themselves to study. Celibacy empowered women by freeing them from childbearing and affording them opportunities for personal development.[99]

In no other part of the world did celibacy become so much a part of the repressive cultural bedrock as in Western Christianity. The staunch resistance of the first martyrs and the brutal asceticism of the early monastics inspired heroic abstinence among Christians. The first monks understood very well the power of sexuality, as revealed in the following regulations against homoeroticism, designed by Pachomius, the founder of the first Christian monastery: monks had to cover their knees, lower their eyes in the presence of colleagues, keep silent during work and meals, avoid being alone with each other, not do or request a favor, and abstain from taking part in the laughter and games of children housed in the monastery. Celibates in early Christianity were angelic compared to the married, who were earthy, unclean, and loathsome. Erections were demonic, and masturbation and wet dreams prohibited; the penis should not be touched or seen. The most radical adherents of celibacy castrated themselves. Eunuchs came to exert considerable power in the Church.[100] As the religious historian Karen Armstrong has observed, Christianity is based on feelings of revulsion about sexuality rooted in deep anxiety and repression. It is also misogynist because of its notion of Original Sin and the view of Eve as the first temptress. Original Sin passes to the next generation through the sexual act, which was contaminated by the desire to take pleasure in creatures and not in God. Western men and women are alienated from themselves because of Christianity's constant denigration of sexuality.[101] Brazilian psychoanalyst Geraldino Ferreira Netto believes that Christianity repressed the mother goddess, whose vagina nevertheless reemerged in the form of the triangular trinity of Father, Son, and Holy Spirit.[102] Nevertheless, the notion of the vagina as the "Gateway to the Devil" persisted. Women were evil, untrustworthy seductresses. A Church struggling to assimilate the belief in the divine conception of Jesus Christ and the lifelong virginity of Mary, the Queen of the World, who had lost her humanity and femininity in Catholic theology, needed to reject the quintessentially human act of sex and uplift virginity and chastity as primary values.[103]

In Max Weber's analysis celibacy is a "symptom of charismatic qualities and a source of valuable ecstatic abilities, which qualities and abilities are necessary instruments for the magical control of the god." Celibacy in Christianity has also been linked to "ethical achievement" and the preservation of Church property because it prevents priests from having heirs.[104] Celibacy receives plentiful justification in the theological statements of the Church hierarchy, which puts chastity on a plane with baptism (the first of the sacraments in a Christian life) and portrays its observance as a battle against the temptations of the flesh, the world, and the devil. Celibacy is also a sign of total dedication to God. It frees priests to conduct pastoral work without the burdens of a family. In the seminaries chastity is the greatest virtue.[105]

Dom Hélder Câmara lived the religious and social ideals of celibacy. He maintained chastity throughout his career despite being surrounded by an assortment of young, attractive, female assistants. He achieved a complete sublimation of his sexual drive in service to the Church. The site of a beautiful woman during an outing with Dom Jaime de Barros Câmara, the cardinal-archbishop Rio de Janeiro, captured Dom Hélder's feelings.

I remember one day when we went out together for a car ride and we passed along Copacabana beach. The first bikinis were starting to appear, and there came a lovely young woman wearing one walking in front of us on her way from the beach. I was dazzled by her beauty: water dripped from her hair, her face, and her arms. I watched her rapt, but I noticed that my cardinal became restless and uncomfortable with my look of beatitude, with my smile of appreciation. Then I said to him: "Look, dear cardinal, it is difficult to judge. . . . In following that woman

with my eyes—I vow to you on the name of Our Lord—I believe that
it must be with the same interior and exterior beauty that we feel at the
end of the Mass. It allows us to submerge into the Spirit of God, and
grace drips from our fingers, from our hands, from our entire body. . . .
I think the human body is admirable, because it is the masterpiece of
creation. And how it is beautiful!"[106]

Dom Hélder was exceptional. As the theologian Edward Schillebeeckx has observed, the celibacy law was the Church's attempt to reactivate, by way of Holy
Orders, the original experience of the Church, which intrinsically led to the
spontaneous practice of celibacy.[107] But most Church leaders held Dom Jaime's
repressive outlook. They wrote the rules for the rest of the clergy.

Although vast numbers of priests, monks, laypeople, and even many popes
flouted the teachings on celibacy, the papacy campaigned to enforce them. In
the Church's first few centuries priests married and procreated just like anybody else. The Church did not seek to impose celibacy until the fourth century. Married priests continued to exercise the ministry, but it became more
difficult for a clergyman to marry after ordination. Nevertheless, priests often
married, in part to form the much-needed viable economic unit afforded by
a family. By the late sixth century most priests no longer married, but compliance with celibacy was poor. For a thousand years, from the fourth to the thirteenth century, in fits and starts the hierarchy would gradually strengthen the
enforcement and extent of the law of celibacy until it included clergymen at
all levels. For instance, reacting to monastics' corruption and disrespect for
celibacy, in the eleventh century Pope Gregory VII launched a great reform. It
largely failed, but celibacy attained greater value among clerics and the faithful.
Trent and the Counter-Reformation reaffirmed celibacy more vigorously than
the Church had ever done before.[108]

The celibacy requirement had spiritual, theological, and economic causes.
It is a historical construct that took centuries to consolidate and enforce. Ultimately it must be seen as an ecclesiastical law and not as a divine institution.

In Brazil celibacy became a primary objective of a Romanizing Church. It
finally distinguished the clergy from the laity in a religious culture in which
priests had rejected chastity. Celibacy reinforced hierarchical discipline and the
creation of an emotional and spiritual allegiance to the institutional Church.
In the seminaries the expression of the sexual drive, whether heterosexual or
homosexual, could disrupt socialization and the establishment of an ecclesiastical esprit de corps. Rectors put a check on the sex drive with a strict code of

behavior. "Any affective manifestation that appeared to be any kind of courtship was taken as sufficient reason for pure and simple expulsion from the seminary," Zildo Rocha, a laicized priest, recollected from his days in the Olinda minor seminary.[109] Seminary programs encouraged sports and frequent exercise as an outlet for sexual energies. Seminarians were prohibited from contact with employees or lay persons in the seminary.[110]

The Church facilitated repression by presenting women as dangerous. Fear of women formed part of a larger campaign by the Church to define their subordinate role in society. The woman was subject to her husband's control. The Church fought constantly against divorce, and it disapproved of women who dressed immodestly or left the seclusion of the home to enter the job market. The one public place that women could frequent was the church. Religion was a feminine domain. In the view of staunch Catholics, women needed to emulate their European counterparts by becoming involved only in safe activities like charitable work. The Church preached against fornication and urged young people to remain sexually pure while developing their religiosity. As the self-proclaimed guardian of the nation's virtues, the Church also sought to reform the Brazilian family. The Church attacked concubinage and aimed to shield the family from the threatening tendencies of modernization. Clerics were not alone in prescribing a model for the family. In trying to establish standards of hygiene and to prevent racial "degeneration," medical reformers and eugenicists studied and issued recommendations about the family and procreation. The bishops were deeply concerned with the influence of the emerging print press on women's roles, sexuality, and the family.[111] They countered by opening Catholic newspapers and periodicals. Father Lacroix, the paragon of the "good press,"[112] wanted Brazil to develop a corps of one thousand sacerdotal journalists and writers to strengthen Catholic publishing. Whereas Brazil had only one Catholic daily newspaper for fifty million people, Holland had twenty-four dailies for only two million inhabitants.[113] The new Catholic publications targeted a female audience and emphasized themes such as the key role of the mother in child-raising. The Church effectively projected its message, but it achieved little in the way of modifying behavior with respect to sexuality and the family.[114]

In a 1935 book Father Lacroix made a case for the "great institution of celibacy" as the basis for the Christian family. Priests and others who chose to live celibately led heroic lives that revealed "a cultural factor of the first order and of the greatest necessity, for individuals as well as society." They set an example of moral behavior. Celibacy, however, everywhere confronted two dangerous concepts: the belief in both the "irresistible sexual need" and the "harmfulness of continence." To solve the "problem" Lacroix advocated vigorous education in morals, devotion to the Sacred Heart of Jesus, monogamy, asceticism, and the avoidance of "bad thoughts," "bad conversations," and "bad company." Boys had to be kept separate from girls in the educational system. "Here in Brazil there is no coeducation, except in Protestant colégios and some small schools of little importance," Lacroix noted.[115]

The accent on sexual continence did not mix well with the Brazilian tradition of clerical concubinage. Some backlands priests resisted change. One clerical defender of Canudos, for example, sired ten children with his lover.[116] Despite their preachments against concubinage among the laity, it is noteworthy that the Vincentian missionaries did not comment on secular priests' attitudes about celibacy. It was better to overlook infractions than to make enemies of priests who assisted the missions.

Inside the seminary celibacy was a cherished ideal. This meant avoidance of all women except those who could be seen asexually: the mother, saints, and the Virgin Mary, who was to be the only element of affection. Seminary staffs promoted an intense devotion to Mary. Saint Theresa, Maria Gorette, and Bernadette of Lourdes were also worthy of devotion. All other women became mere objects, considered culturally inferior and looked upon with disdain and indifference. But at the same time they were dangerous, "the pretty and attractive face of the devil," as one priest said. One of the most popular male saints was São Luís Gonzaga, famous for avoiding the gazes of women, even that of his own mother.[117]

One priest's attempt to entertain the boys at Caraça in the 1950s ended in a collective outpouring of sublimated libido. Father Alpheu showed the 1942 film *Always in My Heart*, a maudlin musical in which a man wrongly convicted of murder wins release from prison only to learn that his wife and daughter have found a new life with another man. The daughter captured the hearts of the seminarians. The day after the screening the entire student body was depressed at the prospect of never being able to be with such a young woman. Their fixation led them to buy the soundtrack and memorize some of its songs.[118]

Seminary professors similarly degraded other threats to celibacy with criticisms or silence. Priests talked as little as possible about families, for instance. If they did, they remembered the inconveniences of conjugal life. Marriage required the sexual act, a necessary evil that tainted people. In Brazil the celebration of marriages was prohibited in seminary chapels.[119]

The policing of sexuality included the repression of homosexual activity and so-called *amizades particulares*, or "private friendships." Both occurred quite naturally in the seminaries' all-male environment. Like all humans, priests needed intimacy. The smothering of this impulse could cause serious psychological difficulties or force the individual to seek intimacy surreptitiously.[120] Homosexuality was no secret in the Church. Since at the least the Middle Ages the priesthood and religious communities held a particular attraction for gay people, providing a refuge from the prejudices of society[121] and a place for engaging in everyday sociability.[122] Late nineteenth-century observers noted that some Brazilian religious clergymen engaged in homosexual activity, and the doorways of convents and church stairways afforded meeting places for gay men. As with its refusal to attack spiritism and Afro-Brazilian religions, however, the Church did not speak out publicly against homosexuality. In line with its policies of modernization, it left this task to the medical and legal communities.[123] But within the disciplinary regime of the seminaries the clergy sought to impose the strictest moral conformity. Sexual activity was motive for immediate expulsion. Private friendships resembled courtship in that the couple established exclusivity, the need of each other's constant company, and feelings such as jealousy. Even if they remained platonic, the friendships were dangerous because they signified a relationship separate from the collective ideal of the priesthood.[124] At Caraça students skirted the prohibition on private friendships by engaging in a practice known as *bonecar,* a neologistical verb derived from *boneca,* or doll. A sixteen-year-old student, for example, would *bonecar* an eleven-year-old by becoming his playmate, grabbing him in jest, or touching him. These relationships took on sexual connotations and were severely scrutinized by seminary professors.[125]

Zildo Rocha's private friendships and struggles with sexuality shed light on the issue of celibacy and sin. In 1946, at the age of eleven, Zildo Rocha entered the minor seminary in Olinda. In contrast with its previous liberal orientation, Olinda now operated in the Tridentine mode. Two of Rocha's brothers also became seminarians. In the minor seminary young Zildo's "bad thoughts" became habitual topics of his weekly confessions. Two incidents involving "semi-declared erotic touches or gestures" with another seminarian left him depressed and repentant to the point that "I cried during confession, considering myself the worst of sinners." In the "artificial" confines of the seminary Rocha began to have a "strong feeling" for another student. He wrote, "I do not remember any censure on the part of my superiors with respect to that friendship. I even have a vague memory of a commentary by Father Arnaldo [Cabral] that the friendship would be advantageous because my friend was an exceptionally gifted person intellectually and spiritually." After Rocha's brother Zeferino left Olinda for Rome, the private friendship intensified. "My affective life would revolve around his, and his presence or absence, his manifestations of indifference or reciprocity would determine the rhythm of my ups and downs." While tension over sexuality and celibacy abounded, Rocha's recollections suggested that a certain tolerance became necessary to accommodate students' feelings.[126]

Years later in Rome seminarian Zildo suddenly could see the "temptations" of the world as he rode the bus daily from the Pio Brasileiro to the Gregorian University. Using English so as to avoid detection of his thoughts by others, he wrote in the diary he had kept since the minor seminary: "How to explain all the temptations against chastity that come to my mind these days? The climate? Yes, but not alone! I read many things that are not bad, but can somehow awake in my mind bad images. I come from the Gregorian University looking at the streets, at the bills that sometimes are so strong and brutal! What must I do from now on?" Later when friends from Recife visited Rocha in Rome, he found himself strongly attracted to their daughter: "I, who for four years had not conversed with a young woman." But such contact was prohibited, and in Rome Rocha had a two-year private friendship with another seminarian.[127]

The conflicts and abuses involving sexuality frequently appeared in Vincentian fathers' letters. Celibacy did more than just discourage vocations. Sexual repression took an unexpected toll on the Church. Priests spent enormous amounts of psychic energy controlling their drive, and sexually active priests had to hypocritically hide their activities while maintaining a public image and warding off potential accusations. Superiors reported in detail on the conduct of individual priests. The fact or even the simple allegation of sexual activity became a weapon that priests could fire against one another. Letters themselves became political arms, whether the pretext was a disciplinary lapse, financial misdeeds, or sexual misconduct. In some instances outsiders got hold of this information and used it against the Church. A look at some difficult examples illuminates the connections among discipline, celibacy, sexuality, and the community.[128]

Systematic sexual repression left profound marks on many priests. Some developed exaggerated scruples with regard to women and sex. In 1909, for example, a Vincentian brother who worked as a doorman at the seminary in São Luís do Maranhão asked to be removed from the "dangerous" position because of having to deal frequently with women.[129] Some years later the rector of the same school, Father Luis de Gonzaga Cunha Marelim, decided to pour out his heart about a "creature who has a very strong inclination towards me." He wrote: "I have already used all means possible to get rid of her, from the mildest to the most harsh (principally), but with no results. A radical measure could cause a scandal, which must be avoided in accordance with priestly character and with my condition as rector, director of associations, assistant to Catholic Action, etc. I know well with whom I am dealing. I have prayed, waited and lost all hope. I think the only solution is my removal."[130] Father Marelim's letter demonstrated how thoroughly Tridentine standards had entered clerical discourse. His beliefs allowed him to resist temptation. More practical incentives were involved, too. At the time of the woman's importunate advances Father Marelim received news that the governor of Maranhão was pushing for his promotion to the episcopal see of another city. The conviction with which he lived his celibacy no doubt contributed to his nomination as bishop two years later at the young age of thirty-seven.

Similar concern about public perceptions occurred during an incident at Mariana in 1949. A member of a spiritist religion spread rumors about the involvement of a Vincentian priest, Father Francisco Trombert, with a fifteen-year-old adolescent girl. "It is clear that I cannot really work here anymore, because the suspicion, even unfounded, against the chastity of a priest makes his ministry useless, as Saint Vincent says," Trombert wrote. Two years later the same priest, now in Diamantina, was "seen kissing and hugging one of the cooks of the seminary!!!"[131]

The examples of the doorman and Father Marelim seem to have been exceptional examples of self-control. Other Lazaristas' letters indicated that yielding to desires was far more frequent. The range of possibilities went from private friendships to overt heterosexual and homosexual contact. At the Mariana seminary in the mid-1940s, for example, cases of priests' involvement with young boys "were not rare," according to Dom Helvécio, who personally witnessed one such incident and complained about it to Father Godinho, the Lazarista superior.[132] Intense controversy marked these occurrences, and the rectors spent considerable time dealing with incorrigible priests and writing detailed letters.[133]

Sexual scandal quickly fueled gossip and even jocular publicity. In 1943 Father Genesco Rabelo denounced an "exaggerated friendship" in Belo Horizonte between Father Laurindo Bicalho and a "certain young woman" who hoped to be a nun. Two years earlier the Church had transferred Bicalho and two other priests out of the Diamantina seminary because of the bad examples they had set. Rabelo maintained that he did not, as Bicalho accused, report the budding romance out of "envy or jealousy," but because people wanted the errant priest disciplined. Father Rabelo stated that Bicalho and his friend had long conversations on the porch of the rectory, alone at night in the sacristy, and during endless bus rides. People called them "os dois namorados" (the two sweethearts). After the priest took the woman to Rio de Janeiro to enter the convent, someone had chalked on the church wall the ironic phrase: "Father Laurindo has gone on a trip. Sunday I will go to Mass."[134]

Father Lázaro Neves, the rector of the Mariana minor seminary, received the "prickly mission" of investigating Bicalho. In a letter to the Lazarista superior he criticized both Bicalho and Rabelo. He reported that one sacristan had apparently heard Bicalho and the woman's "crackling of kisses." Another woman told her confessor that she had seen Bicalho kissing the woman in the sacristy. (Perhaps the secrecy of the confessional was violated.) Neves added that Bicalho had left account books in disarray, given presents to his companion, and abandoned his work except for assisting the feminine branch of Catholic Action. Bicalho later left the Lazarista order, while Neves, showing that obedience and discretion in handling delicate matters earned the confidence of superiors, went on to the episcopacy.[135]

The Church did its best to save face by hiding scandals from the public. In a striking revelation of the Church's strategy of cover-up, the Vincentians attempted to resolve these episodes simply by transferring priests from one seminary or pastoral function to another. There is no record of any other form of disciplinary action. Transfers were routine. The bishops moved the priests like pawns in an enormous, sordid game of ecclesiastical chess.[136] The greatest irony of all lay in the failure to enforce the norms of Romanization. By not punishing the priests more severely or removing them from contact with seminarians and the laity, the Church encouraged immoral behavior and corroded the saintly model of the priesthood it had worked so hard to construct. Romanization did not achieve its goal of a completely celibate clergy. It simply kept sexuality at a low boil.

Abuse of seminarians showed how cover-up worked. Such abuse had occurred since the earliest days of the Church. Ancient documents expressed concern about the mistreatment of minors. The *Didache*, a second-century commentary on the Gospels, commanded that "thou shalt not seduce young boys."[137] "With wine and boys around, the monks have no need of the Devil to tempt them," it was said of some early monastics. By the Middle Ages Western monasticism had become a bulwark of sexual libertinism.[138] Pope Julius III (1550–1555) befriended a fifteen-year-old boy from the streets of Parms and made him a cardinal and secretary of state.[139]

Modern Brazil was no exception. A violent incident took place in 1945, when Father Francisco das Chagas Torres, the rector of the Diamantina seminary, requested the relocation of a certain Father Braga, who "walks down the street conspicuously arm in arm with boys from the town; and during recess he hugs seminarians from the minor seminary and hits those seminarians whom he does not like."[140] Bishops and rectors about to receive disreputable priests fought such transfers but did nothing else.[141] There is no record of any institutional compensation, moral or otherwise, for the victims of priests' advances.[142] Seminarians who caught the eye of priests simply put up with unwanted attention and even physical aggression, or they left the seminary. Whereas seminarians could be expelled en masse for sexual activity, priests remained under the protective wing of the institution. It was an egregious double standard.

And it was disciplinary dysfunction at its worst. The Church made chastity and Christian ethics central to seminary training but ignored them in everyday ministerial reality. Thus could one Lazarista, for instance, advocate in the *REB* that the Church shelter seminarians from evocative dangers such as movie houses, dances, and other diversions and years later be taken out of the Diamantina seminary for having become romantically involved with a young woman.[143]

Complete cover-up, however, was difficult. Actual or alleged sexual indiscretions besmirched the reputation of individual clerics, the Vincentian congregation, and the Church by dragging all into a quagmire with the community. The story of Father Perdigão Sampaio in São Luís demonstrates how the disciplinary system failed morally. His case further illustrates how sexual misdeeds led to, or occurred in tandem with, other infractions. In this and other incidents the Church, which had so much to say about respect for life, revealed its worst hypocrisy.

Father Sampaio had a penchant for intimate friendships with young boys in the minor seminary. Father Marelim, the rector and a stickler for financial probity, hinted in one of his dispatches to Rio de Janeiro that Sampaio, in charge of seminary accounts, had embezzled more than two thousand *mil-réis,* a considerable sum. The priest bragged about the expensive presents he received without permission and others he gave to his favorite seminarians. Sampaio also assumed certain duties and positions without permission.[144]

In detailed letters from 1934 to 1936 Marelim recounted Sampaio's long history of involvement with seminarians. The priest promised to change his behavior but did not. One student at the seminary's primary level boasted to other students that Sampaio liked him so much that he would take him in his lap and kiss him. The errant priest listened to other boys' confessions in a dark room and pressed them against his face. Marelim reported another incident that clearly demonstrated the selective use and abuse of discipline:

The worst is that when his friends grow up and understand things better, they shun him, and the priest then spies on them attentively, exaggerates their faults, accuses them in the council, etc. Just last month he lowered the grade of a boy, who by the way was his *afilhado* [godson], on the pretext that the boy had publicly disobeyed him. . . . In past years he had an enormous friendship with the boy . . . courtesies, presents, caresses, etc., that caused a lot of talk. Even this year there were advances, but the boy has avoided them now that he is no longer so much of a child.

When Sampaio urged Marelim to punish the boy, Marelim replied with the observation that Sampaio demanded too much discipline of students while completely disrespecting his superiors.

The story did not end there. Marelim pressured his Lazarista superiors for Sampaio's removal. "Father Sampaio is a sick man and his presence in Maranhão will continue to hurt the seminary greatly," the rector wrote. Sampaio began to campaign to save his job by complaining to secular priests. He visited families in the town and wrote an unauthorized letter to his *compadres*, who happened to be the parents of abused boys. One of Marelim's worst fears was that the new archbishop of São Luís and Monsignor Pequeno, the papal visitator, would learn about Sampaio. "This will be very ugly for the congregation. I have hidden everything," Marelim wrote. Within days of these confidences of January 1936, Sampaio was on his way to a different position in Fortaleza. There he spent the rest of his career, including positions involving youths and financial matters, until his early death in 1947 at age forty-six.

Former Lazarista Geraldino Alves Ferreira Netto recalled a childhood incident in the Calafate parish of Belo Horizonte. Father José Julho Lino called the nine-year-old boy to his quarters and took him onto his lap for several minutes. Although no sexual activity occurred, young Geraldino was left with an uncomfortable feeling. Later, at Caraça, Geraldino and other boys had to put up with the strange attention of a priest who liked to grab boys' and adolescents' nipples in public. While these and other moral violations took place, seminarians' masturbation was carefully policed. There was even an "emergency confessional" for students to admit their nocturnal autoeroticism in order to be able to receive the Eucharist at morning Mass.[145] Whereas the Church considered self-pleasure a terrible sin, it tolerated sexual abuse as merely an embarrassing inconvenience that might harm an ecclesiastical career.

In 1938 another scandal entangling a Lazarista seminary with the community involved Father Salvador Rubim dos Santos. His situation illustrated how Romanization had thoroughly converted the people's perception of the ideal priest and increased the importance of sexual morality in people's lives. Tolerance and even admiration for the "uncle priest" had given way to a view of the priest as a strict celibate. Sexual gossip raged, attaining a new power, and scandal became a weapon for manipulating the clergy.

At the age of forty-seven, after twenty-three years in the priesthood, Santos suddenly faced an accusation of involvement with a seven-year-old girl in Diamantina. By his own admission Santos had one day inadvertently allowed the child to climb the tower of the basilica and went up himself to save her, but he denied the "exaggerated news" about the incident and the "fears" of rector Avellar as "unfounded." There was even talk of a petition in support of him, Santos affirmed. He pleaded against the Lazarista superior's determination of his transfer. In the process he left it clear that he was also no stranger to the mother of the girl. He wrote, "If I leave, she is capable of losing her mind, . . . of separating from the husband!" The girl's father apparently thought otherwise about the priest's innocence, however. Santos managed to avoid trouble only after sending a friend, whose son studied in the seminary, as an emissary to offer apologies.[146] He clung to his job.

Ten years later the incident still haunted Santos. In a letter to the Lazarista superior he revealed that on the advice of another Vincentian he had given money to the "rascal" father of the girl in order "to avoid any talk on his part, even if it is unproven." Despite the hush money, the girl's father tried unsuccessfully to prosecute the priest. Santos also alluded vaguely to the suicide of a person connected with the girl, who was now engaged to be married. Santos lamented the gossip about himself and other priests in Diamantina and around Brazil: "Here in Diamantina there is much talk, and where today are priests not talked about? If we were to believe in everything, . . . few priests would be able to stay here, beginning with the [diocesan] priests, about whom horrible things have been said. About our own, without sparing the superiors, I know of various disagreeable things that have been said. Naturally, all of this should lead us to the utmost prudence in everything."[147] Three years after his letter Santos, recently removed from the seminary but still near Diamantina, once again dealt with the repercussions from 1938. This time the young woman's fiancé was trying to blackmail the priest. Within months Santos was moved to another city in Minas Gerais. Noting that the tally of clerical scandals had been growing, the Diamantina rector begged the Lazarista superior in Rio de Janeiro to send him priests "capable of wiping out the large black spots that five (!) of the last of our brothers have left and are leaving here. What kind of training can we give the seminarians with such big scandals as these!!!"[148]

More than a decade later sexual scandals still rocked the Brazilian clergy. In 1964 a young priest at Diamantina mocked the traditional model of the ministry defended by some bishops at Vatican II while they ignored the abuses of the clergy: "Cultivate lechery, kiss young women, and abuse children; . . . as long as we are against the 'clergyman' [simplified priestly garb], against the reformed liturgy, against an understanding attitude toward sinners, against everything and everybody. Here, then, is the Saint, the Apostle, the healthy man."[149]

Conclusion

The Romanized Brazilian priest may have seemed a more effective pastor than his predecessor, but the disciplinary system's many drawbacks weakened the Church. The clergy became self-centered and relied too heavily on the seminaries as the founts of ecclesial life. The seminaries lacked creativity and flexibility, and pastoral practice became standardized. The Church thus failed to adapt to societal change. Some priests exploited the interstices of the system. Worse yet, both fathers and the laity turned discipline against the institution. Scandals caused the institution to rot from within. Religion became an endless game of discipline and power. Authentic faith atrophied. In a word, the Tridentine system lacked love.[150]

In the 1950s and 1960s a new generation of seminarians felt dehumanized by discipline. They joined with priests in a revolt against the Tridentine system that generated the biggest crisis in the history of the Brazilian Church.

chapter five

"The Modern Saint Is a Social Saint"

Crisis in the Seminaries and the Search for a New Brazilian Priesthood, 1945–1975

As student protestors manned the barricades in Paris in May of 1968, a large number of angry and confused students at the major seminary at Viamão near Porto Alegre decided to contest the bishops' authority by smashing the kitchen. Singing in Latin, "We want God," they marched toward their objective, only to stop at the sight of the nuns who for years had affectionately watched over the seminary. Not long afterward one hundred seminarians quit Viamão.[1] Several months before his ordination that year Ivo Poletto told his bishop, Dom Benedito Zorzi, that he opposed obligatory celibacy, would advocate against it, and was ready to leave the ministry whenever he could no longer live in chastity. Around the time of his ordination in 1969, Viamão student José Bonifácio Schmidt was booed by his fellow seminarians in the lunchroom, as were others choosing to graduate to the ministry. Another student received his holy orders with the intention of quitting a year later in an act of protest.[2] After his release from prison in 1973, the guerrilla sympathizer Frei Betto refused Holy Orders because the sacrament "would be the first step in rising to power within the Church. I am more convinced every day that any type of power tends to corrupt. Furthermore, the priority is no longer sacramental but rather evangelical and I can continue to evangelize without being ordained a priest."[3] These attacks on the priesthood would have been unimaginable a decade earlier. But as the Church abandoned the Tridentine era and rushed headlong into modernity, the clergy and the seminaries were swept into a maelstrom. This strangest of paradoxes—men preparing for an occupation and then belittling it—arose out of the identity crisis that afflicted the priesthood in the 1960s and 1970s. As Schmidt later recalled, it took courage to delve into a situation so full of unknowns.[4]

The vast changes taking place in the world suddenly transformed growing discontent in the seminaries into a generalized protest against the Tridentine order. The rote theology, languid pedagogy, authoritarian discipline, and sexual repression all appeared obsolete, as people everywhere shed traditional values in favor of modernity, secularism, faith in scientific and technological progress, and a focus on individual accomplishments. New ideas and ecclesial movements from Europe, where the Church had already faced many challenges, further stimulated a rethinking of the Brazilian system. Military rule caused seminarians to become even more radical.

Seminarians and priests strived to construct a new model of the priesthood by undertaking a profound reevaluation of the vocation and its social function. They campaigned to remake the seminary in order to modernize, politicize, and professionalize the ministry, including new forms of theology, pedagogy, and spirituality. Saintliness would no longer reside in the aloof, superior, and asexual seminarian of the Tridentine system but in priests who sought to express their humanity. The new seminarian wanted to abandon the role of *Alter Christus* and come down to the level of the people. Social justice and modernity, and not miracles, were his goal.[5]

Seminarians promoted their goals by organizing into a movement. It quickly became a campaign to start a union. Unprecedented in the hundred-year history of Brazil's seminaries, the movement challenged both the bishops and Brazil's military government. It meant for the Church what student radicalism meant to youth culture: an opening to the world, political protest, and a clamor for social justice, but also the development of an ecclesiastical counterculture and the search for self-fulfillment, including adjustment to the sexual revolution.

This chapter explores the seminarians' movement and the religious and political tensions that shaped it. In the 1960s many new options appeared for the
seminarians. Their choice of paths was not always clear and certainly not inevitable. Which variables most influenced the Church's attempts to change?
What results from the tension between faith and human reality, between individual change and institutional inertia? Was ecclesial democracy possible?
This chapter examines these questions and illustrates how the religious, the
social, the cultural, the political, the occupational, the institutional, and the
personal all became intertwined in the construction of the Brazilian Church's
option for the poor.

Religious and Social Movements and Political Turmoil

Changes in Brazilian society in the post–World War II era gave rise to new social and religious movements that led seminarians to theological innovation
and political activism.

After 1945 Brazil underwent dramatic economic, demographic, and social
transformation. Industrial production more than tripled from 1947 to 1961,
introducing Brazilians to a consumer economy. Juscelino Kubitschek's audacious construction of Brasília deep in the interior symbolized Brazil's capabilities. From 1940 to 1960 the population grew from some forty-one million to
more than seventy million, and the number of city-dwellers rose from 31 percent to 46 percent of the populace. Standards of living and literacy rates went
up throughout the 1950s. Brazil was no longer a static agricultural society,
but a dynamic, modernizing nation. The contrast between haves and have-
nots sharpened. Urbanization stimulated the rise of populism, the demand for
greater democracy and social equality, and social and political mobilization.
Many believed the country was on the path to a "Brazilian revolution," a nationalistic coming of age in which poverty would end and local culture would be
fully valued.

Like their brethren elsewhere, Catholics in Brazil experienced a combination
of malaise and expectation of change in the postwar years. Bishops, priests,
and the faithful felt out of step with—and threatened by—the modernization of a new global society. The spread of Communism increased uneasiness.[6]
The toppling of the dictatorial Vargas regime in 1945 liberalized the political
system and eroded the virtual religious monopoly the Church had enjoyed

under corporatism. Brazil started to become more secular and pluralistic, with competing religions gaining new adherents. Romanization had created an unsure refuge from pluralism, and the Church's stagnation as a missionary organization undermined its ability to appeal to the masses. Massive rural-urban migration reduced the Church's influence by diminishing its traditional base in the countryside. The Church competed with new movements; in the northeast and the interior of São Paulo, for instance, it successfully initiated a network of progressive rural unions as an attractive alternative to peasant organizations and Communist-backed unions.[7]

Pressure for change in the seminaries began with debate over the Tridentine regime in the 1940s and 1950s. Most priests staunchly defended tradition and criticized the idea of a "dynamic priest of the twentieth century."[8] But some began to discuss discipline's harmful effects on priests and their ties to the community.[9] In 1952 a *REB* contributor pointed out that "the masses are no longer obedient and blind." He advocated "a social apostolate that makes people think with their own heads and which puts the priest in touch with current problems in order that he can interpret them with spiritual principles related to them."[10]

In 1950 Pope Pius XII took the extraordinary step of publicly recognizing the difficulties of the disciplinary system. In his apostolic exhortation *Menti Nostrae* the pope suggested that minor seminarians receive training "as near as possible to the normal life of all boys" and in "broad and spacious surroundings that are conducive to health and peace of mind." He further proposed placing newly ordained men in small communities of diocesan priests who could act as mentors. But the Vatican proceeded with extreme caution, upholding the Tridentine model and celibacy.[11] In 1959 the Congregation for Seminaries issued a warning against pedagogical "novelties" that distorted Church teachings.[12]

The Liturgical Movement of the mid-twentieth century challenged tradition and the disciplinary regime. Before Vatican II the Catholic Mass was in Latin and administered entirely by the priest, his back to the people. The congregation could only observe, read prayer books, or pray on their own. In the early 1900s European churchmen began to "democratize the liturgy" by publishing missals in the vernacular and introducing some (still Latin) dialogue between the priest and the people.[13] The movement reached Brazil in the 1930s and expanded after Pius XII approved it in 1947. Brazil's bishops did not unanimously accept the movement until the late 1950s. It split the Church between activists and nonactivists, the forerunners of the progressives and conservatives of the 1970s and 1980s. The activists emphasized social issues and more lay participation. Traditionalists dubbed them as troublesome *liturgicistas* and "liturgy boys."[14] The nonactivists viewed the Mass and discipline as immutable. They rejected the Liturgical Movement as an attempt to lower the clergy's status and to abolish cherished practices like the Rosary.[15]

The seminaries were the *liturgicistas'* "battleground par excellence."[16] *Liturgicista* teachers introduced the works of the controversial French theologian Jacques Maritain, whose "integral humanism" inspired Catholics to radicalize their views on Brazilian social ills.[17] The movement became especially strong at the Belo Horizonte seminary, where Archbishop Dom Antônio dos Santos Cabral supported *liturgicismo* but nearly lost his job after Rome intervened to admonish the bishops to shield seminarians against innovation, leftism, and other errors associated with the movement.[18] The tensions in Brazil's traditionally most Catholic state revealed how deep conflict ran in the Church.

Vincentian *liturgicistas* undermined seminary tradition, attacked the bishops' authority, divided the PBCM, and set a bad example for other priests. Some of the Vincentians' youngest, brightest, and most controversial men joined the movement. The most famous was Padre Lage. Inspired by Maritain, he and other *liturgicistas* developed an unorthodox interpretation of reality. "We reinvented theology and with it our priestly task. We freed ourselves from old taboos, which we ridiculed among ourselves frequently. We even initiated ourselves in para-psychological exercises in our eagerness to learn about everything all over again," Padre Lage recalled in his memoirs.[19] In Bahia the archbishop accused Lage of causing a "revolt" of seminarians.[20] Quitting as a seminary instructor, Lage organized *favelados* and aided the proto-radical Juventude Operária Católica (JOC, or Catholic Youth Workers) under Dom Cabral in Belo Horizonte. Eventually forced out of the PBCM, Lage became one of Brazil's leading radical priests until his exile to Mexico after the 1964 coup.[21] In Mariana *liturgicistas* clashed with the bishop and conservative Lazaristas,[22] and in Fortaleza the archbishop demanded the removal of two capable teachers, Fathers Oscar de Figueiredo Lustosa and Josafá Pinto de Oliveira, for fear they would dominate the seminarians and prompt the secular fathers to leave.[23] These controversies resulted in the departure of about a half dozen top Vincentian intellectuals. Most of them joined the more liberal Dominicans. Two of the new Dominicans—Father Josafá and Father José Rocha—became important leaders of the Catholic Action movement.[24] The departures contributed to the decay of the order.[25]

A major impulse for reform came from Brazilian Catholic Action (ACB). ACB was lackluster until the late 1940s, when Dom Hélder Câmara led a shakeup that created subdivisions based on educational level and occupation. Thereafter it sought to involve lay Catholics more deeply in society, gradually shifting from a cultural, moral, and religious orientation to a focus on political and social activism. The two most prominent groups were the JOC and the JUC, the Juventude Universitária Católica (Catholic University Youth). JUC broke an important barrier by allowing coed groups. The more liberal *assistentes eclesiásticos* (priests who ran ACB for the bishops) promoted lay initiative, encouraged debate, and advised students on both personal and political matters.[26] Adolescents in JEC, the Juventude Estudantil Católica (Catholic Student Youth), had a similar experience.[27] Above all, these groups inspired solidarity with the poor. They adopted phrases from European JOC priests such as "amor de preferência" (preferential love) and "predileção do Senhor pelos pequenos e humildes" (the Lord's predilection for the small and the humble)— strikingly similar to the "preferential option for the poor" of the future Latin American Popular Church.[28]

ACB's great appeal lay in its unique ecclesial culture, which linked religious belief to everyday life and the idea of community. Belgian Father Joseph Cardijn, who had founded JOC in an effort to re-Christianize the European working class, exhorted priests to immerse themselves in workers' reality in order to improve pastoral outreach.[29] He originated ACB's key principles and techniques: *presença no meio* (presence in the milieu), *equipes* (small teams or task forces), and the *ver-julgar-agir* method ("see-judge-act" method), used during meetings to help ACB militants conduct the *revisão de vida* (a review of life's events in a Christian light). Another key element was *formação na ação* (learning through action). ACB's revolutionary methodology replaced the deductive Scholastic method and ecclesial authoritarianism with an inductive method that questioned dogma and hierarchy. It also built a greater sense of fraternity.

To "see" was to identify temporal and eternal purposes,[30] to become conscious of reality, to have concern for fellow humans, to begin to exercise the faith.[31] In Brazil to "see" evolved into critical interpretation of economic, political, and religious realities at the local, national, and international levels.[32] To "judge" involved analysis of historical and structural causes, and interpretation of life in the light of faith in order to specify temporal and spiritual goals more clearly.[33] To "act," the ultimate objective, meant commitment to God and love. It originally aimed at the conversion of the workers to benefit their own class. In Brazil it came to include a wide range of activities, from religious festivals and publications to engagement in union organizing, the student movement, and consciousness-raising. In the Progressive Church to "act" was to construct the Kingdom of Christ by executing God's plan not in the afterlife, but on earth now.[34] "Action" resonated with the priority placed on immediate revolutionary activity by Che Guevara and other guerrilla leaders of the 1960s.[35] The *revisão de vida* was the collective practice of the trilogy by the equipe. It aided the individual in assessing his or her life and helped build group solidarity.[36] In his important 1961 encyclical *Mater et Magistra* Pope John XXIII exhorted young people to use the trilogy.[37] In essence, the *ver-julgar-agir* method gave birth to liberation theology as theory and practice.[38] Rising to the same plane as doctrine, observation and experience became the new tools of theology.

ACB was not a mass movement but a vanguard of the Catholic left. It led to a more critical attitude toward the Church's theology and structures and stimulated innovation. ACB delved into university politics, union organization, and other activities in the late 1950s and early 1960s. *JOCista* fathers proposed that clerics live among the poor.[39] JUC attacked Brazil's economic underdevelopment, criticized capitalism for its anti-Christian abuses, and accepted socialism as a viable option.[40] Significantly, JUC fed other important movements with ideas and volunteers, such as the União Nacional de Estudantes (UNE, or the National Union of Students), the revolutionary Catholic group Ação Popular (AP, or Popular Action), and the Church-sponsored Movimento de Educação de Base (MEB, or the Grassroots Education Movement), a radio literacy program for the poor. The ACB methodology remained a pillar of progressive Catholicism in Latin America into the early 1990s.[41] *Ver-julgar-agir,* for instance, played an important role in the crucial Movement of Landless Rural Workers, discussed below.[42]

The bishops took an organizational cue from ACB to form the CNBB, one of the first bishops' conferences in the world. The CNBB modernized the institutional Church and advocated economic nationalism, essentially representing a "third way" reformist strategy that rejected extreme leftism but also criticized capitalism.[43] The Brazilian bishops wielded considerable influence in the development of another key organization, the Conselho Episcopal Latino-Americano (CELAM, or Latin American Bishops Council). CELAM institutionalized the Latin American Church's preferential option for the poor.

As bulwarks of tradition, the seminaries shirked Catholic Action. The emphasis on the laity threatened the clergy's authority. Even ACB's leading episcopal supporters showed hesitation.[44] At most, seminarians had theoretical discussions about ACB. One Vincentian described AC courses in his seminary as "miserable," and another priest termed them "ridiculous."[45] Nuncio Dom Armando Lombardi, a staunch defender of ACB, scolded the bishops for not promoting it among future clerics, especially because it had the sanction of Pope Pius XII.[46]

One prescient Lazarista proposed the ACB methodology and structure as a way to stir the seminaries out of their lethargy. In a 1956 report to the CNBB, Father Aloísio Deina Goch stated that ACB-style teamwork could reinvigorate seminary life. Students would lose their inhibitions and learn that they were "someone with something to give in the seminary and not just to receive," he wrote. This approach would "heal the tragic problem of boarding schools." Goch's most startling recommendation aimed to alter the hierarchy. He wanted seminarians to think as a national body by holding regional meetings of representatives to discuss their most pressing problems.[47]

The European worker-priests demonstrated the potential and dangers of living the tenets of Catholic Action. Along with practitioners of the social gospel, pro-labor priests, and Dorothy Day's Catholic Worker movement, they practiced liberation theology well before it emerged in Latin America.[48] In 1941 the French Church trained priests for action among the working classes. Later French cardinals and bishops sent 275 priest volunteers in the guise of workers to minister to people in Nazi labor camps. In 1944 a group of priests decided to take full-time factory jobs in order to evangelize the workers. Belgians soon followed their example. The movement quickly radicalized, winning the support of JOC members, labor unions, the Communist Party, and, most significant, Cardinal Emmanuel Suhard of Paris.[49] In 1946 one report foreshadowed the later strategy of the Brazilian clergy: "We desire to plant the church where it has not been, that is, *to insert* Christianity into the natural communities of work, neighborhood and leisure." The fathers met in equipes, lived in poverty, and conducted ACB-style brainstorming sessions. They also embraced a Marxist analysis of reality.[50]

The Vatican was worried about worker-priests who threw themselves into union struggles and other politically sensitive causes. As a result, Rome restricted the movement. Seminarians were forbidden to engage in any kind of work, and priests could spend only three hours per day in the shop. Most obeyed. But the worker-priests had won public opinion, and the suppression of the movement blew up into a major controversy. In 1959 Rome declared the incompatibility of the priesthood with extended manual labor. The situation deepened the malaise within Catholicism and, in fact, was one of the reasons for convening Vatican II. The Council ultimately approved the movement, and the number of worker-priests exploded to nine hundred—3 percent of the French clergy.[51]

Called by Pope John XXIII, Vatican II (1962–1965) opened the floodgates
of innovation. In the assessment of René Latourelle, Vatican II "undoubtedly
constitutes the greatest reform ever carried out in the Church." The council
touched on virtually every aspect of the Church's life, from divine revelation
to the Church's organizational structure to liturgy and the sacraments.[52] More
than 2,200 bishops and hundreds of theologians from around the globe participated in this attempt to end the malaise and bring the Church into the modern world. This process came to be known as *aggiornamento,* or the "bringing
up to date." Theological and pastoral innovators punished before 1962 were re-
habilitated and became inspirational figures for the clergy and seminarians.
The laity moved to center stage in an institution that now defined itself as the
"people of God," and the Mass, now said in the vernacular, became more accessible to the faithful. Although Europeans dominated the Council, Dom Hélder and other Latin Americans played a key behind-the-scenes role in encouraging reform and the adoption of a more humble perspective known as the
"Church of the Poor."[53] In Brazil clergymen, nuns, and seminarians greeted
Vatican II with great enthusiasm, although traditionalist clerics demonstrated
less zeal and sometimes even opposition.

Vatican II's decree on ecclesiastical preparation, *Optatum Totius* (*OT*), furnished powerful justification for overhauling the Tridentine model. *OT* permitted each country to adopt its own method of training as established by the
national conference of bishops and according to local circumstances. Although
OT required that the Holy See periodically review national programs of priestly
training, the nettlesome apostolic visit fell into disuse in Brazil. *OT* thus loos-
ened the straightjacket of Europeanization. Furthermore, *OT* made pastoral
practice the ultimate goal of training and permitted innovations like pastoral
internships. *OT* allowed seminarians to live in small communities, study the
social sciences, and have greater contact with the laity. In addition, it recognized
the pupil's personal needs. *OT* did not completely abandon tradition, however.
OT reaffirmed key elements of training such as piety, silence, and celibacy, although with certain modifications. Discipline was still central, but it was no
longer simply a way to organize community life. Its goal was also to achieve
individual self-control and maturity. Discipline would still foster obedience,
but with the conscious conviction of the individual. In 1970 the CNBB ratified
OT, including the notion of small communities, in a key document on seminary training.[54] *OT* represented a wholesale modernization of the Church's discourse on the seminaries.

Yet for the clergy, reform had mixed results. Vatican II produced a combination of joy, exhilaration, disappointment, confusion, anger, and insecurity among Catholics. Nevertheless, the Council clearly defined the roles of the laity and the bishops. But it did little to address the needs of the Church's middle layer, the hundreds of thousands of priests. The Council fathers failed to inspire in their priests new confidence in the institution, its mission, and its teachings. *OT* and other conciliar documents were improvements, but the new purpose of the clergy was unclear. Parish priests particularly received short shrift.[55] The clergy were caught between tradition and modernity. They remained as God's mediator with the faithful but were also expected to descend to the level of the people. Both the new potential and the acute uncertainty about the clergy's roles plunged the Catholic priesthood everywhere into one of the most profound crises in the history of religion.

Vatican II coincided with political turmoil in Brazil. As the economy stagnated in the early 1960s, politics became polarized between left and right. After President Jânio Quadros took the unusual step of resigning in 1961, Vice President João Goulart, who was opposed by anti-leftist officers, assumed power only after the conflicting military and civilian factions reached a compromise averting civil war. Goulart's government moved leftward, proposing agrarian reform and the nationalization of private oil refineries. Following waves of strikes and pro- and anti-leftist demonstrations, the armed forces overthrew Goulart on March 31, 1964, and installed a national security state. On the day of the coup the Army singled out the student movement for reprisal, as opponents of the UNE burned down its headquarters in Rio de Janeiro. In 1968 the government declared Ato Institucional No. 5 (AI-5, or Institutional Act No. 5), which suspended civil liberties and freedom of the press. The generals closed the National Congress, and torturers routinely plied their skills with impunity. While manufacturing a "miracle" of high rates of economic growth, the military regime efficiently destroyed a plethora of leftist revolutionary organizations and cowed the legal opposition into submission. Only in the mid-1970s did the regime begin to relax the repression. The infamous slow, gradual, and secure transition to civilian rule culminated only in 1985.

The detainment, torture, and assassination of activist clergymen and lay militants produced the worst Church-state (and Church-military) crisis in Brazilian history. The U.S. government and Latin America's authoritarian regimes viewed the progressive clergy as a threat. In 1965 the government of General Humberto de Alencar Castello Branco tried unsuccessfully to banish the

Dominican order from Brazil,[56] as Pombal had done with the Jesuits more than two hundred years before. At first most bishops remained silent about the repression. However, when it became clear in the late 1960s that the institutional Church had become a target, the bishops acted. During the height of the terror in the early 1970s they denounced torture and the regime's unequal economic policies. In a society muffled by the military, the Catholic hierarchy became the "voice of the voiceless." The Brazilian Church of the Poor gained international prominence as a defender of human rights and social justice.

The military's policies reduced the Church's influence by opening the way for new cultural competitors. The drive for national integration and increased consumerism produced cultural industries on a national scale. After remaining stable for two decades, the number of movie theaters doubled between 1967 and 1969. The state spurred publishing, updated the rudimentary telecommunications systems, and linked Brazil to space satellites. This progress favored the formation of television networks, in particular Roberto Marinho's Globo operation, eventually the world's fourth largest, a key supporter of the military and critic of the Progressive Church.[57]

As the military cracked down, the Latin American Church moved left. Discussing the implementation of Vatican II, the 1968 meeting of CELAM in Medellín, Colombia, inspired Catholics to fight for social justice. Medellín marked the birth of liberation theology. It emphasized the eschatological nature of social activism, the social nature of sin, Jesus as liberator of the oppressed, and the creation of a new society.[58] Rejecting capitalism and imperialism, liberation theology used social science, dependency theory, and Marxist concepts such as class struggle to offer a radical critique of socioeconomic structures. Liberation theologians advocated socialism, although they had no concrete plan for achieving it.[59] With the liberalization of authoritarian regimes in the late 1970s and early 1980s, liberation theology shifted from political and economic reductionism to greater emphasis on spirituality and the meaning of liberation. Liberation theology's centerpiece was the preferential option for the poor, who were seen as a privileged source of religious truth. The Church could mobilize the poor through *conscientização,* or consciousness-raising, pioneered in Paulo Freire's famous literacy method. In place of traditional authority his "pedagogy of the oppressed" sought to establish democratic dialogue with students and to focus on their everyday reality.[60] Liberation theology also preached the decentralization of the Church.

In the 1970s the progressive leadership of the CNBB, former ACB members, and other militants consolidated the Brazilian Church of the Poor (or Progressive Church). They established a number of radical pastoral programs, for example, the Comissão Pastoral da Terra (CPT, or Pastoral Land Commission), which clashed with the military regime over agrarian reform. In Miguel Carter's words, "Nowhere in the chronicle of world religion has a predominant religious institution played as significant a role in support of land reform as has the Brazilian Church."[61] Another key Church organization was the Conselho Indigenista Missionário (CIMI, or Indigenous Missionary Council). CIMI defended Native lands and helped push through the idea of a multicultural state in Brazil by ending the colonial-era practice of de-Indianizing Native peoples.[62] Some dioceses set up Peace and Justice Commissions to denounce human rights violations.

Another important innovation was the CEBs, or Grassroots Church Communities. Each CEB had a few dozen members who met to reflect on Bible readings in light of daily struggles. They sought to restore fraternal relations among people, to build faith, and to struggle for social justice among the poor.[63] At the direction of the Church priests and nuns first started CEBs in the 1960s to help alleviate the shortage of clergy and meet the challenge of secularization. They expanded rapidly in the 1970s.[64] Largely a rural phenomenon,[65] they only partially assisted the Church's efforts to give greater attention to city-dwellers.[66] They reflected the strong tendency toward decentralization and experimentalism in post–Vatican II Catholicism. Some saw CEBs as a way to diversify the ministry or even replace the priesthood. As such they indirectly exacerbated the crisis of the clergy.

The new attitudes about society, politics, and authority germinating from the Brazilian student movement also had a profound impact on seminarians. In the late 1950s and 1960s high school and university radicals became stridently anti-imperialist, supported class struggle, and volunteered for literacy and health campaigns in the countryside. Their art and music focused on popular culture and became a form of political expression. The UNE's Centros Populares de Cultura (the Popular Culture Centers), for example, took protest theater to the lower classes. Like their counterparts elsewhere, many Brazilian youths rebelled against family and authority and distrusted anybody over the age of thirty. They discussed the length of hair and skirts, the contraceptive pill, and Marxist philosophy. Their heroes were Fidel Castro, Dom Hélder Câmara, Alceu Amoroso Lima, Ché Guevara, Mao Tse Tung, and Ho Chi Minh.[67]

Student protests and violent crackdowns by the regime became an almost weekly event from 1964 to 1968. The military intervened in the universities and forbade the press from covering student politics. In March 1968 the fatal shooting of a student by the police sparked nationwide protests, including the March of the One Hundred Thousand in Rio de Janeiro. Priests and nuns provided crucial support for the student movement. They gave shelter to students fleeing from the repression. In 1966 and 1967 the clandestine meetings of the proscribed UNE occurred with help from the clergy. Priests, such as a group of Vincentians at the Colégio São Vicente in Rio, and nuns participated in protests.[68] By 1969 the repression severely weakened the movement and most other opposition groups. Some students joined guerrilla organizations fighting the dictatorship. In 1969 two guerrilla organizations kidnapped the U.S. ambassador, who was freed only after the military met a list of demands, including the release of jailed student leaders.

Origins at Viamão

One of the first attempts by seminarians to organize took place at Viamão in 1957. Viamão was a small rural suburb of Porto Alegre, the capital of Rio Grande do Sul. Its recently inaugurated major seminary, named after Nossa Senhora da Conceição (Our Lady of Conception), was the world's third largest and one of the country's best. It was located in the south, arguably the Brazilian Church's most dynamic region.

The south would supply the top leadership of the Brazilian Church of the Poor. Dom Aloísio Lorscheider and Dom Paulo Evaristo Arns, two influential cardinals, and Dom Aloísio's cousin Dom Ívo Lorscheiter all came from the south and played important parts in Church-state relations and the human rights movement. Dom Aloísio and Dom Ivo both served as president of the CNBB. Cardinal Dom Vicente Scherer also hailed from the south.

The Church in Rio Grande do Sul owed its strength and progressivism to the deep religiosity and moral fortitude of the Italian and German immigrant colonies. The institutional Church determined the rhythm of life in Rio Grande do Sul more so than in any other region of Brazil. Church attendance was frequent and fervent. Chapels, cemeteries, and parochial schools dotted the area, and frequent catechism classes instilled a strong sense of faith. The Marian Congregations flourished, and the state had its own devotion to Mary, Nossa Senhora de Medianeira de Todas as Graças (Our Lady, Mediator of All Graces). In the 1950s long trains carried pilgrims to her church in Santa Maria. The travelers spent the night praying and singing, while fathers heard confessions in the aisles. In Porto Alegre the festival of Nossa Senhora dos Navegantes (Our Lady of Navigators) involved the entire city, and in smaller towns novenas and festivals for the patron saint mobilized the populace. Faith in Rio Grande do Sul was linked to a deep, conservative pride in the believers' European backgrounds, a reasonable standard of living, and a sense of superiority with respect to Afro-Brazilians and the rest of Brazil. Fear of breaking habit and the law of God were strong. A feeling of neo-Christendom reigned. Catholics staunchly opposed nontraditional Protestant religions, threw eggs at porn theaters, and held public rallies for their oppressed brethren in the Communist world. Priests stood as guardians over this morally coded universe. People viewed the father as Christ himself and asked for his blessing in public.[69]

The immigrants' spirit of initiative reinforced popular religiosity. The Italians who founded Caxias do Sul in 1875, for example, brought exemplary parish priests from Italy who had traditionally played a role in practically all spheres of life. The combination of initiative and faith made Caxias a socially combative diocese. Bishop Dom Benedito Zorzi's open-minded, personal approach to clerical training was another factor.[70] In the diocese of Passo Fundo the bishop supported the Frente Agrária Gaúcha (Gaúcha Agrarian Front), unions, and other groups aiming to organize workers and improve agricultural techniques in the countryside. In 1970 the diocese of Caxias started the Centro de Orientação Missionária (COM, or Center for Missionary Training), which trained tens of thousands of missionaries sent to work in other regions, especially the north.[71] With heavy support from the Church and the CPT, Rio Grande do Sul gave rise in the 1980s to one of Brazil's most important social movements of the twentieth century, the Movimento dos Trabalhadores Rurais Sem-Terra (Movement of Landless Rural Workers).[72]

Veritable clerical tribes emerged in Rio Grande do Sul. Father Marino Bohn, for example, became the seventy-fifth religious vocation in his mother's family. He was also a distant cousin of Dom Sinésio Bohn, the bishop of Santa Cruz do Sul.[73] Many priests had nuns in their extended families. These vocations blossomed from the German and Italian Catholic traditions, gaúcho families' emphasis on prayer and other domestic devotions, the examples of clergy and sisters, the community's belief in the need to cultivate and financially support vocations, and parents' active involvement in the Church. Most priests came from large families who practiced small-scale agriculture. The unquestioning attitude toward Catholic dogma acted as a further vocational incentive.[74]

In the mid-1990s Rio Grande do Sul was still a throwback to a premodern era in which faith was all-encompassing. During a drive through the countryside,

Dom Sinésio pointed out to me the roadside sanctuaries of the devout. In the picturesque village of Nova Brescia the local leaders warmly greeted Dom Sinésio, and the people packed the church to hear him say Mass during a weekend festival. When I arrived in the town of Rio Pardo to meet Father Zeno Graeff, he sternly questioned the taxi driver to make sure I had not been overcharged. Later, during our interview, Father Graeff explained that in his vocation he made no distinction between human factors and the call from God. They were one.[75]

Viamão shared prestige, history, and rivalry with the Jesuit seminary at nearby São Leopoldo. São Leopoldo had begun in 1913 as an internal seminary for the Society of Jesus, but in 1930 the Vatican designated it as a central seminary along with São Paulo and Salvador. This system remained in force until 1962. Bishops from throughout Brazil sent men to study under the intellectually rigorous Jesuits. (São Leopoldo also continued to train Jesuits until the late 1940s.) In all, more than seven thousand men studied in this seminary from 1913 to 1956. Almost nine hundred were ordained.[76]

After becoming archbishop of Porto Alegre in 1947, Dom Vicente began plans for a new central seminary at Viamão to make room for the growing number of vocations. He invited the Jesuits to teach there when it opened in 1954, but with the proviso that the archdiocese would control administration and finances.[77] The Jesuits declined because of a prior disagreement with the bishops at São Leopoldo[78] and accusations that they were trying to lure diocesan seminarians to the Society.[79] Such infighting typified the pre–Vatican II clergy.

In the late 1950s and early 1960s Viamão clung to the Tridentine regime. Professors taught in Latin. Students met informally at a Porto Alegre bookstore to read and discuss prohibited works. In late 1960 seminarian Luís Casanova dropped out for a year after being accused of leading a student strike in protest of the pedagogical format.[80]

But Viamão quickly developed into a vibrant, cosmopolitan, politicized, and nationally prominent cultural institution. Dom Vicente modeled the studies on the Gregorian University in Rome and sent an entourage of students there to prepare for work as professors. Pressing his students to excel in all areas, Dom Vicente strived to train the best clergy possible for his archdiocese.[81] In the 1960s more than three hundred students from a variety of backgrounds were enrolled annually. Extracurricular activities flourished and included poetry, theater, discussion of classical and contemporary literature, theological symposia, a news mural, talks, and foreign language study groups. Cultural sophistication extended to concern about social issues.[82] The student council for philosophy adopted the name of Tristão de Ataíde, the pseudonym of Alceu Amoroso Lima, who identified with Brazilian student movements and brought new ideas into the Church.[83] The students ran a *cineclube* at which they debated films. The films of Federico Fellini were among their favorites. They projected movies on sheets for small crowds in impoverished neighborhoods. Afterwards they used the films as the basis for discussing political questions.[84] By introducing modern vocabulary and ideas, these events effected a cultural revolution at Viamão and other seminaries in the region.[85]

Viamão produced illustrious intellectuals. One of the most brilliant was Ernildo Stein, a member of the Viamão inaugural class of 1954 who went on to become one of Brazil's top philosophers. Although Stein left before ordination, he kept in touch with former colleagues and became a leading interpreter of the seminarians' movement. He and others demonstrated the importance of the seminaries for the philosophical profession.[86]

Ethnicity affected culture and politics at Viamão. In contrast with São Leopoldo the *gaúcho,* pampas-oriented culture shone through at Viamão.[87] The seminary established a Centro de Tradição Gaúcha (Center for Gaúcho Culture), and students occasionally participated in the celebration of a distinctly *gaúcho* Mass, in which regional vocabulary, dress, and customs replaced the traditional Latin or Portuguese. A bull's horn served as the chalice.[88] Men of Italian, German, Luso-Brazilian, and Polish heritage created a strong religious pluralism in the seminary.[89] Students from Spanish America, North America, and Europe also studied at Viamão.[90] Diversity contributed to the breakdown of ethnic jealousies,[91] although tensions occasionally flared. The mainly Italian and progressive seminarians from Caxias do Sul, for example, clashed with the more conservative group from Porto Alegre.[92] Some students faced prejudice because they spoke Portuguese with an Italian accent. Others spoke specific Italian dialects in secret as a way of asserting a certain feeling of nationalism.[93] The multilingual atmosphere brought advantages for all, however. German- and Italian-speaking students kept their colleagues abreast of theological trends by translating the latest treatises arriving from Europe—for example, the work of the German Jesuit theologian Karl Rahner. Responding to students anxious to form their own ethnic enclave, Dom Benedito Zorzi stated that variety forced seminarians to consider the pluralistic nature of the world and contributed to their holistic formation.[94]

Progressive seminary professors introduced many new texts to their students. The especially qualified staff included Dom Ivo, Father Letos Veit, the psychologist Father Francisco Reis, and Father Hugo Assmann, a JUC advisor and a controversial, prolific theologian who sometimes forgot the fundamentals and went directly to the disputes of the day.[95] Visiting professors included the Jesuits Pedro Beltrão and Henrique Lima Vaz, a leading JUC theoretician. Despite an incipient critique of neo-Scholasticism, at Viamão that method actually exposed seminarians to new ideas through the refutation—and therefore close reading—of authors such as Martin Heidegger, Jean-Paul Sartre, and Karl Marx.[96]

Catholic Action further politicized Viamão. The seminary had strong ties to the Porto Alegre JUC cell, and some students become involved with the radical Ação Popular.[97] ACB sent speakers for guest talks, and students attended meetings of JOC and other ACB groups.[98] ACB exposed seminarians to debates about agrarian reform, the role of the university, and the relationship between ideology and culture.[99] It also created identity with radical politicians. "JUC writes the lyrics, JOC provides the music, and together we will dance the revolution," Leonel Brizola, the fiery leftist *gaúcho* caudillo, would tell young ACB militants.[100]

In 1957 the Viamão students took an important step toward organizing a movement by inviting a nationally recognized Jesuit from São Leopoldo to give a series of lectures on the seminary movement in his native Hungary. Father Géza Kövecses recalled how the dangers of World War II galvanized his colleagues but also how the postwar Communist government suppressed their movement. The Hungarians had aimed for many of the same goals as the Brazilians: clerical unity, greater support from the bishops, and publication of a journal.[101]

The fledgling movement gained steam from discontent over traditional religiosity and teaching methods. Seminarians opposed repetitious, empty forms of prayer such as the Rosary and the breviary. They rejected Scholasticism and its generally authoritarian, nonparticipatory pedagogy. Students wanted to confront it with modern science. Some blamed the Jesuits for this system and the image of the priest as an all-powerful, pedagogical Christ.[102]

Viamão quickly became the informal headquarters of the movement because it already published the monthly *O Seminário,* the official journal of the country's seminaries. *O Seminário* was crucial. With a circulation of 3,700 it reached a large percentage of Brazil's 3,000 major and 22,000 minor seminarians. Since its inception in 1926 it adhered to Catholic doctrine under the guidance of an ecclesiastical censor.[103] In the late 1950s, however, the student publishers transformed *O Seminário* into an organizational tool and a forum for debate for a nationwide organization. Themes such as ecclesiastical problems, pastoral approaches, and seminary training gradually emerged.[104] The student staff assumed greater control over the journal and professionalized and broadened its coverage. By 1968 circulation reached five thousand.[105] Seminarians from Caxias, where the minor seminary had its own journal, brought good writing skills and a profound knowledge of literature to *O Seminário*.[106] In 1963 students from several regions of Brazil met in Rio Grande do Sul and decided to decentralize the journal's administration in order to reflect the movement's national character, although Viamão remained the headquarters.[107] At this point the Palotino order, based in Santa Maria, took over official leadership of the movement. Yet the initiative remained with Viamão. It had the additional advantage of having students from several regions of Brazil, thus facilitating the exchange of news about innovation.[108] Students from São Leopoldo and the Capuchin order in Porto Alegre also played important roles.

In the early 1960s seminarians across Brazil anxiously sought to organize in order to modernize the Church. The Viamão seminarians contacted students from other states who shared their concerns.[109] Seminarians worried about becoming socially irrelevant. They watched as ACB, UNE, the youth sections of political parties, and even Protestants stepped up their activities. "In Brazil everybody is organized. The Communists, the capitalists, the politicians, etc. Only we, only we do not know one another," lamented one seminarian in a 1963 article in *O Seminário*. Seminaries needed to build up "communitarian life" by adopting ACB-style teamwork.[110] Ecclesiastical narrow-mindedness would diminish as students from different schools and regions gathered to discuss their difficulties. Seminarians needed to form a "united and coordinated clergy."[111]

Breaking the ice was not easy after decades of isolation and competition for vocations. In addition, each religious order emphasized its specific characteristics.[112] Once even a fight broke out at a party attended by Jesuit and diocesan seminarians. As Father Irineu Stertz recalled, the different groups almost seemed to belong to distinct religions. During the 1963–1964 summer vacation period he and a team of Viamão seminarians traveled to the interior towns of Ijui and Passo Fundo to promote the movement. In Passo Fundo the group raised suspicions at the diocesan seminary because they had stored their cassocks in suitcases. The Capuchin superiors at Ijui required the Viamão group to work in the fields with the local seminarians in order to earn the right to speak to them about the movement in the evenings. Gradually the barriers of communication broke down as the two groups played games. The Viamão men even tried on the unique Capuchin habits. They then joined in visits to small farmers and helped with the organization of rural unions.[113]

Vatican II provided a key impetus. In São Paulo 350 seminarians from the Movimento de União dos Teólogos de São Paulo (Movement for the Unity of Theologians of São Paulo, or MUT) gathered a few weeks before the Council to discuss "community life" in their schools.[114] When the Council opened on October 11, 1962, some five hundred major seminarians from religious orders and dioceses throughout Rio Grande do Sul gathered for a "little council" of their own, a "day of confraternity." In the ecumenical spirit of Vatican II members of Lutheran and Episcopal theological schools were invited as "observers." The seminarians founded the União dos Seminaristas Maiores do Sul (Union of Major Seminarians of the South, or USMAS). "From the pampas to the Amazon encounters of seminarians are becoming more frequent," *O Seminário* reported.[115]

From 1961 to 1967 organizations sprung up with meetings involving hundreds of men in Espírito Santo, Minas Gerais, Rio de Janeiro, Guanabara, Ceará, Maranhão, Paraíba, Pernambuco, Sergipe, Bahia, São Paulo, Paraná, Santa Catarina, Rio Grande do Sul, and the Colégio Pio Brasileiro in Rome. USMAS was the largest and most influential, with subdivisions known as USMAS-1, USMAS-2, and USMAS-3 spreading into other states. The meetings brought together seminarians from different dioceses as well as from various religious orders. Some organizations also held supra-regional meetings. The walls of prejudice, competition, and regional isolation had begun to fall. The participants discussed the need for unity, adoption of *O Seminário* as a vehicle for the movement, collaboration with UNE, pastoral planning, seminary reform, and the Latin American priest's function in light of Vatican II.

The students made two major demands: the formation of a national organization and the official inclusion of USMAS into the CNBB. In 1963 the movement started planning for a national meeting. In *O Seminário* seminarian Danilo Menezes proposed the formation of USMAB—União Nacional dos Seminaristas Maiores do Brasil (National Union of the Major Seminarians of Brazil). Linking the future of the priesthood to seminary reform, he affirmed that USMAB would play an important part in the renovation of the Church. "Who knows? This will be the road to a USB [União dos Sacerdotes Brasileiros, or Union of Brazilian Priests]?" he wrote.[116] Menezes became the movement's coordinator and visited other seminaries.[117] A few months later the journal launched a proposal to hold the national encounter "possibly in January of 1965, in some place in the center of the country."[118] The seminarians wanted to propose a national seminary curriculum and promote the clergy's engagement in Brazilian social transformation.[119]

The leadership expressed doubts, however, about the seminarians' ability to wage the campaign. The final issue of *O Seminário* in 1963 published the results of a questionnaire to which presidents of four regional organizations responded. All wanted a national meeting, but they wondered whether the rank and file were ready. "Politicization is urgent," wrote one leader. Another observed "intense fermentation" among seminarians, but added that "certain areas are still not well matured." Yet another feared that the most "closed" seminaries would ignore the central issues. The leaders proposed that a national meeting of representatives—not the entire student body—be convened and that regional congresses take place simultaneously. The seminarians needed to convince the bishops to underwrite the cost of a national congress.[120] Dependence on the bishops, who might be less sanguine about change, could compromise the movement. Some seminarians already sensed opposition among the clergy.[121]

The movement first had the hierarchy's approval, but in 1964 the clergy worried about losing control over it. Rectors meeting in São Paulo issued a statement supporting seminarian organizations but opposing a national meeting. The priests urged contact with Catholic Action and the student movement, adoption of the see-judge-act method, the evangelization of the poor, and improved pastoral training. They also supported inclusion of the student organizations in the CNBB's crucial first General Pastoral Plan. But they believed the seminarians needed guidance. Not all students were ready for a national movement, especially because its benefits, goals, and practical operation were not clearly defined. The superiors offered cautionary advice about political activism. Seminarians had a commitment to the priesthood and evangelization and not to "movements of the temporal order." Seminarian organizations had to "remain within the spirit of obedience." The priests recommended that the "competent authority" help plan and implement congresses. The rectors praised *O Seminário* but wanted to reimpose clerical censorship, which had become lax.[122] The priests thus undermined the seminarians' drive for autonomy. Some bishops were upset with the content of *O Seminário*, and in 1965 Viamão rector Dom Ivo Lorscheiter prohibited the circulation of one issue because of disagreement over its content. He had to warn the students to stop slipping articles past the ecclesiastical censor.[123] Some Viamão students involved in the planning for a national meeting were expelled.[124]

The rectors imposed their authority because in 1964 the seminaries still operated within the Tridentine framework and because Vatican II reasserted the existence of an ecclesial hierarchy. Catholicism was liberalizing, but tradition and obedience still counted. Modernization once again had limits. The rectors did not mention the coup. They did not have to. The progressive Catholic groups had already suffered greatly under the new regime's notorious repression. These and other major political events were taboo for O Seminário.[125]

Seminarians were divided over the movement's political goals. Ivo Poletto, a Viamão student and writer for O Seminário, viewed USMAS as the "possible embryo of the unionization of the 'lower clergy.'" The hierarchy "violently combated" this idea.[126] In 1965 Poletto met considerable resistance in his efforts to forge a national strategy. Using O Seminário business as a pretext, Poletto and another seminarian visited more than two dozen seminaries, including Curitiba, Rio de Janeiro, Petrópolis, Belo Horizonte, and Recife. In some schools the reception was cold, even hostile, mainly because the rectors feared the movement. The two men could not even enter the important Ipiranga seminary in São Paulo, ostensibly because they were not wearing cassocks. They had to meet with seminarians at a neutral location. By now Viamão was known as the "red seminary" for its support of the anti-regime UNE.[127]

Irineu Brand, the president of the southern branch of USMAS in 1966, rejected unionization. "It is not a movement of political-syndical scope," Brand asserted in a 1964 interview with O Seminário. The preparation of the first USMAS congress in 1963 had "promised many radical and immediate, almost Messianic, transformations," but when change disintegrated into a series of broad and vague resolutions, disappointment set in, Brand later recalled. He described the movement's objectives as ecclesial mission, unity, and Church renovation through pastoral planning. USMAS could help restructure the seminaries within the bounds of Vatican II and as long as it remained a movement "entirely of the Church."[128]

The careers of Brand and Poletto reflected their different views of the ministry. Brand became a priest in Porto Alegre, whereas Poletto left the formal ministry to become a key leader of the CPT. Regardless of these tendencies, USMAS furnished a democratic forum for debate on regional, national, and international politics as well as issues pertinent to the seminaries and the student movement.[129]

USMAS enjoyed the general support of seminarians. But some did oppose it, either by demonstrating neutrality and indifference[130] or by embracing a conservative position. The conservatives had particular strength among the Jesuits of Germanic origin at the Seminário Cristo Rei in São Leopoldo and in the Porto Alegre group at Viamão, which formed its own association. The conservatives often had the support of the hierarchy but were isolated from the movement's decision-making process.[131]

The rectors' discouragement did not dissuade some of the movement's leaders from seeking to achieve representation in the all-important CNBB. In 1967 the southern wing of USMAS held its fifth congress and discussed "structuring the entity as an organ of the CNBB" on the regional level. This seemed within grasp, for Brazil's new president, General Arthur da Costa e Silva, offered a flicker of hope about liberalizing the regime. Significantly, Dom Ivo Lorscheiter supported the motion.[132] Yet it was far less ambitious than a national organization or seminarians' union. The year 1968 would ultimately decide the fate of these objectives.

The Critique of the Tridentine System and the Identity Crisis of the Priesthood

Despite organizational hurdles, the movement's strong critique of the Tridentine system became a major basis for seminary reform. The movement served as a valuable platform for the articulation of student demands. The lack of clarity in its agenda demonstrated not confusion nor lack of commitment, but complexity. The priesthood was entering its greatest identity crisis since the days of Trent. All topics were legitimate. The seminarians adapted many new ecclesial and political ideas to their particular needs and their vision for a new Church. Seminarians did not fully agree on a single program of change, and experiments varied according to the local setting. And some seminarians and priests rejected change. Nevertheless, the movement represented a generalized protest against the Tridentine system. Seminarians voiced harsh criticisms and proposed alternatives covering the entire spectrum of training and the ministry.[133] In effect, they created what Michel de Certeau called an "antidiscipline."[134] Protests against discipline were an act of courage that both exposed and undermined the system. As they increased, the Church responded by modifying discipline. The movement helped propel the Brazilian Church into *aggiornamento* (the process of bringing the Church "up to date," begun by Vatican II) by introducing new ideas about the cultural, ethical, and pedagogical facets of Catholicism. Brazil's seminarians embarked on a mission to shape a new kind of Brazilian apostle.[135]

Many priests and even some bishops joined the debate. With tensions undermining hierarchical obedience, the priests often sided with the seminarians in protests against the system. Priests (and bishops), after all, shared a unique experience with their colleagues-to-be, first as seminarians and then frequently as professors and rectors. And as priests-in-training seminarians were acutely aware of the issues impinging on the ministry. Focusing on both educational reform and the life of the ministry, priests were fundamental agents in bringing change to clerical training. As one teacher recalled, the student radicals learned prudence from their superiors, who in turn learned from their pupils the need to understand the changing times.[136]

The most common complaint attacked the Tridentine system's social isolation, which prevented seminaries from adapting to the changing times. In 1963 Dom Severino Mariano, the bishop of Pesqueira, Pernambuco, and a founder of *O Seminário,* became the first prelate to publish a letter in the journal. He affirmed the need to open up the seminaries to Brazilian society and the world.[137] In the words of Dom Ivo, the seminary at times had "an appearance of an immutable institution, finished, perfect, and which could now only continue in its normal rhythm of operation, receiving pupils and discharging them for pastoral work." The Brazilian clergy was uniform, mediocre, and uncreative.[138] It was also highly bureaucratic. Many fathers worked in administrative posts or in the education of the elite and seminarians. Fewer than half the clergy actually did direct apostolic work, and the number of parishes was growing faster than vocations.[139]

The movement rejected "massification," or standardization. Many seminaries lacked ethnic diversity, with sons of Italians dominating in some areas.[140] Yet priests and seminarians showed little or no concern about the shortage of Afro-Brazilian vocations.

Isolation distorted seminarians' view of reality and their emotional development. Detachment from family and society at an early age caused "sociological uprooting," and the overemphasis on intellectual training was increasingly out of step with mainstream instruction and culture.[141] In the analysis of ex-seminarian Ernildo Stein, the system robbed the student of "his practical good sense, atrophying his capacity for vigorous initiative."[142] Isolation prevented understanding of the harsh daily existence of most people in an underdeveloped, inflationary economy. Because they were privileged, seminarians developed bourgeois attitudes. The seminarian "does not know how much the dollar is worth, does not know the price of beans," one seminarian wrote in 1967. "The seminarian is like the son born with a silver spoon in his mouth."[143]

Isolation continued after ordination, leading to loneliness, social maladjustment, misunderstanding of the people, and purported sexual problems such as "womanizing" and homosexuality.[144] Unordained former seminarians did not know how to court and lived in "fear that women would trick" them. Seminarians and priests wanted more frequent and natural contact with women, who, after all, represented half of their flocks.[145] Celibacy naturally entered this discussion.

To be a priest in Brazil was not to be celibate. The incidents studied in chapter 4 suggest that both heterosexual and homosexual activity were common in the twentieth century. But it was difficult to measure priests' sexual activity because the Tridentine ethic had forced it deeply underground. The hierarchy opposed learning about priests' sex lives. In the 1960s São Paulo Archbishop Dom Agnelo Rossi and the papal nuncio suspended a research project that included questions about celibacy. Father Godofredo Deelen, a Dutchman, had surveyed three thousand Brazilian clergymen. According to Deelen, the authorities disagreed with the "tendentious and ideological mentality" of his research and considered celibacy and other delicate issues "superfluous." The Church withheld the responses from Deelen and deposited them in the CNBB's secret archive.[146] He speculated that 75 percent of the clergy maintained "illicit relations with women." A later poll of 203 priests by the CNBB's Centro de Estatística Religiosa e Investigações Sociais (CERIS, or Center for Religious Statistics and Social Research) clearly indicated overwhelming opposition to obligatory celibacy (77 percent) and suggested that most priests (67 percent) had great difficulties in remaining chaste.[147] One father affirmed that priests had committed adultery, statutory rape of minors, and abortion. Another calculated that in Rio de Janeiro alone some two hundred men had abandoned the ministry because of celibacy. One bishop reportedly tried to bribe a young man who had recognized him in "a nightclub for loose women."[148] Seminarians also demanded optional celibacy. In one Church survey students generally appreciated the value of celibacy but noted that it was imposed. Many believed it to be unnecessary for the ministry. Others thought it caused psychological disturbances. Yet others said it frightened men away from the priesthood.[149] Celibacy was a utopia.

Between 1965 and 1971 bishops, priests, and seminarians from around the globe engaged in a vigorous debate over celibacy. Brazilian priests openly criticized the obligation. While in psychoanalysis, Father Paulo Eduardo Andrade Ponte, a former student of the Vincentians in Fortaleza, published an article in the *REB* contesting celibacy. He criticized the seminaries' lack of proper theological and psychological orientation on the matter. Ponte criticized Pope Paul VI's traditional defense of celibacy and lamented Vatican II's contradictory conclusions, which described celibacy as a priestly mystery but also a mere "juridical imposition." Celibacy was valuable only if freely chosen, Ponte stated. Making it optional would calm the growing revolt against the hierarchy.[150] Despite colleagues' predictions that he would never be promoted,[151] Ponte became a bishop in 1971, demonstrating how debate could take place in the Church at that time. The Church had little choice when so many men were thinking of quitting. "Celibacy is a question that, in general, interests everybody because of the simple fact of our being men or women, celibate or not," wrote Father Benedito Beni dos Santos, another prominent advocate of optional celibacy. "Speaking of celibacy," he added, "we speak of ourselves, often without knowing it." Celibacy was shaped by historical circumstances, and the "science of sex," secularization, and the study of marriage and sexuality raised questions about its validity. Did people respond more to the symbol of love shown by a celibate or by the love of a couple? Celibacy lost relevance as priests engaged in society and the Church emphasized the laity. Celibacy could now only scare away vocations. It already excluded Afro-Brazilians, whose culture rejected celibacy.[152]

A minority of fathers defended celibacy. They emphasized its spiritual value in upholding the traditional image of the priest as a heroic being with superhuman powers. "Celibacy is our strength, our glory, our honor, our virility, the driving force of our apostolate," one cleric stated. This group offered practical arguments. The cleric was a model for the faithful. If he married, his disobedient children might contradict his preachings. Or he might become involved in a bad marriage. The priest's wife could become jealous of her husband hearing others' private thoughts in the confessional. Priests living on a small salary could not support a family.[153] Celibacy's proponents believed it was a choice, although they ignored the fact that priestly education often began in childhood. In fact, after Vatican II the Church deemphasized the minor seminary and encouraged the once-scorned adult vocations.

Priests' testimonies revealed the tragedy of men who struggled to lead double lives—a public celibacy and a private satisfaction of needs. Tridentine norms had caused priests to dwell in a highly charged environment of forbidden desire. In the post–Vatican II world not only celibacy was in jeopardy; the entire Catholic concept of sexuality and gender relations came into question. Paul VI's controversial encyclicals on celibacy and birth control failed to hold back the flood of new ideas and behavior. Priests made the transition from Tridentine hush to a modern, public discussion of sexuality. For many Brazilian clerics celibacy falsely lived no longer made sense.

Former seminarian Agostinho Both described the discussion of sexual issues as the "liberation from dogmas" and the liberation of the self. In line with religious modernization seminarians replaced guilt and sin with personal reflection as a guide to life. Students began to seek greater contact with women and to discuss and practice masturbation, which the Church considered a mortal sin. The prohibition of masturbation had caused psychological problems for some seminarians. But freedom from guilt meant that young men could now enjoy their sexuality. A general liberalization of seminary life paralleled the changes in sexuality. Ignoring the daily schedule was one example. The arrival of television led students to stay up later, causing them to miss the 5 AM wake-up time. Seminarians abandoned the use of the tonsure, the cassock, and community prayer. The new behavior disturbed the superiors, who tried to preserve at least some of the old customs. But change was like an avalanche, with seminarians suddenly questioning everything in the four-hundred-year-old system.[154]

The movement strongly opposed the Tridentine system's authoritarian stress on discipline and unquestioning obedience. "I will not obey," stated the title of one commentary in O Seminário.[155] These sentiments generated anger toward the bishops. The fathers reported little contact with their superiors, whom they described as cold and uncaring or at best paternalistic. Priests in progressive pastoral programs had to work discreetly. In the clergy's estimation the bishops were better administrators than apostles. One father's commentary summed up many priests' feelings about the Holy See: "I already think it is very serious that laws are made governing the work of the priest without his having been heard on the matter. But I think what really is unjust are the laws governing his *life:* civil status, the breviary, clothing."[156] The students sought control of their lives and a voice in governing the seminaries.[157] Carlos Alberto Libânio Christo (Frei Betto) called for a new discipline resulting from "an interior attitude" rather than a "brake which impedes." Similarly, obedience could occur only after "a lucid and objective dialogue with the superior." Dialogue became a byword of the post–Vatican II era, as the Church accepted a pluralistic world and improved relations both within the institution and with other faiths and philosophies, even Marxism. Seminarians hoped that an "adult" Catholicism would finally shed authoritarianism.[158] In effect, the seminarians advocated the democratization of the seminary.[159]

Tridentine discipline had produced an awkwardness between the clergy and the people because it prohibited pastoral work until after ordination.[160]

A 1962 editorial in *O Seminário* stated that seminarians simply reinforced each other's preconceived ideas about the world, leaving them disoriented once they became priests. The priest "will then find his solutions by escaping. Or he will fanatically and desperately grab the ideas that he has memorized. He will condemn all who do not think as he does. And he will dream of 'the good old days.'... He will be many things, but he will not be a good pastor." The editorial asked how "theoretical" and "dead" ecclesiastical studies could acquire new life. Put "the student in contact with the men who live the problems under study," it replied.[161]

The seminarians thirsted for action in the outer world. In 1963, for instance, students in the northeast held their first Pastoral Week. Father Luiz Gonzaga Sena, a politically controversial ACB intellectual, helped lead the workshop. The students reflected on the role of the seminary in the revolutionary northeast and planned greater contact with the laity, especially the poor.[162]

The demand for an overhaul of the neo-Thomistic program became a central plank of the movement. "The study of philosophy and theology in the seminary is nostalgic; they are for old men and therefore are not useful for young men," one seminarian wrote. "John XXIII said, 'The Church is not a museum.' And I say: neither is the seminary."[163] Philosophy needed to be practical in order to facilitate pastoral outreach.[164] The Church even debated the elimination of philosophy. It survived but lost prestige, pedagogical quality, and the students' interest.

They preferred to explore human sciences such as sociology, anthropology, economics, history, and psychology. Each of these disciplines had helped the Church modernize intellectually. The use of social science fulfilled the movement's goal of putting the study of Brazilian reality into the curriculum. It also prepared students to dialogue with the competing outlooks of secularism and Marxism, both highly influential among the middle classes, particularly intellectuals and university students. Another big step in curricular renovation was to adopt the modernized theology of the post–Vatican II era. "The curriculum of studies, in spite of numerous modifications, still continues to be more apt to train professors of theology than preachers of the gospel," three founders of USMAS, now ordained, observed. The seminarians' movement wanted to "de-intellectualize" theology in order to make it an instrument of pastoral practice and especially to make it more comprehensible to the laity.[165]

Seminarians viewed the outside world as exciting and full of potential for their careers. They anxiously wanted to fall into step with a cosmopolitan culture that propagated the cult of the individual. In Brazil individualism fed on the new ambitions of youths raised in a society filled with both the optimism and the tensions of rapid development. Young people clamored for the expansion of the highly elitist university system. Proponents of development believed the priest had become an "ahistorical being" and the priesthood a symbol of "immobilism." Seminarians feared becoming clergymen "on the margin of the dynamism that animates profane society."[166]

Self-interest and the desire for prestige drove reform. Seminarians lashed out against the highly standardized and stultifying environment of traditional training. Seminaries should train not just for a vocation, but for a range of fulfilling careers from which individuals could freely choose. Seminarians demanded professionalization of the ministry, including the right to have paying jobs and to earn degrees in nonecclesiastical fields such as journalism and psychology. Professionalization assured individual economic stability, especially if a man chose to quit the ministry. Previous generations of ex-seminarians had great difficulties in finding work. Seminarians disliked priests who became financially dependent on the ruling classes in order to supplement incomes based on exploitative religious fees and the goodwill of the impoverished faithful.[167] Professionalization implied ties to the university system and therefore the most upwardly mobile and privileged strata of Brazilian society.[168]

Professionalization could alleviate the class divisions that irritated many priests. While many struggled to survive, others acquired cars, farms, and horses. Many priests reaped profits from the sale of candles and other holy objects. Others lent parish funds at high interest rates. The bishops showed little concern for the less fortunate. The Church largely ignored the health of its pastors, and some vicars went many years without a vacation.[169] Priests eventually won the right to annual vacation, but a social security institute begun in the early 1960s went bankrupt in the late 1970s, leaving a portion of the clergy to depend on Brazil's precarious public-health system.[170] Regular, professional employment would remove the economic risks of the priesthood. It meshed nicely with the Church's need to modernize its workforce and provide it with greater functional diversity and flexibility. But professionalization could endanger traditional values that the Church of the Poor reaffirmed, such as self-sacrifice and poverty. To avoid being overwhelmed by modernity, the clergy needed to balance its necessities with the priestly mission. Professionalization was not an abandonment of the faith, but a survival strategy.[171]

Depending on the job, outside work could actually aid clerical reform and a ministry of poverty. Paid work eliminated financial dependence on the Church and diminished the bourgeois environment of the seminary. It also increased students' contact with society. "Factory life is spectacular; [it's] community life," one worker-seminarian in São Paulo wrote in 1967. "It's great to be paid. It cost sweat to earn it. To eat from wages. To live the life of the people."[172]

Self-fulfillment went far deeper than money, however. The new priesthood required emotionally healthy, well-rounded men. The intellectual, the spiritual, the individualistic, the social, and the political formed interdependent links of a new trend called *formação integral*, or holistic education. Psychological development was another essential link. One bad link could ruin the others: an emotionally frustrated priest would find his evangelical, social, and political work hindered.[173] The emphasis on individual development remedied existential problems by helping personal traits and skills to bloom, and it put intellectual and spiritual life into the context of human and social realities. Above all, the Church needed well-adjusted priests who could deal with key issues such as loneliness, celibacy, homosexuality, and priests' relationship to the laity, especially women.[174]

The seminarians' most radical demand was to live in small communities—inside the seminary or preferably in distant neighborhoods. This model came from the worker-priests and Catholic Action. In 1962 Father Jacques Loew, a leading French worker-priest, had visited Viamão, and an interview with him appeared in *O Seminário*.[175] The small communities combined the notion of proximity to the people with a communitarian critique of modernity and capitalism found in Catholic theological and philosophical writings. They embraced the revolutionary romanticism popular in Brazil at that time.[176] Small communities would soften discipline and stimulate individual development. Community life demanded greater maturity because it required planning and more effective communication among colleagues. "The important thing is that each seminarian be himself, with responsibility, with originality, with authenticity, with his free choice," Dom Ivo Lorscheiter said in an interview with *O Seminário*. "For this to happen, a pedagogy of small groups is indispensable."[177] The new priesthood would be a question of individual conscience.

Priests and students were already experimenting with small communities. At Viamão in the late 1950s seminarians started pastoral activity in miserable working-class areas where radical priests lived in poverty. Using ACB methodology, the students developed Bible study circles for the faithful. The circles helped the people interpret their political activity in labor unions and the construction of housing. These interactions deeply influenced the pastoral outlook of the seminarians.[178] A group of seminarians linked to JOC decided to help organize the poor Luso- and Afro-Brazilian women who worked in abject, sexually exploitative conditions as domestic servants in Porto Alegre. The men and the women prayed together and charted strategy for obtaining the servants' labor rights.[179] Other students gave catechism classes. This experience taught cultural diversity to young men from ethnic enclaves unfamiliar with Luso-Brazilian religiosity. Father Affonso Gregory, a Viamão professor and leading Church sociologist, had students research the social and religious backgrounds of the neighborhoods.[180] Later Viamão divided into several sub-groups of seminarians living in separate residences located in the surrounding community. Viamão still taught philosophy, but theological studies now took place at an institute at the local Catholic university. Thirty-six seminarians from Caxias do Sul, for instance, formed a separate community. The Caxias seminarians even drew up plans for the construction of a new residence.[181] A group of students from the Pio Brasileiro in Rome spent the summer of 1963 working among the poor. Tilden Santiago, a student from Minas Gerais in his final year of theology at the Gregorian University, left the seminary to take up manual labor and subsequently became a worker-priest. He was later imprisoned by the Brazilian military.[182] In another experience forty priests met monthly in small groups of four to eight. The fathers spent the day reviewing and planning their pastoral activities using the *revisão de vida*. They sought unity and familiarity. In some groups the fathers shared their salaries. Others saw in the model the seed for revolutionary change in the structure of the Church.[183] Contact with the people in small groups defined USMAS more than did its drive for a national organization, Ivo Poletto recalled.[184] These experiences prove that priests and seminarians were creating CEBs and practicing liberation theology years before these terms were coined. Using the see-judge-act method, the small groups also served as a method of psychological assistance for the individual seminarian.[185] Chapter 7 studies the concept of the small communities in greater detail.

The new priesthood needed not angels but men of "flesh and blood," as Agostinho Both put it.[186] Fathers and seminarians presented themselves as everyday people. Most replaced the cassock with laymen's clothing or the less obtrusive clerical garb permitted under post–Vatican II norms. This was a simple yet profound way to draw closer to the people. Few gestures symbolized so powerfully the transformation of the priesthood. Today the sight of a man on the street in clerical habit can be as disconcerting as was the priests' shedding of such raiment in the 1960s. Monsignor Darci Domingos Treviso, a director of *O Seminário*, recalled how a Viamão professor expelled him from class one hot day for having removed his white seminarian's collar and loosening the top buttons on his cassock. Seminarians provoked their superiors by taking off their cassocks in class. When the Church finally abolished the requirement, the students celebrated as if Brazil had won the World Cup.[187]

The quest for a humanized priesthood drew seminarians to political causes. One of the most important was nationalism. The movement rejected Romanization. In 1963 *O Seminário* declared that Vatican II marked the end of Westernization in the Church. Noting that even the most nationalist priests still depended on Europe for ideas, Ernildo Stein believed seminarians could learn much from intellectuals and student radicals who sought to create an authentic Brazilian culture.[188] Echoing the seventeenth-century sermons of Father Vieira, Catholic Action leader Father Sena reinforced these sentiments. "Brazil has a vocation as the vanguard within the Church Universal," he told the seminarians of the northeast in late 1963. "It is not Europe but Latin America that is called to give new experiences to the Church Universal. . . . We import everything from Europe as a subproduct. We even import from Europe crises already surpassed, as was the case of the Liturgical Movement, repeated in Brazil ten years after France." Brazil's seminaries needed "originality."[189] Ideas for reform might be European, but their practical application in the context of Latin American poverty could lead to the development of new ecclesial models. As Dom Ivo suggested, seminary innovation could take place more easily in South America because of the region's much younger Catholic tradition.[190] *Optatum Totius*'s emphasis on local innovation encouraged this trend.[191]

The shift to small communities and the crusade for national development led seminarians to implement the preferential option for the poor. In 1965 three former USMAS members declared: "To preach the Gospel in the style of a past era is to row against the current, to ignore all of the new problems of our time and the demand for social justice made in the *self-advancement* of the poor classes. These least favored of people, who form two thirds of humanity, are searching desperately for a solution to their misery."[192] The preferential option became an integral part of the new priesthood as seminarians venerated the poor as a source of wisdom, values, and spirituality.

This commitment required a new empathy for the poor like that of primitive, communistic Christianity. In 1963 seminarians of the northeast meeting in Olinda concluded that ministers must adopt spiritual and actual poverty as a way of life.[193] An article in *O Seminário* recorded an appeal by workers to lower-class seminarians: "Try to study the theology of work, workers' problems, the situation of workers, the psychology of workers. Try to help in the training of new cadres of [JOC ecclesiastical] assistants. Unite yourselves throughout

Brazil around this ideal."[194] Another seminarian wrote that the time had come for the priest to participate in the raising of working-class consciousness by "living as a poor person among the poor and committing himself to them in the struggle for liberation."[195] The spirituality of Charles de Foucauld, a French monk whose life among poor nomads in the Sahara Desert inspired numerous Christians to found small communities, reinforced dedication to the poor in Brazil.[196]

These initiatives refined a new spirituality of social activism. Action and contemplation were no longer separate, but key traditional aspects such as participation in the Eucharist continued. "Prayer demands a strong, virile, and human asceticism," a key CNBB document on priestly spirituality stated in the early 1970s. "It's not enough to be satisfied with the saying 'everything is prayer.'" Pastoral work, the commitment to the poor, politics, and the study of history and social structures generated values that the priest interiorized. Spirituality was no longer at the service of the institution, but the people. The priest was their friend. He publicly defended the oppressed and, as a result, prepared for enduring suffering and persecution.[197]

Listening to the poor, seminarians learned how greatly disaffected many had become toward priests. Highly educated fathers had difficulty in building relationships with rural youths, Father Raimundo Caramuru, a national leader of Catholic Action, told *O Seminário*. "Our authoritarian education often impedes us from having confidence in these simple and unpretentious youths, who are without much instruction, without great horizons, although they possess in themselves the profoundness of life."[198] The comments of urban workers in 1963 revealed yet harsher opinions: "'When he, the father, comes to us it is to ask for something or to complain.' 'We are not loved by him.' 'I don't go to Church, simply because the father is rude.'" *O Seminário* stated that "the poor are not being evangelized!"[199] Four years later a worker-seminarian heard even more devastating statements in a factory:

The priests don't know how to explain the Bible well, and they don't practice what they preach.

Priests should get married so that they can lead the tough life that we lead.

I don't see Christ in the priests: Christ washed the feet of others, and the priests don't follow the example of the Master.

I don't believe that a priest can work in a factory. If he does, it's just for exhibit, to show off.

The student's conclusion echoed a general trend of modern Catholicism: "The Church lost the world of the worker, and the two are increasingly distant from each other."[200] Observed one priest: "Some consider me as useless for society, unless I leave my pastoral function to become a professor, inspector, etc. Others consider me useful for 'those ignorant people' who still need religion. It is necessary to domesticate them. Religion is a brake. It saves on police stations."[201]

Pastors urgently needed to rethink their relationship to the people. The Brazilian priest could no longer administer the Tridentine sacraments like a magician, wrote Monsignor Marcelo Pinto Carvalheira, the head of the new, gigantic seminary at Camaragibe on the outskirts of Recife. Carvalheira exemplified the superior who took up the seminarians' fight for change. Brazilians had stopped expressing unconditional adherence to the clergy and increasingly found Afro-Brazilian cults and Protestant religions more attractive than Catholicism, whose rites had become "hermetic and cold," he affirmed. The priest needed to effect the personal conversion of his followers and to educate them in the faith. The priest had to be a "prophet," a man of dialogue, a servant of the people, and a promoter of community. New circumstances required the "personalization" of priests imbued with greater maturity and creativity. Titles, vestments, and the juridical and official mission were not satisfactory. It was necessary to have content, Carvalheira wrote.[202]

Although Carvalheira and others recognized the growing presence and effectiveness of nontraditional Protestant religions, concern about this issue did not become a theme of the seminarians' movement. There is little evidence in the Brazilian case to support the argument of a number of writers, including rational choice and religious marketplace theorists, that the Church and its clergy changed primarily because of a sense of threat from other religions. The Latin American Church made official statements against Protestantism throughout much of the twentieth century, but the Church was not really concerned about Protestant competition to the point that it took an active and profound interest in learning about the phenomenon and formulating effective ways to counter it. The new Brazilian priesthood had much more to do with modernity, social inequality, and the clergy's personal traumas. The historical context of the 1960s was far different from that of the 1980s and 1990s, when the neo-Pentecostal Protestant boom occurred in Brazil. Clergymen in the 1960s sought to make religion more rational—not the emotive, miracle-oriented model of the Charismatics that gained ground in the 1990s in response to the Protestants.[203] Indeed, the individualistic facet of the seminarians' movement reflected the same individualizing trend of modernity sparked by the Lutheran and Catholic Reformations of the sixteenth century.

Excessive rationalism, however, led seminarians into conflict with popular religion. They tried to impose their view of religion just as the agents of Romanization did in the nineteenth century. Seminarians and young priests opposed the perceived abuse of saintly images. Inspired by the spirit of youth protest, after Vatican II many pastors altered, removed, or even destroyed traditional church fixtures such as saints' statues and paintings. In place of the traditionally ornate altars they put up modernistic, slab-like tables. The new emphasis on the Bible, the rational word, and *conscientização* replaced the Rosary and other traditional rituals.[204] Elite priests such as Hugo Assmann, who believed they stood in the vanguard of reform by embracing a Germanic Catholicism devoid of the saints and processions so revered by Brazilians, scorned popular practices.[205] Most people remained silent in the face of the youths' aggressiveness, but many, especially the elderly, resisted the attack on popular religion.[206] In one *gaúcho* parish the people threatened a violent protest when the vicar tried to remove the statue of Saint George, one of the most important saints in Brazil.[207] But usually the seminarians and young fathers dismissed the defenders of popular religion as "conservatives" or "traditionalists."[208] Popular religion was "superstition," and the people were "alienated," a catch-all term used by seminarians for anything they disagreed with. One student declared to the devout dentist who worked in the seminary that angels did not exist, leading the man to enter a crisis of faith assuaged only after a conversation with the rector.[209] Modernizing reform led to the demythification of Catholicism, which in turn caused the people to become disenchanted and estranged from the clergy.

Ironically, the movement displayed more of a modern theological hubris than a statement of faith. Seminarians' public statements reflected the secularization of the 1960s, but in private or in the family environment they showed great respect for the saints. Publicly they were progressive; privately they could be archconservative. At Viamão they believed that the truly authentic Mass had to be held not in the rational environs of the seminary, but in a poor neighborhood, where traditional symbolism was strongest.[210] Seminarians had practiced a strong traditional religiosity at home and in the minor seminary, where confession and regular devotions were obligatory. Upon entering the major seminary they were suddenly faced with the challenge of adapting to a newly evolving vision of the faith. These self-contradictions revealed the personal ordeal experienced by seminarians of the Vatican II era.[211]

Sharing poverty expanded the seminarian's horizons. One group described contact with the poor as a revelation. Assisting a MEB literacy team in the diocese of Caruaru, Pernambuco, the three seminarians traveled weekly to small villages in the countryside. A 1966 article in *O Seminário* described their newly discovered perception of life as an anxious struggle. They came "face to face" with hunger, ignorance, and the "fatalistic consciousness" inherent in "the sub-human situation of the rural man. . . . We discovered how we were so distant from the man to whose liberation we intended to contribute, how displaced we were from the world that we aspired to transform." They pledged to fight for a more human world by teaching basic literacy and raising the rural dweller's political consciousness so that he could "become the author of his own history." Literacy helped construct "an authentic community" among the poor and end the misery of the "unjust" social order, divided between "dominators and dominated."[212]

The next step for many was political militancy. Seminarians scribbled "Long live activism!" and "Down with alienation" on the blackboards and walls of Viamão. On the door to the chapel they wrote, "This is a place of alienation."[213] "The modern saint is a social saint," *O Seminário* proclaimed. "The seminarian will not be absent when one day the history of the rechristianization of Brazil is told."[214] This declaration echoed the "historical ideal" of JUC, Catholic Action's most radical wing. JUC proposed to form an elite of "saints" who would study the social sciences and, practicing self-sacrifice like the worker-priests, delve into the daily lives of the people. Their goal was to save humanity through revolutionary action.[215] The proposed model for the seminaries resembled university students' vision of the university as a transformative social actor.[216] Seminarians became involved with the UNE as early as 1961,[217] and students from Viamão's philosophy directorate participated in the UNE's national assembly in Rio.[218] Over the years a significant part of the student body came to participate in UNE and regional student politics.[219] Viamão had a rarity among the seminaries: official federal approval of its philosophy and theology courses. This afforded it official voting status in UNE elections.[220] University students urged on the ecclesiastics. In 1962, for example, the Christian Democratic youths of Porto Alegre challenged *O Seminário*'s readers to join them and the Communists to fight for social justice. "Get down from your pedestal of glory," they exhorted.[221] Ex-seminarian Ernildo Stein, president of the State Union of Students in Rio Grande do Sul and linked to the revolutionary AP, stressed that future priests could benefit from "contact with the ideological effervescence" of the university movement.[222] Some seminaries reproduced the model of the *centros acadêmicos,* the secular universities' student councils. In Rio Grande do Sul alone seven centers sprung up with the support of superiors who thought that seminarians should learn about the universities.[223] By the mid-1960s Viamão became a focal point of student activism. Some seminarians joined Catholic Action, while others entered the AP and other radical groups.[224] Seminarians ultimately demanded the fusion of ecclesiastical training with universities.

The seminarians' movement reached its height between 1966 and 1968. *O Seminário* radicalized yet further. In 1966 an USMAS participant at São Leopoldo organized a seminar on the French Jesuit, paleontologist, and evolutionist Pierre Teilhard de Chardin, whose works were prohibited before Vatican II.[225] In 1967 the journal entertained the ideas of Father Ivan Illich, a controversial innovator working in the ultra-progressive diocese of Cuernavaca, Mexico. He believed that the priesthood would disappear as more of the laity ran the Church. Ignoring clerical issues, *O Seminário* aimed to galvanize all Christians for social action. "*O Seminário . . .* cannot be content with abstract formulations," it declared. "It has an appointment with the concrete man."[226]

In 1968 the journal abandoned all ecclesiastical pretense and changed its name to *Ponto Homem* (Point: Man). "Why 'Ponto Homem'?" the first editorial asked.

In the atomic era there is no place for quietism. In the age of engagement, alienation is not possible. The first requirement is to throw oneself into the fray. Because man is threatened. In his liberty. In his dignity. In his salvation. The seriousness of the moment demands of us more than a smiling idealism. It demands of us our all and much more. We live in a time of courage. In an age of risk.

It is the time of Man.

He has become today the point of convergence of all paths. Of all search. There is only one center-point that opens itself to a greatness larger than itself.

That point is *Ponto-Homem.*[227]

As the student movement erupted around the globe, the seminarians' movement had fully embraced the humanism of Vatican II.

Ponto Homem helped plant the seeds of liberation theology. Theologians, priests, and professional writers now dominated its pages. The July–August 1968 issue contained papers from a special assembly at Viamão on the "theology of

development." This meeting gave an intense and wide-ranging preview of liberation theology, born only weeks later at the Latin American bishops' Medellín assembly. Leading speakers included Father Caramuru, an author of
the CNBB's General Pastoral Plan; Dom Ivo Lorscheiter; Belgian Father José
Comblin, a leading liberation theologian; Father Gregory, the religious sociologist and former Viamão professor; and Father Assmann, another important
early liberation theologian. They pondered salvation in the light of history and
Latin American underdevelopment.[228] The final report employed dependency
theory to comment on Latin America's position in the world. Other key themes
included liberation as salvation, life as the source of theological reflection,
theologians' need for an alliance with social scientists, and socialism as a historical necessity.[229] Assmann highlighted the political character of the theology
of development in his presentations on "a theology of revolution" and "elements
for an ethic of the revolutionary option and practice." He noted the powerful
influence that Che Guevara and Colombian priest Camilo Torres, both killed in
guerrilla warfare, held over Latin American youths. He questioned the Church's
preaching of nonviolence because it obscured the existence of institutionalized violence.[230]

Into the Catacombs: Repression, Bishops, and the Suppression of the Movement

Priests, seminarians, and even bishops became the targets of Brazil's national
security state. Catholic media underwent censorship, and across the country
priests faced trial in military courts, imprisonment, torture, and death threats.
Some foreign clergymen were deported, and seven priests were killed.[231] As
the historical Church-state alliance frayed, Brazil's bureaucratic-authoritarian
regime forged ahead with plans for development without the usual moral, intellectual, and political support of the Church. Church and state were aban-
doning their commonly held cosmologies of social domination. Only secret
meetings between the bishops and the generals during the worst years of the
regime prevented a break in relations.[232]

Conservative and traditionalist Catholics helped suppress radical Catholic experiments. Catholic students and militants of the MEB, JOC, JUC, and
other organizations suffered heavy reprisal in the early years of the regime and
experienced increasing conflict with the Church hierarchy. With the approval

of his fellow bishops Dom Vicente Scherer dissolved the dynamic JUC in one of the greatest tragedies in the history of Brazilian Catholicism.

Priests faced accusations related to three kinds of subversion: activities related to poverty and class struggle, abandonment of Catholic practices dear to the military and conservative civilians, and theological radicalism. The accusers went beyond jurisprudence to enter the realm of theological dispute. Priests who did not do the business of the elite were the enemy. Thus, for example, did Father Lage become "the devil's priest," as he titled his memoirs. The generals saw no distinction between revolutionary subversion and calls for Catholic social justice. The search for a new priesthood increasingly resembled the persecuted Church of the catacombs. The repression ultimately spelled the downfall of the seminarians' movement.

A central theme of this book is that clerical opposition to the military regime, the quest for social justice, and the crisis of the priesthood were all interrelated. One priest prosecuted for subversion noted that his conservative enemies tried to associate his activities "with internal problems of the Church, such as the cassock, celibacy, and others."[233] During his trial Father Carlos Gilberto Machado Moraes, once a member of the O Seminário staff, was charged with preaching subversive propaganda in his sermons, talks, and radio programs in Rio Grande do Sul from 1966 to 1970. His accusers focused on the fact that he wore a red T-shirt instead of a cassock. He was concerned "exclusively with earthly and material affairs, such as hunger, peace and all the rest of the things that the reds repeat." Moraes later quit the ministry.[234]

The downfall of the Vincentian fathers best reflected the intertwining of the ecclesial and political crises. In the mid-1960s they and their students experienced a veritable earthquake. The first shocks came with the expulsion of the capable but controversial liturgicistas in the 1950s and continued in the 1960s with the failure to adapt to Vatican II.[235] The fathers abruptly left their seminaries in Mariana, São Luís, Fortaleza, and other cities. The exit from Fortaleza in late 1963 was especially painful. The fathers had taught there for almost one hundred years and trained more than three hundred priests—all the clergy of Ceará and most of the clergy of Rio Grande do Norte. The Fortaleza teachers were unprepared to meet students' demands for reform. The archdiocese eventually put in its own, more modern program.[236]

But the most serious problems struck at the congregation's heart in Minas Gerais. Whereas the Vincentians lagged in Fortaleza, they were too progressive for the hierarchy in Diamantina. The archbishop, Dom Geraldo de Proença

Sigaud, zealously backed Tradition, Family, and Property (TFP), an integralist organization born in 1960 and vehemently opposed to Communism and agrarian reform.[237] His attitude exemplified how the strategy of many bishops to placate the generals and preserve Catholic traditions intensified conflict with radical seminarians and priests. When Dom Sigaud arrived in Diamantina in 1961, the nuncio and bishops from around Brazil exhorted the Lazaristas to defend the seminary from the inevitable ideological onslaught.[238] Dom Sigaud brought in pro-TFP seminarians from other dioceses.[239] In 1964 he became the "ecclesiastical mentor" of the coup in Minas Gerais.[240] The Diamantina students agreed with many points of the seminarians' movement, and the Lazaristas had introduced key innovations, for example, equipes, contact with the poor through sociological research, catechism in the local jail, and extracurricular studies on themes such as Communism.[241] Seven conservative Vincentians complained to their superior about two young radical colleagues and their allies among the seminarians. The two denounced Dom Sigaud and urged students to read *Brasil, Urgente,* a socialist journal founded by Dominican Friar Carlos Josafá, one of the former *liturgicista* Vincentians.[242] Dom Sigaud demanded that the Lazaristas remove the leftist priests and even the moderate rector, Father José Isabel da Silva Campos. Teachers needed to "impregnate the students with love for the social doctrine of the Church and for tradition and with a holy hate against leftism and modernism," Sigaud wrote.[243] One student paraphrased the prelate's maxims: "The problem of the favelas cannot be resolved, because others will appear. You can't end poverty, because if you do we will not have the opportunity to exercise our charity. Why put an end to this lovely Brazilian tradition?"[244]

Dom Sigaud and the military tried to tie the seminarians to Communism. During training at Diamantina in 1962 Father José Dumont, a diocesan priest, had queried Father Lage on the bibliography for a study on Communism sponsored by the seminary's traditional literary guild. After the coup the military found allegedly incriminating correspondence between the two priests and arrested Dumont. He was held incommunicado for forty days in the archiepiscopal palace and released only after considerable public protest.[245] The day of the arrest Dom Sigaud had the police conduct a sweep against seminarians suspected of subversion. The police seized letters, books in Latin, and even North American anti-Communist propaganda. The police interrogated one group of students at the archbishop's home.[246] Using the Lage-Dumont connection as leverage, Dom Sigaud fired the Lazaristas and expelled a number of students. Father Campos denied the allegations against Dumont and the seminarians.[247]

He sent an emergency request to Rome for an apostolic visit. But the Lazarista efforts to keep the seminary failed.

The seminarians' and Father Dumont's correspondence portrays the travails caused by the coup and ecclesial reform. Goulart's overthrow served as a kind of political litmus test for Catholics. It deepened political divisions and especially worried progressives, because anti-Communism included opposition to Catholic Action, aspects of Vatican II, and other Church innovations. One woman wrote Father Dumont about the refusal of priests to assist her youth group for fear of upsetting Dom Sigaud.[248] Father Rogério, a friend, wrote Dumont about the hierarchy's hesitation to change the institution. He lamented the indifference and even hostility some people held toward the clergy. He also commented on the political situation. "Brazil is in revolution: I see in this more the force of money than the Christian spirit," wrote Rogério, an admirer of Dom Hélder. "There was finally a reaction against Communism. But if that is all it does, history will regress."[249] Wanderley Antônio Rodrigues wrote Father Dumont that life in the seminary was tense and "unbearable" because of the Vincentians' expulsion of five politically "advanced" students, resulting in the decimation of the Catholic Action group. Some seminarians were glad. "The happiness increases when the papers announce the arrest of a priest: 'He was working for the C[ommunist] P[arty],'" Rodrigues wrote. Others lamented the loss. "Fortunately, our faith is alive and our hope for better days stronger . . . ," he continued. "Father José, yesterday the soldiers of the Third Infantry Battalion were festively received. At night, at the door of the cathedral, a Mass and a demonstration." Rodrigues added that Catholic activists were being arrested.[250] Another seminarian, Carlos Jurandir, regretted the political polarization taking hold of Brazil and its Church. "There were exaggerations on the right and on the left, if we can say that there is a left here. I stayed out of it," the student wrote. He did not like the impassioned taking of sides or the emotional outbursts about heroes and enemies. "They can even call me remiss. I will express my position without being embarrassed. You know, they wanted me either to be advanced or backward. That I be right there by the radio shouting for or against. I don't like hysteria. I got away from the hysterical people of both sides. . . . I'm looking to walk with the Church."[251]

At Mariana, the "Rome of Minas Gerais," the seminarians nearly revolted because of lack of reform. In 1965 Mariana students were joining Catholic Action and demanding a voice in seminary governance.[252] At year's end tensions exploded. The Lazaristas reported to Rome that a "climate of instability" had produced anguish, discontent, and rebelliousness. The seminarians dealt with psychological difficulties, a lack of individual accommodations, an out-of-date library, the traditional clericalism of the local parish priests, and indecision about celibacy and thus their vocation. As the situation worsened in 1966 the staff faced a dilemma: reestablish discipline and risk revolt, or let the seminary fall into anarchy. After surveying the students, the Vincentians suspended classes in order to rewrite the seminary program in light of Vatican II, *Optatum Totius,* other key Church documents from Latin America and Brazil, and the seminarians' demands. It proposed opening the seminary to society; personal and communitarian orientation and a "functional" lifestyle; a more relevant pedagogy; a student role in decision-making; pastoral internships; establishment of small communities; free afternoons for study, research, and group work; paid outside employment; and "the periodic assistance of a competent psychologist."[253] Eight of the eleven Lazaristas accepted the plan.

Archbishop Dom Oscar de Oliveira and the Vincentians opened a dialogue. Dom Oscar first approved the suspension of classes and the Lazaristas' proposal. Sensationalistic press coverage of the crisis caused him to retreat, however.[254] Himself a former student of the Lazaristas, Dom Oscar staunchly defended the Tridentine regime. He concluded that his highly traditional archdiocese was not ready for change. The Vincentians' dispatch to Rome described him as an aloof man incapable of understanding the new generation. He evaluated the situation as a mere disciplinary matter. The failure to reach a compromise over modifications caused the Vincentians to leave and the seminary to close at the end of 1966. The incident sent shock waves through the institutional Church, because many clerics had looked to Mariana as "a guarantee of hope for priestly formation throughout our country."[255]

Sexuality pervaded the crisis in Mariana. In accordance with *aggiornamento,* in September 1966 the Lazaristas opened the seminary's Art Week to the Mariana community. Finally the seminarians could share their rich cultural background with the public. Seminarians performed plays, sang in a chorale, recited poetry, and exhibited paintings. The pretty teenaged girls of Mariana's all-female Catholic school and the coed public school, some dressed in miniskirts, were enchanted with the intelligent and handsome seminarians. Flirtation led to hand-holding, hugs, and kisses. The boys discussed their fantasies and erections in the confessional. (Such violations were mortal sins before Vatican II.) Not surprisingly, in the student survey most of the seminarians advocated optional celibacy.[256]

By the end of the 1960s the PBCM no longer trained diocesan priests. The Vincentians tumbled from their glorious position as founders of Brazil's Tridentine system. The crisis spread to the congregation's own ranks. In Petrópolis the seminarians vandalized the internal seminary. Moved to Belo Horizonte, it entered chaos. In 1968 and 1969 the entire student body dropped out. So deep and widespread was the crisis that in Holland, which had sent Vincentian missionaries to Brazil, the congregation ceased to exist. An era had ended for both the Church and Brazilian society.[257]

Conflict raged in seminaries across Brazil. In São Paulo, for example, the new Instituto de Filosofia e Teologia (IFT) clashed with Cardinal Rossi and the military authorities. Rossi became enraged at the participation of IFT students in anti-regime protests. He abruptly closed the institute in 1969 after its director, Friar José Freitas Neves, criticized Pope Paul VI and his encyclical *Humanae Vitae* (On the Regulation of Birth) on television.[258] Such turbulence weakened the seminarians' movement. As we will see in chapter 7, seminarians in Recife also protested against the regime.

The movement's challenge to both the bishops and the generals provided the Church with two powerful motives for its suppression. The core of the movement, Viamão and USMAS were especially targeted as a center of student agitation. Viamão seminarians hid university students sought by the police.[259] The priests simply looked the other way.[260] The students put graffiti on the walls denouncing the school's elite status.[261] They also continued to take part in JUC and UNE. In 1967 and 1968 the political police invaded Viamão several times to conduct searches for subversive literature and to interrogate students about political pamphlets and *Ponto Homem*. The interrogators also wanted to know which seminarians participated in the secular student movement. One student's correspondence was opened. The police showed published citations of Marx and the radical Medellín document to Dom Vicente, but the cardinal publicly criticized the incursions into his seminary. Along with other seminarians, Atanásio Orth, a *Ponto Homem* staff member, was jailed during the crackdown on the clandestine UNE congress in Ibiúna, São Paulo, in October of 1968. Orth later became the southern coordinator of VAR-Palmares, an important anti-regime guerrilla organization.[262] In 1968 the Military Tribunal in Porto Alegre called Father Sinésio Bohn, a Viamão student advisor, to testify about two jailed seminarians accused of distributing anti-regime leaflets. Bohn judiciously admitted the students' errors and obtained their release.[263] The Serviço Nacional de Informações, the regime's chief spy agency, also monitored the situation at Viamão.[264] In the hierarchy's eyes the famed seminary resembled a political organization more than a place for training priests.

The tense political climate and the hierarchy's fear of innovation caused the bishops to shut down USMAS. Some advertisers and subscribers had begun to question the content of *Ponto Homem,* and the seminarians had to scrape together funds to keep it going.[265] In early 1969 Dom Vicente Scherer, the papal nuncio, and other bishops decided to close the journal because of its increasingly revolutionary content.[266] Dom Vicente's action came as no surprise. In 1964 he had written a letter to *O Seminário* reaffirming the importance of obedience and rejecting the model of the seminarian as an "agitator of the naïve and ignorant masses."[267] Military censors probably played a role in the shutdown.[268] In the May–June issue the seminarians had reproduced a speech by Dom Antônio Fragoso, bishop of Crateús, Ceará, in which he criticized the regime and called for a popular front of workers and peasants to pressure the state. "It could be that armed struggle will be necessary," the bishop said. "When it is necessary, it can be evangelical." The struggle for justice was not subversion, Dom Fragoso concluded.[269] In the last issue of 1968 a series of articles addressed the controversy over Pope Paul VI's reaffirmation of traditional Church teachings against artificial birth control. "Instead of pills, we underdeveloped countries need revolutions," one author concluded.[270] Although Dom Vicente and the generals might agree with this opposition to the pill, they could not countenance violent struggle. The disappearance of *O Seminário/Ponto Homem* after forty-three years of existence spelled the death knell of the movement. The shutdown coincided with AI-5 and the intensification of torture, growing violence on the left and the right, and the rapid deterioration in Church-state relations. Some seminarians diminished their activities because they feared the same violent reprisal that the regime leveled against the secular student movement. The imprisonment of Cláudio Boeira Garcia, an ex-seminarian and the last president of USMAS, deeply disturbed the students at Viamão. Garcia was accused of links to anti-regime organizations. The departure of the original leaders, some of them to ordination, further weakened the movement. Ironically, the fulfillment of some demands—for example, the formation of small communities within Viamão—led to conflicts in the movement. Another accomplishment—the holding of classes at a new theological institute in 1969— further reduced the need for the movement.[271] His trip to view the innovative seminary in Olinda convinced Dom Ivo to introduce additional changes at Viamão and thus undercut the need for USMAS even more.[272] The creation of small communities terminated Viamão as a key cultural center.[273]

In the early 1970s relations between the hierarchy and the seminarians decayed further, and the police kept Viamão on its watch list. The students wanted the Church to take a tougher stand against the dictatorship. In 1970 seminarians surreptitiously placed political pamphlets in colleagues' and priests' rooms. The leaflets contained denunciations of military oppression and an alleged pact between Dom Vicente and the generals. Seminarians also painted pro-socialist slogans in Viamão's patios. In 1971 a former student was imprisoned and tortured. Another was expelled after the rector discovered a piece of paper pinned on the student's wall with the words: "Viamão 1970—Thirteenth Century. Solidarity with the oppressed and the search for new values."[274] In 1972 four ex-seminarians faced charges of subversion but were found innocent.[275]

Priests and the Hierarchy: Unfulfilled Expectations

The seminarians' movement was part of a "religious rebellion" by radical priests in Brazil and numerous other Latin American countries. Groups of clerics fought for the ouster of unpopular bishops and made other claims on the hierarchy.[276] In Brazil it was in the hierarchy's interest to consider constructive change. The CNBB and individual dioceses were in the midst of renovating the Church under a General Pastoral Plan, and the bishops had pledged at Vatican II to establish dialogue and co-responsibility with the clergy in the Church's mission. Yet the bishops, the Vatican, and the clergy tussled over the latter's demands for change. In the end, the hierarchy largely frustrated the clergy's campaign.

One must revisit the moment to understand how really difficult and bewildering the clerical identity crisis was. The post–Vatican II discourse over the priestly vocation was nebulous. Pope Paul VI seemed as confused as anybody. He emitted vague signals about how to overcome insecurity, appealing to the stark traditions of obedience, faith, and the sanctity of the priesthood. In his view the priesthood did not need redefinition.[277] His analysis typified the hierarchy's lack of bold initiative and imagination.

The priesthood came under intense scrutiny, with people at all levels of the Church producing a large flow of writings, pronouncements, and research projects. Struggling with personal battles of doubt and change, priests answered sociologists' surveys, bared their souls to psychoanalysts, and stripped away the mysterious aura that for centuries had enshrouded their vocation.[278]

Pedro Assis Ribeiro de Oliveira, a lay sociologist for CERIS, coordinated a vast study on priests and analyzed the Church's ambiguity. He observed that "the Church is at the same time 'renovative' and 'conservative': it launches a part of its clergy in new experiences and takes advantages of their positive results, and it protects the rest of the clergy with a conservative attitude in order not to be involved in eventual failures." The clergy, Oliveira concluded, was "an instrument of the Church in its search for malleability. But, providing this service for the Church, the clergy suffers." The lack of a clear missionary role left priests perplexed and insecure.[279]

The rapid transition from pre-Conciliar malaise to post-Conciliar confusion brought on the clerical identity crisis. Older priests could not understand the reforms, and younger ones were impatient.[280] The traditional image of the priesthood was disintegrating. The shifting political, social, and religious foundations of the 1960s made it difficult to reconstruct that image. Archconservatives clung to tradition, while ultra-progressives said the priesthood would wither away. No single, clear path led into the future.

Starting in 1967 Brazilian priests increased pressure for change. Although not as organized as the seminarians, their movement carried great weight. They were ordained ministers with an ongoing role in the life of the Church. Large groups of fathers issued public manifestos criticizing both the bishops and the military regime. They called for a radical reorganization of the Church, including redistribution of power to the clergy, local election of bishops (instead of appointment by the Vatican), local choice in the posting of priests, the right to form organizations of priests and nuns, and the end of obligatory celibacy.[281] The priests urged the politically cautious bishops to speak out against the political and economic atrocities of the government.[282] In one incident in 1969, twenty-seven priests abandoned the diocese of Botucatu after failing to stop the Vatican from installing a new archbishop of a conservative, discipline-oriented bent. Forty thousand people signed a petition supporting the clergymen, and military and civilian officials subscribed to a counter-petition. The press gave heavy coverage to the year-long controversy, which upset much of the Brazilian clergy. Similar confrontations took place in Bahia and elsewhere.[283] One group of 150 conservative priests from a movement called Faith and Discipline took a contrary tack by pledging their obedience to the hierarchy and professing traditional views of the Church and the priesthood.[284]

The progressive clergy's demands initially caused a positive reaction from the CNBB. The bishops organized a nationwide poll of the clergy on the state of the priesthood.[285] This strategy demonstrated the hierarchy's willingness to dialogue and gave it the power to define the crisis. Freelancing radicals thus entered the institutional process. As part of the polling the bishops distributed position papers to the priests. In early 1969 the CNBB sent Dom Valfredo Tepe, a psychologist and the head of the secretariat for the hierarchical ministry, and his assistant, Father José Marins, to meet with elected representatives of the priests throughout Brazil. The priests' conclusions were published as the *Documentos dos Presbíteros* (Documents of the Priests).[286] The *Documentos* said little new about the crisis and conspicuously omitted criticisms of the military and calls for social transformation. Nevertheless, they were significant for their vast canvassing of clerical opinion.[287] They served as a point of departure for the CNBB's historic tenth general assembly, which focused on the crisis of the priesthood, in 1969. Prompted by the priests, the prelates forwarded a copy to the Holy Father. This audacious action demonstrated a certain episcopal independence vis-à-vis the Vatican and undoubtedly inspired Rome's warnings against the campaign to abolish obligatory celibacy.[288]

The *Documentos* advocated ecclesiastical democracy by way of local, regional, and national priests councils that would have voting power in the dioceses and the CNBB.[289] In effect, the priests would have a union. The bishops acted quickly to protect their power. In a preemptive move the CNBB proposed a national, *nonvoting* council as a way to avert a competing "national conference" of priests. The bishops feared an eventual opening of the CNBB to all Catholics as an "Assembly of the People of God." At their 1969 meeting the bishops discussed the national priests' council and the *Documentos*. They were also to vote on the CNBB's crucial new statutes.[290] They postponed a decision on the statutes until 1971, however, because of the need to address AI-5 and the worsening repression. The bishops seesawed, demanding a return to democracy but affirming collaboration with the government. Hundreds of clergymen signed petitions protesting this stance.[291] Dom Marcos Noronha, the bishop of Itabira, and another cleric stopped angry priests from breaking into the assembly to stage a protest.[292] Similarly, the bishops vacillated on the priests' proposals. They approved a national priests' council with just a pro forma voice in the CNBB's assemblies. They overwhelmingly rejected a voting conference of priests and reserved the right to decide on all matters concerning the priesthood.[293]

The tenth general assembly nevertheless took a small step ahead for priests. Both sides compromised in producing the *Documentos,* and together they explored solutions to the clerical crisis. Showing a desire for dialogue, for the first time a CNBB meeting seriously weighed the clergy's opinions. The bishops approved motions to study the decentralization of the parish and create CEBs, two points considered necessary by the priests for ecclesial renovation. Change would occur at the grass roots, not in large structures.[294]

Rome, however, quashed even the modest changes. Quietly and methodi-
cally it prodded the CNBB to reduce the significance given to the new national
priests' council. In 1970 the Vatican's Congregation of the Bishops ordered the
removal of a draft provision in the CNBB's new statutes that raised the status of
priests' council members to *cooperadores* (effective participants in the CNBB).
Before the Vatican's final approval of the statutes, the Congregation forced the
CNBB to reduce the council to a mere "commission" (the Comissão Nacional
do Clero, CNC, or National Commission of the Clergy). The CNC was a con-
sultative agency that could attend CNBB assemblies only by invitation and, of
course, without voting rights.[295]

The reform of celibacy was another critical part of the priests and seminarians' drive to democratize the Church and control their own destinies. After
the announcement of Vatican II by Pope John XXIII in January 1959, speculation arose over the possibility of abolishing obligatory celibacy as a condition
for ordination.[296] For unhappy celibates and priests in clandestine relationships
Vatican II finally brought hope for change. In the late 1960s Brazil's bishops
considered ordaining married men.

But the Roman bureaucracy demonstrated great insensitivity about priests'
difficulties with celibacy. During the fourth and final session of the Council,
Dom Pedro Paulo Koop planned to propose liberalizing the celibacy rule. A
Dutch regular priest who had served for thirty years in Brazil, Dom Koop became bishop of Lins, São Paulo, in 1964. Painfully aware of the priest shortage,
he advocated allowing a subordinate, married clergy to work alongside celibate priests. This idea proved far too controversial for the Vatican and conservative prelates such as Cardinal Jaime Câmara of Rio de Janeiro. He and other
Latin American bishops convinced an assistant to Paul VI to block the question from the otherwise largely unrestricted forum.[297] The pope prohibited discussion of celibacy, restricting the bishops' opinions to written comments. To
quiet rumors that some Latin American bishops disagreed with the canon on
celibacy, Chilean Bishop Manuel Larraín, the head of CELAM, sent a message
of reassurance to Paul VI.[298] The text of Koop's speech was leaked to the press
the day after the pope's order.[299] When the issue came up for a vote, 2,243 bishops reapproved the celibacy law, with only eleven against. The pontiff dashed
any remaining hope of change with his 1967 encyclical *Sacerdotalis Coelibatus*.
But clerical agitation for reform continued at an unprecedented level, prompting cardinals in the Vatican to emit orders to silence the priests, including a
letter to the president of the CNBB in 1969.[300]

Preparing for the ninth assembly of the CNBB and the 1968 Medellín conference, Dom Koop reiterated his support for a married priesthood. He based his argument on the diversification of the ministry and pastoral reform, concepts advocated by the seminarians and trademarks of Vatican II and the Brazilian Church of the Poor. Diversification meant that the Church could supply each community with its own, specially suited minister. There would be workerpriests, rural priests, married and unmarried priests, and full- and part-time priests, Koop stated. Pastoral reform lent particular attention to CEBs and other grassroots communities.[301]

The debate intensified with the approach of the October 1971 synod of bishops on the future of the priesthood. This meeting would draw representatives from across the globe. Preliminary discussions reflected a growing polarization between reformers and conservatives, some of whom rejected Vatican II theology.[302] Pressure for change came from both First World bishops with a plentiful supply of priests and Third World prelates who struggled to staff their dioceses.[303]

Brazil was a leader for change. At the 1969 assembly on the priesthood a majority of the CNBB voted to study the ordination of married men.[304] The CNBB walked a dangerous tightrope between their local needs and obedience to the pope.[305] With widespread support, in August the CNBB's Representative Commission (a mini-assembly of top leaders) voted 26–8 to promote a married clergy at the synod.[306]

The vote drew vociferous reaction from a large number of traditionalist bishops led by Dom Cintra, the former Vatican inspector of the seminaries. He garnered the signatures of seventy-eight bishops—about one quarter of the episcopate—on a petition to the pope criticizing the Representative Commission's "mistake." He asserted that even if carefully regulated, the ordination of married men "will be the end of celibacy, the closing of the seminaries, and the moral decadence of the clergy."[307]

The synod threw sand on the flames of change. A significant minority of the two hundred representatives favored a married priesthood, but the Vatican again intervened to assure that diversification and a married clergy received only superficial attention. The CNBB's Representative Commission registered its disappointment as well as the lack of enthusiasm in Brazil for the synod's "distinctively traditional" conclusions. The synod ignored the "vision of the future" presented by the Brazilians. The Commission nevertheless supported continued debate in Brazil on celibacy, the role of women in the liturgy, and the economic and emotional security of priests.[308]

The CNBB's stance revealed the nationalistic underpinnings of the movement for a new priesthood. The struggle between reformers and traditionalists echoed the earlier confrontation between Father Feijó and the pro-Vatican
bishops. The Representative Commission wanted a Brazil-centered, at least partially noncelibate priesthood, whereas Dom Cintra's camp recalled the criticisms of clergymen who took concubines.

The Great Exodus

Rome's intransigence plunged the priesthood into an even deeper crisis. Priests
everywhere questioned their vocation and began to leave the ministry.[309] According to one study, celibacy was the most important reason for the departures. The unchanging hierarchical structure came in second.[310] In Brazil the
lack of a stronger episcopal stance against the military regime also caused
the exodus.[311] Priests became deeply disappointed when the great expectations
about Vatican II failed to materialize or did not go as far as the clergy had hoped.
As Brazilian Church sociologists put it, "the priest does not properly leave the
sacerdotal ministry but, so to speak, he does not find it."[312] The Brazilian Church
lost many of its best men.[313]

One of them was the brilliant Dom Marcos Noronha. The newly chosen
bishop of Itabira returned to Brazil from Vatican II in 1965 convinced that he
must abandon his Tridentine bookishness and lead the local laity in transforming society. In Itabira he confronted a conservative clergy and a Church
ensconced in the benefits received from the local government, the Companhia
do Vale do Rio Doce, which ran a large mining operation, and the steel company USIMINAS. He moved to reform the diocese by creating a network of
five hundred base communities and preaching a message of holistic salvation
that began in the here and now. In their enthusiasm some of his clerical followers even stopped wearing priestly vestments during the Mass. The traditional clergy and the local bourgeoisie bristled at these changes. Dom Marcos's creativity and progressive ideals cost him dearly. Eight of his priests faced
accusations of subversion and were cleared only after many months of investigation by the military regime. A woman tortured by the political police in
Belo Horizonte took refuge in Dom Marcos's residence. The conservative cardinal Dom Agnelo Rossi falsely denounced him to Rome for sleeping with nuns
in São Paulo. By December 1970 Dom Marcos felt morally and physically ex-

hausted. After Dom Agnelo blocked his transfer to another diocese, Dom Marcos resigned as bishop. That day Itabira's central church collapsed. Many of the faithful believed it was God's punishment against the Church for the departure of Dom Marcos. Six years later he married. Dom Caetano Antônio Lima dos Santos, a Capuchin friar, also quit at the age of fifty-three, after eleven years as bishop of Ilhéus, Bahia. He too married.[314]

In Catholic theology an ordained man remains a priest for eternity. Under canon law a priest can be laicized (reduced to the state of the laity) through the dispensation of one or more of his clerical responsibilities, usually the vow of celibacy. He loses the right to exercise the ministry but retains the sacrament of Holy Orders. Thus the common terms "ex-priests" and "former priests" are incorrect.[315] In Brazil these men are usually called *padres casados,* or married priests. Almost all men who asked for dispensation or who simply abandoned the ministry eventually married. "Laicized priests," "inactive priests," "married priests," and "resigned priests" are the most appropriate terms.

The exodus led to no single promised land. For many it was a figurative migration within the institution. Without resigning, they moved from traditional pastoral structures and activities to *inserção,* or insertion, among the laity and the poor. This group included those who practiced "selective abandonment," for example, leaving teaching or administrative duties to create new activities in the hopes of rebuilding the Church. For most, however, the exodus meant literal departure. This choice was the most difficult because of the need to request the pope's permission, to find employment, to learn to deal with sexuality and women—in short, to adapt to a world from which the men had been sheltered.

This exodus was not the first. After the French Revolution, for instance, numerous pastors left the Church.[316] In the decades before Vatican II, however, laicization was virtually prohibited. The priest who left without permission was subject to excommunication and usually ostracized socially and professionally. Norms issued during and after Vatican II permitted applications for dispensation. By 1971 some 20,000 men worldwide had quit the ministry. Another estimate states that 25,000 left between 1962 and 1970.[317] Table 5.1 shows the Vatican's statistics for the years 1964 to 1989 and laicizations in Brazil for the period 1957–1987. The Vatican's worldwide total comes to 51,451, but the real number is probably closer to 80,000, according to estimates of the laicized priests.[318] This figure equaled one-fifth of the approximately 400,000 priests in the world in the early 1990s. By the start of the new millennium more than 100,000 priests worldwide had resigned, and more than 300,000 nuns had quit.[319] According to Brazilian Church statistics, nearly 3,000 men left the Brazilian ministry between 1958 and 1987. The actual number may be has high as 3,500. The total number of priests in Brazil grew from 11,415 in 1962 to 13,537 in 1987. During this period Brazil's population nearly doubled, increasing the number of people per priest from 6,598 in 1962 to 10,449 in 1987. Without the laicizations, or with a change in canon law to allow formerly active ministers to return (as many desired), the proportion would be lower. The number of dispensations began to drop in the late 1970s. Under Pope John Paul II the Vatican hardened its laicization policy and perhaps contributed to the decline.[320]

Similarly, vocations in Brazil fell in the late 1960s and early 1970s, only to head upward starting in the mid-1970s. Table 5.2 presents these and other vocational trends. The decrease in the number of diocesan seminarians from 1960 to 1964 indicated that the crisis of priestly vocations began before Vatican II. The drop in minor seminarians was especially sharp. Another key trend was the reduction in the proportion of religious seminarians from double the number of diocesan students to parity.[321] From 1965 to 1975, the darkest years of the crisis, the number of seminarians of all categories fell while the population boomed. According to one source, more than one hundred seminaries were closed by the Church in the late 1960s and early 1970s.[322] With certain caveats, Table 5.2 demonstrates the number closed could have reached approximately two hundred. The closures resulted from both lack of students and the restructuring of the training system. Some institutions became dilapidated. The library at the Ipiranga seminary in São Paulo, for instance, was divided up, its card catalogues lost, and many of its collections thrown into a basement where rainwater, dust, and insects damaged the books.[323] The year 1974 marked the nadir of the vocational crisis. That year only 2,005 men were studying in Brazil's major seminaries, a drop of one-third from the 2,998 registered in 1960.

Thereafter the situation for major seminaries showed improvement. Interestingly, the recovery coincided with the slow and gradual political liberalization begun in 1974 by President Ernesto Geisel, the fourth of Brazil's five military dictators, although repression of the Church continued into the 1980s. There is no data to prove a link between liberalization and vocational renaissance.

As the number of departures grew, the resigned ministers began to meet informally for mutual support and to discuss proposals for collective action. In the early 1970s the Movimento dos Padres Casados (MPC, or Movement of Married Priests) organized in several cities.[324] The exodus and the genesis of the MPC led the bishops to put forth several proposals to ease the crisis and

TABLE 5.1

Laicizations among the Clergy, 1957–1989
(Official Statistics of the Vatican and Brazilian Church)

Year	Total Priests	Laicizations Worldwide	In Brazil	Brazil's Percentage
1957	–	–	1	–
1958	–	–	5	–
1959	–	–	4	–
1960	–	–	6	–
1961	–	–	13	–
1962	–	–	37	–
1963	–	–	24	–
1964	–	640	17	2.7
1965	–	1,128	24	2.1
1966	–	1,418	67	4.7
1967	–	1,759	98	5.6
1968	–	2,192	156	7.1
1969	441,199	3,205	167	5.2
1970	439,020	3,504	289	8.2
1971	436,887	3,659	194	5.3
1972	433,396	3,579	180	5.1
1973	429,558	3,690	226	6.1
1974	424,739	3,464	220	6.4
1975	419,410	3,001	240	8.0
1976	414,974	2,679	138	5.2
1977	416,823	2,506	129	5.2
1978	413,967	2,037	91	4.5
1979	416,336	1,576	49	3.1
1980	413,600	1,561	73	4.7
1981	411,074	1,260	81	6.4
1982	408,945	1,226	46	3.8
1983	406,376	1,258	75	6.0
1984	405,959	1,049	118	11.2
1985	403,480	1,002	95	9.5
1986	402,886	1,057	66	6.2
1987	402,243	986	81	8.2
1988	401,930	1,027	–	–
1989	401,479	988	–	–
TOTALS	–	51,451	3010	5.85

Sources: *Annuarium Statisticum Ecclesiae*; "Elementos para reflexão diante dos que abandonaram o ministério" 1974; CERIS, Department of Statistics.

TABLE 5.2
Number of Brazilian Seminaries and Students, 1960–1987

Year	No. of Schools[a]	Diocesan Major	Diocesan Minor	Religious Major	Religious Minor	Total Major Seminarians
1960	605	1,066	–	1,932	–	2,998
1964	–	885	5,020	1,951	10,910	2,836
1965	–	642	4,361	1,923	11,421	2,565
1966	–	898	5,100	1,964	11,539	2,862
1967	–	932	5,548	1,700	11,149	2,632
1968	–	870	4,576	1,665	10,077	2,535
1969	–	936	3,913	1,525	9,220	2,461
1970	393	757	3,424	1,444	7,937	2,201
1971	385	820	2,239	1,292	6,970	2,112
1972	396	801	2,552	1,303	6,117	2,104
1973	387	740	2,121	1,304	5,958	2,044
1974	439	757	3,453	1,248	6,190	2,005
1975	477	1,000	3,259	1,525	6,560	2,525
1976	502	1,083	3,290	1,523	6,375	2,606
1977	508	1,156	3,290	1,577	6,470	2,733
1978	533	1,239	3,280	1,555	6,359	2,794
1979	609	1,466	3,459	1,701	6,536	3,167
1980	648	1,692	3,637	1,847	6,712	3,539
1981	681	2,142	3,877	2,113	6,182	4,255
1982[b]	736	2,381	3,764	2,094	5,606	4,475
1983	806	2,588	3,340	3,048	5,048	5,636
1984	849	2,680	3,252	2,547	5,663	5,227
1985	896	3,067	3,359	2,734	4,212	5,801
1986	905	3,110	3,396	3,296	5,101	6,406
1987	899	3,216	3,149	3,640	4,510	6,856

Sources: On the number of seminaries, *Annuarium Statisticum Ecclesiae,* except for 1960, for which the source is Pérez, Gregory, and Lepargneur 1964:53. See also CERIS, Department of Statistics.
[a] The Vatican's *Annuarium Statisticum* counts the following houses of formation for both diocesan and religious candidates to the priesthood: 1) the minor seminaries; 2) minor seminary residences; 3) philosophical and theological seminaries; 4) and philosophical and theological residences. Because it was taken from a different source, the figure for 1960 may be larger than if it had been counted by Vatican methodology. Thus, the drop between 1960 and 1970 may be less dramatic.
[b] Antoniazzi estimated 2,566 major diocesan seminarians and 2,564 major religious seminarians; see Antoniazzi 1984a:36.

the difficulties of those who left. At the CNBB's 1969 assembly the prelates approved motions allowing married priests to work in certain pastoral activities, although not in their former positions. They suggested to the Vatican that laicization be handled at the national and regional levels.[325] As the crisis lingered, the attention to the married priests grew. At the Fifteenth Assembly of the CNBB in 1974 Dom Koop once again voiced support for married men in the ministry, including "the celebration of the Mass." The bishops learned that some of the faithful had requested married priests as pastors.[326] With the backing of the CNC, the bishops renewed the right of laicized priests to engage in certain activities. An amendment permitted married priests to say Mass in dioceses where the shortage of clergy was especially severe.[327] But only Rome could approve such a radical measure. In the end, only a small minority of married priests actually came to participate in even the nonsacerdotal functions of Church life.[328] Much of the hierarchy ostracized them.

The MPC gained strength in the late 1970s and 1980s. It published a semi-annual bulletin, held national meetings almost yearly, and produced two catalogs listing data on its members. MPC representatives took part in international encounters of former ministers as the movement organized throughout the Catholic world. The wives participated too. High CNBB officials met with the married priests, thus lending the movement further legitimacy. Going against canon law and the wishes of Rome, some Brazilian bishops even allowed the married priests to say Mass.[329]

Conclusion

The seminaries were the fulcrum on which the problems of an outmoded clericalism turned. The seminarians' movement's protest against the Tridentine system revealed the tensions and desires of clerics and students as they sought a footing in the modern world. They transformed the notion of Catholic discipline for the Church and Brazilian society. The movement highlighted the complex interplay of faith, society, politics, profession, Church, and self in the renovation of Brazilian Catholicism.

Military repression and the hierarchy's fear of change halted the seminarians and priests from establishing unions. Seminarians could participate in the Church locally, but the bishops jealously retained power at the national level. For the Church modernization meant only a very timid democratization. The rise of the individual did not mean total freedom of action. Trent did not disappear. For those who found this intolerable, exit from the ministry became a popular option.

Nevertheless, many ideas from the seminarians' movement inspired changes in clerical training in the 1970s and beyond, as the next two chapters demonstrate. The seminarians redefined the Brazilian apostolate. This was an immense achievement.

This generation of seminarians were idealists. They perhaps naively hoped to revolutionize all facets of the priesthood in the flicker of a moment. In the heady 1960s they shared the aspirations of radical youths everywhere who combined modernity and romantic social justice in the attempt to transform society. In Brazil that vision emphasized the search for authentic national identity among the lower classes. In line with previous movements in the Church's history, the seminarians dipped into the past for inspiration. Their ecclesial utopia relied on biblical traditions such as community, the blessedness of the poor, and liberation from oppression. The seminarians' movement produced a healthy discussion about the Tridentine regime and the Church's weakening relationship with the people.[330]

The seminarians wanted to become "modern" and "social" saints. As they embraced scientific rationality and reached out to the people, professionalization and veneration of the poor both seemed possible. But here was a paradox. While the adoption of modernity ostensibly facilitated proximity to an emerging economic elite, the emphasis on the social did not. At a time when secularization and modernization were seen as affecting all of society equally, this contradiction went unnoticed. One of the best examples of this paradox's practical consequences appeared in some progressive priests' rejection of popular religion. Within a few years, however, progressives rescued popular religion because they recognized the potency of traditional religious belief, whose roots reached back to Brazil's colonial experience. The popular and the traditional became characteristics of the option for the poor. This option—and not modernity—gained far greater appeal among progressives because the new clergy ultimately failed to establish an understanding with the modernizing technocratic-military elite, which now considered priests to be irrelevant in the project of national development. Even the presence of Roberto Campos, a prominent former seminarian, at the head of the technocracy did not avoid Church-state misunderstanding.[331]

The seminarians' movement incarnated another set of paradoxical tendencies involving modernity and social sainthood. The students drove to organize *nationally* into a *larger body* in order to fulfill a desire to subdivide their schools into yet *smaller communities* of distinct individuals. Like the Church of the Poor, the seminarians believed that organization would bring the power to re-shape the institution. The seminarians departed from tradition in opposite directions: *inwardly* in the exploration of the professional, the existential, the affective, the psychological, the individual; and *outwardly* in the venture to know Brazilian society, its problems, and its position in the world scheme. The next two chapters explore these paths.

chapter six

"A Special Grace from God"

Experiments in Psychoanalysis and

Liberation Psychology

In the early months of 1967, as seminarians and priests tried to navigate the turbulent post–Vatican II waters of doubt, conflict, and experimentation, Father Géza Kövecses, an authority on clerical training who had helped inspire the seminarians' movement, feverishly composed his memoirs in a race against the cancer destroying his body. The Hungarian Jesuit, who had become a psychotherapist in order to deepen his understanding of the religious vocation, filled pages with spiritual meditations and psychoanalytic ruminations about his life. Géza wrote that one night around the time that he learned of his terminal illness in December 1966, he lay sweating in his bed at the Jesuits' seminary in Rio Grande do Sul and pondering the meaning of two nightmares that seemed to foretell his death. In one a voice called out to him, "Be careful! This is the beginning of the end!" In the second dream, on Christmas Eve, a mysterious hand injected poison from a syringe into his veins.

Géza first judged these dreams to be the "existential reflections" of the "knowledge of the unconscious." But during one of many nights of pain and

FIGURE 8. Father Géza
Kövecses. Courtesy Província
do Brasil Meridional da
Companhia de Jesus.

sleeplessness the devout priest reconsidered his interpretation. After all, he believed that guardian angels had miraculously snatched him away from the gripping perils of Allied bombs and Soviet executioners. Adding the supernatural dimension to the psychoanalytical, Géza concluded that his unconscious was not toiling alone. "I saw clearly that the message was not coming from the 'unconscious' world as such!" Géza wrote. The unconscious could not "consciously" know something, he affirmed. "It became evident to me that the message had arisen from the unfathomable center of my person, from God himself, who lives in the depth of my existence." Géza believed that this kind of experience was universal. Did the Old Testament not present examples of existential dreams? he asked. And in the New Testament did a dream not rouse Joseph out of his sleep to save the Holy Family? God "communicates with each one of us incessantly and sends messages by way of dreams," Géza wrote.[1]

As Géza lay dying, a rebellious young Lazarista took regularly to a psychoanalyst's couch in Rio de Janeiro. Soon he would rise before a crowd of 100,000 people in downtown Rio to declare that the Church was now the people and should side with the student movement in opposing the military regime. Father João Batista Ferreira's striking political and personal odyssey had begun after cracks appeared in his ironclad faith. Father João came from a humble background in Minas Gerais. When he was ten, the Lazaristas requested that he become a live-in sacristan at the Calafate parish in Belo Horizonte. He rang the church bells at five every morning. The following year he enrolled at the venerable Caraça, the first step toward the Vincentian priesthood. As he grew, his faith remained fervent and childlike in its unquestioning acceptance of Catholic teachings. Holding the Eucharist was a magical moment for the young priest, part of a heroic quest to save souls. To him the Church was a perfect institution in which the bishops could do no wrong. But, ordained in late 1963, he had acquired the enthusiasm of the Vatican II era. Presenting Christ in a more clearly human dimension, new theological teachings raised many doubts. Aspects of the treasured seminary began to appear anachronistic. As a teacher at Mariana, Father João brusquely did away with censorship of students' letters. The bishops' conciliar maneuverings and their desire to preserve the Vatican's temporal power especially caused profound disillusionment within Father João. For three nights he could not sleep. He now knew that politics—not the Holy Spirit—guided the Church. His faith in the institution was shaken. Then came the difficult, sexually charged crisis at Mariana that ended in that seminary's abrupt closure (see chapter 5). Father João left Mariana for Rio, where he assumed a position at the Colégio São Vicente, one of the country's most important private Catholic schools and a growing hotbed of opposition to the military government. In Rio the visiting Cardinal Gabriel-Marie Garrone, the prefect of the Vatican's Congregation for Seminary Education, called in Father João and former Mariana rector Father José Pires de Almeida for a tongue-lashing about their liberal attitudes. Surveys about celibacy such as the one at Mariana were unwelcome, the cardinal warned, because they would only encourage more priests to quit. Coupled with the political situation, Father João's crisis of faith left him deeply perturbed. He sought permission to undergo psychoanalysis. The Vincentian superiors assented but required that he keep it a secret. Father João also enrolled in the psychology program at the Federal University of Rio de Janeiro, where he joined the increasingly radical student movement. After speaking as the clergy's representative at the Passeata dos Cem Mil (the March of the 100,000), the largest demonstration against the military to date, he was elected to the ill-fated commission sent to negotiate with President Costa e Silva for the release of political prisoners and the relaxation of the repression. Angry at the students' haughty attitude, one of Costa e Silva's military assistants warned them against "cutucando a onça com vara curta" (poking a cougar with a short stick).[2]

Father João's relations with the official Church deteriorated. His outspokenness led the archdiocese of Rio de Janeiro to prohibit him from saying a Sunday noon Mass that had become a symbol of student resistance. He moved the

FIGURE 9. Flanked by student leaders, Father João Batista Ferreira speaks to the crowd of protesters during the famous March of the 100,000, Cinelândia, Rio de Janeiro, June 26, 1968. Courtesy João Batista Ferreira.

Mass to the basement of the Colégio São Vicente. Father João hid university students sought by the police. In the early morning hours he and other priests ran off student pamphlets on two electric Gestetner machines—ultra-high technology for the time. At night the fathers allowed students to go to the roof of the school in order to capture the signal of Radio Cuba. Some parents complained about Father João's frank conversations with students in civics classes. At the Universidade Santa Úrsula he transformed the usually hated religion class into a forum on modern sexuality. The young women and men asked questions about birth control, masturbation, and premarital sex—all prohibited by Catholic teachings. The only sin, Father João affirmed, was to act without love. The mother superior presented him with an ultimatum: adhere to official doctrine or leave. He left.

Near the end of 1972 Father João had a life-changing dream that he related to his analyst, the renowned Kattrin Kemper. (Kattrin and her analyst husband, Werner, had stayed on in Germany during World War II while he attempted to save psychoanalysis from Nazi prohibitions.) In Father João's dream Kattrin offers him a cup of tea during a session of group analysis. A wasp bites the priest's finger. Kattrin carries him in her arms to her bed in order to care for the finger. Father João witnesses a nocturnal candlelight procession pass by in an adjacent room. This dream, Kattrin explained, symbolized the wounding and imprisonment of Father João's penis. She, the analyst, cured him of this repression as he watched the Church continue its traditional path. He was now free of the Church and his religious vocation. The psychological impact of this interpretation caused Father João's body to break out in blisters. "I was able to understand that I was out of the Church, and it was out of me," Father João later recalled. Not long after the dream he left the Vincentian order and the priesthood. The following year he married a psychologist who had once hidden a political refugee in her parents' home. João too embarked on a career as a psychoanalyst.

The couch and the soapbox largely defined the Brazilian Church of the late 1960s. The experiences of Father Géza and Father João demonstrate how the political, personal, and spiritual crises of the clergy changed the Church. As João later recalled, the search for a new theology and an authentic pastoral experience melded with sexuality. Sexuality gained new importance in the 1960s because of the birth control pill, the sexual revolution, and its rediscovery by the social sciences, psychiatry, and psychoanalysis.[3]

These years gave birth to liberation theology, but also to liberation psychology, whose implications for the Church were even more revolutionary than the new theology. Liberation psychology had a dual significance: it could free people not only from poverty of spirit and mind but also from the repressive structures of Catholicism. Liberation psychology did not gain the fame of its counterpart in theology, but it bore witness to the key role of the psychological in the transformation of the Brazilian priesthood and notions of Catholicity. The adoption of psychology illustrated the complex and lively interplay between Church and society and the way in which the crises of the priesthood helped force the institution to acknowledge the importance of subjectivity in modern life.

This chapter discusses the attempt of the Brazilian clergy to resolve their profound crises through the use of psychotherapy and psychological theory. The clergy hoped that these new tools could improve the recruitment, education, social life, and spirituality of seminarians. Psychological theory and therapy could especially assist with the dire need to reduce the high expenditures of psychic energy caused by the disciplinary overload and social conflicts of the Tridentine seminary. Students and priests repudiated the assembly line–like nature of the seminaries and demanded a focus on the subjective aspects of sacerdotal training: personality development, human relationships, and sexuality. Psychotherapy offered ways of building healthy, well-rounded individuals free of the personal and institutional repression of Catholicism and able to adapt to a rapidly changing world. This fresh perspective made the advent of a new priesthood seem imminent. Many in the Church seized on psychoanalysis as a panacea, and psychobabble rapidly replaced sin in the discourse on ecclesiastical training and pervaded the debate on the crisis of the priesthood. One opponent of obligatory celibacy, for example, referred to it as a "psychic castration." "The clergy suffers from a serious crisis of neurosis," stated another priest.[4] The highest levels of the Brazilian Church at first gave the experiment in psychology their full blessing. Other initiatives expanded the scope of psychotherapy to include social activism among the poor.

The most striking example of psychoanalysis emerged in Christus Sacerdos, a special program for seminary teachers run by Father Géza and a team of psychoanalysts. The dreaming Géza's deathbed search for the link among the unconscious, the spiritual, and the existential exemplified how especially imaginative pioneers dramatically influenced the new model of the priest. Christus Sacerdos was unique in the Catholic Church. One of only two psychology courses in the Catholic world designed specifically for seminary professors, it had the full and official backing of the bishops. Unlike most other initiatives, it went beyond the evaluation of familiar psychological problems to seek the improvement of seminary training. Christus Sacerdos and other experiences in Brazil demonstrated how innovators could experiment freely because of their distance from the center of power at the Vatican. Brazilian adaptability facilitated the creativity of these pioneers. Psychoanalysis served an institutional and social purpose and not merely individual ones. This aspect proved to be its greatest strength—and weakness.

As the liberating power of psychoanalysis became apparent, a fearful hierarchy believed it would subvert discipline and obedience, cornerstones of the Church's institutional strength. Their fears were only magnified by the pall of military repression. Psychoanalysis would meet a tragic end in the Brazilian Church.

Nevertheless, other psychological theories and therapies gained legitimacy in the training of priests. The Church was an important agent in the diffusion of psychology, providing a fascinating case study of how psychoanalysis influenced Brazilian culture.[5]

Historical and Social Context

Psychoanalysis is a product of the modern world. "Simultaneously a theory and a therapy, psychoanalysis shares a boundary with literature, a boundary with psychiatry and medicine and a third boundary with academic psychology," writes Joseph Schwartz. "Psychoanalysis is a science in the sense that it is an attempt to understand human subjectivity in material terms—it locates its understanding of human subjectivity in the world of lived experience rather than in the spirit world of Western religious traditions." Its major themes are the unconscious, repression, childhood sexuality, the interpretation of dreams, and the "resolution of Oedipal tensions as the central feature of human psychological development."[6] Psychoanalysis came onto the stage of history as modernity and the West consolidated their ideological hegemony through urbanization, technological innovation, and imperialism. Modernity heightened the need for introspection. As historian Peter Gay has observed, "The nineteenth century was intensely preoccupied with the self, to the point of neurosis. . . . There were swarms of bourgeois . . . who shared their naked heart with their contemporaries. As was to be expected, specialists in human nature supplied invaluable clues to the search for the self."[7] Modernity accentuated a concept of subjectivity in which public and private identities became split. Psychoanalysis helped to alleviate this gap and to make up for the loss of traditional community feeling and morality.[8] The history of psychoanalysis is also intertwined with the attempt to salvage people's psyches from the ravages of total war, genocide, and torture.

As life became more complex and as people turned from tradition to individualism, they sought professional therapeutic assistance in order to understand their neuroses and inner conflicts and to adjust to the greater psychic demands and variegated stimuli of the modern world. Modernity required a modern mind, one that could function with efficiency and flexibility and independently of traditional notions of faith. Therapy triumphed as the solution, with "psychologizers" replacing "spiritualizers" as the main interpreters of cultural life and the individual's sense of well-being taking priority over corporate interests.[9] Explains Schwartz: "With real markets existing for rapid communications that could reward innovation, the translation of voice signals into electric currents could replace the Morse code. Similarly in psychoanalysis, a new form of human communication grew out of the need for an innovation that could translate previously incomprehensible messages from the human inner world." At the same time, however, psychoanalysis challenges one of the great myths of Western society, "the myth of the Man Alone." Psychoanalysis demonstrates the profound need for human relationships.[10] In addition, the medicalization of the mind meant that diagnosable causes, and not personal failure, stood behind mental illness and many of life's difficulties. Thus the definition of clinical conditions broadened to include many more people. Unlike Catholicism, psychoanalysis did not seek to dictate rules for behavior and desire. It helped the individual to make his or her own choices. Psychoanalysis, however, was not medicine. Based on the understanding of individual desire through the debunking of illusions, it constituted an ethical framework unique in the modern world.[11] It did not concern itself with the question of God but instead with people's perceptions of the divine, seeking to eliminate from religious discourse taboo, fear, guilt, and ignorance.[12]

Historically the care of the mentally ill in Brazil was precarious. Before the mid-nineteenth century they wandered the streets or landed in prisons or hospital wards without any specialized attention. Brazil's first mental hospital, the Hospício Pedro II, was inaugurated in 1852. For nearly four decades the overcrowded facility was staffed by poorly trained nurses and the Daughters of Charity, the Lazaristas' allies in Romanization. In 1890 a reform ended Church control of the Hospício, changed its name, and replaced the Daughters with professional nurses. Around the turn of the century physicians and psychiatrists became increasingly involved in the mental health field. They were the first Brazilians attracted to psychoanalysis. Brazil's first classical analyst was Adelheid Koch, a Jewish physician who had studied at the Berlin Institute for Psychoanalysis before its Aryanization by the Nazis. She arrived in São Paulo in 1936 and began a study group that in 1951 became the Sociedade Brasileira de Psicanálise de São Paulo.[13] Many of Brazil's early analysts had received training in Argentina, one of the world's most psychoanalytically oriented societies, where even the staunchly conservative Church came to accept Freudian ideas.[14]

Psychoanalysis quickly penetrated both the intellectual elite and popular culture. The *modernista* authors of the 1920s assimilated Freudian ideas, and in the 1930s books, radio programs, public education campaigns, and special events introduced Brazilians to the scientific discussion of sex and Freudian concepts. A trend toward self-help coping mechanisms was underway.[15] Brazilians, in fact, showed greater interest in psychoanalysis in the 1910s and 1920s than did Argentines.[16]

The Catholic ministry and classic Freudian psychoanalysis had ample affinity. Sigmund Freud himself, it should be remembered, was a cultural Jew without religious indoctrination. His Catholic nanny took him to Mass, a rite that left an impression on him.[17] Freud frequently used religious history to develop his ideas about the human psyche, and he maintained an important correspondence with the Protestant pastor Oscar Pfister, in which he recognized the importance and beauty of religion.[18] Freud's disciple, Carl Jung, a Swiss Protestant, described religion as an expression of "the deep instincts of race," part of the collective unconscious. Psychoanalysis, Jung believed, could lead Christianity back to its roots in "ecstatic instinctual forces" and away from the "Misery Institute" that classical religions had become.[19] As Erich Fromm noted in 1950, psychoanalysis and religion stood on common ground. Both were concerned with love, reason, and the cure of the soul. Like the priest, he stated, the psychoanalyst was a "physician of the soul."[20]

Father Géza went a step further, blending the two vocations into one. Psychoanalysis served as both a pastoral tool and a way for the priest to improve his own soul-searching. Pierre Sanchis boldly affirms that the Jesuits and psychoanalysis came to have a "privileged relationship" flowing from St. Ignatius's emphasis on individual choice in salvation in his book *The Spiritual Exercises*—albeit always within the traditional hierarchy of the Church.[21] Jesuit Father Eugen Drewermann transformed Jesus into a psychotherapist.[22]

Nevertheless, the psychoanalytic profession and Catholicism lived in constant tension before and even after the Second Vatican Council. Practical political questions played a role. Like other Jews, Freud bore the brunt of Catholic anti-Semitism and witnessed the Church's dubious relationships with fascist governments. He saw the Church as an archenemy of psychoanalysis. Rome did not officially condemn psychoanalysis or Freud's ideas, but the Church opposed them because of profound philosophical differences with neo-Freudian thinkers on questions of religion, the existence of the soul, the nature of humankind, and sexuality.[23] Perhaps the male-dominated Church also had difficulty in accepting psychoanalysis because it represented the formalization of women's roles as builders of human relationships.[24] Whatever the reasons, the Church viewed psychoanalysis as a threat to traditional authority. Modernity increasingly emphasized individual autonomy, which the study of the psyche nurtured, leading the papacy to cast its veto against psychology.[25] Psychoanalysis was also seen as a threat to the family. In Brazil Alceu Amoroso Lima attacked psychoanalysis in the 1920s,[26] while Jesuit Father Leonel Franca attempted to use a Catholic brand of psychology to evangelize the elite during the Church's resurgence in the 1930s.[27] The Brazilian Church reaffirmed the superiority of the moral conscience over instinct. Priests were to be stoics who could completely control their emotions by rational action. Catholic psychologists were primarily amateurs heavily influenced by theology.[28] In the 1930s, after converting to Catholicism, the French analyst Maryse Choisy embarked on a campaign to convince the pope of the benefits of Freudian thought and obtain a Christian status for psychoanalysis. She failed, but pressure from her and other Catholics forced an unofficial dialogue on psychoanalysis to begin within the Church. Meanwhile, priests such as Father Agnostino Gemelli, the founder of the School of Experimental Psychology at the Catholic University of the Sacred Heart of Milan, fought against the acceptance of psychoanalysis. In postwar France psychoanalysis received a greater reception as priests such as the Jesuit Father Louis Beirnaert began to study Freudian ideas, undergo therapy, and practice as analysts. The papacy feared psychoanalysis as much as it did the worker-priests and Marxism. Yet with the anti-Communist struggle taking priority, the hierarchy tolerated experiments with psychoanalysis as long as they did not undermine vocations or faith.[29]

In the interests of modernizing the Church, Popes Pius XII and Paul VI actually encouraged psychological research,[30] opening the door for some to peek into a new world. But Rome frequently shut the door. For example, in the 1950s the Vatican prohibited the French cleric and psychoanalyst Marc Oraison from teaching in seminaries or publishing his writings.[31] Oraison's ideas were potentially explosive: he wanted the Church to arrange for the treatment of seminarians who were psychotics, perverts, "sexually sick," or dangerous to themselves and the institution in some other way. Without acknowledging Oraison's contribution, the Church responded to the need for better evaluation of religious seminarians by requiring psychiatric examinations.[32] As clerical interest in psychoanalysis grew in the late 1950s and early 1960s, Rome reacted strongly. In 1961, after Benedictine monks in Cuernavaca, Mexico entered analysis, the Holy See prohibited priests and nuns from consulting psychoanalysts without their superiors' permission. The edict banned clerics from working as analysts and rejected the opinion of some clergy that psychoanalysis should precede ordination or admission to the seminary.[33]

An ambiguous and uneasy relationship persisted between the Church and Catholic advocates of psychoanalysis. According to historian Elisabeth Roudinesco, the advocates actually succeeded "in having Freudianism penetrate to the heart of the Church while avoiding the wrath of the Holy Office and obtaining from the Pope his 'benevolent neutrality.' Should tempests or experiments deemed provocative occur, the Vatican was free to denounce them." The Church sought to

> assign a status to psychotherapy in which Freudians would have their place on the condition they respect the rules of Christian morality. It mattered little that those rules contradicted the essence of a discovery and a practice; it would suffice, in the worst cases, to maintain appearances, and in the best, to feign belief in a possible compatibility between a discourse and its opposite. . . . Concerned lest it condemn the works of a universally recognized thinker, who was Jewish to boot, the Roman Catholic Church opted to turn against its own

when difficulties with psychoanalysis arose.[34] This was ecclesiastical politics at its best.

Vatican II permitted the use of psychology in the training of priests. But the council included little debate on psychoanalysis. Making no reference to the subject, its final documents demonstrated the Church's fear. During the council the bishop of Cuernavaca, Sérgio Méndez Arceo, defended the "psychoanalytic revolution." He supported the Benedictine experiment, led by Gregoire Lemercier, a Belgian father who had founded the Cuernavaca monastery in 1950 and helped make it the principal center of the Liturgical Movement in Mexico. In 1962, a year after beginning therapy with a non-Catholic analyst, the Mexican Gustavo Quevedo, Lemercier attended the first session of Vatican II as Dom Méndez Arceo's advisor.[35]

As we will see, in Géza's interpretation the lack of non-Catholic analysts was a cause of the Cuernavaca experiment's eventual downfall. Interestingly, while Géza practiced as an analyst in Brazil, Lemercier concluded from the Cuernavaca experience that "it was a contradiction in terms" for a cleric to take the role of therapist because "the functions of the priest and the analyst are totally different." Such a situation "put the patient before a two-headed monster." However, Lemercier and Géza agreed on other points, such as the power of psychoanalysis in spiritual purification.[36] Lemercier probably authored an anonymous, informal document stressing the need of priests to undergo analysis and proposing a dialogue with the international analytic community.[37]

In Vatican II's final session in 1965 Dom Méndez Arceo criticized the antagonism toward psychoanalysis: "The Church, because of the anti-Christian dogmatism of certain analysts, took a position that recalls the case of Galileo; but there is not one field of pastoral work in which psychoanalysis should not be taken into account. Impregnated with excessive mistrust, to this day the interventions of the Church have not exercised any influence over those who devote themselves to this science." Likewise, Dom Méndez Arceo's words had little effect on his fellow bishops.[38]

Psychoanalysis had become a regular part of the Benedictines' community life. From 1961 to 1965 some sixty seminarians and monks entered therapy in Cuernavaca with Quevedo and another non-Catholic, the Argentine Frida Zmund. By 1965 spending on psychoanalysis took up more than half the cloister's budget. The monks worked to help defray the cost. A majority of the men, many of them unordained, left the monastery. Apprehensive about the dropouts and unfavorable publicity, the Vatican opened an investigation, restated its prohibition on analysis, and in 1967 shut down the experiment. Yet psychoanalysis did not cause the departures; the dropout rate was within the norm for seminaries at the time. In fact, the cancellation of the experiment seemed to have the biggest impact: forty of the forty-three remaining monks left the ministry in order to continue in analysis.[39] Lemercier too quit the ministry and married.

Press coverage increased the danger of Cuernavaca becoming an example for other monasteries, convents, and seminaries. While Dom Méndez Arceo supported the experiment, perhaps other Mexican bishops, many of them presiding over psychologically repressed and conservative laities, sent negative signals to the Vatican about psychoanalysis. It did not help matters that Dom Méndez Arceo was frequently attacked by conservatives for the innovations he fostered at Cuernavaca. He removed traditional ornaments from the cathedral, introduced live mariachi music into the Mass, and allowed the controversial Father Ivan Illich to work in his diocese. Illich believed the clergy would disappear. After the Benedictine episode Dom Méndez Arceo became more circumspect about psychoanalysis. He was "worried" about the "danger" that it was a "new panacea, a substitute for religion," a situation that could harm the legitimate use of psychoanalysis in religion.[40]

In Brazil the use of psychoanalysis in ecclesiastical training also ran into doctrinal roadblocks, but it occurred in the peculiarly receptive environment of what Sérvulo Figueira calls Brazil's "psychoanalytic culture." Brazil's first academic psychology program started at the Pontifical Catholic University of Rio de Janeiro in 1953. In 1962 the profession of psychology gained official recognition from the Ministry of Education and Culture. In the late 1960s demand for psychoanalysis boomed, and by the 1980s recourse to psychoanalytic services had grown to levels comparable to those in the United States and France. Ironically, in countries such as England, which has leading theorists and strong institutional support for psychoanalysis, fears still exist with regard to therapy, whereas in Brazil, which has weak institutions and relatively little indigenous theoretical innovation, to undergo analysis became fashionable. In Brazil people openly discussed their therapy and therapists the way they might chat about musical entertainers or soccer players. The demand for psychoanalysis emerged from the tensions and contradictions of rapid modernization in the post–World War II era. While models of the family and gender metamorphosed, traditional attitudes remained strong. Youths faced an increasingly difficult psychological and social transition to adulthood. Psychological strain augmented with the unpredictability of social and economic life, resulting, for instance, from recurrent hyperinflation. While the top economic strata had the easiest access to therapy, even lower social groups became exposed to the psychoanalytic culture, mainly through the mass media.[41]

The politicized counterculture of 1960s Brazil evolved into an emphasis on individual self-knowledge. This trend contributed to the demand for psychoanalysis. The counterculture blossomed into "alternative culture" in which middle-class Brazilians experimented with numerous kinds of psychotherapy inspired in part by Jacques Lacan and Wilhelm Reich, alternative medicine, Oriental medicine, massage, methods of bodily expression, and esoteric or mystical practices such as the ingestion of a hallucinogenic substance extracted from the sacred huayasca, the basis of the religion known as Santo Daime. On the supply side a large number of Argentine psychologists and psychoanalysts entered Brazil upon fleeing their country's military dictatorship.[42] The eclectic nature of Brazilian alternative culture mirrored the great diversity of popular practices within both Catholicism and the growing segment of Protestant Pentecostal religions. Many Brazilian psychoanalysts employ cultural studies in their work and even sometimes encourage patients to try alternative religious treatments such as spiritual cure in Umbanda or Candomblé. Similarly, psychoanalysis has entered the discourse and practices of some popular healers.[43]

In the 1970s the mainstream of Brazilian psychoanalysts supported the Brazilian regime and avoided issues that might offend it. In 1970, for example, the Eighth Latin American Psychoanalytic Congress, held in Porto Alegre, changed its theme from the highly relevant "Violence and Aggression" to the bland "Current Trends in Psychoanalytic Thought." The military, in fact, used psychological tests on political prisoners, and one pro-regime congressman recommended psychotherapy for middle-class youths, whom he deemed susceptible to subversion. In 1980 the Sociedade Psicanalítica do Rio de Janeiro expelled two of its most prominent members, Helio Pellegrino and Eduardo Mascarenhas, for denouncing the collaboration of Army doctor Amilcar Lobo, a psychoanalytic trainee, with the security forces.[44]

The use of psychological theory and therapies in the training of priests meshed with the new psychoanalytic culture. On one level, psychology became an instrument of organizational modernization as it did for corporations, schools, and other establishments.[45] But the singular character of the seminaries also produced an especially urgent demand for psychotherapy. In the eyes of priests and the seminarians' movement, isolation, obligatory celibacy, discipline, and unquestioning obedience engendered psychic crises. In short, the seminaries deformed personality. Psychology appeared as a logical solution for reforming pedagogy and aiding the afflicted.

The German Jesuit theologian and psychoanalyst Eugen Drewermann puts forth an alternative explanation. According to him, the seminary does not warp personalities. Rather, the compatibility of the religious vocation with a fragile psychology leads some men to seek the secure environment of the Church. The subservience expected of the priest attracts such men, whose debilitated egos are the result of a particular psychological constellation produced within the family.[46] North American seminary teacher Father Donald Cozzens provides a similar interpretation by pointing out that priests need to overcome a "presbyteral Oedipal complex" involving "Mother Church" and "Father bishop." The Oedipal complex as the cause of evil is the original sin and inhibits the priest from selflessly serving his flock. The celibate priest, he argues, is an eternally unmarried son enjoying a strong emotional bond with Mother Church.[47]

Drewermann's reliance on psychoanalysis got him into trouble with Rome, which stripped him of his chair at Paderborn University and prohibited him from teaching. He has been called Germany's "new Luther." According to one observer, "Drewermann attempts to go beyond the historical and dogmatic verities of churches, and restore, with the help of psychoanalysis, the power of images, dreams and symbols contained in all religions."[48] His beliefs might be summarized in the profound observation that men who are afraid of love cannot themselves teach others to love.[49] Drewermann reached his conclusions in the 1980s. Twenty years earlier, a similar conclusion was drawn by the psychoanalysts of Brazil's Christus Sacerdos.

In discussing these psychological profiles I do not intend to say that all seminarians shared them. In fact, in the period before Vatican II most probably did not, as the overwhelming majority left the seminary long before ordination. But those who stuck it out were the most likely to suffer the seminary's negative consequences.

The two arguments can be fused: the seminary attracts a specific type whose psychological vulnerability is exploited and exacerbated by the disciplinary structure. Candidates to the priesthood in the pre–Vatican II period were particularly susceptible to this mental molding because of the early age at which most entered the seminary and because of the large number of families that still saw the presence of a son in the priesthood as a sign of prestige. It was these men, virtually consecrated to the institution, who would seek the aid of psychoanalysis.

Pioneers and Experiments

Ecclesiastical pioneers in psychoanalysis helped lay the foundation for Brazil's psychoanalytic culture. In the 1950s, long before the boom, seminary teachers began to study psychology and experiment with therapies specifically with an eye to improving ecclesiastical training.[50] These pioneers helped set the thematic agenda for other priest-psychologists. Others helped introduce psychoanalysis to society without, however, associating with the Church or clerical training.[51]

Relying on foreign authors and the findings of international meetings of Catholic psychologists, the Brazilians first viewed psychology as an aid for prudently helping priests within the Tridentine framework. One widely discussed method was vocational testing, used to measure aptitude for the priesthood. Clergymen saw psychology as an auxiliary in the spiritual direction of students. Enthusiasts of psychology showed great interest in personality development and the treatment of psychological disturbances. They aimed to produce healthy clerics who could serve as amicable models for their flocks. Another key objective was to improve the psychological makeup of seminary teachers.[52]

By publishing articles and receiving promotions, the pioneers carved out a place for psychology in the Church even as the hierarchy combated controversial applications such as psychoanalysis. On the one hand, the pioneers proceeded cautiously by avoiding proposals that would directly threaten the hierarchy. The mere departure from rote scholasticism toward a more dynamic pedagogy worried some bishops. In the early 1960s, for instance, Father Francisco Reis, a psychologist, was expelled from Viamão for his new classroom methods.[53] On the other hand, the pioneers challenged the status quo with their hard assessments of sacerdotal life, and they espoused the institutionalization of psychology in the Church. A 1960 proposal advocated the formation of a national "psycho-pedagogical" institute to be sponsored by the powerful CRB, the Conference of Brazilian Religious.[54]

The foreign status or extensive foreign experience of many pioneers once again highlighted the Brazilian Church's dependence on outside ideas in the process of modernization. But they constantly strived to adapt these ideas to local conditions.

One key trailblazer was Dom Valfredo Bernardo Tepe, the coordinator of the project that led to the *Documentos dos presbíteros* (discussed in chapter 5). A German Franciscan who came to Brazil as a young seminarian in the 1930s, Tepe began to study psychology on his own during his tenure as director of theology students at the Central Seminary of Bahia in the early 1950s. Convinced of its importance for the affective development of the students, Tepe gave weekly lectures on the theme of spirituality and psychology. The talks were published in 1958 as *O sentido da vida* (The Meaning of Life). The book was denounced at the Holy Office (the former Inquisition) for its seemingly unorthodox positions about friendships in the seminaries. The authorities forced Tepe to make corrections in a later edition. Tepe also inserted psychological themes into his talks during courses given in the Movimento por um Mundo Melhor (MMM, or Movement for a Better World). Thousands of priests and nuns took part in MMM. Later, after taking university courses in psychology, Tepe wrote *Prazer ou amor?* (Pleasure or Love?) in which he confronted the orthodox Freudian view of instinctual satisfaction with the Christian ideal of love. In 1967 Tepe became a bishop and a top CNBB official in charge of seminary education. Three years later he was promoted to bishop of Ilhéus, Bahia, and assumed the leadership of the CNBB seminary division. A bishop-psychologist had gained national prominence.[55]

Freud's basic ideas gained currency among the Brazilian clergy through the efforts of Father João Mohana, a physician and author. In the late 1950s five of the young Mohana's newly ordained colleagues from Viamão asked him to give informal classes on psychoanalysis. The priests used the concepts from his presentations to solve personal psychological problems and as a result felt more comfortable as ministers. After the Second Vatican Council two bishops invited Mohana to preach clerical retreats using discussion of psychoanalysis. The clerics again responded positively. Recognizing the high cost and lengthy process of formal analysis, in 1967 Mohana put his simplified version of therapy into a book, *Padres e bispos auto-analisados* (The Self-Analysis of Priests and Bishops).[56] The Vienna-trained Brazilian analyst Norberto Keppe, a former theology student whose practice included priests and former seminarians, wrote a similar work titled *Sexo e religião*, in which he presented atheism, rejection of the Church, and hostile feelings toward religions as the product of unresolved psychological repression. Humans, he concluded, could not live without religion. "Anybody who doubts the existence of the Creator is psychically immature," he wrote. Keppe was influenced by the Austrian analysts Igor Caruso (discussed below) and Viktor Frankl, both of whom sought to demonstrate that humans had a relationship to values and not just instinct. Keppe later developed a therapeutic model based on psychology, philosophy, and theology.[57]

Father João Edênio dos Reis Valle, of the Divine Word order, first studied psychology during his theology program in Germany in the 1950s. Encouraged by Pius XII's desire for greater contact with the human sciences and by his order's need for a professional psychologist in Brazil, Valle obtained a master's degree while still in Europe. After returning to Brazil in 1966, Valle gave presentations and courses on psychology for religious orders, dioceses, Catholic schools, and seminaries around the country, including the controversial IFT in São Paulo. Valle returned to Rome to earn his doctorate in 1973. A prolific author, Valle became an important CNBB advisor on clerical training. In 1989

he rose to the presidency of the CRB, where he worked with the Grupo de Reflexão de Psicólogos a Serviço da Vida Religiosa (Working Group on Psychology
and the Religious Life).[58]

Before the forced closing of IFT in 1969, Valle and a group of psychologists
and physicians wanted to open up a separate, related institute to offer psychological support for candidates to religious orders. They intended to base the
institute on the Association Médicale d'Aide aux Religieux (AMAR, or Association for Medical Assistance to the Religious), which sponsored a ten-
month course in Paris on priestly life in the light of Vatican II, psychology, and
Freudian psychoanalysis.[59] Founded in 1959 by the Dominican Father Robert-
Albert Plé and the Jesuit Beirnaert, AMAR received the backing of the French
confederation of religious orders. AMAR's central goal was to determine a man's
capacity for a life of chastity. Father Plé made the ironic conclusion that "the
more a man seems normal and capable of being a good husband, the better
he can renounce conjugal life by becoming a normal priest, that is, a man like
everyone else." In historian Roudinesco's estimation AMAR demonstrated that
"faith is no longer the same after an adventure with psychoanalysis, and, if
it remains, it is transformed by an attentiveness to the unconscious."[60] Begun
some years later, the AMAR course on clerical life required participants to have
experience in seminary training. They also had to agree to weekly sessions with
a therapist—but only after receiving permission from their superiors. Discussion topics included the moral conscience, celibacy, love, sex, and the danger
of psychoanalysis to faith. AMAR accepted applicants from around the world,
including nuns. Latin Americans were preponderant. Several clerics from Brazil participated, among them a Canadian father who had taken part in group
therapy with Géza. Another was Father Paulo Lisbôa, a Brazilian Jesuit who
later coordinated the Centro de Teologia e Espiritualidade para a Vida Religiosa
(Center of Theology and Spirituality for the Religious Life), a course for professors in religious seminaries.[61] Father Plé agreed to assist Valle and the Brazilians with their psychological institute, but the initiative died after IFT's demise and the escalation of Church-military conflict. A parallel initiative was the
short-lived Associação Brasileira de Psicologia da Religião, founded in 1965. It
joined psychologists, physicians, theologians, and ecclesiastics in the study of
religion from a psychological perspective. It too became a victim of the political climate.[62]

One of the most unusual experiments with psychology involved both clergy
and laity in the south of Brazil. Developed by a São Paulo sociologist and called

Criatividade Comunitária (Communitarian Creativity), this initiative aimed to assist ecclesial reorganization by stimulating creativity and more active leadership. Criatividade divided social life into fourteen different systems, such as kinship, production, loyalty, communication, religion, and politics. In the state of Santa Catarina a number of bishops, priests, nuns, and seminarians adopted the methodology of Criatividade as a way of planning Church activities. One exponent of the movement recommended it as a model for CEBs. The clerics and sisters trained to become Criatividade leaders learned to use psychological techniques to assist their colleagues and lay pastoral workers. Hundreds of people took part in Criatividade seminars,[63] which were led by two hundred trainers, all but twenty of them priests and nuns.[64] Female religious orders participated in Criatividade. Deeply committed to the movement, the Sisters of the Divine Providence took the controversial step of mixing children of the rich and of the poor in their elite private school. The nuns' involvement drew the attention of the Vatican, which intervened to appoint the prim Swiss priest Josef Romer to take charge of the order. Other controversial ramifications included a deemphasis on sin and the encouragement of priests and nuns to pair off in sexual relationships.[65] (In the name of psychology some priests started speaking of a so-called third way—to be neither celibate nor married.[66]) In the assessment of Father Valle, a "naïve psychological euphoria" had taken hold of the movement, ascribing to psychology a magical status.[67] In 1972 the CRB convened a special panel of priests, nuns, and brothers to participate in one of the seminars. The panel's report praised some aspects but found fundamental faults with the program's theological and scientific bases and sharply criticized the lack of up-to-date therapeutic techniques. The panel maintained that Criatividade's method of tracing individuals' personal histories violated privacy and might cause disturbances or depression.[68] The CRB report doomed Criatividade in Church circles. The Church in Santa Catarina, including bishops, entered into a divisive dispute over the program that lasted through the 1970s. Theologians and bishops in Paraná and Rio Grande do Sul quickly condemned Criatividade and banned its seminars.[69]

Other experiments took place elsewhere in the Catholic world. In Brazil Father Décio Zandonade, Father Geraldo Curvo, and Jesuit Father Antônio Benkö joined other pioneers in exploring psychology's benefits for the clergy. Benkö later became a professor at Christus Sacerdos. The demand for psychology was great. One course given by the Salesian fathers in São João del Rei, Minas Gerais, attracted hundreds of priests. Classes on psychology in seminary training were offered in Belo Horizonte. A psychology refresher program in São Paulo drew some five hundred nuns and priests.[70] In Rio de Janeiro an intercongregational team of religious priests and laypersons offered psychological aid to clerics, the faithful, and people of other creeds. In the early 1980s part of this group helped set up the Centro Nacional para a Revitalização da Pessoa (National Center for Personal Revitalization). It used group and individual therapies, relaxation techniques, and other treatments for clergy and the laity. Several fathers directed exercises in the integration of psychology and spiritual life.[71] In Brussels a course entitled "Lumen Vitae" recommended psychotherapy to its priest participants.[72] In the United States the Church turned to psychoanalysts in the 1960s to treat priests with sexual disorders such as pedophilia, and in 1976 the Servants of the Paraclete, a religious order specializing in the ministry to priests, opened a treatment center for clergymen with psychological and emotional difficulties.[73] In Los Angeles the Immaculate Heart Sisters relied on psychologists to help interpret their new directions in the post–Vatican II era. Carl Rogers, for example, conducted workshops aimed at helping the sisters improve communication skills and address the profound changes the order was undergoing.[74] In Rome Father Luís Rulla, an Italian Jesuit who had specialized in psychiatry in the United States, became director of the Gregorian University's psychological institute. His works on psychoanalysis and religious vocations were translated into Portuguese in the 1970s and gained a wide readership in Brazilian ecclesiastical circles.[75] As the Centro Nacional and other examples illustrate, the laity often benefited from the spread of psychology among the clergy.[76]

Father Géza's Discovery of Psychoanalysis

Géza's path to psychoanalysis was circuitous. Although he was European, only after his arrival in far-off Rio Grande do Sul did he delve into psychology. In 1949 Géza made a dramatic escape from his native Hungary to Austria in order to flee the Communist repression of Jesuit seminarians. Géza went to Rome, where he completed his theological program. Studying under difficult circumstances, however, the young Jesuit failed one of his final exams in 1951, causing the order to renege on its promise of postgraduate studies in Europe. The European Church still looked condescendingly on Latin America. The Jesuits demoted Géza to Brazil in 1953. In 1955 he became the spiritual director of the Jesuit seminarians at the Colégio Cristo Rei in São Leopoldo, a suburb of Porto

Alegre. (That same year another Jesuit exile, Pierre Teilhard de Chardin, would die in obscurity in New York City. His works on faith and evolution would soon revolutionize Catholic thinking about science.) Géza's apostolate concentrated on the problems of the clergy and seminarians. He became a specialist in retreats and rapidly built a national reputation as an expert on ecclesiastical training. He also became an internationally known authority on *The Spiritual Exercises* of St. Ignatius, of which he published his own annotated version.[77]

Described by one scholar as a "shock-tactic spiritual gymnastic," the Ignatian meditations were rooted in the Catholic Counter-Reformation and contributed to the rationalistic development of modernity.[78] In the estimation of Ignatius's most recent biographer, John Patrick Donnelly, the writing of *The Spiritual Exercises* was the saint's greatest achievement after the founding of the Jesuit order. The more than five thousand editions of the book since 1548 attest to its immense influence. The exercises' basic model survived over four centuries and is still widely practiced. *The Spiritual Exercises* aimed to help people reproduce Ignatius's mystical experience. The exercises stressed obedience to the Church. Ignatius tried them out on small groups of the faithful, mainly women, including converted prostitutes. They prescribe a rigorous four-week program of prayer and soul-searching for individuals deeply committed to rediscovering a connection with God. A spiritual director with good psychological skills often crafted the exercises according to the participant's individual needs. The director helped the exercitant conduct a thorough examination of conscience. At the end of the first week the exercitants had to make a confession to a priest. This frequently involved a review of sins going back to the start of one's life—a way of diminishing the influence of the past in order to serve God more fully. The exercises were quite practical, helping a person make decisions by putting life in a long-term perspective,[79] and they anticipated much of psychoanalysis. The experience in Ignatian spirituality would heavily influence Géza's thinking.

In 1954 Géza published an article in the *REB* echoing the Tridentine ethic of priestly training but also exploring psychology. He stated the central theological theme that would guide his use of psychoanalysis and prevent him from forming a purely natural, psychological evaluation of the priesthood:

The essence of the Catholic priesthood is the participation in the eternal priesthood of Jesus Christ. Therefore, each priest is equally a priest of Christ: with the same mission, the same power, and the same responsibility. The priest of today is linked to Jesus by the same intimate relation as the priests of the Middle Ages or of the primitive Church; that is, the priestly ideal is the transformation into Jesus Christ. The priest enwraps himself in Christ to the point where he no longer lives himself but at which Christ lives in him.

In accord with Pius XII, Géza believed the world needed an "elite" priesthood—men unconditionally committed, armed with theological principles, and educated at least as well as secular leaders. "Education of the feelings and the heart" was also necessary. The duty of the seminary was to "sublimate in young men the incalculable energies of feelings and to make them noble, elevate them, and put them at the service of God."[80]

Géza then took the monumental step of undergoing a didactic, or training, analysis, considered indispensable for those aiming at a practice in classical psychoanalysis, or depth psychology. Géza cited three reasons. First, he wanted to achieve greater introspection in the quest for spiritual purification. Second, he hoped the experience would enable him to "clarify the difficulties of seminarians and furnish them with more appropriate pastoral orientation." Finally, he sought to understand the new fad among seminarians of "reading books on psychoanalysis and applying it to themselves."[81]

To undergo analysis Géza joined the Brazilian Circle of Depth Psychology in Porto Alegre, the local arm of an organization in Vienna headed by Igor Caruso. Caruso, a member of the Russian Orthodox Church, defended the "spiritualist-existentialist" school of depth psychology and, as Géza stated, "openly confessed the *transcendental view of the world.*" Géza entered the Caruso group by way of Father Malomar Lund Edelweiss, another psychoanalytic pioneer.[82]

Edelweiss brought the Caruso school of psychoanalysis to Brazil. Originally from the diocese of Pelotas, Rio Grande do Sul, Edelweiss studied at the Pio Brasileiro in the late 1940s. Back in Brazil, he heard lectures on Caruso by a Hungarian psychologist visiting from Buenos Aires. After reading Caruso's *Psychoanalyse und Synthese der Existenz* (Existential Psychology), in 1954, Edelweiss went to Vienna to start analysis under him. Caruso went to Brazil twice. In 1956 he visited São Paulo and Porto Alegre, where Edelweiss established the first Brazilian Caruso Circle. Edelweiss translated one of Caruso's articles from German into Portuguese for the journal of the Catholic University of Rio Grande do Sul. In 1968 and 1969 Caruso spent a year in Belo Horizonte, where Edelweiss had resettled. Edelweiss set up another Caruso Circle and practiced psychoanalysis with the support of Dom Serafim Fernandes de Araújo, an auxiliary bishop. Caruso treated patients and trained analysts, and he became the *paraninfo,* or honored spokesman, of the psychology program's class of 1968 at the Catholic University of Minas Gerais.[83]

Published in 1951, *Psychoanalyse und Synthese der Existenz* illustrated how believers held to their faith while adopting modernity. Critically appraising the achievements of Freud, Jung, and the school of existential psychology that arose after World War II, Caruso reached back into pre-Enlightenment history to reunite psychology with its fountainhead in metaphysical philosophy. Caruso lamented the breakdown of the traditional hierarchy of values, in which all philosophical and scientific inquiry had pointed toward the transcendent. Modern man was lost. Freud had rejected the transcendental as an illusion, and Jung had stopped short of finding it with his theory of the collective unconscious. Caruso brought the transcendental back into play. Borrowing from existentialist philosophy, he repudiated the mechanistic determinism of Freudian psychology, which he thought was now totalitarian. Existentialism contributed to the advancement of analysis because it defended freedom and the significance of existence. People were not just psycho-biological beings controlled by impulses, Caruso reminded his readers. They had a spiritual life too. The existence of the conscience, the peculiar quality of humanness, was evidence of the incarnation of the spirit. Human actions were not simply products of the unconscious, but products of one's environment, values, and the desire for the supernatural. Psychoanalysis should aspire to be universal by considering all of these catalysts and by overlapping once again with science and philosophy.[84] Psychology was also a social science that could aid man in adjusting to modern alienation.[85]

Caruso's philosophy dovetailed with Catholic theology and the needs of priests. Psychoanalysis had to run the risk of making value judgments. "The conscience is man's ability to be mindful of a hierarchy of values which was not born of the laws of the flesh," Caruso affirmed. Building on Jung's idea of religious faith as an inborn characteristic, Caruso's psychotherapeutic method focused on the search for the individual's "Christ-archetype," the living truth. Neuroses were "essentially the problem of human relationships with the absolute," for example, the development of false absolutes, including the turning of "myself" into an absolute value. The neurotic lived an "existential lie." "Neurosis searches for a redeemer," Caruso proclaimed.

> The "Christ-archetype" is the central factor in any psychotherapy, making possible psychotherapy for the neurotic, as well as for the analyst. In his search for a redeemer, the neurotic meets his therapist. It is by no

means wholly neurotic to long for a healer, who could assume the burden of neurotic guilt, descend into the neurotic hell in order to redeem finally the neurotic through his triumph over guilt. . . . All human religions, but also all pseudo-religions, such as totalitarian political systems and scientific systems turned into dogmas, are ultimately inspired by the expectation of the future redemption of man. . . . The longing for redemption is based on an eschatological, Messianic archetype. Unless the analyst in some way answers to this longing, his work would be the confirmation of a total illusion, a temptation to total neurosis and thus anything but wholesome. The analyst, then, must in some way correspond to his patient's "Christ-archetype." And this he does. He is able to help in so far only as the "Christ-archetype" is alive within him.

One did not have to choose between psychoanalysis and Christianity. In the psychoanalytic tradition neurosis was always an illness. However, in Caruso's thought it could be the first step on the way to genius, and "for the priest or spiritual adviser the decisive phase on the way towards sanctification." Like Fromm, Caruso saw a fusion of the priestly and medical aspects of analysis. The individual's "existential synthesis," which occurred during the training analysis, was especially valuable for spiritual directors. Psychoanalysis was ultimately an encounter of love "between two unique and equally valuable personalities." Without love there was no cure.[86]

In João Batista Ferreira's opinion, Caruso's ideas represented a first alternative to orthodox Freudian analysis in Brazil. Caruso introduced the notion of a more emotive form of psychoanalysis that resonated with Latin American identity. For a time, discussion of *análise carusiana* became fashionable in Brazilian psychoanalytic circles. Caruso, Father Edelweiss, and Kattrin Kemper and her husband, Werner Kemper, were instrumental in establishing a dissident psychoanalytic society in Rio, the Sociedade Psicanalítica do Rio de Janeiro.[87]

Géza's introduction to the psychoanalytic mode of thinking presented immense emotional and social challenges.[88] First, he had to overcome prejudice and ignorance. Psychoanalysis, he wrote,

was a thing considered to be more than suspect, above all in the seminaries. . . . Especially priests and educators of the clergy would barely hear the subject brought up before thinking of apostasy or, at the very least, deviations, disorientation, perversions, sexuality. . . . In the same way educators and superiors in the seminaries, fearful of their own superiors, would permit no priest to undergo analysis, because—they certainly imagined—this could unleash confusion throughout the seminary. It was the case therefore of a real taboo, which shocked everybody.[89]

Second, Géza had to avoid recrimination from the hierarchy. His analysis remained a secret known to only a few superiors. The situation was doubly ironic. Géza engaged in a practice officially banned by other members of the hierarchy. And, having once risked his life fleeing an anti-religious regime, he now went underground at the behest of the Church.

Discipline had once again blocked the circulation of ideas. Other priests had not the slightest idea that Géza had entered analysis. To keep secrecy he went through "enormous sacrifices," traveling three hours three times a week from São Leopoldo to see his analyst, Father Edelweiss, in Porto Alegre, while maintaining his normal activities in the seminary and lecturing on psychology at a local college. The teaching experience later enabled him to register as a professional psychologist with the Ministry of Education and Culture.[90]

Géza described his training as a process of self-discovery and personal growth. It was, he wrote, an "opening in all directions, towards all horizons of existence." He related his interpretations of dreams involving religious symbolism in the form of Christ, "to which the entirety of the training analysis gravitated: the universal Man, the ideal Man." But he also met his human and animalistic side, "descending into the abyss of life": the id, the passions, the sexual impulse. Géza revealed that he had suffered from depression resulting from a badly resolved sexuality, poorly understood, he believed, because of the isolation of his seminary years and celibacy. Therapy helped him to overcome the problem and to sublimate his sexual drive in the religious mission. "I came to know myself much more," Géza wrote. "I accepted the world and society as they are, not to leave them where they are, in misery, but to carry them with me to the heights in order to liberate them from slavery and from the passions. I opened myself more fully to transcendence." No one with a true priestly vocation need fear psychoanalysis, Géza believed, "because a sincere analysis makes that vocation more authentic, open, intense, and saintly." His experience with therapy was of "inestimable help" in his work with the clergy. Géza considered his analysis to be so extraordinary that he called it a "special grace received from God."[91]

A decisive theme for Géza was the moral conscience. "The 'voice of the conscience' is an undeniable fact, universally experienced in the life of humanity,"

Géza wrote in 1962. Echoing Caruso, he defined the moral conscience as innate and autonomous. It "obliges the person to open himself up to that which is above, to discern between good and evil, towards an ethical attitude."[92] The superego held the therapeutic "key" to the moral conscience. In his evaluation of negative superego development Géza drew conclusions especially relevant to seminary life. The "evolution of a tyrannic superego" resulted in denying a child "the basic conditions of personal evolution: liberty and love." In this case the superego "infantilizes the person, makes him dependent on others, fixes him at a certain level of evolution, forms in him a false moral." This psychological makeup stunted individual development and produced either an "angel complex" or a "scapegoat complex."[93] Caruso's intuitions provided an alternative. Paraphrasing him, Géza stated that the progressive "personalization" of an individual involved a teleological, dialectical evolution, for man "has a historical destiny." Human progress meant ever greater discovery of the self and of one's vocation.[94]

Géza employed his knowledge in group therapy sessions for Jesuit seminarians. His autobiographical statements do not explain how he could do so after keeping his own therapy secret. The students' curiosity and their demand for help no doubt convinced him to go ahead.[95] Géza likely shielded this activity from his superiors, but with time it gained acceptance. By the end of his life the Jesuits had provided him with a consultation room in the seminary.[96]

Géza identified three basic tensions experienced by the seminarians. First was "sexual explosion," the initial revelation of difficulties with sexuality. Second was "conflict with authority," either parents or religious superiors. And third came "problems of religion," often the negation of an "imposed" faith followed by the discovery of "the God of truth, charity, and love." Géza believed that therapy could resolve these tensions.

Group therapy could soften authoritarianism by encouraging the maturation of young men. Wrote Géza: "The seminarians begin to treat their educators in a different way: they seek to converse with them person to person, adult to adult—which can startle unprepared educators. Previously submissive subjects, who accepted determinations, orders, or whatever without discussion, begin, once they become adults, to think, reflect, and often inquire into the motives. They wish to dialogue with their superiors, disposing themselves to accept orders but doing so by way of a free and mature choice." Group therapy altered the structure of seminary life because it triggered the "liberation of individuals from the psychological ties that obstructed them." Even if practiced by only a minority, group therapy could lead the entire institution through a "process of maturation and, consequently, to a more human structure."

Analysis prepared individuals for a greater reception of grace. Even when religion went unmentioned, therapy turned the individual spirit toward Christian openness to others, and it approximated the analysand to the ideal man, Christ. "In sum, this opening to *all* of reality includes the opening to transcendence," Géza wrote. With psychoanalysis, seminary educators could build a "new kind of priest and religious: men made human and divine, men of inner conviction, not of imposition from the outside; active apostles, . . . authentic, generous, the kind our times and society expect of us."[97]

The "modern saint" required psychological stability. But who was the model for that man? And what expectations of gender and culture did Géza perceive in that model? On the theological level, priests needed to emulate a new, humanized version of Christ. But nowhere did Géza's or the seminarians' movement make reference to men or cultural icons. The turn to psychoanalysis made it clear that each seminarian was to develop his own personality—to be his own man.

Géza kept a sober view of psychoanalysis. It had to be integrated with the theological and spiritual aspects of seminary training. In contrast with other innovators, he did not view psychoanalysis as a quick cure-all. Géza agreed with critics that, if left uncontrolled, therapy could lead to unbridled "naturalism." To qualify for work with seminarians, analysts had to work within a Christian framework. A student who focused solely on Freudian anthropological norms would rún the risk of losing both his vocation and his faith.[98]

Géza viewed the Cuernavaca experiment critically. He and other Brazilian clerics were well-informed about the details.[99] The organizers of Christus Sacerdos carefully avoided the Mexican problems. Scientifically speaking, Géza considered the Cuernavaca initiative "good, even notable, but fundamentally defective." The therapists chosen to analyze the monks had little knowledge of religious life, Géza observed, and practically the entire monastery had gone into group therapy at the same time, "saturating the environment of the entire community." The monks too easily embraced a strictly psychoanalytic Weltanschauung (comprehensive worldview) while rejecting "many things which it would be convenient to retain, conserve, and transform as part of a new synthesis."[100] In sum, the Cuernavaca experiment threatened faith. Thus Géza agreed with traditionalists—albeit from a quite different and much more optimistic perspective—that analysis could ruin a priest's vocation.

The Genesis of Christus Sacerdos and Géza's Critique of the Seminaries

In the late 1950s Géza made several requests to organize a permanent enhancement course for seminary professors. The Jesuits welcomed the concept but turned it down for lack of money and qualified personnel. Dom Vicente Scherer and Cardinal Câmara applauded the idea, which received CNBB approval in 1958. Primarily theological, the proposal included ideas from psychology and psychoanalysis.[101] Géza had taken the first step toward establishing Christus Sacerdos.

At the CNBB's behest the rectors and spiritual directors of Brazil's seminaries met in Rio de Janeiro in 1959 to debate priestly training. The priests voted to approve advanced studies for seminary professors, including specialization in psychology. At the meeting Géza underlined the necessity of informing spiritual direction with the advances of scientific psychology. Citing the results of a 1957 survey of 210 seminarians in Rio Grande do Sul, Géza showed that two-thirds affirmed difficulties in speaking to their directors. "'When I talked about my life, the priest decided I was perverted and said there was nothing he could do for me. This was a shock to me, and I just closed up,'" Géza, quoting a seminarian, stated. Others gave similarly critical comments about spiritual directors who were either aggressive or indifferent. Some directors used counseling sessions to vent their own problems rather than focus on the students'. Many of these men lacked familiarity with psychology and displayed "psychic ineptitude," Géza stated. Spiritual directors needed to know themselves before advising others.[102]

From 1960 to 1962 Géza delivered a special three-stage summer course on clerical training. The co-organizer was Father Ivo Lorscheiter, the rector of Viamão. The program had three main areas of study: theology and spirituality, sociology, and psychology. Once again the program had the full approval of the hierarchy, including that of the Vatican's Congregation for the Seminaries.[103]

Vatican II allowed Géza to develop his ideas for a permanent program. In Europe he visited seminaries, universities, and other institutions that trained priests. Géza became convinced that the Brazilian Church should confer degrees as high as the doctorate. However, witnessing the Council's final session, Géza was swept up by the wave of innovation. Perhaps in revolt against his earlier academic rejection in Rome, Géza decided that the Brazilian program would abandon the stress on academic brilliance so important in the ecclesiastical career. There would be no diplomas. Instead the course would concentrate on the "holistic education" of the participants. While in Rome Géza faced an interrogation by Jesuit superiors about his exploration of psychoanalysis as a tool for priestly training, but they did not restrict his work.[104]

In October 1965 Géza felt free to sharpen his critique of the Brazilian priesthood. Psychological factors took center stage as he became more vivid and provocative. Some pastors, he affirmed, completely lacked the essentials. They were "alienated," "infantile," and "anguished." As a group they suffered from general unhappiness, sexual daydreaming, and immoral contact with women. These men lacked "priestly conscience." He stabbed at the heart of the seminaries' problems: the Tridentine distortion of discipline. Géza likened some seminaries in Latin America and Europe to their sister institutions behind the "iron curtain." In the East superiors had little psychological insight and ordained only disciplinary conformists.[105] In a talk to educators that same month, Géza waxed even more radical by comparing seminaries with concentration camps. Of course, Géza stated, the difference was like "the distance between heaven and earth," but a narrow-minded seminary education could breed the same kind of dehumanization found in the camps: depersonalization and isolation; the development of one-sided personalities; sexual repression; an inhuman daily schedule; and psychological and spiritual regression. The Church must avoid cosmetic institutional reform. The spirit of the times demanded a radical change in personal attitudes.[106]

Discipline had come full circle. It had facilitated modernization via Romanization. Now it was being questioned from all sides as a new modernizing project emerged. Psychoanalysis appeared to be the remedy for discipline's negative effects and the tool for building a new kind of seminary.

Géza surprisingly did not scrutinize the question of obligatory celibacy. He seemed to be oblivious to the raging debate. In this respect Géza remained quite traditional. Had he lived longer, he might also have come to question celibacy.[107]

Géza now had the full institutional and financial support of the CRB and the CNBB. Dom Othon Motta, the CNBB's national secretary for the seminaries, sent Géza a letter to "bless, approve, recognize, stimulate, and assume this initiative on a national level." The proposal also had the endorsement of the continent-wide Organization of Latin American Seminaries.[108] In 1966 the Brazilian Church inaugurated Christus Sacerdos. Géza considered this achievement "to be a true miracle."[109]

The Theory and Practice of Christus Sacerdos

Christus Sacerdos took place at the Colégio Cristo Rei, the Jesuit seminary located on a hill overlooking São Leopoldo. The setting encouraged introspection. Surrounded with gardens, Cristo Rei had the rural isolation and self-sufficiency of a medieval monastery, including a library with some fifty thousand books. The course participants shared the intimacy of a small group undisturbed by superiors and the demands of normal priestly life. The idyllic backdrop served to refresh them and smooth over the emotional edges that arose in group therapy and individual analysis. Individual dioceses and the CNBB underwrote most of the cost of lodging and psychotherapy and thus guaranteed financial security. Therapy, even if paid, was a privilege in any society. Ironically, isolation, dependence, and privilege partially reproduced the reality of the seminary, but the priests could come and go as they pleased. Some took up outside activities such as weekend pastoral work.[110]

The centerpiece of Christus Sacerdos was "integral reflection" on the "anguishing" problems of the priesthood and seminary training. To this end the course employed theological, sociological, and psychological perspectives. It aimed for the "integral education" of seminary teachers, "within the limits of orthodoxy," in order to provide "the personal and collective confidence so necessary in times as uncertain as ours." To be able to guide youth effectively, seminary professors needed to familiarize themselves with their own "psychic reactions" and "defense mechanisms." Christus Sacerdos would help the participants attain a "more harmonious structuring of the emotional components of their lives as priests." Ultimately, the priests would help seminarians to cope with their own psychological problems.[111]

The program had both theoretical and practical components. In the theoretical segment the priests studied the latest biblical and theological research, including Vatican II, and focused on the challenges of secularization. Sociological analysis included an examination of contemporary humanity and philosophy as well as a survey of living conditions in Latin America and Brazil. Finally, the priests received a broad introduction to psychology. Professional psychologists and psychoanalysts from the Caruso Circle in Porto Alegre lectured on the psychology of personality, evolutionary psychology, interpersonal dynamics, neuroses, psychopathology, and group psychodynamics.[112]

Some of the lecturers were brutally candid. In a class on neurotic disturbances, psychoanalyst Dr. Alberto Corrêa Ribeiro told the priests that seminary education encouraged homosexual activity among heterosexuals because it presented women as "dangerous," a "temptation" of the devil. "Wherever a person does not have the opportunity to direct his sexual impulse towards the opposite sex, it is natural that he directs it towards people of the same sex," the analyst stated. Homosexuals might enter the seminary because of its all-male population and other favorable conditions for "realizing their homosexuality." Ribeiro also discussed neuroses such as sadism, pedophilia, transvestism, and necrophilia.[113] Such terminology was completely alien to the Tridentine regime. Suddenly the Church allowed priests to hear it. Another psychoanalyst captured the risks of institutionalized repression with a series of questions. Could religion per se cause neuroses? No. Could the *exactions* of religion contribute to neurotic development? Yes. And could neuroses lead to atheism? Yes.[114]

The men of Christus Sacerdos were not a fringe group trying to embarrass the Church into changing the priesthood. On the contrary, the course drew participants and teachers from the ecclesiastical elite. Géza was a respected Jesuit. The course administrator, Father Ivo Lorscheiter, became an auxiliary bishop to Dom Vicente Scherer in 1966 and later secretary-general and president of the CNBB. Another prominent teacher was his cousin Dom Aloísio, a future cardinal and candidate for pope. He lectured on the theology of Vatican II. Table 6.1 gives background on other notables who took part either as teachers or students. All were men of great intellect and power. Some stood in the vanguard of Church renovation.

The team of psychologists and psychoanalysts had connections to the mainstream of the Church in Rio Grande do Sul. The main link was Géza. Another member from the Caruso circle was fellow Jesuit Father Aloysio Arnoldo Koehler. After ordination in 1958 Koehler had studied under Caruso in the graduate program in depth psychology at the University of Vienna. Father Koehler had to convince his superiors that a psychologist could improve seminary education. In Vienna he remained independent by surviving without Jesuit funds. Koehler pushed for a program similar to Christus Sacerdos in the archdiocese of Curitiba. His psychology classes for local seminarians scandalized the bishop, however. Géza sought Koehler's help in the preparation of Christus Sacerdos. (Koehler later left the priesthood and continued work as a professional analyst.)[115] The other analysts from the Caruso Circle were Dr. Ribeiro, Dr. Paulo Brandão, Dr. Ary Wolffenbüttel, and Dr. Siegfried Kronfeld and his wife, Gerda, European Jews who had escaped the Nazis. (Gerda was baptized as a Protestant.) Of German descent, Wolffenbüttel had studied in the Jesuits' private secondary school, the prestigious Colégio Anchieta, in Porto Alegre. His grandfather was

TABLE 6.1
The Men of Christus Sacerdos

Name	Role in Course/Key Career Data
Father Hugo Assmann	Lecturer in theology. Prominent liberation theologian.
Father Antônio Benkö	Lecturer in psychology. Jesuit priest. Professor of psychology at the Pontifical Catholic University of Rio de Janeiro. One of the pioneers of psychology in the Brazilian Church.
Father Raimundo Caramuru de Barros	Lecturer on problems of faith. Assistant to Dom Hélder Câmara. Author of CNBB General Pastoral Plan.
Monsignor Marcelo Pinto Carvalheira	Participant, 1969. Rector of the Northeast II Regional Seminary. Director of Theological Institute of Recife. Assistant to Dom Hélder Câmara. Ordained bishop 1975. Archbishop of Paraíba, 1995–2004.
Father Antônio do Carmo Cheuiche	Lecturer. University professor. Ordained bishop 1969.
Father José Comblin	Lecturer. Belgian diocesan priest. Leading liberation theologian. Involved in seminary experiments in Recife. Expelled from Brazil by military regime.
Father Romeu Dale	Lecturer on moral theology and Vatican II. Dominican friar instrumental in Catholic Action and development of Church communications sector.
Father Afonso Felipe Gregory	Sociological orientation. Director of CERIS, 1963–1980. Ordained bishop 1979. CNBB national social pastoral coordinator, 1983–1991. Author of numerous sociological studies of the Church. Bishop of Imperatriz, 1987–present.
Father Friedrich Karl Laufer	Secretary and spiritual director. German Jesuit father ordained in Brazil. Rector of the Colégio Pio Brasileiro, 1969–1972.
Father João Batista Libânio	Lecturer in theology. Prominent Jesuit liberation theologian.
Father Lucas Moreira Neves	Lecturer on the priesthood in light of conciliar documents. Dominican friar. Auxiliary bishop of São Paulo, 1967–1974. Archbishop of Salvador, 1987–2000. Made cardinal 1988. Leader of Church's conservative wing. President of CNBB, 1995–1998. Secretary of Sacred Congregation of Bishops, Rome, 1979–1987. In 1990s considered a possible successor to Pope John Paul II.
Father José Arlindo Nadai	Participant, 1970. Diocesan priest. Psychology professor. CNBB subsecretary general, 1988–1990.
Father Lauro Palú	Participant, 1968. Vincentian father. Assistant general of the Congregation of the Mission (Vincentians), Rome, 1986–1992.

TABLE 6.1

The Men of Christus Sacerdos (*cont.*)

Name	Role in Course/Key Career Data
Father Paulo Eduardo Ponte	Participant, 1967. Ordained bishop 1971. Coordinator for CNBB national catechism and youth and education sectors. Archbishop of São Luís, 1984–present. Vice-president of CNBB, 1987–1991.
Father José Mário Stroeher	Participant, 1967. Ordained bishop 1983. Bishop of Rio Grande, 1986–present.

Sources: Untitled, undated document, APSB, pasta marked "S. Leopoldo-Cristo Rei. Curso '*Christus Sacerdos,*' Indicações gerais sobre o curso-1970"; pamphlet titled "Curso de Formação para Educadores de Seminários," APSB, pasta marked "S. Leopoldo-Cristo Rei. Curso '*Christus Sacerdos.*' Indicações Gerais sobre o curso-1970"; APSB, pasta marked "S. Leopoldo-Cristo Rei. Curso '*Christus Sacerdos.*' Listas (algumas) dos alunos. 1967, '68, '69, '70"; Carvalheira 1970:257, n. 1; mimeographed document titled "Curso *Christus Sacerdos* (Curso de Formação para Educadores de Seminários)," ACCR; Secretariado Nacional dos Seminários, Comunicado No. 4, "Curso '*Christus Sacerdos,*'" no date, INP Document No. 04663; interviews with Leite and Laufer.

one of the first psychiatrists in Rio Grande do Sul.[116] Father Benkö and another Jesuit, Father Marcos Bach, gave classes on pastoral counseling.

The practical segment of Christus Sacerdos consisted of spiritual exercises and psychotherapy administered by Géza and the team of analysts. In January 1966, a few weeks before the start of the course, Géza led the participants in a retreat that included the Ignatian exercises. During the course the fathers held weekly "life reflection" groups in which they focused on a theme from the Gospels in order to "review, verify, and justify the observations originating in the psychological."[117] Therapy entailed both individual psychoanalysis and group therapy. Each week the Caruso team convened to evaluate its activities. These meetings included self-criticism intended to "orient all in this work towards the supreme goal, sought in all aspects of the course: to liberate man completely in Christ."[118]

Géza designed Christus Sacerdos to provoke strong emotional reactions. He wanted the priests to experience new ways of feeling their personal histories as men of the Church, and he wanted them to explore new paths. He employed Ignatian spirituality to emphasize self-knowledge and control of one's personality.[119] The Ignatian exercises furnished a three-step outline for Christus Sacerdos. The first step brought to consciousness both social and individual problems. It generated internal tensions in the participants because it ended their sheltered existence and revealed a Brazilian reality far different from "the ideal that is put before their eyes," Géza wrote. In the second step the priests studied the problems in large-group meetings and therapeutic sessions. The third step was the sublimation of solutions to the problems. The individual chose a new behavior within the Church, one "marked by authenticity in thought and action." Sublimation was a personal event achieved through prayer, the contemplation of new directions in one's life, and relations with the collective and with God.[120] In effect, Géza used the Ignatian method to assimilate the sociological and the psychoanalytic into Church tradition.

The participants described a variety of experiences. Some focused on the philosophical and theological, including scrutiny of the post–Vatican II Church. Monsignor Marcelo Carvalheira, the director of the seminary in Recife and a close assistant to Dom Hélder Câmara, published an article in the REB based largely on the lectures of Christus Sacerdos. One of the few published references to the course, his essay focused on secularization.[121] But most priests focused on the psychological repercussions.[122]

The sessions of group and individual therapy provided the most jolting moments of Christus Sacerdos. Many of the priests marveled at the process of self-discovery and of building self-esteem. Some believed that they had finally discovered God. Others spoke of resolving deep inner conflicts. And still others recalled that psychoanalysis sparked conflict among the priests. Sexuality and celibacy were frequent themes. Dom Paulo Ponte recalled that the course cleared up questions about sexuality that had been left unanswered in the puritanical environment of the Tridentine seminaries.[123] Regardless of the emotional effect, the exposure to psychoanalysis kindled questioning about these and other challenges of priestly life. Scrutiny of themselves, their vocation, and the institution led the men of Christus Sacerdos to a clearer understanding of their reasons for becoming priests. For some, analysis strengthened the resolve to remain in the ministry. For others, it helped to perceive that a celibate lifestyle was not their true vocation.

Priests testified to the importance of psychoanalysis in statements taken by the CNBB's National Secretariat for the Seminaries after the academic sessions of 1967 and 1969. Of some twenty men registered in 1967, all but one ranked the psychological aspect at the top. No tally was available for 1969, but the priests' remarks underscored the centrality of therapy. In both surveys most of the clerics referred to self-discovery, and all of them gave a positive evaluation of the course:

Because of the classes in theology and psychology and especially the psychotherapy and the profound encounter with my colleagues, this course became a great revelation of God and of man. I discovered myself, my human reality, and my colleagues. [participant, 1969]

· This course was the best present I received on the occasion of my 25th anniversary as a priest, which I celebrated this year. I can only regret not having had this opportunity earlier in my life. . . . I found solutions to problems that had afflicted me since my youth. [participant, 1969]

I think that psychotherapy is extremely useful for priests and candidates to the priesthood, but for those who train the clergy I think it is necessary. [participant, 1967]

I came to the course defeated and lost, in the pits. I was able to get out and discover myself as a person. I believe this course to be the grace of my life. Finding myself and seeing fourteen other colleagues also finding themselves, I saw the most extraordinary ties of love and friendship established that I have ever experienced. [participant, 1969]

For me Christus Sacerdos is so extensive a course that it is difficult to reduce it to terms or expressions. It is a course in which you speak, but especially in which you feel, study, and even more especially, in which you live. It was the most beautiful, the richest, the most authentic year of my entire life. It was the year in which I found myself again as a man. I am 41 years old, but to tell the truth, I feel as if I were only one. I believe that I now know myself better and therefore accept myself more. . . . The analysts, "these silently good men," who speak from a distance without shouting, who open the way without knocking down doors, who sweep through the mind without smashing the person—they made me another person. Among many other things, analysis taught me never to condemn anybody, but to accept all as they are. This was the year of my greatest experience of God. [participant, 1969]

One thing appears clear to me: the value of emotional life. I saw that many conflicts were situated not outside, but inside of me. This helped me to grow. [participant, 1969]

The ideal would be if all the priests of Brazil could take part in this course. [participant, 1967][124]

Years later priests recalled the achievement of emotional tranquility. In the opinion of Father Antônio Juarez de Moura Maia, for instance, all of the participants "put their lives in order."[125] Like him, many discovered how to live celibately without psychological disturbance. Fathers Isidro Sallet, Lauro Palú, and Arlindo Nadai each reaffirmed his option for celibacy with the help of the course.

The crisp testimonies did not impart the anguish and environment of confrontation encountered by at least some of the priests as they struggled to grow beyond their old selves and recognize the paradoxical situations in which they had been living. Many of the problems revolved around sexuality, repression, and celibacy.

Father Maia expressed great personal difficulty with these issues. The rector of the seminary in Manaus, Maia received orders from his bishop to enroll in Christus Sacerdos in 1968. The bishop wanted Maia to renew his priestly commitment and to improve the seminary. Maia felt like a failure and saw no reason for celibacy. He lived the "dubious life" of a minister who watched pornographic films and knew that other priests made love to women without ecclesiastical censure. Maia could act motivated only by the fear generated by the repressive framework of the Church. Strangely, he saw himself as "perfect" in relation to the laity. These many contradictions brought Maia to the verge of leaving the priesthood.[126]

After completing Christus Sacerdos, Maia resettled in Porto Alegre in order to continue his treatment under Dr. Wolffenbüttel. During the analysis Maia achieved self-discovery and transformed his personality—but not before going through a kind of psychological stations of the cross. Maia resisted the efforts of his analyst. At times they argued, and Maia once purposely slept through an entire session. On other occasions Maia cried, and he had bouts of diarrhea, headaches, and insomnia. At one point, thinking his life was destroyed, Maia considered suicide. "I did not want to discover the rotten things inside of me," he recalled. Deeply shaken but now aware of himself, with time Maia built up self-confidence and made a new commitment to his vocation based not on fear, but on personal choice. He learned to improve himself as a minister and to assume fully and comfortably his vow of celibacy. Because of psychoanalysis, Maia believed, he became one of the most beloved priests in the diocese of Porto Alegre.

Other priests experienced similar struggles, suffering, and personal revelations. Some fought with each other. The fathers discussed their relationship of subordination to bishops and religious superiors. As one participant put it, the intense questioning of the self and of the institution led the men to "collective suffering." Most had difficulties with sexuality and experienced "an explosion of sex."

These and other concerns surfaced as priests engaged in free association, told their dreams, and recounted their lives in group therapy. They spoke of problems with parents and school. Some admitted to being homosexuals, although adding that they were celibate. Others remembered that they had been abused as children. Celibacy, of course, came up for debate. Many asked: why not make love? What would it mean for a priest to make love? A few began to court women.[127]

Some rejected celibacy as a personal choice and later left the ministry. Such was the case of Jesuit Father Luiz Osvaldo Leite. A promising career in training seminarians awaited Father Leite. Yet he suffered internal conflict over his vow of chastity. Géza, his former spiritual advisor, suggested in 1967 that he enter analysis. The following year Leite enrolled in Christus Sacerdos. During group therapy sessions the fathers split into camps for and against obligatory celibacy. Leite joined the latter, and the course ultimately helped him to resolve his internal conflict. When he requested laicization from Dom Vicente Scherer in 1970, the archbishop was shocked and wanted to know if Leite had a lover. The Jesuit replied that he did not. After eight years as a priest Leite took off his collar. Shortly thereafter he met and married a woman who had recently left the sisterhood. The couple later had two children.[128]

The psychoanalysts of Christus Sacerdos clearly saw an unconscious element at work among the clergy: their dependence on the Church as a mother figure. According to Dr. Wolffenbüttel, he and the other analysts observed this psychological constellation in almost all of the men. The "common denominator" was a family background in which the mother was predominant and the father only secondary. In the analysts' opinion the priests had experienced the inversion of the traditional patriarchal Brazilian family. These men had great difficulties in identifying with any kind of masculine figure. Many men and women who entered the Church had failed to mature, as if they led their lives still tied to their mothers' apron strings. The many debates and personal agonies over celibacy merely substituted for recognition of the larger problem: those who embraced celibacy did so not out of dedication to a true vocation, but to avoid acting out their roles as men. Priests could wish and dream of being with women, but they were not permitted the right to marry, to start families, and to assume their virility. The only woman with whom they could truly have a relationship was the Church—the great mother that continued caring for them.[129]

The religious vocation was a refuge for people who had difficulties in human relationships and who needed protective isolation. They could dedicate themselves to God, to the sick, to prayer. It was as if they had joined together vocation and the need to sublimate emotional difficulties. This combination, however, often left religious personnel unsatisfied with life. Simply clinging to the vocation was no longer enough in the modern world. Psychoanalysis was needed to unveil the underlying motivations of the vocation to permit the priest to make conscious, healthy choices.

Wolffenbüttel and the other analysts did not mean to say that *all* priests automatically fit this description. There were psychologically healthy men and women who truly saw the religious life as their vocation and were valuable to the community as its spiritual ministers. But Wolffenbüttel could not deny the evidence. During Christus Sacerdos and afterwards, when seminarians from Cristo Rei and other clerics sought his help, he witnessed much mental anguish.[130]

Christus Sacerdos furnished a response to this collective psychological torment, which, as the seminaries so amply demonstrated, was reinforced by the institution's repression of the sexual impulse and by its overemphasis on discipline and obedience at the expense of personal development.

The End of Christus Sacerdos

Military repression and concern about seemingly uncontrollable ecclesial experimentation turned broad institutional support for the course's wide-ranging program of clerical renewal into the kind of skittishness typical of the pre–Vatican II years.

In mid-1970 Dom Ivo called a meeting of the analysts. As Dr. Wolffenbüttel recalled, Dom Ivo very politely hinted that psychoanalysis was causing priests to abandon their ministry. He suggested that the course stick to theory and not therapy.[131] Dom Ivo was clearly carrying a message from his conservative superior, Dom Vicente Scherer, who had become a cardinal in 1969. Dom Ivo had encouraged and then tried to salvage the seminarians' movement, and now he was trying to save Christus Sacerdos in a more moderate form. He embodied the quandary in which progressive bishops found themselves: hoping to introduce innovation while maintaining respect for hierarchy and tradition. Among themselves the members of the Caruso Circle expressed discord with Dom Ivo's proposal. They believed that the priests had made substantial progress in analysis.[132] But after its final session of 1970, Dom Vicente—who had originally backed Christus Sacerdos—abruptly shut down the course. Disgusted with the

Church's "obtuse" decision, Dr. Wolffenbüttel concluded that the issue was psychoanalysis.[133] The reaction against Christus Sacerdos once again illustrated how the Church pulled the levers of discipline to control or eliminate innovations that threatened the structures of power in the institution.

Prima facie Dom Ivo's fears were justified. Priests were indeed quitting after reconsidering celibacy during Christus Sacerdos. Others did not return to their dioceses and stayed on in Porto Alegre to complete their analysis. But the root causes were not Christus Sacerdos or psychoanalysis. As in the case of Cuernavaca, the number of post-course laicizations matched the general rate of exodus. In some instances Christus Sacerdos actually strengthened vocational loyalty. For those who left, the program simply helped clarify preexisting doubts. Decisions had to be made. Christus Sacerdos made them clearer and easier.[134]

Bishops who were alarmed at the revelation of priests' emotional troubles failed to grasp that the aim of analysis was to expose old problems and not to create new ones.[135] Few bishops, in fact, actually visited Christus Sacerdos. They learned about the course by word of mouth or perhaps from the official CNBB reports, which were favorable but nevertheless secondhand evidence. When Dom Afonso Niehues, the CNBB bishop in charge of the seminaries, inspected Christus Sacerdos in late 1970, he issued a positive report.[136] More episcopal visits might have drawn a clearer picture of the benefits of psychoanalysis.

Other novelties disturbed traditionalists. The presence of a Protestant analyst hit like a bombshell. So did the inclusion of some nuns in the course.[137] Priests from the northeast returned to their dioceses with radical new ideas about seminary education and, as a result, clashed with their bishops.[138] The bishops' anxieties increased with the appointment of the deceased Géza's successor, the unorthodox Jesuit Father Oscar Mueller.[139] The bishops unfavorable to Christus Sacerdos waged a "cold war" propaganda campaign against it within the hierarchy and pressed for cancellation.[140]

The course's brush with military repression highlighted the tense climate in which it operated and could only worsen its reputation among conservatives. In November 1969 the police arrested Monsignor Carvalheira after the assassination of Carlos Marighella, Brazil's top anti-regime guerrilla commander. In one of the decisive moments of the Church-state crisis, the police attempted to link Carvalheira and Dom Hélder to Marighella through the Dominican Frei Betto. Betto used the Colégio Cristo Rei, the course's headquarters, as a hideout while helping political refugees and revolutionaries such as Joaquim Câmara Ferreira, Marighella's second-in-command, cross the border into Uruguay. In the hunt for Frei Betto the police arrested eight Jesuits.[141] In addition, some conservatives were upset that Belgian Father José Comblin, a major liberation theologian, lectured at Christus Sacerdos.[142] In 1972 the military government expelled Comblin from Brazil.

Christus Sacerdos's very success was another cause of its downfall. The publicity about its effectiveness led some bishops to misinterpret its purpose or employ it improperly. Instead of sending seminary teachers for a refresher course, they began referring psychologically shaky priests for treatment. Although the Jesuits tried to screen the applicants, the selection became "precarious." It was difficult to know exactly what kind of men the bishops were sending, and, once the problematic priests arrived, the Jesuits had no choice but to accept them.[143] Without Géza's expertise this practice changed the nature of the course. Bishops concerned about the detour complained to the CNBB. During the CNBB assembly in May 1970 the bishops voted for the reorganization of Christus Sacerdos. With new guidelines the coordinators pledged to put the course back on track.[144]

But Cardinal Scherer and the archconservatives prevailed. Dom Vicente's modus operandi was to eliminate Church activities that irritated the regime. He had already closed JUC and *O Seminário*. He showed little sympathy for Frei Betto and the other clerics arrested in his bailiwick.[145] The explosive mixture of allegedly terrorist priests with those who spilled out their feelings on the analyst's couch threatened to blow discipline to bits.

Furthermore, Christus Sacerdos provided a psychological "adjustment which the bishops did not want." The priests who had achieved a new maturity and emotional equilibrium through psychoanalysis "annoyed" their superiors.[146] Emotional security ended psychological dependence, which the hierarchy and its disciplinary regime had thrived on.

Former Ministers and the Clínica Social de Psicanálise

Outside the Church former ministers carried on with psychology and psychoanalysis and established substantial lay clienteles. A sampling of Brazilian laicized priests demonstrated that 1.7 percent went into psychology.[147] This figure translated into a total of more than fifty men. The figure is apparently small—but not for a profession that was in its infancy in the 1960s and early 1970s. For instance, in 1974, the first year of the new Federal Psychology Council, only 895 individuals registered.[148] Furthermore, the intellectual background, social contacts, and pastoral experience of laicized priests provided them with a unique position in the field. Former ministers who entered the profession included Jesuits such as Aloysio Arnoldo Koehler, Milton Paulo de Lacerda, Luiz Osvaldo Leite, Olegário Godoy, Ivan Correia, Jacques Laberge, and Fernando Calsavara. Other priests-turned-analysts were two Dutchmen, Teodoro van Kolk and Ricardo Rozestraten, and Zacarias Carbone, Bernardo Klimsa, Zeferino Rocha, Jorge Ponciano Ribeiro, and Geraldino Alves Ferreira Netto, the older brother of Father João Batista Ferreira, the defiant Lazarista who spoke at the March of the 100,000. Zeferino had been an advisor to the Brazilian bishops at Vatican II. Another inactive priest, Luiz Viegas, had begun analysis at the suggestion of Father Malomar. As a psychoanalyst Viegas reserved two hours per day for priests and sisters who needed therapy. His patients raised such issues as homosexuality, pedophilia and other sexual deviances, and alcoholism.[149]

An ex-Lazarista, Geraldino Alves Ferreira Netto quit the ministry because of deep disappointment with the Church's inflexibility toward sexuality as expressed in *Humanae Vitae*. In the 1970s he studied psychology and became a psychoanalyst. Geraldino underwent psychoanalysis twice. As was typical for a laicized priest, the vocation was a central theme of his analysis. He struggled with feelings of failure, guilt, and treason resulting from the notion of the priesthood as permanent in a man's life. Geraldino was intrigued by the relationship between Freud and Pfister, the analyst-pastor. Geraldino saw a natural bridge between religion and psychoanalytic cure, although the former focused on guilt and traditionally viewed desire as sinful whereas the latter simply sought to help the analysand redirect desire. Geraldino taught for sixteen years in São Paulo at the Instituto Metodista de Ensino Superior (the Methodist Institute for Higher Education) and also chaired its psychology department. He became one of the first analysts to embrace the theory of Lacan in the São Paulo-Campinas region, helping to co-found the (ironically named) Centro de Estudos Freudianos. Joining Geraldino in this enterprise were ex-Franciscan friar Durval Chechinato and the ex-Jesuit Laberge. Other one-time ministers in the São Paulo-Campinas circuit included the ex-Dominican Antônio Rezende and the former Jesuit Miguel de la Puente. In contrast with his brother João, Geraldino became an atheist. Today his religion is psychoanalysis.[150]

Clergy, laity, and former ministers often looked to yet another pioneer, Hélio Pellegrino, as a fundamental reference throughout the psychoanalytic boom. A psychoanalyst and newspaper columnist, Pellegrino became one of the leading intellectual opponents of the military regime. He protested along-

FIGURE 10. Geraldino Alves
Ferreira Netto. Courtesy
Geraldino Alves Ferreira Netto.

side students in the March of the 100,000, was part of the commission that met
with President Costa e Silva, and spent time in jail for his political activities. He
joined other prominent intellectuals and professionals in founding a prayer
group that reflected on the relationship between mysticism and politics. Pellegrino assisted the persecuted, analyzing, for example, Fernando de Brito, one
of the Dominican friars imprisoned and tortured in the plot to assassinate
Marighella. A devout Catholic who believed fervently in the notion of resur-
rection, Pellegrino insisted on the connection between religion and psychoanalysis and embraced liberation theology.[151]

   Pellegrino shepherded Father João Batista Ferreira into psychoanalysis.
Other Lazaristas from the Colégio São Vicente soon followed Father João into
analysis: Father Almeida, Father Marçal Versiani, Father Jorge Soares, Father
Paulo Márcio Grossi, and Father Luciano Castello. Father José Olegário, a diocesan priest from the Mariana seminary and a São Vicente teacher, followed
suit. Castello became an analyst; Grossi and Olegário became psychologists;
and Marçal studied psychology and wrote newspaper articles on the subject.

   Father João's career revealed an especially remarkable combination of religious reflection, social activism, and continuity of pastoral practice. Like most
former ministers, João maintained his faith. Priests and nuns were among his
regular clients. Through his psychoanalytic practice he assisted the politically

persecuted and their relatives. One of his patients, a young militant traumatized for having accidentally killed an innocent person during a guerrilla action, paid in cash and never revealed her name.[152]

In 1972 João, his analyst, Kattrin Kemper, Pellegrino, and other analysts founded a clinic that combined psychoanalysis and liberation theology. It received the name "Clínica Social de Psicanálise." Inspired by Freud's call for clinical outreach to the masses, it harked back to the psychoanalytic center started in Berlin right after World War I. Kemper had worked there. In Brazil the founders acted in protest against the military regime. They aimed to offer therapy to the poor and victims of military repression. The psychoanalysts donated their services. After the first newspaper report about the Clínica more than seven hundred people sought help. Rio had far too few psychoanalysts to meet such demand. But the clinic would become an experimental laboratory for alternative approaches, especially group therapy, which could satisfy the large demand. Kemper designed play groups for children. Psychotics received individual treatment.[153] The Clínica's outlook was primarily Freudian but also borrowed from other theoreticians.

The trademark of the Clínica became its so-called Psychodynamic Encounters, a form of group analysis in which a panel of analysts would discuss psychological and familial dilemmas with large groups of people, usually those unable to afford traditional psychological services. The groups searched for solutions without imposition on the part of the analysts. The experienced lasted until 1991. "Was it psychoanalysis that took place?" João later wrote. "Certainly not, but there was a dynamic created by psychoanalysts."[154]

Despite its populist approach, the Clínica Social attracted very few poor people.[155] Led by João and Pellegrino, a team of analysts decided to carry the Psychodynamic Encounters directly to the poor at the Morro dos Cabritos, a favela located two blocks from the Clínica Social in Rio's Copacabana district. The social barriers were enormous. The *favelados* placed material needs first and were unaccustomed to seeking help with personal and psychological problems related to child-rearing, domestic violence, and sexual abuse. More often than not *favelados* appealed to magic or popular religion to solve existential and familial problems. The analysts, however, were able to convince the local health post to offer care to individuals with psychological difficulties. Some received therapy in the Clínica. A group formed to promote discussion of such fundamental issues as prenatal care and parent-child communication. The analysts worked to bring psychological awareness to the *favelados,* insisting that they were as capable of thoughtfulness as any other human. The Rio

FIGURE 11. Kattrin Kemper. Courtesy João Batista Ferreira.

daily *Jornal do Brasil* described the Clínica as "the first psychoanalytic institution in Brazil to admit therapeutic contact with favelados. For many this is a utopian task. The analysts know that the difficulties are great, but they are convinced that they should not turn their backs on any human."[156]

João later assessed the attempt to synthesize liberation theology and psychoanalysis. The Clínica sought to construct a uniquely Brazilian version of psychoanalysis that served local needs and developed theory based on the social and historical context. Psychoanalysis could have a place among the poor, he stated, as long as the analyst tried "to enter into the linguistic world of that stratum of the population that has no access to the academic world." Psychoanalysis had to be used "as a way of listening, as a way of speaking, as a place of interpretation in the sense of decoding enigmas instead of symptoms."[157] João wrote: "The work of the Comunidades de Base and the research of Paulo Freire on liberating education taught us a great deal. It was necessary to study, to converse with community leaders so that together a way could be found through psychoanalysis to make possible this project in the favela, a project that brought together such unequal worlds."[158] One analyst from the Clínica believed that he and his colleagues had become "arrogant" in assuming the poor wanted psychoanalysis. It also became clear that while helping the poor, psychoanalysis could do little to change their sociological reality.[159] Unsympathetic critics satirized the project. "A poor person should have his intestinal feces [*fezes intestinais*] analyzed, not his libidinal phases [*fases libidinais*]" was one typical commentary. The Clínica Social had upset the comfortable world of the Carioca psychoanalytic elite and spurred debate about the apolitical, socially averse nature of psychoanalytic institutions in Brazil. It thus maintained independence from institutions such as the International Psychoanalytic Association and Brazilian associations. But the Clínica also received prestigious support. During a trip to Brazil Michel Foucault visited the Clínica and urged Kattrin Kemper to carry on. Naum Manella, the owner of the DeMillus lingerie company and a passionate supporter of psychoanalysis, paid the Clínica's rent and other basic costs.[160]

Another prominent experiment in liberation psychology took place through the university course in clinical psychology at the Instituto Sedes Sapientiae in São Paulo. Organized by the nun Mother Cristina (Célia Sodré Dória), the institute looked to liberation theology for inspiration and stressed involvement in grassroots political movements. During the worst years of the dictatorship, the Sedes Sapientiae succored political refugees. In 1975 the institute organized São Paulo's first alternative program in psychoanalysis, thus breaking a monopoly held by the Sociedade Brasileira de Psicanálise de São Paulo.[161]

Conclusion

The Brazilian clergy needed a coping mechanism for overcoming the psychological difficulties of the Tridentine regime and facing new challenges in
a Church seeking to enter the modern world. In the 1960s psychoanalysis exploded onto the ecclesiastical stage. Christus Sacerdos epitomized this trend.
"They wanted to canonize psychoanalysis," Dom Paulo Ponte, one of the course
participants, recalled of the method's more euphoric proponents.[162] In its early
years liberation theology said little if anything about sexuality, gender, and psychology. Domestic violence and the problems of women, for example, were seen
as irrelevant to the struggle for liberation.[163] Christus Sacerdos and other experiments represented an alternative path for the Church that included the attempt to combine the psychological with the theological and social aspects of
liberation. Although lacking the prestige and power of the European branches
of the Church, the Latin American Church—especially the Church in Brazil—
stood out for its courageous desire to transform the traditions of the Old World.
Rejected in Rome, Father Géza flourished in Brazil. If it had continued, Christus Sacerdos would have trained hundreds more priests. A psychological tidal
wave would have been unleashed.

Liberation psychology, however, threatened to replace hierarchy and discipline with individual freedom and a subjectivity of desire.[164] In enhancing
the affective, emotional life of the priest, psychological techniques worked
subtly, if not always to alter, at least to unmask the relations of power within
the Church. In the seminaries, therapy reinforced the trend toward ecclesial
decentralization. It abolished the traditional spiritual directors' and discipli-
narians' job of vigilance and allowed professional psychologists to take on the
task of evaluating seminarians and helping them to discern the values of their
vocation.[165] Similarly, an enlightened view of chastity introduced the value
of choice. Psychoanalysis liberated the individual from mental structures two
thousand years in the making. Independent thought could have eventually
brought pressure to change the Church's structures. Patriarchalism could have
given way to democracy and perhaps even the acceptance of homosexuality,
the ordination of married men, and gender equality. Observes Jochen Kemper: "In the last two millennia man has evolved psychically and culturally and
it is necessary that the Church keep up with that evolution, if it does not want
to lose man."[166]

For the bishops, Catholicism and psychoanalysis proved to be incompatible.
The reaction against Christus Sacerdos by Dom Vicente and other bishops

personified the observation made by Géza on the eve of the course's inauguration in late 1965: "The external behavior of a person is always the projection of his internal structure."[167] An existentialist-spiritualist dreamer and eternal optimist, Géza hoped to use the concept behind this observation to improve the Brazilian priesthood by repairing seminarians' personalities and unshackling their emotional energies. Reactionary discontent swept in quickly to overpower the post–Vatican II hiatus of experimentation. The hierarchy suppressed the course because it feared military repression and did not want to lose control over its priests. Christus Sacerdos thus suffered the same fate as the seminarians' movement, *O Seminário,* and other efforts to renew the Brazilian priesthood. Not since has the Church seen an experiment as broad and integrative as Christus Sacerdos. As Joel Birman has observed, after Vatican II religious discourse no longer repelled psychoanalysis but shared social space with it. But fundamental differences, even a latent hostility, persisted between religion and psychology.[168] The old tension between faith and science remained unresolved. Thus the institutional infrastructure for the diffusion of psychology has remained fragile.

But the cancellation of Christus Sacerdos was not the end of psychotherapy in the training of Brazilian priests. Several Carmelite fathers who had taken the course tried to revive the experience in Belo Horizonte. These men eventually left the ministry, married, and became professional analysts.[169] Since the 1960s hundreds—and perhaps thousands—of priests and seminarians have sought psychotherapeutic help.[170] By the 1980s psychological theory pervaded the discourse on clerical training and was seen in many quarters as indispensable.[171] Interest in psychoanalysis had emerged from the ecclesial grass roots.[172] New programs would crop up using many of the psychoanalytic pioneers' ideas. Even the traditionalists would eventually permit psychoanalysis, although only in a carefully controlled way and sometimes with the intention of disciplining the student.[173] At least some clerics in the 1980s and 1990s still believed that seminarians and their teachers needed to resolve internal conflicts before they could contribute to the Church's mission. They emphasized a holistic development in which the individual assumed discipline as a personal value in service to the community.

The former ministers who became psychologists contributed substantially to Brazil's analytic boom. In exploring psychoanalysis they enjoyed greater freedom than their clerical counterparts. Their ministry lived on in a more modern manner, exhibiting both Christian and Freudian frameworks for understanding human suffering and actions. Whereas Christus Sacerdos mainly dealt with ecclesiastical issues, João Batista Ferreira and the Clínica Social de Psicanálise created a fusion of liberation theology and psychology that transcended the Church. Like a CEB organizer, João took his ideas directly to the poor. Through the Clínica Social psychoanalysts infused tradition with a modernity reinvented in the context of Brazilian popular culture.

If liberation psychology appeared in Brazil, why did a Catholic preferential option for the neurotic not thrive alongside the Church's famed sociological option for the poor? As the case of Christus Sacerdos illustrated, institutional opposition was too strong for official adoption of such an option. In the estimation of João Batista Ferreira, psychotherapy still faced large prejudicial barriers in the Brazilian Church. Ultimately there was a philosophical and methodological impasse between psychoanalysis and religion. The former sought primarily to *listen* to patients, whereas the latter sought to *prescribe* the salvation of souls.[174] Nevertheless, although liberation psychology did not achieve the public notoriety of liberation theology, it slowly and quietly worked changes in the way priests were trained and in how the clergy viewed itself.

Experiments in psychology dealt with the needs of the heart. But they ultimately had ramifications that reached beyond the emotions to institutional concerns: training programs, relations with the hierarchy, and contact with the laity. To change men's minds and sexuality was to change the way they saw themselves and their place in the Church and society. But the hardening of the dictatorship in the late 1960s forced the Church to focus more exclusively on social and political issues. As liberation theology and base communities flourished, the cultivation of the self gave way to the politics of the "other," leading the Church to turn from "therapy to revolution."[175] The look inward ultimately yielded to an emphasis on the community, especially the poor, who represented the norm of Brazilian reality. The turn outward is the topic of the next chapter.

chapter seven

The *Pequenas Comunidades* and the Theological Institute of Recife

In 1967 one of Latin America's largest seminaries shut its doors after only two years in operation. Construction wasn't even finished at the new Regional Seminary of the Northeast, located in the Recife suburb of Camaragibe. For churchmen from three continents the stillborn project represented the last gasp of the century-long campaign to relieve the shortage of priests through large-scale, standardized training.[1] The crisis of the priesthood was deepening. Like the new wine that burst from old wineskins in Christ's aphorism, Camaragibe's first generation of seminarians abandoned the building. The students and their priest-professors broke into small groups and moved into the neighborhoods of Olinda, the traditional sister city of Recife. Soon other seminarians installed themselves in the poor sections of Recife and in the countryside. They had embarked on the world's most radical experiment in seminary education.[2]

In their small groups, known as *pequenas comunidades,* the seminarians forged a new kind of religious life. They not only sought freedom from discipline but looked to create links with the community. While clerics in the more

Eurocentric southern regions of Brazil employed psychotherapy to improve the priesthood, the more Luso-Brazilian, traditional Church of the northeast focused on the question of poverty. Long before Latin America's bishops coined the phrase "preferential option for the poor," these seminarians sought to empathize with the common man and woman. For the academic program, students commuted daily to a new and innovative school, the Instituto de Teologia do Recife (ITER, the Theological Institute of Recife). ITER complemented the opening to the world with an emphasis on the importance of the laity and a curriculum strong in the social sciences and liberation theology.

This chapter traces the history of the *pequenas comunidades* and ITER. It analyzes their internal life, programs, and conflicts as molded by the milieu of the Brazilian northeast. In the archdiocese of Olinda and Recife the seminarians' movement produced concrete results in the form of experiments inspired by Catholic Action, Vatican II, and Brazil's sociopolitical context. The Recife experiments illustrate the fundamental issues faced by seminarians and clerics in the post–Vatican II era. I evaluate the endeavor's strengths and weaknesses, including the cultural, political, and institutional barriers to achieving the movement's ideals.

The Recife experiments epitomized the decentralization of authority taking place throughout the Catholic world. The Brazilian Church had started loosening its hierarchical structure with Catholic Action in the 1950s. Vatican-inspired standardization in seminary education gave way to the design of programs at the national and even the local level. Seminarians' desire to live in small communities further atomized the Church. The genesis of the *pequenas comunidades* illustrated the tensions between, on the one hand, tradition, spirituality, and the authority of Rome and, on the other, innovation, social activism, and nationalistic self-affirmation.

The *comunidades* as well as ITER became the subject of intense controversy between Brazil and Rome. From the start the experiments faced a relentless opposition that ended in their termination by Vatican decree in 1989. Thus the neoconservative reaction that swept over the Church in Brazil in the 1980s had its origins in such tensions and cannot be attributed solely to the election of Pope John Paul II. The dispute over the implementation of liberation theology in Recife strikingly resembled Father Vieira's colonial-era faith in the native laity and the Roman reaction against it. The events of the 1980s were not new but a culmination of the conflict between traditionalists and innovators that predated Vatican II.

Pernambuco: From Social Laboratory to Military Repression

The cradle of slavocracy and sugar monoculture, the northeast is Brazil's most impoverished region. In colonial times sugar barons established their plantations in the *zona da mata,* the low-lying, fertile coastal region. By the mid-twentieth century the situation of laborers had improved little beyond that of the slaves. Sugar workers had once been allowed to cultivate subsistence plots on plantation land, but in the 1900s their situation progressively deteriorated as the industry mechanized and increased its demand for space. Uprooted workers became rural proletarians, or they migrated to the cities,[3] where, in the words of geographer Josué de Castro, the poor lived like crabs in the mud.[4] In the 1960s Brazilian and foreign observers of the northeast witnessed widespread debt peonage, malnutrition, child prostitution, and general poverty.[5] Clergymen propped up the oppressive social structure by favoring the *senhores* over the people.[6] In the 1970s and 1980s the power of the *usineiros* (sugar barons) and *senhores* grew as the military government stimulated the manufacture of cars run on alcohol produced from sugar cane. In their pastoral work seminarians bore witness to the exploitation and harsh conditions. When a seminarian and I visited plantations near Igaraçu in the *zona da mata* in 1987, families still lived in homes made of *pau-a-pique* (wattle and daub), carried buckets to gather water at common spigots, and cooked meals over wood fires. We slept under mosquito nets to avoid being bitten by the *barbeiro,* the insect that transmits the incurable, potentially fatal Chagas's disease, which afflicts millions of people in Latin America.

Further inland lies the *agreste,* a cooler, higher, densely populated transitional zone between the coast and the interior. In the 1960s the *agreste* of Pernambuco was home to subsistence farmers who served as reserve labor for the cutting season in the *zona da mata.* The coastal area and the *agreste* tended to form a single economic block. Seventy percent of the state's land, however, is the *sertão,* the arid backlands.[7]

The frequent droughts of the northeastern sertão have generated human and political problems for the national government since the late nineteenth century. In the drought of 1877–1879 half a million people died in the state of Ceará, which borders on Pernambuco. Corruption and pork-barreling rendered relief efforts largely ineffective. In 1958 bad economic conditions and yet another severe drought distressed the region. Urged by the bishops, the populist-developmentalist government of President Juscelino Kubitschek established the Superintendência do Desenvolvimento do Nordeste (SUDENE, Superintendency for the Development of the Northeast) to coordinate drought assistance and to promote the industrialization of the area, particularly Recife. The initiative enjoyed only limited success.[8]

Politico-religious conflicts have convulsed the northeast since the end of the colonial period. In the nineteenth century revolutionary priests graduated from the seminary of Olinda, the "school of heroes" whose rationalist approach foreshadowed innovation in priestly training in the twentieth century. As Zildo Rocha recalls, in the 1940s students at Olinda, the predecessor of the Camaragibe seminary, still sang the hymns that "impregnated us with the historic responsibility of belonging to that 'crib of warriors,' 'glory of priestly training.'"[9] Millenarianism found able exponents in Antônio Conselheiro and Father Cícero. After World War II exploitation and underdevelopment made the northeast a cauldron of radical politics. Communists organized rural unions, and in 1955 Francisco Julião, a lawyer and politician from Recife, launched the Ligas Camponesas (Peasant Leagues) to help beleaguered sharecroppers defend themselves against large landowners. The Ligas quickly spread across the northeast and to other regions of Brazil. The organization of rural unions increased as the government relaxed its long-standing opposition to them. The Church was not to be left behind. Exploiting its paternalistic relationship with rural dwellers, in 1960 the Church formed its first *sindicato* (peasant union). The clergy initially controlled the Catholic *sindicatos,* but Catholic Action and MEB activists soon joined in to radicalize the peasants.[10]

Pernambuco became the vanguard of leftist political mobilization. In 1962 the voters elected as governor the radical nationalist Miguel Arraes, the former mayor of Recife. Arraes defended peasants and rural workers against the *usineiros* and supported literacy programs. "At this moment Pernambuco is the largest social laboratory and the largest producer of ideas in Brazil. It is the most democratic state in the federation," wrote author Antônio Callado in 1964. Recife, Dom Hélder declared a few years later, "is one of the capitals of the Third World."[11] Under him the Archdiocese of Olinda and Recife established a wide variety of progressive pastoral programs.

The United States feared that the northeast would explode into a larger version of the Cuban Revolution. As a result, it became a required stop for U.S. policymakers. President John F. Kennedy's brother Edward, Peace Corps head Sargent Shriver, former Democratic presidential candidate Adlai Stevenson, and future conservative foreign-policy czar Henry Kissinger all visited the region. Devised to combat Marxism, President Kennedy's Alliance for Progress made assistance to the northeast a priority. In 1962 the U.S. government allocated tens of millions of dollars in aid to the northeast to be administered by SUDENE in conjunction with a large staff from the United States Agency for International Development. Frictions developed, however, because of the political nature of the North American mission and its members' cultural ineptitude.[12] In 1964 the U.S.-supported military coup ousted leftist leaders such as Arraes and SUDENE head Celso Furtado. Recife bore the brunt of military persecution of leftists and Catholic activists.

The Regional Seminary of the Northeast: Early Innovations

Under pressure from the anti-Communist leadership in Rome, in 1960 the bishops of the northeast conceived a regional seminary. Help came from the U.S. bishops, who offered funds for the construction of three large Latin American seminaries. Camaragibe was chosen as one of these sites. Its official name was Seminário Regional do Nordeste (SERENE).[13] It opened in 1965.

Until Camaragibe was ready, the students of SERENE continued at the seminary of Olinda. Although a Tridentine seminary, the Olinda SERENE became embroiled in the campaign for innovation. Catholic Action assistants such as Father Luis Gonzaga Sena and Father Almerry Bezerra had significant influence on the students. Bezerra had encouraged JUC's anti-capitalist radicalization. The coup of 1964 forced Sena and Bezerra into exile.[14] Father Marcelo Carvalheira, another ACB assistant, was rector of SERENE throughout most of the 1960s. JOC founder Father Cardijn and the worker-priest Jacques Loew visited SERENE, as did Father Ivan Illich.[15] As student chronicles revealed, ACB led to a new view of religion as action for change. The students edited their own JOC newspaper and helped direct the organization in Recife. Community life became notably less rigid. The students adopted the see-judge-act method and formed small task forces to organize spiritual life, sports, culture, pastoral work, finances, and relations with the laity. They elected group coordinators to act as representatives before the SERENE administration.[16]

The Olinda SERENE opened up to the world. In 1963 two students spent a month living in a poor neighborhood, where they taught children catechism and sat in on Afro-Brazilian religious services.[17] Students could read newspapers, watch television and movies, go shopping, and even visit the beach. In 1960 it was shocking for students to visit a school only two hundred yards from the seminary; in 1965 they found it quite natural to participate in a "night of bossa nova." Unlike the aridly pious notations of previous generations, the SERENE chronicles made reference to key political events: the Bay of Pigs, the resignation of President Quadros, the assassination of President Kennedy, and the 1964 coup.[18] The military takeover had a profound impact on the life of SERENE. During the first year of the regime the police entered the seminary in search of about a dozen political refugees protected by Father Carvalheira. Two later became revolutionaries and were killed.[19]

Other novelties exposed students to key political and intellectual trends. Important local figures gave talks and classes at SERENE. A personal friend of Carvalheira and a convert to Catholicism, for example, introduced the students to the grassroots theater movement. The seminarians subsequently formed their own theatrical and musical groups. Academic instruction included courses on Marxism, existentialism, cinema, demographic theory, Teilhard de Chardin, and the literacy method of Paulo Freire. Seminarians established links to the UNE and the MEB.[20] They also started practical pastoral training. In 1965 seminarians started spending entire weekends in the field.[21]

Change grated against traditional discipline. The professors began to worry that enthusiasm for modernization could lead students to abandon religious values, and they feared that pastoral activities might become a pretext for avoiding the responsibilities of community life. The teachers noted that the students began to act less formally. They refused to wear cassocks and religious symbols and deemphasized such time-honored regulations as the rule of silence and the need for permission to leave the seminary. Some important visitors were scandalized. Denunciations and anonymous letters criticizing the seminary began to reach the papal nuncio. In 1962 he made a special request for a visitator to review the situation. The visitator recommended that the generally innovative staff be fired. The archbishop of Olinda and Recife, Dom Carlos Coelho, refused to accept the report, and a second visitator, Father Ivo Lorscheiter of Viamão, gave a favorable assessment in 1963.[22] (Olinda, in fact, would inspire further innovation at the indomitable Viamão.[23]) The political struggle over SERENE had begun.

Camaragibe: From Pharaoh to the People

In mid-1965 SERENE moved to Camaragibe. The "Pharaonic project," as rector Zildo Barbosa Rocha described it, was five stories high, 408 meters long, and shaped in the form of a large S for "seminary." Its projected thirty thousand square meters of space could house some five hundred people. The Canadian bishops had joined the Americans in funding the construction, but faults in the project led to cost overruns that burdened the archdiocese of Olinda and Recife with a debt of at least 300,000 German marks. Nevertheless, the Vatican and the American bishops anxiously wanted to see the new structure put to good use.[24] Rome rushed the Brazilians to inaugurate it as soon as possible.[25] The ribbon-cutting ceremony on May 2 was a classical clerical event. Most of the bishops from the northeast attended, for their students would live and study in the new school. The most prominent dignitaries were Dom Hélder, the new archbishop of Olinda and Recife; General Antônio Carlos da Silva Muricy, the commander of the Army's Seventh Military Region; Bishop Antonio Samoré, the president of the Pontifical Commission for Latin America; Archbishop Coleman F. Carroll, who was carrying out his own multi-million-dollar building program in Miami; and Joseph M. Fitzgerald, the president of the international Serra Club, the U.S.-based organization founded to stimulate clerical vocations.[26]

Dom Hélder delivered a politically charged inaugural address. A native of the northeast, he had assumed the direction of the Archdiocese of Olinda and Recife after a long tenure in Rio de Janeiro as Cardinal Câmara's auxiliary bishop, national leader of Catholic Action, and secretary general of the CNBB. Arriving in Recife only eleven days after the coup to replace the deceased Archbishop Coelho, Dom Hélder, already branded as a Communist by ultraconservatives, carefully positioned himself with respect to the new regime by declaring that he was "open to men of all creeds and ideologies." He gave refuge to the sister of the deposed Governor Arraes. The military responded by invading his quarters.[27] At Camaragibe Dom Hélder stressed that while the seminary met Roman criteria, it would be run in the best interests of Brazil. "The seminary opens in the heart of the Brazilian northeast and at a time when the decade of development is starting," he stated. Development, however, was "mutilated in its essence" and "sacrificed in its implications" because of official corruption, speculation, exploitation of the workers, poverty, and the "subtle modalities of neo-colonialism." Camaragibe was to "provide us with an idea of development in all of its broad human significance" and to give it a supernatural dimension. He called for social activism and the radicalization of clerical education. At Camaragibe seminarians would learn philosophy and theology "in light of the experience of the Third World," for example, the study of new paths to socialism and the use of the Bible and traditional Catholic teachings to interpret the dominance of the wealthy nations. The Church had to shield the laity and clergy who had come under attack from the military because of their defense of human rights. At the same time, the clergy had to "save" students and workers from the growing "fascination" with Marxism.[28] Not long after this speech graffiti appeared on Recife's walls with sayings such as "Viva D. Hélder e os comunistas!" (Long live Dom Hélder and the Communists!).[29]

As the SERENE staff prepared for the move to Camaragibe, the seminarians pushed for radical change. The social activists actually opposed leaving Olinda for distant Camaragibe. They also disagreed with the system of internal groups; they wanted to live among the people in *pequenas comunidades*.[30] Encouraged by young rectors such as Carvalheira and Rocha, the students demanded further changes in the educational program. In 1965 and 1966 they deepened their commitment to the secular student movement of Recife. Some enrolled in university night courses and returned to Camaragibe with magazines, newspapers, manifestos, and other documents subsequently copied and distributed by a team of seminarians known as "Protest." The seminarians combed these sources for ideas about a new model of the priesthood. In 1966 Camaragibe had 135 seminarians from thirty-three dioceses across Brazil. Fifty-two were active in the student movement. In September these seminarians marched through the streets with university students to demand that the military respect human rights and release jailed students. Two seminarians were arrested, and a third was beaten. The staff considered the experience to be a "very positive" deepening of the seminarians' commitment to the priestly mission.[31]

Camaragibe delved into other experiments. In May 1966, for example, two psychologists started counseling seminarians. The same month four seminarians in their final year decided to live in a favela, where they bought a shack with money donated by Dom Hélder. Father René Guerre, a professor of pastoral studies, joined them. By day they worked in factories to support themselves, and evenings, Saturdays, and Sundays they took classes under Father José Comblin, a controversial Belgian theologian. Later, groups of younger seminarians did two-week pastoral internships in other poor areas of Recife. In 1967 incoming students were required to participate in a ten-week orientation. During the first month they studied the geography and culture of the *zona da mata* and developed research techniques for understanding the lives of the people. Then the students lived with families in towns in the interior, where they gathered information on the mobility of the populace, housing, educational and cultural facilities, sanitary conditions, the economy, and social, political, and religious

FIGURE 12. Dom Hélder Câmara.
Courtesy Centro de Documentação
Hélder Câmara.

behavior. The students wrote reports and discussed the anthropological implications of their experience and ways of perfecting their research techniques. Contact with women led to debate about celibacy.[32] These examples diverged sharply from the Tridentine regime. Nevertheless, the seminarians maintained a strong spiritual life.[33]

While Brazilian priests played a big role in innovation, a nucleus of European fathers took up the cause of the Recife poor and oversaw the birth of ITER and the *pequenas comunidades.* Guerre directed the orientation for new students in 1967. He was a personal friend of Father Cardijn, and as a worker-priest he had ministered to French coal miners. For thirteen years he was also the national clerical advisor to the French JOC. He came to Camaragibe in 1965 at the invitation of Dom Hélder.[34] Guerre became one of the strongest proponents of the *pequenas comunidades.*[35] The group also included Father Comblin, Father José Servat, a French worker-priest, and Father Eduardo Hoornaert, a Belgian cleric who became a leading historian of Brazilian Catholicism and proponent of liberation theology. All of these men would live with seminarians in *pequenas comunidades*.

The climate of reform made Camaragibe untenable. In a letter to the bishops of the northeast, vice-rector Rocha noted that *Optatum Totius*, the Brazilian bishops, and seminary rectors all recognized the possibility of geographically separate *pequenas comunidades*. A meeting of Latin American rectors in Lima in September 1966 explicitly advocated communities based on the culture of Catholic Action.[36] A year later a leading Brazilian bishop, Dom Avelar Brandão Vilela, affirmed at the synod of bishops in Rome that *pequenas comunidades* were emerging in his country.[37]

The seminarians jumped at the chance to fulfill their goals. In 1967 four teams totaling eighteen seminarians left Camaragibe with the permission of their bishops to live among the people in Recife and João Pessoa, the capital of the neighboring state of Paraíba. In addition to seeking contact with the world, the students hoped to build a greater sense of community through mutual support and the sharing of responsibilities. "This makes us human," the seminarians wrote of the experience. Five of the students went to work in *trabalhos populares* (common people's jobs), while the others taught school. "Salaries shared in common guarantee our subsistence." The seminarians aimed to build a "spirituality of engagement" in which "fundamentally spiritual life should embody everything in our human situation, the center of the Christian perspective." A questionnaire of Camaragibe's students revealed that an overwhelming majority favored the *pequenas comunidades*. Increasing numbers of seminarians, priests, and bishops across Brazil shared this view. After confirming the availability of resources and personnel, the bishops and priests in charge of Camaragibe endorsed the move to the *pequenas comunidades*.[38]

The desire for a new model was not the only reason for the quick approval. The growing crisis of the priesthood jolted the superiors into experimentation. In 1967 nearly a hundred men left the ministry in Brazil, and hundreds more would do so in the coming years. At Camaragibe twenty-nine students dropped out—an ominous portent of the difficult years ahead for SERENE recruitment. The reduction in enrollment, down to ninety-eight from the high of 135,[39] obliged bishops and seminary directors to find new ways to keep young men interested in the priesthood. Greater independence and the opportunity to live among the poor were popular measures with the students. Thus while ideals such as social justice underlay innovation, so did the practical concern of keeping the priesthood alive. As Father Comblin later recalled, the threat of abandonment was "a permanent blackmail of the students" demanding changes in seminary life.[40]

Dispute and Dialogue with Rome

The decision to abandon Camaragibe alarmed the Vatican. Despite Vatican II, Rome clung instinctually to the notion of a centralized seminary. It opposed *pequenas comunidades*. In difficult negotiations the clergy of Recife had to coax Vatican officials into permitting the new system on merely an experimental basis. The tentative status would haunt SERENE and ITER throughout their existence. The seeds of neoconservative reaction in Recife were planted early.

The initial dispute over the *pequenas comunidades*, however, differed sharply from the complaints about SERENE in the early 1960s and the late 1980s, when apostolic visitors were sent in. In 1967 and 1968 the Vatican was willing to dialogue. Of course, dialogue was a central demand of militant seminarians and clergymen. In Recife it began with a series of letters between Cardinal Gabriel-Marie Garrone, the prefect of the Vatican's Congregation for Seminary Education, and Dom Hélder. Their correspondence and subsequent events provide a microcosm of the struggle to transform the priesthood.

Like the rest of the Church, Dom Garrone felt deep uncertainty. Having dealt with worker-priests while a bishop in France, he favored the modernization of ecclesiastical training, but within the Tridentine mold. Dom Garrone believed that priests were different from the laity because of their training in a community with its own internal unity. Any experiment that threatened this unity must be stopped. The central problem was to discover which experiments contributed to *aggiornamento* without endangering the essential, unique characteristics of the Catholic pastor. Caution at the top had to counterbalance radicalization in the ranks. Dom Garrone used his power to allow experimentation in careful doses.

Dom Garrone thus vacillated on the question of *pequenas comunidades*. Like most bishops, he was a good politician. He demonstrated flexibility on the issue when meeting personally with bishops and seminary rectors in Latin America. But back among the leadership in Rome he took a harder line.

In 1966 Dom Garrone traveled to Latin America. He was clear about the need for change and the necessary cooperation of the priests and bishops. "To say that the seminaries must continue as they were is to go against the Council,"

Dom Garrone told Brazilian bishops and rectors gathered in Rio de Janeiro. His Vatican congregation did "not have the responsibility of entering into details, to enter into the life of the seminaries." The duty of the Roman department was only to lay down basic principles. Experimentation, the cardinal observed, was diverse and "inevitable." He singled out Brazil, continental in size, as a country in which no single policy could serve for all seminaries. He left open the question of the communities.[41] Less than a year later, however, Dom Garrone wrote a letter from Rome to a Chilean cardinal expressing his concerns about the dangers of *pequenas comunidades,* for example, the tendency of seminarians to become independent from authority and to resemble the laity too much. Published in the *REB,* the letter concluded that *pequenas comunidades* eliminated part of the essence of "that which the Church calls a seminary." During a 1970 meeting with seminary professors in Caracas, Dom Garrone again softened his position. He advised extreme caution with the communities and recommended against their official adoption by national bishops' conferences. But he also stated that the idea could not be excluded a priori. However, the institution of the seminary had to be preserved, he concluded. In yet another statement, made in Rome, Dom Garrone reversed himself. Seeming to lose patience, he referred to some experiments as "rash" and "reckless."[42]

In the midst of these oscillations Recife started its *pequenas comunidades.* Dom Garrone learned of the plans to abandon Camaragibe from newspaper reports. He wrote to Dom Hélder on December 13, 1967, and included a copy of his forthcoming letter in the *REB.* The cardinal admired the Brazilian for his discreet but highly influential role in moving Vatican II in a liberal direction. However, during his 1966 visit to Rio de Janeiro he became worried about the "radical character" of the seminary reform proposed by the SERENE directors. Dom Garrone and Dom Hélder had also met at the 1967 synod of bishops in Rome, which had been called to discuss the rewriting of norms for seminary education according to Vatican II.[43] The reasons for change were just, Dom Garrone conceded in his letter, but the SERENE superiors risked compromising their goals because they were "simplistic in their audacity."

I am profoundly convinced, Excellency, of the value of the ideas that are at the root of these measures: concern with a personal education and a real education, free of a framework that is narrow-minded and excessively collective. But it appears to me that the measures redound, in fact, to the suppression of the secular instrument that the Church has constructed [the seminary]. It is a return to the period before Trent. And all of the slowly accumulated experience is reduced to nothing. In addition, the problem of conciliating manual labor and studies appears to me to be a chimera. . . . It is impossible to regard as a seminary a system in which the action of the rector is reduced to nothing, in which the community of educators no longer exists, in which the students no longer have the experience of the priestly environment, in which the troubles and fatigue of material labor inevitably compromise true culture, whose requirements the Church has clearly indicated.

By modernizing the seminary, Dom Garrone seemed to be saying, the Brazilians would be taking their Church back to a premodern condition. Stating that he did not want "to become an accomplice to a tragic imprudence," Dom Garrone asked Dom Hélder to reexamine the decision taken in Recife.[44]

Dom Hélder replied on Christmas Eve, December 24. He was diplomatic, but he staunchly defended the *comunidades*. "We would be incapable of acting against a decision or even a simple appeal by Rome," he wrote. Dom Hélder reminded the cardinal that the CNBB had approved the establishment of communities. He responded to Dom Garrone's specific concerns by showing that the experiment was not haphazard but a structured program with many group activities. Dom Hélder affirmed that manual labor would eliminate "the impression of a parasite" that the populace had of the clergy. Each community, he continued, was to have its own priest supervisor, and the seminary would still have a central headquarters where all congregated regularly. The students were to study with the best professors in a new institute, the future ITER, to be set up at the local Catholic university. Countering Dom Garrone's concern that the cultural level of the seminarians would plummet, Dom Hélder affirmed that an open educational system would help students appreciate a Brazil in which two-thirds of the populace were poor, superstitious, ignorant, and fatalist. The new system would also help seminarians adjust better to celibacy. The new program, Dom Hélder concluded, would help the Church discover a new model of the priesthood. His comments echoed the seminarians' movement: "There is a growing multitude of youths who are fighting to discover a new kind of priest, one who is more in touch with real life; who participates in the struggle to liberate man in all his facets; who is freer of 'environment' or 'caste' (sometimes the environment is too *cultivated*); who is more conscious of the human, psychological, and social implications of his consecration to God in the priestly ministry."[45]

Dom Garrone sent another missive on January 9, 1968, in which he again tried to persuade the archbishop to prohibit the *pequenas comunidades*. He carefully couched his words in a spirit of dialogue: he asked that his arguments be considered but left the decision in the hands of the bishops. The cardinal admitted that from a distance it was difficult to discern how much the establishment of the communities would harm the existence of the seminary. He subtly offered an alternative by drawing distinctions between the Recife model and less radical innovations.

In and of itself, the idea of a single educational center around which living centers are distributed undoubtedly causes no reservations. This system already exists in various areas because of the necessity to regroup and select professors. But the living centers constituted around the educational centers are true seminaries, which is not the case when a single seminary is habitually dispersed except during classes and some meetings.

I undoubtedly recognize that the education of a priest cannot be identical from one country to another and that the situation in Latin America is entirely special. But whatever the form of education, it requires time and conditions that cannot be reduced under the present circumstances. Suffice it to say that today essential ideas such as that of the priesthood are threatened. Suffice it to say that the repercussion of ideas such as those of Mons. Illich [who foresaw the end of the clergy] have almost no opposition. If it is necessary to prepare our future priests to know those whom they are going to evangelize and with whom they are going to live, it is also necessary to place them . . . alongside well-prepared witnesses.

Restating his wish to work in "close collaboration" with the Brazilian bishops, Dom Garrone also reminded Dom Hélder that profound transformations in the seminaries could not be made "irreversible."[46] The issue of the Recife experiments involved far more than a personal exchange of letters between two prominent bishops. The *pequenas comunidades* reflected the growing tendency to decentralize the Church on all levels. The controversy was at once a dialogue and a tug of war between a local Church of the periphery and the central power in Rome. On one side stood the Church of the Brazilian northeast, in the throes of political spasm but proudly asserting its regional identity within Brazil vis-à-vis the dominant south and emerging as a leader in the cause for Third World development. With a strong tradition of popular religiosity and opposition to the imposition of European forms of belief and practice, the northeastern Church was once again defending its own interpretation of Catholicism. Clerical nationalism was alive and well. On the other side stood the Vatican, accustomed to intervening in the affairs of the clergy in order to preserve the universality of the faith. The Second Vatican Council had pledged to dialogue and to allow for the adaptation of clerical training according to national needs and circumstances. In practice, however, the logic of tradition and power made the ideals of dialogue and greater local autonomy difficult to implement. In fact, Garrone's position contradicted the liberalizing tendencies of *Optatum Totius,* whereas in 1970 and again in 1984 the CNBB would further legitimize the *pequenas comunidades* by ratifying *OT* and issuing national directives for the seminaries.[47]

The rest of the region's bishops joined in the debate. Dom Hélder revealed the content of Garrone's first letter during a meeting in late 1967 of twelve of the twenty-one bishops of the region, the Northeast II Regional subdivision of the CNBB. The churchmen decided to hold a special plenary session on January 17, 1968, to resolve the disagreement with the Vatican. Most important, they also "felt the necessity of a broader dialogue with Rome." Father Rocha, Camaragibe's vice-rector, communicated this decision to all of the Northeast II bishops. He noted that as the situation stood, the seminarians would have to remain in Camaragibe. "I sincerely fear the repercussion that such news might have among our students," Rocha wrote, adding that the bishops should consider the seminarians' opinions.[48]

The only way to break the impasse was to negotiate. In Father Rocha's words, Dom Garrone had conceded that a "brusque and violent" reversal of the experiment already underway would be "psychologically disastrous for the life of the seminary." Yet the cardinal persisted in cautioning the Brazilians against going too far with innovations. He boldly decided to send Monsignor Fernando Pavanello as his personal representative to the January 17 meeting. Pavanello was the rector of the new Seminary of Our Lady of Guadalupe, established in Verona, Italy, to train diocesan missionaries for Latin America. This maneuver accommodated the Brazilians' wish for greater dialogue, but it also gave the cardinal leverage at the meeting.[49]

A group of seminarians made their own effort to influence events. On the eve of the meeting they presented a letter to the bishops warning of "undesirable consequences" if the *pequenas comunidades* were suppressed.[50] The seminarians no doubt had quitting in mind. They declared: "Given the crisis of the clergy and of those who are considering the priesthood, would it not make sense for the bishops to venture forth with full support for an experiment that has already been judged [in the seminarians' opinion] to be valid? We are facing a very serious problem in the Church. The entire organization is affected. Innumerable vocations are in danger."[51] The seminarians assured the prelates that their desire for a new kind of seminary was rooted in the goal of becoming priests who could meet the new challenges facing the Church.[52]

Monsignor Pavanello arrived in Recife prepared to defend Dom Garrone's position but also to work out a compromise. He carried with him another letter from the cardinal to Dom Hélder that reiterated the French prelate's reservations. "Our exchange of correspondence disturbs me," Dom Garrone wrote. However, once again Dom Garrone admitted that his lack of personal observation made it difficult to understand the situation in Recife. It was, he stated, "impossible . . . to give either an order or even a true piece of advice."[53]

The climate on January 17 was tense. The bishops, Pavanello, and the seminary's superiors met at 8 AM and did not finish until 10 PM. First Pavanello gave a long exposition summarizing Dom Garrone's position mainly as the cardinal had expressed it in his letters to Dom Hélder. As an example of the dangers of *inserção* (insertion) in *pequenas comunidades*, he cited Dom Garrone's observations about the worker-priests: "At a certain point to be a priest—even to exercise priestly functions—was felt to be *an obstacle*, an impediment to *inserção*. Thus many profound misunderstandings and crises had to be confronted."[54] The sixteen bishops present then debated three key issues raised repeatedly by Dom Garrone and Pavanello: how to set up the *acompanhamento*, or supervision, of the seminarians by priests; how to balance work with full-time studies; and how to preserve the specificities of priestly training while seminarians lived among the people. Two general positions emerged. One proposed the return to Camaragibe, while the other advocated locating the communities throughout greater Recife. Unhappy with the first possibility, the rectors considered resigning. Finally, the bishops arrived at a compromise: the *pequenas comunidades* would be approved, but restricted to Olinda, where they would remain close to the main seminary building. The bishops voted fourteen to two in favor of this solution.[55]

All parties involved saw their concerns at least partially addressed. The seminarians would live in *pequenas comunidades,* but in a setup somewhat suggestive of the alternative model proposed by Dom Garrone to Dom Hélder. As the rectors themselves recognized, however, this "unique experience," while "accepted" by Rome, was not "approved" on a permanent basis.[56] In fact, Cardinal Garrone wrote Dom Hélder verifying the experimental status of the *pequenas comunidades*. He stated emphatically that the Recife program could not serve as an example for other seminaries.[57] The Church bureaucracy could easily hamper the new system.

Terror and the "Long Night" of Chaos

Pernambuco was the scene of the greatest post-coup violence in 1964. Stories on torture did not appear in its newspapers, however. By contrast, in the southeast (Rio de Janeiro and São Paulo) the press covered the situation in Recife. In the words of one journalist, the city was a "shroud of silence and suspicion." Headless bodies of peasant leaders turned up on the road from Recife to João Pessoa, and others were burned in furnaces.[58]

The repression against the Church in Recife was among the worst in the country. It radicalized both priests and students. Whereas Dom Hélder himself had once enjoyed harmonious relations with the country's rulers, the new generation of clergymen rejected the state and its interests. Dom Hélder went before the authorities to seek the release of political prisoners and torture victims. He himself became the target of hard-line officers. In 1966 the local commander's verbal attacks on the internationally known archbishop created a political crisis for the government of General Castello Branco, who resolved the problem by promoting the officer to another post.[59] Anita Paes Barreto, the state secretary of education under Governor Arraes, a member of the Movement for Popular Culture, and a psychology instructor at SERENE, was arrested a week after the coup and held for seventeen days.[60] The repression also netted seminarians and priests. In 1969 ITER rector Father Marcelo Carvalheira was jailed and interrogated in Porto Alegre during Christus Sacerdos as part of the security forces' attempt to link Dom Hélder to leftist guerrillas. Afterwards he returned to Recife with the "mark of fire," making him a hero in the eyes of the seminarians.[61]

The same year the repressive forces shocked Recife by torturing and murdering Father Antônio Henrique Pereira Neto, a SERENE graduate ordained in 1965. He was the first priest to lose his life to the dictatorship. Orchestrated to intimidate Dom Hélder, the killing was attributed to the Comando de Caça aos Comunistas (the Communist Hunting Command), a right-wing vigilante group including members of the Tradition, Family, and Property organization embraced by Dom Sigaud, the anti-Communist archbishop of Diamantina and a strident critic of Dom Hélder.[62]

Father Henrique's death horrified the *pequenas comunidades*. Many seminarians had worked with him in a youth program. Father Henrique and a number of seminarians had maintained contact with members of a student group, including ex-JUCistas and Communists, that continued to meet clandestinely after proscription by the military. After the killing, police intimidated seminarians by searching their quarters. Seminarians helped organize Father Henrique's funeral service. The procession to the cemetery attracted several thousand people. The police twice interrupted the twelve-kilometer march, and two men were arrested.[63] Father Henrique's murder and numerous other incidents of repression left seminarians with a sense of persecution, even impending martyrdom.[64]

In 1970 Church-military tensions increased after Dom Hélder publicly denounced torture in Brazil during a speech in Paris.[65] The dictatorship responded by banning mention of Dom Hélder by the media. In 1972 Father Comblin, a key assistant to Dom Hélder, was barred from reentering Brazil. ITER's coordinator of theological studies, in 1968 Comblin had made national headlines when a document he had authored for the CELAM meeting at Medellín was branded as subversive. Seminarians distributed the text to students and in the doorways of movie houses. Now Comblin was accused of employing *conscientização* (consciousness-raising) and associating with Dom Antônio Fragoso, the radical bishop of the diocese of Crateús, Ceará. Comblin's expulsion robbed the Brazilian Church of one of its most critical minds.[66] In the 1970s the government also attempted to link the "rebellious clergy" of the northeast to armed revolutionaries.[67] Tensions with the regime continued into the 1980s.

Meanwhile the clerical crisis sent the seminary population plummeting. The seminarians had proposed reforms in pastoral practice, the theology of the ministry, ecclesiastical training, and celibacy. But the bishops' lukewarm response turned the yearning for activism into deep pessimism about the future.[68] By mandate SERENE absorbed students from a large number of dioceses. Yet the student body decreased from 135 students in 1966 to just twenty in 1974, surpassing one hundred again only in 1985.[69] Ordinations peaked at fourteen in 1966 but averaged only three per year in the 1970s.[70] As the 1970s progressed, SERENE II and ITER took in students who had no experience with Catholic Action or other grassroots ecclesial movements. They lacked knowledge of the previous generation's struggle to leave Camaragibe.[71]

The effort to democratize the archdiocese of Olinda and Recife further blurred clerical identity and mission. Although much of the archdiocese remained conservative,[72] Dom Hélder spurred decentralization in many quarters of the institution. This included diversification of the lay ministry. The archdiocese sponsored radio-transmitted Bible studies, an increase in catechism and leadership programs, assemblies and other structures that stimulated lay participation, and the formation of CEBs and a variety of grassroots movements. The preferential option for the poor and the defense of human rights undergirded this process.[73] In this model the priest lost importance vis-à-vis the laity.

Father Rocha's decision to quit the ministry showed how demoralizing the crisis could be. A well-connected Pio Brasileiro graduate, Rocha took up important posts in the archdiocese and the seminary. In 1968 he became rector of SERENE II, as the seminary became known because of its location in the CNBB's Northeast II region. After Father Carvalheira's departure for Christus Sacerdos, Rocha also assumed the leadership of ITER. Rocha became a central figure in religious circles and Recife society. He maintained good relations with both traditional and progressive priests. Prominence and balance guaranteed him a promotion to bishop. Yet, like so many other men of the Tridentine era, Rocha experienced an explosion of sexuality after ordination. "You have deceived me, Lord, and I have been deceived. . . . It really is difficult to live by the spirit," Rocha wrote in his diary in 1963. That year he suffered profound humiliation when an adolescent orphan revealed to another priest that Rocha had caressed her and touched her breasts. "It was as if a building were collapsing over my person," Rocha wrote of his embarrassment.[74] As repressed feelings surfaced, Rocha questioned the disciplinary system. He favored the seminarians' movement. The attention of women complicated his ordeal. As one colleague recalled, religious women "adored" Rocha. Many of them remained single because of their zealous dedication to Catholic Action,[75] and they undoubtedly liked Rocha not only because he was tall and good-looking, but because his priestly status made him sacred and forbidden. In 1970, "after a period of maturation, prayer, and suffering," Rocha left the priesthood.[76] Shortly thereafter he married, and in 1972 he and his wife had their first of three children. As a layman Rocha later returned to ITER as one of its leading professors and remained there until it closed. Rocha's departure from the formal ministry shocked the clergy, the seminarians, and the public of Recife. As one group of seminarians wrote, it left the experiments in "suspense."[77] Discipline further disintegrated after his exodus.[78]

During the remainder of the 1970s ITER and SERENE II experienced a "prolonged night" of confusion, doubt, and constant shifts in programs.[79] SERENE II and ITER's few students sought even greater independence. With permission from the bishops they set up *pequenas comunidades* outside Olinda, thus violating the accord with the Vatican. Others completely abandoned the *comunidades* and became known as the "equipe da Diáspora." Meetings, study groups, and other activities at SERENE II headquarters in Olinda became irregular.[80] From September 1972 to February 1976 ITER staff did not even bother to record notes of their meetings. Students now received Holy Orders regularly without having completed their degrees. Professors and students constantly debated ITER's programs.[81]

By 1976 the situation at SERENE II had deteriorated so much that the bishops decided to close it. The seminarians' only obligation was to study at ITER. Left to themselves in the *pequenas comunidades* and without adequate finances or systematic supervision, in 1978 the diocesan students initiated their own program. The general state of disorganization lasted until the early 1980s, when ITER reorganized and SERENE II reopened under a new initiative of both the seminarians and the bishops.[82]

ITER and Life in the Pequenas Comunidades, 1968–1980

Amid the chaos students and professors struggled to create a new model of priestly formation. The experiment with *pequenas comunidades* began in earnest in 1968. To furnish academic instruction a group of SERENE II's teachers, bishops, the CRB, and, significantly, members of the laity opened ITER. Its founders included Hoornaert, Comblin, Guerre, and Father Reginaldo Veloso, a leading specialist on the liturgy and a composer of popular religious music.[83] These priests were involved in the communities. The history of ITER and the *pequenas comunidades* was intertwined.

Philosophical-theological institutes such as ITER sprung up wherever students had abandoned the Tridentine system. Institutes operated with varying degrees of success in Fortaleza, Curitiba, Belém, Rio de Janeiro, Belo Horizonte, São Paulo, Porto Alegre, Goiânia, and elsewhere.[84] This structure was not unique; seminarians in Germany, for example, had long experience in taking courses at universities. In Brazil some of the new institutes established links with universities. ITER stood out for its emphasis on interdisciplinary studies and the diversity of its student body, which included both diocesan and religious seminarians, members of the laity, and even Protestants.

Latin America's sociopolitical climate made the Brazilian institutes a crucial forum for debate over the dialectic between theory and practice, between theology and pastoral work. They provided the opportunity for participation in the secular student movement and work among the poor. In effect, they conceptualized and implemented liberation theology. Dom Hélder's inaugural address at ITER reiterated the need to "struggle for development." "The world marches towards socialism," he boldly affirmed, but not without criticizing Marxism for its "mistaken idea that religion annihilates man before God to the point where the death of God appears to be the inevitable price for man's liberation."[85]

At the start ITER experienced serious problems. Conflict arose over the program and lack of academic rigor among the students. From 1968 to 1970 the staff frequently debated course offerings, pedagogical method, and expectations about student performance. The Vatican had little if any input. A debilitating dropout rate and the absence of Tridentine rules meant that ITER students needed special incentives to study. Professors often complained about pupils' intellectual deficiencies, and in administrative meetings student representatives openly criticized the teachers. Both students and teachers arrived late for classes. The frictions resulted from ITER's experimental nature and seminarians' rebelliousness.[86] Difficulties and disputes continued into the early 1980s.

Nevertheless, ITER and other institutes helped the Church advance on a number of fronts. They built the long-sought unity among the clergy, with diocesan and regular seminarians studying together for the first time. By centralizing education the institutes sought to free up priests for pastoral work, although in ITER's case numerous commitments taxed the staff. Significantly, the clergy no longer dominated priestly formation. ITER's staff came to include members of the laity, nuns, a sociologist, and a laicized priest. By 1970 ITER already involved laypersons in new forms of ministry and pastoral work. People took correspondence courses, and roving teams of professors gave classes to adults "in traditional and non-traditional environments." Emphasis on the laity alleviated the crisis in vocations and helped ITER survive the turbulence of the 1970s. ITER developed new apostolic techniques, including the use of the social sciences. Eschewing rote, Eurocentric pedagogy, the institute elaborated a theology based on the culture of the northeast and popular forms of expression. The new theology meshed well with the archdiocese's pastoral priority of building grassroots communities.[87]

Students produced self-evaluations in a new pedagogy designed to stimulate intellectual growth and emotional maturity. Their accounts spoke of improvements over the Tridentine system, but they also revealed a number of unfulfilled expectations and difficulties.

One of the best yardsticks of performance was the ability to establish relationships with the people. The *pequenas comunidades* achieved varying degrees of success in this area. Some seminarians seemed to believe that the process occurred naturally. One equipe, for instance, sought simply to be "a sign" of the Christian faith in the community. They wrote: "Our house always had people from the neighborhood visiting, principally young people who saw in us the friendly support that they did not find in their parents, to the point where they even held parties in our house. Our table always had visitors. Our human relationships were very much emphasized." One seminarian described a similar informality: "In general, I did not try to make an explicit announcement of the faith, as is done in meetings or during services. I simply tried to be an inhabitant of the neighborhood, with no other worry than to reveal Christ through my friendship and happiness."[88]

Other seminarians gave less rosy accounts. Although they embraced the preferential option for the poor, they disabused themselves of what they perceived as the Messianic, perhaps naive belief that students could truly empathize with the poor. Fraternization with different social groups awakened seminarians to the great contrast between themselves and the poor. "We are not bearing witness to poverty. We have a standard of living superior to that which we had in the seminary," one group of seminarians wrote. Another group observed the following: "We try to live a situation of assimilation with the poor, but we have noted a large difference: the people live in constant risk, and we do not run any risk at all. We live in a situation of absolute security. We lack nothing. We are paid to study at the university and to stay at home studying, because the curriculum obliges us to dedicate ourselves to our books. After the books we spend whatever time is left in closer contact with the people. And then the questions come: 'You don't work? Ah! You earn money without having to work.' In short, we are rich because we do not run any material risk. Subsistence is guaranteed. Because of this we recognize that we are currently the most privileged students in Brazil." One student observed that a number of *pequenas comunidades* had female domestic servants—historical fixtures in middle- and upper-class Brazilian households. "My relationship with the servant (three have worked in this house this year) is barely better than the master-slave relationship," the student wrote. Yet another wrote: "We never paid attention to the fact

that the wages we paid the servant were absurdly low. . . . I am certain that we
are committing an injustice, and to continue in this way would be a sin and inconsistent with what we preach. People scream when an *usineiro* pays mi-
serly wages to *camponeses* [peasants], and we do the same thing with Dona
Júlia." Another group admitted that it had fallen into a "paternalistic" treatment of the people: "Many came frequently asking for loans. We seemed to
be 'banks,' or they would come to sell us something when they were in need
of money. . . . And we always helped. . . . We had to do a lot of thinking before
we finally found the right attitude, to avoid indifference while continuing as
friends." Another criticism stated that studies made seminarians "too intellectualized" and had to be reconciled with the need to be closer to the people.
"We are foreigners among the people," one report concluded. [89] The upshot
was that the *form* of seminary life had changed, but much of the social *content*
had not.[90]

Social commitment largely suffered because of the lack of time in the new
model.[91] Devotion to nonacademic activities certainly rose in comparison with
the pre–Vatican II period, but it fell short of the ideal envisioned by the seminarians' movement. Whereas the Tridentine system planned seminarians' lives
to the minute, in the Recife experiments books, jobs, neighbors, household organization, and travel to and from ITER all competed for the precious moments
of the day. As hoped, the need to juggle a number of adult responsibilities made
seminarians more mature. But it also restricted their pastoral and communitarian commitments. Lack of time contributed to inconsistent priestly supervision of seminarians. While some equipes had highly dedicated resident fathers, others complained of infrequent contact with superiors.[92] The dispersion
of the seminarians further reduced the staff's capabilities. And, as the staff focused increasingly on the people, they had less time for the ever less prestigious
function of training priests.

Insufficient time and supervision led to the neglect of spiritual life. The
seminarians' movement advocated an "engaged spirituality" based on *inserção*
in the community, political activism, and the teachings of Vatican II. In theory
the new spirituality built on the foundational elements of the faith such as the
Mass, the sacraments, group prayer, and reading the Bible. But the practice was
far different. "There is no community of prayer," one group of seminarians lamented. The loose structure of the *pequenas comunidades* was another cause.
"Our spiritual life has suffered greatly from the tensions in the group and from
personal tensions," one group stated. Another evaluation complained that seminarians had never received spiritual instruction from the perspective of the

people's milieu. "We continue to demand and teach a classical type of spirituality," it stated.[93]

Differences over spirituality and popular religion caused sharp cleavages at ITER and SERENE II. Priests from Recife had one of Brazil's strongest devotional traditions and knew well the beliefs and practices of the northeast. They had been less affected by Romanization than ecclesiastics taught by the Vincentians, for example.[94] In contrast, the worker-priests and other foreign clerics did not have the same feel for the region.[95] Another rift opened between a segment of Recife's urban-based priests and the seminarians from the *sertão* and *agreste*, where religious tradition was stronger. As one seminarian recalled, in 1973 and 1974 a "clash of mentalities" occurred between the teachings at ITER and what seminarians had learned in their dioceses, where conservative, paternalistic clerics emphasized the liturgy more than their urban counterparts.[96] Even the deeply spiritual Dom Hélder seemed to criticize religious tradition in his remarks on secularization during the inaugural address at ITER. "To the degree that development becomes firmed up in our areas, from them will disappear the naive Christianity of our people," he predicted. The "magical and fatalistic" religion of the people would become transfigured "into a personal and adult encounter with Christ."[97] These words sounded more like Romanization than liberation. Many of the urban priests at ITER wanted to purge popular religion of superstition and replace it with social and political commitment. Some of these priests wounded the feelings of the *interioranos* by demanding a "brusque change" of mind about religiosity. As one former student recalled, this "top-down" approach was "not what was expected" by the seminarians,[98] who wanted dialogue. Thus the historic struggle between the clergy of the coast and the backlands resurfaced as a battle between modern and traditional religiosity. Prejudice against popular religion was highly paradoxical in light of nationalistic defense of the *pequenas comunidades* and ITER's goal of producing a native theology.

In 1975 a dispute over the introduction of liberation theology into the ITER curriculum split the students again. Clerical nationalism and Vatican II's call for Church renewal led to the replacement of European theological bibliography with works by Latin American authors, including liberationists.[99] Men in the *comunidades* already practiced liberation theology. But its formal adoption as the official guideline of seminary education stirred passions. Thirty-three students, many of them new and unfamiliar with ITER's history, signed a document alleging that the director, Father Humberto Plummen, and other professors were turning the program into an institute focusing exclusively on the laity, political and pastoral activism, and the social sciences. They represented the majority.[100] A Dutch Redemptorist, Father Plummen had arrived in the northeast after ordination in 1954. During Vatican II he earned his master's degree in social sciences at Louvain University, a key center of Catholic intellectual ferment in the post–World War II era. A founder of ITER, Plummen took over in 1970 after Father Rocha's departure from the ministry. In his course on sociology and development Plummen lectured favorably on developmentalism and dependency theory. In a letter to the bishops of the CNBB's Northeast II division, the protesting students accused Plummen and other teachers of displaying Marxist tendencies and giving greater emphasis to *Das Kapital* than to the Bible. Two traditionalist priests also opposed Plummen. Sixteen other students countered with their own document in defense of ITER, Plummen, and liberation theology.[101] With ITER in turmoil, Plummen called a meeting of students, professors, and bishops. Liberation theology remained. But tensions smoldered,[102] and the incident harmed ITER's reputation among the bishops. In 1976 the bishops pressured Plummen to resign, in part to assuage the opponents of liberation theology. Similar struggles over liberation theology took place in other Brazilian seminaries.[103]

The vice-director, Sister Ivone Gebara, also left. A liberation theologian, Gebara came from the Dominican order's branch in São Paulo. She broke out of the traditional mold, which relegated nuns to seminaries' domestic chores, and achieved the astonishing feat of being a progressive nun in a key academic position. At ITER Gebara taught a course on the Eucharist. During the conflict over liberation theology she was accused of having made heretical statements. The bishops, who rarely visited ITER and depended on their seminarians for information, did not accept the explanations made in her defense and discriminated against her because she was a woman.[104] Gebara went on to publish important works on feminist liberation theology.[105] In 1993 she gave a controversial interview in the prominent newsmagazine *Veja* defending the legalization of abortion. Her outspokenness led to a punitive silencing by the Vatican for two years—twice the punishment meted out to the famous theologian Leonardo Boff. A number of Brazil's leading bishops rallied to his defense, and he became an international cause célèbre. Only two expressed support for Gebara, whose case went ignored in the media, thus illustrating the enormous sexism still operative in the Church and the Brazilian news corp.[106]

Conflict churned over sexuality as seminarians came into contact with women. The newfound freedom of the equipes led students to vent their feelings and to act on them. Recalled Dom Marcelo Carvalheira, the former

SERENE rector: "People from outside, people who were very good and simple, would march into the homes. This reduced the time for study and ended up causing affairs. For seminary training this was cause for alarm. Some [seminarians] said that the opinion of the bishop was not important, as long as they were working towards liberation. If some were homosexual or had a freer heterosexual life, it was no problem."[107] "Contact with girls made us discover values in the area of affectivity, and at the same time it contributed towards a greater appreciation of celibacy," one seminarian wrote. Another student related the following experience: "At the end of April I began to date. . . . And early on I became aware of the incompatibility of this reality with my commitment. One of the two had to be reviewed. . . . I did so and left the girl. . . . The taboo that has enveloped these problems [for me] has disappeared or at least diminished."[108] During a meeting of two small communities the participants "put the cards on the table": they rejected the "farce" of interpreting cases of dating as isolated examples of faulty vocations; dating, in fact, was a "very common situation among the equipes." It was difficult, as one member of this group concluded, "to live a normal life without wishing for or having a dating experience."[109] One group of seminarians secretly maintained relationships with women in the hopes of establishing a new model for the priesthood that the Church might one day come to accept. They were befriended by a group of young women who developed enthusiasm for liberationist Catholicism and thought celibacy to be a ridiculous requirement for the priesthood. These women called themselves the "Comando de Caça ao Celibato" (CCC, or Anti-Celibacy Command), a play on the name of the right-wing organization that had assassinated Father Henrique. Some of these students were eventually expelled because of their romantic relationships and radical politics. Three ended up marrying women from the CCC. The superiors were especially worried about *forró*, a traditional northeastern dance in which seminarians mingled with women.[110] Desire for personal fulfillment, and not just the Church's mission, occupied the seminarians' minds. Celibacy still circumscribed their existence, making their encounters with women tentative. Despite the freedom to explore sexuality, their worldview still adhered to the Tridentine system's view of the woman as the other, the outsider, the potential danger.

Homosexuality became another issue. At ITER gay and lesbian students openly asserted their sexual orientation. Their aggressive behavior, the prejudice of others, and the Church's difficulty in dealing with sexuality led to intolerance and misunderstanding of sympathetic superiors' attempts to assist gay individuals in need of counseling.[111]

On yet another level, women had a far more pervasive impact on the Church of the northeast. Some sisters pioneered living in *pequenas comunidades* among the poor. This initiative was much bolder than the seminarians'; nuns had to overcome sexism and an existence even more cloistered than that of the Tridentine seminary.[112] Brazilian sisters perceived that they had a special role in pastoral work because of their "peculiar characteristics, especially the capacity for welcoming others, for listening, for being forthcoming, for intuition, for intimacy, for criticism."[113] Sisters' impressive venture out of the convents and into the lives of the people inspired seminarians and priests. Students, clerics, and even bishops such as the highly ascetic Dom Hélder held get-togethers with sisters to recharge themselves spiritually and to renew their sexuality.[114]

Sister Janis Jordan's experience in a Recife favela personified the new commitment of women religious to the poor. A U.S. citizen and member of the order of the Missionary Sisters of the Immaculate Conception, Jordan began her religious work in Houston, Texas, in the mid-1960s working in a hospital and among the poor black population, whose deep faith and poverty she later likened to the situation of the Brazilian poor. After earning a degree in theology, Jordan became involved in research on nuclear weapons. During these formative years she met and read the works of Latin American liberation theologians, who inspired her to go to Brazil to experience *inserção*. Her move into the favela named "Dancin' Days" exemplified both liberation theology's transnational influence and its reliance on foreign personnel. In the 1980s Jordan became an ITER professor and then coordinator of theological studies, bringing her life experience in the favela to bear in the classroom.[115]

In Dancin' Days Jordan immersed herself in a microcosm of Brazilian social, political, and religious reality. Named after a popular Brazilian soap opera, the favela was born in 1979, when a North American priest led a group of squatters to appropriate a patch of swampland belonging to the Brazilian Navy. With landfills and additional occupations over the years the population of the favela grew to as many as five thousand people. In a typical outcome the priest first lived with the people but then had to return to parish responsibilities. In 1981 Jordan moved in to minister to the people's religious needs. She discovered a community without streets, sewage, clean water, adequate housing, a school, or easy access across a small canal to the rest of the city. Jordan encountered youth gangs in Dancin' Days, as well as individuals who smoked marijuana or sniffed glue, the staple drug of poor Brazilian youngsters. Crowded conditions fostered violence among neighbors, and female prostitution was common because of the lack of economic opportunity. Jordan was at first besieged with requests for aid from a people accustomed to clientelistic politicians. The favela had no church, and the people knew little about Catholicism. Their religion consisted of a mixture of Catholicism, Candomblé, Pentecostal Protestantism, and ideas heard on television. Mary, the Mother of God, was the central religious figure, but Jesus was a stranger to these people. In any case, they wanted to have Mass, which a priest occasionally said using loudspeakers in the street in front of Jordan's residence, which she shared with a Brazilian sister.

Jordan believed that without the organization of Dancin' Days' Catholic community, people would simply convert to Protestantism. She hesitated to call her religious community a CEB because of the people's only nascent understanding of the faith. Nevertheless, the group clearly had many elements of a CEB. The size of the community was quite small in comparison to the overall population of Dancin' Days, with Mass drawing from sixty to seventy participants. Outside of Mass Jordan's influence went further. She taught the rudiments of the faith and trained catechism teachers. Doctrinal instruction was holistic, including, for instance, emphasis on hygiene, sex education, and popular medicine. Jordan organized youth and women's groups and baptismal, first communion, and marriage preparation courses. Significantly, three young women from Jordan's community studied introductory courses on the Bible in ITER's training program for lay ministers. In addition, with the sister's help the community organized to obtain a school and a bridge from local politicians. Their own fund-raising campaign stymied by Brazil's high inflation, Jordan and the group got a German Catholic agency to underwrite the building of a religious and community center.

Despite the presence of leaders such as Sister Gebara and Sister Jordan, gender and sexuality received little attention at ITER. Romanization had given the Brazilian Church a primarily male outlook. The *practice* of liberation theology cut against the grain because it was largely female. Yet it failed to transform the Church's gender relations. For all its progressivism, ITER focused almost exclusively on social class as an element of analysis. In the Brazilian context of the late 1970s and early 1980s liberation meant political redemocratization.[116]

The Seminarians of the Hoe

In their quest for contact with the people seminarians set up equipes and engaged in political action in the countryside. The search for popular religion's rural origins—"which we are constantly at risk of betraying," wrote one group—rejected the urban, rationalistic bias of ecclesiastical training.[117] In these rural spin-offs of the Recife experiments, seminarians demonstrated a greater sense of purpose and commitment than their counterparts in the capital.[118] They were a true success.

Responding to the CNBB's call for pastoral innovation, in 1965 Father Servat, a proponent of the Recife *pequenas comunidades,* organized Animação dos Cristãos no Meio Rural (ACR, or Inspiration for Rural Christians). Servat had abandoned his seminary in France during World War II because it had demanded loyalty to the Vichy government. He aided the French resistance effort, and after ordination in 1947 he served as a rural Catholic Action organizer. Servat came to Recife in 1964 as part of the levy of European priests called by John XXIII to serve in Latin America. A personal conversation with Dom Hélder at Vatican II provided further motivation.[119] ACR aimed to transform rural dwellers into "the organized people of God." *Camponeses,* lay activists, priests, and seminarians worked to bring the Christian message, *conscientização,* and technical and financial support to the countryside, including the sugar plantations and the communities of small-scale planters in the *agreste.* In 1967 ACR inaugurated *Um grito no Nordeste* (A Cry in the Northeast), a periodical on the movement and life in the interior. ACR sought to build respect for human rights and called attention to such problems as land conflicts and the accelerating migration to the cities. ACR strongly advocated agrarian reform, and some of its militants organized rural unions. Although it became the target of military surveillance and harassment, unlike many grassroots movements ACR survived the dictatorship, even holding periodic assemblies on problems in the countryside. ACR eventually spread throughout the northeast, Pará, and Minas Gerais, often at the initiative of seminarians. In 1982 ACR's national assembly, held in São Paulo, attracted fifty-five delegates from nineteen states. In the 1980s ACR helped inspire a new generation of seminarians to study the countryside and work with its inhabitants.[120]

ACR radicalized priests such as Father Arnaldo Liberato da Silva. The son of small-property owners, Liberato spent his first eighteen years in the fields of an isolated rural community in Alagoas. At age fifteen Liberato wanted to enter the seminary, but the local priest rejected him because he lacked a primary education. Over the next fourteen years Liberato tried to find a way into the priesthood. To survive he worked as a small shop owner and, following the northeasterner's time-honored route to opportunity, migrated to São Paulo, where he obtained basic education. During his odyssey Liberato crossed the path of

ACR, which led him to study the problems of the northeast's *camponeses*. Rediscovering his roots, Liberato joined ACR and worked alongside its activist seminarians. In 1978 he enrolled in ITER. He exemplified the so-called adult vocations, encouraged after Vatican II and viewed as a way to avoid the youth-distorting Tridentine regime. During his first year Liberato's bishop did not consider him a seminarian because the prelate opposed ITER's materialist outlook. The next year, however, the bishop assented. In 1981 Liberato joined the *pequena comunidade* at Morro da Conceição (Conception Hill, named for Our Lady of the Immaculate Conception), an impoverished Recife neighborhood whose parish was run by Father Reginaldo Veloso. In their residence the seminarians set off a room as a chapel for morning and evening prayers. They held weekly *revisão de vida* meetings with Father Servat, the priest responsible for the equipe. Although located in the city, the equipe spent weekends on the sugar plantations of the *zona da mata*. This pastoral work earned the Morro team a reputation as one of the most radical.[121]

In 1979 Liberato and the Morro equipe helped organize a small strike of sugar cane workers. As the generals allowed a return to democratic politics, Brazil's independent labor movement became stronger. Averting a spread of the strike, the *usineiros* agreed to grant the workers higher pay, two hectares of land to plant crops and raise animals, and free transportation. But then the *usineiros* reneged and paid only the raise. In 1980, forty-three unions representing 240,000 laborers struck anew for two days and won back the concessions, an additional wage hike, and sick pay. Once again the seminarians took part. Shortly after the strike about fifty cane planters, ranchers, and *usineiros* carrying Brazilian flags interrupted a special Mass for the strikers, sang the national anthem, and proceeded to use the flagstaffs to attack some of the fifty-two priests. Yet a third work stoppage occurred in 1982.[122]

Liberato and the Morro equipe mobilized the laborers by identifying issues and passing out pamphlets in the early morning hours. In one strike they obtained the support of the hierarchy. Dom Hélder and a number of priests published letters of solidarity in the press to counteract *usineiros'* propaganda. The students took workers to wealthy parishes to offer testimony about the situation. While the seminarians had Servat's support, their absences from ITER did not sit well with the staff. In 1983 Servat handed over the direction of ACR to Liberato, who was ordained in 1985.

The most remarkable rural experiment was the *teologia da enxada*, or "theology by the hoe." In 1969, on their own initiative, nine seminarians obtained permission from their bishops to live in Tacaimbó, Pernambuco, and Salgado de São Felix, Paraíba, small towns in the *agreste*. The students were all from the interior and had become acclimated to Recife during the first years of their education.[123] But they intended to return to rural pastoral work after ordination. Like their urban counterparts, they believed that the Recife experiments were too intellectual. They studied topics such as atheism and secularization, but learned little about the faithful. Moreover, the rural zone provided a safe haven from the heightening military repression. In 1967, for example, two men who later entered the *enxada* program were kicked out of their factory jobs when it became known that they were seminarians.[124]

The nine students lived among the people, tending crops in the morning, reading theology in the afternoon, and conducting pastoral activities in the evening. They spent much time conducting research in rural anthropology as a basis for discovering the people's religious needs and translating doctrine into understandable language. "Instead of dialoguing with the classic heretics of the history of theology—the traditional method—we thought it better to dialogue with popular religion. In the end, the most important thing is to make popular religion complete," wrote Father Comblin, who supervised the students along with Fathers Guerre and Servat.[125] The students recorded observations about the local inhabitants, from which they formulated questions and interpretations in the light of theology. In the first year they studied the land, the people, gender relations, and culture. In the second year they attempted to gauge the people's understanding of teachings about the life of Jesus, and in the third they did the same for the people's beliefs about life.[126] The seminarians took data on the lack of sanitary and medical facilities, the high rates of illiteracy, and the exploitation of labor in the production of the food staple manioc. They observed that landowners controlled politics and barred the people from contacts with the institutional Church, which was separated from the faithful by "a profound abyss." At the same time, folk religious beliefs were constantly present. Everything was attributed to a vengeful God. "By the majority of our interviewees Jesus is seen as a saint, the head of all the saints, the strongest saint. Placed in the sphere of the saints, Jesus loses completely his humanity," the students wrote.[127] The seminarians witnessed arguments between Catholics and Protestants, and they made note of pilgrims wishing to honor Father Cícero, who had been dead for nearly four decades. From their research the seminarians concluded that the social sciences should be part of the seminary curriculum. "We are not talking about becoming specialists, but about taking advantage of those human instruments that will facilitate evangelization," one equipe stated.[128]

Like their brothers in Recife the rural students had to overcome lack of time and the people's initial skepticism about seminarians deigning to live in their midst. The *teologia da enxada* equipes attempted to dissolve social barriers by joining the people in their own activities, for example, traditional religious feasts, soccer games, and Catholic Action meetings. One duo of seminarians took their main meal of the day in the homes of their neighbors. They also set up a CEB. "Before there were people here who did not even know the names of their neighbors," Servando Cardoso wrote of his involvement. "We had youths kept on the social fringe because of poverty, their color, or the moral status of their family. Today we perceive the beginnings of union, with the people taking small initiatives, such as the celebration of the birthday of one of the poorest of the little girls."[129]

In the mold of the worker-priests the rural seminarians chose physical work as the way to identify with the people and to overcome the fatalism of popular religion. "Until that moment seminarians or 'padres,' as we are known, had never been seen working in the field or in manual labor," wrote João de Almeida. Labor, wrote João Firmino, had two objectives: to produce for consumption and, more important, "to participate in the work of the people, above all learning the suffering and the anguish that they feel. To feel the weight of work as they feel it, the heat of the sun, the danger of the snake." Firmino continued: "In working we have optimal opportunities for dialogue with the *agricultores*. When the caterpillars devour everything, they always say that it is the will of God. In this situation we are much more able to convince them that it is not God that sends the caterpillars." Firmino believed that such contact was one of the best ways of showing the rural laborers "reality" and leading them "to the true God."

Whereas Firmino perhaps shared the presumptuousness of urban priests, João Batista offered a dose of honesty that resonated with the caveats of the more skeptical members of the Recife equipes:

I recognize that after one and a half years of work, I have still not been able to acculturate myself to the fields. That is, I still have not been able to assume work in the fields as something that is mine. One example of this is the fact that I still do not know how to distinguish among the diverse types of beans, or that I sometimes confuse a cotton plant with some other plant. This sometimes makes me fearful that I will never really be able to reach the people. But in spite of everything, I confess to an effort to become loyal to the fields, which I see much more as an act of

witness than as a job in itself. . . . I feel that little by little I am accepting
and integrating the fields into my life. But I also know that it is going to
take some time until I feel the need for them, for example, as I feel the
need to study, to read, or to be up to date with the most important hap-
penings in Brazil and the world (the group calls me "João the reporter").
There are days when it is tough to go to the fields, especially after arriving
from the big city, because it is at that time that I feel the weight of underdevelopment. But this never stopped me from going to the fields. At least
as far as I can remember. I think that this is a victory, isn't it? But I like to
water the plants. I find it to be simple work, but full of revelations. I do
not even feel the weight of the water can on my shoulders.

Despite this critical self-evaluation, João Batista did not escape a certain romanticism about the bucolic setting. The entire experiment resonated with
the revolutionary romanticism of the seminarians' movement and progressive
Catholicism.[130]

The *teologia da enxada* lasted only three years, cut short by the expulsion of
Father Comblin and by lack of support from other priests and seminarians. In
this short period it established itself as one of Brazil's most profound attempts
at reformulating ecclesiastical education. It was a classic example of the liberationist approach of intellectual reflection based on contact with the poor and
Catholic Action's see-judge-act method. It required as much practice as theory
and allowed for ample improvisation.[131] Of the nine seminarians who began
the experiment, seven stayed on until the end in 1971; five became priests, the
other two lay activists. In 1977 Comblin published the seminarians' reflections as
Teologia da enxada, and his four-volume theology treatise, written in the 1980s,
was also based on the experiment.[132] The experiment pointed out the need for
itinerant missionaries,[133] leading Comblin and one of the lay graduates to begin
a similar program in the 1980s at Serra Redonda, Paraíba.

The *teologia da enxada* served as a model for the formation of another radical experiment in liberation theology, the Departamento de Pesquisa e Assesso-
ria (DEPA, or Department of Research and Assistance). Functioning between
1976 and 1990, DEPA trained seminarians who resided in the communities
where they did pastoral work. In fact, pastoral experience was a requirement for
admission. Each student produced a monograph on the religious, political, social, cultural, and economic conditions of his or her area. The maldistribution
of ecclesial power was a frequent theme of discussion. Fourteen priests graduated from the program. DEPA particularly gave nuns access to theological stud-

ies. DEPA's staff included Father Plummen, Sister Gebara, and other key ITER professors. DEPA in turn helped lay the foundations for the important Centro Ecumênico de Estudos Bíblicos (Ecumenical Center for Biblical Studies), a national program for training leaders to assist grassroots communities in Bible studies.[134]

Stabilization and Growth

Although still plagued with numerous problems, in the 1980s ITER and especially SERENE II stabilized their programs, moderated certain innovations, and improved in a number of ways.

Progressivism formed the bedrock of the experiments, although many of its objectives faltered. With lay participation and decentralization dominating the ecclesial agenda, priestly training would have to mold fathers for *service* to the faithful, not tutelage. People in the archdiocese of Olinda and Recife held out hope for the adoption of such innovations as the ordination of lay persons "from a *simple background.*"[135] Yet the institution remained highly clerical. Priests and nuns mainly stimulated reorganization and grassroots experiments. In the words of SERENE II professor Gustavo do Passo Castro, "The Church is still not popular, but it is already by the side of the people . . . and walking with them at their own pace. . . . The Church is still not poor."[136]

The national upswing in vocations of the late 1970s and 1980s provided institutional reinforcement for ITER and SERENE II. A new generation unfamiliar with previous troubles became attracted to the priesthood. Students increasingly came from modest families of the interior, thus reinforcing the dichotomy between the rural and the urban, the traditional and the modern.[137] These seminarians sought a commitment to the poor, but also a career. In the 1980s ITER's philosophical studies earned university equivalency, thus furnishing graduates with greater job opportunities in nonecclesial settings.[138] The influx of new candidates prompted the bishops and the clergy to devote more attention to SERENE II and ITER.

The experiments benefited from the lessons of crisis and the willingness of the directors to synthesize the old and the new. Significantly, the bishops and the clergy restored some elements of traditional discipline, particularly for first-year students. They wanted to strengthen spiritual and academic life and to familiarize rural students with the city. New measures included grouping freshmen in a single building and placing second-year students in larger, more carefully controlled communities, thus making the later transfer to *pequenas comunidades* a less haphazard, more meaningful experience.[139] Other changes were utterly simple but profoundly meaningful, like the director locking SERENE II's door at night. Some older seminarians saw the changes as an attempt to reinstitute Tridentine controls.[140] Their suspicions were clearly justified, but it must be remembered that both ITER and SERENE II retained many of their original goals and structures.

One of ITER's most important innovations was to expand its training course for lay pastoral agents. In the 1980s a number of lay students took courses at ITER, and its special Saturday program for the laity annually enrolled as many as four hundred. The graduates were primarily religion teachers in the public school system and pastoral agents working in poor neighborhoods. They gave the Church a stronger presence in Recife's periphery.[141] The Saturday courses received official recognition from the state of Pernambuco.[142] In addition, ITER sponsored week-long mini-courses in which approximately one thousand people studied the option for the poor, the pedagogy of evangelization, ethics, and theological methodology. The great majority of the participants came from traditional parishes and at times displayed a certain resistance to the lay-based Vatican II model.[143] In other instances the presence of the laity caused hostility and insecurity among some seminarians.[144] ITER's emphasis on the laity represented a certain Protestantization of Catholicism. The idea of poor northeasterners studying theology was previously unthinkable.

ITER's faculty reflected a progressive, diverse, and ecumenical outlook. In 1989 it included a Baptist preacher, a Methodist pastor, seven women, and five laicized priests. Sisters Gebara and Jordan, the laicized Father Rocha, former director Plummen, and other priests and lay professors who had been involved in the experiments since the 1960s continued on the staff.

Father Ernanne Pinheiro anchored the progressive leadership. A diocesan priest who had studied under the Vincentians in the 1950s, Father Ernanne subsequently attended the Pio Brasileiro. Before ordination he spent a year laboring in a French factory with a group of worker-priests. Back in Brazil he was active in Catholic Action, and in the 1970s he served under Dom Hélder in the key post of archdiocesan pastoral coordinator. Starting as ITER director in 1981, he oversaw the school's transition to greater stability. Under Father Ernanne ITER became the northeast's leading center for seminarians, priests, and grassroots lay pastoral agents. Prominent liberation theologians such as Leonardo Boff and Gustavo Gutiérrez spoke to ITER students, and the institute started its own journal, *Perspectivas Teológico-Pastorais*.[145] In the 1980s many ITER and SERENE II seminarians became involved in social movements and the Partido dos Trabalhadores (PT, Workers' Party).[146] The PT, in fact, established a section at ITER.[147] Today a centrist party that rose to power with the election of Luiz Inácio Lula da Silva to the presidency in 2002, the PT of the 1980s was a socialist organization that had built a base of support among former revolutionaries, the vigorous union movement of São Paulo, students, intellectuals, federal bureaucrats, and the progressive wing of the Church, including CEBs and activists such as Frei Betto.

The Vatican Shutdown of the Experiments

In the 1980s post–Vatican II experimentalism and activism gave way to pre-Conciliar orthodoxy and spiritualism. This was the decade of the so-called neoconservative reaction in Latin American Catholicism. In the words of theologian João Batista Libânio, the Church underwent a "volta à grande disciplina," the return to the grand discipline.[148] Under the reign of the enigmatic Pope John Paul II (1978–2005), the Vatican and conservative bishops rolled back many innovations and restricted the clergy's political activities. This reaction had colossal significance.[149] A staunch anti-Marxist, John Paul II helped bring down the Soviet Empire and muted the progressive Church in Latin America.[150]

The Vatican restored discipline in the clerical ranks. Rome punished liberation theologians such as Brazil's celebrated Leonardo Boff, who was silenced by the Vatican for nearly one year in 1985 and 1986 and who ultimately asked for laicization in 1992. It reprimanded progressive bishops, intervened in religious orders, censored publications, and divided the Archdiocese of São Paulo, a progressive stronghold. Locally, bishops suspended activist priests. As one theologian observed, some of these actions sprang more from professional jealousy than from the fear of heresy: liberation theologians garnered more attention than their conservative colleagues.[151] At the fourth assembly of CELAM, held in Santo Domingo in 1992, the Vatican eliminated much of the progressive approach, including the see-judge-act method. In addition, John Paul II appointed more conservative bishops and curtailed the power of the nationalistic CNBB.[152]

Other factors undermined the Brazilian progressives. In the 1980s the return to democracy diminished the need for the Church as the "voice of the voiceless" and caused it to recede from overt political activity. The Church was not a political party and therefore encouraged other groups and movements—unions, political parties, and grassroots organizations—to take the lead, and they assumed much of the work that had been carried out by the Church under the military regime.[153] From moral opponent of the military regime the Church passed to a less aggressive role as moral watchdog of democratic society.[154] Whereas the Church was the glue that held together the left and other opposition groups before the return to civilian rule in 1985, afterward the PT became the glue.

The prestige of the Progressive Church deflated as the political context changed. The collapse of Communism and the retreat of the Latin American left[155] discouraged Catholic progressivism, and disillusionment set in when the Popular Church failed to bring about a deep social transformation.[156] The neo-conservative reaction and the end of the heroic struggle against the dictatorship reduced the enthusiasm and membership of grassroots movements.

As the comments of the seminarians and of Gustavo Castro revealed, the Church had difficulty in bringing itself as close to the people as the rhetoric of priests and seminarians in the 1960s had promised. The Church of the Poor did not attract most of the poor, and the CEBs did not fulfill the heady goals of progressive leaders, some of whom held elitist attitudes toward the poor. Though perhaps not as few as some people estimate, the CEBs included but a fraction of the population.[157] Moreover, their ideology tended to be exclusionary toward such groups as women experiencing domestic strife, youths, and Afro-Brazilians,[158] even though large numbers of the last group did participate.[159] In addition, CEBs came under tighter control by the clergy and were often torn asunder by internal strife produced by the democratic transition. As a result, they became less involved in politics and focused more on religious concerns.[160] They are no longer a major priority of the Church.

Finally, the rapid growth and political ascendancy of Pentecostal Protestant religions in the 1980s posed a threat to the Church's centuries-old politico-religious hegemony. Fed by massive migration, democratic freedom, the growth of the media, and the increasing complexity of an ever more urban society, Pentecostal growth fit into a larger trend of increasing social and religious pluralism. Like the CEBs, Pentecostalism offered a way for the poor to seek economic betterment, social dignity, and political participation, though in a conservative manner.[161] Protestants' share of the population grew from 4 percent in 1960 to approximately 13 percent in 1992.[162] According to the 2000 census, Protestants of all types numbered some twenty-six million, or 15.4 percent of the population.[163]

The Catholic Church responded to this challenge by strengthening its own spiritualistic movements, in particular the Catholic Charismatic Renewal, a "Pentecostalized" organization born in the United States in the 1960s and exported to Brazil in the 1970s. John Paul II strongly encouraged these movements, which stressed prayer and traditional spirituality, expressed loyalty to the pope, and enjoyed the support of many bishops.[164]

The neoconservative reaction had profound implications for priestly training. The Church sought to restore the symbolic power of the hierarchical priesthood and to reaffirm the immutability of Catholic values. In effect, it had initiated a new stage of Romanization.[165] Rome obliged seminaries to revert to a Tridentine-like model. The Vatican deemphasized anthropological, social, and political concerns and accented the study of philosophy and traditional spiritual practices such as prayer, silence, the imitation of Christ, obedience, penance, celibacy, and discipline. In 1980 Cardinal Garrone issued a letter promoting these values in seminary education. Whereas in the 1960s he went on the defensive in meeting demands for more humanistic training, he now positively reaffirmed the old values. Garrone based his argument on the documents of Vatican II but also on Trent.[166]

Recife quickly became suspect. As part of its strategy the Vatican resurrected the pre–Vatican II institution of seminary inspections. Brazil not surprisingly became one of the first countries to undergo inspection. In 1981 Recife, São Paulo, and other key Brazilian schools received visitators.[167] ITER and SERENE II underwent further inspection during a general visit of all of Brazil's diocesan seminaries in 1988 and 1989.[168] Later that year the Vatican brusquely ordered the closing of SERENE II and ITER. It was the most dramatic example of the suppression of seminary experiments in all of the Catholic world. Their demise furnishes an important case study of the neoconservative reaction and the return to discipline in both the local and the international contexts.

As illustrated above, ITER and SERENE II had never received Vatican approval. Nationalist activists and Rome-oriented spiritualists did not achieve consensus over the model of seminary training. After Dom Garrone's initial warnings in the 1960s, in 1976 the Vatican again warned that *pequenas comunidades* threatened the very notion of a seminary.[169] In the 1980s the conservatives finally prevailed. John Paul II alone did not cause the closing; he merely cast the decisive vote in a long power struggle.

Two key moments took place in the mid-1980s. In 1984 Dom Hélder turned seventy-five, the mandatory retirement age for bishops. In his place the Vatican nominated Dom José Cardoso Sobrinho, an archconservative originally from the nearby diocese of Caruarú. Dom Cardoso had spent most of his career in Rome. There he became a professor of canon law, and in 1966 he wrote a doctoral dissertation analyzing the seminarian's option for celibacy from a legal standpoint. In the 1970s Dom Cardoso remained in Rome as an administrator for his religious order, the Carmelites. The Vatican clearly chose Dom Cardoso for Recife because of his orthodoxy and loyalty to the pope. But cloistered in the Vatican bureaucracy, he lacked pastoral experience. He had immense difficulties with the progressive clergy of Olinda and Recife. His supporters were Charismatics and the *Focolares,* a lay organization whose members took religious vows and emphasized obedience to the hierarchy. He was practically a caricature of John Paul II's conservative nominees.[170]

The Vatican appointed Dom Cardoso to dismantle Dom Hélder's innovations. Among many measures, Dom Cardoso forced priests out of the archdiocese; fired the members of the Peace and Justice Commission; suspended Father Reginaldo Veloso for his outspoken criticism; and summoned the police to expel *camponeses* who protested to Cardoso against the removal of their priest. This last action resembled the terror tactics of the military regime.[171]

The second key moment came in late 1986, when the bishops of the northeast withdrew their tacit support from the experiments. Cardinal William Baum, the head of the Vatican's Sacred Congregation for Catholic Education, sent a letter to the Northeast II bishops advising them to reestablish a traditional model of seminary without *pequenas comunidades.* In November the bishops called a special two-day meeting to discuss the letter and proceeded to air accusations against ITER and SERENE II, for example, the occurrence of a classroom debate over celibacy and questions about the juridical status of ITER professors in the Church. The bishops reapproved the schools, but only after the seminarians voted overwhelmingly against the return to a traditional model. In addition, the bishops agreed to reopen the old Olinda seminary in order to train students from the archdiocese of Olinda and Recife in a more orthodox program.[172] (The following year Dom Cardoso transferred his seminarians from ITER and SERENE II to Olinda. He quickly dismissed ten students for questioning celibacy and having pro-union attitudes.) Significantly, the bishops did not protest Cardinal Baum's order nor his assertion that the *pequenas comunidades* were ineffective; in fact, they questioned ITER's capabilities as a clerical training center. Submissive to Rome, they washed their hands of the matter.[173] Although *Optatum Totius* and CNBB directives had asserted the local Church's right to shape training programs, the Vatican had final rights of refusal.[174] The bishops sealed the fate of ITER and SERENE II by sending a copy of their 1986 proceedings, signed by nine prelates, to the Vatican.[175] They in effect cued Rome to investigate further. As vice-rector Severino Vicente da Silva dryly put it, "A bishop is not a progressive. He's a bishop."[176]

For the next several years Recife's seminarians and administrators lived in suspense. By 1989 they had reason to hope the worst was over. In July top Vatican bureaucrats had met with CNBB officials in Brasília to discuss the results of the 1988–1989 inspection of Brazil's seminaries. Not once did they mention Recife. In addition, Dom Vicente Joaquim Zico, the Vincentian bishop who visited ITER and SERENE II, had sent a positive report to Rome. But in August the Vatican surprised progressive bishops and clerics by issuing the order to close. Vatican correspondence stated that the decision *preceded* Dom Zico's report. The Church's own carefully designed procedure of oversight proved meaningless.[177]

In an attempt to save the two schools Dom Luciano Mendes de Almeida, the Jesuit president of the CNBB and the archbishop of Mariana, flew to Rome for a meeting with the Sacred Congregation for Catholic Education and an extraordinary seventy-five-minute audience with John Paul II. Vatican officials indicated to Dom Luciano that they would dialogue on the matter but quickly reversed themselves once the prelate was back in Brazil. Again the bishops of the northeast did not protest. In Recife the closing ignited public protests by priests, sisters, seminarians, and lay activists, and both the local and the national press lent heavy coverage to the situation. The grassroots faithful viewed the closing as a scandal. Young people with fragile faith became distant from the Church.

The ITER and SERENE II students and staff had no choice but to transfer to other seminaries in Recife or elsewhere. Most of the diocesan seminarians moved to the progressive Archdiocese of João Pessoa, where the theological students resided in *pequenas comunidades*.[178] Few ITER professors were invited to participate, however.[179] The members of religious orders studied in regular seminaries in Recife and Olinda.

ITER and SERENE II nevertheless left a highly important legacy. Their proponents continued to affect the religious history of Recife and the northeast, for instance. In the ensuing decade, conflict brewed between Dom Cardoso's group and his progressive opponents, including a small but highly articulate segment of middle-class followers of Dom Hélder known as the "Igreja Nova" (New Church).[180] Many ITER graduates went on to ordination, including three who became bishops in the northeast: Dom Luiz Gonzaga Pepeu, Antônio Muniz Fernandes, and Dom Jacinto Furtado de Brito Sobrinho. A number of other former students went to teach in the theology department of the Pontifical Catholic University of Pernambuco. Many went to work in public and private schools in metropolitan Recife. Another group entered politics and public service.[181] The new model of priestly training, however, seemed to disappear definitively from the northeast. With ITER's closing the Church of the northeast lost its only center of serious intellectual reflection.[182]

Conclusion

Rome's refusal to negotiate on the Recife closings stood in stark contrast to the experience of Dom Hélder and Dom Garrone twenty-one years earlier, when dialogue was the watchword. But even then the Recife experiments could win nothing better than experimental status. Vatican II had endorsed innovation, but also hierarchy. Reaction was simultaneous with innovation. The Church was extremely cautious about innovation, particularly when it affected the clergy, the very core of the institution. Ultimately ITER and SERENE II's ambiguous canonical situation provided a pretext for shutting them down.

The Vatican offered only a vague explanation of the closings in its letter to the bishops of the northeast. It stated that SERENE II "does not correspond to the notion of a major seminary and does not offer the minimum conditions for priestly formation" and that ITER "does not offer intellectual education adequate for future priests, the diocesan clergy as well as the religious clergy."[183] But the decision to close seminaries was an extreme measure for an organization whose main goal since the 1840s had been to alleviate the shortage of priests. Clearly the Roman authorities and their conservative allies in Brazil had very concrete reasons.

The dispute over the closings provided one of the clearest and most tragic examples of how the neoconservative reaction of the 1980s further polarized the Brazilian Church. Each side tendentiously used the shutdown to approve or condemn the past of the *pequenas comunidades* and ITER. However, to write the experiments' history solely from this dualistic perspective would be to ignore the complexities of the seminarians' and clerics' struggles to put their ideas about the new priesthood into practice. After all, the crisis of the ministry was a problem for the entire Church. The Recife experience was a mixture of trials and triumphs.

On one level the experiments simply did not achieve their ideals. The best example was the lack of consistent supervision in the *comunidades*. The progressive clergy recognized this fault and seriously addressed it by selectively re-adopting some Tridentine measures. The underlying difficulty was once again the "shortage" of priests: there simply were not enough to supervise the students properly. The staffs of ITER and SERENE II conscientiously tried to rectify other problems displeasing to the Vatican and the bishops. The inability to eliminate them all provided reasons for disqualifying the schools.

A key sticking point was spirituality. As Dom Marcelo Carvalheira remembered it,

The bishops were alarmed. . . . When a proposal was put forth at ITER to set up a chapel, there was total resistance. A seminarian couldn't pray? How were we supposed to understand that? The only important thing for them was to work towards liberation. If someone wanted to enter the PT, everybody could understand, but to enter a church, no. That was just too much!

The classrooms at ITER even lacked Christian symbols. Dom José Maria Pires, the archbishop of João Pessoa, elaborated on the question of spirituality:

The question should be: am I preparing myself to be a community leader, a political and social leader, or to be a priest? What is the difference? Am I going to preach an ideology or am I going to put myself at the service of the Gospel? If it's for the Gospel, my teacher is Jesus Christ and I must learn with Him. Thus I need to have moments of deep prayer and ample time for meeting with others in order to grow together.

Zildo Rocha, however, pointed out that definitions of spirituality varied:

It depends a lot on what is understood as prayer, as spirituality. If prayer meant holding the breviary in one's hand, they never prayed. But if prayer meant undergoing the *revisão de vida*, meeting in teams, rethinking one's day in light of the principles of the Gospel, analyzing the events of each individual's life, seeing the values and counter-values contained in that life, hearing the call of God—all this was done intensively. I participated as a counselor and can testify to the fact that many times this approach led to a Eucharistic celebration of the things of life.[184]

These descriptions provide a classic example of the different views of spirituality that emerged in the conservative and progressive camps of Brazilian Catholicism (albeit both Dom Marcelo and Dom Pires were progressives). Committed to resolving urgent social and political problems, liberation theology had little time for systematizing its new version of spirituality, thus leaving the strong impression that spirituality lacked priority.[185]

In Rome Dom Luciano heard accusations that some ITER professors had Marxist tendencies and that some students slept outside their *pequenas comunidades*.[186] The allegation of Marxism was unsurprising in the light of the campaign against liberation theology. However, as Sister Jordan pointed out, ITER's program did not endorse Marxism, only its use as an analytical tool. Student embrace of Marxist ideology was not a phenomenon unique to ITER. Youth all across Latin America found it attractive.[187] Furthermore, ITER far exceeded Vatican requirements for Bible-based studies.[188] The second accusation implied that students shirked celibacy. There was probably an element of truth in both allegations. But Marxism and celibacy were merely institutional code words for signaling deeper disagreement on how the Church should be run.

We must then look at two other, interconnected levels of explanation to understand the closing. The first involved the relationship of the clergy to society. In the experiments a number of students became more partisan in their approach to the faithful by living out the option for the poor through *inserção*, or, in some cases, direct political action. Thus, social class—so highly pronounced in Brazil and especially in the northeast—played a role in the closings. The Church in the 1980s began making the transition from the option for the poor to what might be called an option for the middle class. The Tridentine model and administrators such as Dom Cardoso resonated better with this option than did the open system of ITER and SERENE II and radical figures such as Dom Hélder.

The second, and most important, level entailed the model of the priesthood and of the Church envisioned at SERENE II and ITER. The Recife experiments represented a breakdown of the disciplinary regime. They incorporated a search for both greater personal fulfillment and greater contact with the world. In line with Vatican II they attempted to transform the priest from an authoritarian figure into a servant of the people. The Church of Olinda and Recife leaned toward decentralization, with the laity and the clergy to become equal as ministries diversified and diocesan structures democratized. At ITER and SERENE II lay people, Protestant ministers, married priests, and nuns were as important role models as priests. To preserve discipline, obedience, and the male-dominated, hierarchical unity of the Church, the Vatican saw no choice but to bring the experiments to an abrupt conclusion.

In the final analysis the Recife experiments should be judged by their own criteria. They showed success in making seminarians independent, but not without great stress for the institution. At times it seemed that all disciplinary measures were thrown to the winds, leading the bishops and SERENE II's directors to reassert some Tridentine values. The *pequenas comunidades* raised consciousness about Brazilian reality, although a continuing social distance from the people suggested that it was often the *form* rather than the *content* that was changed in clerical education. In addition, ITER and SERENE II became institutionally and politically isolated because they radicalized further than the rest of the Brazilian Church—including many seminarians whose commitment to liberation theology remained shallow or uninformed.[189] In Sister Gebara's estimation, the communities represented an abstract ideal impossible for young men, both sexually and socially inexperienced, to fulfill.[190] The communities most successfully bore fruit in the countryside, the point of origin of Brazilian religious consciousness. But Brazil was becoming an ever more urban society. Like the Brazilian Church as a whole, ITER and SERENE II struggled with the puzzle of pastoral work in the city. Clearly ITER had committed itself to one key solution by putting much energy into the training of lay pastoral workers from the poor neighborhoods. In this sense it worked for the betterment of the Church as "the people of God," but against the logic of clerical power, a development understood only too well by the Roman authorities.

chapter eight

Epilogue

Seminaries and the Clergy in

the New Millennium

This book has examined how Catholic priests in Brazil adapted their vocational calling to different challenges throughout Brazilian history. Important underlying themes in the clergy's life ran throughout the epochs of colony, Empire, and Republic. Priests carried Catholicism to Brazil's shores and *sertão;* stood at the forefront of the nation's economic, social, cultural, and political life; exploited the Native and Afro-Brazilian populations; and both deferred to and defied Rome's demands for absolute obedience and renunciation of sex. These historical patterns and the desires of individual priests often clashed. The personal and social conflicts resulting from priests' central position in the spiritual and temporal realms made their existence a complex and often difficult one. I have examined the inner and outer being of these men in order to highlight this complexity, and I have sought to illustrate how priests provide insight into the human experience because of their unique vocation and their status as intermediaries between God and human, Pope and flock, power and people, and purity and pleasure. The Brazilian priesthood is especially fitting for such reflection, because its conflict-laden history has been part of a colonial and neo-colonial enterprise in which Church and state have attempted to impose religious and social reform on a deeply faithful yet frequently unorthodox populace. The Brazilian priest is a man caught between Europe and America. He wants to preach the Pontiff's beliefs, but he also belongs to a strong tradition of clerical nationalism. The seminary immerses him in a predominantly European world, but the impulse to be Brazilian endures.

Like priests, the seminaries usually served both Church and state. Ordained men frequently turned their attention more toward the concerns of the world—concubines, gold, revolution—than to the things of God—sacraments, piety, and moral behavior. The Portuguese and later the Brazilian imperial state had little interest in allowing the Church to regiment its spiritual soldiers in a way that would allow the institution to organize itself effectively and to improve priests' moral conduct. The example of the Jesuits' state within a state was sufficient reason for the secular state to pursue such a policy. However, when crown and miter agreed on the need for effective social control during the Empire, Dom Pedro II allowed the Vincentian fathers to flourish as missionaries, educators of the lay elite, and instructors of a new clergy molded in the Tridentine framework.

The seminary was an overwhelming response to the age of Feijó. After centuries of false starts the Church was finally able to organize a system of training for its ministers. The isolation of priests from the world produced a new image of the Brazilian padre. The bishops combated the political priest, the "uncle" priest, the *fazendeiro* priest, and the family priest. Purity and holiness became the main standards of the preacher, whom both the bishops and the politically powerful held up as a model of probity for the people. The basis of both the seminaries and the message taught by the fathers was individual discipline, respect for authority, and adherence to orthodoxy. Discipline was the prescription for order and progress—in both the Church and Brazilian society. Transforming the people's and the clergy's perceptions of God and humanity, religious modernization was part and parcel of Brazil's overall socioeconomic modernization. Along the way the Church renewed itself as a formidable intellectual institution. To run the seminaries and purify the priesthood and the people, the bishops initiated a second wave of evangelization of Brazil: the period of Romanization of Brazilian Catholicism, during which dozens of European religious orders set up operations in Brazil. The separation of Church and state during the Republic made the institution independent for the first time in Brazilian history. It was now free to reverse the decay of the clergy evident to all observers in the nineteenth century. However, regionalism, culture, and politics constrained Romanization, which, like Brazil's modernization, was an uneven process. The people clutched to their traditional faith, and many priests resisted celibacy.

Brazil felt the full impact of the modern world after World War II, and so did the Church. Gradually Catholic orthodoxy and the regime of the Tridentine seminaries became obsolete in the eyes of many priests and seminarians. In the 1960s sectors of the Brazilian Church radicalized as they came to share with others a concern for the poor and the problems of underdevelopment. Seminarians and clergymen jettisoned traditional clerical discipline as they sought to construct a modern, professional, and socially conscious priesthood. Romanization, which itself had begun as a modernizing project emphasizing discipline, paradoxically fell victim to a modern critique of discipline. The Tridentine reform that intellectualized the Church prepared the way for a new intellectual movement: liberation theology. Romanization thus illustrated how an essentially conservative movement can lead to political and social change. For the Progressive Church, Catholicism was no longer a religion of passively received sacraments but of social action. During the 1960s—a time of rebellion and ecclesial introspection—Brazilian priests experienced a profound identity crisis, which they attempted to solve by experimenting with new ways of living their vocation and their faith. Some fathers plunged into psychoanalysis, while priests-to-be marched out of the seminary to experience freedom and politics by living among the people. This moment of experimentalism was extraordinary not only in and of itself, but because it took place in the world's oldest, largest, and most rigidly hierarchical institution. Inner sanctum of priestly power and repressed passion, the seminary was forced to open its doors to offer a view of a world in upheaval and, in Brazil, in the throes of economic and demographic transformation, ideological conflict, and political repression. The Brazilian Church's contribution to world Catholicism was its ability to adapt and to innovate in this highly challenging context. In borrowing from Europe it produced new models of faith and action on the ground in Brazil, including the creation of liberation psychology.

Experimentalism was intense but short-lived, outlasted by the crisis of the priesthood, the problems of Brazilian society, and the renewed conservatism of the papacy and its bureaucracy. Political strife and the fear of some leading bishops that change was causing the Church to veer out of control increased tensions. Two camps formed. On the one hand, clerical nationalists aligned with the CNBB and the ideas of *Optatum Totius* to push for experimentalism. On the other, the skeptics of innovation sought to slow its pace or even reverse it. Chapters 5, 6, and 7 showed how opposition to experiments began long before the ascent of John Paul II, the moment commonly perceived as the start of Catholic neoconservatism. Christus Sacerdos was canceled only five years after its inception, and Cardinal Garrone fought to block the *pequenas comunidades* of Recife from the start. (Indeed, as we have seen, conflict between progressives and conservatives had roots in the pre–Vatican II era.) Experimentalism in Brazilian Catholicism became the victim of the Church's abandonment of many of the ideals of Vatican II and a return to the values of universality and discipline. Having taken a strategic retreat for a brief period in the late 1960s and the early 1970s, the post–Vatican II episcopal inheritors of Romanization girded themselves for a new evangelical crusade, perhaps emerging someday as protagonists—or antagonists—of new attempts to reform a Brazilian society that refuses to give up so quickly its colonial past and its own ways of living the faith. Into the fray will jump new ministers, struggling to adapt to new conditions, living their passions, and seeking to define what it means to be a priest in Brazil.

An Uneasy Synthesis

Following the worst years of the clerical crisis, the Brazilian Church moved to end experimentation. Many in the Church felt that some experiments had inadequately addressed the problems of the priesthood. Some experiments relied too much on improvisation, and some innovators, wanting to change everything, failed to retain the positive aspects of the Tridentine era.[1] In the 1980s and beyond, the Church built an uneasy synthesis of pre– and post–Vatican II models.

On the one hand, the Church adhered to Rome's universal directives for priestly education, including elements of the Tridentine seminary. The Catholic ministry remained a hierarchical phenomenon in which the seminary was the most crucial element. On the other hand, the Church adopted many aspects of the experimental phase. It instituted the study of Brazilian reality, permitted the use of the social sciences, and allowed each diocese to adapt philosophical and theological studies to local circumstances. The introduction of lay professors and themes made theological studies less clerical and more Brazilian and Latin American in character. The study of popular religion also became part of seminary curricula. Other innovations included the establishment of electives in pastoral studies, postgraduate courses, internships, and extracurricular activities. Training no longer took place just during the seminary years; it was now considered to be ongoing and holistic, combining spirituality, mission, and personal development. Psychology and sex education became a regular staple of teacher preparation courses (although, as we will see, not always effectively implemented in the seminaries), and psychotherapy became useful in resolving seminarians' personal conflicts. Like nuclear energy, the psychoanalytic technique could serve dual purposes: constructively in the liberation of human potential or repressively in the manipulation of individuals. On the bureaucratic level the CNBB and a group of rectors founded the Organização dos Seminários e Institutos Filosófico-Teológicos do Brasil (OSIB, the Organization of Seminaries and Philosophical-Theological Institutes of Brazil) in order to promote academic exchange and cooperation among seminaries. OSIB emphasized the model of the priest as a modern saint: servant and ally of the poor, activist, and seeker of solutions to the Church's most serious problems, for example, the need to develop an urban pastoral strategy. Encouraging professionalization, OSIB advocated state accreditation of theology courses.[2] OSIB helped keep alive the national vision advocated by the seminarians' movement, although it lacked the spontaneity and political activism of students in the 1960s. OSIB had no voting power in the Church and did not act as a pressure group. The same lack of power afflicted such organizations as the diocesan Priests Councils and the periodic National Priests Congresses.[3] Student participation in the educational process and the life of the local community stood out as another facet of the seminaries in the 1980s and 1990s, although the Church and its seminaries were far from becoming democratic institutions. Without interfering with their studies, students carried out manual tasks within the seminary household.[4]

Despite Rome's disapproval of *pequenas comunidades,* decentralization of seminary studies and the creation of small communities became widespread, although the *comunidades* diminished somewhat in the 1990s. Most diocesan seminarians still lived in traditional seminaries, whereas most candidates to the religious priesthood were in communities.[5] Philosophical-theological institutes and a variation on the *pequenas comunidades* known as *casas de formação* (teaching houses) became a key model for training Brazil's diocesan seminarians. Like the *pequenas comunidades,* the *casas de formação* housed small groups of students interspersed among the populace. These seminarians commuted to the institutes to undertake their academic program. The key difference between the sometimes anarchic *pequenas comunidades* and the generally well-structured *casas de formação* was the regular presence of one or more priests, who provided personal, spiritual, intellectual, and pastoral guidance. The *casas* embodied an emphasis on harmonious communal living and a mature pedagogy developed through the years of experimentalism and crisis. They fulfilled many of the key demands of the seminarians' movement of the 1960s, in particular the calls for psychologically sound personal development, greater contact with the people, and an understanding of modernity in its many ramifications. Discipline remained, but it was now subordinate to love and a sense of personal responsibility. Spiritual direction, abandoned during the experimental years as students turned to psychology and pastoral work, also returned as a central concern. Its purpose was to reinforce communal life. The CNBB and many dioceses adopted the *casas* as the new form of major seminary. By the mid-1990s the debate over *casas* versus the classic Tridentine seminary had given way to discussion over how to implement one model or the other effectively.[6]

Pope John Paul II endorsed the amalgamation of tendencies in an apostolic exhortation titled *Pastores Dabo Vobis* (I Will Give You Shepherds), published in response to the 1990 episcopal synod on the training of the clergy. In this document the pope reaffirmed priests' central role in the hierarchical structure of the Church. He also emphasized the observance of canon law and official Church teachings. Once again a pope identified the shortage of clergymen as one of the principal challenges facing Catholicism. The training of priests and their ongoing sanctification were "one of the most demanding and important tasks for the future of the evangelization of humanity." Much of *Pastores Dabo Vobis* provided clergymen with the traditional reminder that they "must resemble Christ." The system of seminaries had "produced many good results down through the ages and continues to do so all over the world."[7]

But John Paul II also recognized that a new evangelization required "new evangelizers." The document valued the period of experimentalism at the national and local levels, including such innovations as pastoral apprenticeships. The postmodern era presented new challenges, as excessive rationalism, inhuman capitalism, materialism, the breakdown of the family and sexual morals, and individualism threatened to make religion irrelevant. "There is no longer a need to fight against God; the individual feels he is simply able to do without him," John Paul II warned. He did not attack the proliferation of new religious competitors. Rather, he recognized them as a sign of people's search for God and the clergy's need to examine their credibility as preachers. The priest of the new millennium would have to continue to serve the poor and struggle for social justice. In this respect John Paul II demonstrated his adherence to many of the tenets of liberation theology in the context of the Church's traditional social doctrine. The most striking characteristic of *Pastores Dabo Vobis* was its call to rediscover, and regularly cultivate, spirituality in its many ramifications. Christianity, it stated, was not just an ethic, but a spiritual-historical occurrence. John Paul II described the priest as a multidimensional being acting in many spheres. Spirituality was the unifying force, strengthened by celibacy, penance, prayer, asceticism, reflection on the scriptures, the assistance of a spiritual guide, and in some cases even psychological counseling. Daily participation in the Eucharist should be the *"essential moment"* in seminarians' lives. In the loneliness of urban society a priest's essential ability to build a sense of community received reinforcement from the efforts to bring him to an "affective maturity" that is "capable of esteem and respect in interpersonal relationships between men and women." Intellectual formation, including the rigorous study of philosophy and the human sciences, should hold equal importance for a clergy seeking to keep abreast of the latest social developments. The seminary, John Paul II argued, was not so much a structure, but an "*educational community in progress,*" a spiritual place, a way of life.[8]

A substantial change in the vocational profile and a gradual trend toward conservatism after 1975 resulted from and encouraged synthesis. By 1982 the percentage of seminarians in the population had returned to the pre-crisis level of 1960, although in the early 1990s a drop of 5 percent occurred.[9] As in the nineteenth century, the clergy became more Brazilian in the 1980s and 1990s, making the country far less dependent on foreign missionaries. In 1970, for instance, there were 3,866 Brazilians and 1,093 foreigners among the diocesan clergy; in 1987 there were 5,015 Brazilians and only 900 foreigners. Among religious clergy there were 3,788 Brazilians and 4,262 foreigners in 1970, compared with 4,463 Brazilians and only 3,140 foreigners in 1987. In 2003 Brazil had slightly more than 17,000 priests, a striking 84 percent of them natives. The drop in foreign clergymen, a source of new ideas and radicalism in the 1950s and 1960s, might partially explain why seminarians became more conservative in the 1980s and 1990s. A more Brazilian clergy did not necessarily mean a more nationalistic one. Brazil's clergy also became younger and more diocesan. In 1970 secular priests comprised only 38 percent of the clergy. By 1998 they numbered more than half. Between 1980 and 1996 almost 4,800 diocesan fathers received Holy Orders. Thus one half of all diocesan priests had less than fifteen years' experience. Significantly, in the 1980s most students in the major seminaries were inspired by the traditional model of the priesthood. Progressive Catholicism seemed to have relatively little effect on vocations. While many seminarians in the 1980s wanted to work with the progressive CEBs, even more wanted to be traditional parish priests. Interest in the CEBs dropped in the 1990s, and a desire for personal fulfillment endangered pastoral activism. In 2003, for example, only 5 percent of all priests worked with CEBs. Students also rejected political involvement. Furthermore, although Brazil became a predominantly urban nation, the percentage of seminarians from rural agricultural families remained proportionately much larger than the rest of the populace, oscillating from 44.6 percent in 1960 to 56.5 percent in 1982 to 42 percent in 1993. In 1990 less than a quarter of Brazilians worked in the countryside. Few seminarians came from the urban proletariat, the utterly poor, or the wealthy. Most came from families where the father earned between one and five times the minimum wage—an income defining a range from poverty to lower middle-class status.[10]

After Vatican II Brazil's seminaries lost their prominence as great cultural centers. Although the average seminarian was older, more mature, and more likely to have work experience,[11] specialists in clerical training and other observers lamented the drop in students' general intellectual ability and curiosity. The *pequenas comunidades* contributed to this outcome because of their extreme, utilitarian emphasis on pastoral practice, described by one seminary expert as a "pastoralitis" in which studies were seen as a barrier to contact with the people and a waste of time. Seminarians lacked knowledge of such basics as the social doctrine of the Church.[12] Some detected even contempt for theoretical questions and ignorance about culture. Gone are the days of film and literary clubs that played so important a role as recently as the early 1960s. Of course, military repression played a big part in this downfall. Now many seminarians must take remedial courses before beginning philosophical and theological studies. Seminary professors attributed the drop in academic quality not just to the Church's problems but also to the overall decline of the Brazilian educational system, caused in large part by reforms effected by the military regime.[13]

On another front, Afro-Brazilian cultural expression in the Church grew somewhat in the 1980s and 1990s but remained weak overall. Black clergy and activists became more vocal. With great effort Afro-Brazilian students brought their culture onto a par with others in the seminaries. Along with priests, religious women, and other activists, they formed the group Agentes de Pastoral Negros (Black Pastoral Agents).[14] They were part of the Catholic counterculture that started emerging in the 1960s and expressed itself in different styles of liturgical music, alternative forms of the Mass, radical politics, and the support for the landless and indigenous peoples. The overall gains were small, however, and blacks still faced immense prejudice in the Church and society.[15] Of thirteen thousand clergymen in the late 1980s, only two hundred were black.

The latest Church survey of the clergy, released in 2003, did not even ask about ethnicity.[16] The Church still has not assumed the cause of blacks in the same way it came to the aid of Native peoples with its successful Indigenous Missionary Council.[17]

Conservatism also had psychological causes. The vocational call of Brazil's seminarians remained largely rooted in childhood, and the increasing stability of the seminary system after 1975 contributed to a lack of critical analysis of the pedagogical process.[18] The seminaries remained highly paternalistic, with religious orders and dioceses paying a large portion of students' tuition, room and board, and other expenses.[19] The priesthood as a career attracted many youths in search of stable employment and status. Some even requested cars at the moment of their ordination. The mystical notion of self-giving typical of the 1960s and 1970s largely disappeared.[20] This relationship encouraged psychological dependence on the institution and a lack of sense of responsibility. This problem was just one in a panoply of psychological issues that the seminaries had yet to address in a forthright manner.[21] Once in the priesthood, young diocesan fathers have largely had to fend for themselves economically. The Church abandoned the ideas of further professionalization, and few priests adopted the communistic model of pooling income.[22]

The most pessimistic analysis revealed a clergy stagnating in many respects. The clergy and seminarians still struggled with the same structural issues first addressed by the seminarians' movement. At the start of the new millennium Brazil's priests continued to be dissociated from the world of normal work and labor. More and more priests took on administrative jobs, reducing the number of personnel available for teaching and pastoral work, key means to preaching the Christian message. Thus, repeating the problem studied in chapter 4, poor distribution of human energy persisted. Priests continued to come from the lower classes but were alienated from those very classes through the elite nature of seminary training. Despite the new emphasis on spirituality, the clergy's own contemplative experience remained weak. Reflecting the overall character of Roman Catholicism, the Brazilian Church still acted as a hierarchical institution and lacked sufficient discussion of internal democracy.[23]

Synthesis did not bring consensus. In the 1980s and early 1990s the seminaries still struggled with the dual legacy of experimentalism and Tridentine discipline. The Church had to tone down some of the more radical experiments in order to maintain the interest of the new generation of more conservative seminarians.

In other instances the experiments did not go far enough. Some progressive Catholics waited in vain for the new priests to form a pedagogical vanguard that would give the laity greater responsibility in the Church. The Church still struggled to find an adequate method for training seminarians in pastoral work. During this period the job of seminary professor rector lost its pre–Vatican II prestige, leading to shortages and frequent transfer of personnel. As mentioned, the overall academic quality of students also dropped. These trends cast doubt on the Church's ability to keep pace with the modernizing tendencies of Brazilian society. The situation was exacerbated by a continued lack of an official national center for graduate-level clerical education (although the Faculdade de Teologia Assunção in São Paulo and the Pontifical Catholic University of Rio Grande do Sul partially filled this gap by instituting solid graduate programs in theology).[24] The Brazilian Church still depended heavily on institutions in Europe to furnish advanced degrees. Brazilian seminarians also lacked the strong sense of national cohesion and political consciousness achieved prior to 1968 with the publication of *O Seminário* and the flourishing of the seminarians' movement. Ecclesial and military repression snuffed out the seminarians' movement. Nothing comparable has emerged, leaving seminarians isolated and impeding the development of a broad vision of priestly training and Brazil's religious and social challenges. Today's seminarians show less enthusiasm for exploring new ideas.

Another major challenge for all factions was the growing tendency toward individualism. The seminarians' movement had successfully focused greater attention on the individual psychological needs of students and priests. Yet the Church failed to comprehend all of the ramifications of the cultural shifts caused by urbanization and consumerism. The 1979 meeting of the Latin American bishops at Puebla, for instance, defined the clerical crisis in theological terms but failed to examine sociological, psychological, and cultural factors.[25]

Struggling with Sexuality

Another lingering problem is sexuality. Celibacy as a symbol of a priest's commitment to the Church still occupied center stage. In theory the Church made significant advances by proposing celibacy as a freely made choice based on love, sacrifice, and dedication to humanity.[26] In practice the Church and the seminaries in the 1980s and 1990s continued to avoid the question of celibacy and affectivity in general, leaving students to face feelings and conflicts alone. Many seminarians still feared their feelings, and Tridentine guilt persisted. Seminaries were not places of emotional well-being. Students found their teachers unreliable as counselors. While awareness about the psychological permeated the Church's formal discourse at the international and national levels, the practical implementation of psychology, although much further along than in the pre–Vatican II era, still lagged terribly. Instead of relying on greater selectivity in admissions, the Church continued to gamble by allowing in seminarians without carefully examining their psychological background.[27] The Church still thrived on seminarians' emotional dependence. It had little incentive to consider new ideas about sexuality and celibacy, and it stifled debate.[28] The Brazilian Church could be holding a sexual time bomb that could explode like the recent U.S. abuse scandal. Clearly the Church needs a centralized program such as Christus Sacerdos to encourage the discussion of psychological issues and better prepare teachers to assist seminarians with the emotional challenges of priestly life.

A study of one group of priests in the late 1990s demonstrated that only half clearly and consciously chose celibacy. A quarter rejected it, and the rest passively accepted it. Those who valued celibacy believed it challenged priests to grow in both a human and a spiritual sense. Celibacy for these priests fostered self-control and a healthy attitude toward sexuality in general. Celibacy did not deprive men of their sexuality; it ultimately liberated them to love all people. Father Ricardo Rezende, a man frequently threatened with death for his work among the rural poor, likened committed celibates to the Amazonian guerrillas of the 1970s, who forsook sex in their all-out struggle to defeat the military regime. The priestly guerrillas of the reign of God expressed total solidarity with the people. Critics of celibacy saw it as isolating the clergy from others. One priest observed: "When celibacy is an option, the person is happy. When it is imposed, it is frustrating and, most of the time, not possible to maintain."[29] A Church study in 2003 showed 41 percent of Brazilian priests in favor of optional celibacy for diocesan clergy.[30]

As in the North American Church, recent research indicates that priests and the faithful in Brazil have made a distinction between orthodox teachings and actual practice with regard to sexuality and reproduction. In the 1990s Catholics in the poor periphery of Rio de Janeiro engaged in premarital sex, widely used birth control pills, had tubal ligations, and underwent abortions—all practices that directly contradicted some of the Roman hierarchy's most strenuously defended principles. A growing number of teenage and single mothers further challenged the official Catholic worldview. While not necessarily agreeing with these actions, many of the local clergy refused to condemn their followers and, in some instances, even encouraged them to disobey the Church based on their own consciences. Within this approach priests still emphasized the need to nurture basic Christian values such as love and respect.[31] The Church did not fail to exercise its traditional role as moral watchdog, but it also adapted to the people's reality.

The clergy themselves are not saints. Chapter 4 demonstrates that sexual misconduct existed in the Vincentian congregation and damaged its standing in the religious community. Some of the Brazilian cases predated by half a century the North American scandals of the last two decades. The pattern of scandals and cover-ups in Brazil strikingly resembles those in the United States.

The U.S. crisis started in 1983 with the revelation that Father Gilbert Gauthe was abusing minors. Sued, the Church settled the case for $10 million. A long string of allegations and lawsuits followed in the United States and also Canada.[32] The legal settlements have cost the institution over a billion dollars and an estimated $50 million more in psychiatric care. At least 1,500 U.S. priests allegedly engaged in sexual misconduct with minors between the mid-1980s and 2002. (A United States Conference of Catholic Bishops study turned up allegations against more than 4,300 priests for the period from 1950 to 2002.) The victims numbered close to 12,000. Many more incidents probably went unreported. Even priests residing at treatment centers continued their abuses unchecked. One victim committed suicide, and another died in an auto accident caused by a drunk priest.[33] As of 2002 eight American bishops had quit as a result of the revelations.[34] Several foreign bishops also left their posts, including a Polish archbishop close to Pope John Paul II, who was accused of sexually harassing seminarians.[35] In December 2002 Cardinal Bernard Law, the archbishop of Boston and the most influential man in the U.S. Church, resigned after his complicity in the abuses became clear.[36] He was also the first U.S. cardinal questioned under oath for his actions as a leader of the Church. Cardinal Edward M. Egan of New York City was also implicated. In the eyes of one Brazilian cleric, the scandals were the equivalent of the Catholic Church's "September 11," a permanent scar on its reputation.[37]

Instead of defrocking or punishing errant priests, the Church had washed its hands of the problem by transferring them from one diocese to another.

According to one extensive journalistic investigation, the Church's own documents demonstrated that "high-ranking officials had repeatedly put the welfare of their priests ahead of the children." This "betrayal" involved the promotion of abusive priests and a massive cover-up of the perpetrators by Cardinal Law and other leaders. It was the epitome of hypocrisy. Cardinal Law "reacted casually" to complaints about a notorious pedophile who had "publicly endorsed sexual relations between men and boys." This same priest taught teens how to inject drugs. The Vatican knew of the abuses but took no action to stop them. Some clergymen even suggested cleansing Church files in order to avoid prosecution.[38]

Celibacy per se was not a cause of the crisis and the cover-up. Despite heated rhetoric on all sides, the practice of transferring suspected abusers and the failure to stop it had nothing to do with the sharp ideological divisions that emerged after the Second Vatican Council. Neither the proponents of a relaxed celibacy law nor the opponents of gay people could really explain the crisis. After all, sexual exploitation and abuses have also occurred in churches that have a married clergy.[39] The causes could be found elsewhere: the lack of sufficient internal checks and balances, the absence in the past of proper screening of seminarians, a reliance on canon law as opposed to the spirit of Christian ethics, the belief in the Church as a perfect institution, the extreme deference paid the clergy by the faithful and public officials, and the shame of the victims. Another cause was the Church's general failure to come to grips with sexuality. The hierarchy has steadfastly refused to analyze gender issues and the "homosocial" nature of the institution. According to A. W. Richard Sipe, a monk who became a psychotherapist, tolerance for priests' sexual activity flows from a "boys-will-be-boys atmosphere" in the Church. The Church is "like a college fraternity, but with a spiritual aura around it." The hierarchy, including the pope, displayed an aloof and arrogant attitude about the abuses that revealed their primary concern: preserving the image of the Church and therefore their power. In Sipe's words, the crisis revealed the "very, very dark side" of the priesthood. Yet it also had salutary effects. Priests started to organize into mutual support groups. The laity withheld donations as it demanded a greater voice in the government of the church. And calls for the study of taboo subjects—celibacy and the ordination of women—increased. The Church became aware of the need to reform the priesthood more thoroughly.[40]

The greatest cause was the cancer that power became when the Church's disciplinary model became an end in itself. Power, and not the gospel, had become the prime objective of the clergy, namely the episcopate. To keep hold of their power the bishops had needed to snuff out all dissent. Along with power came a sense of moral superiority that made denial of sexual misconduct the only response possible. In the United States it took the work of journalists, television programs, and the legal system to force the Church to reveal its secrets and to begin to understand the psychological and medical implications of child molestation. While some might argue that the Church should be exempt from such scrutiny, others correctly affirm that priests are trusted religious and public figures expected to demonstrate the highest standards of morality.[41]

Ironically, writings on the U.S. crisis reveal a dearth of knowledge about the problem in other countries and completely ignore Brazil, the world's largest Catholic country. They also provide practically no information on the period prior to 1960. But as chapter 4 demonstrates, the crisis is truly long-term. And it is international, despite Vatican attempts to paint it as strictly North American (an assertion the investigative journalists failed to question seriously).[42] The first (and only) significant study of clerical sexual abuse in the post–Vatican II Brazilian Church revealed that the transfer of bad priests continues as the unwritten policy of the bishops. As in the past, the bishops seek primarily to preserve the image of the institution and the priesthood. The Church ignores or even blames the victims. Based on survey research among the clergy and nuns, Father Gino Nasini's book *Um espinho na carne* (A Thorn in the Flesh) estimates that 10 percent of Brazilian priests are involved in abuses against children, teenagers, and adults of both sexes.[43] (Furthermore, an official Church study conducted in 2003 revealed that 41 percent of priests had maintained a relationship with a woman at some point during their ministry.[44]) Macho culture and the complicity of the institutional Church have largely silenced the repercussions of the crisis in Brazil, where media coverage has been practically nil in comparison with North America. Different perceptions of sexuality and sexual abuse and the Church's status as Brazil's semi-official religion have also shielded the institution from greater scrutiny. In the United States the Church currently stands with the sexual abuse scandal where it did a few decades ago when the problem of alcoholic priests came to light. In Brazil the institution is even further behind in recognizing its priests' sexual difficulties. The Brazilian authorities have not yet recognized that weeding out and punishing abusers are paramount in saving victims.[45]

Father Nasini asserts that the phenomenon undermines the credibility of the Church, and he exhorts Brazil's bishops to address it by establishing transparent, national standards for responding to incidents, treating the offenders, aiding victims, and asking forgiveness of the ecclesial community. "By not recognizing the sin of sexual abuse in the lives of its members and ministers, the Church renounces its right to be heard when it expresses ethical concerns," Nasini states. The seminaries have a critical role to play by paying yet greater attention to sexuality, psychology, and the affective life of candidates to the ministry. In the words of one priest, the problem of sexual abuse "demands openness on the question of human sexuality. Without proper orientation, openness, and humility, there is no cure. This is a very arduous task: the Church must orient and raise awareness. She must reconsider the problem of celibacy in the ranks, because, in general, celibacy is non-existent, principally with respect to homosexuality." Father Nasini advocates the establishment of counseling centers for afflicted priests and a national institute for the study of human sexuality and issues in priestly training. Celibacy should be optional so that it signifies a real choice and not an imposition, he asserts. Father Nasini suggests that those who authentically live their vows of celibacy can be loving examples for those who abuse sexuality. By solving the crisis of abuse, the Church can help society in general free itself of the scourge of sexual exploitation and harassment.[46]

Prejudice against gay people has characterized Catholicism everywhere, and Brazil has been no exception, although, as chapter 4 illustrates, abusive gay priests were tolerated within the Vincentian order. Prejudice was not overt. Indeed, it is remarkable that the Church in the past did not more stridently oppose homosexuality. This may simply reflect the fact that homosexuality was taboo. In more recent times, however, the concern about gays has become more explicit both among the tolerant and the less tolerant. In the 1980s some Brazilian clerics began to study homosexuality objectively and to emphasize greater understanding of seminarians' affective formation. In the United States estimates of the percentage of gay priests and seminarians ran as high as 50 percent, leading some to conclude that the Catholic ministry in that country was becoming predominantly gay. There is no survey evidence for the Brazilian clergy, although the clergy have expressed a need for such research. The Brazilian Church has lagged in asking difficult and complex questions about gay seminarians and their impact on training and the institution. A 1985 U.S. vocational directors' publication, for instance, proposed the following questions about gay applicants to the seminary: "Is the applicant's sexual orientation public knowledge? If so, how will this affect his ministry? If not, does the applicant live with anxiety that it might become public? Does the applicant feel it should make no difference? Is this realistic in the setting of the diocese?" Ultimately, how would the grow-

ing number of gay seminarians affect straight priests and seminarians?[47] In Brazil openly and fully gay individuals have faced enormous barriers. As recently as
1989 the Brazilian Church received instructions from Rome to remove from the
seminaries, and block from ordination, gays or persons with homosexual tendencies. But the Brazilians allowed to remain those who could achieve a heterosexual orientation through psychotherapy.[48] By the turn of the century some
religious congregations were showing an increased acceptance of gay persons.
Nevertheless, the general prejudice against homosexuality in Brazil has made it
difficult for gay priests to win social acceptance.[49] The Church's 2003 survey of
Brazil's priests demonstrated that 68 percent still considered homosexuality to
be a pathological condition.[50]

In the Brazilian Church a gay subculture became increasingly apparent in
the 1990s and challenged a reluctant institution to address priests' sexuality
and its ramifications. An explosion of AIDS shed light on gay clerical life and
the Church's ongoing struggle to shape modern sexual morals. One newspaper
report, for instance, revealed a group of priests and seminarians who regularly visited gay saunas in São Paulo. One became HIV-positive and was forced
to leave his religious order.[51] Between 1987 and 1993, twenty-seven priests died
from AIDS in São Paulo. This figure represented 2 percent of that city's clergy.
Nevertheless, AIDS in the Church has remained largely a secret in Brazil.[52]
The Church, in fact, has exercised the most strenuous opposition to government AIDS-prevention programs, although its influence has been minimal,
in part because an internal dispute exists over the correct response to the crisis. Reactions have ranged from fear-mongering to tolerance and understanding. Dom Eugênio Sales affirmed that AIDS is a divine warning. Dom Paulo
Evaristo Arns established Brazil's first AIDS hospice, supported AIDS education, and displayed theological flexibility on the use of condoms to prevent disease.[53] "Christ doesn't want people to have HIV," Dom Paulo stated
during the CNBB's annual assembly in 2000. One São Paulo priest who runs
a program for HIV-positive individuals distributes condoms to the faithful.
The head of the CNBB's pastoral unit on health publicly defended the use of
condoms to prevent AIDS but quickly retracted his statement under heavy
pressure from Rome.[54] Several priests and laicized fathers who were HIV-
positive attended the 2000 meeting, where, to the displeasure of the bishops,
a CNBB clerical advisor criticized the Vatican's blockage of debate on AIDS.[55]
At this same meeting a Vatican official caused further polemic by asserting the
Church's right to test candidates to the priesthood and the sisterhood for HIV.[56]
AIDS among priests diminished in the late 1990s because of greater information

about the disease.[57] In some progressive dioceses AIDS is now discussed as a health issue.[58]

The priests surveyed in Father Nasini's book viewed gay priests—and bishops—as a double-edged sword for the institution. On the one hand, these individuals were perceived as intelligent, creative, and strong performers who easily won over people. On the other hand, their colleagues described them as acting furtively and displaying an affective dissatisfaction and lack of emotional control that were compensated for through frenetic sexual experience, with some dying of AIDS while their bishops failed to act. One priest portrayed gay priests' behavior as violent, lazy, and pharisaical. Seen as well-informed, influential, and unified, the gay clergy sought power, money, and ecclesiastical success. In the eyes of other fathers they were fearful and authoritarian figures. It is difficult to gauge the accuracy of these perceptions. Father Nasini does not give voice to gay priests, and the secretive nature of the subculture combined with the Church's taboo against homosexuality has prevented the collection of anything but anecdotal evidence. Father Nasini urges further study of the issue, in particular whether the environment of the seminaries favored the establishment of the gay subculture.[59]

The growth and increasing acceptance of the gay pride movement could force the Church to liberalize its stance on gays in the priesthood. One of the largest in the world, São Paulo's annual gay pride parade attracts hundreds of thousands of people. As awareness about gay rights spreads, gay priests and seminarians could gain political and moral strength. As Father Donald Cozzens observes about the U.S. clergy, gay priests of the past had little notion of their sexuality. Today they have a better understanding of their orientation and are more likely to reveal it to a trusted circle of friends.[60] The emerging awareness of gays' role in the priesthood in the United States, Brazil, and elsewhere will be one of the key issues facing the Church as it struggles to attract new vocations. Does it matter that the priesthood is becoming a gay profession? To this question Cozzens responds: "Does not the question reveal still another form of homophobia? Is it not another manifestation of discrimination and suspicion? Some would say the issue is best left alone, that we would all be better served not to notice the proverbial elephant in the room. Ignoring the phenomenon would certainly be easier than addressing it; yet closing our eyes to the situation only delays the time when circumstances will demand that it be given attention." At the same time, Cozzens points out the challenge of attracting heterosexual men to the priesthood and maintaining their self-esteem in an increasingly gay institution.[61]

Which Priesthood?

In the new millennium the Brazilian Church's biggest priority was stopping the decrease in the country's proportion of Catholics. In 2000 fewer than 75 percent of Brazilians identified themselves as Catholics—down from over 90 percent a half century earlier. Once again the model of the priesthood would take center stage as the Church sought to rethink its mission.

In the 1990s liberation theology rapidly lost influence among the people as the progressive clergy attempted to institutionalize their ideology and retain control over grassroots movements. Whereas liberationism once represented an effort at radical change in the Church, in some areas it was now a dogmatic tradition that its clerical and intellectual proponents increasingly struggled to defend. Meanwhile, the laity groped to discover new forms of liberation that made sense in the changed sociopolitical context. Those who failed to escape liberationist dogma remained dependent on an intellectually inflexible clergy ensconced in the ecclesiastical bureaucracy. These individuals resorted to pork-barrel politics reminiscent of the heyday of the moral concordat. Liberationism had gotten them nowhere. The more free-spirited laity managed to create new programs and movements such as "pastoral feminism" that emphasized practical solutions to the problems of individuals and the community, although the long-term outcome of these fragile initiatives remained unclear.[62]

At bottom, liberationism was as much about the clergy as about the people, if not more so. It was a response to the clergy's need to rediscover social relevance and to construct a new model of the priesthood.

In fairness to the progressive bishops and their liberationist followers, however, it is important to keep in mind that the attack by the Vatican bureaucracy and its allies in Brazil on experimentalism was overwhelming. Had these experiments and, indeed, the entire Brazilian Church not endured such pressures, where might the progressive project be? Certainly better off than it is today. The large amount of recent literature pointing to the weaknesses of the progressive project often fails to recall this key point.[63]

There were some exceptions to this somber outlook. The Progressive Church did maintain influence among certain downtrodden and discriminated groups, and politically the CNBB continued to carry great weight in national affairs.[64] At the local level the clergy remained active in electoral politics, albeit more out of personal ambition than out of interest in their flocks.[65] Another key Church-backed movement erupted in the countryside. Seminarians schooled in liberation theology backed the land invasions carried out by the Movement

of Landless Rural Workers (MST), Latin America's most successful radical social movement of the past quarter century. João Pedro Stedile, a former seminarian, rose into the MST's top leadership. Like many in the MST, he obtained
his politico-religious outlook from the CPT (discussed in chapter 5). Many
MST militants left the seminary because of the institutional Church's inability
to accommodate men who uncompromisingly embraced the preferential option for the poor.[66] It remained unclear, however, whether the MST could extend
its influence beyond the countryside in an ever more urban nation.

Protestant Pentecostals presented the most serious challenge to the Church.
They first came to Brazil at the start of the twentieth century. They were distinguished from more traditional, so-called mainline Protestants (such as Lu-
therans) by their emphasis on the gifts of the Holy Spirit—for example, speaking in tongues. Pentecostals practice exorcism, emphasize personal morality,
and preach miraculous cures. Additional waves of Pentecostal growth took place
in the 1950s and 1980s. While some denominations expanded with aid from
North American sponsors, causing Catholics to allege an imperialist con-
spiracy, most have become "Brazilianized" and autonomous. The most recent
churches originated in Brazil. They were part of a more dynamic, syncretistic
neo-Pentecostalism. The prime example was the Igreja Universal do Reino de
Deus (Universal Church of the Kingdom of God), which embraced an economically oriented, individualistic "prosperity theology." It relied on the media to
propagate its message, and it was heavily involved in politics. Started in 1977, by
the mid-1990s it had temples across Brazil with several million members; collected as much as $1 billion per year in tithes; and owned Brazil's third-largest
television network, thirty radio stations, two newspapers, a bank, and other
interests. The Igreja Universal rapidly spread to other parts of Latin America,
the United States, Europe, Africa, and Asia. The neo-Pentecostals grew in Brazil
because they developed effective methods for attracting the poor, uneducated,
and politically disenfranchised. Pentecostalism ended the Brazilian Catholic
Church's historical religious and political monopoly. But it fed on the same
forces of modernization that lay behind the growth of the CEBs. Pentecostals
and neo-Pentecostals often displayed anti-Catholic sentiment, but they also resulted from significant qualitative changes in Brazilian society and religion.[67]

The Catholic response to Pentecostalism was at first slow. One key reason
was the Church's preoccupation with internal matters. As the history of the
seminaries demonstrates, the Church had turned in on itself. Enormous energy was expended and political battles fought just to open the Church to the
modern world. Furthermore, it is important to recognize that the Brazilian

Church, which established ecumenical relations with mainline Protestant denominations in the 1970s, has not viewed Pentecostalism through the prism of
pure competition. The life of religious institutions, especially traditional ones
such as the Catholic Church, is far more complex than what can be understood
through a single-variable interpretation such as a zero-sum battle over the faithful. Historically, most Brazilians have been only nominally Catholic and have
had weak links to the clergy. Criticisms and warnings about the Pentecostals
were common in the Catholic message, but only in the 1980s did the Church
begin to study the Pentecostal phenomenon more carefully.[68]

Initiative came from the top. The 1992 CELAM conference at Santo Domingo
began implementing Pope John Paul II's new evangelization. The revival of
pre–Vatican II spirituality and rituals was fundamental. As Father Agostinho
Pretto recalled in the 1990s, the clergy had been "stupid" to give up popular religion in the immediate post–Vatican II era of liberationism and ultra-
rationalism. Only years later did progressive priests correct this error. For example, the Church restored old altars in Passo Fundo that had been destroyed or
taken away in the 1960s.[69] The Lazaristas considered starting a modern version
of their itinerant missions.[70]

Competition from neo-Pentecostals prompted a growing number of conservative Catholic priests and bishops to experiment with new methods for attracting the faithful. In the process the Church sought its roots but also mimicked
the techniques and mass emotional displays of the Pentecostals. Some clerics resorted to miracles and exorcism. The Church also improved its media resources. Despite Pentecostal success, the Church still had Brazil's largest network of religious radio stations and publishing concerns, though it recognized
that it used these tools less effectively than its competitors.

At the core of these initiatives lay Catholic Charismatic Renewal (CCR).
CCR emerged to challenge the hegemony of liberationism in the Brazilian
Church. Based on a mixture of traditional spirituality and elements of moder-
nity, CCR was founded in the United States in the 1960s and subsequently ex-
ported to Brazil. As stated in chapter 7, it is a "Pentecostalized" version of
Catholicism.

In the estimation of religious historian Andrew Chesnut, CCR built the largest and most lively Catholic lay movement in Latin America. It packed soccer
stadiums with spirited followers and dominated Catholic broadcasting with a
new message of liberation—not from political and economic oppression, but
from demons.[71] In São Paulo, for example, the Charismatics filled churches in
both conservative and progressive areas. Charismatics made up approximately

3.8 percent of the population—more than double the number of CEB members. Even some liberationists praised the Charismatics for revivifying faith and
building a sense of community and participation within the Church. Charismatic support was mainly middle class, but the poor also joined. Although the
Charismatics emphasized personal salvation and shunned liberation theology,
they shared the CEBs' interest in the Bible and charitable work.[72]

The rise of CCR renewed the post–World War II intra-church struggle between activism and spiritualism, between terrestrial and heavenly concerns. Because of Charismatics' conservatism, the progressive CNBB bureaucracy waited
until the mid-1990s to grant CCR official status. By then it was clear that CCR
was the best option for competing with Pentecostalism. Even so, the CNBB set
strict controls to keep the movement in line with official post–Vatican II beliefs and practices. The Charismatics also met resistance from some liberationist clergy. Such tensions have kept the Catholic Church from building a
united front against the Pentecostals,[73] although in recent years some liberationists have begun to adopt CCR's approach and even collaborate with the
Charismatic clergy.[74]

CCR adopted a modern entrepreneurial strategy combined with old-time
revivalism. Its clergy viewed the faithful as religious consumers whose demand
for spiritual products could be fulfilled through market research and the use of
the mass media. They borrowed key elements from the neo-Pentecostals. To
affirm the movement's Catholic orientation and to distinguish itself from the
Protestants, CCR embraced the Virgin Mary, Latin America's most powerful
religious symbol.[75] One of the first bishops to employ religious marketing was
the Franciscan friar Dom Fernando Antônio Figueiredo, named bishop of the
new diocese of Santo Amaro after the Vatican separated it and its population of
three million from the archdiocese of São Paulo during the attack on progressivism in the late 1980s. Dom Fernando headed the Instituto Brasileiro de Marketing Católico (Brazilian Institute for Catholic Marketing). "The diocese of
Santo Amaro is like a business. It is organized and knows how to sell its product: salvation," business manager Antonio Miguel Kater Filho, author of a book
on marketing and the Catholic Church and a consultant to the diocese, told a
Brazilian newsmagazine.[76]

In the mid-1990s a Santo Amaro priest, Father Marcelo Rossi, championed
CCR in his meteoric rise as a gospel singer, religious showman, and media
personality who filled large stadiums and appeared on several of the country's
major networks. Trained in physical education, Father Marcelo involved his
followers in the physical, emotional, and musical expression of religious senti-

ments, ending his Masses with a convocation to join in aerobic exercises. Like the neo-Pentecostals, he preached liberation from physical maladies.[77] Father Marcelo developed his own website with numerous links to Church organizations, religious and social news, archives of his television and radio broadcasts, and messages of hope for the faithful. It was but one example of the Brazilian Church's growing presence on the internet.[78] Along with Bishop Edir Macêdo, the founder of the Igreja Universal, Father Marcelo was one of the most controversial figures in Brazilian religion in the 1990s.

The Seminário São João Maria Vianney, the Santo Amaro school where Father Rossi resided as a seminarian, embodied the emphases on spirituality, the new evangelization, and traditional priestly training coupled with modern technology. Inspired by the media appearances of Dom Fernando and Father Marcelo, young men from throughout Brazil sought information about the seminary.[79] In 2002 Cláudio Dias, a Santo Amaro deacon, explained the transformation that took place in the ideal image of the Brazilian seminarian with the rise of CCR. In the past the typical student had long hair and a beard; wore leather sandals, a Ché Guevara T-shirt, and a ring made from the fibers of the *tucum* palm; and ignored the rosary. In the new millennium the seminarian had short hair; wore a clerical collar and cross on his lapel; substituted Ché with illustrations of saints, the Virgin Mary, or Christ; and carried a rosary in his pocket for prayer at a moment's notice.[80] Whereas the Recife experiments, the epitome of liberationism, took place in utterly precarious installations, the Seminário São João Maria Vianney had automobiles, computers, an internet connection, and a vocational director, Father André Eduardo Godoi Lourenço, who readily cited the websites of Father Marcelo, CCR, and related organizations. Psychological evaluations were important, and Father Lourenço demonstrated considerable concern about accepting gay men as candidates. Although the liberationist outlook was tolerated, about half of the seminarians came from CCR. Most were also from the middle class, and many came up through the traditional parish structure. (In just thirteen years Dom Fernando had increased the total number of his parishes from thirty-four to ninety.) The few CEBs in Santo Amaro furnished no vocations. In Father Lourenço's words, the seminary had no political activists, because Brazilian society in the 1990s had generally diminished its interest in politics, although he pointed out that CCR included a focus on the poor and social questions. According to Father Lourenço, the seminary followed CNBB guidelines.[81]

However, the seminaries of CCR and other neoconservative Catholic movements demonstrated little, if any, active cooperation with the CNBB.[82] The Santo

Amaro seminary, for instance, was not even listed in the CNBB's catalogue of seminaries and theological institutes.[83] The decline of the CNBB as the powerful, centralized voice of the Brazilian Church has contributed to the lack of dialogue.[84] Often ignoring the realities of parish life, these seminaries' graduates have attempted to indoctrinate their parishioners in neoconservative spirituality.[85] According to their critics, they have emphasized religious aesthetics over content.

Deacon Cláudio personified what he explicitly described as the connection between a new model of the priesthood and the neoliberal economic model that Brazil and much of Latin America adopted in the 1990s. This outlook reflected the business-oriented approach of Dom Fernando and the Charismatics. At age thirty-five Deacon Cláudio provided a classic example of an adult vocation. He worked for two years in the bodyguard detail of President José Sarney (1985–1990), for which he received training in marksmanship, parachute-jumping, mountain-climbing, and other martial skills. He then spent eight years in the hotel industry, where he learned the importance of keeping clients. Service, not ideology, was the key. The new generation of conservative seminarians was at least minimally informed about the important changes that took place in the Latin American Church in recent decades. During his philosophical and theological studies Deacon Cláudio read Marx, the documents of Vatican II, liberation theology, and writings on bioethics. But instead of philosophy, he believed seminarians needed to study communications. He praised Father Marcelo's ability to inspire enthusiasm for the faith. No other cleric has equaled his massive following. According to Deacon Cláudio, poor Brazilians do not know who Leonardo Boff is, but they definitely know Father Marcelo. Father Marcelo has represented not the faithful's alienation, as many critics have asserted, but their rediscovery of the transcendental. Seminarians still accepted liberation theology's option for the poor, Deacon Cláudio affirmed. In the past, however, that message came without a mystical dimension, and it ignored other social classes or created class divisions. In his interpretation the see-judge-act methodology of progressive Catholicism lacked spirituality. He stated that it was impossible for priests and intellectuals, who live in comfortable settings, to understand truly the situation of the poor. The seminaries' primary concern should not be the people per se, but the training of priests as a paradigm for the people to emulate. This view was informed by pre–Vatican II theology. But it did not mean that the Church should ignore the people. On the contrary, the priest was the psychologist to the poor, ready to help uneducated women in menarche or menopause, for example. Neo-Pentecostal churches have had an advantage because they have the personnel to respond to the problems of the faithful on a twenty-four-hour basis. The Catholic Church does not, thus making the training of more priests a top priority. The neo-Pentecostals were not the enemy, the deacon stated, nor did seminarians need to study them. The Church instead needed to concentrate on ministering to the people's needs. Deacon Cláudio stressed that today's priest must be prepared to work with all social groups, regardless of their financial situation. In his words, why not extend a hand to the homosexual, the AIDS patient, the prostitute, the favela-dweller—but also the governor? The priest must strive to be everything for everybody.[86]

José Joffily's 2000 film *O Chamado de Deus* (The Call of God) beautifully portrays the rediscovery of spirituality in the context of lingering ideological differences among seminarians. Proponents and opponents of the Church's involvement in political questions critique each other's positions in interviews set against the background of the seminarians' humble origins, their families' reactions to their vocational calls, and their approaches to evangelization. Although they do not explicitly identify themselves as followers of liberation theology, the more politicized seminarians clearly adopt its strategy of consciousness-raising, critique of social structures, and construction of grassroots communities. They believe that religion per se is a political act. Similarly, the conservative seminarians see themselves primarily as Catholics, not Charismatics. But they eschew political action. As one seminarian states, the Brazilian president (a military dictator) who told the clergy to remain in the sacristy and to concentrate on purely religious matters was right. The liberationists view their colleagues as retrograde, while the conservatives see their counterparts as narrow-minded. Each side convincingly presents its perspective. Although the film obviously sympathizes with the liberationists, it casts doubt on their strategy by juxtaposing these seminarians' miniscule number of followers with powerful images of vast multitudes worshipping with Father Rossi and other Charismatic priests. Small, primitive, communitarian Catholicism is struck in contrast with the conservative Catholicism of the modern mass market. One of the most telling moments comes when an admirer of Father Rossi prays fervently to God, repeating the words "send us more priests!" The Charismatic movement harks back to the centuries-old theme of the resolution of the clergy shortage as the key to the Church's success.[87]

As the Brazilian Church ventures into the new millennium, debate over the model of the priesthood and the most effective means of evangelization will continue. Unlike the United States and European countries, Brazil has yet to experience a "graying" of its priesthood.[88] Yet the Brazilian Church cannot simply think about ameliorating its own version of the shortage. Many of the complaints voiced by priests and seminarians in the 1960s have not been addressed. And there are new issues. Without serious discussion of women's place in the institution, the dearth of black vocations, celibacy, and the potential role of married priests, for instance, the Brazilian Church is unlikely to see much improvement in its priest-parishioner ratio. The Church will require greater agility and imagination than ever if it is to stanch the decline of Catholics' proportion in the populace and transmit effectively the Christian message. Both the CCR and liberationists will need to learn from each other and be open to the possibility of change and new structures. They must pay special attention to the many dramatic shifts occurring in Brazilian society as it continues to urbanize and participate in the new wave of globalization unleashed in the post–Cold War era. Liberation will undoubtedly remain one of the central themes of Brazilian—and world—religion in the new millennium. But it will no longer be restricted to political radicalism or freedom from traditional sin and temptation. The techno-biological revolution is already redefining human liberation as a struggle against disease and aging. Humanity will overcome many of its limitations—but also encounter new dangers and immoral behaviors. To achieve its goals the Church must reflect more deeply on the history of the clergy and its training not merely as a question of numbers, but also in terms of social and cultural history. In this process the redefinition of priests' social relevance will be crucial. Understanding the rich history of the once-revered Tridentine system and the transition to the radical seminarians' movement of the 1960s can provide the key to future innovation. If there is a central lesson to be learned from those years, it is that priests and seminarians are not only dedicated members of a divinely inspired institution, but also psychological beings who experience all of the many needs of the heart common to the human condition.

Brief Timeline of Important Events

1500	The Portuguese arrive in Brazil.
1545–1563	Council of Trent spurs Catholic Reformation and overhauls seminary education.
1549	First Jesuits arrive in Brazil.
1549–1759	Era of colonial Brazilian Christendom.
1759	Jesuits are expelled from Brazil.
1759–1840	The crisis of Brazilian Christendom.
1800	Seminary of Olinda reestablished under enlightenment doctrine by Dom José da Cunha de Azeredo Coutinho.
1817	"Revolution of the priests" in Pernambuco.
1822	Brazilian independence from Portugal.
1827	Led by Father Feijó, priests in São Paulo call for an end to obligatory celibacy.
1840–1962	Brazilian Catholicism Romanizes by implementing the Tridentine seminaries.
1844–1876	The reformist Dom Viçoso serves as bishop of Mariana.
1851	Imperial decree gives government control over seminaries.
1855	The Empire bans new religious novices and the entry of foreign religious priests.
1858	Pope Pius IX establishes the Pontificio Collegio Pio Latino Americano for the training of Latin American priests in Rome.
1888	Abolition of slavery.
1889	Brazil becomes a republic with the overthrow of Emperor Dom Pedro II.

1890	Church and state become separate for first time in Brazilian history.
1922	Centro Dom Vital founded in Rio de Janeiro.
1930	The revolution led by Getúlio Vargas ends the domination of the rural oligarchy and ushers in a new era of Church-state collaboration.
1934	Colégio Pio Brasileiro inaugurated in Rome. Brazil's new constitution fulfills numerous Catholic demands.
1952	Foundation of Brazil's national conference of bishops.
1954	Brazilian Congress votes to approve funds to construct the National Basilica of Aparecida. Inauguration of the seminary at Viamão.
1955	Church hosts the prestigious Thirty-sixth International Eucharistic Congress.
1962	Foundation of USMAS, the Union of Major Seminarians of the South, the leading organization of the fledgling seminarians' movement.
1962–1965	Second Vatican Council.
1964	The Brazilian Army overthrows President João Goulart, initiating twenty-one years of military rule.
1966–1970	Brazilian priests enter officially sanctioned psychoanalysis in order to improve their performance as seminary teachers.
1967	Seeking social justice and greater personal development, students in Recife abandon their seminary to live in small experimental communities.
1968	Latin American bishops back liberation theology at their historic meeting at Medellín, Colombia. In the spirit of the new theology the Church opens the Theological Institute of Recife. Institutional Act No. 5 deepens the military dictatorship in Brazil.
1969	Under a climate of growing military repression the Church closes the key journal O Seminário and brings the seminarians' movement to an end. In the northeast seminarians begin a new experiment in the countryside called "theology of the hoe."
1985	Brazil returns to democracy with the election of a civilian president. Dom Hélder Câmara, the defender of the Recife seminary experiments, retires as archbishop.
1989	Recife's experimental seminaries are closed by Vatican order.

Abbreviations
and Glossary

ACB	Ação Católica Brasileira (Brazilian Catholic Action). A movement for the Catholic laity (nonclergy) first organized in the 1930s and politically significant in the 1950s and 1960s.
Aldeia	A mission village into which Catholic priests gathered natives.
bishop	The governor of a specific territory within the Catholic Church known as a diocese. The bishop oversees priests, nuns, and members of the laity (nonclergy).
brotherhood	A confraternity of lay Catholics established to pay homage to a particular saint and to assist with the social welfare of its members.
Caraça	The prominent secondary school and seminary founded by the Vincentian fathers in Minas Gerais.
Catholic Action	See ACB above.
CCR	Catholic Charismatic Renewal. A traditional spiritual movement founded in the United States in the 1960s and subsequently exported to Brazil.
CEBs	Comunidades Eclesiais de Base (Grassroots Ecclesial Communities). One of the most important innovations of the Popular Church of the 1970s and 1980s.
CEHILA	Comissão para o Estudo da História da Igreja na América Latina (Commission for the Study of the History of the Church in Latin America).
CELAM	Conselho Episcopal Latino-americano (Latin American Bishops Council). Its second general conference at Medellín, Colombia, in 1968 resulted in a radical document calling for social justice in Latin America.

CERIS — Centro de Estatística Religiosa e Investigações Sociais (Center for Religious Statistics and Social Research).

Christendom — A society or region in which Christianity is the predominant religion.

CM — *Comunicado Mensal* (da CNBB).

CNBB — Conferência Nacional dos Bispos do Brasil (National Conference of the Bishops of Brazil). A national organization of Brazil's bishops that meets regularly to discuss religious, social, and political issues. It became the voice of the Brazilian Church in the 1970s.

concubinage — Cohabitation of a man and a woman without obtaining the sacrament of marriage.

congregation — A religious order.

Congregation of the Mission (C.M.) — The official name of the Vincentian order.

conscientização — Consciousness-raising.

Council of Trent (1545–1563) — Watershed meeting of Church fathers held to respond to the Lutheran Reformation and to reform the Catholic Church from within (the Catholic Reformation). It established the model of seminaries employed by the Church from the sixteenth to the mid-twentieth century.

CRB — Conferência dos Religiosos do Brasil (Conference of Brazilian Religious), a powerful organization of regular priests and nuns established to pool resources and foster greater cooperation among religious orders.

diocesan clergy — Priests who work in dioceses (as distinguished from the religious or regular clergy).

engenho — Sugar plantation.

favela — Shantytown.

favelado — A resident of a shantytown.

inserção — Insertion or introduction of priests, nuns, and seminarians into favelas and other poor communities.

Integralista — A member of Ação Integralista Brasileira (Brazilian Integralist Action), a proto-fascist, pro-Catholic organization that emerged in the 1930s.

irmandade — A brotherhood or confraternity.

ITER — Instituto de Teologia do Recife (Theological Institute of Recife).

Jesuits	A highly prestigious male religious order (also known as the Society of Jesus) of the Catholic Church with special allegiance to the pope and known for its intellectual and educational activities. Very prominent in Brazil.
JOC	Juventude Operária Católica (Catholic Youth Workers). A radical Catholic Action movement criticized by the conservative clergy and attacked by the military regime.
JUC	Juventude Universitária Católica (Catholic University Youth). A radical Catholic Action movement closed by the bishops and attacked by the military.
laity	The members of the Catholic Church who are not clergy or nuns. In the post–Vatican II era referred to as the People of God.
Lazaristas	The Vincentian fathers of Brazil, members of the Congregation of the Mission.
mestiço	A mestizo, or child of Portuguese and native parents.
moral concordat	The informal relationship in which the Catholic Church received semi-official status and public privileges in return for its political support of the state.
neo-Christendom	In modern Brazil the idea of the Catholic Church as the country's sole religion and as a prominent actor in society and politics.
Optatum Totius	A decree of Vatican II that sanctioned the reform of the seminaries.
order	An organization of priests bound to a particular mission, obedient to an elected superior, and, unlike the diocesan clergy, not restricted to a specific territory.
OS	*O Seminário* (see below).
OT	*Optatum Totius* (see above).
padroado	The royal patronage, a relationship in which the Portuguese crown assisted the Church financially and sanctioned its activities in exchange for partial royal control over ecclesiastical appointments and other aspects of Church life.
pastoral agent	A lay Catholic activist or participant in the local missionary efforts of the Church.
pequenas comunidades	Small communities of seminarians living outside the confines of the traditional seminary.
PBCM	Província Brasileira da Congregação da Missão (Brazilian Province of the Congregation of the Mission), the official name of the

	Brazilian province of the Vincentians (and as distinguished from two other provinces of the order established in Brazil in more recent times).
Pio Brasileiro	The Colégio Pio Brasileiro, the school where Brazilian seminarians resided while studying at the Gregorian University or other institutions in Rome.
Popular Church	A wing of the Brazilian Catholic Church that emphasized the struggle for social justice and human rights and peaceful opposition to the military regime.
popular religion	The faith and religious practices of the common people, often in opposition to religious rites and ceremonies as defined by the clergy.
priest	An ordained, celibate minister of the Catholic Church. In traditional Church hierarchy priests command the laity (nonclergy) and pledge obedience to bishops or the heads of religious orders such as the Society of Jesus (Jesuits).
psychoanalysis	A psychological therapy in which the patient meets several times per week with an analyst in the attempt to seek relief from neurotic behavior, to discuss dreams and thoughts, and to rediscover the patient's authentic self.
REB	Revista Eclesiástica Brasileira.
regular clergy	Members of religious orders.
religious clergy	Regular clergy.
Romanization	The conservative modernization and Europeanization of Brazilian Catholicism in the nineteenth and twentieth centuries.
santas missões	Itinerant missions led by the Vincentians and other priests in the interior of Brazil.
secular clergy	Priests who work in dioceses.
SEDOC	Serviço de Documentação.
O Seminário	The official national publication of the seminarians' movement of Brazil.
senhores (de engenho)	Sugar barons of Brazil's colonial era.
SERENE II	Seminário Regional do Nordeste II (Regional Seminary of the Northeast II Region).
sertão	The arid backlands of Brazil, in particular of the northeastern region.

SUDENE	Superintendência para o Desenvolvimento do Nordeste (Superintendency for the Development of the Northeast).
TFP	Tradição, Família e Propriedade (Tradition, Family and Property), an archconservative Catholic organization opposed to agrarian reform.
UNE	União Nacional de Estudantes (National Union of Students).
USMAS	União dos Seminaristas Maiores do Sul (Union of Major Seminarians of the South), the most important branch of the seminarians' movement of the 1960s.
Vatican II	The Second Vatican Council (1962–1965) brought together the world's Catholic bishops in a series of meetings to rethink the life and constitution of the Church. It advocated the most sweeping reforms in the history of the Church.
ver-julgar-agir	The see-judge-act methodology of the Catholic Action movement.
Viamão	The seminary of the archdiocese of Porto Alegre. It took in students from across the southern region of Brazil and was the headquarters of the seminarians' movement of the 1960s.
Vincentians	Members of the Congregation of the Mission, founded by St. Vincent de Paul. Also known in Brazil as "Lazaristas."

Notes

1 Introduction

1. Greeley 1972:69.

2. Notion of brotherhood from Cozzens 2000:47; for additional reflections on the priesthood, see chapter 1 of the same work.

3. See, for example, Miller 2000; Marsden 1997. On the importance of religion in Brazilian millenarianism, see Pessar 2004:5–6, passim. The immense array of writings on religion in Latin America further testifies to religion's importance. For examples, see this volume's bibliography. Brazil and Latin America's contemporary religious effervescence, including African, syncretistic, New Age, and a variety of Protestant religions, illustrates the dynamic, ongoing evolution of religion in the modern world. Furthermore, religion intermingles with gender, ethnicity, politics, economics, and other categories of analysis. See, for example, the discussion in Ricci 2001:190, passim. Religion is not separate from society, but intimately part of it, no matter what our "culture of disbelief" might posit; see Carter 1993. This anti-religious feeling survives in the media and other sectors of American society as an undertone of appalling ignorance about the importance of faith in people's lives. This attitude particularly prospers in academia, whose deeply religious roots withered at lightning speed in the twentieth century. For a general discussion of the secularization of the academy, see Marsden 1994; Marsden and Longfield 1992; also see Dougherty 1994. Secularized scholars perhaps do not like to admit that they have their own emic. Such an attitude hinders the ability to understand the emic of the faithful. On the emic versus the etic, see Harris 1979. See also Kristof 2003. Scholars need to take care in avoiding stereotypes of religion and religious experience. As Certeau has illustrated, methodology and perspective can distort our comprehension. "The concept and the experience of religion do not always refer to the same thing," he states. See Certeau 1988:chap. 3 (p. 141 for the quotation). Similarly, Camp advocates consideration of moral motivation in the study of the Church; Camp 1997:14–15. Carter confirms the importance of value-oriented behavior in his study of the Church and land reform; Carter 2002. The anti-religious outlook further manifests itself in anti-Catholicism, one of the last acceptable prejudices in American life, exemplified by gratuitous pope-bashing and other absurd attacks. The old, conservative

anti-Catholicism, based on class and ethnicity, has reemerged on the left-liberal end of the political spectrum, which focuses on gender and sexuality. The best work on anti-Catholicism is Jenkins 2003; see also Lockwood 2000; Riley and Shaw 1993; Long 1988. For another scholar's personal view of Catholicism, see Vásquez 1998:xi–xv.

4. Members of religious orders and congregations carry their organizations' initials after their names, such as "S.J." in the case of the Jesuits. To simplify matters I refrain from this usage except in the identification of interviewees in the bibliography.

5. For a gripping portrait of Santa Marta, see Barcellos 2003.

6. Interview with Frei Nelson (pseudonym). Frei Nelson is preparing a book manuscript titled "Vida de padre: um grito contra o celibato" (The Life of a Priest: A Cry against Celibacy).

7. Graham 1968.

8. Holston 1999:610–14.

9. Vásquez 1998:22, 23 (adulthood), 24 (emancipation). On modernity see also Thornhill 2000:8 (emancipation), passim. For a survey of modernity, see Hall et al. 1996.

10. Thornhill 2000:24, 31–32, 88.

11. Foucault 1979, esp. part 3. For a fine critique of Foucault and discipline as a concept for understanding Latin America, see Centeno 2001. Centeno rejects the notion of the "unruly" (that is, undisciplined) Latin America, as it might be seen through the eyes of the classic European social theorists, and suggests a research agenda in which the employment and efficacy of discipline should be viewed at the level of institutions such as the military, prisons, and schools.

12. Centeno (2001:289, 294) rightly points out that although discipline and modernity are frequently associated in classical writings on capitalism and democracy (Marx, Weber, Simmel, Elias, Foucault, the Frankfurt school), discipline is rarely defined coherently. He concludes "that discipline is defined by the following special properties: (1) automatic obedience that is (2) maintained by omnipresent surveillance, (3) monitored by internal psychological mechanisms, (4) requiring positive acts and not mere restraint, (5) justified by a hegemonic belief system, (6) and encompassing privileges of equality accompanying responsibility." This definition coincides with the Church's understanding of discipline in the seminaries and my use of the concept in this book.

13. For a discussion of revolutionary romanticism in 1960s Brazil, see Ridenti 2000.

14. Bloch quoted in Gay 1985:7.

15. My focus on psychoanalysis adds to a substantial body of Brazilian writings on the role of that field in Brazilian society. This literature stands in stark contrast to the dearth of material on the psychoanalytic profession in the United States, where until the publication of Luhrmann 2000 the only work was, interestingly, by a Brazilian, Márcia Bandeira de Melo Leite Nunes; see Kracke 2000. For a discussion of the preeminent role of the psychological and the personal in the transformation of the U.S. Jesuits, see McDonough 1992:16–19.

16. Harris 1967.

17. Lacerda 1988.
18. Gay 1985:xiv.
19. Quoted in Miller 1993:19, 92.
20. Miller 1993:30–31.
21. Wills 1971:110, 111 (quotation).
22. Miller 1993:32 (collective practice), 77 (birth, origin), 98 (mad).
23. Teilhard de Chardin paraphrased in Wills 1971:107.
24. Cited in Nasini 2001:76.
25. Weber 1966:162 (monastic, methodologies), 236–237 (relationship, represent).
26. Weber 1966:238.
27. Weber 1966:239, 241–42.
28. On anthropophagy see Johnson 1987.
29. Mintz 1985.
30. Modras 2004:chap. 5.
31. Fitzpatrick-Behrens 2001.
32. See the discussion of Padre Diogo Antônio Feijó's provincialism in Ricci 2001:348.
See also Zolov (1999:184) for a discussion of the introduction of rock music into Mexican culture and rockers' need to create their own original sound.

2   To Be a Priest in Brazil

A note on the chapter title: The title of this chapter was suggested by Mattoso 1982b, whose title in English is *To Be a Slave in Brazil* (Mattoso 1986). Like Mattoso's work, this chapter seeks to draw broad conclusions about long periods.

1. On institutive trends and the idea of a "myth of origin" for the Church, see Sanchis 1992:31–32.
2. Pinheiro 1993. In addition to numerous journalistic accounts of this assembly, see Boff 1992; Hennelly 1993.
3. On protests, see, for example, Lins 2000a, 2000b. For the bishops' statement, see CNBB 2000.
4. On periodization, see Azzi 1983:11.
5. Veiga 1977:140. Also see Rubert 1981. A staunch defender of the secular clergy, Rubert points out historians' excessive, unquestioning dependence on the chronicles of Jesuit critics such as José Anchieta and Manoel da Nóbrega. Many writers also depend on Leite 1938–1950. Aside from Rubert's work there is no published archival study of diocesan priests for the first centuries of the colonial period. An excellent piece based almost entirely on archival research from the nineteenth century is Mattoso 1982a.

6. Donnelly 2004:95.

7. Vainfas and Souza 2000:7–8.

8. Boxer 1969:132–33. On the Church's power in Portugal, see Abreu 1997:14–15.

9. Lima 1990. Spain also had numerous clergy, with two hundred thousand men by the mid-1600s; Delumeau 1977:39.

10. Donnelly 2004:48, 110–12.

11. Nunes 1991:51, 55.

12. Motta 2000:27–28.

13. Freyre 1978:28, note 85.

14. Abreu 1997:157.

15. Rubert 1981:41–42.

16. Rubert 1981:43–44; Freyre 1978:29.

17. Hoornaert et al. 1977:281–84.

18. Veiga 1977:140.

19. Veiga 1977:41–42, 77–78, 139–40.

20. Rubert 1981:75–79, 54–56, 114, 146. In the bishopric of Rio de Janeiro alone the Church had a hundred parishes at the end of the colonial period; see Veiga 1977:63, 70–71, 76, 137, 142–44; Hoornaert et al. 1977:53–54, 277–80, 284–85, 288–89.

21. See Veiga 1977 and Rubert 1981 and 1988.

22. Hoornaert et al. 1977:99 (quotation), 183–85, 288. On parish structure in New Spain, see Taylor 1996.

23. Rubert 1981:88, 179–80.

24. Boxer 1952:165–68; Abreu 1997:107–9.

25. Nunes 1991.

26. Freyre 1978:28, 146–48, 151–53; Azzi 1983:9.

27. On the regulation of customs, see Hoornaert et al. 1977:382–90; Oliveira 1985:141.

28. Vainfas 1997:28–35, 39, 41, 48.

29. Delumeau 1977:60, 89.

30. Hoornaert 1974:47 (Anchieta), 32 (sacred enterprise), 48, 55–56. See also Azzi 1983:11–12.

31. Hoornaert 1974:32–33.

32. Lacombe 1986:51, 54, 55, 57, 60; Bruneau 1974:14–16.

33. Knowles and Obolensky 1974:503; Jedin 1967:275–76. Delumeau (1977:154–59) emphasizes that the lack of religious devotion and knowledge and priests' absence from their parishes—and *not* clerical misconduct such as concubinage—were the main reasons for the Protestant Reformation. There was no "golden age" of Christianity in the medieval era.

34. Previous paragraph and this from Ellis 1965a:1–28, 29 (quotation citing H. Outram Evennett).

35. Freitas 1979:29–30.

36. Cited in Delumeau 1977:21.

37. Moro 1997:259. The Jesuits who trained European diocesan clergy in the sixteenth century also sought to establish a model that included lay students and was attached to a university or other educational institution; see O'Malley 1993:238.

38. Delumeau 1977:185–89.

39. Freitas 1979:54–56, 59, 61, 127, 130–33, 145. Also see Hoornaert et al. 1977:195–200; Pires 1950:303–13; A. Oliveira 2001. On the Jesuits and Malagrida see Tavares 1995. It is difficult to overestimate the impact of the suppression of the Jesuit order. Pombal ordered it expelled from all Portuguese territories. Eighty fathers were executed, hundreds were imprisoned, and a thousand or more deported. In Spain five thousand Jesuits were arrested. See Delumeau 1977:208. On the genesis of the *colégios* and the Jesuits' initial reluctance to train the diocesan clergy, see O'Malley 1993, chap. 6.

40. Kselman 1986:26. For the distinction between Counter-Reformation and Catholic Reformation, see Donnelly 2004:viii.

41. Hoornaert et al. 1977:171; Queiroz 1973.

42. Maués 1987.

43. Russell-Wood 1989:61–89. See also Vainfas and Souza 2000:47–48.

44. Vainfas and Souza 2000:47–56.

45. Levine 1991:1–3.

46. Myscofski 1991 and 1988. For further background on Anchieta, see Motta 2000.

47. Cohen 1991; also see Cohen 1990, 1998.

48. Vainfas and Souza 2000:68.

49. Alden 1996:259.

50. Weber 1966:218–19, 223–25, 232, 235–36.

51. Freitas 1979:150–51.

52. Alden 1987:285–96; Alden 1996:525–26; Schwartz 1982:22 and 1985:90; Rubert 1981:147. Also see Mörner 1953:3–4, 195, 199–200, 202, 206–8.

53. Abreu 1997:152.

54. Delumeau 1977:34.

55. Schwartz 1985:205.

56. Mattoso 1982a:29; Camello 1986:426.

57. Boxer 1969:54 (bad clergymen), 169–70 (between the evils), 255 (Cuiabá). Also see Russell-Wood 1987:209–11, 232.

58. This and next two paragraphs from Schwartz 1985:96, 99, 222, 231–35, 286–87, 292–93, 304, 314, 385–89, 445–46, 489, 493–97, and 1982:18–22.

59. Schwartz 1982:18–22.

60. Schwartz 1985:96, 234 (quotation); Boxer 1952:235 (Vieira), 238–40 (trans-Atlantic trade); Hoornaert et al. 1977:45 (trans-Atlantic trade). On Jesuit dependence on slave labor, see also Mörner 1953:208, 212. For an alternative, though highly polemical and apologetic, discussion of the Jesuit involvement in the slave traffic, see Terra 1984b:114–26.

61. Hauck et al. 1980:160.

62. Schwartz 1985:445–46; Mattoso 1982a:29, 32–33.

63. Boxer 1952:236. Boxer cites Leite 1938–1950 as an example of such apologetical writing. The most recent proponent of Leite's argument is Terra 1984b:66–69.

64. Terra 1984b:69–72, 98–102.

65. Boxer 1952:236–37.

66. Sweet 1995:20, 28.

67. Alden 1996:255.

68. Alden 1996:255 (quotation), 258–61, 267, 271, 295.

69. Lewin 2003a:79.

70. Vainfas and Souza 2000:43–44; see also Socolow 2000:58–59.

71. Warren 2001:65.

72. Vainfas and Souza 2000:12–13, 15–20.

73. Tavares 1995:9, 43.

74. Sommer 2000:32–38.

75. Schwartz 1973:129–38 and 1985:32, 39; Marchant 1942:91.

76. Schwartz 1985:32, 37, 39–40; Freyre 1959:171–72. On the Jesuits in China see Spence 1984.

77. Delumeau 1977:90–92.

78. Alden 1996:265–66, 654–55.

79. Warren 2001:65, 146.

80. Schwartz 1985:39–47; Freyre 1978:109–10, 147–48, 151–53, 417; also see Abreu 1997:96–99, 107–9, 152. For a general overview of the destructiveness of the missions in Latin America, see Langer and Jackson 1995.

81. Hoornaert et al. 1977:78, 86; Mörner 1953:200.

82. Veiga 1977:24; Rubert 1981:286–88.

83. Azzi 1969:9, 25–27; Rubert 1981:289.

84. Rubert 1981:108.

85. Hauck et al. 1980:41–44.

86. Azzi 1976a:46–50; Freyre 1978:109.

87. Azzi 1976a:47–49.

88. Alberigo 1998:550.

89. Mott 1988.

90. Hoornaert et al. 1977:365 (eroticization), 366 ("inclined," according to the Jesuit Jorge Benci).

91. Hauck et al. 1980:64.

92. Vainfas1997:47. In 1745 the Franciscans prohibited the marriage of slaves serving the order; see Vainfas 1997:88.

93. Hauck et al. 1980:208, 270–72; Schwartz 1985:385–89.

94. Vainfas and Souza 2000:22–24.

95. Hauck et al. 1980:268–70.

96. Hoornaert et al. 1977:345.

97. Hauck et al. 1980:52, 146.

98. Not many years later, the bishop of Luanda made somewhat similar observations. He did not believe in the possibility of black vocations, but, noting the lack of white missionaries and their high mortality rates, he accepted mulattoes and mestiços. Proposals also arose to take Indians, blacks, and mulattoes to Europe for clerical training. These plans did not come to fruition. In India the Portuguese allowed both Indians and mestiços to serve as secular priests on the lower rungs of the hierarchical ladder. The pope himself in 1518 went as far as to consecrate a black Congolese bishop, but such a rarity was not to be repeated for several centuries. See Boxer 1963:14 (quotation), 16, 33–35, 66.

99. European Capuchins, for example, portrayed the diocesan clergy of Luanda as concupiscent, simoniacal, and involved in the slave trade. Bishops in East Africa remained hesitant about ordaining local aspirants. In Mozambique the government did not permit the establishment of a seminary until 1761. Not a single priest was ordained in the two centuries leading up to the decision. See Boxer 1963:33–34, 35 (quotation), 56–57.

100. Rubert 1981:182–83; Freitas 1979:130.

101. Foreign travelers in Brazil noted the presence of mulatto and black priests; see Freyre 1978:414. Mulatto and a lawyer, Monsignor Francisco Correia Vidigal was sent to Rome to obtain recognition of Brazil's independence; see Hauck et al. 1980:80.

102. Lewin 2003b:51–53.

103. Souza 1998:625, including note 40 for Rubert citation.

104. Rubert 1981:33–35, 140–43.

105. Hoornaert et al. 1977:399.

106. Hoornaert et al. 1977:398; Hauck, et al. 1980:105, 147–47.

107. Freyre 1978:414; Hoornaert et al. 1977:289–90.

108. Hauck et al. 1980:176.

109. Mott 1988, chap. 1; Azzi 1990.

110. Freyre 1978:93.

111. Vainfas 1997:60–62, 73, 84, 87, 90–94, 99–103.

112. Vainfas and Souza 2000:34–36, 39–40, 49 (cure).

113. Freyre 1978:195 (procreators), 318–19, 442–46, 447 (happy). For additional examples of priests' sexual activity see Hauck et al. 1980: 57, 88, 90, 193; Lustosa 1977:30 and 1985:25–26.

114. Vainfas 1997:83, 85.

115. Lima 1990:2.

116. Vainfas 1997:40.

117. Lima 1990:339–57, 579, 738–79. On the modern confessional, see Vainfas 1997:24. On the Church and concubinage, see also Socolow 2000:11–15, 48–49, 71–73, 154.

118. Azzi 1990:449–65.

119. Donnelly 2004:3.

120. Lima 1990:357–74. Even in Europe the implementation of Trent was far from uniform; see Delumeau 1977:28, passim; Ellis 1965b.

121. Rubert 1988:231–34.

122. Hoornaert et al. 1977:265–81. See also A. Oliveira 2001.

123. Lima 1990:467, 468, 470–86, 751. See chapter 4 of the present work for clerical disputes based on accusations of sexual misconduct in the twentieth century. On the repression of Judaism, see Vainfas and Souza 2000:24–33.

124. This paragraph and previous from Lima 1990:560–87, 588 (mulatto, carnal), 589, 590–91 (Marciana), 592–648, 658 (Sysnando). Also see Mott 1988.

125. Lewin 2003a:43–45.

126. *O clero no Parlamento* 2:167 and 3:358.

127. See, for example, Veiga 1977:114, 139–40, 142–43; Azzi 1969:6–9, 25, 27, 60; Hauck et al. 1980:195; Rubert 1981:114, note 89; Schwartz 1985:286. The parliamentary discourses of priests and bishops who were members of the national assembly make frequent allusion to the low pay of diocesan priests; see *O clero no Parlamento.*

128. Hauck et al. 1980:195; Bruneau 1974:25.

129. Hauck et al. 1980:195.

130. Boxer 1969:179; *O clero no Parlamento* 2:422.

131. Hoornaert et al. 1977:286–87.

132. Mattoso 1982a:28–33.

133. Freyre 1978:414; Hoornaert et al. 1977:210.

134. Freitas 1979:154–55; Hoornaert et al. 1977:190.

135. For Feijó's comments, see *O clero no Parlamento* 2:362–63.

136. Beozzo 1983:94–97.

137. French 2003:55, note 12.

138. Ricci 2001:219–21, 242, 250.

139. Bieber 1999:121.

140. Ricci 2001:307–308.

141. See, for example, Barbosa 1978:13–14; Mattoso 1982a:25, 28; Hauck et al. 1980:88. On the power of the clergy in the interior, see P. Castro 1985:43. On the Instituto, see also Ricci 2001:175, including note 51.

142. *O clero no Parlamento* 2:166, 172–74 and 4:51–52, 448.

143. Hauck et al. 1980:16, 87, 97.

144. De Groot 1996:30.

145. Morel 2000; Souza 1998:627–29 (avid readers).

146. Barman 1988:56–57, 76–77.

147. Hauck et al. 1980:23, 85–86, 97; Barbosa 1978:12, 14, 17–19, 22–23; Maxwell 1978 (Minas). On Pernambuco see also Barman 1988:57–59.

148. Ellis 1965b:44–45.

149. Morel 2000.

150. The best and most recent study of this seminary is Neves 1984. Also see Hauck et al. 1980:82–83, 97; Baratta 1972; Quintas 1985:209–10. See also Silva 1998.

151. Silva 1998:696, 698.

152. Barbosa 1978:12; Hauck et al. 1980:86.

153. Ávila 1978:32–33.

154. On Minas, see Bieber 1999:119–24, 165, 166 (quotation), 173–74.

155. See, for example, Mattoso 1982a:22, 42; Hauck et al. 1980:86; Barbosa 1978:21.

156. Azzi 1983:13–14. On Gallicanism see Ivereigh 2000:10, note 13.

157. Hauck et al. 1980:83; Azzi 1969:68–94.

158. Ricci 2001:346, also see 427.

159. Ellis Júnior 1980:26–28, 77. On the debate over Feijó's genealogy, see Ricci 2001:112–33, passim. On Feijó and other illegitimate clerics, also see Lewin 2003a:78–79, 2003b:108.

160. Lewin 2003a:79.

161. Fleury 1967:88; Lustosa 1977:42–43, 150.

162. Ricci 2001:92.

163. This paragraph and next three from Ricci 2001, passim.

164. P. Castro 1985:43.

165. Ricci 2001:399.

166. Barman 1988:169.

167. P. Castro 1985:43.

168. Ricci 2001:332.

169. Lustosa 1977:36, 51–52, 145.

170. Lustosa 1985:25–26.

171. Freyre 1978:318–19.

172. Lewin 2003b:82, 108.

173. Mattoso 1982a:18–21, 42; Hauck et al. 1980:193 (quotation).

174. Lewin 2003a:80.

175. Lustosa 1977:30.

176. Lewin 2003b:85–86.

177. Freyre 1978:443–44; Hauck et al. 1980:57. For other examples, see Bieber 1999:121, 123.

178. De Groot 1996:33.

179. Mattoso 1982a:21.

180. Ricci 2001:359–60.

181. Ellis Júnior 1980:78–79.

182. Feijó 1828.

183. Ellis Júnior 1980:89–90; Lustosa 1977:86–91, 92–93 (quotation), 94–98, 103.

184. Ricci 2001:346–49.

185. Lustosa 1977:38, 51.

186. Ricci 2001:412.

187. Lewin 2003b:109–14, 214–18.

188. Barros 1985:319–22. On opposition to foreign religious, see *O clero no parlamento* 2:362–63.

189. Barros 1985:319–22. On Jansenism in France, see Tackett 1986:6–7, 9.

190. Cunha 1985:382–97. On the concurrent campaign for juridical nationalism, see Lewin 2003a and 2003b.

191. Ricci 2001:360.

192. Lustosa 1977:68, 80–84.

193. Ricci 2001:348, 375.

194. Azzi 1983:13–14; Lustosa 1977:21–22. On Feijó's argument see Lewin 2003b:112. The liberal-nationalist program further included a revolutionary proposal to institute civil marriage and the civil registry of marriages, births, and deaths. Brazil was the first Latin American nation to consider such a measure. Once again the conservatives, led by Dom Romualdo, held sway, in part by appealing to Catholic religious chauvinism and attacking Protestants, whose presence helped instigate discussion of the need for civil marriage. See Lewin 2003b:115–24.

195. Lustosa 1977:105–10.

196. Quoted in Lustosa 1977:106.

197. Hauck et al. 1980:84.

3 Romanization and the Grand Discipline, 1840-1962

1. On the collective, see de Groot 1996:4–5, 6.

2. Pérez, Gregory, and Lepargneur 1964:53.

3. From a speech published posthumously in 1958 and cited in Silva 1961:116.

4. Oliveira 1985:345. Azzi periodizes Romanization as the reorganization of the Church (1890–1921) in the First Republic and the increase of its political influence during the "Catholic restoration" (1922–1961); Azzi 1983:10, 18–20.

5. The comparison with the Jesuits is suggested in Azzi 1974b:1241–42.

6. Edwards 2002:45.

7. Oliveira 1985:292; Vidler 1971, chap. 13.

8. Bruneau 1974:26; Haring 1958:116–17.

9. Ivereigh 2000:4–6.

10. Bruneau 1974:26, note 46. Pius IX is cited in Camello 1986:471. On the creation and development of the Pio Latino Americano, see Edwards 2002.

11. Hauck et al. 1980:182, 198.

12. See, for instance, Seidl 2003:232–34.

13. White 1989:315.

14. Oliveira 1985:292; Stavrianos 1981:295–98. On Romanization see also Wernet 1987, chap. 4. On religious orders and Catholic revivalism in the United States, see Dolan 1978.

15. De Groot 1996:6.

16. Ivereigh 2000:12.

17. Certeau 1988:141.

18. My interpretation follows the seminal work of Delumeau 1977:194 (quotation), passim.

19. Certeau 1988:128. The reception of Trent's articles by Portugal signified the increasing importance of law in the Luso-Brazilian world and buttressed the monarchy; see Lewin 2003a:xviii, 13–14.

20. Also see Delumeau 1977:175–99.

21. De Groot 1996:6, 7–8, 22, 60, 66.

22. Pessar 2004:2.

23. Quoted in Beozzo 1983:115; see also Oliveira 1985:297–304. The complete title of this document is *Pastoral coletiva dos arcebispos e bispos das províncias meridionais do Brasil.*

24. Serbin 1996b; Oliveira 1985, chap. 7; Maués 1988:1074–79; Borges 1992:171; Miceli 1988:123–30. On First Communion, see de Groot 1996:102–3. On Afro-Brazilian religion in Porto Alegre, see Kittleson 1997, chap. 3. For an interesting comparison with sacraments and rites in Colombia, see Londoño 2000:151.

25. Giumbelli 1997:37–38.

26. De Groot 1996:98–101.

27. On the two camps, see de Groot 1996:92–93. A similar divide would occur between conservative and progressive Catholics in the 1970s and 1980s; see chapters 7 and 8 for a discussion of the neoconservative reaction in Brazilian Catholicism.

28. De Groot 1996:68–69, 73.

29. See, for example, the discussion of the construction of state and Church models for "right behavior" in de Groot 1996:11–13. For a contrasting study of state-building from the bottom up, see Nugent 2002.

30. Bieber 1999:182–83, 194.

31. Borges 1992:166–67.

32. On the growth of other professions, see Graham 1990:66–67, 266.

33. Lustosa 1982:9, 97–98, and 1983:53–79. On Father Cícero see Della Cava 1976b, chaps. 6–8.

34. Hauck et al. 1980:158–59, 164, 201, 278–79.

35. Bruneau 1974:22–25; Haring 1958:115; on funding of diocesan priests, see de Groot 1996:43. For an interesting contrast in attitudes about the Church displayed by Dom Pedro II's devout daughter Princess Isabel, see Barman 2002.

36. Hauck et al. 1980:197 (financial aid, salaries, curricula). On subsidies and government interference, see also Freitas 1979:48–49, 77, 82–83, 87–88, 95, 97–99, 100–105,

124. An example of Church requests for support in *O clero no Parlamento* 2:273, 3:356–57, and 4:263–65, 413, 553–55. On provincial support see Trindade 1951:53–54. Further example of provincial assistance and tensions in Camello 1986:321–28. The Church faced a similar struggle with the German state; see Ellis 1965b:42.

37. Freitas 1979:26, 48–49, 107, 112, 116–17, 121–24; *O clero no Parlamento* 2:273 and 5:259–60 (quotation).

38. Hauck et al. 1980:200–205; Azzi 1975:316; Beozzo 1983:98–101; *O clero no Parlamento* 4:72–74.

39. De Groot 1996:48–50.

40. Bruneau 1974:25–30. Also see Mainwaring 1986:25–26; Borges 1992:168–69; Levine 1992:64; Barros 1985:338–65; Haring 1958:117–25. For an alternative interpretation, see Schneider 1991:58.

41. For comparison with Germany, see de Groot 1996:62.

42. Hauck et al. 1980:200–205; see also Azzi 1975:316; Beozzo 1983:98–101; *O clero no Parlamento* 4:72–74.

43. On institutional expansion see Carrato 1970, chap. 1; Camello 1973:23–24; V. Zico 1981:497–511; Dodin 1981:527–36; Castro 1942. On Saint Vincent's vocation, his pioneering charity, and the origins of the Daughters of Charity in Europe, see Delumeau 1977:4, 37–38, 58–59, 159, 198. On the medal and foreign expansion, see Souza 1999:28, 40.

44. Begg 1985:110–13; "Livro das missões, Diamantina, 1825–1929," Arquivo da Província Brasileira da Congregação da Missão, Rio de Janeiro (hereafter cited as PBCM), 10.

45. Azzi 1974b:1240; also see Souza 1999:146–47.

46. Delumeau 1977:99–128. On Jansenism see also Tavares 1995, chap. 3.

47. Salles 1993:561–62.

48. Pedro Sarneel, "Dados Históricos da PBCM," PBCM, uncatalogued document.

49. Souza 1999:14, 22–23.

50. J. Zico 1981:485.

51. For a skeptical interpretation of Lourenço's noble status, see Souza 1999:15–19; on saintly status, see p. 51. On Lourenço as a prospector, see Salles 1993:324.

52. On the early history of the Lazaristas see Camello 1986 and 1973. Also see J. Zico 1981 and 1988; Carrato 1970; Silva Neto 1965; Salles 1993; "Epítome da Congregação da Missão no Brasil," 1958, PBCM, ME. 1 (1) CC, document 36; Azzi 1974b; Pasquier 2001–2003. In Mexico many leaders also attended seminaries before the consolidation of the Mexican Revolution in the 1920s; see Camp 1997:141–42.

53. Souza 1999:11, 30–36.

54. Both Dom Pedro I and Dom Pedro II had an affinity for the Lazaristas; see J. Zico 1981:485–509. On ultramontane support, see Azzi 1974b:1244–246.

55. Palácios 1987.

56. Santos 1986.

57. Ivereigh 2000:14.

58. Cited in Oliveira 1985:304–5.

59. Borges 1992; de Groot 1996:118–25.

60. Caulfield 2000:3–4, 15, 45–47, 77–78, 97, 189–90.

61. Júlio Maria 1950:237, 244–46. Also see Beozzo 1981:110, 124–26. Because of his charisma as a great preacher, Father Júlio Maria became famous throughout Brazil and was even compared to Father Antônio Vieira, but his style and ideas caused him to fall into disfavor with the conservative clergy. See Salles 1993:550–53.

62. Quoted in Azzi 1981:15

63. Levine 1992:144 (quotations). On Dom Luís and the Vincentians, see Camello 1986:438, 441–42, 443.

64. Levine 1992:150. Also see the classic work of reportage on the confrontation in Cunha 1944. For comparison with a similar episode in Mexico, see Vanderwood 1998. Not all priests opposed Conselheiro; one, in fact, considered himself to be a close friend of the holy man; see Salles 1993:481.

65. Hauck et al.1980:209–10. On the history of the missions in Brazil see Hoornaert et al. 1977:133–35; Hauck et al. 1980:296–306; Levine 1992:33.

66. Delumeau 1977:190.

67. Souza 1999:59, 83–85.

68. Salles 1993:154–56.

69. Delumeau 1977:189–94.

70. Camello 1986:54–56.

71. Azzi 1974b:1238–39 (quotation), 1240.

72. Hauck et al. 1980:103–5; *O clero no Parlamento* 4:214–18, 221, 224–27; Souza 1999:25 (quotation), 49.

73. Salles 1993:85–86.

74. Souza 1999:74, 76.

75. Souza 1999:84. Unless otherwise noted, this and the next four paragraphs are based on "Livro das missões, Diamantina, 1825–1929," PBCM.

76. Delumeau 1977:217.

77. See the photo and accompanying explanation in "Livro das missões, Diamantina, 1825–1929," PBCM, 29.

78. Souza 1999:83, 85.

79. De Groot 1996:78.

80. Cited in Londoño 2000:151.

81. Statistics from Wirth 1982:55–58, 61.

82. On political violence and municipal governance see Bieber 1999, esp. chaps. 5 and 6.

83. Souza 1999:83–84.

84. "Livro das Missões, Diamantina, 1950–1954," PBCM.

85. Bruneau 1974:30; see also Moura and Almeida 1985:324–28; Levine 1992:205, 210. As discussed above and pointed out by Mata (2002:256–67), even before 1889 the Brazilian state began taking lands from the Church.

86. Miceli 1988:59–63. Expansion occurred elsewhere in Latin America; see, for example, Londoño 2000:148.

87. Bruneau 1974:32.

88. Souza 1999:44.

89. Data on national origins of religious orders from Beozzo 1983:120; see also pp. 93–129. Data also from Pérez, Gregory, and Lepargneur 1964:16.

90. Souza 1999:63.

91. Quotation from Hauck et al. 1980:205.

92. Beozzo 1983:127–28.

93. Beozzo 1983:103–6. See also Beozzo 1986:298–99; Nunes 1986:198–202.

94. Passos 1991.

95. Miceli 1988:67–76.

96. Pang 1974. On *coronelismo* see Leal 1977; Lewin 1987.

97. Beozzo 1983; Wirth 1982:144–45. On the embryonic development of Catholicism in Minas, see Mata 2002.

98. Beozzo 1983:110; Azzi 1987. For an overview of immigration, see Petrone 1985:93–133.

99. Beozzo 1983:275, 110. On the northeast, see Levine 1992:125–30.

100. Miceli 1988:76–78; Wirth 1982:142–45; Camello 1986:34, 455–63. On Dom Silvério's phenotype, see Rout 1972.

101. Wirth 1982:143; Miceli 1988:153–54.

102. "Livro das missões, Diamantina, 1950–1954," PBCM.

103. Della Cava and Montero 1991.

104. Bruneau 1974:44–45; Salem 1982:97–134.

105. On Dom Leme, see Bruneau 1974, chap. 2; Mainwaring 1986, chap. 2; Azzi 1977.

106. See the discussion of ecclesiastical unification and "religious *coronelismo*" in de Groot 1996:79, 93; also see the discussion of Church-state relations in the labor arena in J. Souza 2002:208–13.

107. Sanchis n.d. On patriotism see also Serbin 2001b, chap. 1.

108. Beozzo 1986:275, 293–98; Della Cava 1976a:13–14. For a splendid photographic essay on the Cristo Redentor, see Rubinstein 1999.

109. "Livro das missões, Diamantina, 1825–1929," 8.

110. Beozzo 1986:275, 287–89, 293–98, 338–39, 340 (quotation).

111. Schwartzman, Bomeny, and Costa 1984:44–45, 56 (quotation), 60–61. See also Lenharo 1986.

112. Williams 2001:97, 103–9, 114–15, 123.

113. Lima 1936:135–55. On political struggles over religious education, see Dávila 2003. Also on Church-state relations see the discussion of Paraná in Carneiro Junior 2000.

114. Serbin 2000b:25–27.

115. Azevedo 1955:22–23. On chaplains, see also Beattie 2001:168–69.

116. J. Souza 2002; also see Weinstein 1996 passim.

117. J. Souza 2002:211–13, 218.

118. *Coleção das leis de 1954* (Rio de Janeiro: Departamento de Imprensa Nacional, 1954), 3:26. I treat the question of subsidies in detail in Serbin 1991b, 1992b, 1995a, and 1996b. On state funding for the restoration of historic churches, see Williams 2001:109, 123. On patronage and subsidization of the Church in Paraná, see Carneiro Junior 2000:105–6. On Aparecida as a symbol, see Souza 1996.

119. The Lazaristas' private correspondence reveals rich data about the economic life of the seminaries. On subsidies, for example, see Fr. Luis de Gonzaga Cunha Marelim to Fr. Eugênio Pasquier, January 14, 1936, PBCM, 7 (1) CM/5, CR-69; Marelim to Pasquier, October 3, 1936, PBCM, 7 (1) CM/5, CR-73; Marelim to Pasquier, January 12, 1938, PBCM, 7 (1) CM/5, CR-74; Marelim to Pasquier, December 5, 1938, PBCM, 7 (1) CM/5, CR-76; Marelim to Pasquier, January 7, 1939, PBCM, 7 (1) CM/5, CR-77.

120. Untitled documents, Fundação Getúlio Vargas, Centro de Pesquisa e Documentação de História Contemporânea do Brasil (hereafter cited as FGV/CPDOC), Arquivo Gustavo Capanema, GC 35.00.00, folder II, documents 4 and 18, series h.

121. Freitas 1979; Oliveira 1937; Santini 1934; Mendes 1938. For a discussion of these last three works see Veiga 1977:9.

122. Fr. João Bosco Rocha to Hamilton Prisco Paraíso, chief of staff of Clemente Mariani, Minister of Finance in the government of President Jânio Quadros, Rome, August 9, 1961, FGV/CPDOC, Arquivo Clemente Mariani (hereafter cited as ACMa), CMa, 60.12.27, pasta III, document 49, series c. For further discussion, see Serbin 1995a. On subsidies in the 1970s, see Serbin 2000b:153–55. The importance of economics in Latin American religion has reemerged as a central topic and stirred debate about the rationality of religious institutions; see, for example, Gill 1998; http://www.providence.edu/las/discussion.htm; Serbin 1996b and 1999b.

123. Serbin 1996b; Piletti and Praxedes 1997, chap. 23. On priests and social peace see also the film *A Boa Empresa.*

124. Cited in Delumeau 1977:213; also see p. 212.

125. On the monastical model, see Hoornaert 1991.

126. Ellis 1965b:31. See chapter 6 of the current work for a detailed discussion of Saint Ignatius's book *The Spiritual Exercises.* For a detailed study of Saint Vincent's contributions to and ideas about seminary education, see Roche 1964.

127. Salles 1993:331 (establishment), 332–33, 334 (nothing).

128. Frei Aleixo 1943. Among many other laudatory articles on the clergy, see Negromonte 1959; Marinho 1941. In the First Republic the construction of barracks in rural areas led to a similar isolation of Army recruits; see Beattie 2001:265. Isolation of the clergy also took place in the previous European Catholic enlightenment; see Delumeau 1977:179–99.

129. Hoornaert et al. 1977:199–200; Camello 1986:163–65; A. Oliveira 2001, chap. 1.

130. Camello 1986:162, 313–14, 343.

131. Souza 1999:57–58.

132. Hauck et al. 1980:196; Camello 1986:421–23.

133. On Mariana, see Camello 1986:318–19, 359–60; on *De genere et moribus* in the First Republic see Miceli 1988:31–34; see also Azzi 1991:20. On the presence of black priests in Minas, see also Salles 1993:91–92.

134. Salles 1993:277 (monk), 253, 275 (good-bye), 277 (courted).

135. Interview 1 with Pretto.

136. Camello 1986:328–29, 333, 336, 338, 355–58, 366.

137. Camello 1986:346–47, 354–55; "Horário do Seminário Maior de Diamantina," PBCM, 8 (4) CM/6, ED-23. The standard course grid in the diocesan minor seminaries run by the Vincentians included religion, Portuguese, literature, history of Brazil, general history, natural history, science, geography, choralism, mathematics, Latin, French, English, Greek, and apologetics. In the major seminary the philosophy section included courses in logic, metaphysics, history of philosophy, gnosiology (the study of cognition), cosmology, theodicy, ethics, aesthetics, and some notions of sociology and psychology. The theology curriculum introduced students to dogmatic theology, moral theology, fundamental theology, Church history, sacred scripture, exegesis, canon law, biblical Greek, Hebrew, and Gregorian chant. See Souza 1999:89.

138. Souza 1999:89.

139. Salles 1993:391, 406–7, 422–25, 441.

140. See, for example, Campos 1994:135–42.

141. Ellis 1965b:76–77.

142. Camello 1986:328–42, 358–60. For the manual, see *O livro do seminarista* 1959, chap. 2.

143. Camello 1986:367–423, 436, 474–75.

144. Camello 1986:391–92 (quotation), 424, 427–28, 431, 455–69, 473–76.

145. Azzi 1974b:1252.

146. Azzi 1969:60 and 1974b:1251–54.

147. Foucault 1979:209–21.

148. Dom Silvério Gomes Pimenta to Father Pedro Dahaene, Mariana, December 29, 1904, PBCM, 8 (3) CM/7, BI-96. Dahaene, a French Lazarista, was the order's *visitador* (visitor) and thus its supreme authority in Brazil.

149. Azzi 1969:60; 1974b:1251–54; and 1991:2, 35–36; Wernet 1987, chap. 4; on the reform in Rio Grande do Sul, see Hastenteufel 1987; Bohnen and Ullmann 1989.

150. See, for example, Azzi 1976b; Wernet 1987, chap. 3.

151. Camello 1986:438–69; Azzi 1974a:651–52, 656; "Epítome da Congregação da Missão no Brasil," 1958, PBCM, ME. 1 (1) CC, document 36, pp. 25–26. The seminary at Crato closed in 1877 because of the severe drought that plagued the northeast.

152. The Lazaristas made unsuccessful attempts to start seminaries in Pará, Santa Catarina, and São Paulo, where the Italian Capuchins led the reform. A shortage of personnel caused the order to turn down requests to run seminaries in yet other cities.

See, for example, Fr. Luis de Gonzaga Cunha Marelim to Fr. Afonso Maria Germe, São Luís, December 16, 1940, PBCM, 7 (1), CM/5, CR-82.

153. Beozzo 1983:94.

154. Personal correspondence from Father Lauro Palú, February 21, 2005.

155. J. Zico 2000:330–33.

156. For the best prosopograhical analysis of Brazil's modern bishops, see Beozzo 2001a. Historical works on individual prelates are generally lacking. Recent exceptions are Piletti and Praxedes 1997; Calliari 1996; Sydow and Ferri 1999; Arns 2001; Costa, Pandolfi, and Serbin 2001. For a study of bishops in the First Republic, see Miceli 1988.

157. On the military, see Stepan 1971, 1973.

158. The same situation held for rectors in Mexico, Chile, and Colombia; see Camp 1997:155–57, 167.

159. White 1989:266; Ellis 1965b:65.

160. White 1989:265 and chap. 12. On Latin, see also "A pronúncia romana do latim" 1931.

161. Cruz 1996:30–41, 54–57, 73–77, 86, 87. See also Edwards 2002. Figures on Gregorian students are for the 1950s; see Rocha 1972:77.

162. Father João Bosco Rocha to Hamilton Prisco Paraíso, chief of staff of Clemente Mariani, finance minister in the government of President Jânio Quadros, Rome, August 9, 1961, FGV/CPDOC, ACMa, CMa, 60.12.27, pasta III, document 49, series c.

163. Beozzo 1994b.

164. Rocha 1972:26.

165. Azzi 1991:7–8.

166. Pérez, Gregory, and Lepargneur 1964. From the 1940s to the early 1960s the REB and other Church publications carried numerous articles on recruitment, the OVS, papal speeches about the glory of the priesthood, national vocational days, and other related themes. See, for example, Guglielmelli 1941:745–56; Paul VI 1963.

167. Freitas 1979:35.

168. Quoted in Azzi 1991:4.

169. Miceli 1988, chaps. 4 and 5.

170. Pérez, Gregory, and Lepargneur 1964:100–109; CNBB 1984b:90–91.

171. Azzi 1991:5 (quotation), 8.

172. Beozzo 1983:103–4, 108, 123–28. I know of no study that examines in detail the female religious vocation during the First Republic. An article that outlines many of the issues involving nuns is Nunes 1986.

173. Pessoa 1988:31–35.

174. Azzi 1991:8.

175. Barros 1990:413–17. Caramuru and Dom Jaime were not related, nor were Dom Jaime and Dom Hélder. For other examples of mothers' influences, see Rocha 1972:4–15.

176. Buss 1962.

177. Miceli 1988:116. On the lack of primary education for the masses, see J. Nagle 1985:265–69.

178. Trindade 1951:242–44.

179. Bojunga 2001:41–42.

180. Kubitschek 1979:7–9, 10 (quotation). See also Bojunga 2001:52–53. On the tribute to the Vincentians, see "Caraça, Mariana e Diamantina" 1944. On the lack of educational opportunity in Minas and the fathers' influence on Kubitschek, also see Barbosa 1988:191–96, 215–16; Wirth 1982:139–42, 145. On the large number of students of the Diamantina seminary who became prominent laymen, see Mourão 1971:27–32.

181. In the early 1950s Father Geraldo Fernandes estimated the number of ex-seminarians at "many thousands"; see Fernandes 1953:106. Tagliavini (1990:13) estimates the number of nonordained former seminarians in the 1990s at two hundred thousand. Most of these men had probably entered the seminaries before the Second Vatican Council.

182. Campos 1994:28 (quotations), 48; Rocha 1972:44 (stepping-stones). On the accreditation debate, see also "Estudos dos Seminários" 1946; Dom Silvério Gomes Pimenta, archbishop of Mariana, to Dahaene, Mariana, December 23, 1910, PBCM, 8 (3) CM/7, BI-102.

183. Fernandes 1953:106, 108–9, 114; Azevedo 1955:48–49, including note 52; Ribeiro et al. 1990:56.

184. De Boni and Costa 1984:197–98. See also Seidl 2003:230–31, including notes 184 and 185.

185. Cabras 1983:83 (mini-priest), 84–86, 87 (guardian angels); Tagliavini 1990:78–79. As Newton Cabral observes, priests and seminarians stand out in Brazilian literature as figures locked in struggle with sexuality and celibacy; Cabral 2001:138–39. In addition to *O seminarista*, he cites *O Ateneu*, by Raul Pompéia; *O outro caminho*, by João Mohana; *Auto da compadecida*, by Ariano Suassuna; *Em nome do desejo*, by João Silvério Trevisan; *Quarentena*, by Mário Márcio; and *Dom Casmurro*, by Machado de Assis.

186. Cabras 1983:84–85. For contemporary discussions of the debate, see Panzarasa 1948; Azevedo 1960. On selectivity, see White 1989:287–89.

187. "Cópia do termo de visita de Mons. Cintra," September 15, 1946, PBCM, 8 (3) CM/6, ED-39.

188. On obligationists, see Cabras 1983:84–85. On Zenaldo, see Rocha 1972:41–42, 45.

189. Father José Marins cited in Bandeira 2000:256.

190. On the static nature of the system, see, for example, Souza 1999 and Salles 1993. Delumeau (1977) also describes the Tridentine period as one lasting until Vatican II. See also Donnelly 2004:vii, 45, 106; Ellis 1965a:3, 27; Camp 1997:163; Comblin 2000:92.

191. Libânio 1984 (*grande disciplina*).

192. Ivereigh 2000:10, note 13.

193. Souza 1999:54, 100.

194 Cabral 2001:50.

195. Goffman 1974. For Brazilian commentators, see Tagliavini 1990; Cabras 1983. For a critique of the concept of the "total institution" in the study of Brazil's military academy, see Castro 1990:32–34.

196. Azzi 1991:15–16 (Fortaleza, other punishments); Barros 1990:418, 420. See also Barbosa 1988:193.

197. Pessoa 1988:49.

198. Also see the nuanced view of the seminaries provided by Pessoa 1988:40–57. See also the discussion of the complex historicity of the Council of Trent in Alberigo 1998.

199. Salles 1993, passim; on pedagogy of violence, see p. 348; on Boavida, pp. 279, 344, 348, 351, 385–86, 414–16, 435–38; on Dom João Antônio, p. 221.

200. Interview with João Batista Ferreira. A similar view is in Mayrink 2002:22–23.

201. Rocha 1972:33–34.

202. Cited in Delumeau 1977:45.

203. Azzi 1991:9–10.

204. "Estatutos do Seminário Archiepiscopal de Diamantina," 1929, PBCM, 8 (4) CM/6, ED-13.

205. Interview with Marino Bohn.

206. Cabras 1983:79–80; Tagliavini 1990:298.

207. Barros 1990:418–19.

208. Rocha 1972:30–32, 33 (quotation).

209. Azzi 1991:8.

210. Pessoa 1988:39–40 (Mariana); Rocha 1972:70–72 (Rome).

211. See Camello 1986:340–41; "Horário do Seminário Maior de Diamantina," PBCM, 8 (4) CM/6, ED-23, no date, probably 1867; Tagliavini 1990:155; Castro 1990:114 (cadets).

212. Pessoa 1988:49; on Tronson see Delumeau 1977:44.

213. Barros 1990:419; interview 1 with Celso Pedro da Silva (quotation); on readings also see the poignant description in Salles 1993:338, 388–91, 411–12.

214. Azzi 1991:17.

215. Tagliavini 1990:118–20, 133, 160–61 (alarm clocks), 183; Cabras 1983:78–79, 81, 93–97. The observation about the Lazarista is mine.

216. For routines, see Camello 1986:175–76; "Horário do Seminário Maior de São José da Archidiocese de Marianna," PBCM 8 (3) CM/6, ED-29. On Mariana, see Pessoa 1988:41. Data on soccer from interview 1 with Celso Pedro da Silva.

217. Cabras 1983:90–92; Tagliavini 1990:196, 217–19, 278–80. See also Dom Joaquim Silvério de Sousa to Dahaene, Diamantina, January 21, 1908, PBCM, 8 (4) CM/7, BI-51.

218. "Estatutos do Seminário Archiepiscopal de Diamantina," 1929, PBCM, 8 (4) CM/6, ED-13.

219. Barros 1990:419.

220. Azzi 1991:10–11. On Vatican pressure, see also Father Luis de Gonzaga Marelim to Pasquier, São Luís, June 6, 1935, PBCM, 7 (1) CM/5, CR-67. U.S. bishops rejected the European–Latin American model of vacation homes. They preferred that their students have contact with the laity during the off-season. See Ellis 1965b:69.

221. Father José Dias Avellar to Pasquier, Diamantina, October 17, 1939, PBCM, 8 (4) CM/5, CR-359.

222. Interview 4 with Raimundo Caramuru Barros; interview with João Batista Ferreira.

223. "Estatutos do Seminário Archiepiscopal de Diamantina," 1929, PBCM, 8 (4) CM/6, ED-13.

224. See, for example, "Estatutos do Seminário Menor de Mariana," 1927, PBCM, 8 (3) CM/6, ED-37; "Seminário de Diamantina. 1867. Do Diretor," PBCM, 8 (4) CM/6, ED-25; Germe to Lazarista fathers at Diamantina seminary, Rio de Janeiro, January 1, 1943, PBCM, uncatalogued document in folder marked "Corresp. Diversa 1941–43."

225. Interview with José Pires de Almeida; similar data from interview with Hugo Vasconcelos de Paiva. The Lazaristas' intellectual decline had another cause. In order to economize they had decided in the 1920s to stop sending Brazilian Vincentians to study overseas. The decision reduced dependence on the French, but it also removed the Vincentians from the key centers of theological debate.

226. Barbosa 1988:194–95; Avellar to Germe, Diamantina, April 11, 1940, PBCM, 8 (4) CM/5, CR-363.

227. Pessoa 1988:51.

228. Rocha 1972:77, 231.

229. Beozzo 1994b. On Scholasticism see also Wills 1971:22, 25.

230. Interview with Hugo Vasconcelos de Paiva; interview with José Pires de Almeida.

231. Dom Hélder Pessoa Câmara, "Minha passagem pela Ação Integralista Brasileira," unpublished manuscript, 1973, Instituto Nacional de Pastoral (hereafter cited as INP), document 02143. Interview quotation in Câmara 1979:42, 45–46.

232. Rocha 1972:77, 231 (quotation). Catholic Action did not receive adequate attention at the Pio Brasileiro until the early 1960s; see Bratti 1961. In general Brazilian themes received little coverage in the pages of the Pio's periodical, O Pio Brasileiro. On isolation from sociopolitical reality, also see Salles 1993:376. Another example of isolation and conservatism in interview 4 with Luiz Viegas de Carvalho and also in interview with Malomar Lund Edelweiss. Cozzens (2000:72–73) notes a similar lack of critical thinking in the U.S. seminaries for the pre-conciliar period.

233. Bishop Spalding cited in Wills 1971:25.

234. Hesburgh cited in Camp 1997:171–72.

235. Câmara 1979:35, 36 (quotations).

4 The Costs of Discipline

1. Certeau 1988:127.

2. Description of uniformity from Souza 1999:146. In the estimation of de Groot (1996:79), the Church's institutional success led it to become more "impersonal."

3. Adams 1975:103–4, 109–10, 117 (quotation), 137, 235–36. My interpretation here is also supported by Souza 1999:83–84; de Groot 1996:2; Eugen Drewermann as interpreted in Moreira 1995:401.

4. Kemper 1988:177.

5. De Groot (1996:2) arrives at a similar conclusion, describing the post-1930 Church as "paralyzed" and "ossified." Moro (1997:262) describes the seminaries as becoming static.

6. For an overview see Serbin 2000a; Chesnut 2003.

7. The letters are in PBCM, which contains approximately six thousand catalogued documents and hundreds of pages of uncatalogued material. In all I examined nearly seven hundred documents from this collection.

8. See, for example, de Groot 1996:113–17, 149.

9. Neumann 2000:102.

10. Maués 1988:1077, and Maués 1987; Kselman 1986:25; also see Mata 2002; Kittleson 1997:352.

11. De Groot 1996:18, 35, 82–89; on syncretism, also see Kittleson 1997, chap. 3.

12. José Murilo de Carvalho (1987) has described overt dependence on the Brazilian state as "*estadania.*"

13. Forman 1975:221–35. On Holy Cities, see Diacon 1991 and P. Machado 2001; on Pedro Batista, see Pessar 2004. Also on Messianism in the Northeast, see Palácios 1987.

14. Salles 1993:39–40, 61–63, 71–72, 92–94, 129 (heaven and earth), 130–59, 222.

15. Hauck et al. 1980:289–91.

16. Beozzo 1986:294–96.

17. De Groot 1996:135–36; Souza 1996.

18. "Necrologia" 1964. On Brusque see Besen 1977.

19. Lacroix 1936:71–72, 390, 392–93 (quotation), 396, 397.

20. For a fine overview of the most recent history of the priest shortage, see Prien 1985:1026–45. Dozens of articles in the 1940s, 1950s, and 1960s addressed the shortage in Brazil, including many comparing that country's religious demographics with the situation of the Church in European and North American countries. See, for example, "Circular Coletiva do Episcopado Paulista ao Clero" 1943:186–98; "O problema sacerdotal no Brasil" 1943; Ginnetti 1952; Baraúna 1953; Buss 1962. On the priest shortage also see "Mensagem ao nosso clero" 1958; Pizzardo and Staffa 1959:712; Pérez, Gregory, and Lepargneur 1964.

21. For a similar commentary on the earlier failure to employ nuns, see Delumeau 1977:81–82.

22. Beozzo 1987:45. On the race question in this period, see Skidmore 1976; Andrews 1991.

23. Avellar to Pasquier, Diamantina, November 5, 1928, PBCM, 8 (4) CM/5, CR-332.

24. Father José Lázaro Neves to Pasquier, Mariana, May 29, 1938. PBCM, 8 (3) CM/5, CR-156. I found no evidence that either of the tailors entered the order. If they had, they would have worked merely as auxiliaries within the confines of the priests' residence.

25. "Seminário de Sto. Antônio—Maranhão: Condições de Admissão para Alumnos da 'Associação de S. José,'" 1927, PBCM, 7 (1) CM/6, ED-6.

26. Census data from http://www.ibge.gov.br.

27. "O sétimo centenário" 1931:134.

28. "Recrutamento de religiosos entre o elemento de cor" 1960; see also Cloin 1961. On Leite, see Alden 1996:526, including note 117.

29. The export of priests, nuns, and volunteers to Latin America merits a detailed study. Here I summarize the issues relevant to the seminaries and the Brazilian priesthood. On movement of religious personnel see Prien 1985:1040–45; Illich 1967; Ginnetti 1952:376–80; Baraúna 1953; "Falta de Sacerdotes" 1960; "Quase 100 padres para a América" 1961; "Padres espanhois para a América Latina" 1962; "Um Seminário para a América Latina, na Itália" 1963; "A Bélgica tem um centro nacional de vocações" 1964; "Instituto de ciências sociais especializado para sacerdotes" 1960; "Bolsas de Estudos do Centro de Formação para o Clero" 1959; "Bolsas de estudo para sacerdotes Latino-Americanos" 1960; Sousa 1956b; Pius XII 1958b; John XXIII 1959, 1962, 1963; "Missionários canadenses no estrangeiro" 1967; "Sacerdotes espanhois para todo o mundo" 1967; Novais 1957:904–5, 907, 913; Promper 1965. For an overview of flows in private foreign aid during the post–World War II era, see Smith 1990.

30. The themes of the teacher shortage, overwork, and little pay are among those most frequently raised in the Lazarista correspondence. For the examples cited here, see Dom Helvécio to Father François Verdier, superior general (the international head) of the Lazaristas, Turin, October 15, 1925, and to Pasquier, Mariana, January 6, 1926; Avellar to Pasquier, Diamantina, December 12, 1939, PBCM, 8 (4) CM/5, CR-361. For more examples, see Serbin 1993c, chap. 5.

31. See, for example, Avellar to Pasquier, Diamantina, late 1936, PBCM, 8 (4) CM/5, CR-339; Avellar to Pasquier, Diamantina, October 26, 1938, PBCM, 8 (4) CM/5, CR-353; Avellar to Pasquier, Diamantina, November 21, 1939, PBCM, 8 (4) CM/5, CR-354. For a description of the position, see O livro do seminarista 1959, chap. 2.

32. See, for example, Avellar to Pasquier, Conselheiro Mata, July 9, 1938, PBCM, 8 (4) CM/5, CR-349; Avellar to Pasquier, Diamantina, August 3, 1938, PBCM, 8 (4) CM/5, CR-351; Avellar to Pasquier, Diamantina, October 26, 1938, PBCM, 8 (4) CM/5, CR-353. For other examples of difficulties, see Dom Joaquim to Dahaene, Diamantina, January 17, 1909, PBCM, 8 (4) CM/7, BI-49; Neves to Pasquier, Mariana, March 9, 1937, PBCM, 8 (3) CM/5, CR-151.

33. For background on Avellar, see PBCM, "Catálogo dos Coirmãos," 132. For correspondence, see Dom Joaquim to Pasquier, Diamantina, April 28, 1928, PBCM, 8 (4) CM/7, BI-24; Avellar to Pasquier, Diamantina, January 22, 1936, PBCM, 8 (4) CM/5, CR-334; Avellar to Pasquier, Diamantina, January 30, 1936, PBCM, 8 (4) CM/5, CR-335; Avellar to Pasquier, Diamantina, November 16, 1936, PBCM, 8 (4) CM/5, CR-338 (the only reason); Avellar to Pasquier, Diamantina, late 1936, PBCM, 8 (4) CM/5, CR-339 (morally obliged); Avellar to Pasquier, Diamantina, July 22, 1938, PBCM, 8 (4) CM/5, CR-350; "Diamantina," *Ecos da Província* 8:4 (1938), 171–73. For a subordinate priest's view of Avellar's situation see Father Salvador Rubim dos Santos to Pasquier, Diamantina, April 13, 1938, PBCM, 8 (4) CM/5, CR-371. The Jesuits experienced a similar shortage of personnel as they rapidly expanded their educational system in the sixteenth century; see O'Malley 1993:227.

34. Avellar to Pasquier, Diamantina, December 12, 1939, PBCM, 8 (4) CM/5, CR-361; Avellar to Pasquier, Diamantina, January 6, 1940, PBCM, 8 (4) CM/5, CR-362.

35. Bicalho to Pasquier, Diamantina, October 7, 1939, PBCM, 8 (4) CM/5, CR-411. Work alone did not account for all of the complaints. The Vincentians exhibited a degree of hypochondria resulting from the high standards of health and cleanliness that the Tridentine system required of priests and seminarians. At São Luís, for example, the candidate had to show certificates of vaccines and blood tests. See "Seminário de Sto Antônio—Maranhão. Condições de Admissão para Alumnos da 'Associação de S. José,'" PBCM, 7 (1) CM/6, ED-6. Despite long hours, the Vincentians enjoyed great privileges in comparison with most Brazilians and appeared to be healthier. Many lived to a ripe old age. In a sampling of thirty-six priests born between the early 1800s and early 1900s, the average lifespan was seventy-four. Calculation made with data from "Catálogo dos Coirmãos," PBCM. Very few Brazilians lived beyond seventy.

36. Marelim to Pasquier, São Luís, July 24, 1933, PBCM, 7 (1) CM/5, CR-54; Avellar to Pasquier, Diamantina, August 3, 1938, PBCM, 8 (4) CM/5, CR-351; Avellar to Pasquier, Diamantina, September 9, 1938, PBCM, 8 (4) CM/5, CR-352.

37. Among numerous examples, see Dom Silvério Gomes Pimenta to Father Júlio Clavelin, Lazarista visitor, Mariana, June 17, 1900, PBCM, 8 (3) CM/7, BI-92; Dom Joaquim to Pasquier, Diamantina, April 2, 1914, PBCM, 8 (4) CM/7, BI-38; Dom Silvério to Pasquier, Campo Belo, August 26, 1920, PBCM, 8 (3) CM/7, BI-106; Dom Helvécio to Verdier, Turin, October 15, 1925, and to Pasquier, Mariana, January 6, 1926, PBCM, 8 (3) CM/7, BI-77; Dom Serafim to Pasquier, Diamantina, January 23, 1936, PBCM, 8 (4) CM/7, BI-19.

38. Avellar to Pasquier, Diamantina, 1936, PBCM, 8 (4) CM/5, CR-339; Avellar to Pasquier, Diamantina, November 4, 1937, PBCM, 8 (4) CM/5, CR-343; Bicalho to Pasquier, Diamantina, November 7, 1938, PBCM, 8 (4) CM/5, CR-410; Avellar to Germe, Diamantina, April 11, 1940, PBCM, 8 (4) CM/5, CR-363.

39. Antônio Brandão [? name partially illegible], vicar general of Diamantina, to Pasquier, Diamantina, August 1, 1940, PBCM, 8 (4) CM/5, CR-442.

40. Dom Serafim, "Regulamento dos Sres. Padres Colaboradores do Seminário de Diamantina," 1937, PBCM, 8 (4) CM/6, ED-12.

41. Dom Augusto Álvaro da Silva, archbishop of Bahia, to Godinho, Bahia, January 11, 1946, PBCM, uncatalogued document in folder marked "Correspondência 45–66"; Dom Augusto to Godinho, Bahia, November 4, 1947, PBCM, uncatalogued document in folder marked "2 (1) CM, Capelania Militar. Salvador, Correspondência 1953–1954"; Father João Maria Kuenen, rector of Salvador seminary, to Godinho, Bahia, March 27, 1946, PBCM, uncatalogued document; Kuenen to Godinho, Bahia, April 27, 1946, PBCM, uncatalogued document. Also see Dom Augusto to Godinho, Bahia, October 13, 1946, PBCM, uncatalogued document in folder marked "2 (1) CM, Capelania Militar. Salvador. Corrrespondência 1953–54."

42. Father Clóvis Duarte Passos to Godinho, Caraça, August 6, 1956, PBCM, uncatalogued document in folder marked "Correspondência Variada 1951–57."

43. Marelim to Pasquier, São Luís, July 22, 1934, PBCM, 7 (1) CM/5, CR-59.

44. Marelim to Pasquier, São Luís, February 5, 1934, PBCM, 7 (1) CM/5, CR-58; Marelim to Pasquier, São Luís, July 22, 1934, PBCM, 7 (1) CM/5, CR-59; Marelim to Pasquier, São Luís, January 24, 1935, PBCM, 7 (1) CM/5, CR-63; Marelim to Pasquier, São Luís, April 11, 1935, PBCM, 7 (1) CM/5, CR-64 (quotation); Marelim to Pasquier, São Luís, May 26, 1935, PBCM, 7 (1) CM/5, CR-65; Marelim to Pasquier, Bahia, January 27, 1939, PBCM, 7 (1) CM/5, CR-78. On Diamantina, see Avellar to Pasquier, Diamantina, November 4, 1937, PBCM, 8 (4) CM/5, CR-343; Avellar to Pasquier, Diamantina, January 8, 1938, PBCM, 8 (4) CM/5, CR-345; Avellar to Pasquier, July 22, 1938, PBCM, 8 (4) CM/5, CR-350. Also of interest is Avellar to Pasquier, Diamantina, December 5, 1936, PBCM, 8 (4) CM/5, CR-333.

45. Interview with Dom Manoel Pedro da Cunha Cintra. Dom Cintra was the apostolic visitator during the 1940s and 1950s. The idea of the central seminaries arose under Pope Pius XI; also see Azzi 1991. Moro (1997:403, note 13) states that even before this period the Vatican perceived a decline in the quality of seminary studies. As a result, Pope Pius XI introduced a reform that brought the inclusion of college-level studies in the seminaries.

46. Beozzo 1994b.

47. Interview with Dom Manoel Pedro da Cunha Cintra.

48. See, for example, Santos to Pasquier, Diamantina, October 31, 1917, PBCM, 8 (4) CM/5, CR-288; Avellar to Pasquier, Diamantina, July 22, 1938, PBCM, 8 (4) CM/5, CR-350. In this last document Avellar listed the requirements of the "Programa Geral de Estudos dos Seminários do Brasil." Also see Avellar to Pasquier, Diamantina, December 12, 1939, PBCM, 8 (4) CM/5, CR-361. In many other letters I noted that it was the rectors who informed the Lazarista superior of the Holy See's determinations. See also Edwards 2002.

49. Unsigned letter, probably from Dom Augusto da Silva, to Germe, Bahia, April 5, 1944, PBCM, uncatalogued document in folder marked "2 (1) CM. Capelania Militar. Salvador. Correspondência 1953–1954."

50. Interview with Dom Manoel Pedro da Cunha Cintra.

51. Data on Pequeno from interview with Dom Manoel Pedro da Cunha Cintra. For examples of visitators' written reports, see "Cópia do termo de visita de Mons. Cintra," Mariana, September 15, 1946, PBCM 8 (3) CM/6, ED-39, and "Ata da Visita de Mons. Cintra ao Seminário de Diamantina," PBCM, uncatalogued document in folder marked "Corresp. Diversa 1946–1951," September 22, 1945.

52. For examples of preparation, see Marelim to Pasquier, Vitória, January 7, 1939, PBCM, 7 (1) CM/5, CR-77; Rocha 1972:185; Marelim to Pasquier, Bahia, January 27, 1939, PBCM, 7 (1) CM/5, CR-78. For the sexual advances, see Marelim to Pasquier, São Luís, January 4, 1936, PBCM, 7 (1) CM/5, CR-68.

53. Avellar to Pasquier, Diamantina, October 26, 1938, PBCM, 8 (4) CM/5, CR-353; Avellar to Pasquier, Diamantina, November 21, 1938, PBCM, 8 (4) CM/5, CR-354.

54. Interview with Dom Manoel Pedro da Cunha Cintra. On Pequeno, see Marelim to Pasquier, São Luís, January 20, 1934, PBCM, 7 (1) CM/5, CR-57; Marelim to Pasquier, São Luís, April 11, 1935, PBCM, 7 (1) CM/5, CR-64; Marelim to Pasquier, São Luís, June 6, 1935, PBCM, 7 (1) CM/5, CR-67; Avellar to Germe, Diamantina, April 11, 1940, PBCM, 8 (4) CM/5, CR-363.

55. Interview with Dom Manoel Pedro da Cunha Cintra.

56. Father Francisco Lage Pessoa to Godinho, Diamantina, February 5, 1946, PBCM, uncatalogued document in unmarked folder.

57. Father Francisco Delille Pinto Ribeiro to Godinho, São Luís, no date, probably 1945, PBCM, uncatalogued document in folder marked "Corresp. Div. 1945–49."

58. Father José Paulo Sales, rector of Mariana major seminary, to Godinho, Mariana, April 22, 1950, PBCM, uncatalogued document in folder marked "Corresp. Div. 1945–49."

59. Dom Augusto to Godinho, Bahia, October 13, 1946, PBCM, uncatalogued document in folder marked "2 (1) CM, Capelania Militar. Salvador. Correspondência 1953–54."

60. Father José Trombert, rector of Mariana minor seminary, to Godinho, Mariana, November 5, 1946, PBCM, uncatalogued document in unmarked folder. Discipline encouraged backbiting among seminarians. Priests often wished failure for colleagues who took the initiative to improve themselves. The weekly ritual of public accusation at the Vincentians' Petrópolis seminary reinforced the culture of denunciation. The accused kissed the floor and thanked his fellow seminarians for their criticisms. Any error by a seminarian could turn into a cause for his humiliation. The religious life fostered anything but brotherly love. Interview with João Batista Ferreira.

61. Germe to Lazarista fathers at Diamantina, Rio de Janeiro, January 1, 1943, PBCM, uncatalogued document in folder marked "Corresp. Diversa 1941–43."

62. Dom Serafim to Germe, Diamantina, January 16, 1943, PBCM, uncatalogued document in folder marked "Corresp. Diversa 1941–43."

63. Unidentified priest in Diamantina to Godinho, Diamantina, September 25, 1946, PBCM, uncatalogued document in folder marked "Corresp. Div. 1945–49."

64. Dom Helvécio to Verdier, Turin, October 15, 1925 (quotation), and to Pasquier, Mariana, January 6, 1926, PBCM, 8 (3) CM/7, BI-77. See also Trindade 1951:81–82.

65. Lesser 1999.

66. Beozzo 1983:95.

67. Lacroix 1936:71–72, 390, 392–93, 396, 397.

68. Souza 1999:45, 48.

69. De Groot 1996:53, 75.

70. Della Cava 1976b. For a poignant photographic essay of Joaseiro see Santana 2000.

71. Azzi 1987–1988:2:181; Beozzo 1983:122.

72. *Pastoral Collectiva dos Senhores Arcebispos* 1911:299.

73. Dom Joaquim and bishops and archbishops of southern Brazil to the religious orders, São Paulo, October 10, 1910, PBCM, 8 (4) CM/7, BI-44.

74. Azzi 1987–1988:1:356–58, and 2:75–80, 87–88, 89 (quotation), 90, 181–85, 205–7, 256–59.

75. Beozzo 1983:129.

76. Trindade 1979:2–3, 106, 109, 124, 147, including note 16. Dom Hélder, "Minha Passagem pela Ação Integralista Brasileira," unpublished manuscript, 1973, INP, document 02143. Trindade asserts that a study of bishops' and priests' ties to Integralism is still lacking. However, a detailed description of the participation of the clergy in the movement is available in Todaro 1971, chap. 4. This work claims that half of all secular priests were members of the movement, although the evidence is sketchy.

77. Rossi 1951:231. An alternative opinion, denying the existence of friction between foreign and Brazilian priests, can be found in Sousa 1945.

78. Cited in Lacroix 1936:224–27.

79. See *Catalogue des Maisons et du Personnel de la Congregation de la Mission* 1909.

80. Souza 1999:71.

81. "Epítome da Congregação da Missão no Brasil," 1958, PBCM, ME. 1 (1) CC, document 36, pp. 23–24. Similarly, students in sixteenth-century Italy were sensitive to the way in which foreign Jesuits pronounced Latin; see O'Malley 1993:228.

82. Dom Joaquim to Dahaene, Diamantina, March 3, 1908, PBCM, 8 (4) CM/7, BI-50. Emphasis in the original.

83. Dom Joaquim to Pasquier, Diamantina, April 2, 1914, PBCM, 8 (4) CM/7, BI-38.

84. "Catálogo dos Coirmãos," PBCM, 75 (Péroneille in war), 88 (Father Santos's biographical data); Santos to Pasquier, Diamantina, October 31, 1917, PBCM, 8 (4) CM/5, CR-288 (Santos's activities as rector). Hunchbacked condition from verbal communication from Father Clóvis Duarte Passos, February 27, 1989.

85. Santos to Pasquier, Diamantina, November 3, 1917, PBCM, 8 (4) CM/5, CR-289 (he demanded); Santos to Pasquier, Diamantina, October 31, 1917, PBCM, 8 (4) CM/5, CR-288 (much to be sad); Santos to Pasquier, Diamantina, January 29, 1918, PBCM, 8 (4) CM/5, CR-290 (wants to enter, nullity). Emphasis in the original. Also see Dom Joaquim to Pasquier, Diamantina, June 27, 1917, PBCM, 8 (4) CM/7, BI-37.

86. For Santos's career path, see "Catálogo dos Coirmãos," PBCM, p. 88. On Dom Joaquim's support, see Santos to Pasquier, Diamantina, February 27, 1918, PBCM, 8 (4) CM/5, CR-291; Dom Joaquim to Pasquier, Diamantina, July 17, 1917, PBCM, 8 (4) CM/7, BI-36; Dom Joaquim to Pasquier, Caxambu, May 2, 1918, PBCM, 8 (4) CM/7, BI-33.

87. Avellar to Pasquier, Diamantina, December 5, 1936, PBCM, 8 (4) CM/5, CR-333.

88. Barros to Pasquier, Mariana, September 15, 1927, PBCM, 8 (3) CM/5, CR-199 (frequently chastened); Barros to Pasquier, Diamantina, January 9, 1940, PBCM, 8 (4) CM/5, CR-412 (barrack). For Barros's career path, see "Catálogo dos Coirmãos," PBCM, 135.

89. Salles 1993:479–80, 510, 523–25.

90. Antônio Monteiro de Barros to Pasquier, Mariana, December 7, 1919, PBCM, 1 (1) CC/2, VI-545 (first expressed); Barros to Pasquier, Paris, November 22, 1921, PBCM, 1 (1) CC/2, VI-546 (quotations).

91. Barros to Pasquier, Mariana, September 15, 1927, PBCM, 8 (3) CM/5, CR-199 (mischievous); Barros to Pasquier, Mariana, December 29, 1927, PBCM, 8 (4) CM/5, CR-456 (by indulgence). On Barros's problems before ordination, see also Barros to Pasquier, Mariana, November 1, 1927, PBCM, 8 (3) CM/5, CR-200.

92. Barros to Pasquier, Diamantina, January 9, 1940, PBCM, 8 (4) CM/5, CR-412

93. Barros to Pasquier, Diamantina, January 9, 1940, PBCM, 8 (4) CM/5, CR-412; Barros to Pasquier, Diamantina, August 26, 1940, PBCM, 8 (4) CM/5, CR-414.

94. Reference to Integralista movement in Avellar to Pasquier, Diamantina, December 5, 1936, PBCM, 8 (4) CM/5, CR-333. Could Barros conceivably have gone from left to right, from alleged "bolshevist" to Integralista? Yes, because many Brazilian nationalist thinkers underwent similar ideological mutation in the 1920s. See, for example, Trindade 1979:19–34.

95. Barros to Pasquier, Diamantina, August 26, 1940, PBCM, 8 (4) CM/5, CR-414 (overhaul).

96. Interview with Hugo Vasconcelos de Paiva.

97. Moser 2002:537.

98. See also the discussion of the multiple factors shaping the desire for intimacy in Cozzens 2000:32–33.

99. Abbott 2000.

100. Abbott 2000:49, 52, 55–56, 66, 88–90, 100.

101. Armstrong 1993:49–50, 123–25. As Voltaire noted, discussion of the invention of Original Sin is absent from the Holy Scriptures and other early Church writings; cited in Delumeau 1977:230. Only later did Original Sin enter Christian thought.

102. Ferreira Netto 1996:42–43.

103. Abbott 2000:49 (gateway), 17, 56–60.

104. Weber 1966:237–38, and note 7.

105. Cabras 1983:101–5 (hierarchy, seminaries); "Clerical celibacy" 1974 (dedication, pastoral work).

106. Cited in Piletti and Praxedes 1997:287–88.

107. Cited in Nasini 2001:229.

108. Abbott 2000:104–14.

109. Camello 1986:333–36 (hierarchical discipline); Tagliavini 1990:326 (expression of this drive); Rocha 1972:49 (quotation).

110. Rocha 1972:57 (sports); "Seminário de Diamantina. 1867. Do Diretor," PBCM, 8 (4) CM/6, ED-25 (laypersons). See also Pessoa 1988:48.

111. Borges 1992:101 (quotation), passim. On eugenics also see Costa 1989.

112. "Necrologia" 1964.

113. Lacroix 1936:71–72, 390, 392–93, 396, 397.

114. Borges 1992:173–75, 178, 180, 185.

115. Lacroix 1935:125, 236, 239, 503–5, 569–74. In this work Lacroix apparently lashed out at Freud, whom the Church rejected at this time. The psychoanalyst's writings do not appear in the priest's bibliography.

116. Levine 1992:129–30, 134, 136, 127, 134, 147–50, 194–95.

117. On the Virgin Mary and avoidance of women, see Tagliavini 1990:128, 138, 214, 217, 331, 333 (face of the devil), 334, 353. See also Azzi 1991:17 (Marian devotion); Rocha 1972:49 (São Luís Gonzaga); Brandão 1942:673–75 (avoidance of women). Theresa, Gorette, Bernadette from interview with João Batista Ferreira.

118. Interview with João Batista Ferreira.

119. Tagliavini 1990:335 (conjugal life); Cabras 1983:101–7 (necessary evil); Rocha 1972:42 (chapels).

120. On intimacy and smothering, see Cozzens 2000:31, 56.

121. Boswell 1989:105.

122. I am grateful to James Green for this observation.

123. Green 1999:48–49, 113–14. On pp. 135–37, Green recounts the interesting and sad case of Macário S., a German-born priest who spent several periods in the Pinel Sanatorium because of his homosexual activities, considered to be the result of mental illness. As we will see below, however, the Church usually dealt with sexually fractious priests internally.

124. Tagliavini 1990:245–51.

125. Interview with João Batista Ferreira.

126. Rocha 1972:49–50 (bad thoughts, touches, cried), 51 (artificial), 52 (strong feeling, I do not remember), 87 (my affective life).

127. Rocha 1972: 77 (how to explain), 136 (a young woman), 87–96, 103 (private friendship).

128. Denunciation of fellow clerics was not unique to Brazil or the period; it had already taken place in Europe in the Early Middle Ages, for example. See Abbott 2000:110–11. See also the discussion of Eugen Drewermann's Kleriker in Moreira 1995.

129. Father Manuel dos Santos Ferreira, rector of seminary at São Luís, to Dahaene, São Luís, April 27, 1909, PBCM, 7 (1), CM/5, CR-2.

130. Marelim to Germe, São Luís, December 16, 1940, PBCM, 7 (1) CM/5, CR-82.

131. Father Francisco Trombert to Godinho, Mariana, October 6, 1949, PBCM, uncatalogued letter in folder marked "Corresp. Div. 1945-49"; Pereira to Godinho, Rio de Janeiro, February 17, 1951, PBCM, uncatalogued letter in folder marked "Corresp. Div. 1945-49."

132. Dom Helvécio to Godinho, Mariana, no date, probably between 1945 and 1947, PBCM, uncatalogued document in folder marked "Corresp. Diversa 1945-47."

133. See, for example, Deschand to Dahaene, Diamantina, October 16, 1911, PBCM, 8 (4) CM/5, CR-151; Dom Joaquim to Dahaene, Diamantina, January 21, 1908, PBCM, 8 (4) CM/7, BI-51; Marelim to Pasquier, São Luís, May 26, 1935, PBCM, 7 (1) CM/5, CR-65. A number of other sources confirm the existence of priests who had affairs with women or seminarians and who engaged in other kinds of sexual activity. Such data come from: Nasini 2001; interview with José Pires de Almeida; interview with João Batista Ferreira; interview with Geraldino Alves Ferreira Netto; Cabras 1983:107; Rocha 1972:49; Pessoa 1988:40-41; interview with Paviani.

134. Father Genesco Rabelo to Germe, June 12, 1943. PBCM, uncatalogued document in folder marked "Corresp. Diversa 1941-43." For Bicalho's transfer, see Dom Serafim to Germe, Diamantina, January 15, 1941, PBCM, uncatalogued letter in unmarked folder.

135. Neves to Germe, Mariana, June 30, 1943, PBCM, uncatalogued document in unmarked folder; "Catálogo dos Coirmãos," PBCM, pp. 137, 151.

136. Observation on chess from Paul E. Serbin, verbal communication, June 2004.

137. Cozzens 2000:124.

138. Abbott 2000:101 (quotation), 102-4.

139. Cozzens 2000:124.

140. Torres to Godinho, Diamantina, September 29, 1945, PBCM, uncatalogued document in folder marked "Corresp. Div. 1945-49." Also see Dom Helvécio to Godinho, Mariana, no date, probably between 1945 and 1947, PBCM, uncatalogued document folder marked "Corresp. Diversa 1945-47."

141. See, for example, telegram from Torres to Germe, March 7, 1941, PBCM, uncatalogued document.

142. See, for example, Neves to Pasquier, Mariana, April 16, 1943, PBCM, 8 (3) CM/5, CR-145.

143. Guglielmelli 1941:747, 749-52. The same priest wrote other commentaries on the necessity of a rigorous ecclesiastical culture; Guglielmelli 1944a, 1944b. Pereira to Godinho, Rio de Janeiro, February 17, 1951, PBCM, uncatalogued document in folder marked "Corresp. Div. 1945-49"; "Catálogo dos Coirmãos," PBCM, entry on Father Domingos Guglielmelli.

144. This and subsequent paragraphs on Sampaio are based on the following documents: Marelim to Pasquier, São Luís, January 20, 1934, PBCM, 7 (1) CM/5, CR-57;

Marelim to Pasquier, São Luís, October 7, 1934, PBCM, 7 (1) CM/5, CR-60; Marelim to Pasquier, São Luís, May 26, 1935, PBCM, 7 (1) CM/5, CR-65; Marelim to Pasquier, São Luís, June 6, 1935, PBCM, 7 (1) CM/5, CR-67; Marelim to Pasquier, São Luís, June 16, 1935, PBCM, 7 (1) CM/5, CR-66; Marelim to Pasquier, São Luís, January 4, 1936, PBCM, 7 (1) CM/5, CR-68; Marelim to Pasquier, São Luís, January 14, 1936, PBCM, 7 (1) CM/5, CR-69; "Catálogo dos Coirmãos," PBCM, 138.

145. Interview with Geraldino Alves Ferreira Netto.

146. Father Salvador Rubim dos Santos to Pasquier, Diamantina, January 14, 1938, PBCM, 8 (4) CM/5, CR-369 (exaggerated news, unfounded, petition, if I leave, emissary); Salvador Rubim dos Santos to Pasquier, Diamantina, January 16, 1938, PBCM, 8 (4) CM/5, CR-370 (whose son studied). On Avellar's fears, see also Avellar to Pasquier, Diamantina, January 8, 1938, PBCM, 8 (4) CM/5, CR-345. On this case see also Salvador Rubim dos Santos to Pasquier, Diamantina, January 13, 1938, PBCM, 8 (4) CM/5, CR-368. For Santos's career path, see "Catálogo dos Coirmãos," PBCM, 123–24.

147. Salvador Rubim dos Santos to Godinho, Diamantina, August 2, 1948, PBCM, uncatalogued letter in folder marked "Corresp. Div. 1945–49."

148. Pereira to Godinho, Rio de Janeiro, February 17, 1951, PBCM, uncatalogued document in folder marked "Corresp. Div. 1945–49"; "Catálogo dos Coirmãos," PBCM, 123–24. On the historical role of the Church in fomenting local gossip, see Vainfas 1997:99.

149. Father Rogério to Father Dumont, Barra, April 13, 1964, PBCM, uncatalogued document.

150. Eugen Drewermann paraphrased in Moreira 1995:400 (love). For a comparison of Brazilian abuses with the immense scandals of the U.S. Church in the early 2000s, see the epilogue.

5 "The Modern Saint Is a Social Saint"

1. Interview with Dom Sinésio Bohn.

2. Interview with Poletto; interviews 1 and 2 with Schmidt.

3. On Frei Betto's background and attitudes toward the priesthood, see Frei Betto 1977:ix, xi, 229 (quotation). This book was first published in Italy in 1971 under the title *Dai sotterranei della storia.* The first Brazilian edition, entitled *Cartas da prisão,* appeared in 1977.

4. Interview 1 with Schmidt.

5. See Lenz 1992 for a detailed description of the political transformation of popular religion.

6. For an overview of the Church's position in the world from 1945 to the start of Vatican II in 1962, see Martina 1988; Bruneau 1974, chap. 3.

7. For an overview of Church unionization in the early 1960s, including a compelling profile of the activist priest Celso Ibson de Syllos, see Welch 1999, passim.

8. Brandão 1941a:52; see also Siqueira 1942.

9. Medeiros 1941.

10. Morlion 1952:7–8; see also Silva 1983:303.

11. Pius XII quoted in White 1989:286–87.

12. Pizzardo and Staffa 1959:713.

13. Teixeira 1988:211–13. The pre–Vatican II era is frequently characterized as a time when the people were distant from the priest at Mass. This is correct. However, it is important to recall that Trent had brought people and the clergy closer by permitting the raising of altars and the removal of medieval rood-screens that completely isolated the faithful from the altar. See Delumeau 1977:198–99.

14. Luis de Gonzaga Negreiros to Godinho, Fortaleza, March 8, 1950, PBCM, uncatalogued document in folder marked "Corresp. Div."

15. Tradição, Família e Propriedade 1980:422. For a history of the Liturgical Movement, see Silva 1983.

16. Pessoa 1988:65–66.

17. Pessoa 1988:56–80; Silva 1983:318; Souza 1984:154–60.

18. Silva 1983:312–27, 358–63. See also Azzi 1981:51.

19. Pessoa 1988:65–66.

20. Dom Augusto to Godinho, Bahia, November 4, 1947, PBCM, uncatalogued document in folder marked "2 (1) CM. Capelania Militar. Salvador. Correspondência 1953–54." See also Dom Augusto to Godinho, Bahia, October 17, 1947, PBCM, uncatalogued document in same folder.

21. "Catálogo dos coirmãos," PBCM, 163; Pessoa 1988.

22. Aristeu Matos to Godinho, Mariana, October 15, 1948, PBCM, uncatalogued document in folder marked "Corresp. div., 1945–49." Matos referred to Father "D.G.," who was most probably Domingos Guglielmelli, discussed in chapter 4. Ribeiro to Godinho, Mariana, October 16, 1948, PBCM, uncatalogued document in folder marked "Corresp. Div. 1945–49."

23. Dom Antônio de Almeida Lustosa to Godinho, Fortaleza, January 24, 1950, February 6, 1950, and March 29, 1950, PBCM, uncatalogued documents in folder marked "Corresp. Div. 1945–49"; Luis de Gonzaga Negreiros to Godinho, Fortaleza, March 8, 1950, PBCM, uncatalogued document in folder marked "Corresp. Div. 1945–49."

24. Bruneau 1974:95; "Catálogo dos Coirmãos," PBCM, 184.

25. Interview with José Pires de Almeida. And see Salles Júnior 1997:46, 129, 141.

26. Souza 1984:88–89 and chap. 5.

27. Interview with Lesbaupin. And see Frei Betto 2002.

28. "A JOC e o clero" 1950; "O padre e os lares proletários" 1951.

29. Bedoyere 1963:88–147, 163–64, 207–10; Castro 1987:76–77.

30. Bedoyere 1963:163.

31. Guerre and Zinty 1965:100–102; Libânio 1980:137.

32. Wanderley 1984:118, 385, 388, 513–520.

33. Bedoyere 1963; Guerre and Zinty 1965:102; Libânio 1980:138; Wanderley 1984:385.

34. Bedoyere 1963:163–64; Guerre and Zinty 1965:106; Wanderley 1985:386; Castro 1987:84.

35. On action and guerrillas, see Ridenti 2000:212.

36. Carvalheira 1983:17.

37. Souza 1984:86; Carvalheira 1983:17.

38. Numerous primary and secondary sources discuss the theory of *ver-julgar-agir* (see-judge-act). See, for example, Vásquez 1998:26–28.

39. Mainwaring 1986:73–75, 123, 136–37; Wanderley 1984:16, 379–80.

40. Souza 1984:140–41, 144, 154–60, 164; Mainwaring 1986:62.

41. Queiroga 1977:331; Castro 1987:75; Pessoa 1988:76; Souza 1984:121; Carvalheira 1983:20. We lack a comprehensive social and cultural history of Brazilian and Latin American Catholic Action. On the decline of *ver-julgar-agir* in the 1990s, see Serbin 1993b, 1994.

42. V. Machado 2001, passim.

43. Bernal 1989.

44. Queiroga 1977:326; Souza 1984:92, 145.

45. Interview with José Pires de Almeida; interview 1 with Virgílio Leite Uchôa. For further discussion of ACB in the seminaries, see Gonçalves 1943; "Clero e Ação Católica" 1942; Didonet 1941; "Congresso de reitores de seminário" 1948:95; Ortiz 1941.

46. Lombardi cited in Queiroga 1977:332–33, note 10. Lombardi became nuncio in 1954. On his key role in the renovation of the Brazilian Church, see Bruneau 1974:117.

47. Aloísio Deina Goch, "Uma experiência de JEC no seminário," third assembly of the CNBB, November 10–12, 1956, INP Document No. 02795.

48. Arnal 1986:1–6, 171–74; Branch 1989.

49. Martina 1988:23–25; Arnal 1986:53–58, 159–65.

50. Arnal 1986:68, 69 (quotation), 171–72.

51. Martina 1988:23–25. On worker-priests and Vatican II, see Arnal 1986:167, 171, 173.

52. Latourelle 1988:xv. For the official documents of Vatican II, see Kloppenburg 1987. On Vatican II also see Rynne 1963, 1966. On the immediate effects of Vatican II, see Hebblethwaite 1975. For a critical perspective from Brazil, see Libânio 1984. The most recent effort at a comprehensive history of Vatican II is Alberigo 1995–2003.

53. On Brazil's role in the council see Beozzo 2001a.

54. "Decreto 'Optatum Totius' sobre a Formação Sacerdotal," in Kloppenburg 1987:505–26. The Brazilian document is "Complementação para o Brasil das Diretrizes Básicas da Formação Sacerdotal" 1970.

55. See, for example, Rynne 1966:151–52. For other documents on the clergy, see "Decreto 'Presbyterorum Ordinis' sobre o Ministério e a Vida dos Presbíteros," in Kloppenburg 1987:437–83, and "Decreto 'Perfectae Caritatis' sobre a Atualização dos

Religiosos," in Kloppenburg 1987:485–504. A similar interpretation, with particular attention to the U.S. Church, is in Cozzens 2000:18, 129–30.

56. Frei Betto 2000:71; Castro 1984.

57. Ortiz 1988. Also see Della Cava and Montero 1991:12.

58. Smith 1991, chap. 2 and p. 170. On liberation theology's development, see Libânio 1987; Berryman 1987. The classic example of liberation theology is by its most prominent pioneer, the Peruvian Gustavo Gutiérrez; see Gutiérrez 1973. This work first appeared in Spanish in 1971. An important early Brazilian contribution is L. Boff 1972.

59. Sigmund 1990. On the Latin American Church's political and ideological evolution prior to liberation theology see O'Meagher 1997.

60. Mainwaring 1986:68–70; Freire 1970. For a critique of Freire see Paiva 1980.

61. Carter 2002 (citation in abstract); see also V. Machado 2001.

62. Warren 2001:86, 146. This interpretation frontally contradicts Burdick (1993), who views progressivism as uninterested in ethnicity. On ethnic identity and liberation theology, see also French 2003:63, 83, 89–96, 113–33, 140–43, 171–78.

63. Azevedo 1987:57–79.

64. Mainwaring 1986:108–110, 179; Bruneau 1982:129. On the involvement of priests, nuns, and lay pastoral agents in the formation of the CEBs, see Teixeira 1988:307–13.

65. Valle and Pitta 1994.

66. CEBs received great attention from scholars because of their novelty and important role in politics in Central America and Brazil. Like liberation theology, they have influenced the Church worldwide. North American theologian Harvey Cox saw both the new theology and the communities as the first signs of a postmodern Christianity; Cox 1984. In the Brazilian case debate has raged about the CEBs' actual numbers and their real significance in the Progressive Church's option for the poor. While early on a consensus seemed to form that CEBs had reached a total of 60,000 to 80,000 with several million members, other studies have put the number as low as 10,000 with a total membership of 250,000; Hewitt 1991:7–10; Daudelin and Hewitt 1995; Burdick 1993. If the lower figures are accurate, the CEBs' impact has perhaps been far less than earlier claimed. L.A. Souza (2000) disputes the low figures, as do other important studies such as Valle and Pitta 1994. Critics point further to the exclusionary or unpopular nature of the Popular Church—the inability of the progressive message to attract many groups among the poor. See, for example, Burdick 1993; Mariz 1994. For a critique of Burdick and a history of a CEB on the outskirts of Rio de Janeiro, see Vásquez 1998. For a nuanced view of life in a Catholic parish, see C. Souza 2002. See Serbin 2000a:148, including notes 14–17, for a more comprehensive discussion of the literature and themes related to CEBs.

67. On rebels, skirts, and heroes, see Ventura 1988:43–46, 64, 75.

68. Souza 1999:113. On shifts in the Mexican Church resulting from the 1968 massacre of students and others at Tlatelolco, see Camp 1997:80.

69. Description of popular religiosity from interview 1 with Pretto.

70. Interview with Dom Paulo Moretto. And see Beozzo 2001a:292–93.
71. Carter 2002:125, including note 161.
72. Carter 2002; Iokoi 1996, chap. 2.
73. Interview with Marino Bohn.
74. This last point made in interview with Agostinho Both. Other data from numerous interviews with priests from Rio Grande do Sul.
75. Interview 2 with Graeff.
76. On the Jesuits and São Leopoldo, see Bohnen and Ullmann 1989, chap. 9.
77. *A história do Seminário Maior de Viamão* 1979: 9–13, 18, 21–22; Bohnen and Ullmann 1989:281–84.
78. *A história do Seminário Maior de Viamão* 1979:12.
79. Interview with Oscar João Colling; interview with Anúncio João Caldana.
80. Interview with Casanova, including information on bookstore.
81. Interview 1 with Panazzolo.
82. Interview with Paviani. Intellectual creativity and social concern also from interview 1 with Panazzolo.
83. Interview 2 with Benincá.
84. Interview with Casanova; interview with Stertz; interview with Paviani.
85. Interview with Agostinho Both.
86. Interview with Paviani.
87. Interview 1 with Pretto.
88. Interview with Treviso.
89. Interview 2 with Graeff. In 1954, 49 percent of Viamão's philosophy students were of Italian origin, 28 percent of Germanic origin, 20 percent of Luso-Brazilian origin, and 2 percent of Slavic origin. See Seidl 2003:235.
90. Personal correspondence from Cláudio Boeira Garcia, August 13, 2004.
91. Interview with Paviani.
92. Interview with Dom Paulo Moretto.
93. Interview with Paviani. Also, on ethnic tensions see "Será que nosso sacerdócio seria mais rico na formação se fôsse diferente?" Arquivo da Diocese de Caxias do Sul, 5–6.
94. Dom Benedito Zorzi to the major seminarians of the Diocese of Caxias do Sul, Caxias do Sul, May 10, 1965, Arquivo da Diocese de Caxias do Sul.
95. Comment on Assmann from interview with Dom Paulo Moretto.
96. Interview with Paviani.
97. Interview 2 with Benincá.
98. Interview with Casanova.
99. Interview with Paviani.
100. Interview 1 with Pretto.
101. "Os irmãos se encontram" 1958:96; Kövecses 1957.
102. Interview 2 with Benincá.

103. "A redação por dentro" 1956. On the number of seminarians, see Pérez, Gregory, and Lepargneur 1964:53.

104. "Os irmãos se encontram" 1958:100.

105. Interview with Antônio Valentini. Valentini was one of the business managers of *Ponto Homem,* as *O Seminário* was known in its final year of existence.

106. Interview with Paviani; interview with Dom Paulo Moretto.

107. "Relatório da revista 'O Seminário'" 1963; Mourão 1963:99.

108. Interview with Poletto.

109. "Os irmãos se encontram" 1958:96–97.

110. Toldo 1963:24, 28.

111. Menezes 1963a:37–42. In 1953 the students of the Colégio Pio Brasileiro in Rome organized a movement known as Movimento Pro-União Sacerdotal. It remained apolitical, focusing on such traditional themes as the priest shortage. See, for instance, "Movimento Pro-União Sacerdotal" 1953.

112. Interview with Dom Paulo Moretto.

113. Interview with Stertz.

114. Medeiros 1962.

115. Saraiva 1962.

116. Menezes 1963a.

117. Interview 2 with Benincá.

118. "Relatório da revista 'O Seminário'" 1963:8.

119. Interview with Poletto.

120. "Congresso nacional de seminaristas" 1963:9–11.

121. Menezes 1963a:38.

122. "Conclusões da reunião de reitores de São Paulo" 1964:28. Data on ecclesiastical censor's laxity from interview 1 Graeff.

123. Interview 2 with Benincá.

124. Interview with Poletto.

125. Interview 1 with Graeff.

126. Personal correspondence from Ivo Poletto, January 23, 1989.

127. Interview with Poletto.

128. "Irineu vai contar o que foi a USMAS volante" 1964; interview with Brand.

129. Personal correspondence from Cláudio Boeira Garcia, August 13, 2004.

130. Interview 2 with Graeff.

131. Interview with Poletto. Data on the Porto Alegre association from interview with Busanello.

132. Garcia 1967:499.

133. "Os seminários maiores hoje" 1970. In the Catholic world churchmen wrote hundreds of books and articles about change in seminary training. See, for example, the discussion in Libânio 1969. On seminary innovation in Mexico, see Camp 1997:162–63.

134. Cited in Levine 2001:317.

135. Interview with Agostinho Both (*aggiornamento*, new ideas).

136. Interview with Dom Sinésio Bohn.

137. Mariano 1963. Many U.S. priests also reported that their seminary education was "sheltered from the mainstream of life"; see Greeley 1972:46.

138. Trentin, Silva, and Poletto 1966:30–33; on the immutability of the Tridentine system, also see Menezes, Messier, and Frei Eriberto 1965.

139. "A Ocupação do Clero no Brasil" 1967.

140. Saroni 1966:460.

141. On family, see Stein 1963:50 (quotation); Fontanive 1968:177. The study by Fontanive was part of a multi-volume series of sociological and historical investigations directed by the Centro de Estatística Religiosa e Investigações Sociais (CERIS), the research arm of the CNBB set up in the early 1960s. This particular volume was based on a survey in 1965 of seminarians at three of Brazil's leading institutions for clerical education: Viamão in the south, Olinda in the northeast, and Rio Comprido in Rio de Janeiro. One hundred ninety-one students responded. It is a key source for understanding the crisis of the seminaries and the priesthood. Parts of the series were summarized and published in the *REB*. On the issue of overemphasis on intellectual preparation, see "Perspectiva histórica na formação do seminarista" 1964:10; Stein 1963:46.

142. Stein 1963:50.

143. "Uma vida em duas realidades" 1967:35; Robles 1963:82–84; Saroni 1966:464; Pereira 1965:37 (dollar), 42 (silver spoon). Research on U.S. priests demonstrated that seminaries there did not interfere with the emotional development of men; see Greeley 1972:68–69. The kinds of social contrasts between seminary life and the outer world described by Brazilian seminarians were not as sharp as in the affluent U.S. Nevertheless, Greeley also concluded that "the principal emotional problems that are distinctive to the priest are the inability to be sensitive to one's own needs and feelings and particularly the capacity to accept one's own aggressive impulses" (68).

144. Fontanive 1968:50 (quotation), 65–67, 111–12. Also see Saroni 1966:462–64; Toldo 1963:30.

145. Pereira 1965:37.

146. Godofredo Deelen, "O que a pesquisa proibida revelou: política de avestruz e farisaísmo paralizam [*sic*] a Igreja no Brasil," INP Document No. 01190, no date, probably 1967. This document is a translation of an article that Deelen published in a Dutch newspaper.

147. Oliveira 1968a, Appendix, 123, 128, 134, 138, 141, 145. A majority of U.S. priests also opposed obligatory celibacy; see Greeley 1972:312.

148. "Depoimentos sobre o celibato" 1968:21, 24–25, 32, 35–36, 73 (nightclub).

149. Fontanive 1968:112–16, 129, 177.

150. Ponte 1967:547–48, 552 (imposition). The point about the genuine choice of celibacy is also made by Santos 1972:635.

151. Interview with Dom Paulo Ponte.

152. Santos 1972:628–31, 634.

153. "Depoimentos sobre o celibato" 1968:1–18, 6 (our strength).

154. Interview with Agostinho Both.

155. Broetto 1963.

156. "Depoimentos de Sacerdotes" 1968:42–56, 62, 63 (I already think). Emphasis in the original.

157. See, for example, Menezes 1963a:39, 41; Stein 1963:46–51.

158. Frei Betto 1966:181. See also "Será que nosso sacerdócio seria mais rico na formação se fôsse diferente?" Arquivo da Diocese de Caxias do Sul, 3.

159. See, for example, "Do começo de Minas" 1965.

160. See, for example, "Por que mais um ano?" 1967:49. Priests in the United States also reported that seminary courses were "irrelevant to pastoral needs"; see Greeley 1972:46.

161. "Editorial"1962:4.

162. Mourão 1963:99.

163. Fontanive 1968:189.

164. José Comblin cited in Cabral 2001:173–74.

165. The quotation is from Menezes, Messier, and Frei Eriberto 1965:79–80. Also see, for example, Fontanive 1968:178–99; Mourão 1963:97–98; "Por que mais un ano?" 1967:52; "Como deveria o clero encarar o fenômeno marxista no mundo?" 1964. Also see the comments in Libânio 1969:73–74, 84–85, 89–100, 271–72.

166. Schooyans 1968:205–6.

167. "Associação de ex-seminaristas" 1963; see also Pereira 1965:38–43. On financial dependence and ties to elite, see Fontanive 1968:33–34, 65–67, 111–12.

168. Romanelli 1988:91–93; Martins Filho 1987.

169. "Depoimentos de Sacerdotes" 1968:55, 70, 105, 113, 116, 118.

170. I refer to IPREC, the Instituto de Previdência do Clero, on which a copious amount of documentation exists in ecclesiastical publications.

171. Carvalheira 1966b.

172. "Uma vida em duas realidades" 1967:23; also see Libânio 1969:115–16. For a discussion of financial dependence among U.S. clergy, see Cozzens 2000:73.

173. See, for example, Mourão 1963; Menezes, Messier, and Frei Eriberto 1965.

174. See, for example, the statements of seminarians in Fontanive 1968:178–99. Also see Menezes, Messier, and Frei Eriberto 1965:79–80.

175. "Pe. Jacques Loew no seminário de Viamão"1962. On influence of Catholic Action, see also "Entrei para a vida operária," Missão Operária 1:1 (1967), Central de Documentação e Informação Científica "Prof. Casemiro dos Reis Filho," Pontifícia Universidade Católica de São Paulo, JOC, Roll 21. Also see "Como iniciar a Ação Católica" 1958; "O coração da diocese" 1958:109; Silva 1961:14–17; Carvalheira 1966a:346.

176. Ridenti 2000:210–12.

177. Trentin, Silva, and Poletto 1966:33–34.

178. Interview 2 with Benincá. Additional information from interview with Treviso. For a subsequent experience at Viamão, see Zanotelli 1964.

179. Interview with Marino Bohn.

180. Interview 2 with Graeff.

181. "Será que nosso sacerdócio seria mais rico na formação se fôsse diferente?" Arquivo da Diocese de Caxias do Sul, 6.

182. Beozzo 2001a:143. Santiago became Brazil's ambassador to Cuba during the first administration of President Luiz Inácio Lula da Silva (2003–2006).

183. "Depoimentos de Sacerdotes" 1968:90, 115. On sharing, see also Costa, Pandolfi, and Serbin 2001:42–45.

184. Interview with Poletto.

185. Interview with Dom Sinésio Bohn.

186. Interview with Agostinho Both.

187. Interview with Treviso. On the cassock, see also "Batina ou 'Clergyman'?" 1963; "Hábito eclesiástico: consulta nacional em andamento" 1964.

188. Stein 1963:45, 47, 51.

189. Mourão 1963:92–93, 95.

190. Trentin, Silva, and Poletto 1966:33.

191. Saroni 1966:459.

192. Menezes, Messier, and Frei Eriberto 1965:81. Emphasis in the original.

193. Mourão 1963:97. On primitive roots, see also Moro 1997:261–63.

194. Almeida 1964:16.

195. Schmidt 1968.

196. Interview with Dom Marcelo Carvalheira; Beozzo 2001a:143. For background on Foucauld and his influence in Brazil, see Frei Betto 2001.

197. CNBB 1974:43 (quotation), passim.

198. "Pe. Caramuru fala de JAC" 1962:109–10.

199. Aguiar and Gomes 1963:103.

200. "Uma vida em duas realidades" 1967:30. See also "Entrei para a vida operária," *Missão Operária* 1:1 (1967), Central de Documentação e Informação Científica "Prof. Casemiro dos Reis Filho," Pontifícia Universidade Católica de São Paulo, JOC, Roll 21. In the United States one of the main complaints of priests about seminaries was that they failed to teach "how to deal with people"; see Greeley 1972:46 (quotation), 52.

201. "Depoimentos de Sacerdotes" 1968:61, 92. For discussion of the public's perception of the clergy in Brazil in the pre–Vatican II era, see for example "O que pensam de nós Padres" 1957. For an example of the public's view of the clergy in the post–Vatican II years, see "Inquérito entre Leigos sobre a Situação do Padre" 1969:636–44. For examples of internal debate on the crisis of the priesthood, see Marcelo Pinto Carvalheira, "Sobre situações de conflito dos sacerdotes no mundo moderno," 1965, INP Document

No. 01201. For a conservative perspective, see "O padre, figura deslocada?" 1967; "Igreja do futuro sem padres?" 1968.

202. Carvalheira 1966b: 534 (hermetic and cold), 536 (prophet), 537–43, 546–48, 549 (personalization), 550. For more on the psychological aspects of the crisis of the priesthood, see chapter 6; Tepe 1968.

203. For the best rational-choice argument about Catholic progressivism in Latin America, see Gill 1998. For a similar marketplace interpretation, see Chesnut 1997, 2003. For a critique of these approaches, see Serbin 1999b, 2000b:225, 2001a; see also http://www.providence.edu/las/discussion.htm for a debate on rational choice and Latin American religion stimulated by Gill's work; see also Gaskill 2003.

204. Interview 2 with Benincá.

205. Interview with Dom Sinésio Bohn.

206. Interview 2 with Benincá.

207. Interview with Dom Sinésio Bohn.

208. Interview 2 with Benincá.

209. Interview with Busanello.

210. Interview with Dom Sinésio Bohn.

211. Interview with Busanello.

212. Tavares, Lima, and Cabral 1966:390 (struggle), 394 (face to face, fatalistic, sub-human, own history), 395 (authentic community), 396 (unjust, dominators).

213. Interview with Dom Sinésio Bohn.

214. "Editorial" 1963b.

215. Ridenti 2000:214, 215 (quotations), 216.

216. Langland 2004.

217. "Carta de Olinda" 1961:34.

218. Interview 2 with Benincá. Viamão seminarian João Panazzolo took part in the 1962 UNE congress in Petrópolis; interview 1 with Panazzolo.

219. Personal correspondence from Cláudio Boeira Garcia, August 13, 2004.

220. Interview with Poletto.

221. "Escreve o Leitor" 1962:59.

222. Stein 1963:54–55. On Stein, also see Alves 1968:252.

223. "Teólogos capuchinhos fundam centro acadêmico" 1962:44; "Convívio, experiência, vivência" 1964:93–97.

224. Interview with Zeno Hastenteufel; interview 1 with Benincá; interview with Cláudio Neutzling.

225. Interview with Poletto. For an overview of Chardin's significance, see Wills 1971, chap. 5. On Chardin also see Cuénot 1965, Dodson 1984, Vaz 1991.

226. "Artigo-Debate" 1967:517 (quotation), 518–23.

227. "Editorial" 1968.

228. Stein 1968:11.

229. "Relatório" 1968.

230. Assmann 1968a, 1968b. Other articles produced by participants at the theological assembly were Barros 1968a, 1968b; Lorscheiter 1968; Comblin 1968a, 1968b, and 1968c; Gregory 1968; Frei Matias 1968.

231. For an example of the torture of an ex-seminarian who had intended to be a worker-priest, see Marcos Penna Sattamini de Arruda, untitled manuscript, Coleção Marc van Der Weid, Arquivo Público do Estado do Rio de Janeiro, Rio de Janeiro.

232. Serbin 2000b, 2001b.

233. Alves 1968:213–19.

234. Archdiocese of São Paulo 1988:235–36. Background on Moraes from interview 2 with Graeff and interview with Busanello.

235. José Pires de Almeida, "Extrato do relatório enviado ao superior geral," 1966, PBCM, uncatalogued document.

236. On Fortaleza history and statistics, see Zico 1964. Information on Fortaleza crisis from interview with Antônio Gomes Pereira and "Mudanças no Seminário Provincial do Ceará" 1967.

237. On integralism in the 1960s and 1970s, see Antoine 1980; Tradição, Família e Propriedade 1980; Seiblitz 1992. This movement should not be confused with the integralistas of the 1930s.

238. Interview with José Isabel da Silva Campos; also see copy of letter from Campos to Cardinal Pizzardo, Prefect of the Sacred Congregation for Seminaries and Universities, May 26, 1964, PBCM, uncatalogued document in folder marked "Correspond. Variada 1945–63."

239. Zico 2000:238.

240. Interview with José Isabel da Silva Campos; Alves 1968:271. For background on Dom Sigaud and a balanced view of his contributions to the Church and Minas Gerais, including his support for social welfare, see the obituary in REB 59 (December 1999), 966–67.

241. "Minas Gerais vive assim" 1962:62–64; "Os seminários em revista" 1962.

242. José Lima, Manoel Carlos Pereira, Argemiro Moreira Leite, Antenor Pinto de Resende, Eli Carneiro, Felício Fulik, and Hypólito Pena to Dermeval José Mont'Alvão, Diamantina, November 8, 1963, PBCM, uncatalogued document; for background on Brasil, Urgente, see Botas 1983.

243. Dom Geraldo de Proença Sigaud to Mont'Alvão, Rome, December 20, 1963, PBCM, uncatalogued letter in folder marked "Correspond. Variada 1945–63."

244. Carlos Pinto to Father José da Silveira Dumont, March 14, 1963, PBCM, typescript of letter in uncatalogued document in folder marked "Correspond. Variada 1945–63;" see also Carlos Jurandir to Dumont, March 4, 1964, PBCM, typescript of letter in uncatalogued document in folder marked "Correspond. Variada 1945–63." The typescripts of these letters, as well as of others cited below, were apparently made once

the missives came into the hands of Dom Sigaud, as explained below. The typescripts contain the official seal of Dom Sigaud and the signature of the diocesan chancellor, who checked the typed copies with the originals.

245. Alves 1968:271–74.

246. Alves 1968:273; interview with José Isabel da Silva Campos.

247. Interview with José Isabel da Silva Campos; printed copy of letter from Campos to unidentified priest, July 7, 1964, PBCM, uncatalogued document. Compare with Alves 1968:273. Alves's and Campos's accounts differ on some points. I rely on Campos, who was present at the events described here.

248. Virgilene Maria Siqueira to Dumont, Diamantina, February 27, 1964, PBCM, typescript of uncatalogued letter in folder marked "Correspond. Variada 1945–63."

249. Father Rogério to Dumont, April 13, 1964, PBCM, typescript of letter in uncatalogued folder marked "Correspond. Variada 1945–63."

250. Wanderley Antônio Rodrigues to Dumont, April 21, 1964, PBCM, typescript of letter in uncatalogued folder marked "Correspond. Variada 1945–63."

251. Jurandir to Dumont, April 29, 1964, PBCM, typescript of letter in folder marked "Correspond. Variada 1945–63." The typescript of this letter apparently is missing a part of the original, which may have been censored.

252. "Do começo de Minas" 1965.

253. "Rapport de la Direction du Grand Séminaire de MARIANA (Minas Gerais, Brésil) à Son Excellence Mgr. Garrone, Pro-Préfet de la Congrégation des Séminaires," PBCM, uncatalogued document, 1966. I thank Jean Daudelin for his assistance in translating this document.

254. Interview with Lauro Palú. For characterizations of the press coverage and other details on the crisis, see "Mariana, Um Caso Liquidado?" 1968:18. See also "Fato Mariana" 1967. See also "Fechado o Seminário de Mariana" 1966.

255. "Rapport de la Direction du Grand Séminaire de MARIANA," PBCM, uncatalogued document.

256. Interview with João Batista Ferreira.

257. For details on the Vincentian crisis, see Salles Júnior 1997:165–75, 189–90; Souza 1999:107–16.

258. Interview 2 with Gilberto Gorgulho; interview 2 with Ana Flora Anderson.

259. Interview with Treviso. And see Stein 1963:51.

260. Interview with Dom Sinésio Bohn.

261. Interview with Poletto.

262. Interview with Zeno Hastenteufel (JUC, UNE, political police, Marx, Medellín, Orth jailed); interview 1 with Graeff (correspondence opened); interview with Neutzling (JUC, Orth jailed); interview with Neumann (Orth, VAR-Palmares); on VAR-Palmares, or Vanguarda Armada Revolucionária-Palmares (Armed Revolutionary Vanguard-Palmares), see Gorender 1998.

263. Interview with Dom Sinésio Bohn.

264. Interview with Fontoura. See also the secret Army report discussing attempts to confirm Communist infiltration in the seminaries; Ministério do Exército, 10. Exército, 2a. seção, Informação No. 531/71–SC, "Assunto: Infiltração de comunistas nos seminários católicos," 1971, Departamento de Ordem Política e Social da Guanabara, Arquivo Público do Estado do Rio de Janeiro, 268–75.

265. Interview with Treviso.

266. Interview with Zeno Hastenteufel. Interview with Valentini. Information on nuncio from interview with Dom Sinésio Bohn. The official announcement of the closing came on March 15, 1969. No issue was published that year; see Azzi 1981:92.

267. Scherer 1964:5.

268. The hypothesis of military intervention is from the interview with Neumann, an ex-seminarian. Neumann pointed out that the bishops also wanted to close the journal *Mundo Jovem* (Youth World), created as a form of pastoral guide for young people to fill the vacuum left after the suppression of Catholic Action. Its directors, however, saved it by finding ecclesiastical sponsorship outside the seminary. Neumann worked for both *Ponto Homem* and *Mundo Jovem*. With ex-seminarians on its staff, *Mundo Jovem* carried on with some of the initiatives proposed by seminarians in the 1960s. Today it is largely ignored by the bishops. Its mother publication was *Informações Vocacionais*, founded at Viamão in 1963 and succeeded immediately by *S.O.S. Vocações* and then by *Lançai as Redes* in 1964; see, for example, "S.O.S. Vocações—1964" 1963; also see "Novo título para Lançai as Redes" 1967. Started in 1967, *Mundo Jovem* reached a circulation of 120,000 in the 1980s, an extremely high number for any periodical in Brazil; see Neumann 1988; "Juventude em debate: devem os jovens participar na política?" 1968. See also the website http://www.mundojovem.pucrs.br. Yet another publication, *Teocomunicação*, was founded in Porto Alegre in 1971 as a successor to *Ponto Homem*, but its content was strictly ecclesiastical.

269. Fragoso 1968.

270. Ritter 1968:26.

271. Interview with Brand. For the accusation against Garcia, personal correspondence from Cláudio Boeira Garcia, August 13, 2004.

272. Interview with Stertz.

273. Interview with Paviani.

274. Interview 1 with Nilo Buss.

275. "A propósito de 'seminaristas' presos" 1972; see also Moretto 1972.

276. Lernoux 1982:42–44 (rebellion).

277. See, for example, Paul VI 1966a, 1966b.

278. On the crisis of the priesthood and Catholicism in the United States, see, for example, Dolan 1985, chap. 15. In addition to the sociological studies discussed in this chapter, see also Greeley 1972.

279. Oliveira 1968b:890 (quotation); see also Oliveira 1968a:67–69, 71, 77, 79. A detailed summary of the study is also in Marins 1969.

280. Carvalheira 1966b:531–34.

281. CNBB 1969:3; "Aspirações de Sacerdotes de Volta Redonda, São Paulo e Rio de Janeiro" 1968:399.

282. Antoine 1973:126, 132–38; Mainwaring 1986:171, including note 72; Bruneau 1974; "Preocupações que afligem a consciência de padres do Brasil" 1967; "Manifesto de leigos, religiosos e padres de Nova Friburgo" 1968; "Carta aos bispos" 1968; "Sugestões do presbitério da Santa Igreja de Santos à CNBB" 1968; "Cartas de padres à assembléia dos bispos do Brasil" 1968.

283. Antoine 1973:138–41. For reference to the Bahia case and other incidents, see Bruneau 1974:164, note 43. On the repercussion of the Botucatu case among the clergy and allusions to other clashes between the hierarchy and priests, also see CNBB 1969:35–36, 94.

284. "À IX Assembléia Geral Ordinária da Conferência Nacional dos Bispos do Brasil" 1968; "Cartas de padres à assembléia dos bispos do Brasil" 1968:708–9; Antoine 1973:137.

285. "Resposta do episcopado aos sacerdotes" 1968.

286. CNBB 1969:3–5.

287. Radrizzani 1972:1108.

288. See, for example, Lorscheider 1970; Mayer 1969:344; CNBB 1969:101.

289. CNBB 1969:40, 88, 153, 157.

290. Queiroga 1977:263, 267–69.

291. Antoine 1973:260–65, including note 15; Bruneau 1974:223. On seesawing, see also Mainwaring 1986:110–13. On this period, also see Queiroga 1977:268–69.

292. Interview with Marcos Noronha.

293. CNBB 1969:192–94.

294. Antônio Celso Queiroz, "A problemática dos presbíteros na assembléia nacional dos bispos," 1969, INP Document No. 01209, pp. 1, 5, 7, 10–11.

295. Queiroga 1977:279, 280, 284, 296–99.

296. Lynch 1972. Also see Margerie 1962b; Santos 1972.

297. Rynne 1966:148. The Latin text of Koop's projected intervention is available in the archives of the CNBB; see "De ministerio et vita presbyterorum," INP, Document No. 05304; also see Koop's letter to the president and secretary general of the CNBB, November 8, 1965, INP, Document No. 05305.

298. Versaldi 1988:131–33. This work provides a conservative and useful overview of the question of celibacy during and after Vatican II. I do not agree with its interpretation that the expectation about the abolition of obligatory celibacy was a matter only discussed "outside the Church" and simply "fanned by the media." As I demonstrate, celibacy has been central to the priesthood and has been constantly called into question by both open debate in the Church and the sexual activity of priests. Further evidence against Versaldi is in Lynch 1972.

299. Rynne 1966:149.

300. Mayer 1969.

301. Koop 1968.

302. On the 1971 synod see Hebblethwaite 1975:22, 52, 57, 63–64. For a detailed analysis of the issues and debates at the 1971 synod, see Schillebeeckx 1989:287–322. Also see Coriden 1972.

303. "O celibato sacerdotal" 1970a; "O celibato sacerdotal" 1970b; Coriden 1972:1079–83; Radrizzani 1972:1108–13.

304. "Resultado da votação do episcopado sobre o tema 'Presbíteros'" 1969; Antônio Celso Queiroz, "A problemática dos presbíteros na assembléia nacional dos bispos," 1969, INP Document No. 01209. The proposal for married priests was also set forth in a CELAM document written in preparation for the 1971 synod; see "O tema sacerdotal e o clero na América Latina" 1971.

305. Lorscheider 1970.

306. "Comunicado final da presidência" 1971; "Ministério sacerdotal" 1971; "Reflexão da Commissão Representativa e da Commissão Nacional do Clero" 1971; "Visão global dos resultados de estudos regionais sobre o tema 'Sacerdócio Ministerial'" 1971; "Resultado dos grupos de estudo sobre sacerdócio ministerial" 1971.

307. "Ordenação de homens casados"1971. The bishops' declaration was first published in the Rio de Janeiro newspaper O Jornal, October 17, 1971. An earlier protest, aimed at a statement against obligatory celibacy, came from Dom Antonio de Castro Mayer, the traditionalist bishop of Campos and ally of Dom Sigaud; see Mayer 1969.

308. "II reunião da Commissão Representativa da CNBB" 1972. Also see the specific questioning of the synod's conclusions on celibacy in Santos 1972:633–34.

309. Affonso Felipe Gregory, Pedro de Assis Ribeiro de Oliveira, and Maria Hylma Lopes Ceva, "Laicizações do clero do Brasil," INP Document No. 01206, p. 10. Also see Cabras 1983:214, 217, 220.

310. Ribeiro et al. 1990:51–52. Priests in the United States left for the same two reasons; see Greeley 1972:133, 154, 199, 276, 281–83.

311. For an analysis of departures in Brazil, see Cabras 1983:193–214.

312. Gregory, Oliveira, and Ceva, "Laicizações do Clero do Brasil," INP Document No. 01206, p. 15.

313. See, for example, Salles Júnior 1997:141–42. The same cannot be said for the U.S. Church, according to Greeley 1972:312.

314. Interview with Marcos Noronha. Data on Church benefits also from interview with Dom Mário Teixeira Gurgel. On Dom Caetano see Beozzo 2001a:294.

315. Cabras 1983:34.

316. Delumeau 1977:214.

317. Cabras 1983:25; "Dados sobre o movimento de saída de padres" 1971.

318. On the estimate for the worldwide total of laicizations, see Ribeiro et al. 1990:93.

319. Abbott 2000:384, 389.

320. For estimates of the number of worldwide and Brazilian laicizations, see Ribeiro et al. 1990:93, 32. On the demographics of the priesthood, see Pérez, Gregory, and Lepargneur 1964; "Dados Gerais das Circunscrições Eclesiásticas, Paróquias e Presbíteros. Brasil—1970–1987," CERIS, n.d. On dispensations under John Paul II, see Cabras 1983:43. In the 1990s the ratio of priests to the population stabilized, reaching one priest per 10,124 inhabitants in the year 2000; see http://www.ceris.org.br.

321. For a more detailed consideration of these trends, see Serbin 1992a.

322. Locks 1972.

323. Beozzo 1994b.

324. Ribeiro et al. 1990:82–83. Interview 1 with Schmitt.

325. CNBB 1969:201–3.

326. "Padres fora do Ministério" 1975:195–96.

327. "15a. Assembléia Geral. Eleições. Votações e Conclusões" 1974; "Considerações da Comissão Nacional do Clero " 1974.

328. Ribeiro et al. 1990:63.

329. For an overview of the MPC, see Ribeiro et al. 1990:82–105. Additional data from interview 1 with Schmitt, who made the affirmation that in Bahia and the state of Rio de Janeiro bishops have allowed married priests to celebrate Mass. Similar data from interview with Jorge Ponciano Ribeiro. See also Schmitt 1989; Hoornaert 1992. For a critique of the movement's bulletin *Rumos,* see Motta 2002. Regional associations of married priests also formed and published their own bulletins; see, for example, *Sinal,* published by the Padres Casados do Ceará. On married priests in the United States, see Unsworth 1991, chap. 42.

330. On Catholicism and revolutionary romanticism, see Ridenti 2000, esp. 24–25, 50–51, 210–21.

331. On the position of the priest in modern society, see Schooyans 1968. On secularization and popular religion, see Mainwaring 1986:174–78. On the economic technocracy and its rejection of the clergy, see Cabras 1983:132–33. On the technocracy, also see Alves 1985; Schneider 1991. Roberto de Oliveira Campos became the minister of planning and economic coordination under General Castello Branco; see Campos 1994.

6 "A Special Grace from God"

1. Kövecses 1967: 14 (be careful), 15, 16 (existential reflections, knowledge, I saw clearly, incessantly), 18–25 (executioners), 90–94 (Allied bombs).

2. This and the next two paragraphs are based on my interview with João Batista Ferreira. "Vara curta" also cited in Ventura 1988:180.

3. Interview with João Batista Ferreira.

4. "Depoimentos sobre o celibato" 1968:25 (castration); "Depoimentos de sacerdotes" 1969:61, 92 (neurosis).

5. The notion of influence is from Plotkin 2001:4.

6. Schwartz 1999:1, 5, 80.

7. Gay 1995:3. On the history of psychoanalysis, see also Gay 1988, Schwartz 1999, Gaylin 2000.

8. Plotkin 2001:5, 73.

9. On faith and therapy see Rieff 1987:3 (quotations), passim.

10. Schwartz 1999:58, 143.

11. Birman 1988:128–29. Yet psychoanalysis has fallen from favor. The boom in psychopharmacological remedies of the 1990s meant that for millions of people around the world, including Brazil, a pill, and not the couch, became the (much cheaper) way to tranquility. But the effectiveness of these drugs is questionable, and their long-term consequences unclear. See Glenmullen 2000; also see the commentary in Chappell 2000. At the same time psychoanalysis has come under attack from intellectuals who claim that it is unscientific. That point may be irrelevant. Psychoanalysis has helped many people, as have other forms of therapy. In the estimation of Joseph Schwartz, we need "not a sterile debate about whether psychoanalysis conforms to the criteria of past scientific successes but an analysis of the problems of human subjectivity that psychoanalysis has set itself to solve and an evaluation of its successes and failures." See Schwartz 1999:8.

12. Ferreira 1988:150–51, 158.

13. Russo 2002:10–18.

14. Plotkin 2001:1, 3, 70.

15. Russo 2002:22–27. On the introduction of psychoanalysis into Brazil, also see Perestrello 1988; Costa 1989; Villela 2000.

16. Plotkin 2001:8.

17. James, Chalub, and Katz 1992:18.

18. Costa 1988; also see Ferreira Netto 1996.

19. Cited in Schwartz 1999:119, 120.

20. Fromm 1950:4, 7, 99.

21. Sanchis 2005.

22. Paraphrased in Moreira 1995:395.

23. See, for instance, Zilboorg 1969; Gay 1988:30, 132, 604, 617–19; Plé 1974:1200–1201. As Rieff (1987:29) points out, Freud "as a therapist refused to ask the religious question" of consolation or to "proclaim a characterological ideal." On Freud's opposition to the melding of psychoanalysis and pastoral work, see Birman 1988:123, 126.

24. On psychoanalysis and gender see Schwartz 1999:13.

25. Sanchis 2005.

26. Birman 1988:119.

27. Sanchis 2005.

28. See, for example, the attitudes about psychology and its practice expressed in Siqueira 1942; Sousa 1945. On stoicism among the clergy, see Lapenta, Losada, and Almeida 1990:18.

29. Roudinesco 1990:192–95, 198.

30. Plé 1974:1201–2.

31. Oraison 1970. For an interesting example of how psychoanalysis was seen as threatening in the early Soviet Union, see Miller 1985.

32. Roudinesco 1990:199, 201.

33. Plé 1974:1203; also see "Aclaraciones provisionales redactadas por una comisión sobre el caso del padre Lemercier" 1968.

34. Roudinesco 1990:196, 197.

35. Lemercier 1968.

36. Lemercier 1968.

37. Roudinesco 1990:204.

38. Dom Méndez Arceo made his comments in September 1965; see Plé 1974:1203.

39. On the dropout rate, see Lemercier 1968; "Psicanálise e vida religiosa" 1966b:689. Peña and García Labordena (1969) state that nineteen monks left to continue in analysis. See also "O 'caso Lemercier,' do mosteiro beneditino de Cuernavaca" 1967. To my knowledge no historical investigation of the Cuernavaca experience exists. In addition to the documentation cited in this chapter, see the numerous letters, press reports, and other sources in López 1968; also see Ocampo n.d.; also see the obituary on Dom Méndez Arceo by Peter Hebblethwaite in *The Independent* (February 8, 1992; online: http://www.independent.co.uk).

40. Méndez Arceo 1968. Also see Ocampo n.d. In 1969 the Vatican issued a document stating that a psychological study of candidates to the priesthood could be undertaken in difficult cases. Lemercier rejected the interpretation that the statement permitted the use of psychoanalysis. See López Lara 1969; Peña and García Labordena 1969:4/176.

41. Figueira 1992:210, 219–27, and Figueira 1988. On youths, see Valle 1980. For comparison with Argentina's psychoanalytic boom, see Plotkin 2001, chap. 3.

42. Russo 2002:40–42, 47, 57, 58 (quotation), 59–68.

43. On healing in Pentecostal Protestantism see Chesnut 1997; Sanchis 2005. On the Afro-Brazilian religions see, for instance, Kracke 2000.

44. Coimbra 1995:75 (quotations), 94–107, 194–204; on psychology and subversion see also Serbin 2001b:182–83.

45. See, for example, Rozestraten 1960:531.

46. These ideas were presented by Carlo Tursi in a talk entitled "Síndrome do servo sofredor na formação seminarística" at the annual symposium of CEHILA-Brazil, São Paulo, September 11, 1991. Tursi bases his argument largely on the conclusions of Drewer-

mann's controversial *Kleriker* (1990). See Tursi 1990. A similar interpretation can be found in Bowers 1963.

47. Cozzens 2000:5, 49, 54 (quotations), 64.

48. See Tincq 1992. I am grateful to Jeff Weintraub for bringing this article to my attention. See also the fine review of Drewermann's work in Moreira 1995. Also see "Les Évangiles et la Psychanalyse" 1992; Beier 1998.

49. Drewermann paraphrased in Moreira 1995:400.

50. Interview with Dom Valfredo Bernardo Tepe. In the 1950s some priests experimented with parapsychology; see Pessoa 1988:65–66.

51. This observation from interview 5 with Luiz Viegas de Carvalho and interview with Malomar Lund Edelweiss.

52. For these various uses of psychology, see Tepe 1960a, 1960b, and 1961; Azzi 1961; Justo 1963; Rozestraten 1962; Schmieder 1959. Data on practical application of personality, vocational, and intelligence testing from interview with Dom Sinésio Bohn, who used such tests frequently while teaching at Viamão in the late 1960s and early 1970s. Some students were offered access to independent psychologists and psychiatrists. Confirmation of Bohn data in interview with Dom Paulo Moretto.

53. Interview 2 with Graeff; interview with Poletto.

54. Rozestraten 1960.

55. Interview with Dom Valfredo Bernardo Tepe. Tepe 1966 and 1989 [1958].

56. Mohana 1968.

57. Keppe 1968:56, note 1. On Keppe's model see the website http://www.analytical trilogy.org.

58. Interviews 1 and 2 with Valle. See the Bibliography for examples of Valle's numerous writings.

59. Interviews 1 and 2 with Valle.

60. Roudinesco 1990:203.

61. Interview with Lisbôa.

62. Interviews 1 and 2 with Valle.

63. Interviews 1 and 2 with Buss. On the theory of Criatividade Comunitária, see Semprebom 1974.

64. CRB 1973.

65. Interviews 1 and 2 with Buss. In 1975 Father Romer became auxiliary bishop in Rio de Janeiro under Cardinal Sales; CNBB 1991:94.

66. Interview with Dom Paulo Ponte. On the "third way" in the U.S., see Abbott 2000:386–87.

67. Interviews 1 and 2 with Valle.

68. CRB 1973.

69. Interviews 1 and 2 with Buss and 1 and 2 with Valle.

70. Interviews 1 and 2 with Valle.

71. Located in Petrópolis, this center later split, one part moving to São Paulo, another to Maceió, and yet another to nearby Rio de Janeiro. Interview with Joana Costa. Also see "Centro Nacional de Revitalização da Pessoa," promotional flyer of the center, September 4, 1991.

72. Interview with Lisbôa.

73. Investigative Staff of the *Boston Globe* 2002:173–74; Goode 2002.

74. Caspary 2003.

75. See, for example, Rulla 1977. This work was originally published in English in 1971 as *Depth Psychology and Vocation: A Psycho-social Perspective*. For reference to the popularity of Rulla's works in Brazil, see Moser 1989:15, note 1.

76. See, for example, Lacerda 1988.

77. Kövecses 1967:18–25, 41–44. Also see Facchini 1967. On Chardin, see Modras 2004, chap. 5.

78. The scholar is Henry Otram Evennett, cited in Alden 1996:4. Delumeau (1977:55) notes that "we find for the first time in Christian history and the history of the apostolate the spirit of organization." On the *Exercises* and modernity, see also O'Malley 1993:47.

79. Donnelly 2004:19, 34, 52, 78–89.

80. Kövecses 1954:274 (essence), 282 (elite, education, sublimate).

81. Kövecses 1967:56. It is not clear exactly when Kövecses began his training analysis, but his familiarity with psychoanalytic language in his 1954 article suggests that he was already at least interested in, if not already undergoing, analysis.

82. Kövecses 1962:257 (quotation), 258–261; personal correspondence from Malomar Lund Edelweiss, February 7, 1992. Emphasis in the original. Father Malomar was one of the key pioneers of psychoanalysis in Belo Horizonte. Prior to his appearance, Halley Alves Bessa, who converted to Catholicism during his medical studies, started a psychiatric and psychoanalytic practice that included a focus on Christian existentialism. Another influential figure in Belo Horizonte was Pedro Parafita de Bessa (no relation), who was persecuted by the military regime for his educational activities. Both of these men had contact with Fr. Benkö. Influence of these men and contact with Benkö from interview 5 with Luiz Viegas de Carvalho. On Halley Bessa see http://www.cobra.pages.nom. br/ecp-bessa.html. On Pedro Bessa see http://www.ufmg.br/boletim/bol1227/pag5.html and http://www2.metodista.br/unesco/JBCC/jbcc191.htm.

83. Géza also had brief contact with Caruso in Europe. Personal correspondence from Malomar Lund Edelweiss, February 7, 1992, and February 22, 1992. The piece translated by Edelweiss was Caruso 1962. Dom Serafim data from interview with Malomar Lund Edelweiss.

84. I rely here on the English translation; see Caruso 1964:xix–xx, 3–10, 24, 115, 121, 213–16.

85. Caruso 1961.

86. Caruso 1964:xx (myself), 6, 9 (for the priest), 17, 28 (existential lie), 84 (neurosis searches), 101 (essentially the problem), 104 (choice between), 163 (Christ archetype

is the central factor), 171, 172 (between two unique), 209 (existential synthesis), 215 (the conscience), 216. On the "existential lie," also see Kövecses 1962:260.

87. Interview with João Batista Ferreira; and see Coimbra 1995:108–9. On the dissident society, see Russo 2002:28–33.

88. This idea is suggested in part by the psychoanalytic interpretation of graduate education in Loewenberg 1983:63–64.

89. Kövecses 1967:56.

90. Géza did not record the amount of time required for his didactic analysis, but the nature of the activity—in Géza's words a "long process"—and other details of his text suggest that it took at least several years. See Kövecses 1967:57–58. A fellow Jesuit and participant in *Christus Sacerdos* recalled that Géza spent three years in analysis; interview with Sallet.

91. Kövecses 1967:57, 58 (ideal man), 59 (abyss), 60 (opening in all directions, to know myself, accepted the world, sincere analysis, inestimable help, special grace).

92. Kövecses 1962:248 (voice of conscience), 258 (obliges).

93. Kövecses 1962:259.

94. Kövecses 1963:129.

95. The Jesuits expunged references to specific persons and situations from Kövecses' memoirs, but the theoretical outline of his therapeutic experiences with seminarians remains. These missing details might provide clearer answers as to how Kövecses was able to begin conducting group therapy among students. See Kövecses 1967:61–66.

96. Personal correspondence from Malomar Lund Edelweiss, February 22, 1992.

97. Kövecses 1967: 64–65 (sexual explosion, conflict with authority, problems of religion, imposed, God), 61 (the seminarians), 62 (liberation of individuals, process of maturation), 70 (in sum, new kind). Emphasis in the original.

98. Kövecses 1967:63.

99. See "Relación de los documentos presentados al obispo de Cuernavaca (México) en torno a las situaciones-conflicto de los sacerdotes en el mundo moderno," no date, probably 1965, INP, Document No. 15621. See also Kövecses 1967:61; "Psicanálise e Vida Religiosa" 1966a, 1966b. Also see "O 'caso Lemercier'" 1967. Also see Sampaio 1968.

100. Kövecses 1967:63.

101. Kövecses 1967:81–85; "'Christus Sacerdos,' Curso de após-graduação para formadores do clero," 1967, INP, Document No. 04668.

102. "Ecos da reunião de reitores e diretores espirituais dos seminários do Brasil" 1959:7 (perverted), 8 (ineptitude), 9–12. See also Kövecses 1967:81–82.

103. Margerie 1962a:663; on Kövecses's courses also see "Congresso de diretores espirituais" 1957; "Curso intensivo de direção espiritual em Viamão" 1962; "A coleção 'Seminários'" 1962; "Encontro dos diretores espirituais dos seminários do Brasil" 1959; "'Christus Sacerdos.' Curso de após-graduação para formadores do clero," Arquivo da Província Sul Brasileira da Companhia de Jesus (hereafter APSB), in folder marked "S. Leopoldo-Cristo Rei. Curso 'Christus Sacerdos.' Indicações gerais sobre o curso-1970."

104. Interview with Malomar Lund Edelweiss.

105. Kövecses, "Avaliação psicológica da situação atual do clero brasileiro," Secretariado Nacional dos Seminários, Comunicado No. 1, October 1965, INP Document No. 00235, 8 (alienated, infantile, anguished), 9 (iron curtain), 10.

106. Kövecses, "Conferência: 'Como formar o jovem moderno para a vida religiosa?," Secretariado Nacional dos Seminários, Comunicado No. 4, no date, probably 1966, INP Document No. 04663, 11–12, 13 (quotation), 14, 15.

107. For a psychological critique of obligatory celibacy, see Santos 1972:628–31, 634.

108. Kövecses 1967:81–85; "'Christus Sacerdos,' Curso de após-graduação para formadores do clero," 1967, INP, Document No. 04668. For further background on the start of Christus Sacerdos, see Facchini 1967:460.

109. Kövecses 1967:75.

110. Some of these observations about the setting are taken from my own visits to the Colégio Cristo Rei and the surrounding area in August 1989, when the region was far more developed than in the 1960s, yet still semi-rural in appearance. For a description of the setting from the late 1960s, see Frei Betto 2000:76–77. On the funding of Christus Sacerdos, see Secretariado Nacional dos Seminários, Comunicado No. 24, special number, November 1970, INP Document No. 00832, 7; mimeographed document titled "Curso Christus Sacerdos (Curso de formação para educadores de seminários)," Arquivo da Reitoria do Colégio Máximo Cristo Rei de São Leopoldo (hereafter ACCR); interviews with Maia, Leite, Wolffenbüttel, Adami, and Nadai.

111. Kövecses 1967:75 (integral, orthodoxy, confidence); "Curso de formação para educadores de seminários. Finalidade e funcionamento do curso," Secretariado Nacional de Seminários, no date, INP Document No. 04667 (psychic, defense); "Christus Sacerdos. Curso de após-graduação para formadores do clero. Prospecto," no date, probably 1967, INP Document No. 04668. Also see pamphlet entitled "Curso de formação para educadores de seminários," in folder marked "S. Leopoldo-Cristo Rei. Curso 'Christus Sacerdos.' Indicações Gerais sobre o curso-1970," APSB.

112. Kövecses 1967:75–77.

113. "Distúrbios Psicodinâmicos Neuróticos. Notas de aulas, do curso dado pelo Dr. Alberto Ribeiro," p. 9, APSB, in folder marked "S. Leopoldo-Cristo Rei. Curso Christus Sacerdos. Dr. Alberto Ribeiro. Distúrbios psicodinâmicos neuróticos. 1968–parece."

114. "Psicologia educacional. Educação do ser humano nos diversos momentos psicológicos de sua evolução," APSB, in folder marked "S. Leopoldo-Cristo Rei. Curso Christus Sacerdos. Psicologia educacional evolutiva," no date. The author's name is missing.

115. Interview with Koehler.

116. Interview with Wolffenbüttel.

117. Kövecses 1967:77–78. See also pamphlet titled "Curso de formação para educadores de seminários," APSB, in folder marked "S. Leopoldo-Cristo Rei. Curso 'Christus Sacerdos.' Indicações Gerais sobre o curso-1970," 6.

118. Kövecses 1967:78.

119. Manenti 1983:407.

120. Kövecses 1967:79.

121. Carvalheira 1970.

122. Interviews with Adami and Sallet.

123. Interview with Dom Paulo Ponte.

124. Mimeographed document titled "Curso *Christus Sacerdos* (Curso de formação para educadores de seminários)," section titled "Depoimentos sobre o curso *Christus Sacerdos* 1967," ACCR; Secretariado Nacional dos Seminários, Comunicado No. 24, special number, November 1970, "Impressões pessoais sobre o curso em 1969," INP Document No. 00832, 7–10. In these documents the priests' names are omitted.

125. Interview with Maia.

126. This and next two paragraphs from interview with Maia.

127. Interviews with Maia, Leite, and Nadai. Information on the courting of women from interviews with Koehler and Adami.

128. Interview with Leite.

129. Interview with Wolffenbüttel. Similar conclusions in Valle 1984:78–79.

130. Interview with Wolffenbüttel.

131. Interview with Wolffenbüttel.

132. Interview with Wolffenbüttel. On several occasions—by telephone, through correspondence, and in person—I tried to obtain Dom Ivo's version of the events of Christus Sacerdos, but he declined to respond. He similarly avoided my queries about his involvement in secret talks with the military regime; see Serbin 2001b:75.

133. Interview with Wolffenbüttel. While in Porto Alegre I was unable to interview Cardinal Scherer because he was in the hospital. He died in 1996. Other priests and bishops preferred to view psychoanalysis as a cause of the vocational crisis; interview with Oscar João Colling.

134. Interviews with Adami and Nadai.

135. Interviews with Adami and Sallet.

136. Secretariado Nacional dos Seminários, Comunicado No. 24, special number, November 1970, "Visita de D. Afonso [Niehues] ao curso," INP Document No. 00835, 4.

137. Interviews with Adami and Sallet.

138. Interview with Koehler.

139. Interview with Adami.

140. Interview with Maia.

141. Frei Betto 2000; interview with Dom Marcelo Carvalheira.

142. Interview with Maia.

143. Interview with Adami (quotation). Similar data in personal correspondence from Malomar Lund Edelweiss, March 27, 1992.

144. Secretariado Nacional dos Seminários, Comunicado No. 24, special number, November 1970, "Visita de D. Afonso [Niehues] ao Curso," INP Document No. 00835, 4.

145. Frei Betto 2000:127, 146–47, 158.
146. Interview with Maia.
147. Ribeiro et al. 1990:56.
148. Russo 2002:45.
149. Interview 5 with Luiz Viegas de Carvalho. On Zeferino see Beozzo 2001a:384, note 638.
150. Interview with Geraldino Alves Ferreira Netto. For Ferreira Netto's ideas on psychoanalysis and religion, see Ferreira Netto 1996.
151. For background on Pellegrino and his ideas, see Moura 1988; Pellegrino 1988. For another example of assistance to a political activist, see Carvalho 1998:351.
152. Interview with João Batista Ferreira.
153. Ibrahim 1992:14–26.
154. Ferreira 1995a:35–37, 38 (quotation). On the history of the clinic, also see Ibrahim 1992.
155. Ibrahim 1992:44–45.
156. Ferreira 1995b:15–22, 16 (quotation).
157. Cited in Ibrahim 1992:46. On social themes, also see Kracke 2000.
158. Ferreira 1995b:18.
159. Ibrahim 1992:49 (arrogant), 64.
160. Ferreira 1995b:18 (poor person), 19. Data on Manella from interview with João Batista Ferreira.
161. Coimbra 1995:154–56. On Mother Cristina also see Kehl and Vannuchi 1997.
162. Interview with Dom Paulo Ponte.
163. Burdick 1993.
164. Interview with João Batista Ferreira.
165. Manenti 1983:406.
166. Kemper 1988:170, 173.
167. Kövecses, "Avaliação psicológica da situação atual do clero brasileiro," Secretariado Nacional dos Seminários, Comunicado No. 1, October 1965, INP Document No. 00235, 7.
168. Birman 1988:122.
169. Personal correspondence from Malomar Lund Edelweiss, February 22, 1992. See also Sanchis 2005.
170. One analyst alone has treated hundreds of priests, nuns, and seminarians; interview with Joana Costa.
171. See, for example, Lapenta, Losada, and Almeida 1990; Moser 1989; Lapenta 1990. A similar process took place in the Argentine Church, whose schools opened "psychological bureaus" for the faithful in need; see Plotkin 2001:70, 82.
172. Plé 1974:1204.
173. Interview with Joana Costa. On authoritarians' use of psychology, see Coimbra 1995.

174. Interview with João Batista Ferreira.

175. Sanchis 2005. Furthermore, as Donald Cozzens observes, therapies were necessary but insufficient in the pursuit of happiness, holiness, and intimacy. Priests still needed to learn to empty themselves spiritually in order to achieve the selfless love required by divine will. Only through surrender does one actually achieve what one seeks. See Cozzens 2000:28.

7 The *Pequenas Comunidades* and the Theological Institute of Recife

1. Notion of stillborn (*natimorto*) from Zildo Rocha, cited in Cabral 2001:80.

2. On the uniqueness of the Recife experience, see Cabral 2001:109.

3. On the proletarianization of sugar workers, see Singer 1968:308–19; Perucci 1978.

4. Castro 2001.

5. Callado 1964:32; Page 1972, chap. 2. On poverty see also Scheper-Hughes 1992.

6. Broucker 1970:56.

7. Callado 1964:21.

8. For a general description of the geography and economy of the Northeast, see Andrade 1987:26–37. On SUDENE, industrialization, and the problems of drought, see Singer 1968:345–56; Hirschmann 1963, chap. 1. On the bishops' role in the founding of SUDENE, see Broucker 1970:87–89.

9. Rocha 1972:29.

10. De Kadt 1970:107–21.

11. Page 1972; Callado 1964:20; Broucker 1970:193 (capitals).

12. Page 1972; Schlesinger 1965, chap. 7.

13. On the bishops' 1960 decision and the role of Rome, see Rocha, "Seminário de Olinda, 1960–1965. Anotações a partir dos Livros de Crônicas," Arquivo do Seminário Regional do Nordeste II (hereafter Arquivo do SERENE II), box marked "Material para a história do SERENE II," 13. On the Vatican's role in the construction of Camaragibe, also see Câmara 1965:251.

14. On Catholic Action in the seminary, see Rocha, "Seminário de Olinda, 1950–1965. Anotações a partir dos Livros de Crônicas," Arquivo do SERENE II, box marked "Material para a história do SERENE II," 5–7; Santos 1963; Mourão 1963.

15. Rocha, "Seminário de Olinda, 1960–1965. Anotações a partir dos Livros de Crônicas," Arquivo do SERENE II, box marked "Material para a história do SERENE II," 6–7. On Loew's visit see "Pe. Jacques Loew no Seminário de Viamão" 1962.

16. On JOC and newspaper, see Silva 1961:14–17. On community life, see Rocha, "Seminário de Olinda, 1960–1965. Anotações a partir dos Livros de Crônicas," Arquivo do SERENE II, box marked "Material para a história do SERENE II," 3–6.

17. Aguiar and Gomes 1963.

18. Rocha, "Seminário de Olinda, 1960–1965. Anotações a partir dos Livros de Crônicas," Arquivo do SERENE II, box marked "Material para a história do SERENE II," 5–6, 8.

19. Interview with Dom Marcelo Carvalheira.

20. Rocha, "Seminário de Olinda, 1960–1965. Anotações a partir dos Livros de Crônicas," Arquivo do SERENE II, box marked "Material para a história do SERENE II," 3–6, 8; see also "Carta de Olinda" 1961. On MEB, see René Guerre, "As etapas de uma caminhada," 1980 [?], Arquivo do SERENE II, box marked "Material para a história do SERENE II," 1.

21. Rocha, "Seminário de Olinda, 1960–1965. Anotações a partir dos Livros de Crônicas," Arquivo do SERENE II, box marked "Material para a história do SERENE II," 6.

22. Rocha, "Seminário de Olinda, 1960–1965. Anotações a partir dos Livros de Crônicas," Arquivo do SERENE II, box marked "Material para a história do SERENE II," 12–13. Information on students' behavior also from interview with Dom Marcelo Carvalheira; data confirmed in Cabral 2001:75–76.

23. Interview with Stertz.

24. Rocha, "Seminário de Olinda, 1960–1965. Anotações a partir dos Livros de Crônicas," Arquivo do SERENE II, box marked "Material para a história do SERENE II," 13. On the dimensions of the seminary, see *Seminário Regional do Nordeste: Inauguração que vale como um símbolo* 1966. I observed the architecture of Camaragibe on a visit there in September 1990. On the financial problems of the Camaragibe project, also see copy of letter from Dom Hélder Câmara to Franz Hengesbach, archbishop of Essen, Germany, May 5, 1966, Arquivo do SERENE II, folder 3.3.3, "Seminário-Colônia." Data on financing of Camaragibe also from interview 1 with Raimundo Caramuru Barros and interviews 1 and 2 with Zildo Barbosa Rocha.

25. Cabral 2001:78.

26. "Inaugurado o Seminário do Nordeste" 1965:263–64. On Archbishop Carroll, see McNally 1982. For background on Dom Hélder and General Muricy, see Serbin 2001b, chap. 2.

27. Cirano 1983:17 (quotation); Page 1972:214–15; Rocha, "Seminário de Olinda, 1960–1965. Anotações a partir dos Livros de Crônicas," Arquivo do SERENE II, box marked "Material para a história do SERENE II," 10. Dom Hélder denied allegations that the Army forced him to leave Rio de Janeiro; Broucker 1970:193.

28. Câmara 1965:252 (seminary opens, mutilated, sacrificed, provide us), 255 (subtle), 256 (save, fascination), 257 (in light of). This speech also appeared in "O Seminário Regional do Nordeste tem uma missão histórica a cumprir" 1965.

29. Rocha, "Seminário de Olinda, 1960–1965. Anotações a partir dos Livros de Crônicas," Arquivo do SERENE II, box marked "Material para a história do SERENE II," 10.

30. Rocha, "Seminário de Olinda, 1960–1965. Anotações a partir dos Livros de Crônicas," Arquivo do SERENE II, box marked "Material para a história do SERENE II," 13; Guerre, "As etapas de uma caminhada," Arquivo do SERENE II, box marked "Material

para a história do SERENE II," 2. Dom Hélder offered a somewhat different version of events, saying that the seminarians and superiors actually wanted to move to Camaragibe; see Broucker 1970:105–6. Dom Hélder's version is repeated in Cayuela 1969:171. However, the primary documentation supports my interpretation.

31. Guerre, "As etapas de uma caminhada," Arquivo do SERENE II, box marked "Material para a história do SERENE II," 1–4. Guerre wrote that enrollment had reached 125. Ernanne Pinheiro recorded the number at 135; see Pinheiro, "A vida no Seminário Regional do Nordeste em 1969," Arquivo do SERENE II, box marked "Material para a história do SERENE II."

32. Guerre, "As etapas de uma caminhada," Arquivo do SERENE II, box marked "Material para a história do SERENE II," 3–6, and "Roteiro do estágio dos seminaristas de Camaragibe," mimeographed pamphlet, February 20, 1967, Arquivo do SERENE II, folder titled "Avaliações finais." For an outline of the curriculum, see Carvalheira, "Seminário Regional do Nordeste. Projeto para 1967," November 4, 1966, Arquivo do SERENE II, box marked "Material para a história do SERENE II," folder titled "Documentos para a história do SERENE até 1970."

33. Interview with Dom Marcelo Carvalheira.

34. On Guerre, see the preface by Carvalheira in Guerre 1987; Guerre 1983.

35. Cabral 2001:36–37.

36. Father Zildo Barbosa Rocha to the bishops of the Northeast, Recife, November 9, 1967, Arquivo do SERENE II, box marked "Material para a história do SERENE II," folder titled "Documentos para a história do SERENE até 1970." This document includes: "Anexo 1," Rectores de OSLAM, "Sugerencias para una renovación de seminarios mayores, a la hora del concilio," September 4–11, 1966; "Anexo II," "Conclusões do 2º. dia do encontro nacional sobre seminários maiores. São Paulo, 18 a 23 de julho de 1966"; and "Anexo III," CNBB, "Sugestões do Secretariado Nacional de Seminários para a formação de presbíteros," 1967.

37. Cited in Moro 1997:189.

38. Guerre, "As etapas de uma caminhada," Arquivo do SERENE II, box marked "Material para a história do SERENE II," 7 (trabalhos, spirituality), 7–8 (human), 8 (salaries, fundamentally spiritual), 9–11. For views of the pequenas comunidades at the national level, see Nordeste II, Secretariado Regional-CNBB, Serviço de Apostilas, No. 5, "Encontro Nacional de Seminários do Brasil. Relatório do Círculo Final sobre Seminários Maiores," INP Document No. 11706; CNBB, Secretariado Nacional de Seminários, "Conclusões do 2º. dia do encontro sobre seminários," July 18–23, 1966, INP Document No. 00222; CNBB, Secretariado Nacional de Seminários, "Questões sobre seminários a serem debatidos no sínodo episcopal. Sugestões do Secretariado Nacional de Seminários," July 29, 1967, INP Document No. 00245, p. 3; "Sugestões do Secretariado Nacional de Seminários para a Formação de Presbíteros" 1967:33–37. The bishops did not require the communities to have a resident clerical counselor (see Cabral 2001:88).

But this requirement was later included, as the discussion between Dom Hélder and Dom Gabriel-Marie Garrone (see below) illustrates.

39. Guerre, "As etapas de uma caminhada," Arquivo do SERENE II, box marked "Material para a história do SERENE II," 5.

40. Interview with Comblin.

41. "Entrevista de D. Gabriel-Marie Garrone, dd. Pro-Prefeito da Sagrada Congregação dos Seminários e Universidades—Nunciatura Apostólica, Rio, 26 de novembro de 1966. Com os responsáveis pelos Seminários Maiores do Brasil," PBCM, uncatalogued document. Also see "Notas entregues por S. E. Revma. Dom Gabriel-Marie Garrone, pro-prefeito da S.C. dos Seminários e Universidades," INP Document No. 00250; "A visita de Mons. Garrone, da S.C. dos Seminários, ao Brasil" 1967.

42. Garrone 1968; Garrone 1971; Sacred Congregation for Catholic Education 1970:3. See also Comblin 1984b:4–5.

43. Handwritten copy of letter from Dom Garrone to Dom Hélder, December 13, 1967, Arquivo do SERENE II, "Livro de tombo do Seminário Regional do Nordeste, 1962–1975," 64–69. On the encounter of Dom Garrone and Dom Hélder at the 1967 synod, see mimeograph of letter from Dom Garrone to Dom Hélder, January 9, 1968, Arquivo do SERENE II, box marked "Material para a história do SERENE II."

44. Dom Garrone to Dom Hélder, December 13, 1967, Arquivo do SERENE II, "Livro de tombo do Seminário Regional do Nordeste, 1962–1975," 64–69.

45. Handwritten copy of letter from Dom Hélder to Dom Garrone, Recife, December 24, 1967, Arquivo do SERENE II, "Livro de tombo do Seminário Regional do Nordeste, 1962–1975," 65–66. Emphasis in the original.

46. Dom Garrone to Dom Hélder, January 9, 1968, Arquivo do SERENE II, box marked "Material para a história do SERENE II."

47. The CNBB statements are "Complementação para o Brasil das Diretrizes Básicas da Formação Sacerdotal" 1970 and CNBB 1984a:29–32.

48. Copy of letter from Father Zildo Barbosa Rocha to the bishops of the Northeast II Regional of the CNBB, Recife, January 3, 1968, Arquivo do SERENE II, box marked "Material para a história do SERENE II."

49. Mimeograph of letter from Father Zildo Barbosa Rocha to the bishops of Northeast II Region of the CNBB, Recife, January 25, 1968, Arquivo do SERENE II, box marked "Material para a história do SERENE II." On the Verona seminary, see Azevedo 1962–1963.

50. Guerre, "As etapas de uma caminhada," Arquivo do SERENE II, box marked "Material para a história do SERENE II," 11–12.

51. Letter cited in Cabral 2001:100.

52. Guerre, "As etapas de uma caminhada," Arquivo do SERENE II, box marked "Material para a história do SERENE II," 11–12.

53. Dom Gabriel-Marie Garrone to Dom Hélder Câmara, January 15, 1968, Arquivo do SERENE II, box marked "Material para a história do SERENE II."

54. Guerre, "As etapas de uma caminhada," Arquivo do SERENE II, box marked "Material para a história do SERENE II," 12, 14 (quotation), 15. Emphasis in the original.

55. Guerre, "As etapas de uma caminhada," Arquivo do SERENE II, box marked "Material para a história do SERENE II," 15; also see Rocha to the bishops of the Northeast II Region of the CNBB, January 25, 1968, Arquivo do SERENE II, box marked "Material para a história do SERENE II."

56. "Documento de Base," in *SERENE II: Uma caminhada* 1988:96.

57. Cabral 2001:103-4.

58. For a description of these incidents and of other violence and torture in the northeast, see Alves 1967:54 (quotation), passim; Alves 1968; Alves 1973.

59. Alves 1967:29, 109.

60. Alves 1968:11-12, 263.

61. Interview with Dom Marcelo Carvalheira.

62. Alves 1973:159; Cirano 1983:111-21; Dom Hélder Câmara, "Morte, onde está tua vitória? Homilia, pregada por Dom Hélder Câmara, arcebispo de Olinda e Recife, na missa comemorativa do 10°. aniversário do martírio do Padre Antônio Henrique Pereira Neto," INP, document No. 9781. On Dom Sigaud, see chapter 5; Cirano 1983:49-52.

63. Pinheiro, "A vida no Seminário Regional do Nordeste em 1969," Arquivo do SERENE II, box marked "Material para a história do SERENE II"; Absalão 1984; interview with Joana Costa.

64. Cabral 2001:114-15, including note 199 for a detailed list of the acts against the Church.

65. Cirano 1983:69-83.

66. Dom Hélder and Dom José Lamartine Soares to the Brazilian bishops, Recife, March 28, 1972, INP, Document No. 00415; see also Mainwaring 1986:101.

67. "Operação Esperança," Divisão de Segurança e Informações do Ministério da Justiça, Arquivo Nacional (AN, DSI/MJ), Rio de Janeiro, avulso UD093, caixa 3594 (Operação Esperança ano de 1973, anexo B).

68. Pinheiro, "A vida no Seminário Regional do Nordeste em 1969," Arquivo do SERENE II, box marked "Material para a história do SERENE II."

69. Statistics on enrollment in the period 1966-1988 from Ernanne Pinheiro, "A vida no Seminário Regional do Nordeste em 1969," Arquivo do SERENE II, box marked "Material para a história do SERENE II"; Ernanne Pinheiro, "1970," Arquivo do SERENE II, box marked "Material para a história do SERENE II"; "Seminário e formação sacerdotal na Região Nordeste II," March 2, 1974, Arquivo do SERENE II, folder marked "Comunidade e ministérios"; *SERENE II: Uma caminhada* 1988:27.

70. Data on ordinations from "Livro de ordenações," Arquivo do SERENE II; "Ordenações," folders No. 27 and No. 30, Arquivo do SERENE II; *SERENE II: Uma caminhada* 1988:28.

71. Cabral 2001:143.

72. Silva 2003.

73. Castro 1987; Patrick 1984; Comblin 1984a; Guerre 1983; Pinheiro 1984; "A Igreja e a opção pelos pobres" 1982; "A Comissão de Justiça e Paz na Arquidiocese de Olinda e Recife" 1984.

74. Rocha 1972:276-77.

75. Interview with Comblin.

76. Pinheiro, "1970," Arquivo do SERENE II, box marked "Material para a história do SERENE II."

77. "Relatório da vida das equipes—1°. semestre—1970. Seminário Regional do Nordeste," August 25, 1970, Arquivo do SERENE II, box marked "Material para a história do SERENE II," folder titled "Documentos para história do SERENE até 1970" (quotation); perception of shock also from interview with Comblin.

78. Interview with Dom Marcelo Carvalheira.

79. *SERENE II: Uma caminhada* 1988:14.

80. Pinheiro, "1970," Arquivo do SERENE II, box marked "Material para a história do SERENE II"; "Reunião da Comissão Episcopal NE-II com o Secretariado Regional. 26 a 28 de outubro de 1971—Olinda. Sobre o Seminário Regional do Nordeste e a equipe encarregada de formação para os ministérios da Igreja," October 27, 1971, Arquivo do SERENE II, box marked "Material para a história do SERENE II"; Milton Andrade, ex-seminarian, to Father Leônidas da Silva, Olinda, August 30, 1982, Arquivo do SERENE II, box marked "Material para a história do SERENE II" (quotation).

81. "Livro das atas do ITER," Arquivo do Instituto Teológico do Recife (hereafter Arquivo do ITER).

82. *SERENE II: Uma caminhada* 1988:15-16.

83. "Livro das atas do ITER," Arquivo do ITER, 1, 8-10.

84. On institutes in other cities, see "Instituto de Filosofia e Teologia" 1966; Parisse and Pegoraro 1968; CNBB, Eighth General Assembly, "Relatório-síntese das atividades nacionais e regionais (1°. de janeiro de 1966 a 5 de maio de 1967)," May 6-10, 1967, INP Document No. 1443, p. 3; "Faculdade de teologia" 1962; "Instituto Filosófico-Teológico do Paraná" 1967; "Instituto Central de Filosofia e Teologia," no date, probably 1969, INP Document No. 04692; "Centro Teológico de Estudos e Espiritualidade para a Vida Religiosa" 1975; "O Instituto Central de Filosofia e Teologia de Belo Horizonte visto de dentro" 1969; "Instituto Central de Filosofia e Teologia: Estrutura do currículo de seis anos," no date, probably 1967, INP Document No. 16037; Gehlen 1970. For an analysis of the Belo Horizonte experiment, see Serbin 1992a:120-22.

85. Câmara 1989.

86. "Livro das atas do ITER," Arquivo do ITER, 1-42.

87. Pinheiro, "1970," Arquivo do SERENE II, box marked "Material para a história do SERENE II."

88. Guerre, "As etapas de uma caminhada," Arquivo do SERENE II, box marked "Material para a história do SERENE II," 29-30.

89. Guerre, "As etapas de uma caminhada," Arquivo do SERENE II, box marked "Material para a história do SERENE II," 18, 19 (not bearing witness), 21 (we try to live), 24 (intellectualized, foreigners), 29 (paternalistic, many came), 33 (my relationship, we never paid).

90. Similar evaluations in Comblin 1970, 1981.

91. Guerre, "As etapas de uma caminhada," Arquivo do SERENE II, box marked "Material para a história do SERENE II," 21, 31.

92. Guerre, "As etapas de uma caminhada," Arquivo do SERENE II, box marked "Material para a história do SERENE II," 22, 32–33 (maturity); Andrade to Silva, August 30, 1982, Arquivo do SERENE II, box marked "Material para a história do SERENE II" (inconsistency). In São Paulo the experiment with small communities did not bring about a marked increase in the efficiency of clerical training and did little to change pastoral practices; interview 1 with Celso Pedro da Silva.

93. Guerre, "As etapas de uma caminhada," Arquivo do SERENE II, box marked "Material para a história do SERENE II," 23 (engaged), 28 (community, our spiritual life, we continue).

94. Interview with Eduardo Hoornaert.

95. Interview with Dom Marcelo Carvalheira.

96. Andrade to Silva, August 30, 1982, Arquivo do SERENE II, box marked "Material para a história do SERENE II."

97. Câmara 1989:11.

98. Andrade to Silva, August 30, 1982, Arquivo do SERENE II, box marked "Material para a história do SERENE II."

99. Interview with Ernanne Pinheiro.

100. Andrade to Silva, August 30, 1982, Arquivo do SERENE II, box marked "Material para a história do SERENE II"; interview 4 with Severino Vicente da Silva; interview with Plummen. Discrepancies exist among the versions of this incident as recounted in interviews and the letter cited here. I have described the situation as accurately as possible based on my reading of the sources and the historical context. For a similar description, see Cabral 2001:212–25.

101. Andrade to Silva, August 30, 1982, Arquivo do SERENE II, box marked "Material para a história do SERENE II"; interview with Plummen.

102. Interview with Plummen.

103. A notable example was the Faculdade de Teologia Nossa Senhora da Assunção, located on the site of the old Seminário Central de Ipiranga in São Paulo. The student body and the faculty split between conservative modernists, who emphasized the theology of Vatican II, and the proponents of Medellín and liberation theology. Throughout most of the 1970s Assunção's curriculum was mainly a patchwork of theological tendencies. However, with the growing force of radical students, who wanted to study new themes such as human rights and politics, the liberationist persuasion become

predominant. In 1979 liberation theology was formally adopted as the school's curriculum. The growth of the CEBs in São Paulo and the resistance by seminarians and the Church to the military regime played an important part in this shift. Assunção students took an active role in the resurgence of the Brazilian student movement in 1977, for instance. Among the leading proponents of liberation theology at Assunção were Father Gilberto da Silva Gorgulho, a Dominican friar and theological advisor to Dom Paulo Evaristo Arns, and Ana Flora Anderson, a lay professor. Both were kept under police surveillance at the height of the dictatorship. Although a minority, the liberationist faculty and students held sway during this period because of the support of Cardinal Arns, the intellectual excellence of the liberationist professors, and the liberationist faction's ability to organize politically within the seminary. Like ITER, Assunção welcomed numerous laypersons into its program. This description is based on: interviews 1 and 2 with Ana Flora Anderson; interviews 1 and 2 with Gilberto da Silva Gorgulho; interview with José Cardonha; interview 2 with Benedito Beni dos Santos; and interview with José Adriano.

104. Interview 4 with Severino Vicente da Silva.

105. See, for example, Gebara 1992, 2002.

106. Dom Antônio Fragoso and Dom Luciano Mendes de Almeida, the president of the CNBB, privately supported Gebara; interview with Ivone Gebara.

107. Cited in Cabral 2001:112.

108. Guerre, "As etapas de uma caminhada," Arquivo do SERENE II, box marked "Material para a história do SERENE II," 22, 30 (quotations).

109. "Relatório da reunião do dia 18/9/68 das duas equipes da Boa Nova," Arquivo do SERENE II, box marked "Material para a história do SERENE II," folder marked "Relatórios das equipes. 1968."

110. Cabral 2001:134-38.

111. Cabral 2001:130-33.

112. On traditional restrictions on women's participation in the Church, see Lhoëst 1969; Zanlochi 1990; Nunes 1986. On women religious in *pequenas comunidades*, see Brito 1970; "A regional do Recife" 1972:54-58; Tierny 1975; Barreiro 1975.

113. Tierny 1975:18.

114. Interview with Eduardo Hoornaert.

115. This and the following paragraphs are based on interview with Janis Jordan and my own observation of Dancin' Days.

116. On ITER and gender, see Cabral 2001:245-46.

117. "Relatório das duas reuniões feitas pelas equipes que se orientam para a vida do campo," Arquivo do SERENE II, box marked "Material para a história do SERENE II," no date, probably 1968, among documents titled "Equipes rurais. Relatórios."

118. "Reunião da Comissão Episcopal NE-II com o Secretariado Regional. 26 a 28 de outubro de 1971—Olinda. Sobre o Seminário Regional do Nordeste e a equipe encarregada de formação para os ministérios da Igreja," October 27, 1971, Arquivo do SERENE II, box marked "Material para a história do SERENE II."

119. Interview with Servat. On ACR, see Silva 1985:149–50.

120. On ACR, see Servat 1986; Silva 1985; Servat and Father Afrânio 1985; Santos, Silva, and Silva 1984. On surveillance see also "Operação Esperança," AN, DSI/MJ, Rio de Janeiro, avulso UD093, caixa 3594 (Operação Esperança ano de 1973, anexo B). For background on rural union movements in Brazil see Pereira 1997, Houtzager 1998.

121. This and the next two paragraphs from interview with Arnaldo Liberato da Silva. In August of 1987 I visited the Morro da Conceição equipe and spoke with several of its members. For additional background on the Morro, see Nagle 1997.

122. On the strikes, see Silva 1982; see also Castro 1987:130.

123. Comblin 1977:9–10; interview with Comblin; interview with Servat. In addition, three seminarians who had already graduated formed a community in Jupi, Pernambuco. Little is known about this group. See SERENE II: Uma caminhada 1988:13.

124. Interview with Raimundo Nonato de Queiroz.

125. Comblin 1977:9, 11, 12 (quotation). See also SERENE II: Uma caminhada 1988:13.

126. Comblin 1977.

127. João Alves Moura Filho, Raimundo Silva, Francisco Chagas, and Raimundo Nonato, "Relatório dos dias 27 e 28 de setembro em Feira Nova," October 12, 1968, Arquivo do SERENE II, box marked "Material para a história do SERENE II," documents titled "Equipes rurais. Relatórios" (abyss); Comblin 1977:84–85 (Jesus).

128. Moura Filho, Silva, Chagas, and Nonato, "Relatório dos dias 27 e 28 de setembro em Feira Nova," October 12, 1968, Arquivo do SERENE II, box marked "Material para a história do SERENE II," documents titled "Equipes rurais. Relatórios."

129. Quotations in this and next two paragraphs from "Relatório da vida das equipes—1º. semestre—1970. Seminário Regional do Nordeste," August 25, 1970, Arquivo do SERENE II, box marked "Material para a história do SERENE II," folder titled "Documentos para história do SERENE até 1970."

130. On revolutionary romanticism and rural Brazil, see Ridenti 2000:42.

131. Comblin 1977:10.

132. Comblin 1977; Comblin 1983–1986.

133. "Reunião da Comissão Episcopal NE-II com o Secretariado Regional. 26 a 28 de outubro de 1971—Olinda. Sobre o Seminário Regional do Nordeste e a equipe encarregada de formação para os ministérios da Igreja," October 27, 1971," Arquivo do SERENE II, box marked "Material para a história do SERENE II."

134. Cabral 2001:267–91.

135. "Ministérios e vocações. Síntese das sugestões dos grupos apresentadas ao plenário," October 5 and 6, 1976, Assembléia ordinária da CER, Arquivo do SERENE II, file marked "Comunidade e ministérios." Emphasis in the original.

136. Castro 1987:173, 182–86.

137. On vocational increase, see Table 5.2. See also Serbin 1992a:140–44; Antoniazzi 1984b. On cultural differences, see SERENE II: Uma caminhada 1988:86; a similar point made in interview with Ernanne Pinheiro.

138. Cabral 2001:241–42.

139. *SERENE II: Uma caminhada* 1988:23–24.

140. Interview with Arnaldo Liberato da Silva.

141. Interview with Ernanne Pinheiro.

142. Cabral 2001:238.

143. Interview with Ernanne Pinheiro.

144. Cabral 2001:201–2.

145. Interview with Ernanne Pinheiro.

146. Silva 1991.

147. Cabral 2001:244.

148. Libânio 1984.

149. Numerous commentators have dealt with this theme from a variety of perspectives; see, for example, Della Cava 1989; Lernoux 1989; Montero 1992b; Ghio 1991, 1992; M. Martin 1990; Instituto de Estudos da Religião 1990; Mainwaring 1986, chap. 11; Serbin 1993b; Daudelin and Hewitt 1995; Vásquez 1998; V. Machado 2001; Adriance 1995.

150. Bernstein and Politi 1996.

151. Interview 1 with Ana Flora Anderson.

152. A detailed study is needed of the lives and long-term impact of John Paul II's appointees.

153. Mainwaring 1986; Bruneau and Hewitt 1992.

154. Serbin 2000a. Pierucci (1984) observed the São Paulo clergy's embrace of civil liberties in the early 1980s over and above the struggle for socioeconomic justice.

155. Castañeda 1993.

156. Berryman 1996.

157. Pierucci and Prandi (eds.; 1996) estimate CEB membership at 1.8 percent of the population. Also see the important (and methodologically different) statistical study by Valle and Pitta (1994), which counts all types of Catholic communities. For an appraisal of Valle and Pitta's research, see Oliveira 1994. For skeptical views of previous large CEB estimates, see Hewitt 1991 and 1995, Daudelin and Hewitt 1995; Burdick 1993; and Drogus 1992. For an optimistic evaluation of the CEBs see Souza 2000.

158. See Burdick 1993 and 1994 for a critical evaluation of the CEBs' unattractiveness to the poor and for a perceptive essay on the Catholic Church; also see Berryman 1996 and Perani 1987. For a rigorous critique of Burdick's postmodernist, microsocial approach, see Vásquez 1998, which presents a detailed overview of the crisis of the Progressive Church from the perspective of the "macrodynamics" of the capitalist world-system.

159. Pierucci and Prandi, eds. 1996.

160. Vásquez 1997, 1998; Hewitt 1995; Perani 1987.

161. Serbin 2000a:148, 153. See also Fonseca 2002. On the correlation between migration and Pentecostal adherence, see Jacob et al. 2003:215–17.

162. Freston 1993a.

163. See http://www.ibge.gov.br.

164. Serbin 2000a:159. On Charismatics, see also M. Souza 2002.

165. Vásquez 1998:110, 157.

166. Garrone 1980.

167. *SERENE II: Uma caminhada* 1988:18; "História do seminário do regional referente aos anos de 1980–1982," Arquivo do SERENE II, box marked "Material para a história do SERENE II"; "Santa Sé" 1982; "CNBB. Conselho permanente. Atas" 1982; interview with Ernanne Pinheiro. São Paulo received a visitator, Dom Eusébio Scheid, in 1981 and another, Joseph Cardinal Höffner, in 1986. According to Cabral (2001:298, 301), the Vatican built a database of nearly a million items on the situation at ITER. Proof of the size of this database is lacking, however. With the breakup of the Archdiocese of São Paulo in 1989, the Vatican required that the seminary's theology professors have doctorates obtained in Rome. Data on São Paulo from interview with José Adriano.

168. Serbin 1992a:146–49.

169. Moro 1997:190–91, 193.

170. Data on Dom Cardoso from Instituto de Teologia do Recife and Comissão de Justiça e Paz de Olinda e Recife 1989:16; interview with Tenderini, president of the archdiocesan Peace and Justice Commission. On Dom Cardoso's career path, see CNBB 1984b:235. Personal impressions on the archbishop from interview with Dom José Cardoso Sobrinho and from conversations with Brazilian priests in the late 1980s and early 1990s. Data on Focolares from interviews with Ekkehard Schneider and Edmar Alves. On the conservative Catholic movements, see Lernoux 1989; Della Cava and Montero 1991:77–97.

171. On Dom Cardoso's actions in Recife, see Instituto de Teologia do Recife and Comissão de Justiça e Paz de Olinda e Recife 1989 and "Dossiê—crise na arquidiocese de Olinda e Recife" 1990; also see Centro Nordestino de Animação Popular 1989; Silva 1991; Brooke 1989; Serbin 1989c. On Father Reginaldo see Nagle 1997.

172. *SERENE II: Uma caminhada* 1988:25. For details of the 1986 meeting, see Silva 1991:5; data also from interview with Airene José Amaral de Paiva; interview 2 with Severino Vicente da Silva.

173. Cabral 2001:302–23.

174. Serbin 1992a:127–28.

175. Silva 1991. The principal argument of Cabral 2001 is that the closures were the responsibility of the Northeast II bishops; see also Silva 2003.

176. Interview 5 with Severino Vicente da Silva.

177. This and the next paragraph are based on the following: Instituto de Teologia do Recife and Comissão de Justiça e Paz de Olinda e Recife 1989; Serbin 1989a, 1989b, 1989c, 1989d, 1989e, 1989f, 1992a:149–50. Information about reactions among the faithful from interview with Janis Jordan and in conversations with people from grassroots communities during the closing ceremony of ITER and SERENE II, November 12, 1989. For a survey of both the clergy and the faithful, see Guerra Sobrinho 1991. On Vatican opposition to *pequenas comunidades* see also Moro 1997:198, including note 45. In

interview 2, Dom Paulo Evaristo Arns noted the secrecy with which Rome kept information on the review of his own seminary in 1986 by Joseph Cardinal Höffner: "I went to Rome, and there nobody wanted to give me information. I then asked, 'How can I obtain information.' They responded: 'By going to Cologne and directly asking Cardinal Höffner.' I went to Cologne and Cardinal Höffner told me: 'Secretum Pontificium.'" This datum also confirmed in interview 2 with Benedito Beni dos Santos.

178. Moro 1997:373, note 43.

179. Interview with Ivone Gebara.

180. On continued strife see "Briga em nome de Deus" 1993; Lúcia, Tavares, and Andrade 1998. On the Igreja Nova see, for instance, Grupo de Leigos Católicos Igreja Nova 2000. The group publishes a bulletin, *Jornal Igreja Nova,* and a website, http://www. igrejanova.jor.br, with news and commentary on the Church in light of liberation theology. One of the group's founders published a novel recounting the events of the Recife crisis; see Silva Filho 1997. Background on group from interviews with Edelomar Barbosa, Elisabete Barbosa, Assuero Gomes da Silva Filho, and Inácio Strieder.

181. Interview 5 with Severino Vicente da Silva. Data on university professors also from interview 3 with Zildo Barbosa Rocha.

182. Interview with Ivone Gebara.

183. Instituto de Teologia do Recife and Comissão de Justiça e Paz de Olinda e Recife 1989:41.

184. Cited in Cabral 2001:112 (Dom Marcelo), 157 (Christian symbols), 113 (Dom José Maria Pires), 114 (Rocha).

185. Cabral 2001:115-16.

186. Serbin 1989e; also see Cabral 2001:330-31.

187. Interview with Janis Jordan.

188. Cabral 2001:248.

189. This is one of the central arguments of Cabral 2001.

190. Cited in Cabral 2001:139-40.

8 Epilogue

1. Moro 1997:430.

2. Serbin 1992a:131-34. Moro 1997 also posits the idea of synthesis. A similar synthesis took place in Mexican seminaries; see Camp 1997:87. On urban pastoral strategy, see also Comissão Nacional do Clero 1994.

3. For a recent illustration of OSIB's activities and its capacity to draw a national following, see the documentary film *Sereis Minhas Testemunhas.* On the priests' council and congresses, see Antoniazzi 1998:606.

4. Moro 1997:204-7, 212-13, 215.

5. On decentralization and the *pequenas comunidades* in the 1990s, see Antoniazzi 1995a:23, 37; 1995b:62.

6. For a detailed presentation of the model of the *casa de formação* and its theological underpinnings, see Moro 1997. Moro takes a more benign attitude toward the Holy See's position on the *pequenas comunidades*. But, as I sustain in chapter 7, in the larger ecclesial and political context it became clear that the Vatican was working to water down and even eliminate the Brazilian model.

7. John Paul II 1992:5 (important tasks), 13 (resemble Christ), 161 (produced).

8. John Paul II 1992:6 (new evangelizers), 16, 17 (there is no longer), 118, 132 (essential moment), 120 (affective maturity), 121(capable), 161 (educational community). Emphasis in the original.

9. Antoniazzi 1995a:8–9.

10. For the 1970s and 1980s, see Serbin 1992a:140–44; on the 1990s see Antoniazzi 1995a:14–16, 30–32, 36–37; for 2003, see Centro de Estatística Religiosa e Investigações Sociais 2003:10, 13; on youth and diocesans, see Antoniazzi 1998:599–600; on pastoral activism, see J. Valle 1995:51–52. On the rural origins of the clergy even in São Paulo, the continent's most developed capitalist city, see Pierucci 1984:538–40. The sociological background of the clergy mirrors that of the seminarians; see Centro de Estatística Religiosa e Investigações Sociais 2003. On the training of future bishops in Mexico rather than abroad, see Camp 1997:156.

11. Antoniazzi 1995a:18, 20.

12. Moro 1997:245, 320 (pastoralitis), 401. See also Serbin 1992a:138–39, including note 98; Antoniazzi 1995a:18. Not all observers agree with this analysis. Anderson (interview 1) asserted that intellectual training is not as weak as many maintain.

13. Interview with Paviani.

14. Interview with Luiz Fernando de Oliveira. Data on the movement also from interview with Davi Raimundo dos Santos.

15. Myatt 1995.

16. On the 1980s, see Serbin 1992a:142–43; for the latest survey, see Centro de Estatística Religiosa e Investigações Sociais 2003.

17. Interview with Luiz Fernando de Oliveira.

18. J. Valle 1995:41–42, 47, 49–50.

19. Antoniazzi 1995a:25.

20. Interview with José Antônio de Oliveira.

21. J. Valle 1995:51, 55–56.

22. Antoniazzi 1998:607–10.

23. For the clergy see Antoniazzi 1998:610–17. On the seminaries, see Marmilicz 2002:88–89. For a harsh critique of today's seminaries as a continuation of the past, see the anonymous website of "Dom Doca," self-reputed bishop of the poor, http://domdoca. atspace.com. On August 30, 2000, Dom Doca circulated an e-mail article entitled "A instituição 'seminário' no conflito das interpretações," in which he referred to the notion

of seminaries as "absurd." "Dom Doca" is likely a pun on the Portuguese word "dondoca," which signifies a woman of means who spends her time on frivolities—a criticism of the conservative Church.

24. On the graduate program at the Pontifical Catholic University of Rio Grande do Sul, see Seidl 2003:250–52. On the lack of a national training center in Mexico, see Camp 1997:159.

25. On Puebla, see Comblin 1981:321–22, 337–40.

26. See, for example, Moro 1997:294–310.

27. Marmilicz 2002:76 (including note 19), 77, 78 (including note 24), 82–87. Marmilicz is a Vincentian priest. In contrast with the CNBB's own studies, his national survey of seminarians—which covered one quarter of the ecclesiastical student body—posed specific questions about attitudes toward the opposite sex, differences in sexual orientation, acceptance of celibacy, and other psychological themes. Lack of discussion about celibacy was also confirmed in interview with Antoniazzi. A partial exception to this attitude occurred with the completion of a new research project on the background of the diocesan clergy by CERIS. The questionnaire included questions about celibacy, homosexuality, and relationships with women. Oddly, however, it omitted any mention of psychology or professional counseling as options for priests. See Centro de Estatística Religiosa e Investigações Sociais 2003. On the need for greater focus on the psychological, see also Nasini 2001:220–21.

28. Nadai, for example, pointed out that some clerical innovators in the area of sexuality still have difficulty in speaking freely in the Brazilian Church; interview with Nadai.

29. The study is Nasini 2001:67, 71 (quotation). Comment on guerrillas from interview with Ricardo Rezende Figueira.

30. Centro de Estatística Religiosa e Investigações Sociais 2003:19.

31. Ribeiro 2001.

32. See Nasini 2001:167–70. Also see the powerful docudrama *The Boys of St. Vincent* (1993), directed by John N. Smith.

33. Investigative Staff of the *Boston Globe* 2002:8, 42–43, 56, 61, 80, 99, 172. For the bishops conference study, see http://www.usccb.org/nrb/johnjaystudy. On the number of victims, see "Study Reveals One Thousand New Abuse Claims" 2005.

34. "Bishops Who Quit amid Sex Scandals" 2002.

35. Investigative Staff of the *Boston Globe* 2002:7.

36. Belluck and Bruni 2002.

37. Moser 2002:515. For other views of the U.S. crisis, see Cozzens 2000, chap. 8.

38. Investigative Staff of the *Boston Globe* 2002:x (high-ranking officials), 3 (betrayal), 67 (casually), passim.

39. Nasini 2001:227.

40. Investigative Staff of the *Boston Globe* 2002:166 (dark side), 167 (homosocial, atmosphere, fraternity), passim. The *Globe* study makes the interesting observation

that "social science has had little to say about the abuse of minors by priests—neither the Church itself nor academics who study mental health have undertaken a rigorous quantitative study that would shed some light on the frequency or nature of this startling phenomenon. But in the wake of relentless revelations about sexually abusive priests, even the most conservative defenders of the Church have abandoned the argument that the priesthood is no worse than any other profession in which adults work with children" (166). One scholar notes that "the Protestant establishment doesn't tolerate [abuses] the way the Catholic establishment has" (167).

41. Rossetti 1990:1, 4.

42. Serbin 2002a.

43. Nasini 2001:92, 118–22, 127–32, 152–59.

44. Centro de Estatística Religiosa e Investigações Sociais 2003:17.

45. Analogy to the U.S. situation and the need to report abusers suggested by Rossetti 1990:2–3. On macho culture, also see Moro 1997:295, 306; J. Oliveira 2001.

46. Nasini 2001:13 (ethical concerns), 20, 22, 161 (homosexuality), passim. Nasini is a U.S. cleric with considerable experience in Brazil. Although recognizing the important differences in sexual culture between the two countries, he defines sexual abuse in the all-inclusive manner that is characteristic of North America. Thus in his estimation even a relationship between a fully consenting adult and a priest is abusive; see, for example, pp. 88–89, 126–27. Nasini does not consider the fact that some Brazilian priests have regular partners in the same manner that clerics of past eras did. It is hard to see this kind of relationship as abusive, particularly if the priest rejects celibacy and advocates a married clergy. Nasini takes a hard-line approach, yet he does not advocate the "zero tolerance" policy put into effect in the U.S. Church in 2002. Nasini believes in rehabilitation and that each case should be judged separately; see, for example, p. 191. On sexual abuse, also see Alves Filho et al. 1996.

47. U.S. data from Cozzens 2000:98 (quotation), 99, 101–3, 107–9. On Brazilian priests' desire for research on homosexuality, see Nasini 2001:209–10.

48. Interview 2 with Buss. As early as 1981 the CNBB's vocational sector issued a document in which it oriented the seminaries to take in gay men who had "accepted" their problem and demonstrated the possibility of "overcoming" it by "controlling and channeling their sexuality towards the same life objectives that enrich and fulfill the heterosexual candidate." The document recommended therapy before entering the seminary and close personal attention once admitted. See "Pistas para a Ação Pedagógica— Conclusões do Curso sobre 'Moral e Psicologia' (São Paulo, 23–25/10/81), Arquivo/JP [João Pessoa], pasta OSIB," cited in Cabral 2001:130.

49. Interview with José Antônio de Oliveira.

50. Centro de Estatística Religiosa e Investigações Sociais 2003:21.

51. "Aids, tabu na Igreja, é estudada em seminários" 2002; on saunas also see Galhardo 2000b; for other examples of homosexual activity, see Alves Filho et al. 1996.

52. Nasini 2001:81.

53. Schierholz 2001:251–57, 302, 309–10. On Church pastoral programs on AIDS, see Traferetti 2002.

54. Galhardo 2000b (quotation), 2000a; see also D'Azevedo 2000.

55. Interview with José Antônio de Oliveira; and see Galhardo 2000b; J. Oliveira 2001.

56. Galhardo 2000b.

57. Amaral 2000.

58. "Aids, tabu na Igreja, é estudada em seminários" 2002.

59. Nasini 2001:115–16. In interview 2, Buss also mentioned the presumed existence of an extraofficial and informal group of gay priests who were quietly working for a day in which they could make explicit demands on the Church and suggest particular modes of pastoral action. Gay priests have not yet made such demands. However, the AIDS crisis of the late 1980s and 1990s presented the Church with a de facto situation in which at least one key issue—gay health—gained prominence. On the extraofficial group see also Araújo 2002:905–6. Such a subculture clearly exists in the U.S. Church; see Cozzens 2000:100, 109–10.

60. Cozzens 2000:100.

61. Cozzens 2000:107 (quotation), 108–9.

62. Ottmann 2002:143 (pastoral feminism), passim. On the crisis in Brazilian Catholic progressivism, see also Vásquez 1998. For a more optimistic outlook, see Burdick 2004.

63. Two exceptions are Vásquez 1997 and 1998.

64. On the CNBB, see Serbin 2000a.

65. J. Oliveira 2002; see also French 2004.

66. V. Machado 2001. On Stedile as a seminarian, see Cruz and Expedito Filho n.d.; on Stedile, the MST, and the CPT, see Stedile and Fernandes 1999. On the MST and the Progressive Church, see also Burdick 2004.

67. Serbin 2000a:153, 154 (quotations), 155. For a detailed study of the Igreja Universal, see Kramer 2001.

68. Serbin 2000a:158–59.

69. Interview 1 with Pretto; interview 2 with Benincá (Passo Fundo). On the recovery of traditional religiosity, see also Pessar 2004:212–24.

70. Souza 1999:128.

71. Chesnut 2003, chap. 4.

72. Serbin 2000a:159. On Charismatics in São Paulo, see also Singer 2001a, 2001b.

73. Serbin 2000a:160.

74. Ottmann 2002:136, 159–60, 166. On Charismatics, see also Machado 1996; M. Souza 2002; van den Berg 2003; Massarão 2002.

75. Chesnut 2003, chap. 4.

76. Crivellaro 1999:39–41, 42 (quotation).

77. Crivellaro 1999.

78. See http://www.padremarcelorossi.com.br. For the site of CCR, see http://www.rccbrasil.org.br.

79. Interview with André Eduardo Godoi Lourenço.

80. Interview with Cláudio Dias.

81. Interview with André Eduardo Godoi Lourenço.

82. These movements include the seminarians of the Redemptoris Mater (so-called Neo-Catecumenais) in Brasília; the Comunidade Shalom (a Charismatic group) in Salvador, Recife, and Fortaleza; Canção Nova (a Charismatic group) in Cachoeira Paulista; and the Legionários de Cristo (originally a Mexican congregation) in Porto Alegre and Curitiba; interview with José Lisboa Moreira de Oliveira.

83. CNBB 1999.

84. Interview with José Antônio de Oliveira.

85. Interview with José Lisboa Moreira de Oliveira.

86. Interview with Cláudio Dias. On the decline of liberationism and the rise of managerial discourse in Brazilian Catholicism in the 1990s, see Ottmann 2002:160–72.

87. *O chamado de Deus* (2000), directed by José Joffily.

88. On "graying," see Cozzens 2000:20.

References

Seminaries and Theological Institutes Visited (by State and City)

Ceará
Instituto Teológico-Pastoral do Ceará (Fortaleza)
Seminário Regional Nordeste 1 (Fortaleza)

Maranhão
Seminário Interdiocesano Santo Antônio (São Luís do Maranhão)

Minas Gerais
Colégio do Caraça (Santa Bárbara)
Seminário Provincial Coração Eucarístico de Jesus (Belo Horizonte)
Seminário São José (Mariana)

Pará
Instituto de Pastoral Regional (Belém)

Paraíba
Seminário Rural de Serra Redonda (Serra Redonda)

Pernambuco
Instituto Teológico do Recife (Recife)
Seminário Regional do Nordeste II (Recife)

Rio de Janiero
Seminário Arquidiocesano de São José (Rio de Janeiro)

Rio Grande do Sul
Seminário Cristo Rei (São Leopoldo)
Seminário Nossa Senhora da Conceição (Viamão)

Santa Catarina
Convento do Sagrado Coração de Jesus (Brusque)
Pontifício Instituto das Missões (Brusque)

Seminário Filosófico de Santa Catarina (Brusque)
Seminário Menor Metropolitano Nossa Senhora de Lourdes (Brusque [Bairro de Azambuja])

São Paulo
Faculdades Associadas de Ipiranga (São Paulo)
Pontifícia Faculdade de Teologia Nossa Senhora da Assunção (São Paulo)
Seminário Arquidiocesano de São Paulo (São Paulo [Bairro de Tatuapé])
Seminário São João Maria Vianney (São Paulo [Diocese de Santo Amaro])

Interviews

Fr. Jamil Nassif Abib, Rio Claro, July 17, 1987.
Fr. Leopoldo Adami, S.J., São Leopoldo, August 18, 1989.
Fr. José Adriano, São Paulo, May 9, 1990.
Odair Angelo Agostin, São Paulo, July 23, 1987.
Fr. José Pires de Almeida, C.M., Rio de Janeiro, November 13, 1991.
Edmar Alves, Recife, November 23, 1990.
Maria Salete Souza Amorim, São Paulo, July 1, 1986.
Ana Flora Anderson, São Paulo, (1) March 25, 1990, and (2) March 27, 1990.
Fr. Alberto Antoniazzi, Belo Horizonte, August 3, 1987.
Gilbraz Souza Aragão, Recife, November 30, 1989.
Dom Paulo Evaristo Arns, São Paulo, (1) September 10, 1996, and (2) July 29, 1999.
Fr. Marcello de Carvalho Azevedo, S.J., Rio de Janeiro, July 2, 1987.
Riolando Azzi, Rio de Janeiro, June 30, 1987.
Edelomar Barbosa, Recife, June 23, 2001.
Elisabete Barbosa, Recife, June 23, 2001.
Raimundo Caramuru Barros, Brasília, (1) August 1, 1987, (2) February 3, 1990, (3) February 7, 1990, and (4) February 10, 1990.
Fr. Arnaldo Beltrami, Brasília, February 1, 1990.
Fr. Pedro C. Beltrão, S.J., Porto Alegre, August 11, 1989.
Fr. Elli Benincá, (1) Viamão, August 16, 1989, and (2) Passo Fundo, August 5, 1994.
Fr. Bartolomeu Bergese, Nova Iguaçu, October 25, 1988.
Fr. Clodovis Boff, O.S.M., Duque de Caxias, July 14, 1990.
Fr. Marino Bohn, Luziânia, July 27, 1994.
Dom Sinésio Bohn, Santa Cruz do Sul, July 31, 1994.
Agostinho Both, Passo Fundo, August 4, 1994.
Fr. Irineu Brand, Porto Alegre, August 22, 1989.

Paulo Roberto Saraiva de Brito, São Paulo, July 20, 1987.

Fr. Kenneth Brune, O. F. M., Santarém, September 21, 1990.

Mons. Atayde Pedro Busanello, Santa Maria, August 2, 1994.

Fr. Nilo Buss, Brasília, (1) February 6, 1990, and (2) February 16, 1990.

Severino Cadorin, São Luís, August 26, 1987.

Fr. Anúncio João Caldana, Viamão, August 21, 1989.

Fr. José Isabel da Silva Campos, C. M., Belo Horizonte, August 10, 1987.

José Cardonha, São Paulo, March 29, 1990.

Dom José Cardoso Sobrinho, Recife, November 29, 1989.

Raimunda Marilena Freitas Cardoso, São Paulo, July 1, 1986.

Dom Marcelo Pinto Carvalheira, Recife, November 15, 1989.

Luiz Viegas de Carvalho, Rio de Janeiro, (1) August 27, 1996, (2) August 29, 1996,
    (3) March 24, 1997, (4) April 7, 1997, and (5) April 14, 1997.

Fr. Luís Casanova, Santa Maria, August 3, 1994.

Fr. José Alberto Castelo, Fortaleza, (1) August 20, 1987, and (2) August 21, 1987.

Luciano Castelo, Rio de Janeiro, August 2, 2002.

Dom Manoel Pedro da Cunha Cintra, Petrópolis, September 7, 1987.

Fr. Oscar João Colling, Viamão, August 15, 1989.

Fr. Carlo Colombo, P. I. M. E., Brusque, August 8, 1989.

Fr. José Comblin, Serra Redonda, November 26, 1989.

Fr. Hilário Lopes Costa, Xinguara, September 10, 1990.

Joana de Barros Costa, Rio de Janeiro, November 14, 1991.

Fr. Célio Maria Dell'Amore, C. M., Belo Horizonte, August 10, 1987.

José Américo Dias, São Paulo, January 13, 1989.

Humberto Jair Dinato, Santo André, July 23, 1987.

Fr. Malomar Lund Edelweiss, Belo Horizonte, June 5, 1993.

Marcelino da Silva Fernandes, São Paulo, July 19, 1987.

João Batista Ferreira, Rio de Janeiro, July 26, July 30, and July 31, 2002.

Geraldino Alves Ferreira Netto, São Paulo, August 7, 2002.

Fr. Ricardo Rezende Figueira, Conceição do Araguaia, September 6–9, 1990.

Fr. José Antero Floriano, O. S. B., Olinda, November 20, 1989.

General Carlos Alberto Fontoura, Rio de Janeiro, August 12, 1994.

Maria de Socorro de França, Recife, November 12, 1989.

Frei Nelson (pseudonym) (via telephone from San Diego), Registro, February 13, 2004.

Carlos Furlan, Conceição do Araguaia, September 7, 1990.

Fr. Francisco de Assis Gandolpho, São Paulo, July 22, 1987.

Dom Antônio Gaspar, São Paulo, July 2, 1986.

Sr. Ivone Gebara, Recife, June 22, 2001.

Fr. Luiz Girotti, S. S. S., Santo André, July 23, 1987.

Zito Gomes, O. F. M. Cap., São Paulo, July 19, 1987.

Fr. Gilberto da Silva Gorgulho, O.P., São Paulo, (1) March 25, 1990, and (2) March 27, 1990.

Fr. Zeno Graeff, (1) Viamão, August 15, 1989, and (2) Rio Pardo, July 30, 1994.

Dom Affonso Felipe Gregory, Rio de Janeiro, July 10, 1987.

Dom Mário Teixeira Gurgel, Itabira, July 18, 1996.

Fr. Zeno Hastenteufel, Porto Alegre, August 13, 1989.

Eduardo Hoornaert, Olinda, November 3, 1989.

Sr. Janis Jordan, S.M.I.C., Recife, November 7, 1989.

Aloysio Arnoldo Koehler, São Leopoldo, August 18, 1989.

Sr. Agnes Krips, SSpS, São Paulo, July 1, 1986.

Fr. Francisco Pinheiro Landim, Fortaleza, August 21, 1987.

Fr. Frederico Karl Laufer, S.J., Porto Alegre, August 13, 1989.

Luiz Osvaldo Leite, Porto Alegre, August 16, 1989.

Ivo Lesbaupin, Rio de Janeiro, July 14, 1994.

Fr. João Batista Libânio, S.J., Belo Horizonte, August 10, 1987.

Mons. Maurílio César de Lima, Rio de Janeiro, September 2, 1987.

Fr. Paulo Lisbôa, S.J., Rio de Janeiro, August 20, 1990.

Fr. Valentin Loch, Brusque, August 8, 1989.

Sr. Gertrudine Lorenz, SSpS, Rio de Janeiro, July 7, 1986.

Fr. André Eduardo Godoi Lourenço, São Paulo, August 19, 2002.

Fr. Oscar Figueiredo Lustosa, O.P., São Paulo, July 14, 1987.

Fr. Orlando Machado, Belo Horizonte, August 12, 1987.

José Magalhães, Brasília, July 29, 1987.

Fr. Antônio Juarez de Moura Maia, Porto Alegre, August 15, 1989.

Fr. Antônio Luís Marchioni, São Paulo, January 14, 1989.

Fr. José Carlos Melo, C.M., São Luís, August 25, 1987.

Fr. Paulo Meneses, S.J., Recife, November 3, 1989.

Fr. Tarcísio Marques Mesquita, São Paulo, July 20, 1987.

Sr. Fortunata Miniusse, São Paulo, July 22, 1987.

Dom Nei Paulo Moretto, Caxias do Sul, August 6, 1994.

Fr. José Arlindo de Nadai, Campinas, April 20, 1991.

Nivaldo Vieira do Nascimento, Conceição do Araguaia, September 4, 1990.

João Horácio Neto, Conceição do Araguaia, September 5, 1990.

Laurício Neumann, Porto Alegre, August 23, 1989.

Fr. Cláudio Neutzling, Viamão, August 16, 1989.

Marcos Noronha, Belo Horizonte, July 20, 1996.

Delcy Schlottfeldt de Oliveira, Brasília, July 19, 1987.

Fr. Júlio Shinji Ribeiro de Oliveira, São Paulo, August 19, 2002.

Lauro de Oliveira, Recife, June 23, 2001.

Fr. Luís Fernando de Oliveira, São Paulo, March 26, 1990.

Dom Oscar de Oliveira, Mariana, August 6, 1987.

Airene José Amaral de Paiva, Recife, August 15, 1987.

Hugo Vasconcelos de Paiva, Rio de Janeiro, November 14, 1991.

Fr. Lauro Palú, C.M., Rio de Janeiro, September 22, 1989.

Fr. João Panazzolo, (1) Brasília, February 2, 1990, and (2) Luziânia, July 27, 1994.

Jayme Paviani, Porto Alegre, August 7, 1994.

Fr. Antônio Gomes Pereira, C.M., Belo Horizonte, August 8, 1987.

Fr. Ernanne Pinheiro, Brasília, February 9, 1990.

Ana de Souza Pinto, Conceição do Araguaia, September 8, 1990.

Fr. João Humberto Plummen, C.S.S.R., Recife, November 28, 1989.

Ivo Poletto, Luziânia, July 28, 1994.

Dom Paulo Eduardo Ponte, (1) Fortaleza, August 22, 1987, and (2) Belo Horizonte, July 19, 1995.

Everaldo Machado Portela, Rio de Janeiro, April 20, 1989.

Fr. Agostinho Pretto, Nova Iguaçu, (1) July 11, 1994 and (2) July 3, 1996.

Fr. Pierre Primeau, P.S.S., Brasília, February 1, 1990.

Dom Antônio Celso Queiroz, Brasília, February 6, 1990.

Raimundo Nonato de Queiroz, Serra Redonda, November 26, 1989.

Fr. Francisco Manfredo Tomás Ramos, Fortaleza, August 21, 1989.

Fr. Pedro Belisário Velloso Rebello, S.J., Rio de Janeiro, February 21, 1991.

Dom Arnaldo Ribeiro, Belo Horizonte, August 12, 1987.

Jorge Ponciano Ribeiro, Brasília, July 29, 1987.

Sr. Vera Maria Ribeiro, SSpS, São Paulo, July 2, 1986.

Zildo Barbosa Rocha, Recife, (1) August 17, 1987, (2) August 18, 1987, and (3) June 22, 2001.

Fr. Jocy Neves Rodrigues, São Luís, August 25, 1987.

Fr. Wilson de Oliveira Salles, Indaiatuba, May 2, 1990.

Fr. Isidro Sallet, S.J., São Leopoldo, August 18, 1989.

Fr. João Francisco Salm, Brusque, August 8, 1989.

Terezinha Alves Sampaio, São Paulo, March 27, 1990.

Fr. Benedito Beni dos Santos, São Paulo, (1) March 28, 1990, and (2) May 8, 1990.

Fr. Carlos César dos Santos, Nova Iguaçu, October 25, 1988.

Fr. Davi Raimundo dos Santos, Duque de Caxias, June 27, 1989.

Olga Pereira dos Santos, Conceição do Araguaia, September 6, 1990.

Fr. José Bonifácio Schmidt, Viamão, (1) August 15, 1989, and (2) August 17, 1989.

João Basílio Schmitt, Brasília, (1) July 29, 1987, and (2) February 5, 1990.

Sr. Irmhild Schmitz, SSpS, Rio de Janeiro, July 7, 1986.

Ekkehard Schneider, Recife, November 23, 1990.

Fr. Tenário Seibel, Passo Fundo, August 4, 1994.

Fr. Edilberto Sena, Belém, September 16, 1990.

Eunice Sena, Santarém, September 21, 1990.

Fr. José Servat, Recife, November 22, 1989.

Fr. Antônio Wagner da Silva, S.C.J., Brusque, August 7, 1989.

Fr. Arnaldo Liberato da Silva, Recife, November 23, 1989.

Fr. Celso Pedro da Silva, (1) Brasília, July 29, 1987, (2) Brasília, July 29, 1990 and (3) São Paulo, August 3, 2001.

José Ribamar Araújo Silva, São Paulo, March 27, 1990.

Eliane Francisca da Silva, Recife, November 12, 1989.

Severino Vicente da Silva, (1) Recife, August 14, 1987, (2) Recife, August 17, 1987, (3) Recife, November 3, 1989, (4) São Paulo, September 9, 1991, and (5) Recife, June 21, 2001.

Assuero Gomes da Silva Filho, Recife, June 23, 2001.

Fr. Luiz Síveres, S.V.D., Brasília, February 1, 1990.

Fr. Lourenço Pereira de Souza, São Luís, August 24, 1987.

Severino Justino de Souza, Recife, November 12, 1989.

Vagner Barcelos de Souza, Volta Redonda, November 13, 1988.

Fr. José Jacó Spuldaro, Passo Fundo, August 5, 1994.

Fr. Irineu Stertz, Santa Maria, August 3, 1994.

Fr. Orestes João Stragliotto, Belo Horizonte, July 10, 1995.

Inácio Strieder, Recife, June 23, 2001.

Luís Tenderini, Recife, November 8, 1989.

Dom Valfredo Bernardo Tepe, Indaiatuba, April 18, 1991.

Jean Tessier, Conceição do Araguaia, September 7, 1990.

Jovêncio Tibúrcio, Recife, November 12, 1989.

Mons. Darci Domingos Treviso, Passo Fundo, August 5, 1994.

Fr. Virgílio Leite Uchôa, (1) Brasília, September 3, 1990, (2) Brasília, June 10, 1993, and (3) Luziânia, July 26, 1994.

Fr. Antônio Valentini, Viamão, August 17, 1989.

Fr. João Edênio Reis Valle, S.V.D., Rio de Janeiro, (1) August 15, 1990, and (2) October 18, 1990.

Fr. José Maria Vasconcellos, Rio de Janeiro, September 2, 1987.

Florêncio Almeida Vaz Filho, O.F.M., Belém, September 15, 1990.

Fr. Alírio Vicenzi, Brusque, August 7, 1989.

Fr. Décio Weber, Arroio do Meio, July 30, 1994.

Sr. Laeta Weber, SSpS, Belo Horizonte, July 11, 1986.

Fr. Luís Weel, Recife, August 17, 1987.

Ary Wolffenbüttel, São Leopoldo, August 18, 1989.

Films

A Boa Empresa (c. 1962–1964), produced by Instituto de Pesquisa e Estudos Sociais, Arquivo Nacional, QL/FIL.006.

The Boys of St. Vincent (1993), directed by John N. Smith.

O Chamado de Deus (Rio de Janeiro: Coevos Filmes; Rio Filme, 2000), directed by José Joffily.

Como Nascem os Anjos (1996), directed by Murilo Salles.

Sereis Minhas Testemunhas (2000), produced by Organização dos Seminários e Institutos Filosófico-Teológicos do Brasil.

Archives and Collections

Arquivo Clemente Mariani, Fundação Getúlio Vargas, Centro de Pesquisa e Documentação de História Contemporânea do Brasil (FGV/CPDOC, ACMa), Rio de Janeiro.

Arquivo da Diocese de Caxias do Sul.

Arquivo da Província Brasileira da Congregação da Missão (PBCM), Rio de Janeiro.

Arquivo da Província Sul Brasileira da Companhia de Jesus (APSB), Porto Alegre.

Arquivo da Reitoria do Colégio Máximo Cristo Rei de São Leopoldo (ACCR), São Leopoldo.

Arquivo do Instituto de Teologia do Recife (ITER), Recife.

Arquivo do Seminário Regional do Nordeste II (SERENE II), Recife.

Arquivo Gustavo Capanema, FGV/CPDOC, Rio de Janeiro.

Central de Documentação e Informação Científica "Prof. Casemiro dos Reis Filho," Pontifícia Universidade Católica de São Paulo, São Paulo.

Centro Cultural de Documentación (CIDOC) (Cuernavaca) (microfilm on file at University of California, San Diego).

Coleção Marc van Der Weid, Arquivo Público do Estado do Rio de Janeiro, Rio de Janeiro.

Departamento de Ordem Política e Social da Guanabara, Arquivo Público do Estado do Rio de Janeiro, Rio de Janeiro.

Divisão de Segurança e Informações do Ministério da Justiça, Arquivo Nacional (AN, DSI/MJ), Rio de Janeiro.

Instituto Nacional de Pastoral (INP), Conferência Nacional dos Bispos do Brasil, Brasília.

Journals, Periodicals, and Newspapers

America

American Ethnologist

American Historical Review

Anticipation

Boletim de Novidades Pulsional

Cadernos do CEAS

CartaCapital

The Christian Century
Christianity Today
Ciência e Cultura
Coleção das Leis do Brasil
Comunicações do ISER
Comunicado Mensal da CNBB (CM)
Concilium
Convergência
Dados
Época
Estudos Afro-Asiáticos
L'Express
Folha de S. Paulo
O Globo
Grande Sinal
Guardian Weekly
Hispanic American Historical Review (HAHR)
IstoÉ
Jornal do Brasil
Jornal do Commercio
Jornal Igreja Nova
Journal for the Scientific Study of Religion
Journal of Church and State
Journal of Iberian and Latin American Studies
Lançai as Redes
Latin American Perspectives
Latin American Research Review (LARR)
Luso-Brazilian Review (LBR)
Mimesis
Mundo Jovem
National Catholic Reporter (NCR)
New York Review of Books
New York Times
Notícias da CNBB
Novos Estudos CEBRAP
Pergunte e Responderemos
Perspectivas Teológicas
Perspectivas Teológico-Pastorais
O Pio Brasileiro
Ponto Homem
PUC Ciência

Revista Brasileira de Ciências Sociais
Revista da CRB
Revista de Cultura Vozes
Revista do Assistente Eclesiástico
Revista Eclesiástica Brasileira (REB)
Rumos
O São Paulo
São Vicente
O Seminário (OS)
Serviço de Documentação (SEDOC)
Sinal
Slavic Review
Sociology of Religion
The Tablet
Tempo e Presença
Tempo e Sociedade
Teocomunicação
Teoria e Debate
Ultimato
Veja
Veritas
Zero Hora

Books and Articles

"II Reunião da Commissão Representativa da CNBB." 1972. *SEDOC* 5 (November), 548–49.

"À IX Assembléia Geral Ordinária da Conferência Nacional dos Bispos do Brasil." 1968. *SEDOC*, special edition (September), 403–4.

"15a. Assembléia Geral. Eleições. Votações e Conclusões." 1974. *CM* 266 (November), 1065.

Abbott, Elizabeth. 2000. *A History of Celibacy.* New York: Scribner.

Abreu, João Capistrano de. 1997 [1907]. *Chapters of Brazil's Colonial History, 1500–1800.* Trans. Arthur Brakel. New York: Oxford University Press.

Absalão, Sérgio. 1984. "O assassinato do padre Antônio Enrique." *Perspectivas Teológico-Pastorais,* No. 4, Year 3, 84–100.

"Aclaraciones provisionales redactadas por una comisión sobre el caso del padre Lemercier." 1968. In *Cuernavaca: fuentes para el estudio de una diócesis.* Ed. Baltazar López. CIDOC Dossier No. 31, vol. 2, 5/17. Cuernavaca: CIDOC.

Adams, Richard Newbold. 1975. *Energy and Structure: A Theory of Social Power*. Austin: University of Texas Press.

Adriance, Madeleine Cousineau. 1995. *Promised Land: Base Christian Communities and the Struggle for the Amazon*. Albany: State University of New York Press.

Aguiar, Pedro, and Guilherme Gomes. 1963. "Pastoral de dois." *OS*, Year 38, No. 4 (September–October), 101–13.

"Aids, tabu na Igreja, é estudada em seminários." 2002. *Folha de São Paulo* (April 21).

Alberigo, Giuseppe. 1998. "O sentido do Concílio de Trento na História dos concílios." *REB* 58 (September), 543–64.

———, ed. 1995–2003. *History of Vatican II*. 4 vols. Maryknoll, N.Y.: Orbis and Leuven, Belgium: Peeters.

Alden, Dauril. 1987. "Late Colonial Brazil, 1750–1808." In *Colonial Brazil*, 284–343. Ed. Leslie Bethell. Cambridge: Cambridge University Press.

———. 1996. *The Making of an Enterprise: The Society of Jesus in Portugal, Its Empire, and Beyond, 1540–1750*. Stanford: Stanford University Press.

Alecrim, Michel. 2001. "Itália quer que G-8 discuta combate à pobreza." *O Globo* (July 14), Economia-22.

Alencar, Francisco A. S. Duarte de. 1994. *Dom José Lamartine: O pastor do silêncio*. São Paulo: Paulinas.

Alla, Henrique. 1955. *Os congressos eucarísticos internacionais*. Rio de Janeiro: Agir.

Allen, Scott Joseph. 2001. "'Zumbi Nunca Vai Morrer': History, the Practice of Archaeology, and Race Politics in Brazil." PhD dissertation, Brown University.

Almeida, Antônio Lopes de. 1964. "A JOC em Trabalho." *OS*, Year 39, No. 4 (September–October), 7–16.

Almeida, Dalton Barros de. 1998. "A pessoa do presbítero como homem de relações." *REB* 58 (September), 671–82.

Almeida, Dom Luciano Mendes de, and Maria da Conceição Tavares. 1995. *Os excluídos: Debate entre os autores*. Petrópolis: Vozes.

Almeida, Ronaldo. 1996. "A universalização do Reino de Deus." *Novos Estudos CEBRAP* 44 (March), 12–23.

Alonso, Annibal Martins. 1956. *XXXVI Congresso Eucarístico Internacional*. Rio de Janeiro: Companhia Brasileira de Artes Gráficas.

Altemeyer Junior, Fernando. 1996. "A pastoral católica no ano de 1995." *Tempo e Presença* 285 (January–February), 23–25.

Alves, Márcio Moreira. 1967. *Torturas e torturados*. Rio de Janeiro: Empresa Jornalística.

———. 1968. *O Cristo do povo*. Rio de Janeiro: Editora Sabiá.

———. 1973. *A Grain of Mustard Seed: The Awakening of the Brazilian Revolution*. Garden City, N.Y.: Doubleday Anchor.

———. 1979. *A Igreja e a política no Brasil*. São Paulo: Editora Brasiliense.

Alves, Maria Helena Moreira. 1985. *Estado e oposição no Brasil (1964–1984)*. Trans. Clóvis Marques. Petrópolis: Vozes.

Alves Filho, Francisco, et al. 1996. "O pecado do amor." *IstoÉ* 1419 (December 11), 140–44.

Amaral, Luís Henrique. 2000. "Igreja encara infecção pelo virus HIV no clero." *O Globo* (July 30).

Andrade, Manuel Correia de. 1987. *Geografia econômica do Nordeste*. 4th edition. São Paulo: Editora Atlas.

Andrade, Paulo Fernando Carneiro de. 1993. "A condição pós-moderna como desafio à pastoral popular." *REB* 53 (March), 110–11.

Andrews, George Reid. 1991. *Blacks and Whites in São Paulo Brazil, 1888–1988*. Madison: University of Wisconsin Press.

Antoine, Charles. 1973. *Church and Power in Brazil*. Trans. Peter Nelson. Maryknoll, N.Y.: Orbis.

———. 1980. *O integrismo brasileiro*. Rio de Janeiro: Civilização Brasileira.

———. 1999. *Guerre froide et Église Catholique*. Paris: Les Éditions du Cerf.

Antoniazzi, Alberto. 1984a. "O que mudou de 1960 até hoje?" In *Situação e vida dos seminaristas maiores no Brasil*, Estudos da CNBB, No. 40, 35–42. São Paulo: Edições Paulinas.

———. 1984b. "Seminaristas de hoje, padres de amanhã." *Atualização*, Year 15, No. 169/170 (January/February), 71–76.

———. 1995a. "Seminaristas maiores: As diferenças entre diocesanos e religiosos na pesquisa de 1993." In CNBB, *Situação e vida dos seminaristas maiores no Brasil (II)*, Estudos da CNBB, No. 74, 57–66. São Paulo: Paulus.

———. 1995b. "Os seminaristas maiores: Comparação dos resultados das pesquisas de 1982 e 1993." In CNBB, *Situação e vida dos seminaristas maiores no Brasil (II)*, Estudos da CNBB, No. 74, 7–38. São Paulo: Paulus.

———. 1998. "Notas para a história dos presbíteros no Brasil (1969–1998)." *REB* 58 (September), 597–617.

———. 2002. "Faces e fases da Igreja de Belo Horizonte dos anos 50 aos anos 70." In *As veredas de João na barca de Pedro*, 63–142. Ed. Alberto Antoniazzi, Lucília de Almeida Neves, and Mauro Passos. Belo Horizonte: PUC-Minas.

Antoniazzi, Alberto, and Cleto Caliman, eds. 1994. *A presença da Igreja na cidade*. Petrópolis: Vozes.

"A propósito de 'seminaristas' presos." 1972. *O São Paulo* (August 19), 6.

Araújo, Marcelo Conceição. 2002. "Desenvolvimento afetivo, homossexualidade e formação inicial." *REB* 62 (October) 898–910.

Archdiocese of Belo Horizonte. 1994. *Ética: pessoa e sociedade (subsídios para reflexão, Arquidiocese de Belo Horizonte, projeto "Construir a Esperança")*. Belo Horizonte, n.p.

Archdiocese of São Paulo. 1985. *Brasil: Nunca mais*. Petrópolis: Vozes.

———. 1988. *Perfil dos atingidos*. Petrópolis: Vozes.

Armstrong, Karen. 1993. *A History of God: The Four-Thousand-Year Quest of Judaism, Christianity and Islam*. New York: Ballantine.

Arnal, Oscar L. 1986. *Priests in Working-Class Blue: The History of the Worker-Priests (1943–1954)*. New York: Paulist.

Arns, Paulo Evaristo. 2001. *Da esperança à utopia: Testemunho de uma vida*. Rio de Janeiro: Sextante.

Arruda, José Jobson de A. 1980. *O Brasil no comércio colonial*. São Paulo: Editora Ática.

"Artigo-Debate." 1967. *OS*, Year 42, No. 216 (November–December), 517–23.

"Aspirações de Sacerdotes de Volta Redonda, São Paulo e Rio de Janeiro." 1968. *SEDOC*, special edition (September), 394–99.

Assmann, Hugo. 1968a. "Caracterização de uma teologia da revolução." *Ponto Homem*, Year 43, No. 4 (September–October), 6–45.

————. 1968b. "Elementos para uma ética da opção e praxis revolucionária." *OS*, Year 43, No. 4, (September–October), 46–58.

————. 1971a. "The Christian Contribution to the Liberation of Latin America." *Anticipation* 9 (October), 14–27.

————. 1971b. *Opresion-liberación: Desafío a los cristianos*. Montevideo: Tierra Nueva.

————. 1971c. *Teoponte: Una experiencia guerrillera*. Oruru, Bolivia: CEDI.

————. 1986. *A Igreja eletrônica e seu impacto na América Latina*. Petrópolis, Vozes.

Associação Brasileira de História das Religiões. 2001. *Anais eletrônicos do Seminário Internacional de História das Religiões/III Simpósio Nacional da Associação Brasileira de História das Religiões*. CD-ROM. Recife.

"Associação de ex-seminaristas." 1963. *OS*, Year 38, No. 2 (May–June), 19.

Ávila, Fernando Bastos de. 1978. "Sacerdócio e política." In *O clero no Parlamento Brasileiro*, 1:31–35. Brasília: Câmara dos Deputados; Rio de janeiro: Centro João XXIII-IBRADES; Fundação Casa de Rui Barbosa.

Azevedo, Marcello de Carvalho. 1960. "Vocação e Decisão." *REB* 20 (December), 872–87.

————. 1962–1963. "Verona: Um seminário para nós." *O Pio Brasileiro* 13:28, 80–82.

————. 1987. *Basic Ecclesial Communities in Brazil*. Trans. John Drury. Washington, D.C.: Georgetown University Press.

Azevedo, Thales de. 1955. *O Catolicismo no Brasil*. Rio de Janeiro: Ministério da Educação e Cultura.

Azzi, Enzo. 1961. "Contribuição da psicologia no recrutamento dos candidatos à vida religiosa e sacerdotal." *Revista da CRB*, Year 7, No. 72 (June), 341–45.

Azzi, Riolando. 1969. "A vida do clero no Brasil: Síntese histórica." Unpublished manuscript, CERIS.

————1974a. "O movimento brasileiro de reforma católica durante o século XIX." *REB* 34 (September), 646–62.

————. 1974b. "Padres da Missão e movimento brasileiro de reforma católica no século XIX." *Convergência*, Year 7, No. 76, 1237–56.

————. 1975. "Os religiosos e o movimento de reforma católica no Brasil durante o século XIX." *Convergência*, Year 8, No. 82, 301–17.

————. 1976a. "Os Jesuítas e a formação do clero no Brasil." *Convergência*, Year 9, No. 89, 44–60.

————. 1976b. "Os Jesuítas e o movimento brasileiro de reforma católica no século XIX." *Convergência*, Year 9, 491–505.

————. 1981. *Presença da Igreja Católica na sociedade brasileira*. Rio de Janeiro: ISER.

————. 1983. "História dos Religiosos no Brasil." In *A vida religiosa no Brasil: Enfoques historicos*, 9–23. Ed. Riolando Azzi. São Paulo: Edições Paulinas.

————. 1987–1988. *A Igreja e os migrantes*. 3 vols. São Paulo: Edições Paulinas.

————. 1990. "A introdução do celibato eclesiástico no Brasil." *Revista de Cultura Vozes* 84:4 (July–August), 449–65.

————. 1991. "A formação sacerdotal no Brasil (1930–1964)." Unpublished paper.

————. 1992. "O significado das prelazias na segunda evangelização." *REB* 52 (September), 627–54.

Baer, Werner. 1995. *The Brazilian Economy: Growth and Development*. 4th edition. Westport, Conn.: Praeger.

Bandeira, Marina. 2000. *A Igreja Católica na virada da questão social (1930–1964)*. Rio de Janeiro: Vozes; Educam.

Baratta, José do Carmo. 1972. *Escola de heróis*. Recife: Comissão Estadual das Comemorações do Sesquicentenário da Independência.

Baraúna, Guilherme. 1953. "O problema da falta de sacerdotes na América Latina." *REB* 13 (September), 667–69.

Barbosa, Francisco de Assis. 1988 [1961]. *Juscelino Kubitschek: Uma revisão na política brasileira*. Rio de Janeiro: Editora Guanabara.

————. "Síntese Histórica." 1978. In *O clero no Parlamento*, 1:11–30. Brasília: Câmara dos Deputados; Rio de janeiro: Centro João XXIII-IBRADES; Fundação Casa de Rui Barbosa.

Barcellos, Caco. 2003. *Abusado, o dono do Morro Dona Marta*. Rio de Janeiro: Record.

Barman, Roderick J. 1977. "The Brazilian Peasantry Reexamined: The Implications of the Quebra-Quilo Revolt, 1874–1875." *HAHR* 57:3 (August), 401–24.

————. 1988. *Brazil: The Forging of a Nation, 1798–1852*. Stanford: Stanford University Press.

————. 2002. *Princess Isabel of Brazil: Gender and Power in the Nineteenth Century*. Wilmington, Del.: Scholarly Resources.

Barreiro, Álvaro. 1975. "Pequenas comunidades: Anotações sobre um encontro." *Convergência*, Year 8, Nos. 77/78, 27–40.

Barros, Mônica do Nascimento. 1995. "A batalha do armagedon: Uma análise do repertório mágico-religioso proposto pela Igreja Universal do Reino de Deus." MA thesis, Universidade Federal de Minas Gerais.

Barros, Raimundo Caramuru. 1968a. "América Latina, um continente em Desenvolvimento." *Ponto Homem*, Year 43, No. 3 (July-August), 23–40.

―――. 1968b. "A Igreja na América Latina face ao desafio do desenvolvimento." *Ponto Homem*, Year 43, No. 4 (September–October), 70–101.

―――. 1990. "Gratia Dei, sum id quod sum." *Revista de Cultura Vozes* 84:4 (July–August), 410–31.

Barros, Roque Spencer M. de. 1985. "Vida religiosa." In *História geral da civilização brasileira. II. O Brasil monárquico. 4. Declínio e queda do império*, 317–37. Ed. Sérgio Buarque de Holanda. São Paulo: DIFEL.

Bastos, Humberto. 1955. "A Igreja e o desenvolvimento econômico." *Rio Magazine*, No. 249, special edition (July).

"Batina ou 'Clergyman'?" 1963. *Pergunte e Responderemos* (August), 343–48.

Baumann, Fernando. 1951. "Pe. João Batista Reus, S.J., um sacerdote santo dos nossos tempos." *REB* 11 (December), 828–40.

Beattie, Peter M. 2001. *The Tribute of Blood: Army, Honor, Race, and Nation in Brazil, 1864–1945*. Durham, N.C.: Duke University Press.

―――, ed. 2004. *The Human Tradition in Modern Brazil*. Wilmington, Del.: Scholarly Resources.

Becker, Ernest. 1973. *The Denial of Death*. New York: Free Press.

Bedoyere, Michael de la. 1963. *Cardijn, liderança do operário*. Petrópolis: Vozes.

Begg, Ean. 1985. *The Cult of the Black Virgin*. Updated edition. London: Arkana.

Beier, Matthias. 1998. "Embodying Hermeneutics: Eugen Drewermann's Depth Psychological Interpretation of Religious Symbols." Paper presented at the American Academy of Religion (March). Online: http://www.depts.drew.edu/gsadmis/conferences/drewermann/beier.html.

"A Bélgica tem um centro nacional de vocações." 1964. *REB* 24 (March), 226–27.

Belluck, Pam, and Frank Bruni. 2002. "Law, Citing Abuse Scandal, Quits as Boston Archbishop and Asks for Forgiveness." *New York Times* (December 14). Online edition.

Beloch, Israel, and Alzira Alves de Abreu, eds. 1984. *Dicionário histórico-biográfico brasileiro, 1930–1983*. Rio de Janeiro: Forense-Universitária; FGV/CPDOC; FINEP.

Beozzo, José Oscar. 1981. "Pe. Júlio Maria—uma teologia liberal-republicana numa Igreja monarquista e conservadora." In *História da teologia na América Latina*, 107–26. Ed. CEHILA. São Paulo: Paulinas.

―――. 1983. "Decadência e morte, restauração e multiplicação das ordens e congregações religiosas no Brasil, 1870–1930." In *A vida religiosa no Brasil: Enfoques históricos*, 85–129. Ed. Riolando Azzi. São Paulo: Edições Paulinas.

―――. 1984. *Cristãos na universidade e na política*. Petrópolis: Vozes.

―――. 1986. "A Igreja entre a Revolução de 1930, o Estado Novo e a redemocratização." In *História Geral da civilização brasileira. III. O Brasil republicano. 4. Economia e cultura (1930–1964)*, 271–341. Ed. Boris Fausto. São Paulo: DIFEL.

―――. 1987. "O clero italiano no Brasil." In *A presença italiana no Brasil*, 34–62. Ed. Luis Alberto De Boni. Porto Alegre: Escola Superior de Teologia.

———. 1994a. *A Igreja do Brasil*. Petrópolis: Vozes.

———. 1994b. "Reformulação curricular—Faculdade de Teologia N. S. da Assunção." Photocopy.

———. 1997. "Sinais marcantes na pastoral católica." *Tempo e Presença* 291 (January-February), 20–23.

———. 1998. "Os atores do sínodo." *REB* 58 (March), 176–85.

———. 2001a. "Os padres conciliares brasileiros no Vaticano II: Participação e prosopografia, 1959–1965." PhD dissertation, Universidade de São Paulo.

———. 2001b. "Os resultados da discussão historiográfica na CEHILA." *História das religões no Brasil*, 1:372–409. Ed. Sylvana Brandão. Recife: Editora Universitária da UFPE.

Bernal, Sergio. 1989. *CNBB: Da Igreja da cristandade à Igreja dos pobres*. São Paulo: Edições Loyola.

Bernardes, Ernesto. 1995. "Na linha de frente da Guerra." *Veja* (20 September), 72–76.

Bernstein, Carl, and Marco Politi. 1996. *His Holiness: John Paul II and the Hidden History of Our Time*. New York: Doubleday.

Berryman, Phillip. 1987. *Liberation Theology*. Philadelphia: Temple University Press.

———. 1996. *Religion in the Megacity: Catholic and Protestant Portraits from Latin America*. Maryknoll, N.Y.: Orbis.

Besen, José Artulino. 1977. *Azambuja*. Brusque, Santa Catarina: Seminário de Azambuja.

Besse, Susan K. 1996. *Restructuring Patriarchy: The Modernization of Gender Inequality in Brazil, 1914–1940*. Chapel Hill: University of North Carolina Press.

Bieber, Judy. 1999. *Power, Patronage, and Political Violence: State Building on a Brazilian Frontier, 1822–1989*. Lincoln: University of Nebraska Press.

Bingemer, Maria Clara Lucchetti. 2004. "Vocação sacerdotal e fragilidade humana." *Informativo Rede de Cristãos*. Online: http://wwwusers.rdc.puc-rio.br/agape.

Bingemer, Maria Clara Lucchetti, and Roberto dos Santos Bartholo Jr., eds. 1997. *Exemplaridade ética e santidade*. São Paulo: Edições Loyola.

Birman, Joel. 1988. "Desejo e promessa, encontro impossível: O discurso freudiano sobre a religião." In *Hélio Pellegrino: A-Deus*, 116–43. Ed. João Carlos Moura. Petrópolis: Vozes.

Birman, Patrícia. 1992. "Modos periféricos de crença." In *Catolicismo: Unidade religiosa e pluralismo cultural*, 167–96. Ed. Pierre Sanchis. São Paulo: Edições Loyola.

"Bishops Who Quit amid Sex Scandals." 2002. *New York Times* (December 15). Online edition.

Blay, Eva. 1993. "Em cinco anos, nada de novo." *Teoria e Debate* 22:73–75.

Boechat, Walter. 1988. "A psicologia de Jung e o sentido religioso." In *Hélio Pellegrino: A-Deus*, 160–64. Ed. João Carlos Moura. Petrópolis: Vozes.

Boff, Clodovis. 1984. *Teologia pé-no-chão*. Petrópolis: Vozes.

———. 1987. *Feet-on-the-Ground Theology*. Maryknoll, N.Y.: Orbis.

———. 1992. "Lições da primeira evangelização." *REB* 52 (September), 517–37.

Boff, Leonardo. 1972. *Jesus Cristo Libertador: Ensaio de cristologia crítica para o nosso tempo.* Petrópolis: Vozes.

———. 1981. *Igreja, carisma e poder: Ensaios de eclesiologia militante.* Petrópolis: Vozes.

Boff, Leonardo, and Clodovis Boff. 1984. *Salvation and Liberation.* Trans. Robert R. Barr. Maryknoll, N.Y.: Orbis.

Bohnen, Aloysio, and Reinholdo Aloysio Ullmann. 1989. *A atividade dos Jesuítas de São Leopoldo, 1844–1889.* São Leopoldo, Rio Grande do Sul: UNISINOS.

Bojunga, Claudio. 2001. *JK: O artista do impossível.* Rio de Janeiro: Objetiva.

"Bolsas de estudo para sacerdotes Latino-Americanos." 1960. *REB* 20 (December), 1041.

"Bolsas de estudos do Centro de Formação para o Clero." 1959. *CM* 82 (July), 22–23.

Borges, Dain. 1992. *The Family in Bahia, Brazil, 1870–1945.* Stanford: Stanford University Press.

Boswell, John 1989. "Homosexuality and Religious Life: A Historical Approach." In *Homosexuality in the Priesthood and Religious Life,* 3–20. Ed. Jeannine Gramick. New York: Crossroad.

Botas, Paulo Cezar Loureiro. 1983. *A benção de abril.* Petrópolis: Vozes.

Bowers, Margaretta K. 1963. *Conflicts of the Clergy: A Psychodynamic Study with Case Histories.* New York: Thomas Nelson.

Boxer, Charles R. 1952. *Salvador de Sá and the Struggle for Brazil and Angola, 1602–1686.* London: Athlone.

———. 1963. *Race Relations in the Portuguese Colonial Empire.* London: Oxford University Press.

———. 1969. *The Golden Age of Brazil, 1695–1750.* Berkeley: University of California Press.

Boyer, Richard. 2001. *Lives of the Bigamists: Marriage, Family, and Community in Colonial Mexico.* Abridged edition. Albuquerque: University of New Mexico Press.

Branch, Taylor. 1989. *Parting the Waters: America in the King Years, 1954–1963.* New York: Simon & Schuster.

Brandão, Ascânio. 1941a. "Cartas a um neo-sacerdote." *REB* 1 (March–June), 52–58.

———. 1941b. "Três desordens." *REB* 1 (September), 573.

———. 1942. "Cartas a um neo-sacerdote. III. Ministério exterior—leitura espiritual—perigos e ilusões." *REB* 2 (September), 667–68.

Brandão, Carlos Rodrigues. 1992a. "A partilha do tempo." In *Catolicismo: Cotidiano e movimentos,* 89–153. Ed. Pierre Sanchis. São Paulo: Edições Paulinas.

———. 1992b. "Crença e identidade, campo religioso e mudança cultural." In *Catolicismo: Unidade religiosa e pluralismo cultural,* 7–74. Ed. Pierre Sanchis. São Paulo: Edições Loyola.

Brandão, Sylvana, ed. 2001. *História das religiões no Brasil,* vol. 1. Recife: Editora Universitária da UFPE.

Bratti, Paulo. 1961. "Círculo de Ação Católica." *O Pio Brasileiro* 11:26 (June), 33–37.

Brett, Donna Whitson, and Edward T. Brett. 1988. *Murdered in Central America*. Maryknoll, N.Y.: Orbis.

"Briga em nome de Deus." 1993. *Veja* (April 14), 69.

Brito, Sebastiana R. de. 1970. "Pesquisa sobre as pequenas comunidades." *Convergência*, No. 28 (October), 2–12.

Broetto, Délcio. 1963. "Não obedeço." *OS*, Year 38, No. 4 (September–October), 76–78.

Brooke, James. 1989. "Two Archbishops, Old and New, Symbolize Conflict in the Brazilian Church." *New York Times* (November 12), 14.

Broucker, José de. 1970. *Dom Helder Camara: The Violence of a Peacemaker.* Trans. Herma Briffault. Maryknoll, N.Y.: Orbis.

Brown, Diana DeG. 1994. *Umbanda: Religion and Politics in Urban Brazil.* New York: Columbia University Press.

Bruneau, Thomas C. 1974. *The Political Transformation of the Brazilian Catholic Church.* New York: Cambridge University Press.

———. 1982. *The Church in Brazil.* Austin: University of Texas Press.

Bruneau, Thomas C., and W. E. Hewitt. 1992. "Catholicism and Political Action in Brazil: Limitations and Prospects." In *Conflict and Competition: The Latin American Church in a Changing Environment,* 45–62. Ed. Edward L. Cleary and Hannah Stewart-Gambino. Boulder: Rienner.

Burdick, John. 1993. *Looking for God in Brazil.* Berkeley: University of California Press.

———. 1994. "The Progressive Catholic Church in Latin America: Giving Voice or Listening to Voices?" *LARR* 29:1, 184–97.

———. 2004. *Legacies of Liberation: The Progresssive Church in Brazil at the Start of a New Millennium.* Burlington, Vt.: Ashgate.

Burdick, John, and W. E. Hewitt, eds. 2000. *The Church at the Grassroots in Latin Ameica: Perspectives on Thirty Years of Activism.* Westport, Conn.: Praeger.

Burke, Peter. 2002. "The Art of Re-Interpretation: Michel de Certeau." *Theoria* 49:2 (December), 27–37.

Buss, Tito. 1962. "Perseverança e desistência nos seminários." *REB* 22 (March), 50–65.

Butler, Kim D. 1998. *Freedoms Given, Freedoms Won: Afro-Brazilians in Post-Abolition São Paulo and Salvador.* New Brunswick, N.J.: Rutgers University Press.

Cabral, Newton Darwin de Andrade. 2001. "Báculos no meio dos caminhos: Modelos eclesiais em conflito no Regional Nordeste II (1965–1990)." PhD dissertation, Universidade Federal de Pernambuco.

Cabras, Alessio. 1983. "Os anjos querem ser homens: Um estudo sobre a laicização de padres no Brasil." MA thesis, University of Sao Paulo.

Callado, Antônio. 1964. *Tempo de Arraes: Padres e comunistas na revolução sem violência.* Rio de Janeiro: José Alvaro.

Calliari, Ivo. 1996. *D. Jaime Câmara: Diário do cardeal arcebispo do Rio de Janeiro.* Rio de Janeiro: Léo Christiano Editorial.

Câmara, Dom Jaime de Barros. 1954. *Trigésimo sexto Congresso Eucarístico Internacional: Décima sétima carta pastoral de D. Jaime de Barros Câmara.* Petrópolis: Vozes.

Câmara, Hélder. 1965. "Dom Hélder: Padres para um Brasil brasileiro." *OS,* Year 40, No. 204 (July–August), 251–59.

———. 1979. *The Conversions of a Bishop: An Interview with José de Broucker.* Trans. Hilary Davies. Cleveland: Collins.

———. 1989. "Eu sou o caminho . . ." In *Faz escuro mas eu canto . . . risco e esperança no caminho da Igreja no Nordeste,* 10–11. ITER and Comissão de Justiça e Paz de Olinda e Recife. Recife: ITER; Comissão de Justiça e Paz de Olinda e Recife.

Camello, Maurílio José de Oliveira. 1973. *Caraça, centro mineiro de educação e missão (1820–1830).* Belo Horizonte: Imprensa Oficial.

———. 1986. "Dom Antônio Ferreira Viçoso e a Reforma do Clero em Minas Gerais no Século XIX." PhD dissertation, Universidade de São Paulo.

Camp, Roderic Ai. 1997. *Crossing Swords: Politics and Religion in Mexico.* New York: Oxford University Press.

Campos, Roberto de Oliveira. 1994. *A lanterna na popa: Memórias.* Rio de Janeiro: Topbooks.

Cancian, Renato. 2001. "Comissão Justiça e Paz de São Paulo: Gênese e atuação política (1972–1985)." MA thesis, Universidade Federal de São Carlos.

"Caraça, Mariana e Diamantina são marcos definidores de uma civilização: A homenagem aos padres lazaristas." 1944. *São Vicente,* Year 13, No. 4, 230–33.

Carneiro, Leandro Piquet. 1997. "The Church as Political Context: Civic Culture and Political Participation Among Protestants." Paper delivered at the LASA Twentieth International Congress, Guadalajara, Mexico (April).

Carneiro Junior, Renato Augusto. 2000. "Religião e política: a Liga Eleitoral Católica e a participação da Igreja nas eleições, 1932–1954." MA thesis, Universidade Federal do Paraná.

Carrato, José Ferreira. 1963. *As Minas Gerais e os primórdios do Caraça.* São Paulo: Companhia Editora Nacional.

———. 1970. "O Caraça português." Undergraduate thesis, University of São Paulo.

"Carta aos Bispos." 1968. *SEDOC,* special edition (September), 399–401.

"Carta de Olinda." 1961. *OS,* Year 36, No. 2 (May–June), 34–35.

"Cartas de Padres à Assembléia dos Bispos do Brasil." 1968. *REB* 28 (September), 706–9.

Carter, Miguel. 2002. "Ideal Interest Mobilization: Explaining the Formation of Brazil's Landless Social Movement." PhD dissertation, Columbia University.

Carter, Stephen L. 1993. *The Culture of Disbelief: How American Law and Politics Trivialize Religious Devotion.* New York: Basic.

Caruso, Igor. 1961. "A psicologia, ciência do homem histórico e ciência social da pessoa." *Veritas,* Year 6, No. 2 (August), 125–42.

———. 1962. "A situação psicanalítica, modêlo micro-social." *Veritas,* Year 7, No. 3 (September), 211–30.

———. 1964. *Existential Psychology.* New York: Herder and Herder.

Carvalheira, Dom Marcelo Pinto. 1966a. "Formação em seminário?" *OS,* Year 41, No. 210 (September–October), 334–49.

———. 1966b. "O Tipo de Padre que a Igreja Espera após o Concílio Vaticano II." *REB* 26 (September), 529–51.

———. 1970. "Aspectos Culturais da Crise na Igreja." *REB* 30 (June), 257–81.

———. 1983. "Momentos históricos e desdobramento da Ação Católica Brasileira." *REB* 43 (March), 10–28.

Carvalho, José Murilo de. 1987. *Os bestializados: O Rio de Janeiro e a república que não foi.* São Paulo: Companhia das Letras.

Carvalho, Luiz Maklouf. 1998. *Mulheres que foram à luta armada.* São Paulo: Editora Globo.

Casanova, José. 1994. *Public Religions in the Modern World.* Chicago: University of Chicago Press.

———. 1997. "Globalizing Catholicism and the Return to a 'Universal' Church." In *Transnational Religion and Fading States,* 121–43. Ed. Susanne Hoeber Rudolph and James Piscatori. Boulder: Westview.

"O 'caso Lemercier,' do mosteiro beneditino de Cuernavaca." 1967. *REB* 27 (September), 769–70.

Caspary, Anita M. 2003. *Witness to Integrity: The Crisis of the Immaculate Heart Community of California.* Collegeville, Minn.: Liturgical.

Castañeda, Jorge G. 1993. *Utopia Unarmed: The Latin American Left after the Cold War.* New York: Knopf.

Castro, Celso. 1990. *O espírito militar.* Rio de Janeiro: Jorge Zahar Editor.

Castro, Gustavo do Passo. 1987. *As comunidades do Dom: Um estudo de CEB's no Recife.* Recife: Fundação Joaquim Nabuco; Editora Massangana.

Castro, Jerônimo Pedreira de. 1942. *S. Vicente de Paulo e a magnificência de suas obras.* Petrópolis: Vozes.

Castro, Josué de. 2001. *Homens e caranguejos.* Rio de Janeiro: Civilização Brasileira.

Castro, Marcos de. 1984. "Os caminhas da Igreja." In *Retrato do Brasil* 2:328. São Paulo: Política Editora.

———. 1985. *A Igreja e o autoritarismo.* Rio de Janeiro: Jorge Zahar Editora.

Castro, Paulo Pereira de. 1985. "A 'experiência republicana,' 1831–1840." In *História geral da civilização brasileira. II. O Brasil monárquico. 2. Dispersão e unidade,* 9–67. Ed. Sérgio Buarque de Holanda. São Paulo: Difel.

Catalogue des Maisons et du Personnel de la Congregation de la Mission. 1909. Paris: n.p.

Caulfield, Sueann. 2000. *In Defense of Honor: Sexual Morality, Modernity, and Nation in Twentieth-Century Brazil.* Durham, N.C.: Duke University Press.

Cayuela, José. 1969. *Hélder Câmara: Brasil, un Vietnam católico?* Barcelona: Editorial Pomaire.

"O celibato sacerdotal." 1970a. *SEDOC* 2 (March), 1105–40.

"O celibato sacerdotal." 1970b. *SEDOC* 3 (July), 41–60.

Centeno, Miguel Angel. 2001. "The Disciplinary Society in Latin America." In *The Other Mirror: Grand Theory through the Lens of Latin America*, 289–308. Ed. Miguel Angel Centeno and Fernando López-Alves. Princeton: Princeton University Press.

Centeno, Miguel Angel, and Fernando López-Alves, eds. 2001. *The Other Mirror: Grand Theory through the Lens of Latin America.* Princeton: Princeton University Press.

Centro de Estatística Religiosa e Investigações Sociais [CERIS]. 2003. "Perfil do presbítero brasileiro." Rio de Janeiro: CERIS.

Centro Nordestino de Animação Popular. 1989. *O pastor e seu rebanho.* Recife: Centro Nordestino de Animação Popular.

Centro Nordestino de Pastoral and Instituto de Teologia do Recife. 1987. *ITER, ano letivo 1987.* Recife: ITER.

———. 1989. *ITER, ano letivo 1989.* Recife: ITER.

"Centro Teológico de Estudos e Espiritualidade para a Vida Religiosa." 1975. *REB* 35 (June), 450–51.

Cerejeira, Manuel Gonçalves. 1949. "O padre e as exigências do nosso tempo." *REB* 9 (March), 1–7.

Certeau, Michel de. 1986. "The Laugh of Michel Foucault." In *Heterologies: Discourse on the Other*, 193–98. Ed. Michel de Certeau. Minneapolis: University of Minnesota Press.

———. 1988. *The Writing of History.* Trans. Tom Conley. New York: Columbia University Press.

Chappell, David L. 2000. "Salvation by Serotonin? The Prozac Priests and Other Medicine Men Face 'Inessential Suffering.'" Review of T. H. Luhrmann's *Of Two Minds: The Growing Dis-order in American Psychiatry* and Joseph Glenmullen's *Prozac Backlash* (July). Online: http://www.beliefnet.com.

Chesnut, R. Andrew. 1997. *Born Again in Brazil: The Pentecostal Boom and the Pathogens of Poverty.* East Rutherford, N.J.: Rutgers University Press.

———. 2003. *Competitive Spirits: Latin America's New Religious Economy.* Oxford: Oxford University Press.

Cipriani, Gabriel. 1994. "The Catholic Church and Religious Pluralism in Brazil." *Notícias da CNBB* (International Edition) 6:16 (January–March), 1–4.

Cirano, Marcos. 1983. *Os caminhos de Dom Hélder.* Recife: Editora Guararapes.

"Circular Coletiva do Episcopado Paulista ao Clero." 1943. *REB* 3 (March), 186–98.

Cleary, Edward L. 1997. "The Brazilian Catholic Church and Church-State Relations: Nation Building." *Journal of Church and State* 39:2 (Spring), 253–72.

Cleary, Edward L., and Hannah Stewart-Gambino, eds. 1992. *Conflict and Competition: The Latin American Church in a Changing Environment.* Boulder: Rienner.

"Clerical Celibacy." 1974. *New Catholic Encyclopedia* 16:81–82 (supplement 1967–1974). New York: McGraw-Hill.

"Clero e Ação Católica." 1942. *REB* 2 (September), 772–74.

O clero no Parlamento Brasileiro. 1978–1980. 5 vols. Brasília: Câmara dos Deputados; Rio de Janeiro: Centro João XXIII-IBRADES; Fundação Casa de Rui Barbosa.

Cloin, Tiago G. 1961. "Documentos pontifícios esclarecendo problemas relacionados com o recrutamento de vocações entre gente de cor." *Revista da CRB*, Year 7, No. 68 (February), 71–74.

CNBB [Conferência Nacional dos Bispos do Brasil]. 1963. *Plano de emergência para a Igreja do Brasil.* Rio de Janeiro: Livraria Dom Bosco Editora.

———. 1969. *Documentos dos presbíteros.* Rio de Janeiro.

———. 1974. *Espiritualidade presbiteral hoje.* Estudos da CNBB, No. 1. São Paulo: Edições Paulinas.

———. 1984a. *Formação dos presbíteros na Igreja do Brasil: Diretrizes básicas.* Documentos da CNBB, No. 30. São Paulo: Edições Paulinas.

———. 1984b. *Membros da Conferência Nacional dos Bispos do Brasil.* São Paulo: Edições Paulinas.

———. 1984c. *Situação e vida dos seminaristas maiores no Brasil.* Estudos da CNBB, No. 40. São Paulo: Edições Paulinas.

———. 1989. *Exigências éticas da ordem democrática.* Documentos da CNBB No. 42. São Paulo: Edições Paulinas.

———. 1990. *Participação popular e cidadania: a igreja no processo constituinte.* Estudos da CNBB No. 60. São Paulo: Edições Paulinas.

———. 1991. *Membros da Conferência Nacional dos Bispos do Brasil.* Brasília: CNBB.

———. 1993. *Ética: Pessoa e sociedade.* Documentos da CNBB No. 50. São Paulo: Edições Paulinas.

———. 1994a. *Brasil: Alternativas e protagonistas—por uma sociedade democrática.* Petrópolis: Vozes.

———. 1994b. *Orientações pastorais sobre a Renovação Carismática Católica.* Documentos da CNBB No. 53. São Paulo: Paulinas.

———. 1995a. *Formação dos presbíteros da Igreja no Brasil. Diretrizes básicas.* Documentos da CNBB, No. 55. São Paulo: Paulinas.

———. 1995b. "Pronunciamento sobre a conjuntura nacional." Mimeograph (18 May).

———. 1995c. *Situação e vida dos seminaristas maiores no Brasil (II).* Estudos da CNBB, No. 74. São Paulo: Paulus.

———. 1996. "Nota da Conferência Nacional dos Bispos do Brasil, sobre o massacre de Eldorado dos Carajás, Estado do Pará." *Revista de Cultura Vozes* 3 (May–June), 3–5.

———. 1997. *A fraternidade e os encarcerados: Cristo liberta de todas as prisões.* São Paulo: Editora Salesiana Dom Bosco.

———. 1999. *Catálogo da OSIB.* Brasília: CNBB.

———. 2000. *Brasil—500 anos: Diálogo e esperança.* São Paulo: Paulinas.

————. 2002. *Membros e endereços.* Brasília: CNBB.

"CNBB. Conselho permanente. Atas." 1982. *CM* 359 (August), 782.

"CNBB diz que país sucumbiu à desordem." 1994. *Zero Hora* (July 26), 13.

Cohen, Thomas. 1990. "The Fire of Tongues: Antonio Vieira and the Christian Mission in Brazil." PhD dissertation, Stanford University.

————. 1991. "Millenarian Themes in the Writings of Antonio Vieira." *LBR* 28:1 (summer), 23–46.

————. 1998. *The Fire of Tongues: António Vieira and the Missionary Church in Brazil and Portugal.* Stanford: Stanford University Press.

Coimbra, Cecília. 1995. *Guardiães da ordem: Uma viagem pelas práticas psi no Brasil do 'Milagre'.* Rio de Janeiro: Oficina do Autor.

"A coleção 'Seminários.'" 1962. *Revista da CRB,* Year 8, No. 89 (November), 729–33.

Comblin, José. 1968a. "Desenvolvimento—vocação cristã." *Ponto Homem,* Year 43, No. 3 (July–August), 53–66.

————. 1968b. "Igreja e Desenvolvimento." *Ponto Homem,* Year 43, No. 3 (July–August), 67–81.

————. 1968c. "Teologia do desenvolvimento." *Ponto Homem,* Year 43, No. 3 (July–August), 82–99.

————. 1970. "Significado das pequenas comunidades." *Convergência,* No. 28 (October), 13–17.

————. 1977. *Teologia da enxada.* Petrópolis: Vozes.

————. 1979. *The Church and the National Security State.* Maryknoll, N.Y.: Orbis.

————. 1981. "Algumas reflexões sobre a formação sacerdotal hoje." *REB* 41 (June), 320–45.

————. 1983–1986. *Breve curso de teologia.* São Paulo: Edições Paulinas.

————. 1984a. "Dom Hélder e o novo modelo episcopal do Vaticano II." *Perspectivas Teológico-Pastorais,* Year 3, No. 4, 23–45.

————. 1984b. "A formação sacerdotal depois de Vaticano II." Mimeograph.

————. 1993. "A Nova Evangelização." In *Santo Domingo: Ensaios teológico-pastorais,* 206–24. Ed. Clodovis Boff et al. Petrópolis: SOTER; Vozes; Ameríndia.

————. 1996. *Cristãos rumo ao século XXI.* Petrópolis: Vozes.

————. 2000. "Dom Hélder, bispo do terceiro milênio." In *Hélder, o Dom: Uma vida que marcou os rumos da Igreja no Brasil,* 3rd edition, 91–94. Ed. Zildo Barbosa Rocha. Petrópolis: Vozes.

"A Comissão de Justiça e Paz na Arquidiocese de Olinda e Recife." 1984. *Perspectivas Teológico-Pastorais,* Year 3, No. 4, 109–15.

"Comissão Episcopal Pró Colégio Pio Brasileiro." 1961. *CM,* No. 108 (September), 25–29.

Commissão Nacional do Clero. 1994. *O presbítero no processo de urbanização.* Brasília: Conferência Nacional do Bispos do Brasil.

"Como deveria o clero encarar o fenômeno marxista no mundo?" 1964. *OS,* Year 39, No. 5 (November-December), 43–46.

"Como iniciar a Ação Católica." 1958. *OS*, Year 33, No. 2 (May–June), 88–91.

"Complementação para o Brasil das Diretrizes Básicas da Formação Sacerdotal." 1970. *CM* 216–17 (September–October).

"Comunicado final da Presidência." 1971. *SEDOC* 4 (October), 401–4.

"Conclusões da reunião de reitores de São Paulo." 1964. *OS*, Year 39, No. 5 (November–December), 27–29.

Conferência dos Religiosos do Brasil [CRB]. 1973. "Parecer sobre Criatividade Comunitária." *CM* 244 (January), 54–60.

"Congresso de diretores espirituais." 1957. *REB* 17 (December), 972–79.

"Congresso de reitores de seminário." 1948. *Revista do Assistente Eclesiástico*, Year 1, No. 6 (March), 88–95.

"Congresso nacional de seminaristas." 1963. *OS*, Year 38, No. 5 (November–December), 9–15.

Conrad, Robert. 1972. *The Destruction of Brazilian Slavery, 1850–1888*. Berkeley: University of California Press.

Conselho Episcopal Latino-Americano [CELAM]. 1982. *Elementos para su historia*. Bogotá: CELAM.

"Considerações da Comissão Nacional do Clero." 1974. *CM* 266 (November), 1128.

"Convívio, experiência, vivência." 1964. *OS*, Year 39, No. 2 (May–June), 93–97.

"O coração da diocese." 1958. *OS*, Year 33, No. 5 (November–December), 109–15.

Coriden, James A. 1972. "O celibato, o direito canônico e o sínodo de 1971." *Concilium* 8:1079–92.

Costa, Célia Maria Leite, Dulce Chaves Pandolfi, and Kenneth Serbin, eds. 2001. *O bispo de Volta Redonda: Memórias de Dom Waldyr Calheiros*. Rio de Janeiro: FGV Editora.

Costa, Emília Viotti da. 1966. *Da senzala à colônia*. São Paulo: Difusão Européia do Livro.

Costa, Jurandir Freire. 1988. "Sobre psicanálise e religião." In *Hélio Pellegrino: A-Deus*, 85–94. Ed. João Carlos Moura. Petrópolis: Vozes.

———. 1989. *História da psiquiatria no Brasil*. 4th edition. Rio de Janeiro: Xenon.

Cox, Harvey. 1984. *Religion in the Secular City*. New York: Simon and Schuster.

———. 1988. *The Silencing of Leonardo Boff*. Bloomington, Ind.: Meyer-Stone.

Cozzens, Donald B. 2000. *The Changing Face of the Priesthood: A Reflection on the Priest's Crisis of Soul*. Collegeville, Minn.: Liturgical.

Crespo, Samyra. 1992. "Escolas católicas renovadas e a educação libertadora no Brasil." In *Catolicismo no Brasil: Modernidade e tradição*, 153–218. Ed. Pierre Sanchis. São Paulo: Edições Paulinas.

Crivellaro, Débora. 1999. "O encantador de almas." *Época* (March 15), 39–42.

"Crônica Eclesiástica." 1973. *REB* 33 (September), 734–37.

Cruz, Angélica Santa, and Expedito Filho. N.d. "Vontade radical," *Veja Educação*. Online: http://veja.abril.com.br/idade/educacao/pesquise/mst/1459.html.

Cruz, Mário Luís Cardoso da. 1996. "Origens e fundação do Pontifício Colégio Pio Brasileiro (1927–1934)." History thesis, Gregorian University.

Cuénot, Claude. 1965. *Teilhard de Chardin: A Biographical Study.* Trans. Vincent Colimore. Baltimore: Helicon.

Cunha, Euclides da. 1944. *Rebellion in the Backlands.* Trans. Samuel Putnam. Chicago: University of Chicago Press.

Cunha, Pedro Otávio Carneiro da. 1985. "A fundação de um império liberal: Primeiro reinado, reação e revolução." In *História geral da civilização brasileira.II. O Brasil monárquico. 1. O processo de emancipação,* 135–78. Ed. Sérgio Buarque de Holanda. São Paulo: DIFEL.

"Curso intensivo de direção espiritual em Viamão." 1962. *Revista da CRB,* Year 8, No. 81 (March 1), 187–90.

"Dados sobre o movimento de saída de padres." 1971. *REB* 31 (June), 515.

Dassin, Joan, ed. 1986. *Torture in Brazil.* Trans. Jaime Wright, New York: Vintage.

Daudelin, Jean, and W. E. Hewitt. 1995. "Latin American Politics: Exit the Catholic Church?" In *Organized Religion in the Political Transformation of Latin America,* 177–94. Ed. Satya Pattnayak. Lanham, Md.: University Press of America.

Dávila, Jerry. 2003. *Diploma of Whiteness: Race and Social Policy in Brazil, 1917–1945.* Durham, N.C.: Duke University Press.

D'Azevedo, Erica Luísa. 2000. "AIDS—um desafio para a Igreja no Brasil." *REB* 60 (September), 669–71.

Dean, Warren. 1969. *The Industrialization of São Paulo.* Austin: University of Texas Press.

De Boni, Luis Alberto, and Rovílio Costa. 1984. *Os italianos no Rio Grande do Sul.* Porto Alegre: Escola Superior de Teologia de Sao Lourenco de Brindes; Caxias do Sul: Universidade de Caxias; Correio Riograndense.

Degler, Carl N. 1971. *Neither Black nor White: Slavery and Race Relations in Brazil and the United States.* New York: Macmillan.

de Groot, C. F. G. 1996. *Brazilian Catholicism and the Ultramontane Reform, 1850–1930.* Latin America Studies 75. Amsterdam: CEDLA.

de Kadt, Emanuel. 1970. *Catholic Radicals in Brazil.* London: Oxford University Press.

Della Cava, Ralph. 1970. *Miracle in Joaseiro.* New York: Columbia University Press.

———. 1976a. "Catholicism and Society in Twentieth-Century Brasil." *LARR* 11, 7–50.

———. 1976b. *Milagre em Joaseiro.* Trans. Yedda Linhares. 2nd edition. Rio de Janeiro: Paz e Terra.

———. 1985. *A Igreja em flagrante: Catolicismo e sociedade na imprensa brasileira, 1964–1980.* Rio de Janeiro: ISER; Editora Marco Zero.

———. 1989. "The 'People's Church, the Vatican, and Abertura." In *Democratizing Brazil,* 143–67. Ed. Alfred Stepan. New York: Oxford University Press.

———. 1992a. "Política do Vaticano 1978–1990: Uma visão geral." In *Catolicismo: Unidade religiosa e pluralismo cultural,* 231–58. Ed. Pierre Sanchis. São Paulo: Edições Loyola.

———. 1992b. "Vatican Policy, 1978–90: An Updated Overview." *Social Research* 59:1 (Spring), 171–99.

————. 1993. "Thinking about Current Vatican Policy in Central and East Europe and the Utility of the 'Brazilian Paradigm.'" *Journal of Latin American Studies* 25:257–81.

Della Cava, Ralph, and Paula Montero, 1991. . . . *E o verbo se faz imagem: Igreja católica e os meios de comunicação no Brasil, 1962–1989*. Petrópolis: Vozes.

Delumeau, Jean. 1977. *Catholicism between Luther and Voltaire: A New View of the Counter-Reformation*. Trans. Jeremy Moiser. Philadelphia: Westminster.

"Demônios do fim do século (Análise da prática do exorcismo na Igreja Universal do Reino de Deus)." 1993. *REB* 53 (September), 693–95.

"Depoimentos de sacerdotes." 1968. In "O papel do padre. Volume II. Documentos e ensaios." Unpublished manuscript. Rio de Janeiro: CNBB and CERIS.

"Depoimentos sobre o celibato." 1968. In "O papel do padre. Volume II. Documentos e ensaios." Unpublished manuscript. Rio de Janeiro, CNBB and CERIS.

Desrochers, Georgette, and Eduardo Hoornaert, eds. 1984. *Padre Ibiapina e a Igreja dos Pobres*. São Paulo: Edições Paulinas.

Diacon, Todd A. 1991. "The Search for Meaning in an Historical Context: Popular Religion, Millenarianism, and the Contestado Rebellion." *LBR* 28:1 (summer), 47–57.

Dias, Rosinha Borges. 1994. "Projeto pastoral 'Construir a Esperança.'" In *A presença da Igreja na cidade*, 36–47. Ed. Alberto Antoniazzi and Cleto Caliman. Petrópolis: Vozes.

Didonet, Frederico. 1941. "Primeira semana de Ação Católica do clero diocesano de Santa Maria (Rio Grande do Sul)." *REB* 1 (March-June), 232–35.

————. 1957. "O sacerdote e sua doação total às almas." *REB* 17 (December), 873–75.

"Do começo de Minas." 1965. *OS*, Year 40, No. 204 (July–August), 268–69.

Dodin, André. 1981. "A misteriosa oração de 'Monsieur Vincent.'" *Grande Sinal* (September), 527–36.

Dodson, Edward O. 1984. *The Phenomenon of Man Revisited: A Biological Viewpoint on Teilhard de Chardin*. New York: Columbia University Press.

Doimo, Ana Maria. 1992. "Igreja e movimentos sociais pós-70 no Brasil." In *Catolicismo: Cotidiano e movimentos*, 275–308. Ed. Pierre Sanchis. São Paulo: Edições Paulinas.

————. 1995. *A vez e a voz do popular: Movimentos sociais e participação política no Brasil pós-70*. Rio de Janeiro: Relume-Dumará.

Dolan, Jay P. 1978. *Catholic Revivalism: The American Experience, 1830–1900*. Notre Dame, Ind.: University of Notre Dame Press.

————. 1985. *The American Catholic Experience*. Garden City, N.Y.: Doubleday.

Dominian, Helen G. 1958. *Apostle of Brazil: The Biography of Padre José de Anchieta, S.J. (1534–1597)*. New York: Exposition.

Donnelly, John Patrick. 2004. *Ignatius of Loyola: Founder of the Jesuits*. New York: Pearson Longman.

Donoghue, Denis. 2002. "Brotherhood without Fatherhood." *New York Review of Books*, 46:16 (October 24), 52–54.

"Dossiê—crise na arquidiocese de Olinda e Recife." 1990. *SEDOC* 22 (May–June), 693–747.

Dougherty, Jude. 1994. "What Was Religion? The Demise of a Prodigious Power." In *Modernity and Religion*, 131–44. Ed. Ralph McInerny. Notre Dame, Ind.: University of Notre Dame Press.

Drewermann, Eugen. 1990. *Kleriker: Psychogramm eines Ideals*. Olten, Switzerland: Walter-Verlag.

Drogus, Carol Ann. 1992. "Popular Movements and the Limits of Political Mobilization at the Grassroots in Brazil." In *Conflict and Competition: The Latin American Church in a Changing Environment*, 63–86. Ed. Edward L. Cleary and Hannah Stewart-Gambino. Boulder: Rienner.

———. 1997. *Women, Religion, and Social Change in Brazil's Popular Church*. Notre Dame, Ind.: University of Notre Dame Press.

Dussell, Enrique. 1981. *A History of the Church in Latin America*. Grand Rapids, Mich.: Eerdmans.

"Ecos da reunião de reitores e diretores espirituais dos seminários do Brasil." 1959. *CM*, No. 83 (August), 1–14.

"Editorial." 1962. *OS*, Year 37, No. 5 (November–December), 4–5.

"Editorial." 1963a. *OS*, Year 38, No. 1 (March–April), 4–5.

"Editorial." 1963b. *OS*, Year 38, No. 3 (July–August), 3–4.

"Editorial." 1968. *Ponto Homem*, Year 43, No. 1 (March–April), 10.

"Editorial: 'Mundo quebrado.'" 1967. *OS*, Year 42, No. 214 (July–August), 210–13.

Edwards, Lisa Marie. 2002. "In Science and Virtue: The Education of the Latin American Clergy, 1858–1967." Ph.D. dissertation, Tulane University.

"Elementos para reflexão diante dos que abandonaram o ministério." 1974. *CM*, No. 226 (November), 1126.

Ellis, John Tracy. 1965a. "A Short History of Seminary Education: I—The Apostolic Age to Trent." In *Seminary Education in a Time of Change*, 1–29. Ed. James Michael Lee and Louis J. Putz. Notre Dame, Ind.: Fides.

———. 1965b. "A Short History of Seminary Education: II—Trent to Today." In *Seminary Education in a Time of Change*, 30–81. Ed. James Michael Lee and Louis J. Putz. Notre Dame, Ind.: Fides.

Ellis Júnior, Alfredo. 1980. *Feijó e a primeira metade do século XIX*. 2nd edition. São Paulo: Editora Nacional; Instituto Nacional do Livro.

"Encontro dos diretores espirituais dos seminários do Brasil." 1959. *CM*, No. 81 (June), 8–12.

Engelke, Dom Inocêncio. 1959. "Pastoral de D. Inocêncio Engelke: Conosco, sem nós ou contra nós se fará a reforma rural." *Revista do Assistente Eclesiástico*, Year 4, No. 37 (November–December), 76–83.

"Eras Tu, Senhor? (A fraternidade e os excluídos)." 1995. *REB* 55 (March), 198–200.

REFERENCES
420

Erickson, Kenneth Paul. 1977. *The Brazilian Corporative State and Working-Class Politics.* Berkeley: University of California Press.

"Escreve o Leitor." 1962. *OS,* Year 37, No. 5 (November-December), 58–59.

"Estudos dos Seminários." 1946. *São Vicente,* Year 15, No. 4, 205–7.

"Les Évangiles et la Psychanalyse." 1992. *L'Express* (April 24), 26, 28–30.

Evans, Peter. 1979. *Dependent Development.* Princeton: Princeton University Press.

Facchini, Natal. 1967. "Na casa do Pai." *Revista da CRB,* Year 13, Nos. 146–47 (August– September), 454–63.

"Falta de Sacerdotes." 1960. *REB* 20 (December), 1039–40.

"Faculdade de teologia." 1962. *OS,* Year 37, No. 5 (November–December), 45.

"Fátima." 1967. In *New Catholic Encyclopedia,* 5:855–56. New York: McGraw-Hill.

"Fato Mariana." 1967. *OS,* Year 42, No. 212 (March–April), 80–81.

Fausto, Boris. 1976. *Trabalho urbano e conflito social.* São Paulo: DIFEL.

"Fechado o Seminário de Mariana." 1966. *REB* 26 (December), 980–81.

Feijó, Diogo Antonio. 1828. *Demonstração da necessidade da abolição do celibato clerical pela Assembleia Geral do Brasil, e da sua verdadeira e legítima competência nesta matéria.* Rio de Janeiro: Tipografia Imperial e Colonial.

Feitosa, Antônio. 1952. "Grandeza do sacerdote." *REB.* 12 (June), 266–73.

Fernandes, Bob, and Mino Carta. 2000. "Paulo Evaristo Arns: História do Brasil." *Carta-Capital* (April 26), 64–68.

Fernandes, Geraldo. 1953. "O problema dos ex-seminaristas." *REB* 13 (March), 105–14.

Fernandes, Rubem César. 1992a. *Censo Institucional Evangélico 1992: Primeiros Comentários.* Rio de Janeiro: ISER.

———. 1992b. "Imagens da paixão, a Igreja no Brasil e na Polônia." In *Catolicismo: Modernidade e tradição,* 67–89. Ed. Pierre Sanchis. São Paulo: Edições Paulinas.

Ferreira, João Batista. 1988. "Caminhos da utopia e da esperança." In *Hélio Pellegrino: A-Deus,* 144–59. Ed. João Carlos Moura. Petrópolis: Vozes.

———. 1995a. "Encontros psicodinâmicos: primeiros passos da Clínica Social de Psicanálise." *Boletim de Novidades Pulsional,* Year 8, No. 71 (March), 35–38.

———. 1995b. "Luxo no lixo ou a psicanálise tem lugar fora do asfalto?" *Boletim de Novidades Pulsional,* Year 8, No. 71 (March), 15–22.

———. 2002. "Trajetórias de formação clerical." *Ciência e Cultura* 31:208 (December), section titled "Horizontes Novos," 3.

Ferreira Netto, Geraldino Alves. 1996. "Deus é inconsciente." Boletim de Novidades Pulsional, Year 9, No. 85 (May), 41–46.

Figueira, Ricardo Rezende. 1986. *A Justiça do lobo.* Petrópolis: Vozes.

Figueira, Sérvulo A. 1988. "Psicanalistas e Pacientes na Cultura Psicanalítica Brasileira." In *Efeito psi: A influência da psicanálise,* 131–49. Ed. Sérvulo A. Figueira. Rio de Janeiro: Campus.

———. 1992. *Nos bastidores da psicanálise.* Rio de Janeiro: Imago.

———, ed. 1988. *Efeito psi: A influência da psicanálise.* Rio de Janeiro: Campus.

Fitzpatrick-Behrens, Susan. 2001. "Of Divine Import: The Maryknoll Missionaries in Peru, 1943–2000." PhD dissertation, University of California, San Diego.

Fleet, Michael, and Brian H. Smith. 1997. *The Catholic Church and Democracy in Chile and Peru.* Notre Dame, Ind.: University of Notre Dame Press.

Fleury, Renato Sêneca. 1967. *O Padre Feijó.* São Paulo: Melhoramentos.

Flynn, Peter. 1978. *Brazil: A Political Analysis.* Boulder: Westview.

Follmann, José Ivo. 1992. "O cotidiano religioso católico numa paróquia suburbana da região metropolitana de Porto Alegre." In *Catolicismo: Cotidiano e movimentos,* 155–208. Ed. Pierre Sanchis. São Paulo: Edições Paulinas.

Fonseca, Alexandre Brasil Carvalho da. 1996. "Uma igreja na política: Voto, clientelismo e mediação na Igreja Universal do Reino de Deus." *Cadernos do CEAS* 164 (June/August), 66–88.

———. 2002. "Secularização, pluralismo religioso e democracia no Brasil: Um estudo sobre evangélicos na política nos anos 90." PhD dissertation, Universidade de São Paulo.

Fontanive, Dalcy. 1968. "O papel do padre. Volume III: Formação no seminário." Unpublished manuscript. Rio de Janeiro: CNBB and CERIS.

Forman, Shepard. 1975. *The Brazilian Peasantry.* New York: Columbia University Press.

Foroohar, Manzar. 1986. "Liberation Theology: The Response of Latin American Catholics to Socioeconomic Problems." *Latin American Perspectives* 13:3 (summer), 37–57.

Foucault, Michel. 1979. *Discipline and Punish.* Trans. Alan Sheridan. New York: Vintage.

Foweraker, Joe. 1981. *The Struggle for Land.* Cambridge: Cambridge University Press.

Fragoso, Dom Antônio. 1968. "O evangelho e a justiça social." *Ponto Homem,* Year 43, No. 2 (May-June), 10–25.

Frei Aleixo. 1943. "Pró-seminário." *REB* 3 (December), 1013–17.

Frei Betto [Carlos Alberto Libânio Christo]. 1966. "Um diálogo impossível ou necessário?" *OS,* Year 41, No. 208 (May–June), 176–83.

———. 1977 [1971]. *Against Principalities and Powers.* Trans. John Drury. Maryknoll, N.Y.: Orbis.

———. 1981. *Cartas da prisão.* Rio de Janeiro: Civilização Brasileira.

———. 1985. *Das catacumbas.* Rio de Janeiro: Civilização Brasileira.

———. 1987 [1982]. *Batismo de sangue.* Rio de Janeiro: Editora Bertrand Brasil.

———. 1989. *Lula: a biografia política de um operário.* São Paulo: Estação Liberdade.

———. 2000. *Batismo de sangue: A luta clandestina contra a ditadura militar.* Revised and augmented edition of *Batismo de sangue* [1982]. São Paulo: Casa Amarela.

———. 2001. "Charles de Foucauld, Homem de Deus." *América Latina em Movimento.* Online: http://alainet.org/active/show_text.php3?key=1407.

———. 2002. *Alfabetto: Autobiografia escolar.* São Paulo: Editora Ática.

Frei Betto, and Afonso Borges Filho. 1988. *Sinal de contradição.* Rio de Janeiro: Espaço e Tempo.

Frei Betto, and Paulo Freire. 1985. *Essa escola chamada vida.* São Paulo: Editora Ática.

Frei Matias. 1968. "Comunidade Eclesial para o Desenvolvimento." *Ponto Homem*, Year 43, No. 4 (September–October), 46–58.

Frei Nelson (pseudonym). N.d. "Vida de padre: Um grito contra o celibato." Unpublished manuscript.

Freire, Paulo. 1970. *Pedagogy of the Oppressed*. Trans. Myra Bergman Ramos. New York: Herder and Herder.

Freitas, José Higino de. 1979. *Aplicação no Brasil do decreto tridentino sobre os seminários até 1889*. Belo Horizonte: Editora São Vicente.

French, Jan Hoffman. 2003. "The Rewards of Resistance: Legalizing Identity among Descendants of *Índios* and Fugitive Slaves in Northeastern Brazil." PhD dissertation, Duke University.

———. 2004. "A Tale of Two Priests and Two Struggles: The Shifting Landscape of Church-State Relations from Dictatorship to Democracy (Sergipe 1970–2000)." Paper delivered at the international symposium "The Cultures of Dictatorship: Historical Reflections on the Brazilian Golpe of 1964," University of Maryland, October 14–16, 2004.

French, John D. 1991. "The Origin of Corporatist State Intervention in Brazilian Industrial Relations, 1930–1934: A Critique of the Literature." *LBR* 28:2 (winter), 13–26.

———. 1992. *The Brazilian Workers' ABC*. Chapel Hill: University of North Carolina Press.

Freston, Paulo. 1993a. "Protestantes e política no Brasil: Da constituinte ao impeachment." PhD dissertation, Universidade Estadual de Campinas.

———. 1993b. "Brother Votes for Brother: The New Politics of Protestantism in Brazil." In *Rethinking Protestantism in Latin America*, 66–110. Ed. Virginia Garrard-Burnett and David Stoll. Philadelphia: Temple University Press.

Freyre, Gilberto. 1959. *A propósito de frades*. Bahia: Universidade da Bahia.

———. 1978. *Casa-grande e senzala*. 19th edition. Rio de Janeiro: José Olympio Editora.

Fromm, Erich. 1950. *Psychoanalysis and Religion*. New Haven: Yale University Press.

Gabeira, Fernando. 1980. *O que é isso, companheiro?* Rio de Janeiro: CODECRI.

Galhardo, Ricardo. 2000a. "CNBB divulga nota condenando camisinhas." *O Globo* (June 15). Online edition.

———. 2000b. "Igreja pode exigir teste de HIV em seminários." *O Globo* (June 15). Online edition.

Garcia, Cláudio. 1967. "Encontro e reflexões." *OS*, Year 42, No. 216 (November–December), 496–99.

Garfield, Seth. 2001. *Indigenous Struggle at the Heart of Brazil: State Policy, Frontier Expansion, and the Xavante Indians, 1937–1988*. Durham, N.C.: Duke University Press.

Garrone, Cardinal Gabriel-Marie. 1968. "Carta do Cardeal Garrone sobre o seminário dividido em *pequenas comunidades* dispersas." *REB* 28 (March), 172–76.

———. 1971. "Formación y vida sacerdotal en la Iglesia actual." In *Seminarios,* 49–53. Ed. Conselho Episcopal Latinoamericano. Bogotá: Departamento de Ministerios Jerárquicos del CELAM.

———. 1980. "Carta circular sobre alguns aspectos mais urgentes da preparação espiritual nos seminários." *SEDOC* 12 (June), 1171–74.

Gaskill, Newton J. 1997. "Rethinking Protestantism and Democratic Consolidation in Latin America." *Sociology of Religion* 58/1 (spring), 69–91.

———. 2003. "Religion and Religious Scholarship in Changing Social Contexts." *LARR* 38:3, 189–99.

Gaspari, Elio. 2002a. *As ilusões armadas: A ditadura envergonhada.* São Paulo: Companhia das Letras.

———. 2002b. *As ilusões armadas: A ditadura escancarada.* São Paulo: Companhia das Letras.

———. 2003. *O sacerdote e o feiticeiro: A ditadura derrotada.* São Paulo: Companhia das Letras.

Gay, Peter. 1985. *Freud for Historians.* New York: Oxford University Press.

———. 1988. *Freud: A Life for Our Time.* New York: Anchor.

———. 1995. *The Naked Heart.* Vol. 4 of *The Bourgeois Experience: Victoria to Freud.* New York: Oxford University Press.

Gaylin, Willard. 2000. *Talk Is Not Enough: How Psychotherapy Really Works.* New York: Little, Brown.

Gebara, Ivone. 1992. *Vida religiosa: Da teologia patriarcal à teologia feminista.* São Paulo: Edições Paulinas.

———. 2002. *Out of the Depths: Women's Experience of Evil and Salvation.* Trans. Ann Patrick Ware. Minneapolis: Fortress.

Gehlen, Ivaldo. 1970. "IT: Dois anos de presença." *Teocomunicação,* Year 1, No. 1 (November), 2–5.

Ghio, José-Maria. 1991. "The Latin American Church in the [*sic*] Wojtyla's Era: New Evangelization or 'Neo-Integralism'?" Helen Kellogg Institute for International Studies Working Paper No. 159 (May).

———. 1992. "The Latin American Church and the Papacy of Wojtyla." In *The Right and Democracy in Latin America,* 183–201. Ed. Douglas A. Chalmers, Maria do Carmo Campello de Souza, and Atilio A. Boron. New York: Praeger.

Gill, Anthony. 1995. "The Politics of Religious Regulation in Mexico: Preliminary Observations." Paper presented at the Latin American Studies Association Nineteenth International Congress, Washington, D.C. (September 28–30).

———. 1998. *Rendering Unto Caesar: The Catholic Church and the State in Latin America.* Chicago: University of Chicago Press.

Ginnetti, Mario. 1952. "O problema das vocações sacerdotais na América Latina." *REB* 12 (June), 374–81.

Giumbelli, Emerson. 1996. "Da religião como problema social: Secularização, retorno do sagrado, liberdade religiosa, espaço e comportamento religioso." Unpublished paper.

———. 1997. *O cuidado dos mortos: Uma história da condenação e legitimação do espiritismo.* Rio de Janeiro: Arquivo Nacional.

Glenmullen, Joseph. 2000. *Prozac Backlash: Overcoming the Dangers of Prozac, Zoloft, Paxil, and Other Antidepressants with Safe, Effective Alternatives.* New York: Simon & Schuster.

Goffman, Erving. 1974. *Manicômios, prisões e conventos.* São Paulo: Perspective.

Gomes, Dom Fernando. 1982. *Sem violência e sem medo: Escritos, homilias e entrevistas.* Goiânia: Universidade Católica de Goiás, 1982.

Gomes, Flávio dos Santos. 1995. *História de quilombolas: Mocambos e comunidades de senzalas no Rio de Janeiro—século XIX.* Rio de Janeiro: Arquivo Nacional.

Gomes, Wilson. 1992. "Cinco teses equivocadas sobre as novas seitas populares." *Cadernos do CEAS* 139 (May–June), 39–53.

Gonçalves, Martins. 1943. "A preparação dos seminaristas em ordem a Ação Católica." *REB* 3 (September), 781–94.

Goode, Erica. 2002. "Abusive Priests Are Varied, But Treatable, Center Found." *New York Times* (April 26). Online edition.

Gorender, Jacob. 1980. *Escravismo colonial.* São Paulo: Editora Ática.

———. 1998. *Combate nas trevas.* 2nd edition. São Paulo: Editora Ática.

Graham, Richard. 1968. *Britain and the Onset of Modernization in Brazil, 1850–1914.* Cambridge: Cambridge University Press.

———. 1990. *Patronage and Politics in Nineteenth-Century Brazil.* Stanford: Stanford University Press.

Greeley, Andrew M. 1972. *The Catholic Priest in the United States: Sociological Investigations.* Washington, D.C.: United States Catholic Conference.

———. 1986. *Confessions of a Parish Priest: An Autobiography.* New York: Simon & Schuster.

Green, James N. 1999. *Beyond Carnival: Male Homosexuality in Twentieth-Century Brazil.* Chicago: University of Chicago Press.

Gregory, Affonso. 1968. "Aspectos socio-religiosos da Igreja na América Latina (1)." *Ponto Homem,* Year 43, No. 3 (July–August), 100–14.

Grings, Dadeus. 1978. "Os seminários na formação sacerdotal." *Teocomunicação,* Year 8, No. 39, 39–40.

Grupo de Leigos Católicos Igreja Nova. 2000. *III Jornada Teológica Dom Helder Camara.* Recife: n.p.

Guerra Sobrinho, Lemuel Dourado. 1991. "A reação neoconservadora na Igreja católica de Pernambuco." MA thesis, Universidade Federal de Pernambuco.

Guerre, René. 1983. "O impulso teológico-pastoral provocado pela ação de Cardijn e da JOC." *Perspectivas Teológico-Pastorais,* Year 2, No. 3, 37–46.

———. 1987. *Espiritualidade do sacerdote diocesano.* São Paulo: Edições Paulinas.

Guerre, René, and Maurice Zinty. 1965. *Padres para o meio operário*. Rio: Agir.

Guglielmelli, Domingos. 1941. "O pároco e o problema do recrutamento sacerdotal." *REB* 1 (December), 745–56.

———. 1944a. "Cultura eclesiástica." *REB* 4 (September), 541–62.

———. 1944b. "A união do clero à luz da doutrina do corpo místico de Cristo." *REB* 4 (March), 1–18.

Guillermoprieto, Alma. 1991. *Samba*. New York: Vintage.

Guimarães, Bernardo. 1967. *O seminarista*. Rio de Janeiro: Edições de Ouro.

Gutiérrez, Gustavo. 1973. *A Theology of Liberation*. Trans. Caridad Inda and John Eagleson. Maryknoll, N.Y.: Orbis.

"Hábito eclesiástico: Consulta nacional em andamento." 1964. *CM*, No. 136 (January), 9–13.

Hagopian, Frances. 1996. *Traditional Politics and Regime Change in Brazil*. Cambridge: Cambridge University Press.

Hall, Stuart, David Held, Ron Hubert, and Kenneth Thompson, eds. 1996. *Modernity: An Introduction to Modern Societies*. Oxford: Blackwell.

Haring, Clarence. 1958. *Empire in Brazil*. Cambridge: Harvard University Press.

Harris, Marvin. 1979. *Cultural Materialism: The Struggle for a Science of Culture*. New York: Random House.

Harris, Thomas A. 1967. *I'm OK, You're OK*. New York: Avon.

Hastenteufel, Zeno. 1987. *Dom Feliciano na Igreja do Rio Grande do Sul*. Porto Alegre: Acadêmica.

Hauck, João Fagundes, Hugo Fragoso, José Oscar Beozzo, Klaus Van Der Grijp, and Benno Brod. 1980. *História da Igreja no Brasil*, Tome II, Vol. 2 of CEHILA, *História Geral da Igreja na América Latina*. Petrópolis: Vozes.

Hebblethwaite, Peter. 1975. *The Runaway Church: Post-Conciliar Growth or Decline*. New York: Seabury.

Hemming, John. 1978. *Red Gold: The Conquest of the Brazilian Indians*. London: Macmillan.

Hennelly, Alfred T., ed. 1993. *Santo Domingo and Beyond: Documents and Commentaries from the Fourth General Conference of Latin American Bishops*. Maryknoll, N.Y.: Orbis.

Hess, David J., and Roberto A. DaMatta, eds. 1995. *The Brazilian Puzzle: Culture on the Borderlands of the Western World*. New York: Columbia University Press.

Hewitt, W. E. 1991. *Basic Christian Communities and Social Change in Brazil*. Lincoln: University of Nebraska Press.

———. 1995. "Religion and the Consolidation of Democracy in Brazil: The Role of the Comunidades Eclesiais de Base." In *Religion and Democracy in Latin America*, 44–58. Ed. William H. Swatos Jr. New Brunswick, N.J.: Transaction.

Hirschmann, Albert O. 1963. *Journeys towards Progress*. New York: Twentieth Century Fund.

A história do Seminário Maior de Viamão. 1979. Porto Alegre, n.p.

"Histórias fascinantes de padres que já não são padres." 2003. *Ultimato* 285 (November–December).

Holston, James. 1989. *The Modernist City: An Anthropological Critique of Brasília.* Chicago: University of Chicago Press.

———. 1999. "Alternative Modernities: Statecraft and Religious Imagination in the Valley of the Dawn." *American Ethnologist* 26:3 (August), 605–31.

Hoornaert, Eduardo. 1974. *Formação do Catolicismo Brasileiro, 1500–1800.* Petrópolis: Vozes.

———. 1991. "A relação entre a formação ministerial e o ideal monástico na tradição católica." Paper delivered at the CEHILA symposium entitled "Formação ministerial nas igrejas e sociedade brasileira." São Paulo (September 11).

———. 1992. *A novidade dos padres casados.* Brasília: Serviço de Editoração Rumos.

Hoornaert, Eduardo, Riolando Azzi, Klaus Van Der Grijp, and Benno Brod. 1977. *História da Igreja no Brasil. Primeira Epoca,* Tome II, Vol. 1 of CEHILA, *História Geral da Igreja na América Latina.* Petrópolis: Vozes.

Houtzager, Peter P. 1998. "State and Unions in the Transformation of the Brazilian Countryside, 1974–1979." *LARR* 33:2, 103–42.

Ibrahim, Cesar Mussi. 1992. "As clínicas sociais psicanalíticas do Rio de Janeiro: Um estudo sobre a possibilidade da expansão social da psicanálise." MA thesis, Pontifícia Universidade Católica do Rio de Janeiro.

"Igreja do futuro sem padres?" 1968. *Pergunte e Responderemos* 101, 195–205.

"A Igreja e a opção pelos pobres." 1982. *Perspectivas Teológico-Pastorais,* Year 1, No. 1 (entire issue).

Illich, Ivan. 1967. "The Seamy Side of Charity." *America* 116:3 (January 21), 88–91.

"Inaugurado o Seminário do Nordeste." 1965. *OS,* Year 40, No. 204 (July–August), 263–64.

"Inquérito entre leigos sobre a situação do padre." 1969. *REB* 29 (September), 636–44.

"O Instituto Central de Filosofia e Teologia de Belo Horizonte visto de dentro." 1969. *SEDOC* 12 (June), 1619–47.

"Instituto de ciências sociais especializado para sacerdotes." 1960. *REB* 20 (June), 501–2.

Instituto de Estudos da Religião [ISER]. 1990. "Estação de seca na Igreja." *Comunicações do ISER,* Year 9, No. 39 (entire issue).

"Instituto de Filosofia e Teologia." 1966. *Revista da CRB,* Year 12, No. 127 (January), 59–60.

"Instituto Filosófico-Teológico do Paraná." 1967. *REB* 27 (June), 484–85.

Instituto de Teologia do Recife and Comissão de Justiça e Paz de Olinda e Recife. 1989. *Faz escuro mas eu canto . . . risco e esperança no caminho da Igreja no Nordeste.* Recife: ITER; Comissão de Justiça e Paz de Olinda e Recife.

Investigative Staff of the *Boston Globe.* 2002. *Betrayal: The Crisis in the Catholic Church.* Boston: Little, Brown.

Iokoi, Zilda Márcia Grícoli. 1996. *Igreja e camponeses: Teologia da libertação e movimentos sociais no campo, Brazil e Peru, 1964–1986.* São Paulo: Editora HUCITEC.

Ireland, Rowan. 1991. *Kingdoms Come: Religion and Politics in Brazil.* Pittsburgh: University of Pittsburgh Press.

"Irineu vai contar o que foi a USMAS volante." 1964. *OS,* Year 39, No. 1 (March–April), 78–86.

"Os irmãos se encontram." 1958. *OS,* Year 33, No. 1 (March-April), 96–100.

Ivereigh, Austen. 2000. "Introduction: The Politics of Religion in an Age of Revival." In *The Politics of Religion in an Age of Revival,* 1–21. Ed. Austen Ivereigh. London: Institute of Latin American Studies.

———, ed. 2000. *The Politics of Religion in an Age of Revival.* London: Institute of Latin American Studies.

Jacob, Cesar Romero, Dora Rodrigues Hees, Philippe Waniez, and Violette Brustlein. 2003. *Atlas da filiação religiosa e indicadores sociais no Brasil.* Rio de Janeiro: Editora PUC-Rio; São Paulo: Loyola.

James, Carlos, Miguel Chalub, and Chaim Samuel Katz. 1992. *Religião e psicanálise: Aliança ou conflito?* Atualidade em Debate, Caderno 18. Rio de Janeiro: Centro João XXIII.

Jarschel, Heidi. 1991. "Aborto: Entre a fome e o desejo." *Tempo e Presença* 256 (March–April), 37–39.

Jedin, Hubert. 1967. "Trent, Council of." In *New Catholic Encyclopedia* 14:271–78. New York: McGraw-Hill.

Jenkins, Philip. 2003. *The New Anti-Catholicism: The Last Acceptable Prejudice.* Oxford: Oxford University Press.

"A JOC e o clero." 1950. *Revista do Assistente Eclesiástico,* Year 3, No. 30 (March), 46–53.

John XXIII. 1959. "Discurso de S. S. o Papa João XXIII ao Conselho Episcopal Latino-Americano." *REB* 19 (March), 176–82.

———. 1962. "Carta de João XXIII ao episcopado da América Latina." *REB* 22 (June), 461–63.

———. 1963. "Carta ao episcopado canadense em favor da América Latina." *REB* 23 (June), 482–84.

John Paul II. 1992. *I Will Give You Shepherds* [*Pastores Dabo Vobis*]. Washington, D.C.: United States Catholic Conference.

———. 1999. *The Church in America.* Washington, D.C.: United States Catholic Conference.

Johnson, Randal. 1987. "Tupy or Not Tupy: Cannibalism and Nationalism in Contemporary Brazilian Literature and Culture." In *On Modern Latin American Literature,* 41–59. Ed. John King. New York: Noonday.

Jones, E. Michael. 1999. "Carl Rogers and the IHM Nuns: Sensitivity Training, Psychological Warfare, and the 'Catholic Problem.'" *Culture Wars* (October). Online: http://www.culturewars.com/CultureWars/1999/rogers.html.

Júlio Maria. 1950. *O Catolicismo no Brasil (Memória histórica)*. Rio de Janeiro: Agir.

Justo, Henrique. 1963. "Papel da psicologia nas comunidades religiosas." *Revista da CRB*, Year 9, No. 94 (April), 207–13.

"Juventude em debate: Devem os jovens participar na política?" 1968. *Mundo Jovem*, Year 6, No. 31 (November–December), 18–19.

Kehl, Maria Rita, and Paulo Vannuchi. 1997. "Madre Cristina." In *Rememória: Entrevistas sobre o Brasil do século XX*, 153–71. Ed. Ricardo de Azevedo and Flamarion Maués. São Paulo: Editora Fundação Perseu Abramo.

Kemper, Jochen. 1988. "Subsídios psicanalíticos para uma teologia da libertação." In *Hélio Pellegrino. A-Deus*, 165–79. Ed. João Carlos Moura. Petrópolis: Vozes.

Keogh, Dermot, ed. 1990. *Church and Politics in Latin America*. New York: St. Martin's.

Keppe, Norberto R. 1968. *Sexo e religião (estudo psicanalítico)*. São Paulo: Livrex.

Kieser, Ellwood E. 1991. *Hollywood Priest: A Spiritual Struggle*. New York: Doubleday.

Kingstone, Peter R., and Timothy J. Power. 2000. *Democratic Brazil: Actors, Institutions, and Processes*. Pittsburgh: University of Pittsburgh Press.

Kittleson, Roger Alan. 1997. "The Problem of the People: Popular Classes and the Social Construction of Ideas in Porto Alegre, Brazil, 1846–1893." PhD dissertation, University of Wisconsin.

Kloppenburg, Dom Boaventura. 1987. *Compêndio do Vaticano II*. Petrópolis: Vozes.

Knowles, David, and Dimitry Obolensky. 1974. *Nova história da Igreja. II. A Idade Média*. Trans. João Fagundes Hauck. Petrópolis: Vozes.

Koop, Dom Pedro Paulo. 1968. "Comunidade de base e novo ministério sacerdotal." *SEDOC*, special edition (September), 407–10.

Kövecses, Géza. 1954. "Formação do clero adaptada à época." *REB* 14 (June), 274–84.

———. 1957. "Sinais de uma época mais nova (um movimento dos seminaristas)." *OS*, Year 32, No. 1 (March-April), 71–77.

———. 1962. "O descobrimento progressivo da consciência moral." *Veritas*, Year 7, No. 3 (September), 248–74.

———. 1963. "Ontogênese da consciência moral." *Veritas*, Year 7, No. 1 (March), 104–33.

———. 1967. "Comunicações." Unpublished manuscript.

Kracke, Waud. 2000. "Some Anthropological Observations on Psychoanalysis in Brazil: 1999." Paper presented at Les États Generaux de la Psychanlyse, Paris (July 5–8). (Also published in Portuguese online: http://www.estadosgerais.org/gruposvirtuais/kracke-algumas_observacoes.shtml#.)

Kramer, Eric W. 2001. "Possessing Faith: Commodification, Religious Subjectivity, and Collectivity in a Brazilian Neo-Pentecostal Church." PhD dissertation, University of Chicago.

Kristof, Nicholas D. 2003. "Believe It, or Not." *New York Times*. August 15. Online edition.

Kselman, Thomas A. 1983. *Miracles and Prophecies in Nineteenth-Century France*. New Brunswick, N.J.: Rutgers University Press.

————. 1986. "Ambivalence and Assumption in the Concept of Popular Religion." In *Religion and Political Conflict in Latin America*, 27–41. Ed. Daniel H. Levine. Chapel Hill: University of North Carolina Press.

Kselman, Thomas A., and Steven Avella. 1986. "Marian Piety and the Cold War in the United States." *The Catholic Historical Review*, 72:3 (July), 403–24.

Kubitschek, Juscelino. 1979. "Juscelino Kubitschek (depoimento, 1976)." FGV/CPDOC-História Oral, E-19.

Lacerda, Milton Paulo de. 1988. *Lições de Incoerência. Amor, sexo e . . . vida de padre*. Petrópolis: Vozes.

Lacombe, Américo Jacobina. 1986. "A Igreja no Brasil colonial." In *História geral da civilização brasileira. I. A época colonial. 2. Administração, economia e sociedade*. Ed. Sérgio Buarque de Holanda. São Paulo: DIFEL.

Lacroix, Pascoal. 1935. *Solução do problema sexual*. Petrópolis: Vozes.

————. 1936. *O mais urgente problema do Brasil, o problema sacerdotal e sua solução*. Petrópolis: Vozes.

Langer, Erick, and Robert H. Jackson, eds. 1995. *The New Latin American Mission History*. Lincoln: University of Nebraska Press.

Langland, Victoria. "Geração Muda? University Student Politics after Institutional Act No. Five." Paper delivered at the international symposium "The Cultures of Dictatorship: Historical Reflections on the Brazilian Golpe of 1964," University of Maryland, October 14–16, 2004.

Lapenta, Victor Hugo Silveira. 1990. "Uma pesquisa sobre a afetividade dos religiosos do Brasil." *Convergência*, Year 15, No. 229 (January/February), 31–47.

Lapenta, Victor Hugo Silveira, Manuel Maria Rodriguez Losada, and Dalton Barros de Almeida. 1990. *Afetividade e vida religiosa*. Rio de Janeiro: CRB.

Lathan, Michael E. 2000. *Modernization as Ideology: American Social Science and "Nation Building" in the Kennedy Era*. Chapel Hill: University of North Carolina Press.

Latourelle, René. 1988. "Introduction." In *Vatican II: Assessment and Perspectives: Twenty-Five Years After (1962–1987)*, 1:xv–xix. Ed. René Latourelle. New York: Paulist.

————, ed. 1988. *Vatican II: Assessment and Perspectives: Twenty-Five Years After (1962–1987)*. New York: Paulist.

Leal, Victor Nunes. 1977 [1949]. *Coronelismo: The Municipality and Representative Government in Brazil*. Trans. June Henfrey. Cambridge: Cambridge University Press.

Lee, James Michael, and Louis J. Putz. 1965. *Seminary Education in a Time of Change*. Notre Dame, Ind: Fides.

Leite, Serafim. 1938–1950. *História da Companhia de Jesus no Brasil*. 10 vols. Lisbon: Livraria Portugalia.

Lemercier, Gregoire. 1968. "Un monasterio benedictino en psicoanálisis." In *Cuernavaca: fuentes para el estudio de una diócesis*. Ed. Baltazar López. CIDOC Dossier No. 31, vol. 2, 5/36–5/39. Cuernavaca: CIDOC.

Lenharo, Alcir. 1989. *Sacralização da política.* 2nd edition. Campinas: Editora da UNI-CAMP/Papirus.

Lenz, Matias Martinho. 1992. "Festas religiosas, CEBs e mudanças." In *Catolicismo: Unidade religiosa e pluralismo cultural,* 121–65. Ed. Pierre Sanchis. São Paulo: Edições Loyola.

Leoni, Brigitte Hersant. 1997. *Fernando Henrique Cardoso: O Brasil do possível.* Trans. Dora Rocha. Rio de Janeiro: Editora Nova Fronteira.

Lernoux, Penny. 1982. *Cry of the People: The Struggle for Human Rights in Latin America—The Catholic Church in Conflict with U.S. Policy.* New York: Penguin.

———. 1989. *People of God: The Struggle for World Catholicism.* New York: Viking.

Léry, Jean de. 1990. *History of a Voyage to the Land of Brazil, Otherwise Called America.* Trans. Janet Whatley. Berkeley: University of California Press.

Lesser, Jeffrey. 1999. *Negotiating National Identity: Immigrants, Minorities, and the Struggle for Ethnicity in Brazil.* Durham, N.C.: Duke University Press.

Levine, Daniel. 1992. *Popular Voices in Latin American Catholicism.* Princeton: Princeton University Press.

———, ed. 1986. *Religion and Political Conflict in Latin America.* Chapel Hill: University of North Carolina Press.

Levine, Robert M. 1991. "The Millenarian and Messianic Legacy." *LBR* 28:1 (Summer), 1–4.

———. 1992. *Vale of Tears: Revisiting the Canudos Massacre in Northeastern Brazil, 1893–1897.* Berkeley: University of California Press.

———. 2001. "Michel de Certeau and Latin America." In *The Other Mirror: Grand Theory through the Lens of Latin America,* 309–28. Ed. Miguel Angel Centeno and Fernando López-Alves. Princeton: Princeton University Press.

Lewin, Linda. 1987. *Politics and Parentela in Paraíba: A Case Study of Family-Based Oligarchy in Brazil.* Princeton: Princeton University Press.

———. 2003a. *Surprise Heirs.* Vol. 1: *Illegitimacy, Patrimonial Rights, and Legal Nationalism in Luso-Brazilian Inheritance, 1750–1821.* Stanford: Stanford University Press.

———. 2003b. *Surprise Heirs.* Vol. 2: *Illegitimacy, Inheritance Rights, and Public Power in the Formation of Imperial Brazil, 1822–1889.* Stanford: Stanford University Press.

Lhoëst, Bernadete. 1969. *O apostolado das religiosas.* Cuernavaca: CIDOC.

Libânio, João Batista. 1969. *Estudos teológicos.* São Paulo: Edições Loyola.

———. 1980. *Formação da consciência crítica. 2. Subsídios sócio-analíticos.* 2nd edition. Petrópolis: Vozes.

———. 1984. *A volta à grande disciplina.* São Paulo: Edições Paulinas.

———. 1987. *Teologia da libertação.* São Paulo: Edições Loyola.

———. 1992. "VIII encontro intereclesial das CEBs (eventos no evento)." *REB* 52 (December), 789–800.

Lies, William M. 2004. "Caught between Shepherd, Sheep and Wolves: Assessing the Preaching Tenor of Chilean Catholic Clergy." Paper delivered at the Twenty-fifth

International Congress of the Latin American Studies Association, Las Vegas, Nevada, October 9–11, 2004.

Lima, Alceu Amoroso. 1936. *Indicações políticas: Da revolução à constituição.* Rio de Janeiro: Civilisação Brasileira.

Lima, Délcio Monteiro de. 1987. *Os demônios descem do norte.* Rio de Janeiro: Francisco Alves.

Lima, Haroldo, and Aldo Arantes. 1984. *História da Ação Popular.* São Paulo: Editora Alfa-Omega.

Lima, Lana Lage da Gama. 1990. "A confissão pelo avesso: O crime de solicitação no Brasil colonial." PhD dissertation, Universidade de São Paulo.

Lins, Letícia. 2000a. "Cimi denunciará governo brasileiro à OEA por violência contra índios." *O Globo* (April 25). Online edition.

———. 2000b. "Manifestação Brasil: Outros 500 quer reunir 40 mil em marcha de protesto." *O Globo* (April 22). Online edition.

O livro do seminarista. 1959. São Paulo: Ed. Ave Maria Ltda.

Locks, José. 1972. "A Crise dos Seminários." *REB* 32 (December), 937.

Lockwood, Robert P., ed. 2000. *Anti-Catholicism in American Culture.* Huntington, Ind.: Our Sunday Visitor.

Loewenberg, Peter. 1983. *Decoding the Past: The Psychohistorical Approach.* New York: Knopf.

Londoño, Patrcia. 2000. "The Politics of Religion in a Modernising Society: Antioquía (Colombia), 1850–1910." In *The Politics of Religion in an Age of Revival,* 141–65. Ed. Austen Ivereigh. London: Institute of Latin American Studies.

Long, Kevin G. 1988. *Anti-Catholicism in the 1980s.* Milwaukee: Catholic League for Religious and Civil Rights.

López, Baltazar, ed. 1968. *Cuernavaca: Fuentes para el estudio de una diócesis.* CIDOC Dossier No. 31. Cuernavaca: CIDOC.

López Lara, Abraham. 1969. "Razón de Lemercier: Inconsistencia clerical." In *México: "Entredicho" del Vaticano a CIDOC, 1966–1969.* Ed. Tarcisio Ocampo V. CIDOC Dossier No. 37, 4/201–4/202. Cuernavaca: CIDOC.

Lorscheider, Dom Aloísio. 1970. "Celibato Sacerdotal." *CM,* Nos. 210–11 (March–April), 37.

Lorscheiter, Dom Ivo. 1968. "Bíblia e desenvolvimento." *Ponto Homem,* Year 43, No. 3 (July–August), 41–52.

Love, Joseph L. 1971. *Rio Grande do Sul and Brazilian Regionalism, 1882–1930.* Stanford: Stanford University Press.

———. 1980. *São Paulo in the Brazilian Federation, 1889–1937.* Stanford: Stanford University Press.

Lowden, Pamela. 1996. *Moral Opposition to Authoritarian Rule in Chile, 1973–90.* Basingstoke: Macmillan.

Löwy, Michael. 1996. "A teologia da libertação acabou?" *Teoria e Debate* 31 (April-May-June), 75–77.

"D. Lucas quer a CVRD para brasileiros." 1997. *Jornal do Brasil* (March 21), 20.

Lúcia, Nara, Fabíola Tavares, and Juracy Andrade. 1998. "O pastor sem rebanho." *Jornal do Commercio* (December 6), "Cidade," 1–4.

Luhrmann, T. M. 2000. *Of Two Minds: The Growing Disorder in American Psychiatry.* New York: Knopf.

Lustosa, Oscar de Figueiredo. 1977. *Reformistas na Igreja do Brasil-Império.* São Paulo: Universidade de São Paulo.

———. 1982. *Política e Igreja: O partido católico no Brasil, mito ou realidade?* São Paulo: Edições Paulinas.

———. 1983. *Igreja e política no Brasil.* São Paulo: Edições Paulinas/CEPEHIB.

———. 1985. *Reformismo da Igreja no Brasil.* São Paulo: Loyola.

———. 1991. *A Igreja Católica no Brasil República.* São Paulo: Edições Paulinas.

Lynch, John. 1972. "Crítica da Lei do Celibato na Igreja Católica." *Concilium* 8:1032–47.

———. 1986. "The Catholic Church in Latin America, 1830–1930." In *The Cambridge History of Latin America,* 4:527–95. Ed. Leslie Bethell. Cambridge: Cambridge University Press.

Macaulay, Neill. 1986. *Dom Pedro: The Struggle for Liberty in Brazil and Portugal, 1798–1934.* Durham, N.C.: Duke University Press.

Macedo, Carmen Cinira. 1992a. "Catolicismo e sexualidade." In *Catolicismo: Cotidiano e movimentos,* 81–88. Ed. Pierre Sanchis. São Paulo: Edições Paulinas.

———. 1992b. "Todo dia é dia." In *Catolicismo: Cotidiano e movimentos,* 209–39. Ed. Pierre Sanchis. São Paulo: Edições Paulinas.

Machado, Maria das Dores Campos. 1996. *Carismáticos e pentecostais: Adesão religiosa na esfera familiar.* Campinas: Editora Autores Associados.

———. N.d. "Da teologia da prosperidade à participação no debate sobre a campanha de planejamento familiar—a Igreja Universal do Reino de Deus em perspectiva." Rio de Janeiro.

Machado, Paulo Pinheiro. 2001. "Um estudo sobre as origens e a formação política das lideranças sertanejas do Contestado, 1912–1916." PhD dissertation, Universidade Estadual de Campinas.

Machado, Vitor Barletta. 2001. "Agentes religiosos, motivação política: A influência da Igreja Católica na organização do movimento dos trabalhadores rurais sem-terra do Assentamento II de Sumaré no Estado de São Paulo." MA thesis, Universidade de São Paulo.

Mainwaring, Scott. 1986. *The Catholic Church and Politics in Brazil, 1916–1985.* Stanford: Stanford University Press.

———. 1995. "Brazil: Weak Parties, Feckless Democracy." In *Building Democratic Institutions: Party Systems in Latin America,* 354–98. Ed. Scott Mainwaring and Timothy R. Scully. Stanford: Stanford University Press,.

Mainwaring, Scott, and Paulo Krischke. 1986. *A Igreja nas bases em tempos de transição.* Porto Alegre: L&PM Editores.

Mainwaring, Scott, and Alexander Wilde. 1989. *The Progressive Church in Latin America.* Notre Dame, Ind.: University of Notre Dame Press.

Manenti, Alessandro. 1983. "Para um novo projeto de formação." *Convergência* 165 (September), 404–12.

"Manifesto de Leigos, Religiosos e Padres de Nova Friburgo." 1968. *SEDOC,* special edition (September), 289–394.

Maram, Sheldon. 1977. "Labor and Left in Brazil, 1890–1921: A Movement Aborted." *HAHR* 57:2 (May), 254–72.

Marchant, Alexander. 1942. *From Barter to Slavery: The Economic Relations of Portuguese and Indians in the Settlement of Brazil, 1500–1580.* Baltimore: Johns Hopkins University Press.

Marega, Marisa. 1999. *O livro de Madre Teresa de Jesus: Petrópolis, Juiz de Fora, Itaguaí.* São Paulo: Musa Editora.

Margerie, Bertrand de. 1962a. "A coleção 'Seminários.'" *Revista da CRB,* Year 8, No. 88 (October), 663–68.

———. 1962b. "Luzes antigas e novas sobre o celibato." *REB* 22 (September), 616–37.

Maria, Joaquim Parron. 2002. "Igreja e escândalos sexuais: Elementos éticos para uma reflexão." *REB* 62 (July), 656–64.

Maria, José. 1943. "A missão do sacerdote à luz da missão do verbo incarnado." *REB* 3 (June), 273–85.

"Mariana, um caso liquidado?" 1966. *São Vicente,* Year 36, No. 5., 18.

Mariano, Ricardo. 1995. "Neopentecostalismo: Os pentecostais estão mudando." MA thesis, Department of Sociology, Universidade de São Paulo.

Mariano, Dom Severino. 1963. "Seminário . . . uma casa fechada?" *OS,* Year 38, No. 1 (March–April), 14–18.

Marinho, Benedicto. 1941. "Sacerdos alter Christus." *REB* 1 (March–June), 6–11.

Marins, José. 1969. "Pesquisa sobre o clero no Brasil." *REB* 29 (March), 121–38.

Mariz, Cecília. 1994. *Coping with Poverty: Pentecostals and Christian Base Communities in Brazil.* Philadelphia: Temple University Press.

Marmilicz, André. 2002. "O ambiente educativo nos seminários maiores do Brasil: Uma pesquisa." Extract of PhD dissertation, Pontifical Salesian University.

Marsden, George M. 1994. *The Soul of the American University.* New York: Oxford University Press.

———. 1997. *The Outrageous Idea of Christian Scholarship.* New York: Oxford University Press.

Marsden, George M., and Bradley J. Longfield, eds. 1992. *The Secularization of the Academy.* New York: Oxford University Press.

Martin, David. 1990. *Tongues of Fire: The Expansion of Protestantism in Latin America.* Cambridge, Mass.: Blackwell.

————. 1999. "Bear Market for Base Communities: Pentecostalism, Power Shifts, and Competition in Latin American Religion." *Christianity Today* (January/February). Online edition.

Martin, Malachi. 1990. *The Keys of This Blood: The Struggle for World Dominion between Pope John Paul II, Mikhail Gorbachev, and the Capitalist West.* New York: Simon & Schuster.

Martina, Giacomo. 1988. "The Historical Context in Which the Idea of a New Ecumenical Council Was Born." In *Vatican II: Assessment and Perspectives Twenty-Five Years After (1962–1987)*, 1:3–73. Ed. René Latourelle. New York: Paulist.

————. 1992. "As CEBs e a cultura popular." Unpublished paper.

Martins, Heloisa Helena T. de Souza. 1994. *Igreja e movimento operário no ABC, 1954–1975.* São Caetano do Sul: Editora HUCITEC.

Martins Filho, João Roberto. 1987. *Movimento estudantil e ditadura militar.* Campinas: Papirus.

Massarão, Leila Maria. 2002. "Combatendo no espírito: A Renovação Carismática na Igreja Católica (1969–1998)." MA thesis, Universidade Estadual de Campinas.

Mata, Sérgio da. 2002. *Catolicismo popular, espaço e proto-urbanização em Minas Gerais, Brasil: Séculos XVIII-XIX.* Berlin: Wissenschaftlicher Verlag Berlin.

Mattoso, Kátia M. de Queirós. 1982a. "Párocos e vigários em Salvador no século XIX: As múltiplas riquezas do clero secular da capital baiana." *Tempo e Sociedade* 1:1 (January/June), 13–47.

————. 1982b. *Ser escravo no Brasil.* São Paulo: Brasiliense.

————. 1986. *To Be a Slave in Brazil.* Trans. Arthur Goldhammer. New Brunswick, N.J.: Rutgers University Press.

Maués, Raymundo Heraldo. 1987. "A tensão constitutiva do catolicismo: Catolicismo popular e controle eclesiástico." PhD dissertation, Federal University of Rio de Janeiro.

————. 1988. "Impasses da romanização e da teologia da libertação na Amazônia: O choque com a lógica do catolicismo popular." *Ciência e Cultura* 40:11 (November), 1074–79.

————. 1992. "Catolicismo popular e pajelança na região do Salgado: As crenças e as representações." In *Catolicismo: unidade religiosa e pluralismo cultural*, 197–230. Ed. Pierre Sanchis. São Paulo: Edições Loyola.

Mauro, Frédéric. 1991. *O Brasil no tempo de Dom Pedro II (1831–1889).* Trans. Tomás Rosa Bueno. São Paulo: Companhia das Letras.

Maxwell, Kenneth R. 1978. *A devassa da devassa: A Inconfidência Mineira, Brasil-Portugal, 1750–1808.* Rio de Janeiro: Paz e Terra.

Mayer, Dom Antônio de Castro. 1969. "Reflexões e conclusões de padres 'progressistas.'" *SEDOC* 2 (September), 344–46.

Mayrink, José Maria. 2002. *Vida de repórter.* São Paulo: Geração Editorial.

McDonough, Peter. 1981. *Power and Ideology in Brazil.* Princeton: Princeton University Press.

————. 1992. *Men Astutely Trained: A History of the Jesuits in the American Century.* New York: Free Press.

McInerny, Ralph, ed. 1994. *Modernity and Religion.* Notre Dame, Ind.: University of Notre Dame Press.

McNally, Michael J. 1982. *Catholicism in South Florida, 1868–1968.* Gainesville: University Presses of Florida.

Medeiros, Roberto Saboia de. 1941. "Crise na direção espiritual aos moços." *REB* 1 (March–June), 171–76.

Medeiros, Tito de. 1962. "Encontro dos teólogos." *OS*, Year 37, No. 5 (November–December), 30–34.

Medina, C. A. de, and Pedro A. Ribeiro de Oliveira, 1972. *Autoridade e Participação: Um estudo sociológico da Igreja Católica.* Rio de Janeiro: CERIS.

Mendes, Agostinho. 1938. "A Bula Inter Coetera." Thesis, Gregorian University.

Méndez Arceo, Dom Sergio, 1968. "Reflexión del señor obispo de Cuernavaca con todo el pueblo de Dios en su diócesis sobre el monasterio de Nuestra Sra. de la Resurreción." In *Cuernavaca: fuentes para el estudio de una diócesis.* Ed. Baltazar López. CIDOC Dossier No. 31, vol. 1, 4/75. Cuernavaca: CIDOC.

Mendonça, Antônio Gouvêa, and Prócoro Velasques. 1990. *Introdução ao protestantismo no Brasil.* São Paulo: Edições Loyola.

Menezes, Danilo Inácio de. 1963a. "Iniciativa e passivismo." *OS*, Year 38, No. 2 (May–June), 37–58.

————. 1963b. "Iº. encontro regional USMAS II (Sta. Catarina e RGS)." *OS*, Year 38, No. 2 (May–June), 16–18.

Menezes, Danilo Inácio de, Marcel Messier, and Frei Eriberto. 1965. "A primeira reflexão: USMAS 2." *OS*, Year 40, No. 1 (March–April), 78–93.

"Mensagem ao nosso clero." 1958. *REB* 18 (September), 641–44.

Métraux, Alfred. 1979. *A religião dos Tupinambás.* Trans. Estevão Pinto. 2nd edition. São Paulo: Companhia Editora Nacional; Editora da Universidade de São Paulo.

Miceli, Sergio. 1979. *Intelectuais e classe dirigente no Brasil (1920–1945).* São Paulo: DIFEL.

————. 1988. *A elite eclesiástica brasileira.* Rio de Janeiro: Editora Bertrand Brasil.

Miller, James. 1993. *The Passion of Michel Foucault.* New York: Simon & Schuster.

Miller, Martin A. 1985. "Freudian Theory under Bolshevik Rule: The Theoretical Controversy during the 1920s." *Slavic Review* 44:4 (winter), 625–46.

Miller, Maureen C. 2000. "Religion Makes a Difference: Clerical and Lay Cultures in the Courts of Northern Italy, 1000–1300." *American Historical Review* 105:4 (October), 1095–130.

Milpacher, Pio. 2002. "Rumo ao nono encontro nacional dos presbíteros." *REB* 61 (December), 877–92.

"Minas Gerais vive assim." 1962. *OS*, Year 37, No. 4 (September–October), 61–78.

"Ministério sacerdotal." 1971. *SEDOC* 4 (October), 403–15.

Mintz, Sidney. 1985. *Sweetness and Power.* New York: Viking.

Miracapillo, Vito. 1985. *O caso Miracapillo.* Trans. José Duran y Duran. Recife: Nordestal/ Comunicarte.

"Missionários canadenses no estrangeiro." 1967. *REB* 27 (June), 502.

Modras, Ronald. 2004. *Ignatian Humanism: A Dynamic Spirituality for the Twenty-first Century.* Chicago: Loyola.

Mohana, João. 1968. *Padres e bispos auto-analisados.* 2nd edition. Rio de Janeiro: Livraria Agir.

Montero, Paula. 1992a. "O papel das editoras católicas na formação cultural brasileira." In *Catolicismo: Modernidade e tradição,* 219–50. Ed. Pierre Sanchis. São Paulo: Edições Paulinas.

———. 1992b. "Tradição e modernidade: João Paulo II e o problema da cultura." *Revista Brasileira de Ciências Sociais,* Year 7, No. 20 (October), 90–112.

Moraes, Dênis de. 1989. *A esquerda e o golpe de 64.* Rio de Janeiro: Espaço e Tempo.

Moraes Junior, Antônio d'Almeida. 1941. "Torturas do Padre do século XX." *REB* 1 (December), 709–11.

Moreira, Alberto. 1942. "Torturas do padre do século XX: A tortura do catecismo." *REB* 2 (June), 286–89.

Moreira, Alberto. 1995. "Eugen Drewermann e a psicanálise da Igreja clerical." *REB* 55 (June), 395–405.

Morel, Marco. 2000. *Frei Caneca: Entre Marília e a pátria.* Rio de Janeiro: Editora FGV.

Moretto, Nei Paulo. 1972. "Esclarecimento da reitoria do Seminário Maior de Viamão sobre a trágica morte de Valtair Bozan." *O São Paulo* (August 19), 6.

Morlion, Félix. 1952. "Realismo no apostolado de penetração no Brasil." *REB* 12 (March), 1–9.

Mörner, Magnus. 1953. *The Political and Economic Activity of the Jesuits in the La Plata Region.* Stockholm: Library and Institute of Ibero-American Studies.

Moro, Celito. 1997. *A formação presbiteral em comunhão para a comunhão: Perspectivas para as casas de formação sacerdotal.* Aparecida: Editora Santuário.

Morse, Richard, ed. 1965. *The Bandeirantes: The Historical Role of the Brazilian Pathfinders.* New York: Knopf.

Moser, Antônio. 1989. *Integração afetiva e compromisso social na América Latina.* Rio de Janeiro: CRB.

———. 2002. "Igreja: Desafios inusitados. Pedofilia: primeiras reações e interpelações." *REB* 62 (July), 515–47.

Mott, Luiz. 1988. *O sexo proibido: Virgens, gays e escravos nas garras da Inquisição.* Campinas: Papirus.

Motta, Lauro. 2002. "Rumos de um jornal: Uma leitura crítica do jornal *Rumos.*" Fortaleza. Mimeograph.

Motta, Marcus Alexandre. 2000. *Anchieta, dívida de papel.* Rio de Janeiro: FGV Editora.

Motta, Othon. 1950. "Santificação do clero." *REB* 10 (June), 297–303.

Moura, João Carlos, ed. 1988. *Hélio Pellegrino: A-Deus*. Petrópolis: Vozes.

Moura, Sérgio Lobo de, and José Maria Gouvêa de Almeida. 1985. "A Igreja na Primeira República." In *História da Civilização Brasileira. III. O Brasil republicano. 2. Sociedades e instituições (1889–1930)*, 321–42. Ed. Boris Fausto. São Paulo: DIFEL.

Mourão, Paulo Krüger Corrêa. 1971. *O Seminário de Diamantina de 1867 a 1930*. N.p.

Mourão, Vicente Tôrres. 1963. "Pastoral da marca registrada 'Olinda.'" *OS*, Year 38, No. 5 (November–December), 87–99.

Mousinho, Dom Luis. 1950. "A vocação sacerdotal e a família." *REB* 10 (June), 321–32.

"Movimento Pro-União Sacerdotal." 1953. *O Pio Brasileiro* 3:8 (July), 57–59.

"Mudanças no Seminário Provincial do Ceará." 1967. *REB* 27 (March), 193.

Muls, Nair Costa, and Telma de Souza Birchal. 1992. "Campesinato: modernização e catolicismo." In *Catolicismo: Unidade religiosa e pluralismo cultural*, 75–120. Ed. Pierre Sanchis. São Paulo: Edições Loyola.

Muraro, Rose Marie. 1999. *Memórias de uma mulher impossível*. Rio de Janeiro: Editora Rosa dos Tempos.

Myatt, Alan Doyle. 1995. "Religion and Racial Identity in the *Movimento Negro* of the Roman Catholic Church in Brazil." PhD dissertation, Iliff School of Theology and University of Denver.

Myscofski, Carole A. 1988. *When Men Walk Dry: Portuguese Messianism in Brazil*. American Academy of Religion Academy Series 61. Atlanta: Scholars.

———. 1991. "Messianic Themes in Portuguese and Brazilian Literature in the Sixteenth and Seventeenth Centuries." *LBR* 28:1 (summer), 77–94.

Nachman, Robert G. 1977. "Positivism, Modernization, and the Middle Class in Brazil." *HAHR* 57:1 (February), 1–23.

Nagle, Jorge. 1985. "A Educação na Primeira República." In *História geral da civilização brasileira. III. O Brasil republicano. 2. Sociedade e instituições (1889–1930)*, 259–92. Ed. Boris Fausto. São Paulo: DIFEL.

Nagle, Robin. 1997. *Claiming the Virgin: The Broken Promise of Liberation Theology in Brazil*. New York: Routledge.

Nascimento, Elimar Pinheiro do. 1994. "A exclusão social no Brasil: algumas hipóteses de trabalho e quatro sugestões práticas." *Cadernos do CEAS*, 152:57–66.

Nasini, Gino. 2001. *Um espinho na carne: Má conduta e abuso sexual por parte de clérigos da Igreja Católica no Brasil*. Aparecida: Editora Santuário.

"Necrologia." 1964. *REB* 24 (March), 240–41.

Negrão, Lísias Nogueira. 1996. *Entre a cruz e a encruzilhada: Formação do campo umbandista em São Paulo*. São Paulo: Editora da Universidade de São Paulo.

Negromonte, Álvaro. 1959. "A salvação do Brasil depende do clero." *REB* 19 (March), 1–7.

Neumann, Gerson Roberto. 2000. "A Muttersprache (língua materna) na obra de Wilhelm Rotermund e Balduíno Rambo e a construção de uma identidade cultural híbrida no Brasil." MA thesis, Universidade Federal do Rio de Janeiro.

Neumann, Laurício. 1988. "A educação e a imprensa alternativa: A experiência do jornal Mundo Jovem." MA thesis, Pontifícia Universidade Católica do Rio Grande do Sul.

Neves, Guilherme P. D. Pereira das. 1984. "O Seminário de Olinda: Educação, cultura, e política nos tempos modernos." MA thesis, Universidade Federal Fluminense.

Novaes, Regina. 1992. "Uma greve sacramental: A catolicidade no fio da navalha." In *Catolicismo: cotidiano e movimentos,* 241–73. Ed. Pierre Sanchis. São Paulo: Edições Paulinas.

Novais, Fernando. 1975. *Estrutura e dinâmica do sistema colonial.* Lisbon: Livros Horizonte.

Novais, Germano de. 1957. "O movimento por um mundo melhor." *REB* 17 (December), 890–915.

Novak, Michael. 1986. *Will It Liberate? Questions about Liberation Theology.* New York: Paulist.

"Novo título para Lançai as Redes." 1967. *Lançai as Redes,* Year 5, No. 23 (September), 20.

Nugent, David. 2002. "Erasing Race to Make the Nation: The Rise of 'the People' in the Northern Peruvian Andes." In *Locating Capitalism in Time and Space: Global Restructurings, Politics, and Identity,* 137–74. Ed. David Nugent. Stanford: Stanford University Press.

———, ed. 2002. *Locating Capitalism in Time and Space: Global Restructurings, Politics, and Identity.* Stanford: Stanford University Press.

Nunes, Clarice. 1991. "Os jesuítas na educação brasileira: presença polêmica." *PUC Ciência* 6:51–55.

Nunes, Maria José F. Rosado. 1986. "Prática político-religiosa das congregações femininas no Brasil—uma abordagem histórico-social." In *Os religiosos no Brasil: Enfoques históricos,* 188–218. Ed. Riolando Azzi and José Oscar Beozzo. São Paulo: Edições Paulinas.

Ocampo, Tarcisio V., ed. N.d. *México: "Entredicho" del Vaticano a CIDOC, 1966–1969.* CIDOC Dossier No. 37, 4/176–4/178. Cuernavaca: CIDOC.

"A ocupação do clero no Brasil." 1967. *REB* 27 (December), 1013–14.

Oliveira, Alcilene Cavalcante de. 2001. "A ação pastoral dos bispos da diocese de Mariana: Mudanças e permanências (1748–1793)." MA thesis, Universidade Estadual de Campinas.

Oliveira, José Lisboa Moreira de. 2001. "Abuso sexual cometido por padres." *REB* 61 (June), 420–24.

———. 2002. "A candidatura de presbíteros a cargos políticos." *REB* 62 (April), 259–96.

Oliveira, Oscar de. 1937. "Os dízimos eclesiásticos do Brasil nos períodos da Colônia e do Império." Thesis, Gregorian University.

Oliveira, Pedro A. Ribeiro de. 1968a. "O Papel do Padre. Volume I. Pesquisa de Campo." Unpublished manuscript. Rio de Janeiro, CNBB/CERIS.

———. 1968b. "Sumário da pesquisa sobre o clero no Brasil." *REB* 28 (December), 890.

————. 1985. *Religião e dominação de classe: Gênese, estrutura e função do catolicismo romanizado no Brasil.* Petrópolis: Vozes.

————. 1992. "Estruturas de Igreja e conflitos religiosos." In *Catolicismo: Modernidade e tradição,* 41–66. Ed. Pierre Sanchis. São Paulo: Edições Paulinas.

————. 1994. "CEBs: O que são? Quantas são? O que fazem?" *REB* 54 (December), 931–34.

————. 1999. "O catolicismo: Das CEBs à renovação carismática," *REB* 59 (December), 823–35.

————. 2002. "Perfil social e político das lideranças de CEBs no Brasil," *REB* 62 (January), 172–84.

O'Malley, John W. 1993. *The First Jesuits.* Cambridge: Harvard University Press.

O'Meagher, Matthew. 1997. "Before Liberation Theology: Catholicism, Development, and the 'Christian Revolution' in Latin América, 1959–68." *Journal of Iberian and Latin American Studies* 3:2 (December), 55–78.

Oraison, Marc. 1967. *The Celibate Condition and Sex.* Trans. Leonard Mayhew. New York: Sheed & Ward.

————. 1970. *Strange Voyage: The Autobiography of a Non-conformist.* Trans. J. F. Bernard. Garden City, N.Y.: Doubleday.

"Ordenação de homens casados." 1971. *SEDOC* 4 (December), 675–77.

Organização dos Seminários e Institutos Filosófico-Teológicos do Brasil. 1999. *Aplicação das diretrizes básicas da formação presbiteral da Igreja no Brasil.* Brasília: CNBB.

Oro, Ari Pedro. 1994. "O 'expansionismo' religioso brasileiro para os países do Prata." *REB* 54 (December), 875–95.

————. 1996. *Avanço pentecostal e reação católica.* Petrópolis: Vozes.

Ortiz, Carlos. 1941. "A nova ordem na vida paroquial." *REB* 1 (March–June), 393–94.

Ortiz, Renato. 1988. *A moderna tradição brasileira.* São Paulo: Editora Brasiliense.

Ottmann, Goetz Frank. 2002. *Lost for Words? Brazilian Liberationism in the 1990s.* Pittsburgh: University of Pittsburgh Press.

Owensby, Brian. 1999. *Intimate Ironies: Modernity and the Making of Middle-Class Lives in Brazil.* Stanford: Stanford University Press.

Packenham, Robert A. 1992. *The Dependency Movement.* Cambridge: Harvard University Press.

"O padre e os lares proletários." 1951. *Revista do Assistente Eclesiástico,* Year 4, No. 42 (September–October), 67–80.

"O padre, figura deslocada?" 1967. *Pergunte e Responderemos* 87:125–33.

"Padres espanhois para a América Latina." 1962. *REB* 22 (March), 254.

"Padres fora do Ministério." 1975. *REB* 35 (March), 195–96.

"Padres sem castidade," *Ultimato* 277 (July–August 2002) (entire issue). Online edition.

Page, Joseph A. 1972. *The Revolution that Never Was: Northeast Brazil, 1955–1964.* New York: Grossman.

Paiva, Vanilda Pereira. 1980. *Paulo Freire e o nacionalismo-desenvolvimentista.* Rio de Janeiro: Civilização Brasileira and Edições UFC.

———, ed. 1985. *Igreja e questão agrária.* São Paulo: Edições Loyola.

Palácios, Guillermo. 1987. "Campesinato e escravidão: Uma proposta de periodização para a história dos cultivadores pobres livres no nordeste oriental do Brasil. C. 1700–1875." *Dados,* 30:3,325–56.

"'Palavra Viva' na telinha." 1993. *REB* 53 (September), 684–85.

Palazzolo, Jacinto de. 1943. "A vida eucarística identifica o sacerdote com Cristo. Hora santa do clero." *REB* 3 (September), 584–91.

Pang, Eul-Soo. 1974. "The Changing Roles of Priests in the Politics of Northeast Brazil." *The Americas* 30:3 (January), 341–72.

Panzarasa, Valentim. 1948. "Liberdade na Escolha da Vocação." *REB* 8 (March), 139–58.

Parisse, Luciano, and Olinto Pegoraro. 1968. "Os jovens 'anciãos' de amanhã." *Convergência,* No. 1 (January/February), 28–32.

Parker, Phyllis R. 1979. *Brazil and the Quiet Intervention, 1964.* Austin: University of Texas Press.

Pasquier, Eugênio. 2001–2003. *Os primórdios da Congregação da Missão no Brasil e a Companhia das Filhas da Caridade.* 2 vols. Trans. Joaquim Meireles Maia et al. Rio de Janeiro: Província Brasileira da Congregação da Missão and Província das Filhas da Caridade de Belo Horizonte.

Passos, Mauro. 1991. *A classe trabalhadora em Minas Gerais e a Igreja Catolica: A ponta de uma memoria (1900–1930).* São Paulo: Edições Loyola.

Pastoral Collectiva dos Senhores Arcebispos e Bispos das Provincias Ecclesiasticas de S. Sebastião do Rio de Janeiro, Marianna, S. Paulo, Cuyuabá e Porto Alegre. 1911. Rio de Janeiro: Typographia Leuzinger.

Patrick, Maria Bernarda. 1984. "Dom Hélder: Dados biográficos de um pastor, profeta universal." *Perspectivas Teológico-Pastorais,* Year 3, No. 4, 9–21.

Pattnayak, Satya, ed. 1995. *Organized Religion in the Political Transformation of Latin America.* Lanham, Md.: University Press of America.

Paul VI. 1963. "Radiomensagem do papa às mães do Brasil." *REB* 23 (June), 469–70.

———. 1966a. "Mensagem de Paulo VI aos sacerdotes." *REB* 28 (September), 698–99.

———. 1966b. "Sentimentos de incerteza nos padres de hoje." *REB* 26 (March), 171–74.

"Pe. Caramuru fala de JAC." 1962. *OS,* Year 37, No. 3 (July–August), 104–12.

"Pe. Jacques Loew no seminário de Viamão." 1962. *OS,* Year 37, No. 2 (May–June), 104–12.

Pellegrino, Hélio. 1988. *A burrice do demônio.* Rio de Janeiro: Rocco.

Peña, José A., and Fernando García Labordena. 1969. "La iglesia tendrá que renovarse: Lemercier." In *México: "Entredicho" del Vaticano a CIDOC, 1966–1969.* Ed. Tarcisio Ocampo V. CIDOC Dossier No. 37, 4/176–4/178. Cuernavaca: CIDOC.

Perani, Cláudio. 1987. "Novos rumos da pastoral popular." *Cadernos do CEAS* 107 (January–Febuary), 37–46.

Pereira, Anthony. 1997. *The End of the Peasantry: The Rural Labor Movement in Northeast Brazil, 1961–1988.* Pittsburgh: University of Pittsburgh Press.

Pereira, Antônio Aparecido. 1982. "A Igreja e a Censura Política no Brasil." MA thesis, International Center for the Study of Public Opinion.

Pereira, Jayme. 1965. "De como ligar uma ilha a um continente." *OS,* Year 40, No. 1 (March–April), 34–48.

Perestrello, Marialzira. 1988. "Primeiros Encontros com a Psicanálise: Os Precursores no Brasil (1889–1937)." In *Efeito psi: a influência da psicanálise,* 151–81. Ed. Sérvulo A. Figueira. Rio de Janeiro: Campus.

Pérez, Gustavo, Affonso Gregory, and François Lepargneur. 1964. *O Problema Sacerdotal no Brasil.* Rio de Janeiro: CERIS; Bogotá: CIS; Brussels: FERES.

"Perspectiva histórica na formação do seminarista." 1964. *OS,* Year 39, No. 1 (March–April), 6–15.

Perucci, Gadiel. 1978. *A República das usinas: Um estudo da história social e econômica do nordeste, 1889–1930.* Rio de Janeiro: Paz e Terra.

Pessar, Patricia R. 2004. *From Fanatics to Folk: Brazilian Millenarianism and Popular Culture.* Durham, N.C.: Duke University Press.

Pessoa, Francisco Lage. 1988. *O padre do diabo.* São Paulo: EMW Editores.

Petersen, Douglas. 1996. *Not by Might Nor by Power: A Pentecostal Theology of Social Concern in Latin America.* Oxford: Regnum.

Petrone, Maria Tereza Schorer. 1985. "Imigração." In *História geral da civilização brasileira. III. O Brasil republicano. 2. Sociedade e instituições (1889–1930),* 93–133. Ed. Boris Fausto. São Paulo: DIFEL.

Pierucci, Antônio Flávio de Oliveira. 1984. "Democracia, Igreja e voto: O envolvimento dos padres de paróquia de São Paulo nas eleições de 1982." PhD dissertation, Universidade de São Paulo.

———. 1996. "Liberdade de cultos na sociedade de serviços: Em defesa do consumidor religioso." *Novos Estudos CEBRAP* 44 (March), 3–11.

Pierucci, Antônio Flávio de Oliveira, Beatriz Muniz de Souza, and Candido Procópio Ferreira de Camargo. 1986. "Igreja católica: 1945–1970." In *Historia geral da civilização brasileira, tomo III, O Brasil republicano, Vol. 4, Economia e cultura (1930–1964),* 343–80. Ed. Boris Fausto. São Paulo: DIFEL.

Pierucci, Antônio Flávio de Oliveira, and Reginaldo Prandi. 1996. "Religiões e voto: A eleição presidencial de 1994." In *A realidade social das religiões no Brasil: Religião, sociedade e política,* 211–38. Ed. Antônio Flávio de Oliveira Pierucci and Reginaldo Prandi. São Paulo: Editora HUCITEC.

———, eds. 1996. *A realidade social das religiões no Brasil: Religião, sociedade e política.* São Paulo: Editora HUCITEC.

Piletti, Nelson, and Walter Praxedes. 1997. *Dom Hélder Câmara: Entre o poder e a profecia.* São Paulo: Editora Ática.

Pinheiro, Ernanne. 1984. "Dom Hélder Câmara, como arcebispo de Olinda e Recife." *Perspectivas Teológico-Pastorais,* Year 3, No. 4, 46–55.

———, ed. 1993. *Santo Domingo: Uma leitura pastoral.* São Paulo: Edições Paulinas.

Pires, Heliodoro. 1950. "Professores de teologia no Brasil colonial." *REB* 10 (June), 303–13.

Pius XII. 1957. "Carta de Pio XII sobre o sacerdote, homem de deus e da Igreja." *REB* 17 (June), 468–70.

———. 1958a. "Exortação de Pio XII ao Colégio Pio-Brasileiro." *REB* 18 (September), 809–11.

———. 1958b. "Exortação de Pio XII aos reitores dos seminários maiores da América Latina." *REB* 18 (December), 1090–93.

Pizzardo, Cardinal J., and Dino Staffa. 1959. "Carta da S.C. dos Seminários sobre a formação dos sacerdotes." *REB* 19 (September), 711–16.

Plé, Robert-Albert. 1974. "Mudança da Igreja em relação à psicanálise." *Concilium* 9:1200–204.

Plotkin, Mariano Ben. 2001. *Freud in the Pampas: The Emergence and Development of a Psychoanalytic Culture in Argentina.* Stanford: Stanford University Press.

———. 2003. *Mañana es San Perón: A Cultural History of Perón's Argentina.* Trans. Keith Zahniser. Wilmington, Del.: Scholarly Resources.

Poerner, Artur José. 1979. *O poder jovem.* 2nd edition. Rio de Janeiro: Civilização Brasileira. .

Poletto, Ivo. 1995. "Desenvolvimento social: o bem-estar como prioridade absoluta." *REB* 55 (March), 161–66.

Ponte, Paulo Eduardo Andrade. 1967. "Celibato sacerdotal e lei do celibato." *REB* 27 (September), 545–69.

Pope, Clara. 1985. "Human Rights and the Catholic Church in Brazil, 1970–1983." *Journal of Church and State* 27:3 (autumn), 429–52.

"Por que mais um ano?" 1967. *OS,* Year 42, No. 212 (March–April), 46–52.

Prado Júnior, Caio. 1967. *The Colonial Background of Modern Brazil.* Trans. Suzette Macedo. Berkeley: University of California Press.

Prandi, Reginaldo. 1996. "Religião paga, conversão e serviço." *Novos Estudos CEBRAP* 45 (July), 65–77.

Prandi, Reginaldo, and André Ricardo de Souza. 1996. "A carismática despolitização da Igreja Católica." In *A realidade social das religiões no Brasil: Religião, sociedade e política,* 59–91. Ed. Antônio Flávio de Oliveira Pierucci and Reginaldo Prandi. São Paulo: Editora HUCITEC.

"Preocupações que afligem a consciência de padres do Brasil." 1967. *REB* 27 (December), 1014–16.

Pressburger, Miguel, and Maria Tereza de Araújo. 1989. "A conjuntura ecclesial." *Cadernos do CEAS* 124 (November–December), 42–55.

Prien, Hans-Jürgen. 1985. *La historia del cristianismo en América Latina.* Salamanca: Ediciones Sígueme; São Leopoldo: Editora Sinodal.

"O problema sacerdotal no Brasil." 1943. *REB* 3 (March), 232–33.

Promper, Werner. 1965. *Priesternot in Lateinamerika.* Louvain: Latein-Amerika-Kolleg der Katholischen Universität.

"A pronúncia romana do latim é ardentemente desejada pelo Santo Padre." 1931. *OS,* Year 5, Nos. 5 and 6 (October–November), 144–45.

"Psicanálise e vida religiosa." 1966a. *REB* 26 (June), 460–63.

"Psicanálise e vida religiosa." 1966b. *Revista da CRB* 137 (November), 689–92.

"Quase 100 padres para a América." 1961. *REB* 21 (September), 798.

Queiroga, Gervásio Fernandes de. 1977. *Conferência Nacional dos Bispos do Brasil: Comunhão e corresponsabilidade.* São Paulo: Edições Paulinas.

Queiroz, Maria Isaura Pereira de. 1973. *O campesinato brasileiro.* Petrópolis: Vozes.

"O que pensam de nós padres." 1957. *REB* 17 (March), 107–11.

Quintas, Amaro. 1985. "A agitação republicana no Nordeste." In *História geral da civilização brasileira. II. O Brasil Monárquico. 1. O processo de emancipação,* 207–37. Ed. Sérgio Buarque de Holanda. São Paulo: DIFEL.

Radrizzani, Juan F. 1972. "O celibato sacerdotal na América Latina." *Concilium* 8:1108–13.

Rahner, Karl. 1959. *Free Speech in the Church.* New York: Sheed & Ward.

"Recrutamento de religiosos entre o elemento de cor." 1960. *REB* 20 (December), 1023.

"A redação por dentro." 1956. *OS,* Year 31, No. 5 (November–December), 278–80.

"Reflexão da Comissão Representativa e da Comissão Nacional do Clero." 1971. *SEDOC* 4 (October), 416–22.

"A regional do Recife." 1972. *Convergência,* No. 44 (April), 54–58.

"Relatório." 1968. *Ponto Homem,* Year 43, No. 3 (July–August), 115–28.

"Relatório da revista 'O Seminário.'" 1963. *OS,* Year 38, No. 4 (September–October), 5–8.

"Resposta do Episcopado aos Sacerdotes." 1968. *SEDOC,* special edition (September), 404.

"Resultado da Votação do Episcopado Sobre o Tema 'Presbíteros.'" 1969. *SEDOC* 2 (October), 469–78.

"Resultado dos Grupos de Estudo sobre Sacerdócio Ministerial." 1971. *CM* 227 (August), 104–14.

Ribeiro, Ivete, and Ana Clara Torres Ribeiro. 1994. *Família e desafios na sociedade brasileira: Valores como um ângulo de análise.* Rio de Janeiro: Centro João XXIII.

Ribeiro, Jorge Ponciano Ribeiro, et al. 1990. *Padres casados: Depoimento e pesquisa.* Petrópolis: Vozes.

Ribeiro, Lúcia. 1994. "A experiência do aborto entre as mulheres católicas." *Cadernos do CEAS* 153 (September-October), 70–76.

———. 2001. *Sexualidade e reprodução: O que os padres dizem e o que deixam de dizer.* Petrópolis: Vozes.

Ribeiro Júnior, José. 1976. *Colonização e monopólio no nordeste brasileiro: A Companhia Geral de Pernambuco e Paraíba (1759–1780).* São Paulo: HUCITEC.

Ricci, Magda. 2001. *Assombrações de um padre regente: Diogo Antônio Feijó (1784–1843).* Campinas: Editora da Unicamp.

Ridenti, Marcelo. 2000. *Em busca do povo brasileiro: Artistas da revolução, do CPC à era da tv*. Rio de Janeiro: Editora Record.

Rieff, Philip. 1987. *The Triumph of the Therapeutic: Uses of Faith after Freud*. Chicago: University of Chicago Press.

Riley, Patrick, and Russell Shaw, eds. 1993. *Anti-Catholicism in the Media*. Huntington, Ind.: Our Sunday Visitor.

Ritter, Affonso, 1968. "Pílulas para os subdesenvolvidos." *Ponto Homem*, Year 43, No. 5 (November–December), 11–27.

Robles, Orivaldo. 1962. "Jocistas no seminário de Curitiba." *OS*, Year 37, No. 1 (March– April), 84–89, 94–95.

————. 1963. "Problema instalado." *OS*, Year 38, No. 3 (July–August), 82–84.

Rocha, Zildo Barbosa. 1972. "Anotações à margem das lembranças: Ensaio auto-interpretativo." Unpublished manuscript.

————, ed. 2000. *Helder, o Dom: Uma vida que marcou os rumos da Igreja no Brasil*. 3rd edition. Petrópolis: Vozes.

Roche, Maurice A. 1964. *St. Vincent de Paul and the Formation of Clerics*. Studia Friburgensia 39. Fribourg, Switzerland: University Press.

Rodrigues, Sérgio Henrique da Costa. 2004. "Tensão e diálogo: Relações diplomáticas entre a ditadura brasileira e o vaticano (1964–1985)." Paper presented at the conference "Seminário ditadura militar e resistência no Brasil," Rio de Janeiro, March 22–26, 2004.

Rolim, Francisco Cartaxo. 1985. *Pentecostais no Brasil: Uma interpretação sócio-religiosa*. Petrópolis: Vozes.

————. 1992. "Teologia da libertação no Brasil 1980–1986." In *Catolicismo: Cotidiano e movimentos*, 9–79. Ed. Pierre Sanchis. São Paulo: Edições Paulinas.

————. 1994. *Pentecostalismo: Brasil e América Latina*. Petrópolis: Vozes.

Romanelli, Otaíza Oliveira. 1988. *História da educação no Brasil*. Petrópolis: Vozes.

Romano, Roberto. 1979. *Brasil: Igreja contra estado*. São Paulo: Kairós.

Rossetti, Stephen J. 1990. "Introduction." In *Slayer of the Soul: Child Sexual Abuse and the Catholic Church*, 1–8. Ed. Stephen J. Rossetti. Mystic, Conn.: Twenty-Third.

————. 1996. *A Tragic Grace: The Catholic Church and Child Sexual Abuse*. Collegeville, Minn.: Liturgical.

————, ed. 1990. *Slayer of the Soul: Child Sexual Abuse and the Catholic Church*. Mystic, Conn.: Twenty-Third.

Rossi, Agnelo. 1951. "Dez anos da Revista Eclesiástica Brasileira." *REB* 11 (June), 225–31.

Roudinesco, Elisabeth. 1990. *Jacques Lacan & Co.: A History of Psychoanalysis in France, 1925–1985*. Trans. Jeffrey Mehlman. Chicago: University of Chicago Press.

Rout Jr., Leslie B. 1972. "The 'Black Bishops' Mystery." *LBR* 9:1 (summer), 86–92.

Rozestraten, Ricardo. 1960. "Utilidade e necessidade de uma instituição psico-pedagógica da vocação religiosa ligada à CRB." *Revista da CRB*, Year 6, No. 63 (September), 527–35.

———. 1962. "Os critérios psicológicos para a vocação sacerdotal e religiosa." *REB* 22 (March), 65–74.

Rubert, Arlindo. 1981. *A Igreja no Brasil. Vol. 1: Origem e desenvolvimento.* Santa Maria, Rio Grande do Sul: Livraria Editora Pallotti.

———. 1988. *A Igreja no Brasil. Volume 3: Expansão territorial e absolutismo estatal (1700–1822).* Santa Maria, Rio Grande do Sul: Editora Pallotti.

Rubinstein, Mauro. 1999. *O Cristo do Rio.* Rio de Janeiro: n.p.

Rulla, Luís M. 1977. *Psicologia do profundo e vocação: As instituições.* São Paulo: Edições Paulinas.

Russell-Wood, A. J. R. 1982. *The Black Man in Slavery and Freedom in Colonial Brazil.* London: Macmillan.

———. 1987. "The Gold Cycle, c. 1690." In *Colonial Brazil,* 190–243. Ed. Leslie Bethell. Cambridge: Cambridge University Press.

———. 1989. "Prestige, Power, and Piety in Colonial Brazil: The Third Orders of Salvador." *HAHR* 69:1 (February), 61–89.

Russo, Jane. 2002. *O mundo PSI no Brasil.* Rio de Janeiro: Jorge Zahar Editor.

Rynne, Xavier. 1963. *Letters from Vatican City—Vatican Council II, First Session: Background and Debates.* New York: Farrar, Straus.

———. 1966. *The Fourth Session: The Debates and Decrees of Vatican Council II, September 14 to December 8, 1965.* New York: Farrar, Straus and Giroux.

"Sacerdotes espanhois para todo o mundo." 1967. *REB* 27 (June), 502–3.

Sacred Congregation for Catholic Education. 1970. *The Basic Plan for Priestly Formation.* Washington, D.C.: National Conference of Catholic Bishops.

Salem, Tânia. 1982. "Do Centro Dom Vital à Universidade Católica." In *Universidades e instituições científicas no Rio de Janeiro,* 97–134. Ed. Simon Schwartzman. Brasília: CNPQ.

———, ed. 1981. *A Igreja dos oprimidos.* São Paulo: Editora Brasil Debates.

Salles, Joaquim de. 1993. *Se não me falha a memória.* São Paulo: Instituto Moreira Salles.

Salles Júnior, José Paulo. 1997. *Recordações.* Rio de Janeiro: N.p.

Sampaio, Maurílio. 1968. "Carta a Mons. Méndez Arceo con ocasión de la declaración de Mons. sobre el caso del P. Lemercier." In *Cuernavaca: Fuentes para el estudio de una diócesis.* Ed. Baltazar López. CIDOC Dossier No. 31, vol. 2, 4/286. Cuernavaca: CIDOC.

Sanchis, Pierre. 1992. "Introdução." In *Catolicismo: Modernidade e tradição,* 9–39. Ed. Pierre Sanchis. São Paulo: Edições Loyola.

———. 2005. "A Igreja Católica no Brasil e a dimensão do 'sujeito.'" In *A psicologização no Brasil: Atores e autores,* 15–37. Ed. Luiz Fernando Dias Duarte, Jane Russo, and Ana Teresa A. Venancio. Rio de Janeiro: Editora Contracapa.

———, ed. 1992a. *Catolicismo: Cotidiano e movimentos.* São Paulo: Edições Loyola.

———, ed. 1992b. *Catolicismo: Modernidade e tradição.* São Paulo: Edições Loyola.

————, ed. 1992c. *Catolicismo: Unidade religiosa e pluralismo cultural.* São Paulo: Edições Loyola.

Santana, Tiago. 2000. *Benditos.* Fortaleza: Tempo d'Imagem.

"Santa Sé." 1982. *CM* 352 (January), 10–18.

Santini, Cândido. 1934. "De regio Jure Patronatus in Brasilia." PhD dissertation, Gregorian University.

Santos, B. Beni dos. 1972. "Celibato em questionamento." *REB* 32 (September), 625–35.

Santos, Carmil Vieira dos. 1963. "O padre, o nordeste, e o cristão." *OS,* Year 38, No. 1 (March–April), 343–7.

Santos, Carmil Vieira dos, Drance Elias da Silva, and Arnaldo Liberato da Silva, 1984. "Práticas pastorais na Igreja do Nordeste." *Perspectivas Teológico-Pastorais,* Year 3, No. 5, 13–24.

Santos, João. 1986. "Os franciscanos no Rio Tapajós." In *Os religiosos no Brasil: Enfoques históricos,* 127–45. Ed. Riolando Azzi and Oscar Beozzo. São Paulo: Edições Paulinas.

Saraiva, Genival. 1962. "Pré-regional sul." *OS,* Year 37, No. 5 (November–December), 23–29.

Sarmento, Walney Moraes. 1984. *Nordeste: A urbanização do subdesenvolvimento.* 2nd edition. Porto Alegre: Mercado Aberto.

Saroni, Fernando. 1966. "Reflexões sobre o seminário menor." *OS,* Year 41, No. 211 (November–December), 454–64.

Scheper-Hughes, Nancy. 1992. *Death without Weeping: The Violence of Everyday Life in Brazil.* Berkeley: University of California Press.

Scherer, Dom Vicente. 1964. "Cartas novas." *OS,* Year 39, No. 1 (March–April), 4–5.

Schierholz, Thomas W. 2001. "Imagining Public Health: Ideas and the Politics of Making AIDS Prevention Policy in the United States and Brazil." PhD dissertation, Columbia University.

Schillebeeckx, Edward. 1989. *Por uma Igreja mais humana.* Trans. Isabel Fontes Leal Ferreira. São Paulo: Edições Paulinas.

Schlesinger Jr., Arthur M. 1965. *A Thousand Days: John F. Kennedy in the White House.* Boston: Houghton Mifflin.

Schmidt, José Bonifácio. 1968. "Posição Igreja-Operário." *Ponto Homem,* Year 43, No. 2 (May–June), 92–99.

Schmieder, Godofredo. 1959. "Testes psicológicos para a vida religiosa e sacerdotal." *OS,* Year 34, No. 1 (March–April), 67.

Schmitt, João Basílio. 1989. *Associação Rumos: Catálogo nacional.* 2nd edition. Brasília: Associação Rumos.

Schneider, Ronald M. 1991. *"Order and Progress": A Political History of Brazil.* Boulder: Westview.

Schooyans, Michel. 1968. "O Padre Frente a um Mundo em Desenvolvimento." Unpublished manuscript. In "O Papel do Padre. Volume II. Documentos e Ensaios," 200–220. Rio de Janeiro: CNBB/CERIS.

Schwartz, Joseph. 1999. *Cassandra's Daughter: A History of Psychoanalysis.* New York: Viking.

Schwartz, Stuart B. 1973. *Sovereignty and Society in Colonial Brazil.* Berkeley: University of California Press.

————. 1982. "The Plantations of St. Benedict: The Benedictine Sugar Mills of Colonial Brazil." *The Americas* 39:1 (July), 1–22.

————. 1985. *Sugar Plantations in the Formation of Brazilian Society: Bahia, 1550–1835.* Cambridge: Cambridge University Press.

Schwartzman, Simon, Helena Maria Bousquet Bomeny, and Vanda Maria Ribeiro Costa. 1984. *Tempos de Capanema.* Rio de Janeiro: Paz e Terra; São Paulo: Editora da Universidade de São Paulo.

Seiblitz, Zélia. 1992. "Conflito na diocese de Campos." In *Catolicismo: Modernidade e tradição,* 251–303. Ed. Pierre Sanchis. São Paulo: Edições Paulinas.

Seidl, Ernesto. 2003. "A elite eclesiástica no Rio Grande do Sul." PhD dissertation, Universidade Federal do Rio Grande do Sul.

"Semana Rural da Diocese de Campanha." 1950. *Revista do Assistente Eclesiástico,* Year 4, No. 37 (November–December), 85–99.

Semeraro, Giovanni. 1994. *A primavera dos anos 60: A geração de Betinho.* São Paulo: Edições Loyola.

Seminário Regional do Nordeste: Inauguração que vale como um símbolo. 1966. Recife: Imprensa Universitária.

"O Seminário Regional do Nordeste tem uma missão histórica a cumprir." 1965. *Revista da CRB,* Year 11, No. 121 (July), 391–98.

"Os seminários em revista." 1962. *OS,* Year 37, No. 3 (July–August), 82.

"Os seminários maiores hoje." 1970. *SEDOC* 2 (April), 1301–12.

Semprebom, Rinaldo. 1974. "A Criatividade Comunitária, um método eficiente para a criação de comunidades eclesiais de base (CEB)." MA thesis, Foundation School of Sociology and Politics of São Paulo.

Serbin, Kenneth P. 1988. "Five Brazilian Bishops Condemn Government Policy." *NCR* (November 25), 35.

————. 1989a. "Brazilians to Start New Seminaries." *NCR* (October 13), 7.

————. 1989b. "Brazil's Bishops Accept Recife Closings." *NCR* (October 20), 9.

————. 1989c. "Recife Archbishop Fires Peace and Justice Commission." *NCR* (December 22), 8.

————. 1989d. "Vatican Softens Position on Brazil Seminary Flap." *NCR* (September 29), 7.

————. 1989e. "Vatican Stands Firm on Closing Recife Seminaries." *NCR* (October 6), 11.

————. 1989f. "Which Gospel for Brazil's Poor? Vatican-ordered Seminary Closings Threaten Schism." *NCR* (September 22), 8–9.

————. 1990. "Dom Antônio Celso Queiroz (entrevista)." *Comunicações do ISER* 9:38, 77–79.

————. 1991a. "Brazil Bishops' Vote May Mask Future Power Shift." *NCR* (May 3), 12.

————. 1991b. "Igreja, estado, e a ajuda financeira pública no Brasil, 1930–1964: Estudos de três casos chaves." *Textos CPDOC.* Rio de Janeiro: FGV, CPDOC.

————. 1992a. "Os seminários: Crise, experiências e síntese." In *Catolicismo: Modernidade e tradição,* 91–151. Ed. Pierre Sanchis. São Paulo: Edições Loyola.

————. 1992b. "State Subsidization of Catholic Institutions in Brazil, 1930–1964: A Contribution to the Economic and Political History of the Church." Notre Dame, Ind.: Helen Kellogg Institute for International Studies. Working Paper no. 181.

————. 1993a. "Collor's Impeachment and the Struggle for Change." *North-South Focus* 2:2.

————. 1993b. "Latin America's Catholic Church: Religious Rivalries and the North-South Divide." *North-South Issues* 2:1.

————. 1993c. "Priests, Celibacy, and Social Conflict: A History of Brazil's Clergy and Seminaries." PhD dissertation, University of California, San Diego.

————. 1994. "Re-creating the Brazilian Church in the Post-Santo Domingo Era." Paper presented at the Latin American Studies Association Eighteenth International Congress, Atlanta, Georgia (March 10–12).

————. 1995a. "Brazil: State Subsidization and the Church since 1930." In *Organized Religion in the Political Transformation of Latin America,* 153–75. Ed. Satya R. Pattnayak. Lanham, Md.: University Press of America.

————. 1995b. "Simmering Abortion Debate Goes Public in Brazil." *The Christian Century* (March 8), 266–71.

————. 1996a. "Brazilian Church Builds International Empire." *The Christian Century* (April 10), 398–403.

————. 1996b. "Church-State Reciprocity in Contemporary Brazil: The Convening of the International Eucharistic Congress of 1955 in Rio de Janeiro." *HAHR* 76:4 (November), 721–51.

————. 1996c. "O diálogo secreto de bispos e generais nos anos da repressão." *O Estado de São Paulo* (March 3), Caderno X.

————. 1998a. "Anatomia de um crime: Repressão, direitos humanos e o caso de Alexandre Vannucchi Leme." *Teoria e Pesquisa* 20–23, 1–23.

————. 1998b. "The Anatomy of a Death: Repression, Human Rights, and the Case of Alexandre Vannucchi Leme in Authoritarian Brazil." *Journal of Latin American Studies* 30:1–33.

————. 1999a. "Religious Tolerance, Church-State Relations and the Challenge of Pluralism in Brazil." In *Evangelization and Religious Freedom in Latin Ameica: The Challenge of Religious Pluralism,* 204–19. Ed. Paul Sigmund. Maryknoll. N.Y.: Orbis.

————. 1999b. Review of *Rendering Unto Caesar: The Catholic Church and the State in Latin America. Journal of Interamerican Studies and World Affairs* 41:2 (summer), 136–40.

―――. 2000a. "The Catholic Church, Religious Pluralism, and Democracy in Brazil." In *Democratic Brazil: Actors, Institutions, and Processes*, 144–61. Ed. Peter R. Kingstone and Timothy J. Power. Pittsburgh: University of Pittsburgh Press.

―――. 2000b. *Secret Dialogues: Church-State Relations, Torture, and Social Justice in Authoritarian Brazil.* Pitt Latin American Studies. Pittsburgh: University of Pittsburgh Press.

―――. 2001a. "'Bowling Alone,' Bishops' Biographies, and Baptism by Blood: New Views of Progressive Catholicism in Brazil." *Latin American Politics and Society* 43:4 (winter), 127–41.

―――. 2001b. *Diálogos na sombra: Bispos e militares, tortura e justiça social na ditadura.* São Paulo: Companhia das Letras.

―――. 2002a. "De volta à pedra de Pedro." *Valor* (May 24–26), weekend supplement "Eu & Fim de Semana," 3:101:16–17.

―――. 2002b. "Dom Hélder Câmara: Pai do catolicismo progressista brasileiro." In *Perfis cruzados: Trajetórias e militância política no Brasil do século XX*, 141–74. Ed. Beatriz Kushnir. Rio de Janeiro: Imago.

―――. 2004. "Dom Hélder Câmara: The Father of the Church of the Poor." In *The Human Tradition in Modern Brazil*, 249–66. Ed. Peter Beattie. Wilmington, Del.: Scholarly Resources.

SERENE II: Uma caminhada. 1988. Recife: Seminário Regional do Nordeste II.

Servat, José. 1986. "Um grito no nordeste: A experiência da A.C.R. no Brasil, 1965–1986." Unpublished manuscript.

Servat, José, and Father Afrânio. 1985. "Um grito no nordeste." In *Igreja e questão agrária*, 153–59. Ed. Vanilda Paiva. São Paulo: Edições Loyola.

"O sétimo centenário de Santo Antônio e o Seminário de Maranhão." 1931. *OS*, Year 6, No. 5 (September), 134–35.

Shannon, William H. 1997. *"Something of a Rebel": Thomas Merton. His Life and Works. An Introduction.* Cincinnati: St. Anthony Messenger Press.

Sigmund, Paul E. 1990. *Liberation Theology at the Crossroads.* New York: Oxford University Press.

―――, ed. 1999. *Evangelization and Religious Freedom in Latin Ameica: The Challenge of Religious Pluralism.* Maryknoll. N.Y.: Orbis.

Silva, Arnaldo Liberato da. 1982. "Greves na cana em Pernambuco (uma leitura de fé)." *Perspectivas Teológico-Pastorais*, Year 1, No. 2, 58–64.

Silva, Belchior Cornélio da. 1961. "Diretrizes da Santa Sé para os Seminários." *REB* 21 (March), 116–20.

Silva, Carlos Alberto da Costa. 1998. "Aprender do passado: A formação do clero segundo Azeredo Coutinho (1795–1802)." *REB* 58 (September), 695–700.

Silva, Gerson Flávio da. 1985. "Animação Cristã no Meio Rural (ACR)." In *Igreja e questão agrária*, 149–52. Ed. Vanilda Paiva. São Paulo: Edições Loyola.

Silva, José Ariovaldo da. 1983. *O Movimento Litúrgico no Brasil.* Petrópolis: Vozes.

Silva, José Cícero da. 1961. "Seminaristas preparam-se para a JOC." *OS,* Year 36, No. 2 (May–June), 14–21.

Silva, Severino Vicente da. 1991. "Pequeno panorama da formação presbiteral no NE-II, 1960–1990." Unpublished paper.

———. 2002. "Dom Hélder: Um sopro progressista na arquidiocese de Olinda e Recife." *REB* 62 (January), 133–49.

———. 2003. "Entre o Tibre e o Capibaribe: Os limites do progressismo na arquidiocese de Olinda e Recife." PhD dissertation, Universidade Federal de Pernambuco.

Silva Filho, Assuero Gomes da. 1997. *Réquiem para um bispo.* Recife: Bagaço.

Silva Neto, Belchior J. da. 1965. *Dom Viçoso, Apóstolo de Minas.* Belo Horizonte, n.p.

Singer, André. 2001a. "D. Cláudio transita em correntes opostas." *Folha de S. Paulo* (May 20), A-10.

———. 2001b. "'Mercado favorece os fortes,' diz cardeal." *Folha de S. Paulo* (May 20), A-11.

Singer, Paul. 1968. *Desenvolvimento econômico e evolução urbana.* São Paulo: Companhia Editora Nacional/Editora da Universidade de São Paulo.

Siqueira, A. A. de. 1942. "Pasce oves meas!" *REB* 2 (June), 273–80.

Skidmore, Thomas E. 1967. *Politics in Brazil, 1930–1964: An Experiment in Democracy.* New York: Oxford University Press.

———. 1976. *Preto no branco: Raça e nacionalidade no pensamento brasileiro.* Rio de Janeiro: Paz e Terra.

———. 1988. *The Politics of Military Rule in Brazil, 1964–85.* New York: Oxford University Press.

Smith, Anne-Marie. 1997. *A Forced Agreement: Press Acquiescence to Censorship in Brazil.* Pittsburgh: University of Pittsburgh Press.

Smith, Brian H. 1982. *The Church and Politics in Chile.* Princeton: Princeton University Press.

———. 1990. *More than Altruism: The Politics of Private Foreign Aid.* Princeton: Princeton University Press.

Smith, Christian. 1991. *The Emergence of Liberation Theology.* Chicago: University of Chicago Press.

Socolow, Susan Migden. 2000. *The Women of Colonial Latin America.* Cambridge: Cambridge University Press.

Sommer, Barbara. 2000. "Negotiated Settlements: Native Amazonians and Portuguese Policy in Pará, Brazil, 1758–1798." PhD dissertation, University of New Mexico.

"S. O. S. Vocações—1964." 1963. *S.O.S. Vocações,* Year 1, No. 2 (November), 2.

Sousa, Silvano de. 1945. "Caridade fraterna entre sacerdotes. Psicologia de suas dissensões." *REB* 5 (March), 1–12.

———. 1951. "A santidade sacerdotal." *REB* 11 (September), 529–35.

———. 1956a. "A situação do clero no Brasil." *REB* 16 (September), 561–68.

———. 1956b. "Vocações sacerdotais. Uma solução prática." *REB* 16 (June), 411–12.

Souza, César Augusto Martins de. 2002. "Quando a 'Santa Teresinha' é o ponto de encontro: Sociabilidade, amor e família na paróquia de Jurunas, Belém-Pará." MA thesis, Universidade Federal do Pará.

Souza, Jessie Jane Vieira de. 2002. *Círculos Operários: A Igreja Católica e o mundo do trabalho no Brasil.* Rio de Janeiro: Editora UFRJ.

Souza, José Evangelista de. 1999. *Província Brasileira da Congregação da Missão: 180 anos dos lazaristas no Brasil.* Belo Horizonte: Santa Clara.

Souza, Juliana Beatriz Almeida de. 1996. "Mãe negra de um povo mestiço: Devoção a Nossa Senhora Aparecida e identidade nacional." *Estudos Afro-Asiáticos* 29 (March), 85–102.

Souza, Laura de Mello e. 1982. *Desclassificados de ouro: A pobreza mineira no século XVIII.* Rio de Janeiro: Edições Graal.

Souza, Luiz Alberto Gómez de. 1984. *A JUC: Os estudantes católicos e a política.* Petrópolis: Vozes.

———. 2000. "As CEBs vão bem, obrigado." *REB* 60 (March), 93–110.

Souza, Maurício Rodrigues de. 2002. "'A Igreja em movimento': Um estudo sobre identidades religiosas carismáticas em Belém, Pará." MA thesis, Universidade Federal do Pará.

Souza, Ney de. 1998. "A formação do clero no Brasil colonial e a influência do iluminismo." *REB* 58 (September), 618–33.

Spence, Jonathan D. 1984. *The Memory Palace of Matteo Ricci.* New York: Viking Penguin.

Stark, Rodney, and James C. McCann. 1993. "Market Forces and Catholic Commitment: Exploring the New Paradigm." *Journal for the Scientific Study of Religion* 32:2, 111–24.

Stavrianos, L. S. 1981. *Global Rift: The Third World Comes of Age.* New York: William Morrow.

Stedile, João Pedro, and Bernando Mançano Fernandes. 1999. *Brava gente: A trajetória do MST e a luta pela terra no Brasil.* São Paulo: Editora Fundação Perseu Abramo.

Steigenga, Timothy. 1997. "'Jesus Christ Is Lord of Guatemala': Religious Freedom and Religious Conflict in Central America's Most Protestant Nation." Paper presented at conference on "Evangelization and Religious Freedom in Latin America," Princeton University (October 24–25).

Stein, Ernildo. 1963. "Universidade X seminarista." *OS,* Year 38, No. 2 (May–June), 43–58.

———. 1968. "Horizontes críticos para uma teologia do desenvolvimento." *Ponto Homem,* Year 43, No. 3 (July–August), 9–22.

Stein, Stanley J. 1957. *Vassouras: A Brazilian Coffee County, 1850–1900.* Cambridge: Harvard University Press.

Stepan, Alfred. 1971. *The Military in Politics: Changing Patterns in Brazil.* Princeton: Princeton University Press.

———. 1973. "The New Professionalism of Internal Warfare and Military Role Expansion." In *Authoritarian Brazil: Origins, Policies, and Future,* 47–65. Ed. Alfred Stepan. New Haven: Yale University Press.

———. 1988. *Rethinking Military Politics: Brazil and the Southern Cone.* Princeton: Princeton University Press.

Stoll, David. 1990. *Is Latin America Turning Protestant?* Berkeley: University of California Press.

"Study Reveals One Thousand New Abuse Claims." 2005. *The Tablet* (February 26). Online edition.

"Sugestões do presbitério da santa Igreja de Santos à CNBB." 1968. *SEDOC,* special edition, (September), 402.

"Sugestões do Secretariado Nacional de Seminários para a formação de presbíteros." 1967. *CM,* Nos. 176–77 (May–June), 33–37.

Swatos Jr., William H. ed. 1995. *Religion and Democracy in Latin America.* New Brunswick, N.J.: Transaction.

Sweet, David. 1995. "The Ibero-American Frontier Mission in Native American History." In *The New Latin American Mission History,* 1–48. Ed. Erick Langer and Robert H. Jackson. Lincoln: University of Nebraska Press.

Sydow, Evanize, and Marilda Ferri. 1999. *Dom Paulo Evaristo Arns: Um homem amado e perseguido.* Petrópolis: Vozes.

Tackett, Timothy. 1986. *Religion, Revolution, and Regional Culture in Eighteenth-Century France.* Princeton: Princeton University Press.

Tagliavini, João Virgílio. 1990. "Garotos no túnel—um estudo sobre a imposição da vocação sacerdotal e o processo de condicionamento nos seminários." MA thesis, University of Campinas.

Tavares, Célia Cristina da Silva. 1995. "Entre a cruz e a espada: Jesuítas e a América portuguesa." MA thesis, Universidade Federal Fluminense.

———. 2002. "A cristandade insular: Jesuítas e inquisidores em Goa (1540–1682)." PhD dissertation, Universidade Federal Fluminense.

Tavares, J. Batista, A. Almeida Lima, and J. Augusto Cabral. 1966. "Uma posição a tomar." *OS,* Year 41, No. 210 (September–October), 390–99.

Tavares, Maria da Conceição. 1972. *Da substituição de importações ao capitalismo financeiro.* Rio de Janeiro: Zahar Editores.

Taylor, Kit Sims. 1978. *Sugar and the Underdevelopment of Northeastern Brazil, 1500–1970.* University of Florida Social Sciences Monograph 63. Gainesville: University Presses of Florida.

Taylor, William B. 1996. *Magistrates of the Sacred: Priests and Parishioners in Eighteenth-Century Mexico.* Stanford: Stanford University Press.

Teixeira, Faustino Luiz Couto. 1988. *A gênese das ceb's no Brasil: Elementos explicativos.* São Paulo: Edições Paulinas.

"O tema sacerdotal e o clero na América Latina." 1971. *REB* 31 (June), 457.

"Teologia pastoral América Latina." 1964. *OS,* Year 39, No. 1 (March–April), 90–93.

"Teólogos capuchinhos fundam centro acadêmico." 1962. *OS,* Year 37, No. 5 (November–December), 44–45.

Tepe, Valfredo. 1960a. "Formação psicológica e social dos religiosos educadores." *Revista da CRB,* Year 7, No. 64 (October), 601–9.

———. 1960b. "Formação psicológica e social dos religiosos educadores." *Revista da CRB,* Year 7, No. 65 (November), 649–57.

———. 1961. "Exame psicológico dos candidatos à vida religiosa." *Revista da CRB,* Year 7, No. 72 (May), 295–300.

———. 1966. *Prazer ou amor?* Salvador: Editora Mensageiro da Fé.

———. 1968. "A Personalidade do Presbítero." In "O Papel do Padre. Volume II. Documentos e Ensaios," 280–321. Unpublished manuscript. Rio de Janeiro: CNBB/CERIS.

———. 1989 [1958]. *O sentido da vida.* Petrópolis: Vozes.

Terra, João Evangelista Martins. 1984a. *Frei Boff e o neogalicanismo da igreja brasileira.* 2nd edition. São Paulo: Militia Christi.

———. 1984b. *O negro e a Igreja.* São Paulo: Edições Loyola.

Theije, Marjo de. 1997. "Conservative CEBs and Liberated Charismatics." Paper presented at the Brazilian Studies Association Fourth Congress, Washington, D.C. (November 12–15).

Theisen, Ilfio José Theisen. 1968. "Semana do desenvolvimento." *Ponto Homem,* Year 43, No. 1 (March–April), 84–86.

Thornhill, John. 2000. *Modernity: Christianity's Estranged Child Reconstructed.* Grand Rapids, Mich.: Eerdmans.

Tierny, Jeanne Marie. 1975. "Pequenas comunidades empenhadas na pastoral." *Convergência,* Year 8, Nos. 77/78, 5–26.

Tincq, Henri. 1992. "Drewermann: A Rebel with a Cause." *Guardian Weekly* (March 1), 15–16.

Todaro, Margaret Patrice. 1971. "Pastors, Prophets and Politicians: A Study of the Brazilian Catholic Church, 1916–1945." PhD dissertation, Columbia University.

Toldo, Plínio. 1963. "II encontro regional dos seminaristas maiores de São Paulo." *OS,* Year 38, No. 1 (March–April), 20–31.

Topik, Steven. 1987. *The Political Economy of the Brazilian State, 1889–1930.* Austin: University of Texas Press.

Torres-Londoño, Fernando. *A outra família: Concubinato, Igreja e escândalo na colônia.* São Paulo: Edições Loyola, 1999.

Tradição, Família, e Propriedade [TFP]. 1980. *Meio século de epopeia anticomunista.* São Paulo: Editora Vera Cruz.

Traferetti, José. 2002. "AIDS e pastoral familiar: Informação, conscientização e saúde." *REB* 623 (October), 823–44.

Trentin, Ary, Golias Silva, and Ivo Poletto. 1966. "Dom Ivo Lorscheiter, um episcopado em Nova et Vetera." *OS,* Year 41, No. 207 (March–April), 27–37.

Trindade, Hélgio. 1979. *Integralismo.* 2nd edition. São Paulo-Rio de Janeiro: DIFEL.

Trindade, Raimundo. 1951. *Breve noticia dos seminários de Mariana.* Mariana: Archidiocese of Mariana.

Tursi, Carlo. 1990. "Isto é meu corpo que é dado por vocês." Undergraduate thesis, Instituto Teológico-Pastoral do Ceará.

Uchôa, Virgílio Leite. 1998. "Análise de conjuntura, julho-agosto de 1998." Brasília: CNBB. Mimeograph.

"Um Seminário para a América Latina, na Itália." 1963. *REB* 23 (March), 226–27.

Unsworth, Tim. 1991. *The Last Priests in America*. New York: Crossroad.

Vainfas, Ronaldo. 1997. *Trópico dos pecados: Moral, sexualidade e Inquisição no Brasil*. Rio de Janeiro: Editora Nova Fronteira.

Vainfas, Ronaldo, and Juliana Beatriz de Souza. 2000. *Brasil de todos os santos*. Rio de Janeiro: Jorge Zahar Editor.

Valentini, Dom Demétrio. 1998. "Reflexões sobre o sínodo da América." *REB* 58 (March), 16–33.

———. 2004. "42a. assembléia da CNBB." Online: http://www.diocesedejales.org.br.

Valle, João Edênio Reis. 1965. "As etapas psicológicas da motivação à vocação sacerdotal: Um projeto de pesquisa." MA thesis, Pontifical Atheneum of the Salesians, Rome.

———. 1980. "Juventude, análise de uma opção." *Convergência*, No. 131 (April), 156–75.

———. 1984. "Observações psicossociológicas." In *Situação e vida dos seminaristas maiores no Brasil*, 65–80. CNBB, Estudos da CNBB No. 40. São Paulo: Edições Paulinas.

———. 1995. "Observações psicopedagógicas sobre a pesquisa de 1993." In *Situação e vida dos seminaristas maiores no Brasil (II)*, 39–56. CNBB, Estudos da CNBB, No. 74. São Paulo: Paulus.

———. 1998. "Dimensão psico-afetiva da vida e do ministério do presbítero." *REB* 58 (September), 683–90.

Valle, Rogério. 1995. "Tecnoestruturas e exclusão social." *Perspectivas teológicas* 27, 37–44.

Valle, Rogério, and Marcelo Pitta. 1994. *Comunidades eclesiais católicas: Resultados estatísticos no Brasil*. Petrópolis: Vozes; CERIS.

van den Berg, Irene de Araújo. 2003. "As representações do mal no discurso da Renovação Carismática Católica." MA thesis, Universidade Federal do Rio Grande do Norte.

Vanderwood, Paul. 1998. *The Power of God against the Guns of Government: Religious Upheaval in Mexico at the Turn of the Nineteenth Century*. Stanford: Stanford University Press.

Van Young, Eric. 2001. *The Other Rebellion: Popular Violence, Ideology, and the Mexican Struggle for Independence, 1810–1821*. Stanford: Stanford University Press.

Vasconcelos, José Antonio. 2001. *Quem tem medo da teoria? A história intelectual e a ameaça do pós-modernismo nas páginas da American Historical Review*. PhD dissertation, Universidade Estadual de Campinas.

Vásquez, Manuel A. 1997. "Structural Obstacles to Grassroots Pastoral Practice: The Case of a Base Community in Urban Brazil." *Sociology of Religion* 58:1, 53–68.

————. 1998. *The Brazilian Popular Church and the Crisis of Modernity.* New York: Cambridge University Press.

Vaz, Henrique de Lima. 1991. "O itinerário inaciano de Teilhard de Chardin." *PUC Ciência* 6:35–39.

Veiga, Eugênio de Andrade. 1977. *Os párocos no Brasil no período colonial, 1500–1822.* Salvador: Universidade Católica de Salvador.

Ventura, Zuenir. 1988. *1968: O ano que não terminou.* Rio de Janeiro: Editora Nova Fronteira.

————. 1994. *Cidade partida.* São Paulo: Companhia das Letras.

Venturin, Teresinha. 2001. *Formação religiosa para o século XXI—freira, mulher cidadã.* Petrópolis: Vozes.

Versaldi, Giuseppe. 1988. "Priestly Celibacy from the Canonical and Psychological Points of View." In *Vatican II: Assessment and Perspectives: Twenty-Five Years After (1962–1987),* 3:131–57. Ed. René Latourelle. New York: Paulist.

"Uma vida em duas realidades. Comunidade operária, Santo André, S.P." 1967. *OS,* Year 42, No. 212 (March–April), 19–37.

Videla, Gabriela. 1984. *Sergio Méndez Arceo, un señor obispo.* Mexico City: Ediciones Nuevomar.

Vidler, Alec R. 1971. *The Church in an Age of Revolution: 1789 to the Present Day.* Pelican History of the Church, vol. 5. Baltimore: Penguin.

Villela, Lúcia. 2000. "Psychoanalysis in São Paulo, Brazil: Controversies, History and Discourse." Paper presented at the American Psychoanalytic Association meeting (December 17).

"Visão global dos resultados de estudos regionais sobre o tema 'Sacerdócio ministerial.'" 1971. *CM* 227 (August), 88–104.

"A visita de Mons. Garrone, da S.C. dos Seminários, ao Brasil." 1967. *CM,* No. 174/175 (March/April), 20–28.

Wagley, Charles. 1971. *An Introduction to Brazil.* New York: Columbia University Press.

Walsh, William Thomas. 1947. *Our Lady of Fatima.* New York: Macmillan.

Wanderley, Luiz Eduardo. 1984. *Educar para transformar.* Petrópolis: Vozes.

Wanderley, Luiz Eduardo, and Clodovis Boff. 1992. "Os novos movimentos eclesiais." *REB* 52 (September), 702–6.

Ward, Graham, ed. 2000. *The Certeau Reader.* Malden, Mass.: Blackwell.

Warren, Jonathan W. 2001. *Racial Revolutions: Antiracism and Indian Resurgence in Brazil.* Durham, N.C.: Duke University Press.

Weber, Max. 1966. *The Sociology of Religion.* Trans. Ephraim Fischoff. London: Social Science Paperbacks and Methuen.

Weinstein, Barbara. 1990. "The Industrialists, the State, and the Issues of Worker Training and Social Services in Brazil, 1930–50." *HAHR* 70:3 (August), 379–404.

————. 1996. *For Social Peace in Brazil: Industrialists and the Remaking of the Working Class in São Paulo, 1920–1964.* Chapel Hill: University of North Carolina Press.

Welch, Cliff. 1999. *The Seed Was Planted: The São Paulo Roots of Brazil's Rural Labor Movement, 1925–1964*. University Park: Pennsylvania State University Press.

Wernet, Augustin. 1987. *A Igreja paulista no século XIX: A reforma de D. Antônio Joaquim de Melo (1851–1861)*. São Paulo: Editora Ática.

Weschler, Lawrence. 1990. *Um milagre, um universo*. Trans. Tomás Rosa Bueno. São Paulo: Companhia das Letras.

White, Joseph M. 1989. *The Diocesan Seminary in the United States: A History from the 1780s to the Present*. Notre Dame, Ind.: University of Notre Dame.

Williams, Daryle. 2001. *Culture Wars in Brazil: The First Vargas Regime, 1930–1945*. Durham, N.C.: Duke University Press.

Wills, Garry. 1971. *Bare Ruined Choirs: Doubt, Prophecy, and Radical Religion*. Garden City, N.Y.: Doubleday.

———. 2002a. "The Bishops at Bay," *New York Review of Books* 49:13 (August 15), 8–11.

———. 2002b. "High Fidelity," *New York Review of Books* 49:19 (December 5), 40–43.

———. 2004. "God in the Hands of Angry Sinners," 51:6 *New York Review of Books* (April 8), 68–74.

Wirth, John D. 1970. *The Politics of Brazilian Development, 1930–1954*. Stanford: Stanford University Press.

———. 1982. *O fiel da balança: Minas Gerais na Federação Brasileira, 1889–1937*. Trans. Maria Carmelita. Rio de Janeiro: Paz e Terra.

Wolfe, Joel. 1991. "Anarchist Ideology, Worker Practice: The 1917 General Strike and the Formation of São Paulo's Working Class." *HAHR* 71:4 (November), 809–46.

Zanlochi, Terezinha Santarosa. 1990. "A participação das comunidades religiosas femininas na pastoral diocesana em Bauru, de 1964 a 1968." *Mimesis* 11:1, 187–201.

Zanotelli, Jandir. 1964. "Cristoperto: Viamão vai à Vila." *OS* Year 39, No. 1 (March–April), 61–66.

Zico, José Tobias. 1979. *Caraça: Ex-alunos e visitantes*. Belo Horizonte: Editora São Vicente.

———. 1981. "Os lazaristas do Caraça." *REB* 41 (September), 485–509.

———. 1988. *Caraça, peregrinação, cultura, turismo*. 5th edition. Belo Horizonte: Ed. Líttera Maciel.

———. 2000. *Congregação da Missão no Brasil: Resumo histórico (1820–2000)*. Belo Horizonte: Santa Clara.

Zico, Vicente Joaquim. 1964. "Deixando o Ceará." *São Vicente*, Year 34, No. 3, 26–27.

———. 1981. "São Vicente de Paulo, há 400 anos e hoje." *Grande Sinal* (September), 497–511.

Zilboorg, Gregory. 1969. *Psicanálise e religião*. Petrópolis: Vozes.

Zolov, Eric. 1999. *Refried Elvis: The Rise of the Mexican Counterculture*. Berkeley: University of California Press.

Index

In this index names of people, organizations, and movements are alphabetized, where appropriate, by the Portuguese, rather than the English translation.

KENNETH P. SERBIN

is an associate professor of history at the University of San Diego.